THE CAMBRIDGE HISTORY OF
THE SECOND WORLD WAR

War is often described as an extension of politics by violent means. With contributions from twenty-eight eminent historians, Volume II of *The Cambridge History of the Second World War* examines the relationship between ideology and politics in the war's origins, dynamics and consequences. Part I examines the ideologies of the combatants and shows how the war can be understood as a struggle of words, ideas and values, with the rival powers expressing divergent claims to justice and controlling news from the front in order to sustain morale and influence international opinion. Part II looks at politics from the perspective of pre-war and wartime diplomacy, as well as examining the way in which neutrals were treated and behaved. The volume concludes by assessing the impact of states, politics and ideology on the fate of individuals as occupied and liberated peoples, collaborators and resistors, and as British and French colonial subjects.

RICHARD J. B. BOSWORTH is Senior Research Fellow at Jesus College, Oxford.

JOSEPH A. MAIOLO is Professor of International History in the Department of War Studies at King's College London and Visiting Research Professor at the Norwegian Defence Intelligence School, Oslo.

THE CAMBRIDGE HISTORY OF
THE SECOND WORLD WAR

GENERAL EDITOR

EVAN MAWDSLEY, *Honorary Professorial Research Fellow and formerly Professor of International History at the University of Glasgow.*

The Cambridge History of the Second World War is an authoritative new account of the conflict that unfolded between 1939 and 1945. With contributions from a team of leading historians, the three volumes adopt a transnational approach, to offer a comprehensive, global analysis of the military, political, social, economic and cultural aspects of the war. Volume I provides an operational perspective on the course of the war, examining strategies, military cultures and organization, and the key campaigns, whilst Volume II reviews the 'politics' of war, the global aspirations of the rival alliances, and the role of diplomacy. Volume III considers the war as an economic, social and cultural event, exploring how entire nations mobilized their economies and populations, and dealt with the catastrophic losses that followed. The volumes conclude by considering the lasting impact of the Second World War and the memory of war across different cultures of commemoration.

VOLUME I
Fighting the War
EDITED BY JOHN FERRIS AND EVAN MAWDSLEY

VOLUME II
Politics and Ideology
EDITED BY RICHARD J. B. BOSWORTH AND JOSEPH A. MAIOLO

VOLUME III
Total War: Economy, Society and Culture
EDITED BY MICHAEL GEYER AND ADAM TOOZE

THE CAMBRIDGE
HISTORY OF
THE SECOND WORLD WAR

*

VOLUME II
Politics and Ideology

*

Edited by
RICHARD J. B. BOSWORTH
and
JOSEPH A. MAIOLO

Contributors to Volume II

KLAS ÅMARK is Professor Emeritus in History at Stockholm University. He was coordinator for the research programme 'Sweden's relations to Nazism, Nazi Germany and the Holocaust', funded by the Swedish Research Council.

DONALD BLOXHAM is Richard Pares Professor of European History at the University of Edinburgh.

RICHARD J. B. BOSWORTH is Senior Research Fellow at Jesus College, Oxford.

STEVEN CASEY is Professor in International History at the London School of Economics and Political Science.

PATRICIA CLAVIN is Professor of International History at the University of Oxford, and Zeitlyn Fellow and Tutor in History, Jesus College.

MARK EDELE is Professor of History at the University of Western Australia.

Jo Fox is Professor of Modern History at Durham University.

ROBERT GERWARTH is Professor of Modern History at University College Dublin, and Director of the university's Centre for War Studies.

NORMAN J. W. GODA is Norman and Irma Braman Professor of Holocaust Studies at the University of Florida.

KEN'ICHI GOTO is Professor Emeritus in the Graduate School of Asia Pacific Studies at Waseda University, Tokyo.

WILLIAM I. HITCHCOCK is Professor of History in the Corcoran Department of History at the University of Virginia, and Director of Research and Scholarship and Randolph Compton Professor at the Miller Center, also at the University of Virginia.

THE CAMBRIDGE
HISTORY OF
THE SECOND WORLD WAR

*

VOLUME II
Politics and Ideology

*

Edited by
RICHARD J. B. BOSWORTH
and
JOSEPH A. MAIOLO

CAMBRIDGE
UNIVERSITY PRESS

University Printing House, Cambridge CB2 8BS, United Kingdom

Cambridge University Press is part of the University of Cambridge.

It furthers the University's mission by disseminating knowledge in the pursuit of education, learning and research at the highest international levels of excellence.

www.cambridge.org
Information on this title: www.cambridge.org/9781107034075

© Cambridge University Press 2015

This publication is in copyright. Subject to statutory exception and to the provisions of relevant collective licensing agreements, no reproduction of any part may take place without the written permission of Cambridge University Press.

First published 2015
Reprinted 2018

Printing in the United Kingdom by TJ International Ltd. Padstow Cornwall

A catalogue record for this publication is available from the British Library

ISBN 978-1-107-03407-5 Hardback
ISBN 978-1-108-40640-6 Paperback

Cambridge University Press has no responsibility for the persistence or accuracy of URLs for external or third-party internet websites referred to in this publication, and does not guarantee that any content on such websites is, or will remain, accurate or appropriate.

Contents

Contents

Contents

Illustrations

The color plates can be found between pages 366 and 367

Figure

Every effort has been made to contact the relevant copyright-holders for the images reproduced in this book. In the event of any error, the publisher will be pleased to make corrections in any reprints or future editions.

Maps

Contributors to Volume II

Klas Åmark is Professor Emeritus in History at Stockholm University. He was coordinator for the research programme 'Sweden's relations to Nazism, Nazi Germany and the Holocaust', funded by the Swedish Research Council.

Donald Bloxham is Richard Pares Professor of European History at the University of Edinburgh.

Richard J. B. Bosworth is Senior Research Fellow at Jesus College, Oxford.

Steven Casey is Professor in International History at the London School of Economics and Political Science.

Patricia Clavin is Professor of International History at the University of Oxford, and Zeitlyn Fellow and Tutor in History, Jesus College.

Mark Edele is Professor of History at the University of Western Australia.

Jo Fox is Professor of Modern History at Durham University.

Robert Gerwarth is Professor of Modern History at University College Dublin, and Director of the university's Centre for War Studies.

Norman J. W. Goda is Norman and Irma Braman Professor of Holocaust Studies at the University of Florida.

Ken'ichi Goto is Professor Emeritus in the Graduate School of Asia Pacific Studies at Waseda University, Tokyo.

William I. Hitchcock is Professor of History in the Corcoran Department of History at the University of Virginia, and Director of Research and Scholarship and Randolph Compton Professor at the Miller Center, also at the University of Virginia.

TALBOT IMLAY is Professor of History in the Département des sciences historiques at Université Laval, Québec.

ASHLEY JACKSON is Professor of Imperial and Military History in the Defence Studies Department at King's College London, and Visiting Fellow at Kellogg College, Oxford.

PETER JACKSON is Professor of Global Security at the University of Glasgow.

GREGOR KRANJC is Assistant Professor in the Department of History at Brock University, St Catharines, Ontario.

PAUL H. KRATOSKA is Publishing Director for NUS Press at the National University of Singapore.

JOSEPH A. MAIOLO is Professor of International History in the Department of War Studies at King's College London and Visiting Research Professor at the Norwegian Defence Intelligence School, Oslo.

JÜRGEN MATTHÄUS is a historian and Research Director at the Jack, Joseph and Morton Mandel Center for Advanced Holocaust Studies of the United States Holocaust Memorial Museum in Washington DC.

PETER MAUCH is Senior Lecturer of International History at the University of Western Sydney, Australia.

DAVID MOTADEL is a Research Fellow in History at Gonville and Caius College, University of Cambridge.

SILVIO PONS is Professor of Contemporary History and East European History at the University of Rome 'Tor Vergata', and Director of the Gramsci Foundation, Rome.

PAUL PRESTON is the Príncipe de Asturias Professor of Contemporary Spanish History at the London School of Economics.

DAVID REYNOLDS is Professor of International History at the University of Cambridge.

DAVIDE RODOGNO is Professor in the International History Department at the Graduate Institute of International and Development Studies, Geneva.

NICHOLAS STARGARDT is Professor of Modern European History at Oxford University.

MARTIN THOMAS is Professor of Imperial History at the University of Exeter.

JONATHAN WATERLOW is a British Academy Postdoctoral Fellow in History at St Antony's College, University of Oxford.

MARGHERITA ZANASI is Associate Professor of Chinese History at Louisiana State University.

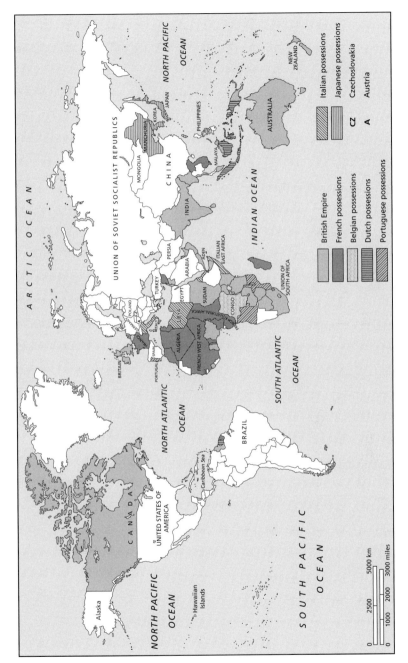

0.1 The old world order, 1937

British Empire
French possessions
Belgian possessions
Dutch possessions
Portuguese possessions

Italian possessions
Japanese possessions
CZ Czechoslovakia
A   Austria

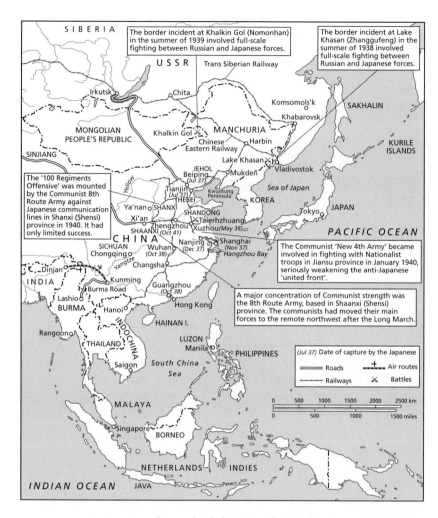

The border incident at Khalkin Gol (Nomonhan) in the summer of 1939 involved full-scale fighting between Russian and Japanese forces.

The border incident at Lake Khasan (Zhanggufeng) in the summer of 1938 involved full-scale fighting between Russian and Japanese forces.

The '100 Regiments Offensive' was mounted by the Communist 8th Route Army against Japanese communication lines in Shanxi (Shensi) province in 1940. It had only limited success.

The Communist 'New 4th Army' became involved in fighting with Nationalist troops in Jiansu province in January 1940, seriously weakening the anti-Japanese 'united front'.

A major concentration of Communist strength was the 8th Route Army, based in Shaanxi (Shensi) province. The communists had moved their main forces to the remote northwest after the Long March.

SIBERIA

USSR Trans Siberian Railway

Irkutsk Chita Komsomols'k SAKHALIN

Khabarovsk

MONGOLIAN PEOPLE'S REPUBLIC Khalkin Gol MANCHURIA Chinese Eastern Railway Harbin KURILE ISLANDS

SINJIANG

JEHOL Lake Khasan Vladivostok

Beiping (Jul 37) Mukden

Tianjin (Jul 37) Kwantung Peninsula Sea of Japan

HEBEI KOREA

Ya'nan SHANXI SHANDONG Tokyo JAPAN

Xi'an Taierhzhuang

Zhengzhou Xuzhou (May 38)

SHAANXI (Oct 41)

PACIFIC OCEAN

CHINA Nanjing (Dec 37) Shanghai (Nov 37)

SICHUAN Wuhan (Oct 38) Hangzhou Bay

Chongqing

Dinjan Yangtze Changsha

INDIA Kunming

Burma Road Guangzhou (Oct 38)

Lashio Hong Kong

BURMA Hanoi

HAINAN I.

Rangoon

THAILAND LUZON Manila PHILIPPINES

Saigon South China Sea

(Jul 37) Date of capture by the Japanese

Roads Air routes
Railways Battles

MALAYA

Singapore BORNEO

NETHERLANDS INDIES

INDIAN OCEAN JAVA

0 500 1000 1500 2000 2500 km
0 500 1000 1500 miles

0.2 Japanese advances by diplomacy and conquest, 1937–41

The following text labels appear within the map:

Scale bars:
0 150 300 450 600 750 km
0 150 300 450 miles

Legend:
Mannerheim line
Maginot line
Curzon line
Luleå–Kiruna–Narvik railway
Westwall

Annotation boxes:

The Russian invasion of Finland was mounted north and south of Lake Ladoga. Field defences of the Mannerheim line. One of best-known Red Army defeats was at Suomussalmi where a Russian division was cut off in a forest and destroyed.

Swedish iron ore deposits, located near Gällivare and Kiruna, were a resource of great importance. In the summer the ore was moved by rail to Luleå, but in the winter, when the Baltic was frozen, it was sent through Narvik in Norway.

WESER. Invasion of Norway, Apr 40.

Sep 39, Oct 39: Baltic states accept Russian bases. Jun 40: annexed by USSR.

The Curzon line demarcated regions that were predominantly Polish and regions that were predominantly Belorussian or Ukrainian. It was laid out by the British Foreign Secretary, Lord Curzon, in 1920 and played an important part in determining the boundary between Poland and the USSR in 1939 and 1945.

German invasion of Poland and Norway
German advances

Place labels:
Petsamo, Murmansk, Narvik, Kiruna, Gällivare, Luleå, Oulu, Suomussalmi, Namsos, Trondheim, Adalsnes, NORWAY, SWEDEN, FINLAND, Tampere, Viipuri, Lake Ladoga, Bergen, Oslo, Helsinki, Karelian Isthmus, Leningrad, Stavanger, Hanko, USSR, ESTONIA, North Sea, LATVIA, DENMARK, Copenhagen, Baltic Sea, Memel, LITHUANIA, Polish Corridor, Danzig, EAST PRUSSIA, Wilhelmshaven, Berlin, NETHERLANDS, GERMANY, POLAND, Warsaw, BELGIUM, Rhine, GENERAL GOVERNMENT, Vistula, Bug, SILESIA, SUDETENLAND, UPPER SILESIA, RHINELAND, SAAR, Prague, BOHEMIA-MORAVIA, CZECHOSLOVAKIA, FRANCE, Westwall, Munich, SLOVAKIA, Vienna, Bratislava, SWITZERLAND, AUSTRIA, HUNGARY, ROMANIA, ITALY

0.3 German advances by diplomacy and conquest, 1936–41

Introduction to Volume II

RICHARD J. B. BOSWORTH AND JOSEPH A. MAIOLO

The editors of Volume II of *The Cambridge History of the Second World War* accept as a starting point Carl von Clausewitz's famous definition of war as a continuation of politics by violent means.[1] While the unbound savagery and destruction of the war may have appeared like violence for its own sake, the opposite was true. Why war came and expanded, the way the war was fought and its world-dividing consequences can only be understood if we accept that politics guided thought and action. It is sobering to reflect that across the globe so much inhumanity was done for human purposes.

What determined those purposes? In earlier periods, religious conflict, dynastic glory, state interests and imperial expansion defined the reasons for battle, but the twentieth century was distinctly the time of ideological war. Although the First World War began as a typical geopolitical struggle between the great powers of East Central Europe over the Balkans, its unforeseen duration, magnitude and intensity transformed international relations and domestic politics and blurred the distinction between them.[2] Industrial total war destroyed empires and sparked revolutions. War waged with increased implacability recast existing ideas of national political, economic and social order, which had shaped the identity of states before, but which now became central to the way in which political leaders and elites understood the world. Ideological affinity or antipathy became the way to identify friends and foes.[3] Of the ideologies that configured the great conflicts of the twentieth century, from 1914 to the end of the Cold War in 1990,

1 Carl von Clausewitz, *On War*, ed. and trans. Michael Howard and Peter Paret (Princeton University Press, 1976).
2 Christopher Clark, *The Sleepwalkers: How Europe Went to War in 1914* (London: Penguin Books, 2012).
3 Mark L. Haas, *The Ideological Origins of Great Power Politics, 1789–1989* (Ithaca, NY: Cornell University Press, 2005).

conservatism, liberalism and socialism had roots in the nineteenth century, but fascism emerged from the political, social and cultural trauma of the First World War.[4] Its rise would be an explosive ingredient in the making of the Second World War, and its legacy would pervade the Cold War. Not dissimilar would be the communist variant of socialism, which had been hardened by its birth in the First World War in 1917 and in its Russian continuation into the murderous civil war.

When we think of the two decades before the outbreak of the Second World War in Europe, the word ideology prompts images of the vast industrial complexes of the Soviet Union's Five-Year Plans and massed marching ranks of Italian Fascist and German National Socialist paramilitaries. These regimes and Japan's ultra-nationalists sought to reshape their nations and remake the world according to expansionist visions of race and nation that included the destruction and subjugation of enemy states and peoples.[5] Even if the policy elites of the aggressors could not agree on a single revisionist international order, nor thought it essential to do so, leaders in Tokyo, Rome and Berlin found common cause in their antagonism to liberalism, socialism and communism. The friend–foe orientation that ideology provides as a framework for understanding the world and for evaluating and changing it worked both ways. The liberal democracies, France, Britain and the United States, emerged from the First World War as the victors, but their wartime unity did not survive disputes over the terms of the peace settlement, including the purpose of the most iconic of all the liberal peace projects, the League of Nations. Yet, even in the crisis years of the 1930s, when quarrels over trade, finance and foreign policy divided them, political elites in France, Britain and the United States shared an interest in upholding the status quo against the threat of the revisionists, and a common identity defined around individual liberty, anti-collectivism and market economics. The response of the liberal democratic powers to the domestic political, diplomatic and strategic challenge of German and Italian fascism and Japanese imperialism was prefigured and complicated by an antipathy to the Bolshevik revolution of 1917 and the consolidation of Stalin's dictatorship in the 1930s. After all, it was the Soviet Union in the early 1930s that led the international effort to isolate Berlin by forming the Popular Front of

---

4 Robert O. Paxton, *The Anatomy of Fascism* (London: Penguin Books, 2005); Alan Kramer, 'The First World War as Cultural Trauma', in Richard J. B. Bosworth (ed.), *The Oxford Handbook of Fascism* (Oxford University Press, 2009), pp. 32–6.
5 Eric D. Weitz, *A Century of Genocide: Utopias of Race and Nation* (Princeton University Press, 2003).

centre-left political parties across Europe, and by concluding security pacts with France and Czechoslovakia.

The Great Depression intensified the ideological conflict. The crisis of global capitalism undermined faith in parliaments, markets and international trade as the true path to modernity. Among the smaller states of Europe, for instance, the ambiguity of the relationship between liberalism and nationalism brought crisis upon crisis as the decade wore on. Outside that fringe of Europe that ran from France to Scandinavia, every continental state began to curb the freedoms of its peoples under some form of authoritarian governance. The justification was almost always 'ethnic'. Nation states, it was proclaimed, must not allow subject nationalities to flourish too mightily. In the late 1930s, the future, so it seemed, belonged to an emerging international order of dictatorships, corporatism, command economies and autarchic empires.

From 1936 onward, the spiralling arms race in Europe and Asia reinforced the growing sense of a world accelerating toward epoch-making change. According to the accepted military theory of the day, arming for total war required the mobilization of all national resources, state control of industry and regimented societies. Future war would thus be 'totalitarian war'. Anxious that building a war economy in peacetime would buy security at the price of liberty, the liberal powers resisted the totalizing trend by adopting deterrence strategies of limited armaments. With varying degrees of success, the 'totalitarian' states embraced all-out social and economic mobilization. The Soviet leadership saw the Great Depression, the rise of fascism in Europe and Asia, and the race to mobilize war economies as the 'crisis of capitalism' that Marxism-Leninism had foreseen and which would trigger the final showdown between capitalist imperialism and communism. Many liberal thinkers feared that if total war came, the whole world would quickly succumb to a totalitarian nightmare of permanent war and perpetual mobilization.[6] When it did come, and then expanded and reached the culminating point of 1941, the Western Allies and the Soviet Union adjusted their ideological outlooks to the pragmatic politics of jointly vanquishing the forces of fascism. Once that objective was accomplished, the ideological conflict resumed, but this time between the United States and the Soviet Union as the rival centres of global power.

Considering the central role of ideology in the politics of the Second World War and the legacy of Cold War it bequeathed, this volume examines

6 Joseph A. Maiolo, *Cry Havoc: How the Arms Race Drove the World to War, 1931–1941* (New York: Basic Books, 2011).

the complex and sometimes paradoxical relationship between ideology and politics in the war's origins, dynamics and consequences. The twenty-four chapters, organized here into three parts, are written by leading historians who offer readers up-to-date and thought-provoking syntheses of the latest research. In Part I, the first three chapters examine the ideologies of the combatants: the Axis powers, the Western Allies and the Soviet Union. Wars are more than a mere contest between opposing armed forces and a test of national endurance; they are also a struggle of words, ideas and values. The editors have therefore included chapters on propaganda and censorship, the means through which the combatants expressed their rival claims to justice and controlled news from the front, to sustain morale and influence international opinion. All wars come to an end, and waging war purposefully entails the formulation of war aims and a programme for post-war order.[7] Germany, Italy and Japan waged war with visions of conquest and revolution, but few fixed ideas about how to build a new international system, other than that it should be dominated by their empires.[8] For the Nazi regime, as Chapter 7 shows, waging total war also meant the radicalization of their pre-war persecution of German Jews to the industrial and bureaucratic mass murder of all European Jewry, known as the 'Final Solution'. For Churchill, Roosevelt and Stalin, negotiating the post-war peace settlement was as vital to the making of the Grand Alliance as was strategic decision-making. Despite the perceived failure of the League of Nations and collective security, their negotiations included the resurrection of institutionalized international cooperation in the form of the United Nations Organization, which was intended by Roosevelt to have at its core the wartime allies as a global directorate. For the Western powers, one condition of post-war stabilization was the reconstruction of the world monetary system and the restoration of international trade. Building a stable post-war international system and capitalism's rebirth are explored in Part I, as well as the international effort to hold individuals to account for their wartime conduct by the prosecution of war crimes. Although historians now debate how important the revelations of Nazi crimes against civilians were to the codification of human rights in post-war international law, the coinage of the term 'genocide' by the Polish refugee jurist Raphael Lemkin, to define

7 Fred C. Ikle, *Every War Must End* (2nd edn, New York: Columbia University Press, 2005).
8 Richard J. B. Bosworth, 'Visionaries of Expansion', in Thomas W. Zeiler and Daniel M. DuBois (eds.), *A Companion to World War Two* (2 vols., Oxford: Wiley-Blackwell, 2013), vol. I, pp. 77–90.

the systematic attempt by Hitler and his regime to exterminate Europe's Jews provided an important conceptual tool for understanding this distinctively twentieth-century form of state violence globally.[9]

Part II of this volume looks at politics from the perspective of pre-war and wartime diplomacy. The modern practice of diplomacy originated in the Renaissance, when the warring city states of Italy established embassies to monitor each other's courts and the resident ambassador emerged as a fixture in international relations.[10] Many historians credit the long peace of the nineteenth century to the norm of great-power cooperation established through the diplomatic practices of the Concert of Europe. The erosion of those practices is also often cited by scholars as a contributing factor to the outbreak of war in 1914.[11] Could better diplomacy have halted the breakdown of the international system in the 1930s and prevented the slide into war in Europe and Asia-Pacific? Answering this question once again underscores the importance of ideology in understanding the conflicts of the interwar years. Diplomacy can serve as a useful tool for governments that seek to resolve their disputes peacefully. Yet the First World War not only discredited the 'old diplomacy' of military alliances and secret treaties rooted in imperialism and nationalism, it also produced the political challenges of Wilson's liberalism and Lenin's Communism, both of which posited the ideological uniformity of all states as the only way to universal peace.[12] The outcome of the 1914–18 war and the impact of the Great Depression also opened up the divide between those great powers that had a stake in the existing world order – Britain, France and the United States – and those which did not – Germany, Italy, Japan and Russia. This status quo versus revisionist strategic orientation corresponded with the ideological divide in world politics. The former powers had renounced war as a means of resolving international disputes, and the latter powers regarded war as the engine of internal and external revolutions. As Japan's war in China and the European crisis escalated, bridging these divides with diplomacy was

---

9 G. Daniel Cohen, 'The Holocaust and the "Human Rights Revolution": A Reassessment', in Akira Iriye, Petra Goedde and William I. Hitchcock (eds.), *The Human Rights Revolution: An International History* (Oxford University Press, 2012), pp. 53–71; Mark Mazower, 'Violence and the State in the Twentieth Century', *American Historical Review* 107:4 (2002), 1158–78.

10 M. S. Anderson, *The Rise of Modern Diplomacy, 1450–1919* (London: Routledge, 1993).

11 Paul W. Schroeder, 'World War I as Galloping Gertie', *Journal of Modern History* 44:3 (1972), 319–45.

12 David C. Engerman, 'Ideology and the Origins of the Cold War, 1917–1962', in Melvyn P. Leffler and Odd Arne Westad (eds.), *The Cambridge History of the Cold War*, vol. I: *Origins* (3 vols., Cambridge University Press, 2010), pp. 20–43.

impossible, because the great powers did not share a common interest in upholding the existing global order and could not possibly agree a common vision for building a new one.[13]

When cannons speak, diplomats do not remain silent. In wartime, the task of diplomacy is to build alliances and to influence neutral states. Alliance diplomacy was crucial to the outcome of the Second World War in Europe and Asia. As historians have long understood, Germany, Japan and Italy were economic featherweights compared to the industrial might and human resources of the British Empire, the Soviet Union, the United States and China.[14] As Richard J. Overy has shown, so long as the Allies fought together, their victory was virtually certain. Despite decades of distrust between London, Washington and Moscow, the Grand Alliance pooled its resources and coordinated its strategies with success. By contrast, the Axis was not an alliance at all. The revisionist powers each fought their own regional wars against an overwhelming global coalition.[15]

Part II also examines the ideological paradoxes of diplomacy and strategy by examining the way in which neutrals were treated and behaved.[16] For instance, although France and Britain went to war to defend the rights of small powers, their war plans included violating the neutrality of Scandinavian states to cut Sweden's iron ore trade with Germany. As it happened, the Germans beat them to it by invading Denmark and Norway in May 1940.[17] The pretext for the Franco-British operation in Scandinavia was to help Finland fight Soviet aggression in the Winter War of 1939–40. In 1941, however, authoritarian Finland launched its own 'continuation war' alongside the Axis states against the Soviet Union. As noted earlier in the case of the Soviet Union, which signed a Non-Aggression Pact with Germany in August 1939 and later aligned itself with the capitalist powers in an anti-fascist coalition, ideological thinking does not preclude pragmatic calculation. The same practical means–ends calculations shaped Spanish policy during

---

13 Donald C. Watt, 'Diplomacy and Diplomats', in Robert Boyce and Joseph A. Maiolo (eds.), *The Origins of World War Two: The Debate Continues* (Basingstoke: Palgrave, 2004), pp. 331–41.

14 Mark Harrison (ed.), *The Economics of World War II: Six Great Powers in International Comparison* (Cambridge University Press, 2000).

15 Richard J. Overy, *Why the Allies Won* (London: Jonathan Cape, 1995).

16 Neville Wylie (ed.), *European Neutrals and Non-Belligerents* (Cambridge University Press, 2002).

17 Joseph A. Maiolo, '"To Gamble All on a Single Throw": Neville Chamberlain and the Strategy of the Phoney War', in Christopher Baxter, Michael L. Dockrill and Keith Hamilton (eds.), *Britain in Global Politics* (Basingstoke: Palgrave Macmillan, 2013), pp. 220–41.

the war. Despite an ideological affinity between General Franco's regime and the Axis powers and Vichy France, as well as a debt to Hitler and Mussolini for assistance in the civil war, Spain was not drawn into a European war fought for German purposes.

In Part III, the volume turns to the influence of states, politics and ideology on the fate of individuals as occupied and liberated peoples, collaborators and resistors, and as British and French colonial subjects. In the opening phase of the war, Axis victories in Europe and Asia, and the advance of the Red Army into Poland, the Baltic states and Karelia, brought tens of millions under the control of foreign armies. The unfolding of the harsh, punitive and genocidal occupations, especially in Eastern Europe, China and East Asia, offers an insight into what the future would have looked like had the Axis powers realized their visions of expansion. The occupation policies of the aggressors reflected their ideological objectives, and they also reflected a deeper century-long normative shift in world politics, from a focus on demarcating frontiers to managing populations. After the French Revolution and the Napoleonic Wars, the Vienna peace of 1815 supported dynastic rule over multi-ethnic, multi-confessional empires. After the Ottoman, Romanov and Habsburg Empires collapsed, the Paris Peace of 1919 endorsed national self-determination in Eastern Europe; and the peace treaty with Kemalist Turkey, the Treaty of Lausanne of 1923, sanctioned the forced deportations of a million Christians from Anatolia to Greece and 350,000 Muslims from Greece to Turkey. By affirming the principle of national self-determination and the ideal of national, ethnic and racial homogeneity within a sovereign state, post-war international relations legitimized what Eric D. Weitz has called 'population politics'.[18] In the making of the Paris Peace, the liberal variant of population politics expressed itself in the international protection of minority rights and the establishment of the League of Nations mandates to legitimize the acquisition by the victors of former Ottoman and German colonies. During the Second World War, for the aggressors, the politics of treating whole population groups, however defined, as assets to be expended or dangerous minorities requiring solutions found expression in the wartime practices of forced labour, what would later be called 'ethnic cleansing' and genocide.

Ideology also shaped the liberation-occupation policies of the Soviet Union and the Western Allies. For Stalin, the imposition by advancing armies of

---

18 Eric D. Weitz, 'From the Vienna to the Paris System: International Politics and the Entangled Histories of Human Rights, Forced Deportations, and Civilizing Missions', *American Historical Review* 113:5 (2008), 1313–43.

competing socio-economic systems on occupied territories made the Second World War distinct from earlier conflicts.[19] The Kremlin's first wartime experiment in the Sovietization of occupied states occurred in 1940, when Moscow imposed communist regimes on the Baltic states under the terms of the Molotov–Ribbentrop Pact of August 1939. British and American policy-makers framed the occupation of their Axis foes as one of liberating captive populations from the enslavement of dictatorial regimes to allow democratic politics and markets to flourish. Incompatible Western and Soviet policies clashed most tellingly in the post-war joint occupation of Germany, the breakdown of which was as much a cause as a consequence of the Cold War, but was also evident in the occupations of Italy and Japan and the partition of Korea.[20] As in international politics, Moscow, London and Washington made pragmatic choices to support irregulars fighting the Axis. In the Sino-Japanese War, Stalin sent aid to Mao Zedong's communist guerrillas and what he thought would be the more effective nationalist army of Generalissimo Chiang Kai-shek. Britain sent military aid and offered training to communist partisans in Yugoslavia, Greece and Malaya. The United States helped the communist-dominated Viet Minh to fight the Japanese. Of course, that did not mean that London and Washington wanted this military support to assist communists in power. In December 1944, for instance, British troops intervened in Greece to back the anti-communist government. In a similar fashion, the Red Army eagerly supported partisan formations behind German lines to pave the way for the advance to Berlin. However, Moscow did not offer support to the Polish Home Army, which was loyal to the Polish government-in-exile in London, because it would resist the Soviet Union's post-war domination of Poland and the radical redrawing of its frontiers westward.[21]

For the Poles, the Red Army's liberation of 1944 was no less brutal than the Soviet occupation of 1939–40. The experiences of Axis occupation varied. In Eastern Europe, the Balkans, most of China and East Asia, the Axis occupiers responded to resistance with savage repression. Where the resistance formed irregular armies that inflicted losses on the occupiers and disrupted their communications, the violence meted out to civilians in reprisals was greatest. Ideology made a difference as well. In Poland and

19 Milovan Djilas, *Conversations with Stalin* (London: Hart-Davis, 1962), p. 90.
20 Hans-Peter Schwarz, 'The Division of Germany, 1945–49', in Leffler and Westad, *The Cambridge History of the Cold War*, vol. 1, pp. 133–53.
21 Evan Mawdsley, 'Anti-German Insurgency and Allied Grand Strategy', *Journal of Strategic Studies* 31:5 (2008), 695–719.

the Soviet Union, the German invaders arrived as a master race intent not only on ruthless economic exploitation, but also on mass murder and mass deportations to change the demographics of their eastern 'living space'. Planners cheerfully talked of the death of '30 million' people in the immediate term and implied more later. Everywhere the Axis found collaborators among local peoples to act as auxiliary police and even to fight as fraternal combatants in the Waffen-SS. The Croatian Ustaša acted as a ruthless Axis proxy in Yugoslavia. In France, the collaborationist Vichy government espoused authoritarian values and sought a place in the Nazi New Order. As occupiers, the Japanese likewise employed mass violence and terror to prevent unrest, and collaborationist regimes to control the Chinese and the other conquered peoples of East Asia. In exacting moral and material support from local populations and punishing collaborators, resistance groups could be as brutal as the occupiers in their use of terror and violence. Ideological disputes, local feuds and private vendettas often resulted in fighters from different national guerrilla organizations turning their guns on each other. In Greece, the conflict between nationalists and communists escalated into a very bloody civil war. On the scale of the small local wars of collaboration, resistance, repression, reprisal and retribution, which brings into sharp focus individuals as victims, perpetrators and witnesses, Clausewitz's definition of war as purposeful political violence loses much of its clarity.

In the final three chapters, Part III examines the French and British empires and surveys the varied experiences of Islamic peoples, most of whom were under European colonial rule at the start of the European war. One way to look at the British and French empires is in the same way that pre-war planners in the metropoles did, as sources of men and raw materials to feed the imperial war machines. In this respect, the British Empire was more beneficial to Britain's war than the French Empire was to France. After France's sudden defeat in May–June 1940, its empire splintered and became the arena for a civil war between Vichy and Free France. Another way to view the empires is from the perspective of imperial peoples, who suffered starvation, mass migration, economic exploitation and repressive violence and terror from colonial security forces. There was, of course, no singular experience of the war in the empires or reactions to British and French imperial rule, which could equally inspire loyalty, stir resistance and inflict great suffering. India, for example, fielded a huge volunteer army, witnessed violent and non-violent resistance to British rule, and lost millions to famine because of the colonial regime's extraction of resources and mismanagement. From a wider perspective, a crisis of legitimacy that predated the war, but which was exposed by it, was fundamental to the end of the British and French Empires. In 1919, the Paris Peace settlement affirmed the principle of ethnic self-determination, but the peacemakers did not apply it to their colonies. The League of Nations mandate system instead recast the expansion of British and French imperial rule as an international trusteeship to elevate backward colonial populations to modernity. The hollowness of this 'civilizing mission' provoked violent insurgency, repression and organized political opposition, from Africa to the Middle East and Asia. By the outbreak of the war in Europe, political unrest and economic deprivation had rendered large parts of the British and French Empires ungovernable. Wartime mobilization, imperial defeats and the Axis occupation of colonial territories fuelled the political crisis. In victory, London and Paris would fight to rebuild their empires against the opposition of nationalist movements, but a world war fought to liberate Europeans from fascist tyranny had underscored the illegitimacy of the prolongation of French and British colonial rule.[22]

22 Martin Thomas, *Fight or Flight: Britain, France, and their Roads from Empire* (Oxford University Press, 2014).

PART I

*

IDEOLOGIES

Introduction to Part I

RICHARD J. B. BOSWORTH AND JOSEPH A. MAIOLO

It is the long-lived, leftist and populist American historian Louis ('Studs') Terkel (1912–2008) who has provided what might be agreed as the 'name brand' of the global conflict fought between 1939 and 1945. In 1984 he published *The Good War*.[1] The next year, it won the Pulitzer Prize for non-fiction. Terkel aimed to recover the reaction of 'ordinary' Americans (and only them), whether they were civilians or military, to their years of battle from 1941 to 1945. A critic might find his book 'wromantic', to deploy the *1066 and All That* term (it means mistakenly sentimental). In Terkel's mind, virtue was deeply inscribed in the American people, whatever might be thought of their passing leaders, their nation's high politics and its capitalist devotion. The title stuck.

After all, the narrowness of its American base was irrelevant when, for example, it seemed clearly to endorse the British view that they had fought a 'people's war' of sacrifice, dedication and unity, an experience that was given some permanency in the social democracy of the welfare state, pioneered by Attlee's Labour government once peace returned. Already, in 1969, Angus Calder (1942–2008) had published a book with that emblematic title.[2] It was critically acclaimed and, even if Calder himself spent quite a bit of time thereafter qualifying sentimental readings of his work,[3] it has remained the standard British interpretation of their war experience. The Second World War in the British version remains astonishingly popular in that country; no public event, royal, sportive or political, is imaginable without an evocation of it, while wartime leader, Winston Churchill (despite his manifold

---

1 S. Terkel, *The Good War: An Oral History of World War II* (New York: Pantheon, 1984).
2 Angus Calder, *The People's War: Britain, 1939–45* (London: Jonathan Cape, 1969).
3 See, notably, Angus Calder, *The Myth of the Blitz* (London: Jonathan Cape, 1991).

failings during the rest of his career before and after 1945), holds top position of great Britons throughout history in every poll on that matter.[4]

Across the European continent in Russia, the war, even if badged there as the 'Great Patriotic War', is similarly unshaken as a glorious victory and a time when the 'nation' endured its most severe test. Joseph Stalin's many other sins are frequently obscured by his 'success' in leading his country to victory, although it is also widely assumed that huge credit belongs to the peoples of (most of) the Russias. Only historians remember that Stalin's USSR was not a nation and that the Communist regime was deeply troubled by the task of finding a proper line on the nationality question.[5]

What can be the reason for this remarkable unanimity? Why is it all but universally accepted that the Second World War, unlike the First World War, the Crimean, the Napoleonic Wars, Vietnam, Iraq, Afghanistan (in either the Soviet or Western versions) and every other armed struggle throughout history, was simply a 'good war'? In a nutshell, the answer, and it is highlighted in this segment of the new Cambridge University Press history, is ideology. Elite and popular opinion in the USA, UK and ex-USSR[6] is still sure that their wartime enemies, Adolf Hitler and Nazism, were wicked beyond doubt and redemption. Consensus agrees that, had Germany not been defeated, civilization by any definition would have been destroyed. In most reckonings, the Nazis were fundamentalists in the absolute literal meaning of that word, bent on genocide, certainly of the Jews, very probably of much of the population to their East, and perhaps of that of the Americas, since their ambitions were both total and global.[7] Nothing could appease them or alter the fact that they were hell-bent on war and devastation. As Ian Kershaw concluded in his magisterial biography of the Führer, Hitler was 'mad';[8] his violence, therefore, could only be met and destroyed by violence and war.

---

4 For approving description, see Mark Connelly, *We Can Take It! Britain and the Memory of the Second World War* (Harlow: Pearson Longman, 2004).
5 See, notably, Terry Martin, *The Affirmative Action Empire: Nations and Nationalism in the Soviet Union, 1923–1939* (New York: Cornell University Press, 2001); Ronald Grigor Suny and Terry Martin, *A State of Nations: Empire and Nation-Building in the Age of Lenin and Stalin* (Oxford University Press, 2001).
6 For the war myth and the post-1945 'nation', see Yitzhak M. Brudny, *Reinventing Russia: Russian Nationalism and the Soviet State, 1953–1991* (Cambridge, Mass.: Harvard University Press, 1998). Cf. Nina Tumarkin, *The Living and the Dead: The Rise and Fall of the Cult of World War II in Russia* (New York: Basic Books, 1994).
7 On this last matter, see Adam Tooze, *Wages of Destruction: The Making and Breaking of the Nazi Economy* (London: Allen Lane, 2006).
8 Ian Kershaw, *Hitler, 1889–1936: Hubris* (London: Allen Lane, 1998); *Hitler, 1936–1945: Nemesis* (London: Allen Lane, 2000).

It is indeed a decisive conclusion, one highly unusual for sceptical, relativist and argumentative historians to approve. Should it be amended? After all, in reality, Germany was not the only enemy of the 'United Nations', as they came to be called somewhat inaccurately, given that Britain was a fading empire, the USA a rising one, and the USSR a confused tyranny. Historiography remains critical of Fascist Italy and of that Japan which sought a Greater East Asian Co-Prosperity Sphere, but neither is viewed as approaching Nazism in a totality of evil. Yet of Germany's lesser friends and allies, quite a number have found historical resuscitation since the collapse of the Soviet Union. Slovakia and Croatia have become established nation states, as have the Baltic republics, Kosovo and Ukraine, quite a few of whose leaders did not utterly reject German support before and after 1939. Francoism may have collapsed in Spain with remarkable rapidity after the dictator's death in 1975, yet the current Spanish government does not wholly renounce those policies which sent 'volunteers' off to fight alongside Germans on the Eastern Front. In Italy, Silvio Berlusconi pronounced that Mussolini never killed anyone. In Japan, a patriotic reading of the war survives at the Yasukuni Shrine in Tokyo and lingers in many Japanese minds. Moreover, in most countries that experienced Nazi, Fascist or Japanese occupation, ex-collaborators returned swiftly to politics after 1945; in Asia, many of them immediately after 1945. In other words, a number of the little Second World Wars have in their time been revised in meaning, and current historiography no longer agrees that they can be summarily read as a conflict between good and bad.

As the chapters in this part of the Cambridge University Press history display, historical research may have amplified our knowledge of the ideological basis of the conflict and to some extent frayed the virtue of the wartime stances of the decidedly disunited nations in their campaigns across the globe. Yet the big picture has not altered: Nazism remains the common enemy of humankind, blessedly defeated in battle.

Robert Gerwarth leads off with a restatement of what held Germany, Italy and Japan together: anti-communism, anti-liberalism, authoritarian governance somehow defined, a leadership cult, a variety of populism, and an expansionism that saw no need to be checked in its brutality and murder. Yet, he explains, 'mutual irritations', whether practical or reflecting ideological incomprehension and incompatibility, undermined the Tripartite Alliance 'from its inception'. In the Nazi-led coalition, he adds, 'a coherent transnational belief system', like Marxism or even liberal democracy, failed to emerge. Indeed, Gerwarth concludes, the 'thinness' of the alliance's ideological base was a major explanation of why the warmongering alliance went down to utter defeat.

Talbot Imlay and Silvio Pons explore the belief systems of the anti-Nazi alliance, with a focus on Britain, the United States and France on the one hand, and the USSR on the other. Here is scarcely a simple story of mutually agreed goodness. As Imlay immediately reminds us, in any case, the 'national ideologies' in the liberal democratic combatant states were the 'subject of frequent and sometimes fierce dispute, not only within each country, but also between countries'. Governments, with at least a formal commitment to reflect the views of their peoples, had to ask and keep answering the 'vital question. . .: what are we fighting for?' This demand inevitably engaged with time: the Allies had to explain away how they had got into the war and provide some sort of sketch of a happier, post-war future, when war could be overcome or avoided. The practical effect of this situation was paradoxical. The British Empire (and the French), with Churchill the very definition of a recalcitrant and 'Eurocentric' imperialist, hoped to avoid too much international revisionism, but did accept more readily government-sponsored welfare at home. F. D. Roosevelt and the American leadership had no nostalgia for European-style empires, but their country had few reasons to doubt that the post-New Deal version of capitalism needed much re-tooling. The Atlantic Charter was the key document expressing the Alliance's war aims, but the UK and the USA read the Charter's meaning differently. Nazism, in sum, certainly was bad. Deciding precisely what might be good remained a contested matter.

Such debate was naturally enough widened when Stalin's USSR was added to the equation. Here was a state that, since the imposition of Communist rule, had been committed to its own 'revolutionary' transnationalism, however much damaged in August 1939 by the cynical realpolitik of the Molotov–Ribbentrop Pact. Nonetheless, once the Germans launched Operation BARBAROSSA and ensured thereafter that the war's epicentre, the arena where the greatest number (military and civilian) died, lay in the East, Stalinist war acquired a virtue and sometimes even a glamour that would have been hard to predict in 1940. There were contradictions. As Silvio Pons explains, the Stalinist regime was, if anything, more ruthlessly realistic in shoring up and then expanding the security zone of its empire than was Churchill's UK. In 1945, the USSR stood victorious. Yet the communists of Yugoslavia and China had fought (and in the latter case were still fighting) wars that differed from the Stalin version.

Furthermore, the gap between 'Soviet state interests' (sometimes reduced to little more than Russian nationalism) and 'world policy' already existed and would grow more yawning as the USSR tried, with declining success, to proclaim that it had been the only real repository of good in the war.

After the three general chapters, the focus of our other authors switches to the issue of how the rival ideologies in conflict could be marshalled in wartime. Jo Fox and Steven Casey examine propaganda, or the selling of the war. Fox focuses mostly on governments, especially in the liberal democracies, sometimes on other agencies, in their attempts to explain or command the peoples who had to fight it. In her view, the latter states made praiseworthy efforts to render their propaganda 'fit for democracy', and in so doing bested their rivals, be they on the Nazi-Fascist side or in the USSR. Yet, she adds, 'information' was 'controlled' also on this side of the front, and its recipients were perfectly capable of recognizing that 'truth' was the first casualty of war. Such sensible scepticism, none-theless, did not mean that the wartime campaigns did not provide 'key narratives' that 'shaped the subsequent representations' of the war, at least among the victors. 'Propaganda' lingered beyond its immediate setting.

Casey, by contrast, reviews what has come to be called 'embedded' journalism, exploring the relationship between newspapermen and women at or near the front and the military (as well as with government, notably in the Axis states, which had policed reporting severely also in peacetime). Naturally, he traces much squabbling between individual correspondents and those who sought to direct or exploit them (Montgomery and MacArthur were ever alert to self-boosting). Yet in the final analysis, journalists on all sides did not quarrel with their nations' war efforts. 'Censorship, in short, worked', Casey concludes emphatically.

Patricia Clavin returns the volume to issues sketched in the chapters on the war aims of the combatant states, in her case with the special emphasis being the drive to some form of international organization. After 1945, it was to be formalized into the United Nations and its associated bodies. Although the Nazis, the USSR and various naturally transnational bodies, the Vatican being one, flirted with their own forms of international-ism, in practice, the war somewhat ironically maintained and even expanded the situation that had existed during the interwar period. Then, the League of Nations (however Eurocentric and imperial) was liberal in its theory and practice, still prosecuting the battles of 1918–19 between

Wilson and Lenin,[9] and those with Hitler to come. Now, as Clavin argues, 'the years between 1939 and 1945 marked the most energetic period of global institution building in modern history'. The artificers of this project were certainly not the people, nor even necessarily their leaders, but rather a group of bureaucrats and experts, many with experience in the League. Continuities were as evident as was change, and the United Nations, with its offices in New York and so at the epicentre of American liberal capitalism, faced a future that had scarcely been given cut-glass certainty by the defeat of Nazi fascism.

In the final two chapters of this part of the Cambridge history, Jürgen Matthäus illuminates the detail of the Nazi genocides, and then Donald Bloxham and Jonathan Waterlow assay the efforts after 1945 to apply legal process to the perpetrators. For Matthäus, quite a few Nazi designs in combating 'Judeo-Bolshevism' 'dovetailed with traditional goals' favoured by much of the German right. Neither racism nor its marriage with (pseudo-) science in eugenics nor obsessive anti-communism was unknown in other societies, including those that would fight Nazi fascism. Yet only for the Nazis was war the ideal opportunity to extend and cement what was in any case, already by 1939, a growing radicalization of their ideas and practice. Once engaged in battle, the German regime became ever more fundamentalist, moving viciously to achieve the 'Final Solution' and dreaming of the killing of 30 to 50 million Slavs. Its limitless aim was 'the physical elimination of millions of people deemed "harmful influences" or "useless eaters", on a historically unprecedented scale' and could not be appeased except by complete military conquest. In its commitment to murder, Hitler's Germany indeed had a total war aim.

Liberal (and Soviet) attempts to prosecute those killers who, unlike Hitler, did not die before the war's end, were, by contrast, messy and incomplete. Such a situation was perhaps natural in the practice of ideologies that retained enough humility not to be total, even if, as Bloxham and Waterlow report, 'the number of trials and convictions under Soviet courts was far greater than in the West', given that law 'was ever an instrument of the Revolution' and that the war had reached its maximum harshness on the Eastern Front. In any case, the war over, peacetime politics resumed. Politicians on both sides of the Cold War had to reckon with what they discerned might be the future, as well as what their peoples believed to

9 For the classic statement, see Arno J. Mayer, *Wilson vs Lenin: Political Origins of the New Diplomacy* (New York: World Publishing Company, 1959).

matter in the recent past. Already, history books rather than courts were becoming the key repository of vivid debates about the Second World Wars in their full global extent. Despite, since the 1990s, 'the end of history', the withering away of communism, and the achievement of global neoliberal hegemony, such intellectual (and political) disputation is not yet stilled. But, in almost every sense, the ideology of Nazism is dead and buried. Only lunatics regret this prime result of the Second World War.

I

The Axis

Germany, Japan and Italy on the road to war

ROBERT GERWARTH

In a famous speech in Milan's cathedral square in November 1936, the leader of Fascist Italy, Benito Mussolini, used a metaphor first invented by Hungary's former Prime Minister, Gyula Gömbös, to describe the newly intensified German-Italian relations: an 'axis' had been forged between Berlin and Rome, he insisted, with a reference to the Treaty of Friendship signed between the two powers on 25 October 1936, 'around which all those European states which are animated by a desire for collaboration and peace can revolve'.[1]

In Italian and German propaganda, the 'axis' was celebrated as the joining of forces between two long suppressed but now re-emerging empires, with shared histories and superior cultures, as well as common foes who sought to prevent them from assuming their rightful place among the world's great powers. For the West, the axis promised anything but 'peace'. Instead, it raised the spectre of a combined threat to European collective security by two expansionist powers under the leadership of dangerous dictators.[2]

The threat became global when, within weeks of the formation of the Axis, Hitler entered into a further pact with Japan that was soon to be known as the Anti-Comintern Pact. Despite Hitler's racial prejudices against the Japanese as an Asian people allegedly incapable of 'creating culture', he viewed the country as having similar geopolitical (and predominantly anti-Soviet) interests. On 27 November 1936, Hitler formally approved the

I am grateful to Sebastian Conrad, Gustavo Corni and the editors of this volume for the constructive criticism they provided on an earlier draft of this chapter.

1 Mussolini, as quoted in Elizabeth Wiskemann, *The Rome–Berlin Axis: A History of the Relations between Hitler and Mussolini* (New York: Oxford University Press, 1949), p. 68. See, too, Jens Petersen, *Hitler-Mussolini: Die Entstehung der Achse Berlin-Rom 1933–1936* (Tübingen: Niemeyer, 1973), p. 60.
2 Ian Kershaw, *Hitler, 1936–1945: Nemesis* (London: Allen Lane, 2000), p. 26.

Anti-Comintern Pact, which Italy joined a year later. The pact's main provision – recorded in a secret protocol – was that neither of the signatories would assist the Soviet Union in any way in the event of it attacking either Germany or Japan.[3] As Ian Kershaw has noted, the pact was more important for its symbolism than for its actual provisions. The full military alliance that was to confront the Western powers (and the Soviet Union) in the Second World War was yet to be formalized through the 'Pact of Steel' of May 1939 between Germany and Italy, and the Tripartite Pact of September 1940 (subsequently joined by Hungary, Romania and Slovakia in November 1940 and Bulgaria in March 1941). Yet it was the Anti-Comintern Pact of 1936–37 that first sent a very clear and alarming message to the rest of the great powers: the most staunchly revisionist, militaristic and expansionist powers in the world had found their way to each other.[4]

Such an alliance would have been difficult to predict when Hitler first came to power in Germany in 1933. For much of the early 1930s, Mussolini and his foreign policy advisors deeply distrusted Hitler's geopolitical ambitions, notably his unconcealed aim to incorporate the German-Austrian rump state created by the Treaty of St Germain into the Greater German Reich. More worryingly, the Duce suspected that Hitler's ambitions to swallow up all ethnic German minorities currently living under foreign rule would not stop at Italy's borders, which contained the predominantly German-speaking population of Alto Adige / South Tyrol.[5] Bilateral relations between the two countries only improved in the mid-1930s, largely due to Hitler's support for Italy's invasion of Ethiopia and subsequent cooperation during the Spanish Civil War.[6]

German-Japanese relations in the first years of the Third Reich were also anything but straightforward. Traditionally, Germany's (and indeed Italy's) sympathies and economic interests lay in China, a source of indispensable raw materials for armaments production. For that reason alone, an alliance with Japan was vigorously opposed by influential Nazis such as Hermann Göring, and powerful industrialists such as the armaments magnate Gustav Krupp von Bohlen und Halbach, who rightly feared that

---

3 Ibid., p. 27.
4 Ibid.; Mario Toscano, *The Origins of the Pact of Steel* (Baltimore, Md.: Johns Hopkins University Press, 1967).
5 R. J. B. Bosworth, *Mussolini* (London: Arnold, 2002), pp. 264ff.
6 Angelo Del Boca, *The Ethiopian War, 1935–1941* (University of Chicago Press, 1969); David Nicolle, *The Italian Invasion of Abyssinia, 1935–1936* (Westminster, Md.: Osprey, 1997).

any rapprochement with Japan would drive China into the camp of the Western Allies.[7]

For much of the 1930s, the Japanese government and the country's military elites had not been wholeheartedly supportive of an alliance with Berlin either, largely because it was feared that an understanding with Hitler would alienate Japan's traditional Western ally, Britain. The primary goal of any rapprochement with Hitler was to weaken German links with China and to gain a potential ally against the Soviet Union.[8] Even after a meeting between the Japanese diplomat Oshima Hiroshi and Joachim von Ribbentrop in Berlin in 1935, it remained unclear what a potential agreement between the two powers might entail. While some politicians in Tokyo sought to limit the alliance to an anti-Soviet pact, there were also increasingly influential circles – notably the so called reform bureaucrats and intellectuals of the Showa Research Association – that were pushing for a more inclusive alliance with Hitler. Led by such individuals as Shiratori Toshio, the Japanese ambassador to Rome until late 1939, the pro-Axis camp favoured a full alliance with Germany and Italy that would be directed against the Soviet Union on the one hand, and against Britain, France and the United States on the other.[9]

Yet even after the signing of the Anti-Comintern Pact, the alliance was anything but frictionless. Throughout the Second World War, the Axis remained a far less coherent alliance than that formed by Britain and France (and subsequently joined by the United States). To be sure, the beginning of the Japanese war in China in July 1937 convinced Prime Minister Konoe Fumimaro that his country needed closer cooperation with other revisionist powers, and that it was in Japan's interest to intensify relations with Italy and Germany. But neither before nor after 1939/41 did Japan, Germany and Italy produce a concerted plan of action to challenge the liberal world order that had been created in Paris in 1919 (and which all three states were eager to revise in their favour). There were no concrete agreements about global war aims or even functioning mechanisms of coordinating the war effort against the Grand Alliance.[10]

7 Bernd Martin, 'Die deutsch-japanischen Beziehungen während des Dritten Reiches', in Manfred Funke (ed.), *Hitler, Deutschland und die Mächte: Materialien zur Aussenpolitik des Dritten Reiches* (Düsseldorf: Droste, 1976), pp. 454–70.

8 Gerhard L. Weinberg, *A World at Arms: A Global History of World War II* (2nd edn, Cambridge University Press, 2005), p. 31; John Fox, *Germany and the Far Eastern Crisis, 1931–1938: A Study in Diplomacy and Ideology* (Oxford: Clarendon University Press, 1982), pp. 175–6; Theo Sommer, *Deutschland und Japan zwischen den Mächten 1935–1940. Vom Antikominternpakt zum Dreimächtepakt* (Tübingen: Mohr, 1962), pp. 21–2.

9 Weinberg, *A World at Arms*, p. 83.

10 Jürgen Förster, 'Die Wehrmacht und die Probleme der Koalitionskriegsführung', in Lutz Klinkhammer, Amedeo Osti Guerrazzi and Thomas Schlemmer (eds.), *Die 'Achse'*

Indeed, mutual irritations undermined the Axis from its inception. In 1939, for example, Hitler had anticipated that when he attacked Poland, Italy would fulfil its obligations under the terms of the Pact of Steel. However, while Mussolini was happy to use the international distraction caused by the German-Polish war as an opportunity to occupy Albania, the Duce felt unprepared for a more general war with the West, which Berlin was clearly willing to risk.[11]

Japan, meanwhile, was shocked by the proclamation of the Hitler–Stalin Pact that preceded the German attack on Poland, and which looked to them like a violation of the Japanese-German Anti-Comintern Pact at a time when Tokyo was still engaged in active hostilities with the Soviet Union. Caught by surprise, the Japanese government concluded an armistice with Moscow that came into effect on 15 September. The Japanese reluctance to open up a second major front on the Soviet Union's eastern border in 1942, in turn, put Hitler under serious pressure, as the Wehrmacht was now facing a numerically far superior enemy, whose attention was not diverted by a Japanese offensive on the Soviet Union's eastern borders.

Against this background of continuing friction and half-hearted coordination between the principal Axis powers, this chapter will discuss what it was that actually held the 'axis' together. Was it an alliance simply based on common geopolitical interests and common enemies? Or was there such a thing as an 'Axis ideology', a set of core beliefs shared by the three major Axis powers, Germany, Italy and Japan? The answer to the latter question is likely to be 'no', if by 'Axis ideology' we mean a coherent transnational belief system similar to that offered by Marxism-Leninism, or even a shared minimum consensus about the intrinsic superiority of a certain political system over that offered by the West. After all, there existed considerable differences between the fascist regimes in Berlin and Rome, while wartime Japan can only be described as 'fascist' if we stretch the definition of that ideology to the point of meaninglessness.[12] Unlike Germany and Italy, Japan

im Krieg. Politik, Ideologie und Kriegführung 1939–1945 (Paderborn: Schöningh Verlag, 2010), pp. 108–21.
11 Weinberg, A World at Arms, p. 73.
12 Stanley Payne, A History of Fascism, 1914–1945 (Madison: University of Wisconsin Press, 1995), pp. 328–37; Rikki Kersten, 'Japan', in R. J. B. Bosworth (ed.), The Oxford Handbook of Fascism (Oxford University Press, 2009), pp. 526–44; Hans Martin Krämer, 'Faschismus in Japan. Anmerkungen zu einem für den internationalen Vergleich tauglichen Faschismusbegriff', Sozial.Geschichte 20 (2005), 6–32.

24

lacked the essential fascist attribute of a single mass-based party, and no comparable attempts to those in Italy and Germany were made to violently 'cleanse' the body politic from broadly defined internal enemies.[13]

Nonetheless, it is possible to identify a number of comparable features between the Axis powers. Most importantly, perhaps, there was a common ideological rejection of the liberal political order on the one hand and Soviet-style Bolshevism on the other, as well as an attempt to provide authoritarian alternatives to that liberal order. In addition, all three countries harboured bitter antagonism toward 'the West' for the imposition of the 1919 peace treaties, which they considered detrimental to their geopolitical ambitions (or, in the case of Germany, outright criminal), notably their intention to establish imperial spheres of influence outside their existing borders, thereby achieving economic autarchy: Japan's violent expansion into China and Southeast Asia and Hitler's ambitions to carve out a *Lebensraum* in the vast space between the 1919 eastern German borders and the Urals had their functional equivalents in Mussolini's ambitious plans for Italian dominance over northern Africa and the Mediterranean. The Fascist dream of an empire for a newly reinvigorated nation, the conquest of the *spazio vitale*, was Italy's equivalent of Hitler's fantastic plans for 'living space' in the East, even if the German variant proved much more deadly during the war itself.[14] Racism was at the core of all three Axis powers' expansionism and empire-building, as it legitimized the conquest of territories inhabited by 'inferior' races – be they Slavs, Chinese or apparently lesser Mediterranean (Greek) and African peoples – and the killing or rape of enemy civilians at will. Despite the rhetoric about its ambition to create a pan-Asian 'sphere of co-prosperity', the Japanese regime allowed its soldiers to massacre Korean and Chinese civilians en masse. And Mussolini adopted a policy of liquidating large sections of Ethiopia's intelligentsia as a means of 'pacifying' the newly conquered territory. Biological racism certainly went furthest in Germany, where wartime anti-Semitism posed a unique case in its ambition to murder each

---

13 Payne, *Fascism*, pp. 333–6.
14 MacGregor Knox, *Common Destiny: Dictatorship, Foreign Policy, and War in Fascist Italy and Nazi Germany* (Cambridge University Press, 2000); Davide Rodogno, *Fascism's European Empire: Italian Occupation During the Second World War* (Cambridge University Press, 2008); Gustavo Corni, 'Impero e spazio vitale nella visione e nella prassi delle dittature (1919–1945)', *Ricerche di Storia Politica* 3 (2006), 345–57; Aristotle Kallis, *Fascist Ideology: Territory and Expansionism in Italy and Germany, 1922–1945* (London: Routledge, 2000).

and every Jew in Nazi-occupied Europe, but Hitler's genocidal ambitions and policies should not distract from the murderous racism that drove policies in wartime Japan or Fascist Italy.[15]

The historian Masao Maruyama, perhaps the most important advocate of the idea that Japan experienced 'fascism from above', has identified several additional features that wartime Japan shared with Fascist Italy and Nazi Germany, notably a positive view of foreign expansion, the glorification of the military, and the firm belief that modernity had obscured a mythical 'national essence' (in Japanese, *kokutai*) that could be revived through war.[16] It is certainly true that all three regimes sought to counter the challenges of modernity (and the ills of modern capitalism in particular) with the promise of a national rebirth that would strengthen the mythic historical core of the nation. War was endorsed by the political elites as a means to regenerate the respective 'warrior nations'.

One important common feature that should be added to Maruyama's list is the centrality of charismatic leadership, whether hereditary or through popular support, in all three countries. Although the Führer, the Duce and Emperor Hirohito certainly represented three different types of autocratic leaders – two dependent on 'success' and popular support to legitimize their rule, one consecrated by divine will – and three very different personalities, their role as leaders was crucial for the outbreak and course of the Second World War.

As in Nazi Germany, the Duce and the Emperor bridged social, cultural, generational and regional differences to help bind the nation together. Hitler's ability to draw on cross-sectional support from the German people, well beyond the point where it had become clear that the Nazis were losing the war, is well documented by historians. And at least until the war took a bad turn for Italy, Mussolini, too, seemed to be a sacrosanct figure, however much his subordinates were reviled. Hirohito was unique in the sense that he remained beyond criticism even after the military defeat of 1945, when his subordinates accepted responsibility for the war and Japanese atrocities (and were promptly executed by the Allies), while Hirohito remained on

---

15 Paul Brooker, *The Faces of Fraternalism: Nazi Germany, Fascist Italy, and Imperial Japan* (Oxford University Press, 1991). On Japanese racism (and even anti-Semitism), see John Dower, *War Without Mercy: Race and Power in the Pacific War* (New York: Pantheon Books, 1986); Isaiah Ben-Dasan, *The Japanese and the Jews* (New York: Weatherhill, 1972).

16 On Maruyama and his arguments, see Kersten, 'Japan'; Sebastian Conrad, *Auf der Suche nach der verlorenen Nation* (Göttingen: Vandenhoeck & Ruprecht, 1999), pp. 165–9.

the throne until the mid-1980s. Unlike the post-Great War leadership cults around Hitler and Mussolini, the emperor-based ideology of wartime Japan dated back to the 1889 Meiji Constitution, which constituted an attempt to unite the nation in response to the 'Western challenge' and positioned the emperor at the apex of spiritual and legal authority in Japan, while at the same time leaving space for political actors to rule without reigning. The 'Emperor System', as described in the ideological tract *Kokutai no Hongi* (Cardinal Principles of National Polity), was built around several core principles: the divine origins of the imperial family; the essential racial and spiritual homogeneity of the Japanese; the notion of the emperor as father of the nation; and the mythical idea of a continuous line of emperors from ancient times.[17] While Hitler and Mussolini depended on 'success' to sustain their charismatic leaderships, Hirohito did not.

But this is not the only reason why the argument of structural similarities between the three regimes should not be pushed too far. Neither Hirohito nor his wartime Prime Minister, General Tojo, was a comparable dictator to Hitler or Mussolini, and their rule is better described as conservatively authoritarian rather than fascist, even if ultra-nationalism motivated the decision of all three regimes to go to war. Once they embarked on the path to total war, Japan became a military dictatorship, while the power in Nazi Germany and Fascist Italy always remained firmly in the hands of the civilian dictators.

The key question to be addressed by this chapter, then, is how the three rather different societies and regimes arrived at a historical juncture where a military alliance against the Soviet Union and 'the West' was considered desirable and put into practice. In order to answer that question, this chapter will place less emphasis on the war after 1941 than on the evolution of historical paths that temporarily converged in 1941. Any such structural analysis has to go back as far as the Paris Peace Conference, which opened in December 1918 and ended in the summer of 1919. Here, the victorious powers of the Great War aimed to produce a lasting settlement of the international order. Having fought a 'war to end all wars', however, the peacemakers created more problems than they solved.[18]

The key issue, of course, was Germany, and how to prevent it from becoming a threat to European collective security again. In that respect,

---

17 Kersten, 'Japan', p. 531.
18 Margaret MacMillan, *Peacemakers: The Paris Conference of 1919 and its Attempt to End War* (London: J. Murray, 2001).

the Treaty of Versailles turned out to be a complete failure. There was not a single party in Germany, either right or left, that did not reject the main provisions of the treaty. Revision of the settlement remained a powerful cause in German politics, and one of the fatal weaknesses of the Versailles Treaty was that it had been too harsh to be accepted by anyone in Germany, but not harsh enough to prevent the Reich from rising again.[19]

Revisionism was not only an issue in Germany. The successor states of the collapsed Habsburg and Hohenzollern Empires, created on the basis of Wilson's promise of national self-determination, were anything but ethnically homogeneous. Inevitably, this fed irredentism. Successor states sought expansion to include lands inhabited by 'exiled' ethnic minorities across Central and Eastern Europe. For Hitler and the Nazis, the 'return' of these minorities under German rule was imperative and laid the groundwork for the imperial project that Nazi Germany embarked on during the Second World War.[20] But Germany was not alone in this. Hungary – Germany's past and future wartime ally – lost 75 per cent of its pre-war territory in the Trianon settlement, and almost 3 million Hungarians were forced to live under Romanian, Czech and Yugoslav rule. Bulgaria, which had fought alongside Germany in the Great War, suffered a similar fate: a million ethnic Bulgarians lived under foreign rule after 1919. Austria, the German-speaking heartland of the Habsburg Empire, became a small republic. Its imperial territories were handed over by the Allies to the successor states of Poland, Czechoslovakia and Yugoslavia.

In contrast to Germany and the other Central Powers of the First World War, Italy and Japan were nominally victors of the Great War. But neither Rome nor Tokyo was entirely satisfied with the results of Paris. The Empire of Japan had been contemplating its peace aims for some time. As early as September 1915, the Japanese established the *Kowa Junbi Iinkai* (Peace Preparation Commission) to coordinate planning among the military, the Cabinet and the Diet.[21] The Japanese delegates to an inter-allied conference

---

19 On Versailles and its impact, see Manfred F. Boemeke, Gerald D. Feldman and Elisabeth Gläser (eds.), *The Treaty of Versailles: A Reassessment after 75 Years* (New York: Cambridge University Press, 1998). See, too, Jörg Duppler and Gerhard P. Gross (eds.), *Kriegsende 1918: Ereignis, Wirkung, Nachwirkung* (Munich: Oldenbourg, 1999).
20 See Mark Mazower, *Hitler's Empire: How the Nazis Ruled Europe* (New York and London: Penguin Press, 2008).
21 See Thomas W. Burkman, *Japan and the League of Nations: Empire and World Order* (Honolulu: University of Hawaii Press, 2008), pp. 30–1.

in late 1917 received instructions for peace aims that prefigured more or less exactly what Japan would obtain from the Paris Peace Conference: despite its minimal involvement in actual fighting, Tokyo secured the formerly German-governed Shandong and control over the German Pacific islands north of the equator. Far less successful, however, was Japan's proposal for the inclusion of a 'racial equality' clause in the Covenant of the League of Nations, as it felt itself to be the victim of racial discrimination. Strident opposition from the US government (concerned about Japanese immigration to California) and the British Dominions (notably from the Australians, fixated on maintaining Australia as a 'White' dominion) meant that Tokyo was left deeply frustrated and offended.[22]

The Italian government felt that it was left even worse off. Italy had entered the Great War against Germany and Austria-Hungary in 1915 and paid a high price for doing so: over 600,000 men were killed and many Italians had high expectations for compensation once the Central Powers had been defeated in 1918. In the peace treaty, some territory was won from Austria, most notably the partly German-speaking region of South Tyrol/ Alto Adige, but nationalists were outraged by what the war poet Gabriele d'Annunzio called a 'mutilated victory' that prevented the country from taking control over 'historically Italian' territories in the Adriatic, now handed over to the new Kingdom of Serbs, Croats and Slovenes.[23]

None of this augured well for the future. While Britain and France absorbed new territories into their respective empires (under mandates from the League), including the captured German colonies in Africa, and the formerly Ottoman territories in the Middle East (Syria, Lebanon, Jordan, Palestine and Iraq), Italy and Japan felt that they had been short-changed.

The immediate post-war period was important for the future formation of the Axis in yet another sense. The Great War had opened the floodgates of social revolution, most notably in Russia, where an extraordinarily violent civil war cost more than 3 million lives; but also in Germany, Austria and Hungary, where monarchies were toppled and replaced with fragile democratic states. The Russian Revolution was a key event, both as a

22 Shimazu Naoko, *Japan, Race and Equality: The Racial Equality Proposal of 1919* (London: Routledge, 1998), esp. ch. 5, 'Australia Overwhelms the British Empire Delegation', pp. 117–36.

23 Oliver Janz, 'Nationalismus im Ersten Weltkrieg. Deutschland und Italien im Vergleich', in Oliver Janz, Pierangelo Schiera and Hannes Siegrist (eds.), *Zentralismus und Föderalismus im 19. und 20. Jahrhundert. Deutschland und Italien im Vergleich* (Berlin: Duncker & Humblot, 2000), pp. 163–84; Mark Thompson, *The White War: Life and Death on the Italian Front, 1915–1919* (London: Faber & Faber, 2008).

game-changer in international politics now confronted with the first Bolshevik regime openly hostile to Western liberal democracy and capitalism, and as a fantasy that mobilized anti-revolutionary forces well beyond those countries where a triumph of Bolshevism was probable.[24]

In Germany and Italy, the successful consolidation of power by a determined revolutionary minority of Bolsheviks in Russia quickly injected a powerful new energy into politics and triggered the emergence of determined counter-revolutionary forces, for whom the violent repression of revolution, and more especially of revolutionaries, constituted their overriding goal. Not dissimilar to the situation in the late eighteenth century, when Europe's horrified ruling elites feared a Jacobin 'apocalyptic' war, many Europeans after 1917 suspected that Bolshevism would spread to 'infect' the rest of the old world, prompting violent mobilization and action against the perceived menace. Fear of 'Russian conditions' resulted in a right-wing counter-mobilization that bred charismatic leaders such as Mussolini and Hitler.[25]

During Italy's so-called *biennio rosso* (the 'Two Red Years' of 1919 and 1920), strikes, factory and land occupations were common, while clashes with government forces led to more than 200 deaths. In the general elections of 1919, the socialists made major gains and the middle classes became increasingly worried about the possibility of a communist takeover and the inability of the liberal post-war Italian state to prevent it.[26] This was the context in which Fascism became a mass movement in Italy. In March 1919, Mussolini, a former socialist, founded the Italian Fascist movement, *Fascio di Combattimento*, which programmatically promoted a combination of nationalism, anti-socialism and anticlericalism, and which initially drew most heavily on the support of war veterans, but quickly attracted others as well.[27]

---

24 Robert Gerwarth and John Horne, 'Bolshevism as Fantasy: Fear of Revolution and Counter-Revolutionary Violence, 1917–1923', in Gerwarth and Horne (eds.), *War in Peace: Paramilitary Violence after the Great War* (Oxford University Press, 2012), pp. 40–51. On Italy, see Emilio Gentile, 'Paramilitary Violence in Italy: The Rationale of Fascism and the Origins of Totalitarianism', in ibid., pp. 85–106.

25 Gerwarth and Horne, 'Bolshevism as Fantasy'.

26 See Douglas Forsyth, *The Crisis of Liberal Italy: Monetary and Financial Policy, 1914–1922* (Cambridge University Press, 1993).

27 Several very good general and local studies have been published on this. See, among others, MacGregor Knox, *To the Threshold of Power, 1922/33: Origins and Dynamics of Fascist and National Socialist Dictatorships* (2 vols., Cambridge University Press, 2007), vol. 1; Adrian Lyttelton, *The Seizure of Power: Fascism in Italy, 1919–1929* (London: Weidenfeld & Nicolson, 1973); Frank M. Snowden, *The Fascist Revolution in Tuscany, 1919–1922* (Cambridge University Press, 1989); on paramilitarism in Italy (and

In the summer of 1922, when membership in the Fascist movement reached a quarter of a million, grass-roots Fascist pressure for the capture of power intensified, and in the autumn, plans for a 'March on Rome' were laid. The liberal Italian government faced a difficult choice. If they resisted, the army and police (who had proved rather ambivalent in their attitude toward the government) might refuse to fight the Fascists. Even if the Fascists were defeated, the radical left might profit. Politicians, business and the army agreed that it would be safest to bring the Fascists into the government. On 29 October 1922, Mussolini became the first fascist Prime Minister worldwide, and his ascent to power did not go unnoticed in either Japan or Germany.[28]

Hitler, at the time still the leader of a tiny fringe group of right-wing extremists with significantly less popular appeal than the Italian Fascists, tried to emulate Mussolini's 'March on Rome' in 1923, when he attempted a putsch in Munich. The adventure ended in disaster, and Hitler was imprisoned in Landsberg where he had time to consolidate his ideological convictions and rethink his strategies for obtaining power.

By the time he came out of prison, Hitler had assembled the ideology of Nazism from disparate elements of anti-Semitism, pan-Germanism, eugenics and so-called racial hygiene, geopolitical expansionism, hostility to democracy and opposition to cultural modernism, which had been circulating in Germany for some time, but had not so far been integrated into a coherent whole. His political manifesto, *Mein Kampf*, with its emphasis on race and the quest for living space, did not, however, turn the Nazis into a mass movement. As late as the general elections of May 1928, the Nazi Party only secured 2.6 per cent of the popular vote, and a grand coalition of centrist and leftist parties, led by the Social Democrats, took office in Berlin. In October 1929, however, the Wall Street crash brought the German economy tumbling down with it. American banks withdrew the loans on which German economic recovery had been financed since 1924. German banks had to call in their loans to German businesses in response. Within little more than two years, more than one German worker in three was unemployed, and millions more were on short-term work or reduced wages.

Germany), see Sven Reichardt, *'Faschistische Kampfbünde': Gewalt und Gemeinschaft im italienischen Squadrismus und in der deutschen SA* (Cologne: Böhlau, 2002).

28 Giulia Albanese, *La Marcia su Roma* (Rome: Laterza, 2006). On the impact of Mussolini's rise on intellectual debates in Japan, see Reto Hofmann, 'The Fascist Reflection: Japan and Italy, 1919–1950' (unpublished PhD thesis, Columbia University, 2010).

The economic and political crisis in Germany undermined popular faith in democracy and benefited the radical parties of the left and right, which – without government responsibility – could make populist promises without having to put them to the test. By 1932, the Nazis were the strongest party in the Reichstag, but not strong enough to form a government of their own. It was only in January 1933, at a time when popular support for the Nazis began to wane, that Hindenburg – encouraged by conservative friends who believed they could control and instrumentalize the Nazis in a coalition government – decided to appoint Hitler to the Chancellorship. Although the Nazis had not created Germany's economic and political crisis, they proved to be its main beneficiary.

The rise to power of Mussolini and Hitler (and the basis of their dictator-ships) therefore differed substantially from the situation in Japan, largely because the political system there remained largely unchanged, and because the Emperor was neither 'appointed' nor a commoner, like the two fascist leaders whose power rested on a combination of public support and repres-sion.[29] Hitler's talent as a demagogue and orator, and his ability to sway the masses is well documented. But Mussolini, too, was a charismatic leader. When Mussolini spoke in public, he was greeted by 'fanatical scenes, delirious, mad'; of crowds 'weeping, kneeling, shrieking, arms stretched out'.[30]

At the same time, there was an extraordinary degree of surveillance imposed on real or potential dissenters in both countries – far more so in Germany and Italy than in Japan, where the political police (the *tokubetsu koto keisatsu*) operated a less systematic regime than its European counterparts.[31] The Nazis had very consciously used terror tactics from the moment of Hitler's appointment as German Chancellor, in order to frighten the opposition into acquiescence. For Hitler, the purpose of 'cleansing' the nation of potential and real 'internal enemies' was to prepare the nation for war, without having to fear a repeat of November 1918, when – in his view – a small minority of revolutionaries on the home front had betrayed the German war effort and caused the military collapse. Open SA terror on

29 For public opinion in Italy, see Christopher Duggan, *Fascist Voices: An Intimate History of Mussolini* (Oxford University Press, 2013); Paul Corner, *The Fascist Party and Popular Opinion in Mussolini's Italy* (Oxford University Press, 2012).
30 Duggan, *Fascist Voices*. See, too, Emilio Gentile, 'Mussolini's Charisma', *Modern Italy* 3 (1998), 219–35.
31 Richard H. Mitchell, *Thought Control in Prewar Japan* (Ithaca, NY: Cornell University Press, 1976).

German streets in the early months of the Third Reich ultimately gave way to more sophisticated and 'silent' means of intimidation and suppression, largely orchestrated by the SS and, more specifically, the Gestapo. Although the Gestapo was never a huge organization – wartime Berlin, for example, a city with 4.5 million inhabitants, never had more than 800 Gestapo officers and operatives, or, in other words, one agent for 5,600 Berliners[32] – it succeeded in creating a pervasive atmosphere of fear and suspicion. Making up for its relatively small size, its leaders suggested in public interviews and journalistic pieces that it was an omnipresent and omnipotent organization, rightly feared by the enemies of the state. This perception did not reflect the actual strength of the Nazis' political police force, but it nonetheless success-fully created a situation in which citizens refrained from committing 'crimes' out of fear of the Gestapo.[33]

In Italy, too, critics of Mussolini's regime were targeted long before the outbreak of war. Arrests, intimidation through violence and forced resettle-ment to remote parts of southern Italy affected outright political opponents, but also other 'troublemakers', such as homosexuals and petty criminals. The Gestapo's Italian equivalent was the political police or 'PolPol', formed in 1926. It worked closely with local police and the Organization for Vigilance and Repression of Anti-Fascism (OVRA), which monitored the correspondence of dissidents. Similar to the Gestapo, OVRA employed former political enemies who were recruited under the threat of arrest. Some of them were former socialists or communists. The result of all this was a pervasive atmosphere of suspicion and distrust; even schoolchildren were wary of expressing criticism of the regime. As in Germany, many people sent denunciations to the police when they witnessed imprudent remarks or behaviour.[34]

Japan's path toward political radicalization bore a distant resemblance to the crisis of interwar Germany and pre-Fascist Italy, but it led to different results. Here, too, interwar domestic politics were profoundly affected by the crisis of the world economy, though in different ways from Germany or Italy. Japan had experienced a major economic boom during the Great War,

32 Roger Moorhouse, *Berlin at War* (New York: Basic Books, 2010), p. 224.
33 The image of the Gestapo as an omnipresent and universally intrusive institution was challenged by Robert Gellately, 'Allwissend und allgegenwärtig? Entstehung, Funktion und Wandel des Gestapo-Mythos', in Gerhard Paul, Klaus-Michael Mallmann and Peter Steinbach (eds.), *Die Gestapo: Mythos und Realität* (Darmstadt: Wissenschaftliche Buchgesellschaft, 1995), pp. 47–70.
34 See diaries quoted in Duggan, *Fascist Voices*.

when it gained predominance in the Asian markets previously dominated by the European colonial powers. Shortly after the war, however, foreign demand for Japanese goods collapsed, creating a deep recession and causing skyrocketing prices for basic foodstuffs and violent resistance against this development (as in the 1918 Rice Riots). The 1920s in Japan, the period of the so-called Taisho democracy, thus saw the rise of strikes and labour unrest, though never at a comparable level to post-war Italy and Germany. Following a major banking crisis in the mid-1920s and the beginning of the Great Depression, unemployment rates soared to 15 per cent of the Japanese workforce. Violence – after 1918 primarily directed against external enemies (as during the Japanese intervention in the Russian Civil War or in China) – became internalized, epitomized by various assassination attempts against Japanese Prime Ministers in 1930, 1932 and 1936. In that respect, Japan shared with post-First World War Germany and Italy the fatal weakness of liberal democracy in the face of socio-economic instability and increasing domestic violence. Public debates during this period revolved around how the country could confront the challenges of capitalist modernity.[35] During the 1920s, Japanese statesmen had further been torn between different visions of the future of the empire, and whether Japan as a great power should pursue a *datsu A* ('escape Asia' or pro-Western) policy or an *ajia shugi* (pan-Asian) policy.[36] But during the slump after 1929, Japan was increasingly denied access to markets and sources of raw materials. Not dissimilar to Germany and Italy, the Japanese military faced a particular tactical problem, in that certain critical raw materials – especially oil and rubber – were not available within the Japanese sphere of influence. Instead, Japan received most of its oil from the United States and rubber from British Malaya. Japanese nationalists reacted to Japan's economic isolation with calls for a crusade against the West and the creation of a new order in world politics. Some intellectuals, such as Kita Ikki, or politicians like Nakano Seigo, advocated that Japan should follow the example of Fascist Italy in its attempt to create that new order.

Political radicalization in response to economic hardship was not specific to Japan, but a global phenomenon. The Great Depression ended the brief era of internationalist collaboration for which the treaties of Locarno and the

---

35 Harry Harootunian, *Overcome by Modernity: History, Culture, and Community in Interwar Japan* (Princeton University Press, 2000).
36 Ionoue Kiyoshi, *Geschichte Japans* (Frankfurt and New York: Campus, 1994), pp. 497–580; Shimazu, *Japan, Race and Equality*, pp. 92–5.

Kellogg–Briand Pact stand. The dire economic and social consequences of the slump undermined confidence in liberal capitalism and parliamentary democracy, and pushed populations in many economies toward political extremism. In much of East Central Europe as well as in Japan, anti-democratic parties and elites built on popular resentments by articulating demands for some kind of new order in domestic as well as international politics.[37]

Leading circles in the Japanese military called for Japanese conquests to provide Japan with secure areas for colonization and economic exploitation, and an empire to match those of Britain and France. For Japan, the natural area of expansion was northern China. For years, large Japanese conglomerates (the *zaibatsu*) had operated the coalmines and iron deposits of Manchuria. Tokyo kept strong forces there – the so-called Kwantung Army – to protect Japan's economic interests. Deteriorating relations with China and the growing Soviet threat from the north endangered those interests. At the instigation of right-wing leaders of the Kwantung Army, Japanese forces seized the whole of Manchuria in September 1931. After the Manchurian Incident, the puppet state of Manchukuo was established.[38]

The Manchurian crisis and the League of Nations' lack of determination in its response to a Chinese plea for help showed that no state could expect to be protected by Geneva if it were attacked. This lesson was not lost on Mussolini. In Italy, as elsewhere, the Great Depression triggered a shift in foreign policy. Italian nationalists, like their Japanese counterparts, argued for an expansionist foreign policy in the Mediterranean and northern Africa. They planned to achieve this by enlarging Italy's small colonial inheritance – Libya, Somalia, Eritrea – into a second Roman Empire.[39]

In 1932, the Italian Foreign Ministry began planning for the conquest of Ethiopia, one of the few countries in Africa not under colonial administration. Italian trade and investment were prominent in the country. To Mussolini and his closest advisors the seizure of Ethiopia seemed highly desirable. In October 1935, Italian forces invaded and victory was secured the

---

37 Richard J. Overy, *The Interwar Crisis, 1919–1939* (Harlow: Pearson, 1994), pp. 44ff, 75ff.

38 For Japan's fatal involvement in China, see Edward L. Dreyer, *China at War, 1901–1949* (London: Longman, 1995); Louise Young, *Japan's Total Empire: Manchuria and the Culture of Wartime Imperialism* (Berkeley: University of California Press, 1998); Prasenjit Duara, *Sovereignty and Authenticity: Manchukuo and the East Asian Modern* (Lanham, Md.: Rowman & Littlefield, 2003). On Manchukuo, see also Yoshihisa Tak Matsusaka, *The Making of Japanese Manchuria, 1904–1932* (Cambridge, Mass.: Harvard University Press, 2001).

39 Dennis Mack Smith, *Mussolini's Roman Empire* (London: Longman, 1976).

following spring.[40] Similar to Hitler, whose popularity increased with every foreign policy 'success', Mussolini reached the height of his popularity with the successful invasion of Ethiopia, despite the indiscriminate use of poison gas and aerial bombing against military and civilian targets alike.[41] The war in Ethiopia not only provided Mussolini with cause for optimism that Italians could be remoulded into aggressive, well-disciplined and fanatical members of a more 'odious, tough and implacable' new master race; Hitler's support for Mussolini's Ethiopian adventure also marked a turning point in the relationship between the two dictators and ultimately paved the way for the formation of the Axis in Europe. Mussolini now began to view the Germans as a kindred race – in contrast to the peoples of the West. In private conversations with his lover, Clara Petacci, the Duce insisted that only the Italians and Germans were able to 'love that supreme, inexorable violence which is the chief motor force of world history'.[42]

Hitler and Mussolini indeed both saw warfare as a positive way of bringing out the racial essence of their people. In the long-run, war, for Hitler, was inevitable, an existential necessity, and in that, Mussolini agreed. Mussolini himself described Italy's intervention against the Western Allies as a war against 'the plutocratic and reactionary democracies of the West who have invariably hindered the progress and often threatened the very existence of the Italian people'.[43]

Hitler's initial step toward what he considered an inevitable war with Soviet Russia (and, if necessary, the West) was to begin Germany's rearmament in defiance of the Versailles Treaty. Italy and Japan acted more cautiously than the Third Reich, but certainly abandoned the course of expansion. If anything, the Manchurian Incident increased scepticism in Japan as to whether liberal democracy and party cabinets were capable of protecting Japanese interests in China. In November 1937, following a series of assassinations and even a putsch attempt in Tokyo, Japan began a more general war with China, mobilizing Japanese society long before the beginning of hostilities in the Pacific in late 1941. In January 1938, Japanese troops

---

40 Overy, *Interwar Crisis*, n. 79; George W. Baer, *The Coming of the Italo-Ethiopian War* (Cambridge, Mass.: Harvard University Press, 1967); George W. Baer, *Test Case: Italy, Ethiopia and the League of Nations* (Stanford, Calif.: Hoover Institution Press, 1976); H. James Burgwyn, *Italian Foreign Policy in the Interwar Period, 1918–1940* (Westport, Conn.: Praeger, 1997).
41 Alberto Sbacchi, *Ethiopia under Mussolini: Fascism and the Colonial Experience* (London: Zed Books, 1985).
42 Mussolini, as quoted in Duggan, *Fascist Voices*.
43 Knox, *Common Destiny*, p. 124.

moved swiftly and seized the Chinese capital at Nanjing. By the end of the year, most of northern and eastern China was in Japanese hands. In Italy, Mussolini found himself under pressure from his own party to extend Italian interests in the Mediterranean, the Mare Nostrum. He complied with these demands.[44]

The key reason for the escalation of the international crisis in the late 1930s, however, was Nazi Germany. While some sympathies existed in Western Europe for Berlin's demands to 'right the wrongs' of the Versailles settlement and few objected even to the annexation of Austria in 1938, the mood changed in the autumn of 1938. Hitler had set his eyes on the Sudetenland, a territory in the west of Czechoslovakia, where some 3 million ethnic Germans lived. Although a European war was narrowly avoided at the Munich Conference in September 1938, London and Paris made it clear that they were prepared to fight if Hitler went any further. Meanwhile, Hitler's gaze turned to Poland, a country whose legitimacy as a state he had never accepted in the first place. When the Polish government resisted Nazi pressure to renegotiate the country's border with Germany, Hitler decided to resolve the issue once and for all through war.

In this situation, Mussolini proved to be a less reliable partner than Hitler had hoped. The conquest of Ethiopia in 1935, Italy's military intervention in the Spanish Civil War (1936–39)[45] and the long-term effects of the Great Depression had left the Italian state coffers empty. Given these pressures, further investments in the poorly equipped armed forces were impossible, leaving Italy woefully unprepared for a war against Britain and France. When it broke out, Mussolini had no alternative but to adopt a stance of 'non-belligerence', to the relief of most Italians. This proved to be extraordinarily popular among most Italians[46]

As soon as the Nazis' military campaign turned out to be a success, however, Mussolini grew increasingly irritated at his countrymen's evident distaste for war: 'I have to say they nauseate me. They are cowards and weaklings . . . It's disappointing and soul-destroying to see that I've failed to change these people into a people with steel and courage!' The popular reaction to Italy's

---

44 On Italian expansionist visions, see R. J. B. Bosworth, 'Visionaries of Expansionism', in Thomas Zeiler and Daniel DuBois (eds.), *A Companion to the Second World War* (2 vols., Chichester: Wiley-Blackwell, 2013), vol. 1.

45 J. F. Cordale, *Italian Intervention in the Spanish Civil War* (Princeton University Press, 1975).

46 H. Cliadakis, 'Neutrality and War in Italian Policy, 1939–1940', *Journal of Contemporary History* 9 (1974), 171–90.

declaration of war on France and Britain on 10 June 1940, which set Italy on a path of 'common destiny' with Nazi Germany, was mixed.[47]

Mussolini's anxiety grew when the Italian invasion of Greece in October 1940 turned out to be a catastrophe. Instead of the anticipated lightning victory, the poorly prepared Italian forces were humiliated by superior Greek troops, while the British quickly routed the Italians in Libya and Ethiopia. Hitler had to step in to rescue the situation, and the ease with which the Germans drove the British out of Greece, combined with Rommel's stunning victories in North Africa, only added insult to injury from the Italian perspective.[48]

Japan proved to be a more formidable military ally, even if the Japanese never opened up the second front in Russia that Hitler had hoped for. The Japanese, in fact, benefited more from the Nazis than vice versa. Even before the Japanese attack on Pearl Harbor, German military successes in Europe allowed Japan to increase pressure on European colonial territories in Southeast Asia. The Dutch government agreed to provide Japan with oil supplies from the Dutch East Indies, while Vichy France agreed to an outright Japanese occupation of French Indochina. By the spring of 1940, according to Akira Iriye,

> a conscious decision was made in Tokyo to take advantage of the develop-
> ments [in Europe] and to reorient its policy once again, this time not only to
> conclude an alliance with Germany and Italy, but also to effect a rapproche-
> ment with the Soviet Union. Tokyo's grandiose scheme for establishing a
> worldwide coalition of non-democratic and anti-democratic nations pitted
> itself against an alliance of democratic powers, led by the United States and
> Britain.[49]

But the gains Japan made from the Tripartite Pact and the Soviet pledge of neutrality in Asia through the Neutrality Pact were lost when Germany attacked the Soviet Union. In response, China and the Western Allies became even more resolute and ready to act in cooperation, even with the Soviet Union. 'Rarely', Iriye argues, 'did a diplomatic initiative end in a more complete fiasco'.[50] Events in Europe left the Japanese leadership in the late

---

47 Knox, *Common Destiny*, p. 47.
48 J. J. Sadkovitch, 'Italian Morale During the Italo-Greek War of 1940–1941', *War and Society* 12 (1994), 97–123; J. J. Sadkovitch, 'The Italo-Greek War in Context: Italian Priorities and Axis Diplomacy', *Journal of Contemporary History* 28 (1998), 439–64.
49 Akira Iriye, *The Origins of the Second World War in Asia and the Pacific* (London and New York: Longman, 1987), p. 83.
50 Ibid., p. 113.

summer of 1941 in a remarkable state of uncertainty and indecisiveness; a consensus between the army, the navy and the civilians was hard to achieve.[51]

By the autumn of 1941, and after the appointment of General Tojo Hideki as Prime Minister, the hawks had won the upper hand and Hirohito gave his consent to a war with the West in early November.[52] Following the December 1941 attack on Pearl Harbor and the declaration of war in the South Pacific, Japan managed to conquer vast territories in the region – from Burma to Malaya, from the Dutch East Indies to Singapore and the Philippines. It was in this period, during which a one-party state (the Imperial Rule Assistance Association of 1940) was established and repression at home and violence abroad intensified, that Japan began to resemble its European allies more closely than before.[53] The Japanese military's overconfidence in its own abilities during the coming years was partly rooted in these easy early victories and partly in its racial stereotypes of other Asian peoples as inferior. Although the Japanese were initially welcomed in some Asian colonies by the indigenous populations as 'liberators' from European domination, the racial prejudices and extreme violence displayed by the Japanese military governments in these nations created great resentment and hostility that outlived the end of the Second World War. The stunning early Japanese victories over unprepared opponents had a negative side effect for Tokyo as well: they left Japan overextended and vulnerable to Allied counter-attacks that would ultimately drive the Japanese out of all of the territories they had conquered since 1941.[54]

With the expansion of a regional war into a worldwide conflict in December 1941, the inability of the Axis to develop a global strategy became even clearer. At the time of the conclusion of the Tokyo–Berlin alliance, each side had reasons for a rapprochement that were in part strategic (the German desire for a means to offset British naval preponderance) and partly material (the Japanese interest in acquiring cutting-edge naval technology, now that access to such technology was severely restricted by the Anglo-American naval powers). From the beginning of the war, however, it was clear that great issues persisted, from enormous geographic distance to cultural and

---

51 Bernd Martin, *Japan and Germany in the Modern World* (Oxford University Press, 1995).
52 Margaret Lamb and Nicholas Tarling, *From Versailles to Pearl Harbor: The Origins of the Second World War in Europe and Asia* (Houndmills: Palgrave, 2001).
53 Hofmann, 'Fascist Reflection', pp. 19–20.
54 H. P. Willmott's *The Second World War in the Far East* (London: Cassell, 1999).

linguistic barriers; from incompatible strategic aims to the absence of any direct contact by the top leadership of either country with that of the other.[55]

When one reflects on the dearth of opportunities for real strategic coordination between Germany and Japan in the Second World War, a counterfactual question inevitably arises: was there no strategic theatre in which real coordination was possible, no vital moment when the two nations, had they coordinated their strategies, might have dealt a serious blow to the Allied cause? Some historians have speculated that an all-out effort by the Japanese to thrust into India and to seize Britain's Indian Ocean bases at the same time that German forces drove south through the Caucasus and east through Suez might have knocked Britain or Russia out of the war.[56] Such ideas even circulated among German navy circles in the spring of 1942. But such plans were delusional, as they were simply beyond the capacities of either nation to achieve.[57]

The most that was achieved through the efforts at cooperation by the German and Japanese navies was long-range exchanges of technology, strategic resources, intelligence and personnel. At first, these exchanges were undertaken by surface blockade runners, mostly German, slipping past Allied blockades in the Atlantic. For Germany, this blockade-running effort offered the possibility of obtaining vital resources from Japan's empire of conquest: rubber, tin, magnesium and other materials unavailable in Europe. But with the increasing control achieved by Allied navies over the Atlantic, the Axis powers were reduced to transporting such materials by submarines.

For the Japanese, communication and transportation by submarine offered the possibility of acquiring German technologies and technical expertise. But in the later stages of the war, the ability of the Allies to read both German and Japanese naval communications traffic, and the ever-expanding effectiveness of Allied anti-submarine warfare, made even submarine voyages a thing of terrible risk for the German and Japanese navies.

By 1943, the fortunes of war were decisively turning against the Axis. The costly German defeat at Stalingrad, the loss of control over northern

---

55 These barriers to an effective coalition have been explored in Johanna Menzel Meskill, *Hitler and Japan: The Hollow Alliance* (New York: Atherton Press, 1966), and, more recently, by Martin, *Japan and Germany in the Modern World*. See, too, Hans-Joachim Krug, Yoichi Hirama, Berthold J. Sander-Nagashima and Axel Niestle, *Reluctant Allies: German-Japanese Naval Relations in World War II* (Annapolis, Md.: US Naval Institute Press, 2001), p. 77.

56 See, for example, H. P. Willmott, *Empires in the Balance: Japanese and Allied Pacific Strategies to April 1942* (Annapolis, Md.: Naval Institute Press, 1982), pp. 437–8.

57 Krug et al., *Reluctant Allies*.

Africa, as well as the Allied landing in Southern Italy and American victories in the Pacific, indicated the fatal weakness of the Axis once it had lost the surprise momentum of swift attacks. While in Germany and Japan the public continued to support the war effort, war enthusiasm in Italy collapsed quickly. When Mussolini was eventually overthrown in 1943, Italians welcomed the subsequent surrender. However, soon their former German allies started arresting Italian troops, sending them to the Reich as forced labourers. Over the following months the country experienced vicious fighting. The former Duce was rescued from captivity by German parachutists and installed in the puppet regime of Salò in the north, at the same time as a resistance movement emerged, meeting with brutal reprisals from Mussolini's remaining followers and their German allies.[58] More than 50,000 people were killed. Mussolini himself was shot by partisans while trying to flee, his body strung upside down outside a petrol station in the suburbs of Milan.

His principal Axis partner, Hitler, did not survive him for long, committing suicide in his bunker under the rubble that was left of the capital of the Third Reich. Hitler had been more 'successful' in mobilizing the Germans to fight until the bitter end, even after they had given up hope of military victory. A combination of brutal repression and propaganda, amplifying widespread fears of Soviet revenge and fatal loyalty to an ailing regime led to soaring casualty rates in the endgame of Nazi Germany.[59] Japan, too, was to suffer its highest casualties in the final months of the war, but was only prepared to surrender after the dual nuclear strikes at Hiroshima and Nagasaki convinced Hirohito of the inevitability of defeat. Japan surrendered on 2 September 1945, but was unique among the Axis powers in at least one sense: the military defeat of Japan did not lead to the removal of the head of state. Unlike Hitler and Mussolini, whose charismatic leadership depended (as Max Weber pointed out and Mussolini discovered in 1943) on constant re-consecration by success, the Japanese Emperor seemed immune to the penalties of failure. In a controversial move, he was spared the public humiliation of a war criminal's trial, and General MacArthur even decided that Hirohito should stay on as head of state to ensure the Japanese public's acceptance of the US occupation. He continued to act as head of state until his death in 1987.

---

58 L. Quartermaine, *Mussolini's Last Republic: Propaganda and Politics in the Italian Social Republic, 1943–45* (Exeter: Elm Bank Publications, 2000).

59 Ian Kershaw, *The End: Hitler's Germany, 1944–45* (London: Allen Lane, 2011).

So looking back from the vantage point of the Axis's total defeat, what can be said about the inner coherence of this alliance? It has been argued here that wartime Germany, Italy and Japan were not united by a shared and coherent ideological belief system similar to Marxism-Leninism, or by a desire to defend the values of a specific political system (such as liberal democracy in the case of Britain, France and the United States). The Axis was based on little more than fundamental opposition to those values represented by their military opponents during the Second World War. Yet all three regimes shared a common belief in the superiority of some kind of authoritarianism over liberal democracy and the desire to create new orders, both at home and abroad, notably through an expansionist foreign policy that would revise the Paris Peace system established in 1919. In all three countries between the later 1930s and 1945, 'empire-building' played a significant role, either as a source of radicalization (as in Japan) or the result of it (as in Germany and Italy). This comparatively thin platform of common ideological ground was one of many reasons why the Axis ultimately failed to achieve its objectives. Apart from serious economic, strategic and demographic disadvantages vis-à-vis the Western Allies and their Soviet partners, the lack of a concrete vision regarding their common post-war objectives undermined the efforts to defeat a well-coordinated global alliance of enemies.

2

Western Allied ideology, 1939–1945

TALBOT IMLAY

This chapter discusses the wartime ideology of the Western Allies, chiefly Britain and the United States, but also France. A difficulty immediately arises in trying to define ideology. There is no scholarly consensus on the meaning of the term: available definitions include beliefs rooted in material realities, worldviews, political doctrines, belief systems, philosophies of life, everyday practices, hegemonic discourses, instruments of domination and the process by which meaning is ascribed. In this chapter, ideology refers to the mix of principles, beliefs and perceived interests that inform without necessarily determining national policy. Whatever its limits, this definition draws attention to the point that each nation possesses a dominant ideology and that this ideology has practical consequences. These national ideologies, it is worth adding, are not fixed, but contested. For the Western Allies, ideology was a subject of frequent and sometimes fierce dispute, not only within each country, but also between countries. The context of war, moreover, provided a key framework for these disputes. Each of the Western Allies felt the need to justify its involvement in the conflict by endowing it with purpose and meaning. The vital question throughout was: what are we fighting for? The question interested not only governments, but also a variety of political actors within each of the Western Allies. Ideological considerations, moreover, were omnipresent, for the question's reach extended well beyond the achievement of military victory to encompass the foundations of the post-war political order both at home and abroad.

Although there were numerous other Western allies, most notably but not solely the British Dominions, each of which merits study, this chapter limits itself to France, Britain and the United States, partly because of space constraints, but also because these three allies exerted the greatest influence.

Accordingly, this chapter considers ideology through the prism of war aims. The latter are defined broadly to include not only precise demands, such as the liberation of occupied territories, but also the question of how the Western Allies understood the stakes involved in the war. If these stakes would influence the post-war order, they also helped to shape the nature of the conflict itself. Here, it is useful to distinguish between status quo and revisionist aims. Broadly speaking, proponents of the status quo sought to limit the war's impact both at home and abroad, a goal which at least initially meant downplaying any ideological differences with enemy countries. Proponents of revisionism, by contrast, conceived of the conflict as a crusade against a politically and morally repugnant foe, a conception that worked against attempts to restrain the war's disruptive effects. Indeed, implicit and sometimes explicit in this conception was the prospect of significant changes to domestic and international politics. To be sure, the revisionism of the Western Allies had nothing to do with that of the Axis powers, most notably Nazi Germany, whose programme of racial and territorial conquest was breathtaking in its scope and inhumanity. Nevertheless, the revisionist and status quo labels highlight important dynamics and differences at work in the war aims of the Western Allies.

The chapter is divided into two parts. The first part examines the war aims of Britain and France from the outbreak of the European war in September 1939 to Germany's military victories in the West in 1940. Both countries entered the war as status quo powers. Governed by centre-right political coalitions, Britain and France aimed to defeat Germany as painlessly as possible and to avoid major political reforms at home and in their empires. Challenging this limited approach, however, was the emerging belief that Nazi Germany was anathema and that it must therefore be defeated and Nazism destroyed. The British and French governments soon came under mounting political pressure for a greater war effort – for a more thorough mobilization of national and societal resources, as well as for active military operations. Significantly, in both countries, much of this pressure came from the opposition parties on the centre-left, which viewed the war as an opportunity to reshape the political order at home and, to a lesser extent, abroad. During 1939–40, domestic politics worked to widen the perceived ideological divide separating the Western Allies from Nazi Germany, which in turn influenced the nature and meaning of the war for Britain and France.

The second and longer part considers the war aims of Britain and the United States from 1940 to 1945. A shared commitment to the defeat of the Axis powers could not conceal the deep differences between the American and British conceptions of the war. From the beginning, the United States framed the war as a moral crusade aimed not simply at defeating its enemies, but also, more ambitiously, at recasting international relations along broadly liberal internationalist lines. Leading American statesmen defined this project in opposition to what they perceived as the pre-war international order of shackled political and economic freedoms. At home, meanwhile, the war blunted what remained of the New Deal's reformist energies, creating a disjuncture between domestic and international aims: the Americans would fight to remake the world and not the United States. Britain, by comparison, presented something of a mirror image. Ongoing developments on the home front fuelled popular calls for a 'people's war', prodding the government to promise that the warfare state would become a welfare state once peace had returned. On the international front, however, Britain appeared to be far more of a status quo power: as Churchill repeatedly indicated, the British waged war to maintain their great-power and imperial positions and not to reorder international politics. The interaction of these cross-cutting ambitions in the domestic and international realms would help to determine the war aims of the Western Allies. Yet because the United States enjoyed a growing preponderance of power within the alliance, it would have the greater say in defining the meaning of the war – at least when it came to international politics.

The Phoney War: 1939–1940

Britain and France went to war in September 1939 with considerable reluctance. For much of the 1930s, the two countries had striven to prevent another European conflict. Only during 1938–39, when it became clear that Hitler's territorial ambitions had not been satisfied at Munich with the annexation of the Sudetenland, did London and Paris accept the need to oppose German aggression, if necessary by force. Even then, hopes persisted that Nazi Germany might be deterred by a show of determination, which included last-minute efforts to ally with the Soviet Union – a power the British and French governments had hitherto shunned, largely on ideological grounds. The Wehrmacht's unprovoked attack on Poland, however, left Britain and France with no choice but to declare war. As the French premier, Édouard Daladier, explained in a radio address on 3 September 1939:

> France and England have made countless efforts to safeguard peace. This very morning they made a further urgent intervention in Berlin in order to

address to the German Government a last appeal to reason and request it to stop hostilities and to open peaceful negotiations. Germany met us with a refusal... I am conscious of having worked unremittingly against the war until the last minute.[1]

Across the Channel, the British Prime Minister, Neville Chamberlain, lamented that '[t]his is a sad day for all of us, and to none is it sadder than to me. Everything that I have worked for, everything that I have hoped for, everything that I believed in during my public life, has crashed into ruins.'[2]

The reluctant entry into the conflict coloured the discussion of war aims in London and Paris. Viewing war as an unmitigated disaster, the British and French governments conceived of the conflict in narrowly defensive terms. 'Neither France nor Britain has entered the war to conduct a kind of ideological crusade', Daladier announced in October 1939. Two months later, Lord Halifax, the British Foreign Secretary, elaborated on this point:

> We desire peoples who have been deprived of their independence to recover their liberties. We desire to redeem the peoples of Europe from this constant fear of German aggression, and we desire to safeguard our own freedom and security... We do not seek aggrandizement, and we do not seek to redraw the map in our own interests, and still less...are we moved by any spirit of vengeance.[3]

The overriding goal was a return to the pre-war status quo – to a time before Germany had become a menace to its neighbours. In effect, the Germans would have to be persuaded to abandon their expansionist ambitions. To be sure, it remained unclear whether this goal required the end of the Nazi regime. For Chamberlain and his closest advisors, it probably did not: during the Phoney War, they hinted at the possibility of negotiations with German leaders, though perhaps not with Hitler himself.[4] For Daladier, however, Hitler and his acolytes would have to go before a lasting peace

---

1 'Statement by Edouard Daladier, Premier, to the Nation, September 3, 1939'. http://avalon.law.yale.edu/wwii/fr3.asp (accessed 29 October 2014).

2 'Address by Neville Chamberlain – September 3, 1939'. http://avalon.law.yale.edu/wwii/gb2.asp (accessed 29 October 2014).

3 'Edouard Daladier, Prime Minister: Broadcast from Paris, October 10, 1939', and 'Lord Halifax, Secretary of State for Foreign Affairs: Speech to the House of Lords in Answer to Viscount Cecil's Request for a Statement on War Aims, December 5, 1939', both reproduced in Louise W. Holborn and Hajo Holborn (eds.), *War and Peace Aims of the United Nations: September 1, 1939 – December 31, 1942* (Boston, Mass.: World Peace Foundation, 1943), pp. 170–2, 560–1.

4 Peter W. Ludlow, 'The Unwinding of Appeasement', in Lothar Kettenacker (ed.), *Das 'Andere Deutschland' im Zweiten Weltkrieg* (Stuttgart: Klett, 1977), pp. 9–46.

could be secured. Yet whatever the proposed fate of Hitler's regime, the British and French governments studiously refrained from framing the war in political-moral terms. The Germans might have to furnish what the French Foreign Ministry called 'effective material guarantees' against future aggression, but such demands were rooted more in traditional power-political considerations than in any uncompromising ideological antagonism to Nazi Germany.[5]

The desire to return to a pre-war status quo, in turn, shaped the way Britain and France waged war. In principle, Anglo-French planners conceived of a long conflict. Because Nazi Germany's head start in rearmament gave it an immediate military advantage, the Allies would initially remain on the defensive, repelling German attacks while mobilizing their latent yet superior resources. Eventually, when the balance of military and economic power had shifted decisively in their favour, the British and French would launch a military offensive to defeat Germany.[6] In reality, however, the Allies appeared to be less than fully committed to this strategy. One reason was that a lengthy war might prove to be unnecessary: the British and French hoped that economic and political warfare would bring victory, perhaps through an internal overthrow of the Nazi regime. But another reason was that neither the British nor the French government welcomed the political, social and economic costs implied in a massive mobilization of resources. The greater the overall effort, the more difficult it would be to preserve the status quo at home and abroad.

Chamberlain was acutely aware of the link between war and political change. A lengthy and demanding conflict risked augmenting the influence of the Labour Party and of the trade unions, both of which demanded far-reaching reforms in order to wage war more effectively and to lay the basis for a better future. The current conflict, argued Harold Laski, a leading Labour intellectual, in November 1939, must lead to 'Socialist reconstruction, national and international'. Three months later, a Labour statement proclaimed that the war was being fought to forge a 'new world order' in which national sovereignty would be conditional, global wealth redistributed, and

5 Frédéric Seager, 'Les buts de guerre alliés devant l'opinion, 1939–40', *Revue d'histoire moderne et contemporaine* 32 (1985), 617–38 (quotation at 629).
6 François Bédarida, *La stratégie secrète de la Drôle de guerre. Le Conseil suprême interallié. Septembre 1939 – avril 1940* (Paris: Presse de la Fondation nationale des sciences politiques, 1979); and Robert J. Young, 'La Guerre de longue durée: Some Reflections on French Strategy and Diplomacy', in Paul Preston (ed.), *General Staffs and Diplomacy Before the Second World War* (London: Croom Helm, 1978), pp. 41–64.

colonial empires progressively dismantled.[7] In response, Chamberlain and his supporters resisted pressure to enlarge the government to include Labour and other members. Equally telling, they also sought to curb the country's war effort. Britain's military contribution, the government maintained, should focus on the navy and air force, with the army retaining its status as the junior service. In the autumn of 1939, Chamberlain thus fiercely opposed proposals for a large-scale expansion of the army. If this opposition reflected bitter memories of trench warfare during 1914–18, no less important a factor was the Prime Minister's fear of the financial, industrial and political price of creating a mass army. Similarly, when it came to mobilizing industry for war, the government remained attached to the principle of 'business as usual', which it increasingly defined in opposition to Labour Party and trade union calls for tripartite corporatist arrangements (between employers, organized labour and state officials) at all levels of industry. Such arrangements, Chamberlain rightly recognized, risked transforming the balance of industrial and political power in Britain.[8]

Daladier pursued a similar course in France. Although no one proposed to restrain the size of the French army, which confronted the vast bulk of the Wehrmacht in the West following Poland's rapid defeat, the French government set its teeth against fundamental reforms at home. In the political realm, this meant marginalizing the centre left and non-communist left, which, as in Britain, lobbied for a greater mobilization of national resources with all that this implied. 'It will be necessary', Léon Blum, the socialist leader, explained in January 1940, in order 'to resist and to defeat [Germany], that France be inspired more and more by collective organization, that she regulate the economy more and more strictly around collective needs by removing it from the [working] of so-called laws of "liberty"...[and] that she ensures the notion of collective good over that of private interest.'[9] In the economic realm, meanwhile, the government's resistance to reform manifested itself in a dogmatic attachment to non-interference, which effectively handed over the task of organizing France's emerging war economy to industry groups. In addition to excluding organized labour from any influence, this approach aimed at immunizing the country against a recrudescence

7 Harold J. Laski, *The Labour Party, the War, and the Future* (London: The Labour Party, 1939), p. 5; and Labour Party, *Labour, the War, and the Peace* (London: The Labour Party, 1940).
8 Talbot C. Imlay, *Facing the Second World War: Strategy, Politics, and Economics in Britain and France, 1938–1940* (Oxford University Press, 2003), pp. 299–353.
9 Léon Blum, 'Voeux au parti', *Le Populaire de Paris*, 2 January 1940, p. 1.

of the pre-war Popular Front – the political and social movement that aimed to recast the industrial and political orders. The threat of war during the late 1930s had allowed the Popular Front's opponents to undo many of its specific measures, while also curbing organized labour's political influence. Nevertheless, during 1939–40, the centre right and right feared that a lengthy and demanding conflict would usher in reform and perhaps even revolution. Significantly, in the early months of 1940, Paul Reynaud, the Finance Minister, urgently demanded sizeable reductions in overall spending for the war, despite his well-earned reputation as a hardliner toward Nazi Germany.[10]

Britain and France sought to safeguard the status quo not only at home, but also in their dependent empires. Although liberating peoples from foreign occupation and oppression constituted an Allied war aim, it was one that applied solely to Europe. Both the British and French governments were strongly committed to maintaining control over their empires. During the 1930s, the fear of war's disruptive impact on the structures of imperial rule had factored into the pre-war efforts to appease Germany, especially on the British side. With the advent of war, Allied propaganda trumpeted empire as a major source of confidence and strength. The Western Allies quickly set about mobilizing imperial resources and manpower in particular: in September 1939, for example, over 10 per cent of France's mobilized soldiers came from the colonies. Yet behind the apparent show of strength, the British and French empires were politically shaky. In India, the British confronted a powerful independence movement, while in Palestine, efforts to keep a lid on the violence between Jews and Arabs absorbed scarce British military resources. During the interwar years, as Martin Thomas has shown, France faced mounting labour and political opposition within its empire, starkly revealing the precariousness of French rule.[11] One did not have to be clairvoyant to understand that a lengthy war in Europe would place additional pressures on the British and French empires – pressures that might prove overwhelming.

It was on the home front, however, that the two Allied governments faced the biggest challenge in their attempts to preserve the status quo. In Britain, the growing criticism of Chamberlain's conduct of the war prompted a

---

10 Talbot C. Imlay, 'Paul Reynaud and France's Response to Nazi Germany, 1938–1940', *French Historical Studies* 26 (2003), 508–15.

11 Martin Thomas, *Violence and Colonial Order: Police, Workers and Protest in the European Colonial Empires, 1918–1940* (Cambridge University Press, 2012); and Martin Thomas, *The French Empire Between the Wars: Imperialism, Politics and Society* (Manchester University Press, 2005).

reconfiguration of parliamentary politics, paving the way for the coalition that would attain power in May 1940 under Churchill's leadership. Labour's prominent place in this coalition all but ensured that the foundations of Britain's domestic political order would be renegotiated. Indeed, this was already happening. During the early months of 1940, employers' organizations and trade unions worked out agreements for the joint management of industry, which promoted organized labour to the role of partner in industrial policy. Although unhappy with these developments, Chamberlain's government could do little to prevent them, having become an unwitting victim of its earlier decision to limit intervention in industrial matters. In France, meanwhile, criticism of the government led to Daladier's replacement by Reynaud in March 1940. Almost immediately, the new premier found himself caught between those who demanded a greater war effort and those who resisted this demand, partly for fear of its longer-term political consequences. In a bid to reconcile the two competing positions, Reynaud championed immediate military action by the Allies to bring the war to a rapid and victorious end. The desperate search for an elusive short cut to military victory fuelled a dangerous radicalization of French and Allied military strategy. This was most apparent in the gathering support for military operations against the Soviet Union, particularly its oil industry in the Caucasus, the likely result of which would have been to provoke the Soviet Union's entry into the war on the side of Nazi Germany.[12] The Phoney War had witnessed a rising tide of anti-communist sentiment in France and Britain, egged on by the Molotov–Ribbentrop Pact, Moscow's diplomatic and economic aid to the Germans, and the Red Army's unprovoked attack on Finland. For some observers, Soviet belligerence promised to reconfigure the emerging ideological bases of the war. Instead of an effort to defeat Nazism, the conflict would become an anti-communist crusade.[13]

Nazi Germany's stunning military victories in the summer of 1940 brought an abrupt end to the radicalization of Allied strategy. France lay defeated and partially occupied, while Britain stood isolated; the latter's short-term war aims consisted of survival, and its longer-term aims of waiting and hoping for the intervention of outside powers – the United States most obviously,

---

12 Talbot C. Imlay, 'A Reassessment of Anglo-French Strategy during the Phony War, 1939–1940', *English Historical Review* 481 (2004), 333–72.

13 For the French, see Jean-Louis Crémieux-Brilhac, *Les Français de l'An 40*, vol. 1: *La guerre oui ou non* (2 vols., Paris: Gallimard, 1990); for the British, see Robert Crowcroft, '"What Is Happening in Europe?" Richard Stokes, Fascism, and the Anti-War Movement in the British Labour Party During the Second World War', *History* 93 (2008), 514–30.

but also (ironically) the Soviet Union. But though brief, the Phoney War period helped to shape the ideological aspects of the war. Britain and France initially strove to frame the conflict in limited terms. Rather than a crusade against Nazism and Nazi Germany, the war would be fought to thwart the latter's expansionist ambitions as a prelude to a return to a pre-war status quo. The underlying aim was not to transform the political orders at home and abroad, but to preserve them. At the same time, it proved increasingly difficult to limit the conflict in this sense, as political developments inside Britain and France highlighted the potential links between war and change. The United States' entry into the war would strengthen these links.

The global war

For the British, the wait for new allies after France's defeat proved to be long, but ultimately successful. In June 1941, Operation BARBAROSSA propelled the Soviet Union into the war; six months later, the United States entered the conflict, following the Japanese attack on Pearl Harbor and Nazi Germany's declaration of war. Churchill greeted the latter event, in particular, with immense relief, rightly viewing American belligerence as a guarantee of final victory. But at the end of 1941, victory in Europe lay well in the future. Though animated by a shared determination to defeat Nazi Germany and Fascist Italy (and then Japan), the Anglo-American alliance would be subject to considerable strain over the coming months and years. If strategic questions provoked considerable tensions between the two Western Allies, so too did the subject of war aims.

That the United States would conceive of the war as a crusade to remake international relations was apparent even before December 1941. In his State of the Union address the previous January, Roosevelt had famously announced that Americans 'look forward to a world founded upon four essential human freedoms' (freedom of speech, freedom of worship, freedom from want and freedom from fear), adding that they applied 'everywhere' and 'anywhere in the world'.[14] Notwithstanding their vagueness, the four freedoms reflected a vision of a post-war international order – a vision whose contours were defined in reaction to the challenges posed by the Axis

14 The 'Four Freedoms', Franklin D. Roosevelt's Address to Congress, 6 January 1941. www.wwnorton.com/college/history/ralph/workbook/ralprs36b.htm (accessed 29 October 2014).

powers, particularly Nazi Germany and Imperial Japan. The Roosevelt administration believed that the Germans and Japanese were embarked on a similar project, to create by war and conquest closed political-economic blocs (empires) on a continental scale. In response, the Americans envisaged an interdependent world in which countries and peoples, free from direct foreign rule, engaged in open commerce with one another. Rather than empires, the world would comprise politically independent nation states integrated into a global economy. That this world would benefit the United States first and foremost did not bother Roosevelt any more than it had Woodrow Wilson, his ideological predecessor, as both men assumed that American and global interests were identical. Admittedly, during 1940–41, American visions of the post-war international order remained embryonic. Nevertheless, it was clear that if and when the United States entered the war, it would do so as a revisionist and not as a status quo power.

Britain, by comparison, remained more attached to the status quo, especially in the international realm. Although the wartime governing coalition now included Labour, which continued to call for a 'new world order' to emerge from the war, Churchill and his closest advisors treated Roosevelt's revisionist impulses with suspicion. Although the Prime Minister knew better than anyone that Britain desperately needed the United States to enter the war, he hoped to limit the longer-term effects of American belligerence. For Churchill, the imperative was to win the war with the least possible damage to Britain's great-power and imperial status. If the prospect of a lengthy war constituted a threat to this imperative, so too did the United States' immense strength, both actual and potential. The longer the war lasted, the more the balance of power within the Western alliance would shift toward the Americans, placing Washington in a dominant position to shape the post-war international settlement. The challenge for Churchill after December 1941 was to forge the closest possible alliance with the United States, which was necessary both to win the war and to support Britain afterwards, while at the same time reining in Washington's revisionist ambitions.

Britain and the Atlantic Charter

That Churchill's challenge would be difficult is apparent from the history of the Atlantic Charter, the single most important statement of Allied war aims. The charter was the product of a meeting between Churchill and Roosevelt off the coast of Newfoundland in August 1941. Consisting of eight brief points, it pledged Britain and the United States not to seek territorial aggrandizement or territorial changes without the consent of the people concerned; to respect the right to self-government; to promote open trade between countries, as well as global progress and prosperity; and to establish a peace based on disarmament as well as on freedom from foreign aggression and on freedom of the seas.[15] Many contemporary observers viewed the charter as an ideological broadside against the Axis powers. As Felix Frankfurter, Supreme Court Justice and trusted presidential advisor, wrote to Roosevelt soon afterwards: it 'give[s] meaning to the conflict between civilization and arrogant brute challenge, and give[s] promise. . .that civilization has claims and resources that tyranny will not be able to overcome, because it will find that force and will and the free spirit of man are more powerful than force and will alone'.[16] A clear ideological divide supposedly separated the Allies from the Axis. Reflecting this view, in January 1942, twenty-six nations signed a Declaration of the United Nations that not only endorsed the charter, but also announced that 'complete victory' over the Axis powers was 'essential to defend life, liberty, independence and religious freedom, and to preserve human rights and justice in their own lands as well as in other lands'.[17]

Other observers, however, were more circumspect when it came to the Atlantic Charter. W. Arnold-Forster, a Labour Party expert on foreign policy, remarked that '[s]ome of its Points seem inconsistent with others, so that a reconciling explanation is needed'.[18] The remark is astute. From the outset, the charter was a document to be interpreted, argued over and endowed with precise content. It was less a declaration of war aims than it was a spur for the Allies – and for the British and Americans in particular – to define and impose their own views regarding the stakes of the conflict.

In the autumn of 1941, it was probably Churchill who possessed the most clear-cut position concerning the stakes of the war. The Prime Minister viewed the Atlantic Charter principally through the lens of Nazi tyranny. The Allies were fighting to defeat Hitler's Germany and to restore freedom to the nations and peoples of Europe whom the Nazis had brutally subjected.

---

15 For the text, see http://avalon.law.yale.edu/wwii/atlantic.asp (accessed 29 October 2014).
16 Cited in M. S. Venkataramani, 'The United States, the Colonial Issue, and the Atlantic Charter Hoax', *International Studies* 13 (1974), 2.
17 For the text, see http://avalon.law.yale.edu/20th_century/decade03.asp (accessed 29 October 2014).
18 W. Arnold-Forster, 'The Atlantic Charter', *Political Quarterly* 13 (April 1942), 159.

Although this restoration might involve some adjustments of territory and population, Churchill basically envisaged a return to the pre-1939 map of Central and Western Europe. Admittedly less clear were the future borders of Eastern Europe. The Soviet Union, the third pillar of the Grand Alliance and signatory of the January 1942 Declaration, insisted on the recognition of its 1940 borders, which meant leaving the Baltic states and a considerable part of Poland under Soviet rule. The Soviet Union's massive military contribution to the war, and the sympathy that this effort engendered among the British (and American) public, made it wiser for the time being to ignore the possible contradiction in opposing Nazi but not Soviet expansionism. That said, Churchill's emphasis on tyranny within Europe meant that the principles espoused in the Atlantic Charter could easily be turned against the Soviet Union if circumstances changed.

While undoubtedly genuine, Churchill's Eurocentric understanding of the Atlantic Charter had the effect of downplaying some of its less attractive implications. The promotion of free trade and freedom of the seas pointed to a liberal international economic order that Britain had largely turned its back on in the early 1930s with the policy of imperial preference. Determined to preserve the latter, Churchill persuaded Roosevelt to add the caveat 'with due respect for their existing obligations' to the Atlantic Charter's fourth point, regarding open access to trade and resources. This is not to say that the British envisaged the kind of closed and exploitative economic blocs that the Axis powers strove to impose. After the war, the Empire-Commonwealth would be open to outside commerce, partly because this was in the perceived interest of various groups within Britain and partly because the 'White Dominions' – its most influential members – would undoubtedly oppose such a bloc. Nevertheless, during the war, British officials viewed a liberal international economic order as a potential menace. Even before September 1939, it was questionable whether British industries were competitive enough and Britain's financial situation sound enough to prosper without some protection. Once at war, the British quickly found themselves compelled to mortgage their economic future, as industries focused on the short-term goal of maximizing production while the country's external debt skyrocketed. Not surprisingly, this situation reinforced existing doubts about the wisdom of economic liberalism as an international programme. Within Whitehall, it was understood that post-war British governments would require the power to protect sterling and to ensure privileged access to external resources and markets. Indeed, as early as December 1940, John Maynard Keynes drew a parallel between

Britain's needs for an economic bloc and Nazi Germany's plan for continental Europe. What we propose, he mischievously admitted, 'is the same as what Dr Funk [the German Economics Minister] offers, except that we shall do it better and more honestly'.[19]

But for Churchill, perhaps the most troubling aspect of the Atlantic Charter concerned the future of the British Empire. The charter, the Prime Minister insisted, applied to Europe alone. 'At the Atlantic meeting', he explained to the British parliament in September 1941, 'we [Roosevelt and himself] had in mind, primarily, the restoration of the sovereignty, self-government and national life of the States and nations of Europe now under the Nazi yoke', adding that 'that is quite a separate problem from the progressive evolution of self-governing institutions in the regions and peoples which owe allegiance to the British Crown'.[20] Elsewhere, Churchill described British policy more succinctly as 'Hands off the British Empire'.[21] Several reasons explain this determination to preserve the empire. One was economic: as already noted, Britain's projected post-war difficulties made the empire an indispensable financial and commercial asset. Over the course of the conflict, Britain would become increasingly dependent on its empire, a situation underscored by the rapidly accumulating sterling holdings of its various members, most notably India. Another reason stemmed from a sense of responsibility mixed with more than a sprinkling of paternalism. It was widely assumed that many colonies would not be ready for self-government before a period lasting at least several decades, during which Britain would provide the necessary political guidance and development aid. Premature transfers of power under the principle of self-government – a principle echoed in the Atlantic Charter – would be irresponsible. It would, Herbert Morrison, a Labour politician and Home Secretary, remarked in 1943, 'be like giving a child of ten a latch-key, a bank account, and a shot-gun'.[22]

Great power considerations also factored into the attachment to empire. For many British observers, the future appeared to lie with large political organizations that transcended national borders. Addressing an American audience in 1943, Quintin Hogg, a British MP and close political ally of

---

19 John Maynard Keynes, 'Proposals to Counter the German New Order', 1 December 1940, reproduced in Donald Moggridge (ed.), *The Collected Writings of John Maynard Keynes*, vol. xxv: *Activities, 1940–1944* (30 vols., London: Macmillan, 1980), pp. 7–10.
20 For the full text, see http://hansard.millbanksystems.com/commons/1941/sep/09/war-situation (accessed 29 October 2014).
21 Wm. Roger Louis, *Imperialism at Bay, 1941–1945: The United States and the Decolonization of the British Empire* (Oxford: Clarendon Press, 1977), p. 433.
22 Ibid., p. 14.

Churchill, claimed that international politics 'are moving into a world in which the Nation State is no longer the standard political institution'. Prevailing trends instead pointed 'toward larger groupings in continents, areas and groups of states'. Although Hogg spoke vaguely of 'federations' and of 'economic interdependence', these were synonyms for empire. If it were to have any chance of keeping up with the two emerging superpowers, Britain would need the 'British Commonwealth' – 'a world area, based on the sea'.[23] To be sure, not everyone was as wedded to empire as Churchill and his supporters. In 1941, Clement Attlee, the Labour leader and Deputy Prime Minister, remarked that the Atlantic Charter included '[c]oloured peoples, as well as whites'.[24] More generally, Labour was committed to the principle of eventual self-government for colonies when (and if) they were judged ready. Yet if the nature of the future relationship between Britain and its empire remained a matter for debate throughout the war, none of the principal political parties could imagine the rapid decolonization that would occur after 1945.

The United States and the Atlantic Charter

The American President's understanding of the Atlantic Charter differed notably from Churchill's. Currents of Wilsonian internationalism flowed through the Roosevelt administration, helping to ensure that the charter would be conceived as a guide for reordering international politics. The charter's invocation of freedom of international trade and of the seas not only echoed Wilson's 'Fourteen Points'; they were also meant to be applied globally. Cordell Hull, Secretary of State during most of the war, believed in the beneficent workings of economic liberalism as a matter of faith. After the war, he announced in May 1941, a 'broad program of world economic reconstruction' would be needed based on a 'system of open trade', for otherwise 'there will be chronic political instability and recurrent economic collapse', leading to further wars.[25] From this perspective, Britain's regime of

---

23 Quintin Hogg, 'British Policy: A Conservative Forecast', *Foreign Affairs* 1 (October 1943), 33–5.
24 Cited in Marc Matera, 'Black Internationalism and African and Caribbean Intellectuals in London, 1919–1950' (unpublished PhD thesis, Rutgers, The State University of New Jersey, 2008), p. 353.
25 'Radio Address by Secretary of State Cordell Hull on Danger to Free Nations (May 18, 1941)'. www.jewishvirtuallibrary.org/jsource/ww2/hull051841.html (accessed 29 October 2014).

imperial preference was simply anathema. Hull's voice, of course, was not the sole one on the subject of the post-war international economic order. Others within or close to the administration lobbied for a more intervention-ist approach that looked to transpose the New Deal onto the international stage. The leading industrial countries of the world, argued Alvin Hansen and Charles Kindleberger, two prominent economists, should work out a 'comprehensive program of international economic development, the promotion of full employment and the raising of living standards both of production and consumption throughout the world'.[26] Such a global New Deal would require significant doses of international cooperation, coordination and management.

If Hansen and Kindleberger's call for a global development programme went well beyond Hull's free trade vision, several points are worth under-scoring. First, everyone agreed that the United States would have to assume a leading role in recasting the post-war international economy. The United States, Hansen and Kindleberger concluded, must 'take the lead'.[27] Second, this recasting would be along more open and multilateral lines: in the economic sphere, Roosevelt commented in 1941, the United States must tear down 'Chinese walls of isolation' between nations.[28] Fuelling this liberal internationalist impulse was an awareness of waxing American strength. In many ways, a more liberal economic order served the interests of countries with dynamic and expanding economies, which had been the case for Britain during the nineteenth century and was now for the United States. Third, regardless of the debates within the administration over the details of the post-war international economic order, in practice, American wartime diplomacy worked to prevent Britain from preserving a tariff and sterling bloc. The United States thus bargained hard over the terms of Lend-Lease – the programme by which Washington 'lent' war materiel and other goods to its allies. Signed in February 1942, Article VII of the preliminary Anglo-American agreement committed Britain to 'the elimination of all forms of discriminatory treatment in international commerce, and to the reduction

---

26 Alvin H. Hansen and C. P. Kindleberger, 'The Economic Tasks of the Postwar World', *Foreign Affairs* 3 (April 1942), 466–7; and Elizabeth Borgwardt, *A New Deal for the World: America's Vision for Human Rights* (Cambridge, Mass.: Harvard University Press, 2005).
27 Hansen and Kindleberger, 'The Economic Tasks of the Postwar World', 476.
28 Roosevelt, '"We Choose Human Freedom" – A Radio Address Announcing the Proclamation of an Unlimited National Emergency', 27 May 1941, reproduced in Samuel I. Rosenman (ed.), *Public Papers and Addresses of Franklin D. Roosevelt, 1941* (New York: Harper, 1950), p. 184.

of tariffs and other trade barriers'.[29] Afterwards, the Americans used the periodic negotiations over the terms of renewal not only to remind their allies of their commitment, but also to limit Britain's wartime sterling balances, effectively increasing London's financial and hence political dependence on the United States.

An equally, if not more contentious issue between the two Western allies concerned the future of European empires. Unlike Churchill, Roosevelt did not confine the Atlantic Charter's reach to Europe. The charter, he publicly announced in February 1942, 'applies not only to the part of the world that borders the Atlantic but to the whole world'.[30] That this implied support for the 'self-determination' of colonial peoples was evident from Roosevelt's comments at a press conference the previous year: 'There never has been, there isn't now, and there will never be any race of people on earth fit to serve as masters over their fellow men... We believe that any nationality, no matter how small, has the inherent right to its own nationhood'.[31] Generally speaking, the American President looked upon European empires with considerable disapproval, remarking on several occasions that the imperial powers had exploited their colonies while doing little to improve the lives of colonial peoples. France aroused particular scorn in this regard, with Roosevelt expressing hostility to the idea of a French return to Indochina following Japan's defeat.

But the British also came under pressure from Washington to place their empire more clearly on the path to self-government. American officials repeatedly pointed to the Philippines, which was due to become independent in 1946, as a model for Britain to follow. American policy toward the Philippines, Hull typically lectured in 1942, was a 'perfect example of how a nation should treat a colony or dependency in cooperating with it...in making all necessary preparations for freedom'.[32] Early on, moreover, the Americans considered British policy toward India as something of a test case. Backed by congressional and public opinion, which tended to view the British as unrepentant imperialists, Roosevelt urged Churchill to grant India immediate self-government and even Dominion status, arguing that this

---

29 For the text, see http://avalon.law.yale.edu/20th_century/decade04.asp (accessed 29 October 2014).

30 Cited in Venkataramani, 'The United States, the Colonial Issue, and the Atlantic Charter Hoax', 26.

31 Cited in Eric S. Rubin, 'America, Britain, and *Swaraj*: Anglo-American Relations and Indian Independence, 1939–1945', *India Review* 10 (2011), 47.

32 Cited in Christopher Thorne, *Allies of a Kind: The United States, Britain, and the War Against Japan, 1941–1945* (Oxford University Press, 1979), p. 160.

would help to ensure Indian cooperation in the war against Japan. Churchill's undisguised resentment at such interference compelled Roosevelt to tread carefully. Nevertheless, ignoring British protests, the Americans began to develop independent contacts with Indians, a policy that included the establishment of 'limited quasi diplomatic relations'.[33] In London, such measures were rightly perceived as signs of American opposition to a return to the pre-war colonial order in Asia and beyond.

Both Britain and the United States viewed the Atlantic Charter as an important statement of the war's purpose – and thus of its ideological underpinnings. The two allies, however, ascribed different meanings to the charter. Whereas for the British government the charter expressed a commitment to defeat Nazi Germany and to restore freedom to the peoples and nations of Europe, for the American government it encapsulated several broad principles for reordering international politics and economics. Which of the two meanings would prevail would be decided by the interplay of several factors, the most important of which was the shifting balance of power between the two allies in favour of the United States.

War aims: Britain

In defining what the war was being fought for, the United States would enjoy the greater say in the international realm. Washington took the lead in revising the pre-war international political and economic order along liberal internationalist lines, dragging a reluctant London along. But in the domestic political sphere, it was the British who were more revisionist, waging war to transform their own society, while the Americans sought to preserve the status quo at home.

If a domestic equivalent to the Atlantic Charter existed in Britain it was the Beveridge Report. Published in December 1942, the report, or plan as it quickly became known, was the product of an interdepartmental committee chaired by William Beveridge, a leading economist and social reformer. The report identified five great social evils (squalor, ignorance, want, idleness and disease) before going on to propose a comprehensive scheme directed by government: among the elements were full employment, a national health service, family allowances and social insurance. Although individually the proposals had roots in pre-war debates and policies, taken together they

---

33 Rubin, 'America, Britain, and *Swaraj*', 52.

constituted a project for recasting the political and social order at home. The relationship between the state, society and the individual would be reconfigured by the creation of a durable safety net designed to protect people from the uncertainties and risks associated with modern capitalism.[34] Not surprisingly, perhaps, Churchill looked askance at the proposals, dismissing them as 'airy visions of Utopia and Eldorado'. In addition to distracting attention from the immediate goal of winning the war, the Beveridge plan would usher in a socialist transformation of Britain.[35] Yet notwithstanding Churchill's ill-humour, the government was soon compelled to commit itself publicly to implementing some version of the proposals after the war.

Pressure on the government came from several sources. One was the governing coalition itself. Labour, predictably, enthusiastically endorsed the Beveridge plan, as did the Trades Union Congress, despite reservations about the nature and scope of the benefits. As the second largest party in the coalition after the Tories, Labour could not easily be ignored. Meanwhile, the Liberals, together with several backbench Tory MPs, also backed the plan. Another source of pressure was the Ministry of Information, which seized on Beveridge's proposals as a means to bolster popular morale. The Ministry published the report in a cheap edition, stimulating interest and discussion. Yet another source of pressure was public opinion. Although the latter is notoriously amorphous, various organized pressure groups lobbied in favour of the plan. No less importantly, opinion polls suggested that a majority of people soon came to perceive the stakes of the war through the lens of Beveridge's proposals. As a Mass Observation report remarked in this sense:

> Security, equality of opportunity and a reasonable standard of comfort and provision or everyone's needs within a planed [sic] state. This is roughly what people want of the post-war world, what they want to know they are fighting for. . . Social security. . .is the keystone of this post-war world.[36]

The result was the emergence of a broadly based political and popular movement that demanded fundamental change at home as a counterpart to wartime effort and sacrifice. It quickly became clear, moreover, that Churchill (and his political allies) had lost control over the debate on domestic war aims

---

34 José Harris, *William Beveridge: A Biography* (Oxford: Clarendon Press, 1977), pp. 378–418.
35 Stephen Brooke, *Labour's War: The Labour Party During the Second World War* (Oxford: Clarendon Press, 1992), p. 171.
36 Paul A. Thomas, 'Mass-Observation in World War II: Post-War Hopes & Expectations and Reaction to the Beveridge Report' (University of Sussex, 1988), accessed online at: www.massobs.org.uk/downloads/MOWW2_Post_War_Hopes.pdf (accessed 29 October 2014).

to this movement. Although the Beveridge Report did not create the demand for change, it played a vital role in crystallizing diffuse expectations and hopes concerning the post-war future into a tangible project to remake British society.

War aims: The United States

In early 1943, Beveridge undertook a publicity tour in the United States. The tour was immensely successful, as Beveridge and his plan attracted supportive crowds and commentary at various stops. But this success did not presage far-reaching changes to the domestic order. Political developments within the United States followed a different course from those in Britain. To be sure, the war proved to be a potent force for change. Economic mobilization put an end to the Depression, stirring a boom that provided millions of Americans with jobs and relatively high wages. Among the beneficiaries were women and minorities, especially African Americans, as labour shortages prompted companies to look beyond a white male workforce. That many of the best jobs were in the northern states contributed to a migratory wave from the south of both white and African Americans, which would alter the country's demographic landscape.

Just as importantly, however, none of these developments amounted to a reform programme. Aside from an executive order outlawing discrimination in defence industries or government, whose reach proved extremely limited, the administration did little to end the entrenched institutional racism in the United States, which, as Mahatma Gandhi impishly pointed out in a letter to Roosevelt, contradicted claims to be fighting for individual freedom and democracy.[37] More generally, Roosevelt effectively abandoned reform ambitions, insisting that winning the war took priority: Dr New Deal became Dr Win the War. As Paul Koistinen has argued, Dr Win the War oversaw a notable power shift toward business, and especially corporate interests, and away from organized labour, which found itself increasingly shut out from any political influence.[38] Meanwhile, following the 1942 elections, Congress proceeded to eliminate or debilitate several of the major New Deal agencies set up during the 1930s, including the National Resources Planning Board, the

---

37 Lloyd C. Gardner, 'The Atlantic Charter: Idea and Reality, 1942–1945', in Douglas Brinkley and David R. Facey-Crowther (eds.), *The Atlantic Charter* (New York: St Martin's Press, 1994), p. 61.

38 Paul A. C. Koistinen, 'Mobilizing the World War II Economy: Labor and the Industrial-Military Alliance', *Pacific Historical Review* 42 (1973), 443–78.

Farm Security Administration and the Rural Electrification Administration. It is true, as David Kennedy writes, that Congress left alone the 'New Deal's core achievements', such as social security, agricultural support and minimum wage laws.[39] But though an important point, it is also worth noting that the politics of reform during the war quickly assumed a more defensive hue, as the primary goal became to limit the rollback of previous gains rather than to conceive of new advances.

Change on the scope outlined in the Beveridge plan was simply inconceivable in the wartime American political context. Unlike the British, the Americans would not wage war to transform the order at home. Abroad, however, the roles were reversed. On the international front, the British sought to preserve a good deal of the pre-war order. Weakness explains much of this. Economically – and especially financially – Britain faced daunting post-war prospects that fostered a wariness toward major political and economic changes. The need to pay for Beveridge's proposed domestic reforms reinforced this cautious attitude. Imbued with a sense of immense strength, the United States, by contrast, looked to remake the international order in line with American principles and interests. If anything, the blunting of reform impulses at home created a need for an outlet for reformist ambitions, strengthening the tendency to look abroad.

The United States' revisionist impulses were clearly evident on the issue of the post-war international financial order. The conference at Bretton Woods in New Hampshire in July 1944 has understandably attracted considerable scholarly attention, as it established a framework that would endure for the next three decades. The conference is often portrayed as a duel between two prominent economists-cum-government officials: the brilliant and flamboyant Keynes for the British, and the reserved and methodical Henry Dexter White for the Americans.[40] Each one drew up plans for the post-war world, and of the two, Keynes's was the most ambitious. Aware that Britain would emerge from the war as a net debtor and facing sizeable balance of payments deficits, Keynes imagined an international bank or clearing institution, together with a new international currency (bancor) to replace gold. If both measures were designed to help correct international payments imbalances, it is worth adding that the burden of adjustments would fall more heavily on

39 David M. Kennedy, *The American People in World War II* (Oxford University Press, 1999), pp. 357–8.
40 For the most recent version, see Benn Stell, *The Battle of Bretton Woods: John Maynard Keynes, Harry Dexter White, and the Making of a New World Order* (Princeton University Press, 2013).

creditor states than on debtor states (like Britain); the former would be compelled to transfer surpluses to the bank and to pursue expansionist policies at home. Another proposed measure, also meant to protect Britain, was national controls on capital movements to prevent destabilizing capital flows.

White's initial plan envisaged the creation of an international bank and a stabilization fund. Attention, however, soon centred on the fund, which would have two purposes. The first, mirroring Keynes's plan, was to introduce a measure of collective management into the functioning of the international economy. White was no apostle of unbridled laissez-faire: the belief that 'international economic adjustments, if left alone, would work themselves out toward an "equilibrium" with a minimum of harm to world trade and prosperity', he dismissed as nonsense.[41] Yet significantly, White applied his interventionist leanings to the service of a larger project of economic liberalism. Whereas Keynes sought to protect Britain, above all, from the harsh realities of post-war economic weakness, White's plan aimed to prod and push states to integrate into a global international economy. The fund would promote economic liberalization by compelling members to limit trade barriers (such as imperial preference), to abandon controls on foreign exchange, to forego exchange rate manipulations, and to avoid domestic policies that would impact their balance of payments. Not surprisingly, American officials rejected Keynes's proposal that the United States, as the leading creditor state, should be obliged to finance debtor states such as Britain.

Several scholars have argued that the post-war international financial order that emerged from Bretton Woods amounted to a compromise between the British and American conceptions.[42] But if the final accords reflected some give-and-take between London and Washington, as well as a shared belief in the benefits of institutionalized international cooperation, in the end they conformed far more to American than to British proposals. For all Keynes's persuasive genius, he largely failed to impose his views on the Americans. As White reported of the Bretton Woods accords: 'It is a part of a compromise, but much more like the American plan'.[43] Rather than an international

---

41 Cited in Harold James, 'The Multiple Contexts of Bretton Woods', *Past & Present*, supplement 6 (2011), 300.

42 In addition to ibid., see G. John Ikenberry, 'A World Economy Restored: Expert Consensus and the Anglo-American Postwar Settlement', *International Organization* 46 (1992), 289–321.

43 Cited in Robert Skidelsky, *John Maynard Keynes: Fighting for Britain* (London: Macmillan, 2001), p. 320.

bank, there would be a fund in which American liabilities were strictly limited; the United States would not underwrite debtor nations such as Britain. Also in conformity with American wishes, the accords restricted the ability of countries to manipulate their exchange rates, thereby blunting what in the past had been a handy economic tool for national governments. And finally, Keynes's idea of creating an international currency for accounting purposes was set aside in favour of the US dollar, which would be the sole national currency directly linked to gold and which became the international reserve currency.

The Bretton Woods accords underscore a basic point: the balance of economic power by 1944–45 greatly favoured the United States, giving it the whip hand over Britain. In negotiations, remarks Robert Skidelsky, 'the British proposed, the Americans disposed. This was the inevitable consequence of the asymmetry of power'.[44] Still more to the point, the Americans used this imbalance of power to reduce barriers to exchanges and to constrain the ability of states like Britain to manage and limit their integration into the international economy. Animating these efforts was a keen sense of American interests, but also a highly idealist vision of international politics in which open and multilateral exchanges would foster prosperity and peace for all. It was a revisionist vision, moreover, that deliberately set itself against pre-war trends favouring economic nationalism and exclusive economic blocs.

Much the same dynamics were at work on the issue of empire. As already mentioned, the Roosevelt administration looked askance at Britain's goal of preserving its empire. In March 1943, the State Department issued a 'Declaration for National Independence for Colonies', promising that the 'opportunity to achieve independence for those peoples who aspire to independence shall be preserved, respected, and made more effective'. Going further, the declaration called on imperial powers to fix timetables for independence. The British understandably felt threatened. 'The whole tenor of it', noted one Foreign Office official of the declaration, 'is to look forward to the end of the British Empire and the substitution for it of a multiplicity of national sovereignties'.[45] At the same time, as the British realized, countervailing forces were at work on American policy. Like their European counterparts, American officials questioned the fitness of many British (and other) colonies for independence in the near or even long-term future. India was

---

44 Ibid., p. 310.
45 Both cited in Matthew C. Price, *The Advancement of Liberty: How American Democratic Principles Transformed the Twentieth Century* (Westport, Conn.: Praeger, 2008), p. 99.

one thing, most of Africa another. Equally important, American military leaders were eager to acquire military bases in the Pacific, coveting in particular several island groups captured from the Japanese. As the British gleefully intimated, such ambitions could not easily be reconciled with the United States' anti-colonial pretensions.

In order to reconcile their anti-colonialist principles with the 'realities' of power, including their own imperial ambitions, the Americans proposed to internationalize empires through the creation of what the March 1943 declaration called an 'International Trusteeship Administration'. Under a trusteeship system, countries would be responsible to an international organization for the administration of their imperial territories. For some within the Roosevelt administration, trusteeship offered a convenient fig leaf for control of territories in the Pacific and beyond. Sumner Welles, the Under-Secretary of State, thus insisted in 1943 that any trusteeship system must exclude the western hemisphere; for Welles, trusteeship also offered a possible means to force open closed economic spaces to American business interests.[46] But for others, trusteeship would help to ensure that colonial rule functioned in the best interests of local inhabitants, while also providing a means to pressure imperial powers to prepare their colonies for eventual self-government and even independence. Britain, in any case, predictably resisted proposals for trusteeship, balking at the prospect of outside interference in the running of its empire. The British, as Churchill sternly informed Roosevelt and Stalin in 1943, 'intended to hold on to what they had'.[47]

Once again, differences between the two Western allies led to negotiations and compromise. And once again, the outcome reflected American more than it did British wishes. At the Yalta Conference in February 1945, the British reluctantly agreed that trusteeship would be applied to all mandated territories (i.e. the colonies of the defeated powers entrusted to the victors after the First World War), and not just to those of the Axis countries. In effect, the British Empire through its colonial mandates would be subject to international scrutiny. Three months later, at the San Francisco Conference, which established the United Nations, the delegates agreed to create a Trusteeship Council, with the authority to examine annual reports from the imperial powers on colonial administration, to dispatch missions to investigate local

---

46 Thorne, *Allies of a Kind*, p. 215; and Patrick J. Hearden, *Architects of Globalism: Building a New World Order During World War II* (Fayetteville: University of Arkansas Press, 2002), pp. 93–118.

47 Cited in Ronald Ian Heiferman, *The Cairo Conference of 1943: Roosevelt, Churchill, Chiang Kai-shek and Madame Chiang* (Jefferson, NC: McFarland, 2011), p. 127.

conditions (though only at the invitation of colonial authorities) and, perhaps most importantly, to receive petitions from local inhabitants. The council's extensive authority constituted a defeat for the British, who had sought to de-fang any trusteeship system by excluding provisions for formal accountability. Equally unpleasant for London, Chapter xi of the UN Charter clearly indi-cated that independence was the end goal for all colonies. The imperial powers, it read, had an obligation 'to develop self-government, to take due account of the political aspirations of the peoples, and to assist them in the progressive development of their free political institutions, according to the particular circumstances of each territory and its peoples and their varying stages of advancement'.[48] That the Soviets and the Chinese quickly emerged as outspoken proponents of colonial independence within the United Nations only added to the pressure on Britain – and other imperial powers.

To be sure, there is no direct link between the trusteeship system created in 1945 and the rapid post-war decolonization of the British Empire. Never-theless, trusteeship did embody the principle that all colonies were destined for independence, however selectively the United States might apply this principle in practice. For the Americans, political independence for colonies was part and parcel of a larger vision of a post-war world in which individual nations were bound together in a multilateral web of free and open exchanges. Although it would be wrong to view the British as unrepentant imperialists, the wartime British government rejected the assumption that the 'empire project' was doomed.[49] The future of empire was thus at stake in the efforts of the two leading Western allies to define the meaning of the war. And in imposing a fairly extensive trusteeship system, the Americans succeeded in nudging developments in the direction of decolonization. 'In retrospect', concludes the leading historian of the subject, 'the American concept of trusteeship helped to set the colonial world on a different course towards self-determination, independence, and fragmentation'.[50]

Conclusion

It would be misleading to conclude that the war aims of Britain and the United States differed in all respects. Most obviously, the two Western allies

---

48 For the text, see www.un.org/en/documents/charter/chapter11.shtml (accessed 29 October 2014).

49 John Darwin, *The Empire Project: The Rise and Fall of the British World-System, 1830–1970* (Cambridge University Press, 2009), pp. 514–65.

50 Roger Louis, *Imperialism at Bay*, pp. 463–4.

were committed to the defeat of the Axis powers, a grouping of enemies whose aims and guiding principles were judged abhorrent. Common ground also existed between the British and Americans on some aspects of the post-war international order: in the form of the United Nations, Washington and London cooperated in creating an institution capable of providing collective security to individual states, as well as a collective direction to international politics. Nevertheless, the British and the Americans disagreed on the political-economic underpinnings of this order. The United States worked to recast international politics in a broadly liberal Wilsonian mould, a project that threatened Britain's position as an economic and imperial power. And because of its immense resources and strength, the Americans succeeded to a large extent in imposing their preferences on the British, thereby ensuring that the war would be fought to remake international politics.

At least two important qualifiers should be attached to this conclusion. The first is that American success was more evident in the international than in the national sphere. In response to the popularity of the Beveridge Report, the British government promised a profound reform of the domestic order after the war. Beginning in 1945, the British would construct a welfare state in which one guiding principle was to protect people from the uncertainties of market forces – a principle that stood uneasily beside the American emphasis on free and unbridled competition both at home and abroad. The second qualifier concerns the Soviets. During the war, the Americans said little about the Soviet Union's place in a post-war liberal international order, despite Moscow's well-known ideological and practical opposition to many of its aspects. After 1945, Soviet opposition would quickly manifest itself as part of the emerging Cold War. One result is that the Americans found themselves forced to adapt their pursuit of a liberal international order to the new post-war realities. Ironically for the British, this process of adaptation included a more sympathetic attitude toward European empires, as well as considerable financial support for European welfare states.

3

The Soviet Union and the international left

SILVIO PONS

On the eve of the Second World War, the Soviet Union and the communist movement had reached their lowest point in terms of prestige, support and ideological influence. The pact between Stalin and Hitler of August 1939 cancelled what was left of the anti-fascist legitimacy after defeat in Spain. Relations between communists and socialists – already jeopardized by the Great Terror and by anti-Trotskyite persecutions in Spain – were in ruins. The honeymoon between many intellectuals and the Soviet Union of the mid-1930s seemed lost forever. Even Marxist dissidents, former communists and left-oriented intellectuals increasingly labelled Stalin's USSR as a totalitarian power. By the end of the war, all this had changed and the situation seemed largely reversed. Stalin's personal prestige and the Soviet Union's role as a great power were internationally acknowledged far beyond the communist ranks. Soviet socialism embodied an alternative model and a major challenge to liberal capitalism, both in Europe and in the non-European world. The communist movement achieved spectacular growth in Europe and China. In East Central Europe, socialist transformation could be enforced by the presence of the Red Army. The communists seemed ready to overcome the minority positions they held in the interwar period, when compared with the main socialist parties. The main purpose of this chapter is to assess how such a dramatic change took place during the war, and to show how its ideological and political bases were consistent and durable at the start of the post-war era.

The aftermath of the Molotov–Ribbentrop Pact

One year before the outbreak of the war, the bases of Soviet ideology and political culture were fixed in the *Short Course of History of the VKP(b)* – a new handbook published in the autumn of 1938 and the tool of a gigantic propaganda campaign, establishing the orthodox Stalinist version of Marxism-Leninism and Soviet history. The *Short Course* immediately became the gospel for rank-and-file communists, supporting their faith in Lenin and Stalin; it was also a shameful example of how memory was falsified and manipulated in the USSR. The handbook was intended to forge a new generation of communists after the Great Terror – combining Stalin's personal cult, state idolatry and ideological conformity. Its omissions were no less remarkable than its narrative. One of them – reflected in Zhdanov's report and Stalin's intervention at the Politburo session of 11 October 1938 – was that it lacked any significant reference to anti-fascism as an international phenomenon, even though it aimed to provide a guide not only for the Soviet Communist Party, but also for communist parties abroad.[1]

In fact, the Soviet effort to influence European anti-fascist political opinion by promoting popular fronts, writing a new constitution and supporting Republican Spain had failed. In Spain, the very effects of the Great Terror – the witch-hunt against Trotskyites, anarchists and other left-oriented groups, as well as the reduction in Soviet military involvement – undermined the internationalist authority of the Soviet Union. Though the popular fronts had implicitly discarded the theory of 'social fascism' – applied to social democracy before Hitler took power – any prospect of coalition building in the European left was lost. The Molotov–Ribbentrop Pact hugely damaged the residual credibility of the Soviet Union as an anti-fascist power. Consequently, there was no longer any need for restraint in criticizing the Soviet Union because of its role in challenging international fascism. Anti-communist feelings already running high among European liberals and socialists grew abruptly. Many saw the Pact as a confirmation of the similarities between the Nazi and Soviet regimes. The notion of totalitarianism employed in recent years by liberal and Catholic thinkers, as well as Marxist dissidents – to denounce the convergence of the two regimes in spite of their ideological opposition – acquired considerable legitimacy. Left-oriented intellectuals, such as Rudolf Hilferding, Franz Borkenau and George Orwell, helped to establish the comparison between Stalin's Russia and Hitler's Germany.[2]

---

1 *Stenogrammy zasedanii Politburo CK Rkp(b)-Vkp(b) 1923–1938gg.* (3 vols., Moscow: Rosspen, 2007), vol. III, pp. 677–82, 690–7.
2 W. D. Jones, *The Lost Debate: German Socialist Intellectuals and Totalitarianism* (Urbana: University of Illinois Press, 1999), pp. 118–24, 134–7.

The alliance between Stalin and Hitler was something extremely hard for communists to swallow. Their blind faith and unbending sense of loyalty underwent its most difficult test, even more so than with the Great Terror. While non-communist anti-fascists had felt at least very sceptical about the Moscow trials and their miserably incongruous script, this was hardly true of the communists. After all, terror was in tune with the European revolutionary tradition originated by the French Revolution. Furthermore, the threat of a fascist war would justify, to their mind, persecution against any 'fifth column' of traitors. But the Pact was a different matter. It undermined the anti-fascist identity that had been the main *raison d'être* for the communists after Hitler's rise to power. It did not recall any serious precedent in terms of revolutionary tradition. It could be defended only by invoking the priority of avoiding the Soviet Union's involvement in the war. This was what most communists did. But as a result of the Pact, the communist movement was shocked and isolated. The Comintern could not provide any clear directive for more than two weeks. Georgi Dimitrov's idea that his anti-fascist line could survive the Pact only added to the confusion and proved to be a naive delusion.[3]

After the outbreak of the war, on 7 September 1939, Stalin instructed Dimitrov on how the new situation should be understood. In particular, he maintained that

> A war is now on between two groups of capitalist countries... We see nothing wrong in their having a good hard fight and weakening each other... Before the war, opposing a democratic regime to fascism was entirely correct. During war between the imperialist powers that is now incorrect. The division of capitalist states into fascist and democratic ones no longer makes sense... Maintaining yesterday's position (the United Popular Front, the unity of the nation) today means slipping into the position of the bourgeoisie.[4]

Stalin's logic was clear enough, as it followed the old Bolshevik undifferentiated approach to the imperialist world. Nevertheless, the new line took time to be defined and implemented. Before Stalin's instructions to Dimitrov, the first moves of the European communist parties had followed the anti-fascist stance. French and British communists voted in Parliament in

---

3 A. Dallin and F. Firsov (eds.), *Dimitrov and Stalin, 1934–1943: Letters from the Soviet Archives* (New Haven, Conn., and London: Yale University Press, 2000), doc. 27, p. 150; N. S. Lebedeva and M. M. Narinskii (eds.), *Komintern i Vtoraia Mirovaia Voina* (2 vols., Moscow: Pamiatniki Istoricheskoi Misly, 1994–98), vol. 1, docs. 1–8.

4 I. Banac (ed.), *The Diary of Georgi Dimitrov, 1933–1949* (New Haven, Conn., and London: Yale University Press, 2003), pp. 115–16.

favour of wartime mobilization in their own countries. When this position was abruptly reversed, they found themselves in real trouble, which in France led to an earthquake. The adoption of the anti-imperialist attitude imposed by the Comintern and the subsequent condemnation of France's involvement in the war provoked the banning of the French Communist Party. In a few days, the last mass-membership European communist party dissolved and its leadership was disbanded and arrested. Maurice Thorez escaped to Moscow.[5] By October 1939, the communists had no legal existence in Europe – the only exceptions being Britain and Sweden. Even in Britain, however, the leadership was sharply divided and Harry Pollitt resisted the anti-imperialist policy change before capitulating to the orthodox component grouped around R. Palme Dutt.[6]

Stalin was quite possibly unconcerned about the developments in France. He did not intend to promote any revolutionary upsurge, but only to prevent the communist parties from defending positions at odds with the interest of the Soviet Union. The Comintern eventually established its new policy under the supervision of Andrei Zhdanov and of Stalin himself.[7] Though the European parties were at best reduced to a few thousand cadres, their unyielding loyalty and capacity to create covert networks, operating in close connection with Moscow, would be enhanced by the state of war. What mattered to Stalin was the primacy of Soviet interests. The revision imposed on Dimitrov showed its basic logic in the imperial expansion of the Soviet state, the occupation of eastern Poland, and the consequent gains in terms of territorial security by means of violence, repression and mass murder.[8]

However, the crisis of the European communist parties at the end of the decade signalled that Soviet outside influence was in steep decline, while nobody could see how this could be reversed by Stalin's alliance with Hitler. The separation between dogmatic loyalties and the appeal of Soviet Communism increased sharply. The attempt to justify the war against Finland by creating a fictitious communist government failed and was soon forgotten.[9]

5 S. Courtois and M. Lazar, *Histoire du parti communiste français* (Paris: Puf, 2000), pp. 169–70.
6 A. Thorpe, *The British Communist Party and Moscow, 1920–1943* (Manchester University Press, 2000), pp. 258–60.
7 Dallin and Firsov (eds.), *Dimitrov and Stalin*, doc. 29, p. 164; Banac (ed.), *Diary of Georgi Dimitrov*, pp. 119–20.
8 T. Snyder, *Bloodlands: Europe Between Stalin and Hitler* (New York: Basic Books, 2010), pp. 128–30.
9 N. S. Lebedeva et al. (eds.), *Komintern i Finlandiia, 1919–1943* (Moscow: Nauka, 2003), docs. 116–118.

At the same time, the Winter War provoked further escalation in the heated relations with Britain and France – and with the European socialists. To be sure, the Socialist left was much more in trouble than the Comintern was. By June 1939, the Socialist International had been dissolved as a consequence of unresolved political conflict between Frederick Adler – the last political heir of the once powerful German and Austrian tradition – and the Labour Party.[10] Nevertheless, this was cold comfort for the disbanded European communists. Although the communist movement maintained its well-known discipline, the risk of insignificance could not be discounted, while dissenting voices were more likely to be heard. Continuing persecution against prominent dissidents even outside Soviet borders revealed Stalin's fears rather than his confidence. The obvious case was the assassination of Trotsky in exile in Mexico by the hand of an NKVD (predecessor of the KGB) emissary, in August 1940.[11] The mysterious death of Willi Münzenberg – the architect of Soviet propaganda in the West and even in the non-European countries, who distanced himself from Moscow and became a public critic of Stalinism after the Molotov–Ribbentrop Pact – coincided with Trotsky's murder.[12] The monolithic image of communism had thus been reaffirmed by means of violence – not necessarily a sign of strength.

No ideological mobilization was carried on during 1940 and early 1941. The communist movement did not even try to resist Hitler's conquest of the European continent. This passivity was an obvious consequence of its lack of mass influence. But it also showed the paralysing effect of the Soviet alliance with Nazi Germany. In the aftermath of France's collapse in June 1940, the French communists even entertained for some time ambiguous negotiations with the German occupiers, following the Comintern's advice. Such moves were soon ended, but serious damage had been done to the French Communist Party's credibility.[13] Although tensions emerged later between Moscow and Berlin in the Balkans, all Dimitrov's faint efforts to obtain Stalin's consent to launch some kind of mobilization were frustrated.

10 L. Rapone, 'La crisi finale dell'Internazionale Operaia e Socialista', in *I socialisti e l'Europa* (Milano: Angeli, 1989), pp. 68–93.
11 B. M. Patenaude, *Trotsky: Downfall of a Revolutionary* (New York: HarperCollins, 2009).
12 S. McMeekin, *The Red Millionaire: A Political Biography of Willi Muenzenberg, Moscow's Secret Propaganda Tsar in the West* (New Haven, Conn., and London: Yale University Press, 2003), pp. 295–307.
13 Dallin and Firsov (eds.), *Dimitrov and Stalin*, doc. 32, pp. 175–81; Lebedeva and Narinskii (eds.), *Komintern i Vtoraia Mirovaia Voina*, vol. I, docs. 110, 113, 116; B. H. Bayerlein, M. M. Narinski, B. Studer and S. Wolikow, *Moscou-Paris-Berlin: Télégrammes chiffrés du Komintern, 1939–1941* (Paris: Tallandier, 2003), docs. 160–161.

At the end of November 1940, after Molotov had returned from his talks with Hitler in Berlin, Dimitrov asked him whether the line 'of demoralizing the German occupation troops in the various countries' would interfere with Soviet policy. Molotov replied that such goal should be pursued, though 'quietly'.[14] In late March 1941, on the eve of the German invasion of Yugoslavia, Molotov instructed Dimitrov in the same manner: 'Not raise a stink, not shout, but firmly carry out your position'. Accordingly, Dimitrov advised Tito to confine his followers 'at this stage to an energetic and skillful explanation of the position you have adopted among the masses, but without organizing any street demonstrations, and taking all pains to avoid armed clashes between the masses and the authorities'.[15] After the German attack and the fall of the pro-Soviet government in Belgrade, Zhdanov told Dimitrov that 'the events in the Balkans do not alter the overall stance we have taken as regards the imperialist war and both of the combatant capitalist alignments'.[16] Thus the communists were requested to restrict themselves to strengthening their covert organization in Yugoslavia, Greece and Bulgaria.

The only idea cultivated by the Stalinist leadership between 1939 and 1941 was to combine the ideological orthodoxy established at the end of the Great Terror with a patriotic appeal to the country, while apparently discouraging communists abroad from any significant move – other than maintaining their strict association with Moscow. In fact, however, Soviet institutions did not really promote popular mobilization for the prospect of war even inside the Soviet Union. Propaganda and indoctrination were scarcely active and effective in the Red Army.[17] The desire to appease Hitler prevailed over all other attitudes within Stalin's inner circle. Military preparations were carried on discreetly. Only in May 1941 did Stalin speak openly in public about preparing the Red Army in an 'offensive' mode, but even then his words were abridged in the press and no propaganda campaign actually started.[18]

The Soviet leaders understood that communists had to adjust their vague anti-imperialistic rhetoric. In February 1941, Zhdanov acknowledged that

14 Banac (ed.), *Diary of Georgi Dimitrov*, p. 136.
15 Ibid., pp. 152–3.
16 Ibid., p. 154.
17 D. Brandenberger, *Propaganda State in Crisis: Soviet Ideology, Indoctrination, and Terror under Stalin, 1927–1941* (New Haven, Conn., and London: Yale University Press, 2011), pp. 244–8.
18 Banac (ed.), *Diary of Georgi Dimitrov*, p. 160; V. A. Nevezhin, *Sindrom nastupatelnoi voiny. Sovetskaia propaganda v preddverii "sviashchennykh boev" 1939–1941 gg.* (Moscow: Airo-XX, 1997).

'We got off track on the national question. Failed to pay sufficient attention to national aspects'.[19] On 20 April, Stalin told Dimitrov that the Comintern prevented the parties 'from developing independently and resolving their own problems as national parties'.[20] The argument was by no means controversial. Dimitrov realized that the very existence of the International was in question, and discussed with Togliatti and Thorez the prospect of abolishing its Executive Committee. On 12 May, Dimitrov agreed with Zhdanov on the principles underlying the dissolution of the Comintern, to begin with the idea of 'combining a healthy, properly understood nationalism with proletarian internationalism'. They expected that the parties would especially benefit from weakening 'the bourgeoisie's highest trump card, that the communists are subjects of a foreign center, hence "traitors"'.[21] As far as we know, these ideas were not followed up, though the door was left open on the decision to dissolve the Comintern, which came two years later. However, any communist discourse about the 'nation' in Nazi Europe seemed scarcely effective in light of the alliance between the Soviet Union and Germany. After all, Stalin in person had maintained as early as September 1939 that the 'unity of the nation' could no longer be enhanced by the communists, at a time when they were supposed to relaunch their anti-imperialist tradition. Only the unexpected resumption of anti-fascism would change such a state of affairs.

The aftermath of the German invasion

The Nazi attack of 22 June 1941 had the immediate effect of radically changing the official language and image of the Soviet Union and the Comintern. The patriotic appeal became convincing because of the invasion and was quite rapidly exploited by the regime – despite the shocking impact of Stalin's failure to appease Hitler. Anti-fascist propaganda was relaunched as if nothing had happened in the last couple of years and soon showed its effect in terms of mobilization. The combination of patriotism and anti-fascism was destined to leave its stamp on Soviet and communist wartime ideology, although the emphasis shifted between the Soviet Union – where the patriotic thrust against the German enemy largely obscured any other concept – and the European countries – where resistance against the Nazi order provided the main identity tool. A few hours

19 Banac (ed.), *Diary of Georgi Dimitrov*, p. 150.
20 Ibid., p. 156.
21 Ibid., pp. 162–4.

after the German attack, on 22 June, Dimitrov wrote in his diary that 'The issue of socialist revolution is not to be raised. The Soviet people are waging a patriotic war against fascist Germany'.[22] Such words would remain a major source of inspiration in the following years.

Pressured by Moscow, many communist parties soon issued statements that reversed their former anti-war rhetoric into a pro-war line. The French Communist Party was better positioned, as an effort to come out of isolation by invoking France's 'independence' had already been outlined in May–June. In July 1941, the party began approaching the other political forces about the prospect of a national coalition – though it would take time to overcome the bad blood created by the Molotov–Ribbentrop Pact.[23] Other parties followed the same pattern. Obscured by patriotic appeals and deprived of any public profile, the Comintern focused its activities on propaganda and the organization of 'covert operations' in connection with Soviet security agencies.[24]

The development of a well-defined strategy for post-war scenarios took time to be accomplished. When the basic security objectives of the Soviet Union for the post-war period were established – in the meeting between Stalin, Molotov and Eden of December 1941 – the political perspective of the communist movement had yet to be defined. Only at the end of 1942 and the beginning of 1943 – at the height of the regime's patriotic appeal in the aftermath of the Battle of Stalingrad – did Moscow instruct the French and Italian parties to embrace more concretely the prospect of 'national unity'.[25] This line meant collaboration with all forces fighting against fascism and rejection of civil war as a way to power – at least until after victory occurred. In this respect, the idea was not simply to rescue the popular fronts, but also to enlarge the scope of coalition building, even beyond the borders of the international left. After Stalin's approval, the French Communist Party joined the resistance movement led by General de Gaulle in January 1943.[26]

Soon after that, the idea that the Comintern should disappear – put forward by Stalin two years earlier – emerged again and was discussed along the same lines. This time, the decision was taken and implemented quickly.

22 Ibid., p. 167.
23 S. Wolikow, *L'Internationale communiste (1919–1943). Le Komintern ou le rêve déchu du parti mondial de la révolution* (Paris: Les Éditions de l'Atelier, 2010), pp. 138–42.
24 N. A. Rosenfeldt, *The "Special" World: Stalin's Power Apparatus and the Soviet System's Secret Structures of Communication* (2 vols., Copenhagen: Museum Tusculanum Press, 2009), vol. II, p. 249.
25 Lebedeva and Narinskii (eds.), *Komintern i Vtoraia Mirovaia Voina*, vol. II, doc. 101.
26 F. Firsov, *Sekrety Kommunisticheskogo Internatsionala. Shifroperepiska* (Moscow: Rosspen, 2011), p. 381.

On 21 May, the Politburo approved the relevant resolution. Stalin stressed how the end of the Comintern prevented accusations against the communists of 'supposedly being agents of a foreign state'.[27] The eventual dissolution of the Comintern in June 1943 was clearly intended to provide an image of the Soviet Union as a 'normal' state, detached from the original ideal of world revolution, and leaving the communist parties to follow their own destiny. No doubt this choice helped to strengthen the war coalition with the Western powers. In this sense, Stalin's initiative could be seen as purely tactical. In fact, the communist parties maintained their close relations with Moscow through the apparatus of the Communist Party of the Soviet Union (CPSU).[28] Nevertheless, Stalin seemed to take seriously the project to 'nationalize' the parties, by combining the concepts of class and nation on the pattern followed by the CPSU, namely using national appeal – even Russian nationalism, despite the multinational structure of the Soviet Union – as a means for mobilization and legitimization. From this moment on, the line of 'national fronts' became central to the communist movement and accompanied the reversal of the military struggle on the Eastern Front.

Visions and projects for the post-war era

Over the next two years, the international standing of the Soviet Union and the fate of the communists changed completely. The overlap between the counter-offensive of the Red Army and the growth of anti-fascist resistance – especially in the Balkans, Italy and France – revived the Soviet myth and favoured the recruitment of a new generation of communists. When Stalin, Churchill and Roosevelt met at Tehran in December 1943, there was already the prospect of Soviet expansion and communist influence in the heart of the continent, which would have been unthinkable in 1939, and even more so in 1941. For most communists – and anti-communists too – the challenge was now the relaunch of the universal mission originated by the October Revolution, after an era of isolation, modernization and terror. However, Stalin and the Soviet ruling elite understood their mission primarily in terms of power. Ideological conformism and the use of patriotism were seen as functional and integrated parts of the scenario of imperial expansion. Soviet wartime myth-making was supposed to provide the proper synthesis of

27 Banac (ed.), *Diary of Georgi Dimitrov*, p. 276.
28 G. M. Adibekov, E. N. Shakhnazarova and K. K. Shiriniia, *Organizacionnaia struktura Kominterna 1919–1943* (Moscow: Rosspen, 1997), pp. 228–41.

national appeal and class vision. Consequently, no universalist thinking was felt necessary to support Soviet projects for the post-war era. Stalin's plans would focus essentially on (1) outlining the spheres of interest in Europe, with the aim of establishing the largest achievable influence of the Soviet Union in the East Central and Southern part of the continent; (2) re-imposing political pedagogy in the Red Army in order to prevent the military from unwanted ideological contamination as they advanced westward beyond the country's borders; (3) defining both the political line of the communist parties and the profile of the regimes to be established in the countries occupied by the Red Army, in accordance with the Soviet Union's interests and, if possible, in a manner acceptable to its allies.[29] Those trends were already at work in Moscow by late 1943 and early 1944.

The main Soviet document we know at this stage about post-war planning is Ivan Maisky's memorandum to Molotov of January 1944. Maisky imagined post-war Europe under the shared influence of Great Britain and the Soviet Union. In this respect, his document only reflected already established claims and the expectation that Soviet security could be achieved by cooperation between the Big Three – a view that prevailed in the Commission on post-war arrangements chaired by Maxim Litvinov. Yet Maisky's memorandum was not only remarkable for the issue of the spheres of influence. It also revealed speculation about the future of socialism in Europe. Maisky had lived in London up to May 1943, where he exchanged views with prominent personalities of the British political and intellectual left. In his writing, he confirmed the idea that social revolution was unlikely, whereas transformation could occur 'in the spirit of the popular front'. Such an expression was possibly his way of translating the European zeitgeist for the Soviet political elite.[30]

---

29 On Soviet wartime plans about spheres of influence in Europe, see S. Pons, 'In the Aftermath of the Age of Wars: The Impact of World War II on Soviet Security Policy', in S. Pons and A. Romano (eds.), *Russia in the Age of Wars, 1914–1945* (Milan: Annali Feltrinelli, 2000), pp. 277–307; G. Roberts, *Stalin's Wars: From World War to Cold War, 1939–1953* (New Haven, Conn., and London: Yale University Press, 2006), pp. 229–34. On the shift in Soviet wartime propaganda, see D. Brandenberger, *National Bolshevism: Stalinist Mass Culture and the Formation of Modern Russian National Identity, 1931–1956* (Cambridge, Mass.: Harvard University Press, 2002); K. C. Berkhoff, *Motherland in Danger: Soviet Propaganda During World War II* (Cambridge, Mass., and London: Harvard University Press, 2012), pp. 206–7. On the political line of the communist parties, see S. Pons, *La rivoluzione globale. Storia del comunismo internazionale (1917–1991)* (Torino: Einaudi, 2012), ch. 3.

30 T. V. Volokitina (chief ed.), *Sovetskii faktor v Vostochnoi Evrope 1944–1953. Dokumenty* (2 vols., Moscow: Rosspen, 1999–2002), vol. 1, doc. 1, pp. 23–48.

However, Maisky was too optimistic in his popular front hint. In fact, a basic ambivalence lay behind the impending triumph of the Red Army. Communists and many anti-fascists saw the prospect of Soviet victory over Nazism and revolutionary change in Europe as obviously converging events. But imperial expansion and revolution might also entail tension and opposition. The feelings of suspicion and hostility widespread in the non-communist left before June 1941 were not dissolved, and the emergence of the Soviet Union as a major power in East Central Europe produced dissimilar reactions and forecasts about the post-war settlement – to a large extent associated with European perceptions of communism as either a legitimate actor or a dangerous menace. European socialists were a diaspora that could not be said to represent an international force in its own right. Many experienced either emigration, particularly Germans and Italians, or compromise with Nazi occupiers, as with the French. Only in Great Britain – after the formation of the coalition government under Churchill's leadership in May 1940 – and in neutral Sweden were they in government. Nevertheless, the socialists' political ideas were relevant to the formation of Western European opinion. One of the major problems was how to define the relationship with the communists. For a quarter of a century, antagonism and struggle had largely prevailed over shared cultures and visions. Once again, the dilemmas of potential alliance and real competition, proximity and distrust, came onto the agenda, especially after the dissolution of the Comintern.

The issue mainly concerned perceptions of and prognoses for the evolution of Stalin's regime and the Soviet Union's future international role. In this respect, the Labour Party was clearly in the leading position, as it represented both the main Allied European power and the major socialist force in wartime Europe, besides being historically much stronger than the local communists. Internationalism was not a distinctive feature of the party. Even relations with other socialist parties were difficult, particularly with the German exiles – harshly treated as nationalists reluctant to accept the unconditional surrender of Germany and marginalized in wartime London.[31] Nevertheless, the views of Labour leaders covered the spectrum of all possible attitudes to Soviet Communism in the non-communist left. They ranged from the combination of realism and ideological hostility that characterized the party establishment – primarily Clement Attlee and Ernest Bevin – to the more or less pronounced

31 A. Glees, *Exile Politics During the Second World War: The German Social Democrats in Britain* (Oxford: Clarendon Press, 1982).

empathy and critical understanding typical of personalities of the left like Aneurin Bevan, G. D. H. Cole and Harold Laski.[32]

The two political and intellectual poles were probably best represented, however, by Laski and Orwell – though the latter was in many ways a complete outsider. Both had firmly criticized the Communist Party of Great Britain (CPGB) for its alignment to the Molotov–Ribbentrop Pact and its inclination to put British imperialism on a par with Nazi Germany. Orwell's peremptory definition of British communists as 'Russian publicity agents posing as an International Socialist' was shared by most socialists.[33] But after June 1941, their respective positions increasingly diverged over the role of the Soviet Union. By 1943, Laski assumed that the Soviet Union was bound to become a crucial player not just because of its power, but also because of its contribution to the prospect of economic planning and social justice. After the dissolution of the Comintern, he decided that the Labour Party should take on the task of founding a new Socialist International based in London, which would include the Soviet Union. He held on to such an idea up to the end of the war and even later – followed by such other socialists as the Austrian Julius Braunthal, the Italian Pietro Nenni and the Russian Menshevik Fedor Dan.[34] Laski was no 'fellow traveller', but he admired the Soviet image of modernity, and hoped that the post-war years would bring about a transformation of the regime. Orwell adopted a totally different stance. To his mind, great power politics was the only real motivation of Soviet Communism. He maintained that Stalin's Russia was a menace to democratic socialism and that the end of the Comintern made no substantial difference. He complained that Trotsky-inspired criticism 'in a wide sense' of the Soviet Union was silenced because of the war alliance, and criticized Laski for ignoring Stalin's dictatorship and the hierarchical nature of Soviet Communism. Orwell kept faith with the principle that 'the destruction of the Soviet myth was essential if we wanted a revival of the socialist movement' – as he would famously write after the war.[35]

---

32 T. D. Burridge, *British Labour and Hitler's War* (London: André Deutsch, 1976). S. Brooke, *Labour's War: The Labour Party During the Second World War* (Oxford: Clarendon Press, 1992).

33 J. Newsinger, *Orwell's Politics* (London: Macmillan, 1999), p. 113. See also V. Gollancz, *The Betrayal of the Left: An Examination and Refutation of Communist Policy from October 1939 to January 1941, with Suggestions for an Alternative and an Epilogue on Political Morality* (London: V. Gollancz, 1941).

34 I. Kramnik and B. Sheerman, *Harold Laski: A Life on the Left* (New York: Allen Lane, 1993), pp. 467–8; H. Laski, *Reflections on the Revolution of Our Time* (London: Allen & Unwin, 1943).

35 Newsinger, *Orwell's Politics*, p. 115; S. Ingle, *The Social and Political Thought of George Orwell* (New York: Routledge, 2006), p. 115; Kramnick and Sheerman, *Harold Laski*,

As a prominent figure in the Labour Party – though not really involved in decision-making – and as a teacher at the London School of Economics, Laski had followers not only in Britain, but also abroad. His influence on non-European leaders – especially on Nehru and the Indian post-war political elite – is well known, but he also interacted with American liberals. Much more than his ideas about socialism, his view of the Second World War as a 'democratic revolution', the expectation that the Soviet Union could play a progressive role, and fear that isolating Moscow might lead to a new war were shared in the United States by the intellectuals grouped around such journals as *The Nation* and *The New Republic*.[36] On the other hand, Orwell had no relations with the political establishment and was a loner, even detached from the radical leftist groups he had joined in the pre-war years. But his influence was potentially quite important. The totalitarian paradigm he applied to the Soviet Union and kept alive in left-wing public discourse would regain acceptance in the last phase of the war – in light of Soviet and communist behaviour in East Central Europe. The Labour leadership would stick closely to this stance, and influenced other European socialists.[37]

Behind closed doors in the summer of 1944, Soviet ideologists grouped around Zhdanov worked on scenarios that failed to take into account the perceptions and hopes of European political opinion. In order to re-establish ideological orthodoxy – which implied interpreting the war as a victory of the 'Soviet system', and not only of the Russian people – they debated the future international role of the two systems – the socialist and the capitalist. The class struggle between them was expected to define the post-war era and was seen as the authentic basis for defining Soviet interests. Consequently, the ideologues foresaw the emergence of the Soviet Union's power in Europe as one that would establish a 'new type' of state and social structure in its own sphere of influence. They were concerned much less with the alliance of the Big Three than with the building of a unilateral framework for the post-war arrangements under Soviet influence. While their view of relations with the Western powers as intrinsically antagonistic obviously differed from that of leading diplomats, it nonetheless represented a crucial development inside Soviet political elites. The idea of 'popular democracy'

pp. 470–1; *The Complete Works of George Orwell*, ed. Peter Hobley Davison, Ian Angus and Sheila Davison (20 vols., London: Secker & Warburg, 1986–98), vol. xv, pp. 106–8, vol. xvi, pp. 122–3, vol. xix, p. 88.

36 F. A. Warren, *Noble Abstractions: American Liberal Intellectuals and World War Two* (Columbus: Ohio State University Press, 1999), pp. 162–8.

37 Burridge, *British Labour and Hitler's War*, p. 161.

mainly stemmed from such thinking, adapting a political term born during the Spanish Civil War to a vision of how the Soviet Union would exert its own hegemony in post-war East Central Europe.[38]

The aftermath of the war

All communist parties embraced the line of 'national fronts'. Though a centralized organization did not exist anymore, the strategies followed by communists were still scarcely distinguishable under the guidelines provided by Soviet foreign policy and its proclaimed aim to maintain the war coalition. In the United States, Earl Browder openly presented support for President Roosevelt as a reflection of the 'Tehran principles', and on that premise he even proposed dissolving the party – a radical measure, perplexing to Dimitrov.[39] In Britain, Harry Pollitt was more cautious, but the CPGB's request for affiliation to the Labour Party was intended to exploit, albeit in vain, the political meaning of the war alliance.[40] In any case, little could have been expected of communists in Britain and in the United States, and the best they could do was to free themselves of the label 'agents of Moscow'. However, communists would soon take on a more significant role in continental Europe.

Here they implemented the 'national front' line within the resistance movements, as they did in the countries liberated from Nazi occupation where new coalition governments had to be created – the first of which was Italy, after the fall of Mussolini and the armistice of September 1943. During 1944, the aim to subvert fascist or collaborationist regimes was largely overcome by military events – with some remarkable exceptions, like Slovakia, Yugoslavia, Greece and northern Italy. As the Nazi empire collapsed under the offensive of the Allied armies, the communist leaders returning to their countries after exile in Moscow were invariably committed to the establishment of national coalition governments. After considerable uncertainty over whether to encourage or contain the radical thrust of local anti-fascists, Stalin's instructions to Togliatti eventually established the pattern of the 'moderate' solution in March 1944.[41] Social revolution and civil war were not on the agenda, even in the final phase of the war. Both in Western and

38 Pons, 'In the Aftermath', p. 297.
39 Banac (ed.), *Diary of Georgi Dimitrov*, p. 307.
40 Thorpe, *The British Communist Party and Moscow*, pp. 270–1.
41 Banac (ed.), *Diary of Georgi Dimitrov*, pp. 303–4.

in East Central Europe, that same pattern was adopted in the second half of the year, contributing to the expansion of the communist parties.

Plans to define the spheres of influence in Europe did not seem to affect the fundamental political line that Moscow prescribed the communists. After the meeting between Stalin and Churchill in October 1944, a memorandum of Litvinov to Molotov and Stalin sketched an extended Soviet zone of interest, conceived as a product of their collaboration with the British. Moscow was following a twofold strategy of influence: outlining a division of Europe largely favourable to its interest, while pushing communist partners to refrain from revolutionary action that could endanger relations with the West and prevent them from enhancing their political weight.[42] As in Italy, the formulation of the communists' political line in France was governed by Moscow's diplomatic relations. Stalin ordered Thorez in November to avoid challenging de Gaulle and to prevent the party from being isolated.[43] The line was no different in Eastern European countries. Czechoslovak communists were the first to be instructed to enter a coalition of national forces. In Poland, Bulgaria, Romania and Hungary in the autumn of 1944, the communists were instructed to build large political coalitions.[44]

However, 'national unity' did not entail moderate behaviour everywhere. Leaving aside political formulas, the very logic of the spheres of influence created a clear difference between the two halves of Europe. When Stalin met Churchill, he provided reassurance about the goals of the communists in the West by hinting at Togliatti's prudent conduct in Italy.[45] But the same was not necessarily true in the East. With the partial exception of Bulgaria, the communists of that area had no significant part in the resistance movements. The Polish communist wing of resistance founded in Moscow had little credibility, even though the basic nucleus of anti-Nazi rebellion made up of anti-communist nationalists had suffered badly under Nazi repression in July 1944 – while the Red Army stalled its march before Warsaw. Though the communists were restrained from embracing radical social goals, it was the dominance of the Red Army that guaranteed their central role in any political coalition. The obvious frailty of the party in Poland – combined with

---

42 Pons, 'In the Aftermath', pp. 299–304.
43 Banac (ed.), *The Diary of Georgi Dimitrov*, pp. 342–3.
44 E. Mark, *Revolution by Degrees: Stalin's National-Front Strategy for Europe, 1941–1947* (Washington DC: Cold War International History Project, working paper 31, February 2001).
45 O. A. Rzheshevskii, *Stalin i Cherchill. Vstrechi. Besedy. Diskussii. Dokumenty, kommentarii 1941–1945* (Moscow: Nauka, 2004), p. 426.

the country's past and its anti-Soviet role in the interwar years – was the premise for a wave of persecutions against non-communist forces launched by Soviet agencies as early as the second half of 1944. The Nazi empire's strategy of annihilation (and, to a lesser degree, also the Soviet occupations of 1939–40) had already destroyed the pre-war ruling classes and educated strata of society in the region. The role of revolutionary forces could be limited to planning structural reforms like nationalizations – largely shared by other political forces and progressive public opinion – and maintaining a firm grip on state power. In this respect, Poland was no exception. In fact, the violent behaviour of Soviet agencies prefigured a pattern to be followed from the end of 1944. Accordingly, local communists attained power in spite of their unpopularity – paradoxically enhanced by their Soviet partner, as they themselves understood without being able to find alternative solutions.[46] Although the obsession with security and the related practices of repression in the occupied Polish and Baltic territories had jeopardized Soviet security on the borders with Hitler's empire, that same security pattern was put forward by Stalin at the end of the war.[47]

Yet not everything was under Soviet control. Although the combination of the Soviet Union's foreign policy and the communists' new national line worked quite well, there were important exceptions in the Balkans and China – where the implementation of Moscow's directives depended not so much on leaders coming back from exile, as on those emerging from the liberation struggle. Here, the balance between loyalty to Soviet imperatives and the ideological tradition of the movement proved to be very different. This was clearly the case of Tito and the Yugoslav communist leadership, who did not perceive their struggle exclusively as a 'national revolution'.[48] Moscow criticized more than once the Yugoslavs' poor commitment to

---

46 I. Iazhborovskaia, 'The Gomułka Alternative: The Untravelled Road', in N. Naimark and L. Gibianskii (eds.), *The Establishment of Communist Regimes in Eastern Europe, 1944–1949* (Boulder, Colo.: Westview Press, 1997).

47 V. Tismaneanu (ed.), *Stalinism Revisited: The Establishment of Communist Regimes in East Central Europe* (Budapest and New York: Central European University Press, 2009); Naimark and Gibianskii (eds.), *The Establishment of Communist Regimes in Eastern Europe.* See also K. Kersten, *The Establishment of Communist Rule in Poland, 1943–1948* (Berkeley and Los Angeles: University of California Press, 1991); M. Mevius, *Agents of Moscow: The Hungarian Communist Party and the Origins of Socialist Patriotism, 1941–1953* (Oxford University Press, 2005); P. Kenez, *Hungary from the Nazis to the Soviets: The Establishment of the Communist Regime in Hungary, 1944–1948* (New York: Cambridge University Press, 2006); V. Dimitrov, *Stalin's Cold War: Soviet Foreign Policy, Democracy and Communism in Bulgaria, 1941–48* (London: Palgrave Macmillan, 2008).

48 M. Djilas, *Wartime* (New York: Harcourt Brace, 1980), p. 59. See also G. Swain, 'Tito and the Twilight of the Comintern', in T. Rees and A. Thorpe (eds.), *International*

creating a 'national front'.[49] Tension surfaced again at the end of 1943, when the Yugoslav Liberation Committee decided to ban the king's return to the country – an uncompromising position that Tito had not agreed with Dimitrov. Stalin reacted angrily, complaining of the resultant complications for his talks in Tehran.[50] The dispute soon faded, but the divergence remained. In April 1944, Molotov explained to Djilas the national unity line chosen for Italy, making clear, at the same time, that Moscow opposed any 'sovietization' of Yugoslavia.[51] However, in September 1944, when Tito went to Moscow asking for military help to liberate Belgrade, the Yugoslav communists had already emerged as the leading force of an autonomous revolution, thus creating a fait accompli.

The revolutionary flair of the Yugoslavs was not confined to their own struggle. They also supported the Greek communists, providing them with assistance and backing their confrontational approach to relations with other components of the liberation movement. By late 1943, the Yugoslavs were in charge of developments in Greece, and Moscow contacted them for information. By mid-1944, the communist component of the liberation movement had become a mass force, reluctant to maintain an alliance with monarchist and pro-British forces. Though alerted that the Soviet Union was not going to provide aid, the Greeks still believed that the Yugoslav pattern could be replicated – unaware that their country had been assigned to Britain by the agreement between Stalin and Churchill. They engaged themselves in a political conflict that eventually led to mass mobilization, quickly followed by bloody repression in Athens in early December 1944.[52] Quite significantly, a few weeks later, Stalin commented to Dimitrov that 'I advised not starting this fighting in Greece. The ELAS [Ellenikós Laikós Apeleftherotikós Stratós – Greek People's Liberation Army] people should not have resigned from the Papandreou government. They've taken on more than they can handle. They

Communism and the Communist International (Manchester and New York: Manchester University Press, 1998).

49 Lebedeva and Narinskii (eds.), *Komintern i Vtoraia Mirovaia Voina*, vol. II, doc. 68, pp. 216–17; Banac (ed.), *Diary of Georgi Dimitrov*, pp. 211, 234.

50 Djilas, *Wartime*, p. 367.

51 G. P. Murashko (chief ed.), *Vostochnaia Evropa v dokumentakh rossiiskikh arkhivov 1944–1953* (2 vols., Moscow and Novosibirsk: Sibirskii Khronograf, 1997–98), vol. I, doc. 2, p. 34.

52 Lebedeva and Narinskii (eds.), *Komintern i Vtoraia Mirovaia Voina*, vol. II, doc. 198, p. 474; P. J. Stavrakis, *Moscow and Greek Communism, 1944–1949* (Ithaca, NY: Cornell University Press, 1989); I. O. Iatrides, 'Revolution or Self-Defense? Communist Goals, Strategy, and Tactics in the Greek Civil War', *Journal of Cold War Studies* 7:3 (summer 2005); A. Gerolymatos, *Red Acropolis, Black Terror: The Greek Civil War and the Origins of Soviet-American Rivalry, 1943–1949* (New York: Basic Books, 2004), pp. 122–8.

were evidently counting on the Red Army's coming down to the Aegean. We cannot do that. We cannot send our troops to Greece, either. The Greeks have acted foolishly'.[53] In other words, Stalin considered what had happened in Greece to be an act of insubordination and obviously understood that such a policy was linked to the radical thrust of the Yugoslavs in the Balkans – he directly complained to Hebrang about this.[54]

The civil conflict in Greece would soon become the context against which the role and perspectives of the communist movement had to be defined. The Italian and French leaders publicly declared that they rejected the 'Greek model' and its catastrophic consequences. Thus, a strategic divergence surfaced among major partners of the movement – one that would endure throughout the early post-war years. In the following months, this divergence increasingly focused on the Trieste question. Tito pressured Stalin for a decision in favour of the annexation of the city to Yugoslavia, while Togliatti asked for its internationalization, trying to prevent huge damage to the national image of the Communist Party of Italy. Stalin was less consistent than he had been some months earlier. He let the Yugoslavs occupy Trieste in late May 1945 and informed the Italians that they must yield. But when he realized that the confrontation with the Western powers over the city was becoming dangerously heated, he forced Tito to withdraw.[55] Tension between Moscow and Belgrade grew sharply for some time and left a sense of resentment. The Yugoslavs clearly represented an autonomous revolution, and though they considered themselves loyal to the Soviet Union no less than others, their idea of loyalty somewhat differed. They did not find great-power geopolitics acceptable, while revolution was to be pursued in the interest of the whole movement.

The case of the Chinese communists was no different. In principle, they were the best example of the implementation of 'national unity' outside Europe – as in China that line predated wartime formulations and was adopted soon after the Japanese invasion of the summer of 1937. Nevertheless, their behaviour was hardly consistent with 'national unity'. Mao Zedong's reluctance to follow Moscow's directives on collaboration with

53 Banac (ed.), *Diary of Georgi Dimitrov*, pp. 352–3.
54 Murashko (chief ed.), *Vostochnaia Evropa v dokumentakh rossiiskikh arkhivov*, vol. I, doc. 37, p. 130.
55 Banac (ed.), *Diary of Georgi Dimitrov*, p. 371; F. Gori and S. Pons (eds.), *Dagli archivi di Mosca. L'URSS, il Cominform e il PCI* (Rome: Carocci, 1998), docs. 9–10; M. Djilas, *Rise and Fall* (New York: Harcourt Brace, 1985), p. 106. See also S. Pons, *L'impossibile egemonia. L'URSS, il PCI e le origini della guerra fredda (1943–1948)* (Rome: Carocci, 1999), pp. 175–82.

the Guomindang was already apparent before the outbreak of the Second World War. In late 1940 and early 1941, the Chinese communists stood on the brink of armed confrontation with the Guomindang. After June 1941, Moscow made clear that the alliance with Chiang Kai-shek was even more crucial to Soviet interests.[56] By 1942, the obvious analogy between the Nazi order in Europe and Japanese expansion had reinforced the line of 'national unity' in Asia. The communists endorsed that line in Southeast Asia and even in India – where they had to face the problem of how to reconcile the pro-war stance with the arrest of the Congress leaders, including Gandhi, by the British administration in August 1942.[57] However, Mao's strategy was always to avoid integration into the Guomindang and to maintain his forces for the confrontation with the nationalists that was likely to come sooner or later. In December 1943, Dimitrov wrote to Mao that he considered 'politically mistaken the tendency to wind down the struggle against China's foreign occupiers, along with the evident departure from a united national front policy'.[58] Mao did not reject such criticism, but neither did he accept it unreservedly.

By early 1945, the statements of the Chinese Communist Party were totally aligned with Moscow's instruction for a coalition government and for maintenance of the war alliance with the United States. But Mao expected that the end of the war would lead the Soviet Union to provide decisive support for the communists. In July–August 1945, he planned civil war with the nationalists after Japan's surrender. Stalin's decision to conclude a treaty with Chiang and prevent the communists from fighting him was seen by Mao as a betrayal of the Chinese Revolution.[59]

Mao was an original political thinker and strategist, as was apparent from his policies and writings in the pre-war decade. Nevertheless, his wartime experience did not lead to heresy, but a greater assimilation of Stalinist methods and language.[60] The *Short Course* was widely read among Chinese communists. Rivals in the leadership were rudely dismissed in the name of orthodoxy. In his main principles and worldviews, Mao was no less loyal to Moscow than Tito. However, his understanding of the Chinese Revolution,

56 Dallin and Firsov (eds.), *Dimitrov and Stalin*, docs. 23–24, pp. 135–41.
57 D. N. Gupta, *Communism and Nationalism in Colonial India, 1939–45* (New Delhi: Sage, 2008), pp. 211–37.
58 Banac (ed.), *Diary of Georgi Dimitrov*, p. 290.
59 O. A. Westad, *Cold War and Revolution: Soviet-American Rivalry and the Origins of the Chinese Civil War, 1944–1946* (New York: Columbia University Press, 1993), pp. 65–85.
60 F. C. Teiwes, *The Formation of the Maoist Leadership* (London: Contemporary China Institute, 1994).

and possibly world revolution, brought him close to conflict with Stalin's power politics. Thus, behind the monolithic facade of the communist movement, new fissures were emerging from the development of the autonomous revolutions originated by the Second World War. This situation would put a strain on relations between centre and periphery, as it would on realists and radicals across the movement, given the Yugoslav influence in Europe and the Chinese influence in Asia. Soviet victory in the war concealed all these tensions. Stalin's authority was undisputable. But the establishment of Soviet control over all the components of the communist movement could not be taken entirely for granted.

Conclusions

Before and after the Yalta Conference, Stalin seemed willing to emphasize – though not publicly – the notion that, as a consequence of the Second World War, the Soviet model was no longer the imperative and different forms of socialist transition might be viable. His statement that 'perhaps we are making a mistake when we think that the Soviet form is the only one leading to socialism' could be applied in principle both to Eastern and Western Europe.[61] The experience of the 'national fronts' could now generate new forms of 'popular democracy' in the Soviet zone of influence. Stalin even admitted that 'an anti-fascist democracy' would be preferable to the Soviet system in Germany.[62] In other words, the idea of 'popular democracy' endowed with social content was intended to provide a communist response to Europe's post-war arrangements – one that allowed competition with traditional liberal democracy and avoided scaring people with an endorsement of the Soviet model. There was, however, no grand design in this response. What was actually emerging was a blend of power politics pattern based on spheres of influence and slightly adapted axioms from Soviet political culture, as outlined by Zhdanov's ideologues. Popular democracies were part of a short-term policy aimed at expanding Soviet influence while maintaining cooperation with the West. But they were also seen to side with the Soviet Union in a world likely to be divided in the long run – the opposite vision to Roosevelt's 'one world'.

Stalin's famous prophecy to Djilas that each great power would establish its own system in its sphere of influence – while representing an obvious

---

61 Banac (ed.), *Diary of Georgi Dimitrov*, p. 358.
62 Ibid., p. 372.

warning against autonomous moves outside the Soviet sphere of influence –
should be understood in such light.[63] Stalin continued to look at future
developments in terms of opposition between the socialist and capitalist
worlds, as he himself confessed to Dimitrov.[64] From his point of view, the
basis for post-war peace was precarious. The rise of the Soviet Union as a
great power in the aftermath of victory over Hitler might, in principle, lead
to a downplaying of the pre-war obsession with total security – as major
threats had vanished and East Central Europe stayed under Moscow's influence. But it could also inspire a sense of self-sufficiency and enforce antagonism against the outer world. Much depended on international developments,
but the cultural and ideological premises for choosing the second option
were quite compelling. The impact of the American use of the atomic bomb
in Japan in August 1945 would bring renewed insecurity and fuel the antagonistic trend much more rapidly than Stalin himself could have prophesied
earlier in the year.[65]

Certainly, the prestige of the Soviet Union had never been so high and,
unlike the pre-war years, the communist movement had become a powerful
international factor. Almost everywhere, communist parties were increasing
their membership to levels never attained before in their history. While in
France and Czechoslovakia the parties recovered their pre-war numbers,
new mass parties counting several hundred thousand members were being
built in Yugoslavia, Italy and Greece. Memberships increased substantially in
Finland and Bulgaria. Even in countries where the communist presence had
always been very weak, like Poland or Romania, the parties grew considerably in numbers. And there was reason to expect similar developments in
Germany. By the spring and summer of 1945, all of this was significantly
changing the pre-war political map of Europe. Furthermore, the communist
movement – though still basically Eurocentric – had developed during the
war crucial non-European extensions. Besides north China – an obvious
stronghold – communists achieved a monopoly of power in the north of
Korea and of Vietnam. The communist parties of India and Indonesia were
becoming mass organizations. Even in Central Asia, the Communist Party of
Iran (*Tudeh*) had grown considerably under Soviet occupation. Though the
movement was mainly expanding along the Eurasian periphery of the Soviet

63 M. Djilas, *Conversations with Stalin* (New York: Harcourt, Brace and World, 1962).
64 Banac (ed.), *Diary of Georgi Dimitrov*, p. 358. See also *Sto sorok besed s Molotovym. Iz dnevnika F.Chueva* (Moscow: Terra-Terra, 1991), p. 78.
65 D. Holloway, *Stalin and the Bomb: The Soviet Union and Atomic Energy, 1939–1956* (New Haven, Conn., and London: Yale University Press, 1994).

Union, or in the European 'outer empire', its global ambitions seemed more justified now than ever before.[66]

However, the grounds for such spectacular growth were quite dissimilar. The parties enjoying mass support in their respective societies were those playing a leading role in their resistance movements. Where this did not happen – in most East European countries – increased membership was mostly connected to the presence of the Red Army and represented no guarantee for future leadership in those societies. Such a difference had crucial consequences for post-war developments, as the weakness of local communist parties was a cause of violence and repression in the Soviet sphere of influence. Had communists become a legitimate force in the political nation in Europe? The answer was not straightforward. In fact, there could be no doubt that this was the outcome in France, Italy, Czechoslovakia and Yugoslavia. But it seemed unlikely in Poland, Romania and Hungary – while in Germany, the punitive and violent behaviour of the Red Army worked against such an objective.[67] This mismatch was hardly a minor detail, since the principal weaknesses lay at the heart of the Soviet sphere. As for the non-European world, widespread feelings of sympathy for the Soviet Union among the national anti-colonialist leaders were very often combined with hostility toward communism. In any event, Stalin showed little interest in the colonial and post-colonial countries. His focus was on Europe.

Though hardly apparent at the time, weaknesses and conflicting trends undermined the prospect of an ideological, cultural and political hegemony of Soviet Communism in the post-war era. The experience of the Second World War had sown seeds of internal contradictions, while not eliminating the legacy of isolation. The basic duality between Soviet state interests and world revolution could not be averted – despite the Stalinist identification of the two concepts – and depending on their own experience, communists themselves came to different understandings of how such duality could be reconciled, exposing diversity in the monolithic self-representation of the movement. The ideological orthodoxy that was being re-established in the Soviet Union – after its virtual disappearance in wartime, the *Short Course* was again printed in millions of copies in 1945 – did not provide any universal message. At the same time, though a remarkable shift on the left was appreciable in European public opinion, as a reaction to the tragedy wrought

66 Pons, *La rivoluzione globale*, pp. 154–60.
67 N. M. Naimark, *The Russians in Germany: A History of the Soviet Zone of Occupation, 1945–1949* (Cambridge, Mass.: Harvard University Press, 1995).

by Hitler's war, the main political force to benefit from this was the Labour Party – which came to power in Great Britain in July 1945 announcing an uncompromising anti-communist stance. Future developments in Germany were unpredictable, but the propensity of communists to conceive alliances with other leftist forces in terms of dominance and incorporation had already emerged in the Soviet zone of occupation, instigating negative perceptions in the West. By the end of the war, the political significance of anti-fascism was already dissolving, and efforts by communists to claim their own monopoly over that same notion only increased division and suspicion. Their ambition to establish political hegemony over the European progressive forces was disputed, and their supremacy would materialize only in the Soviet sphere of influence by authoritarian means.

4

The propaganda war

JO FOX

By December 1918, the dismantling of Britain's first Ministry of Information was complete. Across the Atlantic, eight months later, Executive Order 3154 closed the United States' Committee on Public Information. The demise of these agencies prompted a public debate about the use of propaganda by the modern state. Some commentators, including Campbell Stuart in *The Secrets of Crewe House* and George Creel in *How We Advertised America*, both published in 1920, glorified the activities of Allied propagandists, while pacifists, notably Arthur Ponsonby in *Falsehood in Wartime* (1928), condemned the arrogance of governments which beguiled their peoples into participating in mass slaughter. The German General Erich Ludendorff, embittered by defeat, argued that propaganda had caused the German collapse, 'hypnotizing' the troops and civilians 'as a snake does a rabbit'.[1] Such publications established assumptions about propaganda that became difficult to dislodge: propaganda was a hidden force in society that could shape the thoughts and behaviour of the vulnerable masses. It could be deployed to persuade these masses to mobilize, fight and die; and it possessed an insidious ability to undermine civilian and military morale. These assumptions have subsequently been challenged by historians seeking to understand propaganda as a complex and multifaceted phenomenon.

While propaganda has the potential to mobilize and contain mass opinion, to structure and order social relationships, and to channel and shape attitudes and behaviour, it also operates through a series of intricate and flexible interactions between the propagandist and the recipient. The observation that 'public opinion and propaganda mutually limit and influence each other' captures both the power of persuasion and the power of the public to accept

---

1 Erich Ludendorff, *My War Memories* (London: Hutchinson and Co., 1920).

or reject it.[2] As such, propaganda becomes a reciprocal transaction, an 'ongoing process involving both persuader and persuadee', responding to individual practical, spiritual or philosophical needs and contributing to the process of community formation.[3] It is a dynamic and responsive process. This, in part, explains why it is most successful when crystallizing or sharpening pre-existing beliefs, when it is credible (but not necessarily truthful) or when it responds to a critical popular need, such as hope, or to an emotional response, such as fear.

Propaganda during the Second World War operated within these parameters. Governments undoubtedly believed that propaganda was critical to their justification of war, to their vilification of the enemy, and to the persuasion of the fighting and producing peoples to unite in sustaining their sacrifice until ultimate victory. However, they also understood its limits. Sir Reginald (Rex) Leeper, Director of the headquarters of Britain's Political Warfare Executive, conceded in 1942 that 'the propagandist must be content to be the forerunner of those who will claim the prize'.[4] This statement recognized that words alone could not win battles, and that propaganda could only achieve its objectives when underpinned by military victories. Moreover, state propaganda circulated in a complex and unpredictable environment, alongside rumours, gossip, informal news networks and enemy propaganda, all of which affected the reception of particular appeals. Its success was also determined by its correlation with fundamental values, ingrained belief systems and individual subjectivity. This applied in both liberal democracies and totalitarian dictatorships. As such, historians are beginning to use the study of propaganda as a means not only to understand how the grand narrative of the war as an ideological struggle was constructed, but how ordinary people interpreted local, national and international events and identified with the world around them.

Agents, organization and approaches

Wartime propaganda was not the sole preserve of government organizations. All media were mobilized (or self-mobilized) in support of the war

---

2 Marlis Steinert, *Hitler's War and the Germans: Public Mood and Attitude During the Second World War* (Athens: Ohio University Press, 1977).

3 Dan Nimmo quoted in Terence Qualter, *Opinion Control in the Democracies* (London: Macmillan, 1985), p. 110.

4 Reginald Leeper quoted in Charles Cruickshank, *The Fourth Arm* (Oxford University Press, 1981), p. 185.

effort, creating a vast but ill-defined network of potential propagandists. The demands of war blurred the distinctions between forms of communication: political speeches, radio addresses by monarchs and statesmen, newspaper editorials, popular songs and even church sermons were all used to convey a sense of national urgency and unity, as part of a 'rich and sophisticated propaganda diet'.[5] Not only was propaganda received by the masses within this complex environment, but it also formed the context for the activities of the centrally controlled propaganda or information agencies: both propagandist and target had to contend with numerous groups and individuals (to a greater or lesser degree, depending on the nature of government) intent on making public statements about the war. The official organs of state propaganda had the task of coordinating these appeals and producing a consistent national wartime narrative. Their work was complicated not only by a burgeoning mass media, but also by popular perceptions of propaganda following its use during the First World War.

State-controlled propaganda occupied an uneasy position within liberal society. Claims that governments deliberately misled their own people and those of other nations during the Great War through the 'fabrication' of atrocity stories in order to vilify the enemy and justify the conflict had a profound effect in both Britain and the United States.[6] The growth of social-scientific and psychological research into propaganda and its effects was, in part, a response to the debates of the 1920s and 1930s that struggled to reconcile 'the right to persuade with the right of the public to free choice'.[7] The rhetoric that characterized propaganda as deviant and anathema to liberal democracy only intensified with the rise of Europe's 'propaganda dictators', who, contemporary commentators noted, deployed centralized state communications in pursuit of power at the expense of individual freedoms and the rights of the citizen. While the liberal democracies continued to endorse 'soft' national 'publicity' campaigns in the interwar period, and while their capitalist economies benefited from a growing advertising industry to promote domestic and international trade, they could not afford to ignore popular unease over state involvement in active and overt publicity campaigns.

---

5 Richard Toye, *The Roar of the Lion: The Untold Story of Churchill's World War II Speeches* (Oxford University Press, 2013), p. 72.
6 On these atrocity stories, see John Horne and Alan Kramer, *German Atrocities, 1914: A History of Denial* (New Haven, Conn.: Yale University Press, 2001).
7 Michael J. Sproule, *Propaganda and Democracy: The American Experience of Media and Mass Persuasion* (Cambridge University Press, 1997), p. 271.

For these reasons, in both Britain and the United States, the revived wartime propaganda agencies (created in 1939 and 1942 respectively) faced considerable difficulties, their establishment the subject of vigorous government and public debate. The British Ministry of Information (MoI), despised by the press, who objected to its attempts to control news, outmanoeuvred by other government departments, and sidelined by the two wartime Prime Ministers, Neville Chamberlain and Winston Churchill, lacked political power.[8] The Minister of Information did not hold a Cabinet seat and, on occasion, Ministry staff were forced to attend the press conferences of the armed services to elicit information on military operations. While the appointment in July 1941 of Brendan Bracken, a close associate of Churchill and former journalist, afforded the MoI some legitimacy and stability, three successive Ministers (Lord Macmillan, Sir John Reith and Duff Cooper) had either resigned or been dismissed within the first twenty-one months of war. As the BBC's advisor on home affairs, A. P. Ryan, recognized, a fundamental problem remained: 'Statesmen, civil servants and leaders in the fighting services' could not openly admit that 'news is a nuisance and propaganda a cheapjack charlatan game': they sought instead to deny propaganda recognition and authority.[9] Even Reith, the second Minister of Information, considered propaganda to be an 'exotic' and doubted that it 'could be grafted on to the democratic machinery'.[10] His successor, Duff Cooper, constantly attacked by the press, in the House of Commons and by other Ministries, was weakened by the '[continual] squabbling' and lack of support from Churchill, who, he claimed, 'was not interested in the subject'.[11]

Cooper would find no solace on a visit to the United States. Defying the official 'no propaganda' policy, a British response to counteract the widespread belief that the US government had been duped into entering the First World War, he embarked on a speaking tour of major cities in January 1940 as part of the British attempt to transform neutral governments into allies. In San Francisco, he was greeted by an angry mob brandishing giant lollipops, with the slogan 'Don't be a Sucker for War Propaganda'.[12] In the same year, librarians at the New York public library found several books

---

8 Frederick Winston Birkenhead, *Walter Monckton* (London: Weidenfeld & Nicolson, 1969), pp. 185–6; Ian McLaine, *Ministry of Morale: Home Front Morale and the Ministry of Information in World War II* (London: Allen and Unwin, 1979), p. 18.

9 McLaine, *Ministry of Morale*, p. 37.

10 John Reith, diary entry, 27 March 1940, in Charles Stuart (ed.), *The Reith Diaries* (London: Collins, 1975), p. 244.

11 Duff Cooper, *Old Men Forget* (London: Hart Davis, 1953), p. 279.

12 Nicholas J. Cull, *Selling War: The British Propaganda Campaign Against American 'Neutrality' in World War II* (Oxford University Press, 1995), p. 35.

defaced with protestations over British influence.[13] Such protests reflected a deep suspicion of propaganda that proved just as problematic for Franklin D. Roosevelt, as he initiated a campaign to alert the American public to the dangers of Nazism and its threat to American security. His attempt to establish a central propaganda agency was complicated by the memory of the Committee on Public Information during the First World War, public and congressional hostility to state control of the media, and a vocal isolationist lobby. As a result, argued Richard W. Steele, 'the President's efforts were slow, confused, and ultimately ineffective'.[14]

Archibald MacLeish, the Librarian of Congress and Director of the Office of Facts and Figures (OFF – the first major national information agency) from October 1941, struggled with assuming responsibility for two seemingly inconsistent tasks: ensuring freedom of information on the one hand and curtailing and directing it on the other. He felt uncomfortable that he was 'often on the verge of propaganda'.[15] Like British Ministers of Information, MacLeish was 'hampered by a distinct lack of authority'. He received little direct support from the President and was reliant on the armed services for the release of relevant information. The OFF ultimately became little more than a 'domestic information clearing house'.[16] In a further striking parallel to the MoI, attacks by the press and Congress led to the perception that the OFF was 'ineffective in dealing with the morale-building needs of wartime America', and resulted in its closure in June 1942.[17]

The OFF's successor, the Office of War Information (OWI), under the direction of the former radio commentator Elmer Davies, fared little better. Critics alleged that the OWI was open to political exploitation by the 'New Dealers', and serious divisions emerged as advertisers were drafted in to direct campaigns. This led to a series of disputes in April 1943 over increased exhortation, 'ballyhoo' and 'slick salesmanship', culminating in the public resignation of prominent members of the OWI.[18] According to Gerd Horten, this marked the 'privatization' of American propaganda: national and

13 Todd Bennett, 'The Celluloid War: State and Studio in Anglo-American Propaganda and Film-making, 1939–1941', *International History Review* 24 (2004), 64.

14 Richard W. Steele, 'Preparing the Public for War: Efforts to Establish a National Propaganda Agency, 1940–41', *American Historical Review* 75 (1970), 1653.

15 Brett Gary, *The Nervous Liberals: Propaganda Anxieties from World War I to the Cold War* (New York: Columbia University Press, 1999), pp. 131–3, 152.

16 Sproule, *Propaganda and Democracy*, p. 158.

17 Steele, 'Preparing the Public for War', 1652.

18 Allan M. Winkler, *The Politics of Propaganda: The Office of War Information, 1942–1945* (New Haven, Conn., and London: Yale University Press, 1978), pp. 64–5.

corporate interests merged and signalled an increased 'intimacy between free-enterprise and government' that was to characterize both wartime appeals and the shape and nature of the media after 1945.[19]

The employment of the private advertisers opened the floodgates for the OWI's critics, who regarded this as evidence of its inefficiency, and seemingly confirmed that private industry, not the state, was best placed to conduct propaganda. Republicans in Congress and the Senate unleashed their fury on the OWI, which was decried as 'a haven of refuge for the derelicts', its propaganda 'a stench in the nostrils of a democratic people'. In June 1943, the House Appropriations Committee cut the Domestic Branch's budget by 40 per cent – just enough, remarked Davis, to prevent 'the odium of having put us out of business, and carefully enough not to let us accomplish much'. This amounted to the agency's 'emasculation', and responsibility for specific campaigns passed largely to the Treasury and the State Department.[20]

Despite these difficulties, democratic propagandists achieved a remarkable degree of success. They could exploit established liberal traditions, and later the skills of Madison Avenue advertising executives, to generate a unifying propaganda based on Nazism's threat to the civilized world. Moreover, the conduct of propaganda, superficially at least, was made fit for democracy. The rhetoric surrounding the 'strategy of truth' concealed the more clandestine and subversive psychological warfare operations (or 'black' propaganda), conducted through underground radio broadcasts, the distribution of leaflets and the circulation of rumours ('Sibs') in enemy territory. Simultaneously correcting the 'misdemeanors' of the First World War and attempting to distinguish themselves from the aggressive propaganda of the dictators, official 'white' propagandists crafted the image of a propaganda free from 'deception, lies, disinformation, atrocity stories and the creation of false expectation'.[21] Even the titles of their agencies announced the intention to provide information rather than 'propaganda'. Mayor of New York Fiorello La Guardia declared in October 1941 that the OFF was 'not a propaganda agency': 'There are three reasons why it is not. The first is that we don't believe in this country in artificially stimulated high-pressure, doctored nonsense, and since we don't, the other two reasons are

19 Gerd Horten, *Radio Goes to War: The Cultural Politics of Propaganda During World War II* (Berkeley: University of California Press, 2002), p. 7.
20 Winkler, *The Politics of Propaganda*, pp. 70–1; Steven Casey, *Cautious Crusade: Franklin D. Roosevelt, American Public Opinion, and the War Against Nazi Germany* (Oxford University Press, 2001), pp. 156–7.
21 Gary, *The Nervous Liberals*, p. 153.

unimportant'.[22] That the young cadre of propagandists in the OWI resigned in April 1943 because, in their view, it had become increasingly difficult to 'tell the full truth' appeared to be powerful evidence that the 'strategy of truth' was central to their approach.[23] This fitted neatly with the overarching propaganda narrative that explained what the Allies were fighting for.

Despite this rhetoric, the public knew that official information and news reports were subject to a degree of omission or censorship, and remained sceptical of the reach and purpose of national propaganda agencies. While the public and the press accepted the suppression of operational details in the interests of national security, they also suspected that the authorities took the opportunity to smother less favourable stories and feared an escalation from restricting news to restricting opinion. While liberal governments publicly stated that censorship was 'voluntary', in reality, the fighting services and other government departments tightly controlled the release of informa-tion.[24] In this sense, war forced a certain convergence between democracies and dictatorships on the function of propaganda, and, as Aristotle Kallis has argued, 'clear distinctions between allegedly free and controlled information flow became increasingly blurred'.[25]

The control of information was a primary objective of dictatorships. By September 1939, mechanisms had long been in place to ensure the coordin-ation of the media. Fascist Italy's Ministry of Popular Culture, formed in 1937 out of the Under-Secretariat for Press and Propaganda, regulated the press, radio, the arts, literature and film. The Nazi Party established the *Reichsministerium für Volksaufklärung und Propaganda* (RMVP) in Germany just under three months after the 'seizure of power' in 1933, and embarked upon a systematic *Gleichschaltung* (coordination) of state and party communi-cations. Although full nationalization was complete only in 1942, this process created an intricate system that connected the propaganda of the Party and the state in order to mobilize the population and to silence alternative channels of information. All major Party organizations, such as the youth, women's and labour movements, conducted 'cascading' publicity campaigns designed to intensify the propaganda environment.[26] Soviet propaganda was

22 Steele, 'Preparing the Public for War', 1652.
23 Winkler, *The Politics of Propaganda*, p. 65.
24 See Steven Casey's Chapter 5 in this volume, on news censorship.
25 Aristotle Kallis, *Nazi Propaganda and the Second World War* (Basingstoke: Palgrave, 2005), p. 7.
26 David Welch, *The Third Reich: Politics and Propaganda* (London: Routledge, 2002), pp. 28–58; Kallis, *Nazi Propaganda*, pp. 16–62; Steinert, *Hitler's War*, p. 11.

centralized under the Central Committee's Directorate of Propaganda and Agitation, responsible to the Politburo, Orgburo and Secretariat, and supplemented by a complex system of political agitation in which propaganda was conducted by multiple state agencies and organizations. That it was seamlessly integrated into every state association and union signalled the leadership's intention to reach into and to order the private lives of its citizens.

Yet the success of these extensive propaganda operations depended on a complex interaction between the state and its people. Richard Bosworth's research into 'deep belief' in Fascist Italy reveals that the Party's 'control over its subjects' mental world was always partial', in spite of its ever more insistent propaganda. The Fascist state was, in part, created, sustained and indeed challenged 'from below', through the population's construction of 'an "everyday Mussolinism"....on their own terms'.[27] Equally, despite rhetoric designed to smooth the transition to dictatorship and establish Nazism as the de facto representative of the 'national will', Goebbels' observation that the RMVP was 'the living contact' between the state and the people' reflects a deeper, more ambiguous relationship that lay at the heart of the Nazi regime.[28] Nazi propaganda, argues Robert Gellately, 'was not, and could not, be crudely forced on the German people. On the contrary, it was meant to appeal to them, and to match up with everyday German understandings'.[29] Those understandings were not situated within the false dichotomy of consent and coercion: they owed more to the coalescence of pre-existing beliefs and traditions, a broad consensus regarding the benefits of fascist rule and the promise of a national revival, and the persistence of private, individual and personal opinions that remained beneath a public veneer of compliance.

This reciprocal relationship between state and people was also crucial to the success of Japanese imperial propaganda. From early in the Showa era, Japanese propagandists understood that, due to the diversity and breadth of their empire, total control of communications would be impossible. They devised a system that Barak Kushner likened to 'a spoked wheel', where the state 'provided the centre hub of...plans and programmes', while the population 'provided the structure that supported and reinforced'. Both elements were mutually dependent. Directives from the Cabinet Board of

27 Richard Bosworth, 'War, Totalitarianism and "Deep Belief" in Fascist Italy', *European History Quarterly* 34:4 (2004), 498–9.
28 Richard Taylor, 'Goebbels as Propagandist', in David Welch (ed.), *Nazi Propaganda* (London: Croom Helm, 1983), pp. 35–7.
29 Robert Gellately, *Backing Hitler. Consent and Coercion in Nazi Germany* (Oxford University Press, 2001), p. 259.

Information were re-interpreted from 'below' through local non-government agencies, such as the Imperial Rule Assistance Association. National exhibitions and competitions to design campaigns stripped propaganda of its pejorative connotations and enlisted the population as participants in Japan's *shisosen* ('thought war').[30]

Not only was propaganda in the dictatorships subject to and influenced by popular opinion, but the systems established to control information did not ensure consistency and conformity. With numerous ministries and state organizations claiming some responsibility for propaganda, tensions were inevitable and simply exacerbated by war.[31] Such tensions exposed propagandists to even deeper scrutiny and an increasing suspicion of the official message. Centralization and strict censorship created dry and repetitive copy. Its uniformity and blandness alienated audiences and established a 'permanent climate of propaganda and mass integration [which generated] a certain degree of fatigue':[32] radio listeners in the Soviet Union walked away from public speakers when the Bureau Bulletin aired, while film-goers in Nazi Germany attempted to avoid the *Wochenschau* by sneaking into cinemas just as the main feature started. Such was the extent of the problem that in 1943 Goebbels decreed that the doors to cinemas were to be locked at the beginning of each programme.[33]

War also had the potential to disrupt publicity campaigns. In Germany, aerial bombardment destroyed film stock, studios, print works and cinemas: a significant proportion of film production was transferred to Prague in the final months of war.[34] The Soviet Union experienced problems from the outset. Radio was not received in many parts of the vast Soviet empire. Film attendance dropped significantly, due to shortages in equipment, personnel, cinemas and mobile film units, since much was requisitioned for war purposes. Some kolkhozes did not receive a single film during the war. Increased work hours curtailed leisure time. Paper shortages, poor distribution networks and the reallocation of existing supplies to the military for forces

---

30 Barak Kushner, *The Thought War. Japanese Imperial Propaganda* (Honolulu: University of Hawaii Press, 2006), pp. 6–35.
31 For further details of these tensions, see Steven Casey's Chapter 5 in this volume.
32 Clemens Zimmermann, 'From Propaganda to Modernization: Media Policy and Media Audiences under National Socialism', *German History* 24 (2006), p. 434.
33 Karel C. Berkhoff, *Motherland in Danger: Soviet Propaganda During World War II* (Cambridge, Mass., and London: Harvard University Press, 2012), p. 277; Oron J. Hale, *The Captive Press in the Third Reich* (Princeton University Press, 1964); David Welch, *Propaganda and the German Cinema* (London: I. B. Tauris, 2001), p. 170.
34 Jo Fox, *Film Propaganda in Britain and Nazi Germany* (Oxford: Berg, 2007), p. 260.

newssheets led to a significant decline in newspaper circulation. In the absence of an efficient mass media, the Party became increasingly reliant on local agitprop, which was notoriously unreliable. The Party message was open to local interpretation and distortion. Reacting to formulaic directives, some agitators even speculated on the outcome of war based on 'spin the bottle' or reading tea leaves. They played down Soviet military might in favour of the effect of the Russian winter, and sheer land size, in repelling the invader. They embellished official propaganda and infused it with local stories and customs, while some agitators simply read out dry copy regardless of the target audience, quoting verbatim from the *Bloknot agitatora* ('Agitators' Notebook'), to disinterested comrades.[35]

Authoritarian regimes did not, then, have an iron grip on propaganda. State publicity campaigns were not 'total' in their reach or effect, and the state was not immune from inter-agency conflict and the circulation of inconsistent messages. Despite attempts to control how propaganda was received, populations continued to invest state publicity with their own meaning. Nor were the liberal democratic nations the innocent purveyors of truth that they claimed to be. They were, after all, propagandists with the aim of shaping perception and manipulating information to suit their purpose. That purpose was to present the case for war and to sustain the armed forces and the home front through the hardships that would follow.

Justifying war

Propagandists faced a difficult task in September 1939: the memory of the Great War contributed to a lack of enthusiasm about the prospect of another, and most people entered with a sense of 'reluctant loyalty'.[36] All protagonists claimed that the war was defensive and unavoidable. Performing a remarkable volte-face after the Non-Aggression Pact with the Soviet Union in August 1939, Nazi propagandists fell silent on 'Jewish Bolshevism' and openly confronted Poland, whose belligerence, they claimed, had been roused by warmongering plutocrats in London and Paris. The *Volksdeutsche* (ethnic Germans) in the East were the victims of atrocity at the hands of the Poles. 'Perfidious Albion' stood aside in the knowledge that a German defensive

---

35 Richard J. Brody, *Ideology and Political Mobilization: The Soviet Home Front During World War II* (Pittsburgh, Pa.: Center for Russian and East European Studies, University of Pittsburgh, 1994).

36 Helmut Krausnick quoted in Steinert, *Hitler's War*, p. 50.

action would provide a pretext for a long-awaited war, the opportunity to destroy a rival who had challenged its imperial dominance and cynically denied self-determination to the peoples of the Dominions and colonies, while claiming to be the protector of freedom and democracy. The expansionist rhetoric of *Lebensraum* (living space), the rejection of democratic principles and virulent anti-Semitism coalesced around the Nazi identification of a 'Jewish capitalist world enemy' determined to encircle and 'exterminat[e] the German people'.[37] In the face of such provocation, a peace-loving Führer had made every effort to avoid conflict, an image that persisted into the Polish campaign, with Hitler's 'peace offer' in early October.[38]

The speed of victory in Poland served to emphasize Hitler's image as a decisive military strategist and to raise popular hopes of a short Blitzkrieg, temporarily allaying fears of a protracted war of attrition. The first major film of the war, Hans Bertram's 'documentary' of the eighteen-day campaign in Poland, *Feuertaufe* ('Baptism of Fire'), was a potent combination of justification, power and threat that appealed to such hopes. It set out the German case and provided a visual record of Warsaw's destruction, 'the land ablaze' and 'resistance ruthlessly crushed'. The Luftwaffe, the film's commentary informed the audience, 'knows how to seek out the guiltiest of the guilty... What have you got to say now, Herr Chamberlain?... Here you can see the results of your pointless war policies. This is all your work!' Screened in Rome, Copenhagen, Oslo, Brussels and The Hague in April 1940, *Feuertaufe* was not simply a justification of war for home audiences: it was an aggressive weapon designed to encourage capitulation.[39]

Britain's initial propaganda was more modest, consisting of reassuring messages from the King and select government ministers, and an appeal to citizens to serve the nation, be alert to enemy propaganda and remain resilient until an assured final victory arrived. The King's broadcast of 3 September 1939 implored his people to 'make our cause their own' and to 'stand firm, calm and united' in the face of Hitler's unprovoked aggression and 'primitive doctrine' that would end 'all hopes of...the security of justice and liberty among nations'. Yet early propaganda, such as A. P. Waterfield's poster that told the nation that 'Your Courage, Your Cheerfulness, Your Resolution will

---

37 Jeffrey Herf, *The Jewish Enemy: Nazi Propaganda During World War II and the Holocaust* (Cambridge, Mass., and London: Belknap Press of Harvard University Press, 2006), p. 64.
38 Monthly report of the *Regierungspräsident* for Upper and Middle Franconia, 7 November 1939, in Steinert, *Hitler's War*, p. 59.
39 Fox, *Film Propaganda*, pp. 39–59.

bring us victory', seemed more to divide than to unite: far from being a 'rallying war cry' that would put Britons in 'an offensive mood at once', it was interpreted as confirmation that the ordinary people would be required to make the necessary sacrifices from which the privileged would benefit. The government failed to clarify its war aims beyond the broad rhetoric of defeating fascism. Consequently, its propaganda lacked the immediacy and penetrating potency of its adversary's opening salvos.[40]

In the face of popular and congressional intransigence over formal intervention (the United States did not enter the war until December 1941), Roosevelt waged a 'complex, subtle' and 'cautious crusade' to undermine isolationism, expose the direct threat that Nazism posed to US interests and provide assistance to American allies.[41] As Edward Murrow from September 1940 brought the Blitz into the living rooms of America through his radio broadcasts, Roosevelt pledged that the United States would become the 'arsenal of democracy'. This marked an escalation of Roosevelt's interventionist campaigns: he mentioned Nazism directly only five times in his speeches before December 1940. This increased to 152 times throughout 1941. Despite Roosevelt's determined attempt to persuade Americans that the war in Europe was being fought for universal concerns, intervention secured relatively little popular support, with the consequence that the United States was 'mentally unprepared to enter the war'. It was only the attack on Pearl Harbor on 7 December 1941 that delivered the 'miracle which no amount of logic or persuasion had previously been able to achieve'.[42] To the Japanese, Pearl Harbor was presented as a challenge to the support of the Western powers for Chiang Kai-shek and their mobilization in the Pacific, which threatened Japanese economic, military and territorial expansion. The assault on Pearl Harbor, claimed the Imperial Rescript on the Declaration of War, was an act of 'self-defence' requiring an 'appeal to arms' and the determination to 'crush every obstacle in [our] path'.[43]

Friend and foe

Liberal democratic propagandists struggled to find a consistent and universally accepted way to portray their opponents, in particular Germany and the

40 McLaine, *Ministry of Morale*, pp. 27–60.
41 Casey, *Cautious Crusade*, p. 37.
42 Horten, *Radio Goes to War*, p. 37; Casey, *Cautious Crusade*, pp. 37–9, 44–8.
43 David C. Earhart, *Certain Victory: Images of World War II in the Japanese Media* (Armonk, NY: M. E. Sharpe, 2009), p. 220.

Soviet Union. Responding to a perceived lack of public urgency and a failure to appreciate the consequences of an Axis victory, in June 1940, Britain's MoI devised an 'anger campaign', which sought to inflame the masses, unleashing their 'primitive instincts' against 'Europe's gangsters. . .and German lust for world domination': the 'sophisticated and educated classes' were to be given 'more restrained and factual' proof of the 'fundamental "rottenness" of the German character. . .[and] the German bully complex'.[44] BBC politeness was to be set aside and Nazi leaders labelled as villains: Churchill's characterization of Hitler as a 'bloodthirsty guttersnipe' after the Nazi invasion of the Soviet Union in June 1941 continued appeals in this vein.[45] The public was to be divested of any impression of German invincibility. The radio broadcaster J. B. Priestley captured the mood of the proposed campaign, warning of 'Europe's secret beast', vulnerable to 'hero worship' and 'folly' and 'roused to senseless fury. . . He will rage and destroy. He will slaughter the women and children. But in the end, he will run from the men as he has always run in the past.'[46]

Such emotive and explicit incitement to hate the enemy, however, conflicted with a number of appeals by politicians, the King and religious leaders from 1938 onward, which stressed the defence of Christian civilization against Nazi barbarism and invoked 'the constitutional and historical, the loyalties to family, locality, nation and Empire, conceptions of national character,. . .the ethic of "service". . .[and] spiritual values'.[47] These appeals contrasted rational liberal thought with the irrationality of totalitarianism. The June 1940 initiative promised to destabilize this shared and powerful narrative. Ultimately, the MoI chose instead to focus on 'What Would Happen If Hitler Won'. Playing on deeply ingrained beliefs in the importance of 'freedom. . .a liberal constitution,. . .democratic and Parliamentary government,. . .Magna Carta and the Petition of Right', articulated in a speech by Churchill in May 1938, Duff Cooper stressed that Nazi domination 'would take away all our liberties which we have fought so many centuries to obtain'.[48] Britons' anger, if aroused at all, was to be simmering, not excessive or disproportionate. This national 'characteristic' survived in propaganda that captured the growing antagonism toward the Nazis at the height of the Blitz. The 1941 short film

44 McLaine, *Ministry of Morale*, pp. 142–7.
45 Toye, *The Roar*, p. 103.
46 McLaine, *Ministry of Morale*, pp. 142–7.
47 Philip Williamson, 'Christian Conservatives and the Totalitarian Challenge, 1933–40', *English Historical Review* 115 (2000), 609–10.
48 McLaine, *Ministry of Morale*, p. 148.

Words for Battle, for example, effectively set Kipling's poem 'The Beginnings', a stolid but determined expression of resentment, against scenes of devastation following the aerial bombardment of London from September 1940.

Just as British propaganda drew upon presumed national and imperial identities to form the basis of its publicity, US propagandists mobilized expressions of American values, such as the Declaration of Independence and the memory of 1776, to emphasize the contrast to Nazism, continuing the prioritization of Roosevelt's 'Atlantic First' policy.[49] The OWI found particular success with its slogan 'You Can't Do Business With Hitler', based on a book by Douglass Miller, commercial attaché to the American Embassy in Berlin, and an associated poster campaign and fifty-six-episode radio series that ran throughout 1942–43. Not only was this propaganda 'emotionally restrained', but it presented the war as a battle for 'two alternative settlements for a future world' – a German 'stranglehold' over the global economy, or American free enterprise and its associated 'way of life'.[50]

The British and American home publicity campaigns were, in general, directed against Hitler and the 'Nazi criminal conspiracy'. This was a carefully designed strategy to reinforce propaganda to the German people intended to encourage internal resistance in the Reich and, in so doing, bring a speedy end to the war. The success of these appeals depended on a consistent message at home and abroad: Nazi propagandists exploited any vindictive or vitriolic statements by the Allies. Lord Vansittart's pamphlet *Black Record*, published in 1941, was considered a 'gift for Goebbels'.[51] Kenneth Clark, Director General at the MoI, denounced Vansittart's condemnation of the 'incurable' German character as 'disastrous from the point of view of propaganda': it alienated dissenters in Germany and created 'a sense of hopelessness...in the mind of the average thoughtful man', who would be in perpetual anticipation of the next act of aggression by 'the same old Hun'. Learning from the failures of atrocity campaigns of the First World War, which proved counter-productive in the longer term, British propagandists placed blame squarely on the shoulders of the Nazi leadership, with the 'good' German providing the obvious counterpoint.[52]

49 Casey, *Cautious Crusade*, p. 62.
50 Susan Brewer, *Why America Fights: Patriotism and War Propaganda from the Philippines to Iraq* (Oxford University Press, 2009), p. 106; Horten, *Radio Goes to War*, pp. 55–9; Casey, *Cautious Crusade*, p. 63.
51 Robert Vansittart, *Black Record: Germans Past and Present* (London: Hamish Hamilton, 1941), p. 53; Heinrich Fraenkel, *Vansittart's Gift for Goebbels*, Fabian Society Tract 254 (London: Fabian Society, 1941).
52 Fox, *Film Propaganda*, pp. 137–59.

This approach was replicated in early American propaganda campaigns, which represented the conflict as 'Hitler's personal war', broadly corresponding to public opinion that saw the German people as 'essentially peace loving and kindly, [but] misled, too often, by ruthless and ambitious rulers'. American propaganda attempts broadly reflected Roosevelt's private views on war guilt, and increasingly succumbed to diplomatic pressure from the Soviet Union following the Tehran Conference in 1943. In 1942, Roosevelt drew a sharp distinction between 'the Nazi gang and the German people', resisting calls for propaganda to deepen and broaden popular anger against Germany in order to 'accelerate the process of political change there'. However, as the possibility of internal revolt against Nazism receded, by August 1944, he declared that 'too many people here and in England hold the view that the German people are not responsible for what has taken place – that only a few Nazi leaders are responsible. That unfortunately is not based on fact'. They were now implicated in 'a lawless conspiracy against the decencies of modern civilization'. While some critics, such as Rex Stout in *The New York Times Magazine*, openly began to pursue a Vansittartist line, this view did not find unambiguous expression in American propaganda, nor did it significantly alter the distinction in the public mind.[53]

No distinctions were afforded to the Japanese, however. They were denied, as John Dower observes, 'even the merest semblance of pluralism', confirming the persistence of racial, imperial and Eurocentric hierarchies. The only 'Good Jap', as a popular song went, was 'a dead Jap', a phrase that became part of the American wartime lexicon, repeated by adults and children alike.[54] Racial characterization featured prominently, and, whereas the Nazis possessed the worst human characteristics, the Japanese were not considered to be human at all, depicted as 'monkeys, baboons, gorillas, dogs, mice and rats, vipers and rattlesnakes, cockroaches, vermin, or..."the Japanese herd"'. This distancing, a sense that the Japanese were subhuman or, at best, distinctly different from Americans and Europeans, permitted a far more direct and violent form of propaganda: popular songs encouraged the troops to 'Mow the Japs Down', 'Do a Job on the Japs' and even 'Slap the Dirty Jap'.[55]

---

53 Casey, *Cautious Crusade*, pp. 19–22, 55–9, 130, 144.
54 See, for example, the Library of Congress American Folk Life Center's Rumor Project Collection, AFC1945/001.
55 John W. Dower, *War Without Mercy: Race and Power in the Pacific War* (New York: Pantheon, 1986), pp. 79–82.

Historic animosities provoked similarly aggressive, ferocious and dehu-
manizing propaganda. Although Soviet propagandists initially distinguished
between Nazi leaders and the German people, characterizing the war as an
expression of international class struggle, the impact of total war invoked
memories of traditional German *zakhvatchiki* (conquerors) and *okkupanty*
(invaders), and prompted a fierce and intense propaganda offensive. The
invaders were frequently referred to as 'killers (*ubiitsy*) and child-killers
(*detoubiitsy*), butchers (*palachi*), man-eaters (*liudoedy*), cannibals (*kannibaly*),
vermin (*gada*)', and their victims as the innocent women and children of the
Soviet Motherland.[56] Drawing attention to the destruction of culture and
the barbarity of the occupier, Soviet propagandists recalled atrocity in
graphic detail. Nazi attacks on villages and homes, the violation of sweet-
hearts, wives, mothers and even children represented the 'suffering nation'
and personalized the war, reducing it to a series of individual, deeply
resented acts that compelled citizen and soldier to exact a brutal revenge.[57]
Propaganda and popular sentiment collided in what Richard Stites has
described as a united, 'implacable, [pulsating] loathing'. Alexei Surkov's
poem 'I Hate' encouraged citizens to 'strangle' the invader with their bare
hands, a singularly personal act, while Konstantin Simanov's verse 'Kill Him'
left no doubt as to the course of action every patriotic citizen had to take:
'If you do not want to have / The girl you courted / But never dared to
kiss / Because your love was pure– / If you don't want fascists to bruise and
beat / And stretch her naked on the floor / In hatred, tears and blood / And
see three human dogs despoil / All that you hold dear /... Then kill a
German, kill him soon / And every time you see one – kill him'.[58]

For liberal democratic propagandists, however, demonizing the Western
enemy by publicizing their atrocities was problematic. While British propagandists may have looked for 'another Edith Cavell' in the campaigns of June
1940, they were, like their American counterparts, bound by the memory of
'false' atrocity stories of the First World War. 'If they wanted to cry wolf
again', argues Horten, 'propagandists had to make sure they had documentation on which to base their charges'.[59] In general, atrocity repelled

56 Argyrios K. Pisiotis, 'Images of Hate in the Art of War', in Richard Stites (ed.), *Culture
and Entertainment in Wartime Russia* (Bloomington: Indiana University Press, 1995),
p. 141.
57 Jeffrey Brooks, *Thank You, Comrade Stalin! Soviet Public Culture from Revolution to Cold
War* (Princeton University Press, 2000), pp. 178–80.
58 Richard Stites, *Russian Popular Culture: Entertainment and Society Since 1900* (Cambridge
University Press, 1992), pp. 99–100.
59 McLaine, *Ministry of Morale*, p. 145; Horten, *Radio Goes to War*, p. 58.

audiences and potentially acted as a barrier to peace. Consequently, liberal propagandists avoided excessive descriptions of the atrocities committed in Europe, with the obvious consequence that the plight of the Jews and others was largely ignored. Where atrocity featured in propaganda, it was often confined to specific, verifiable and credible incidents, one example being Nazi reprisals following the assassination of Reinhard Heydrich. MacLeish described the execution of Lidice's men and the deportation of its women and children as a 'single act' symbolizing 'the full frightfulness...the utter immorality of the Nazi system'. In the United States, a Lidice Lives Committee formed, with a prestigious membership including Albert Einstein and Thomas Mann, while in Britain, the documentary film-maker Humphrey Jennings re-enacted the event in a small mining town (Lidice was also a mining community) in Wales in *The Silent Village* (1943). Lidice became 'an "immortal" symbol', 'told and re-told' countless times to press home Nazi barbarity in a personal and direct way. Its impact, as *The New York Herald* recognized, derived from the fact that 'it was restricted enough to be comprehensible'; it was 'Hitlerism in capsule form', a distillation of the unimaginable apocalypse that was unfolding in Eastern Europe.[60]

The Nazis perceived this reticence in propaganda as a vulnerability. Goebbels frequently characterized his British counterparts as weak, indecisive 'dilettantes', who could not seize opportunities when they arose.[61] Goebbels' own conception of the enemy rested on demonstrating the disadvantages of liberal democracy, the perfidy of the Jewish plutocratic caste, and Britain's ruthless suppression of its own people and its empire. In his 1940 Empire Day address, George VI confronted this accusation. 'There is a word our enemies use against us', he stated, '– imperialism. By it they mean the spirit of domination, the lust of conquest... Our object has always been peace – peace in which our institutions may be developed, the condition of our peoples improved'.[62] However, the rhetoric alluding to peaceful, 'civilizing' missions and new imperial 'partnerships' increasingly rang hollow at home and abroad, and collided with campaigns that served to reinforce national and racial hierarchies (the 'Together' poster, for example, positioned white Australians, Canadians and Britons leading their Indian and African counterparts). Propaganda simply exposed the fragility of empire. The fall of

60 Casey, *Cautious Crusade*, pp. 64–71.
61 Goebbels diary, 14 May 1941, in E. Fröhlich (ed.), *Sämtliche Fragmente*, vol. IV: *Die Tagebücher von Joseph Goebbels* (4 vols., Munich: K. G. Saur, 1987), pp. 640–1.
62 Cited in Wendy Webster, *Englishness and Empire, 1939–1965* (Oxford University Press, 2005), p. 26.

Singapore in February 1942 prompted *The Times* to urge the abandonment of 'misguided conceptions of racial prestige and narrow obsolete interpretations of economic interest if democracy is to have any meaning or appeal for the colonial peoples'.[63] As Siân Nicholas argues, empire propaganda found itself 'fatally hamstrung by the political sensitivities' of and popular disengagement from the imperial idea: the 'Kiplingesque Neverland' receded in the British popular imagination in favour of new priorities over Britain's place in Europe and the Anglo-American relationship.[64] The latter was complicated by the commitment to self-determination embodied in the Atlantic Charter, the persistence of British colonial control, particularly in India, and a powerful national memory of British imperial domination resulting in the American Revolution.

Empire provided an ideal opportunity for Goebbels to exploit divisions in the alliance, to aggravate tensions within Britain and to foment unrest in Britain's colonies. However, he was careful to confine his propaganda to 'the British plutocracy alone', in order to sow 'mistrust of the...ruling caste'.[65] In pursuit of this aim, he drew on atrocities past and present, from the concentration camps of the Boer War to the suppression of independence movements in Ireland, India and the Middle East, to evoke contempt for Britain's false superiority and merciless imperial mission. He undertook wide-ranging publicity campaigns in British imperial territories in India, the Middle East and North Africa, presenting 'the Nazi regime as a champion of secular anti-imperialism': in Muslim countries, Nazi propagandists '[selectively appropriated] the traditions of Islam' to engender a sense of ideological affinity, not least in a shared hatred of the Jews.[66]

Goebbels' condemnation of the plutocratic caste's expansionist aims, contempt for the masses and financial greed all emanated from the Nazi worldview that the conflict was primarily a 'Jewish war', orchestrated as part of an international conspiracy that, by 1941, united the Soviet Union and its Western allies. As Jeffrey Herf argues, this was 'simultaneously a cynical, utilitarian political instrument as well as a fanatical and deeply believed interpretative framework'. Such was the vehemence with which this was

63 Ibid.
64 Siân Nicholas, '"Brushing up your Empire": Dominion and Colonial Propaganda on the BBC's Home Services, 1939–45', *Journal of Imperial and Commonwealth History* 31 (2003), 225.
65 Fröhlich, *Tagebücher*, 24 July 1940, p. 70, 2 June 1940, p. 49.
66 Jeffrey Herf, 'Nazi Germany's Propaganda Aimed at Arabs and Muslims During World War II and the Holocaust: Old Themes, New Archival Findings', *Central European History* 42 (2009), 709.

pursued that leading Nazis eschewed the euphemism so frequently associated with the language of the Holocaust in favour of outright statements that pitted Nazi Germany against Judaism, in a war of 'annihilation' and 'extermination'.[67]

Changing allegiances had a profound effect on enemy propaganda. This applied, in particular, to the Soviet Union. Early Nazi anti-Bolshevik propaganda was suppressed with the announcement of the Nazi-Soviet Pact. The launch of Operation BARBAROSSA in June 1941 was initially portrayed as an 'act of liberation'. Only when popular opinion on the home front stabilized did Goebbels renew his tirade against Bolshevism.[68] Anti-Soviet propaganda reached a crescendo with German losses in the East and the imminent threat of the 'Bolshevization of Europe'. Goebbels' February 1943 'Total War' speech predicted the descent of brutal Jewish-Bolshevik *Liquidationskommandos* (liquidation squads), hell-bent on the annihilation of the German people, claims that were seemingly confirmed by the discovery of the mass graves of Polish Officers at Katyn, a find that propagandists exploited to the full at home and in the occupied territories. Such propaganda, targeted at all sections of the community, including children, played on deep-seated fears of the consequences of invasion from the East, fears that only intensified as that possibility drew closer.[69]

The alliance between Britain and the Soviet Union from June 1941, and the Anglo-American–Soviet alignment after December 1941, threatened to disrupt the liberal propaganda narrative. Propagandists were forced to recast Stalin as an enlightened and benevolent leader, commanding a determined, brave and defiant Red Army on the Eastern Front. The 1943 film *Mission to Moscow*, based on a book by Joseph E. Davies, US ambassador to Moscow, went as far as to suggest that those accused in the 'show trials' of the 1930s were guilty of treason.[70] 'An affiliation of nations not ideologies' presented a more credible and comfortable explanation for the unlikely union, however. Churchill's speech of 22 June 1941 depicted

---

67 Jeffrey Herf, 'The "Jewish War"': Goebbels and the Anti-Semitic Campaigns of the Nazi Propaganda Ministry', *Holocaust and Genocide Studies* 19 (2005), 54–5; Herf, *The Jewish Enemy*.

68 Jürgen Matthäus, 'Controlled Escalation: Himmler's Men in the Summer of 1941 and the Holocaust in the Occupied Soviet Territories', *Holocaust and Genocide Studies* 21 (2007), 221.

69 Kallis, *Nazi Propaganda*, pp. 77–83; John P. Fox, 'Der Fall Katyn und die Propaganda des NS-Regimes', *Vierteljahrshefte für Zeitgeschichte* 30 (1982), 462–99.

70 Clayton R. Koppes and Gregory D. Black, *Hollywood Goes to War: How Politics, Profits and Propaganda Shaped World War II Movies* (London: I. B. Tauris, 1988), pp. 185–208.

a 'pre-revolutionary past', in which Russia and the West were 'natural allies'. The threat of fascism provided the opportunity for a 'mythic past [to merge] with the present,...[revealing] the true soul of Russia and [rendering] Stalinist ideology irrelevant'.[71] This sentiment also found expression in the MoI's propaganda campaigns. Fearful of anti-Soviet sentiment and the Communist Party of Great Britain's exploitation of the new alliance, the Ministry prioritized the image of heroic military and civilian resistance over ideological comment on communism. In February 1943, all churches held special prayers (at government request) 'for the people and church of Russia', and the twenty-fifth anniversary of the Red Army was marked with a concert at the Albert Hall that included readings by Laurence Olivier and John Gielgud; that September, factories screened *The USSR at War* to 1.25 million workers, and the BBC produced thirty programmes on the subject. The MoI urged publishers to avoid reprinting George Orwell's *Animal Farm* for the foreseeable future.[72]

Propagandists, then, were forced to respond to a rapidly evolving situation, while attempting to preserve their fundamental wartime narratives. Appeals benefited from the exploitation of existing stereotypes, but they also had the potential to expose tensions. Propaganda justifying war and identifying the enemy were inextricably bound: together they provided the motivation to fight and to endure the sacrifices that war demanded. Although Duff Cooper contended in July 1941 that propaganda's central role was to 'press the results of victory miles further', arguably its success was best tested, and its limitations revealed, at times of crisis.[73] While its effects were heightened when accompanied by military success, propaganda needed to prepare the home front and front lines for the prospect of a war of attrition, requiring resilience and sacrifice. News of military success or setbacks provoked a range of emotions. The role of propaganda was to stabilize or at least to contain fluctuations in morale and mood, to conceal or divert the reality of disunity, to contextualize events and to galvanize the nation. As such, propaganda had particular significance at times of uncertainty.

71 Toye, *The Roar*, p. 35.
72 McLaine, *Ministry of Morale*, pp. 200–3; 1943 ES-1, in Philip Williamson, Stephen Taylor, Alasdair Raffe and Natalie Mears (eds.), *National Prayers: Special Worship Since the Reformation*, vol. III: *Worship for National and Royal Occasions in the United Kingdom, 1871–2012* (Woodbridge: Church of England Record Society/Boydell, forthcoming).
73 Cooper in Cruickshank, *The Fourth Arm*, p. 185.

Crisis, resilience and loss

The success of Churchill's speeches to the House of Commons on 4 and 21 June 1940, following the evacuation of Dunkirk and the fall of France, owed more to realism than to idealism. As Richard Toye observes, Churchill's speeches 'worked their effects in complex ways', one element of a broader propaganda offensive designed to emphasize resilience against the odds.[74] Churchill's invocation of the elect nation defending Christian civilization and preventing the emergence of a 'new Dark Age' fused with J. B. Priestley's 'little pleasure steamers' of Dunkirk to create a nostalgic, characteristically 'English epic' that 'snatched glory out of defeat'.[75] Herbert Mason's photograph of St Paul's Cathedral rising out of the smouldering embers of London, and the MoI short film *London Can Take It* captured Britons' plucky determination to prevail. Together these embodied the emerging propaganda narrative of the war: this was a people's war that drew individuals within the community together in their will to defeat fascism and protect liberal values. Underpinned by the 'rhetoric of association between war sacrifice and peace-time reward', such propaganda attempted to conceal division based on class, gender, race or region.[76] But evocations of the English rural heartland and the plight of blitzed Londoners had the potential to alienate those in the regions, while references to pre-war unemployment and slum housing within progressive propaganda encouraging community spirit (such as the 1941 short film *Dawn Guard*) exerted pressure on the old elites, held responsible for the policy of appeasement and the effects of economic depression in the 1930s, to make post-war concessions. 'People's war' propaganda was marked by tension and could simultaneously unite and divide: it was vague enough to appeal to most, but sufficiently volatile to have potentially damaging consequences.[77] Propaganda attempted to erode such frictions through the retelling of Britain's wartime story, '[lending] the desperate months of 1940, in retrospect, a "terrible beauty" built of nostalgia', and demonstrating that propaganda's most profound effects may be felt in the longer term rather than in the moment.[78]

74 Toye, *The Roar*, pp. 9, 55–9, 71.
75 Penny Summerfield, 'Dunkirk and the Popular Memory of Britain at War', *Journal of Contemporary History* 45 (2010), 788–811.
76 Mark H. Leff, 'The Politics of Sacrifice on the American Home Front in World War II', *Journal of American History* 77 (1991), 1316.
77 Sonya Rose, 'Sex, Citizenship, and the Nation in World War II Britain', *American Historical Review* 103 (1998), 1175; Sonya O. Rose, *Which People's War? National Identity and Citizenship in Wartime Britain, 1939–1945* (Oxford University Press, 2003).
78 Toye, *The Roar*, p. 71.

Britain's central wartime narrative contained universal values that united the liberal democracies and that were inflected according to national circumstance. Norman Rockwell's 1943 visual representations of Roosevelt's Four Freedoms were forceful articulations of liberal principles played out in small-town America. Forming the basis of war-bond poster campaigns, radio shows, newsreels and exhibitions, Rockwell's portraits fused the absolute human rights to free speech, free worship and freedom from fear with the economically determined freedom from want.[79] 'Freedom of enterprise' quickly became the unofficial fifth freedom, allowing 'the "miracle" of production and promised consumption [to] take center stage' in US wartime propaganda.[80] That African Americans were denied civil rights, despite their contribution to the war effort, and that Japanese American citizens (Nisei) were interned, complicated the democratic rhetoric that underpinned the OWI's propaganda. While African American activists launched the 'Double V' campaign (victory in the fight against fascism and victory in the campaign for civil rights), OWI propaganda directed at the African American community was considered to be 'a holding action. . ., a mixture of honeyed words and star-spangled symbolism. . ., subtle threats if co-operation were not forthcoming, and occasional concessions granted tardily and grudgingly'.[81] However, propaganda featuring boxer Joe Louis, who had famously knocked the German Max Schmeling to the floor in 1938, and the 1944 film *The Negro Soldier* simply laid bare the vulnerability of propaganda that sought to enforce unity by hinting at 'the possibilities of race advancement', and contributed to a growing recognition that 'black people could not be ignored as American citizens'.[82]

Soviet wartime propaganda was also borne of crisis. The Nazi invasion of the Soviet Union initiated the 'Great Patriotic war' (a term first used by *Pravda* on 23 June 1941). Propagandists attempted to bind the Soviet peoples in the common task of repelling the invader through the 'vertical ties' to the state (the *Sovetskiii stroi*), and by encouraging 'horizontal ties' through the 'fraternal co-operations [of] its nations and peoples', subduing ethnic identities and adopting a Russocentric approach.[83] The Red Army was frequently portrayed as tackling the liberation of Soviet territories alone. When Churchill

79 Brewer, *Why America Fights*, pp. 119–21.
80 Leff, 'The Politics of Sacrifice', pp. 1317–18.
81 Clayton R. Koppes and Gregory D. Black, 'Blacks, Loyalty, and Motion Picture Propaganda', *Journal of American History* 73 (1986), 388–90.
82 Lauren R. Sklaroff, 'Constructing G.I. Joe Louis: Cultural Solutions to the "Negro Problem" of World War II', *Journal of American History* 89 (2003), 982.
83 Berkhoff, *Motherland in Danger*, pp. 202–9; Brooks, *Thank You, Comrade Stalin!*, p. 160.

attempted to delay the opening of the Second Front in August 1942, Stalin demonstrated that he was unafraid of destabilizing the alliance and chose instead to use propaganda as an instrument to bring pressure to bear on the Allied leaders. He instructed the media to reinvigorate its anti-British propaganda, showed support for Roosevelt by offering extensive coverage of his envoy's (Wendell Willkie) visit to the Soviet Union, and used Associated Press briefings to point to the Allies' lack of aid. He turned every public message of congratulations to Britain and the United States as they advanced through Africa and Italy from 1943 into a reminder of the absence of the Second Front, eventually calling for the Allies to finally 'join the action' in February 1944. They did so in June. He repaid them for the delay by consistently refusing to report British and American losses. This underpinned his broader narrative of the Soviets' disproportionate sacrifice in pursuit of victory.[84]

An estimated 28 million Soviets lost their lives by 1945. One of the unique characteristics of Soviet wartime campaigns, according to Karel Berkhoff, was the 'wilful neglect of the suffering of one's own citizens in the hinterland', and the reduction of sacrifice to a 'simplistic dilemma of death or treason'. Death became an expected and rather ordinary sacrifice.[85] This approach contrasted sharply with the focus on exceptional acts of bravery elsewhere. The 'Fighting Sullivans' of Iowa, killed at Guadalcanal in November 1942, were the subject of poster and war bond campaigns and a 1943 film, while Japanese propaganda glorified the 'Nine Warrior Gods of the Showa era', the men of the midget submarines killed in the attack on Pearl Harbor. In a paean to the 'The Nine Pillars, [the] Warrior Gods of Incomparably Pure Loyalty', the Navy Information Bureau celebrated their bravery in 'protecting the nation by scattering their lives like petals of manhood in full bloom'. They were accorded an elaborate funeral in Hibiya Park, Tokyo, 'enshrined for all eternity as a fiercely strong shield of gods', their birthplaces turned into memorials.[86] In effect, this was pre-propaganda for individual and collective suicide actions (*banzai*, *kamikaze* and *gyokusai*), thought by the military authorities to have a devastating effect on the morale of Allied troops. These missions fused Japan's fighting and producing peoples: they were not only the product of military bravery, but a feat of engineering performed by the 'kamikazes of production' on the home front.[87]

84 Berkhoff, *Motherland in Danger*, pp. 250–4.
85 Ibid., pp. 270, 274.
86 Earhart, *Certain Victory*, pp. 414–23.
87 Ibid., pp. 430–41.

Such sacrificial propaganda gave meaning to and mitigated defeat: it was a reminder that victory was not assured, an inducement to greater effort, and offered spiritual reassurance that the losses were not in vain. Japanese propagandists used the defeat at Iwo Jima in 1945 to encourage Japan's 'One Hundred Million' to emulate 'the brave warriors'.[88] Death was preferable to capture. Nazi Germany's failure to report the surrender of General Paulus's troops at Stalingrad indicated a similar preference for *Heldentod* (heroic death). The RMVP daily directive on 5 February 1943 instructed the press to emphasize the 'sublime example of heroism, this ultimate, self-sacrificing dedication to Germany's final victory [that will] blaze forth like a sacred flame'. Reminiscent of appeals to Japanese civilians, the RMVP instructed Germans to 'draw...on those spiritual and material forces which assure the nation of the victory it is now more fanatically than ever resolved to win', in homage to 'the deathless heroism of the men of Stalingrad'. Stalingrad was reinvented, in the words of Herman Göring, as a defence 'to the last man', a 'powerful heroic song of an unparalleled battle' reminiscent of the Battle of the Nibelungen or the Spartans at Thermopylae.[89] Later, the religious and secular motif of empowering sacrificial death was resurrected to pay tribute to the dead during the fire-bombing of major German cities.[90]

Goebbels' 1943 'Total War' speech in Berlin's Sportspalast, just fifteen days after the announcement of the defeat at Stalingrad, was designed to counteract the increasingly apparent tensions between Nazi propaganda and lived reality in the Reich. Admitting that the military had suffered setbacks on the Eastern Front, Goebbels emphasized that victory was now conditional on total mobilization and further self-sacrifice. An echo of the hopes expressed following the Polish campaign, the slogan for 1943 read *Totaler Krieg – kürzester Krieg* (Total War – Shortest War). While the SD (*Sicherheitsdienst –* Nazi Party security service) reports recorded that the German people were 'grateful to the leadership for speaking frankly at last', the speech only 'confirmed the fear of many that there was no question of stabilizing the eastern front, that the series of setbacks was not yet at an end and that the war could still take a serious turn'.[91]

88 Ibid., p. 404.
89 Jay W. Baird, 'The Myth of Stalingrad', *Journal of Contemporary History* 4 (1969), 197–8.
90 Nicholas Stargardt, 'Beyond "Consent" or "Terror": Wartime Crises in Nazi Germany', *History Workshop Journal* 72 (2011), 196.
91 Jeremy Noakes (ed.), *Nazism, 1919–1945*, vol. IV: *The German Home Front in World War II* (University of Exeter Press, 1998), p. 545.

Stalingrad and the call to total war heralded a series of 'plural, dynamic and transformatory' crises that resulted in significant fluctuations in the popular mood.[92] Allied bombardment and the devastation of German cities revived earlier propaganda, casting Washington's and London's plutocrats as 'war criminals'. This led to the promise of *Vergeltung* (revenge) to be delivered by new weapons of 'retaliation', the V1 and V2 rockets. The mere mention of these weapons 'conjured up mystical and apocalyptic visions of the future', and became the focus of hopes for a final victory. The uplift in morale was only matched by profound disappointment when the decisive blow failed to materialize. It was clear by 1944 that there would be no miracle, and 'Nazi propagandists could do precious little to counter this feeling of having been let down'.[93] After the firestorm in Hamburg in July 1943, rumour had already begun to circulate about other forms of retaliation: Allied bombing was increasingly interpreted as retaliation for the war and retribution for the suffering inflicted upon the Jews.[94]

As Germany's war drew to a close, Goebbels fused the propaganda of fear, struggle and myth. Germans were now required to display their character and will: this was no longer simply a battle for the survival of the Reich, but a fight to preserve the soul of Germany. The concluding sequences of the Reich's last major film, *Kolberg*, a testament to the spirit of total war and resilience in the face of imminent collapse, promised resurrection. *Kolberg* imagined a future emerging from the devastation of war, just as popular emotions responded to the 'sharply oscillating hopes and fears' of the final years of the war by '[focusing] less on state and society and more on personal futures', as Nicholas Stargardt has argued.[95] For those who could not imagine such a future, perhaps through loyalty to the Reich, fear induced by the ominous propaganda that accompanied the threat of Soviet invasion, the effects of Allied bombing, guilt or loss of hope, there was another alternative. A 'suicide epidemic' emerged in response to a desperate fear for the days, months and years ahead. Ultimately, it was also the choice made by the architects of the war, as Soviet troops entered Berlin in April 1945.[96]

---

92 Ibid., 190–1, 197; Kallis, *Nazi Propaganda*, p. 159.
93 Gerald Kirwin, 'Waiting for Retaliation – A Study in Nazi Propaganda Behaviour and German Civilian Morale', *Journal of Contemporary History* 16 (1981), 565–83.
94 Stargardt, 'Wartime Crises', 197–8.
95 Ibid., p. 202.
96 Christian Goeschel, 'Suicide at the End of the Third Reich', *Journal of Contemporary History* 41 (2006), 153–73.

Conclusion

The significance of propaganda in the Second World War cannot be found in its contribution to victory or defeat, but in the way key narratives shaped the subsequent representation of the war, particularly for the victors. A 'Great Patriotic War' for the Soviet Motherland requiring unprecedented sacrifice; a 'People's War' in which divisions of class, gender and region were set aside to defend liberal democracy, a war that required a special kind of spirit which dictated that no matter how remote the possibility of success, Britons could remain resilient and calm; a 'good war' for the 'American way of life', for the small-town America embodied in Rockwell's depiction of the four freedoms, for the right to free enterprise and the American Dream. These narratives assume a particular power because they represent a crisis overcome. At the time, they were contested and ambiguous, and exposed tensions. However, those tensions were gradually eroded to form a central component of post-war national identities. They serve to stabilize, anchor and explain the present. After 1945, propagandists re-mobilized the master narratives of the war in the service of new conflicts or to mitigate change: for example, as a reminder of prestige and power after the loss of empire, to cultivate the image as a defender of freedom or to sustain an ideological position. When contemporary crisis looms, and the future is uncertain, it is to these national stories that we turn. This remains the enduring legacy of the propaganda of the Second World War: it gave meaning to the war from 1939 to 1945, and it holds meaning today.

5

Reporting from the battlefield

Censorship and journalism

STEVEN CASEY

In the autumn of 1940, at the height of the London Blitz, Robert Casey, a war correspondent for the *Chicago Daily News*, compiled a mock dispatch in a vein he thought would most appeal to the British censor. 'An undetermined number of bombers', he wrote,

> came over an unidentified portion of an unmentioned European country on an unstated day. There was no weather. Had there been it would have been considered a military secret. The alert sounded at no particular hour because the enemy – one hesitates to label them with a proper name – are not supposed to know the right time. The bombs fell on a golf course killing seventy-five unnamed rabbits.[1]

Casey's sarcasm typified the hostility that reporters, accustomed to working in a system with no overt controls, often directed toward military censorship. In their view, the censors' cuts were invariably excessive; they also prevented journalists from doing their job, which was to relay fairly accurate depictions of the fighting to the home front. At a deeper level, moreover, such stringent censorship undermined these reporters' professional self-image. War correspondents like Casey were heirs to a long tradition that dated back to the Crimean War and the colonial conflicts of the nineteenth century. It was a tradition that emphasized glamour, danger and the prospect of fortune and fame. A war correspondent, as one of the most illustrious once observed, 'was a more romantic figure, more dependent on his own resources, initiative, daring, imagination, and audacity' than other types of journalist. At the start of the Second World War, many reporters headed for the front with images like these fixed firmly in their minds. And on arrival, they did not take

---

1 'Casey Ribs Censors', *Editor and Publisher*, 30 November 1940.

kindly to being told by overly officious censors that they could only write anodyne and antiseptic dispatches.[2]

To be sure, long before the Second World War, the war correspondents' self-image had clashed with the reality of increasingly systematic military control. Ever since the 1904–5 Russo-Japanese War, when the Japanese army had successfully chaperoned reporters, military organizations had honed their methods of censorship and control. In the First World War, frontline censorship had been particularly systematic. Both the British and French armies had only allowed a small number of correspondents at their Western Front headquarters, and had placed them under close military supervision. On the other side, the German army had ruled that all war news gathered by individual papers had to be cleared with the respective local military commands, which were rarely known for their openness.[3]

The British censors that Casey confronted in 1940 were thus following a long-standing tradition of their own, but they had a particularly strong reason for making savage cuts now. Since the threat of a German invasion had not yet passed, the British were determined to deny the enemy any information of military value. More immediately, precise details of where bombs had fallen and how much damage they had wrought might provide the Luftwaffe with useful intelligence about where to direct their next raids. Censorship, therefore, was crucial. Not for the last time, it was about more than trying to manipulate war reporters into producing vague copy that verged on the meaningless. Instead, restricting the publication of sensitive information was crucial to the success of the whole war effort.

But censorship was by no means the only way that military organizations interacted with war correspondents. In fact, Casey's attack on overzealous British censorship is particularly interesting because it came at a time when the British government was engaged in one of the most famous efforts to try to publicize war news. Working with radio broadcasters like Edward R. Murrow, British officials in the autumn of 1940 relaxed many of their controls to enable US journalists to air live descriptions of London's suffering directly into American homes. In this instance, British motives were

2 Philip Gibbs, 'Introduction', in Frederic Villiers, *Days of Glory: The Sketch Book of a Correspondent at the Front* (New York: G. H. Doran, 1920), p. vii. See also Joseph J. Matthews, *Reporting the Wars* (Minneapolis: University of Minnesota Press, 1957), pp. 241–8; Mark Pedelty, *War Stories: The Culture of Foreign Correspondents* (New York: Routledge, 1995), pp. 6–8, 29, 72–6.

3 Martin J. Farrar, *News from the Front: New Correspondents on the Western Front, 1914–18* (Stroud: Sutton Publishing, 1998), pp. 13, 23, 44, 68; Ross F. Collins, 'The Development of Censorship in World War I France', *Journalism Monographs* 131 (1992), 1–25.

transparent: by emphasizing that the stubborn and determined Londoners could take everything the Nazis threw at them, they hoped to cement US support for their war effort.[4] On other occasions, governments had a range of additional motives for balancing publicity against censorship, including not just appealing to neutral opinion, but also celebrating battlefield success and, above all, motivating their home fronts to keep up the fight. As a result, although war correspondents were frequently frustrated by stringent controls, many still had some space to relay vivid descriptions of the war to their audiences back home. Just how much space they had at various stages of the war – and why this fluctuated over time – is the focus of this chapter.

Expanding war, 1939–1941

Although all belligerents sought to control what war correspondents wrote, precisely how they did this depended largely on the nature of the regime. The democracies initially struggled. In Britain, a series of Defence Notices established the legal framework for censorship, with Regulation 3 stating that only information of military value would be cut; 'censors had no right to interfere with opinion, comment, speculation, or matter which the enemy might find useful in his propaganda'. The new Ministry of Information hastened to reassure the press that anything not of direct value to the enemy would be passed. But the services remained the final arbiter of what information was of military value, and they tended to err on the side of caution. To make matters worse, many of the new censors had a naval background, and, as one close observer explained, they treated journalists 'as potentially mutinous naval ratings who should be instantly put in chains if they disobeyed an order'.[5]

British journalists reacted scornfully. As the Phoney War set in, most became frustrated by the lack of eye-catching news stories. And they rapidly recoiled at the notion that they were in some way adjuncts of the state who ought to be disciplined if they rebelled. True, there were important pressures that ensured that the British media did not get too far out of line. Along Fleet Street, the vast majority of newspapers patriotically supported the war and eagerly pledged to do their bit to defeat Hitler. On the airwaves, the semi-independent BBC was subjected to close government supervision, including

4 Nicholas J. Cull, *Selling War: The British Propaganda Campaign Against American 'Neutrality' in World War II* (Oxford University Press, 1995), pp. 101–4.
5 Ian McLaine, *Ministry of Morale: Home Front Morale and the Ministry of Information in World War II* (London: George Allen & Unwin, 1979), pp. 34–7; Michael Balfour, *Propaganda in War, 1939–1945* (London: Routledge, 1979), pp. 59–60.

'continuous policy censorship'.[6] But the nature of the free media was bound to cause problems for the censors. For one thing, the British government had to forge relationships with a large variety of news organizations with different demands, from wire services who focused on providing instant, breaking 'spot news', to commentators and magazine writers who had more freedom to contextualize what they witnessed. For another, these news organizations all saw the war as a major opportunity to boost circulation. Facing relentless daily deadlines, they demanded constant information, either communiqués from military authorities or stories – perhaps even scoops – from their own reporters. And they were highly impatient with delays and restrictions.

By contrast, totalitarian and authoritarian regimes had an obvious edge when trying to control war news. For a start, they had been restricting information for years and already had the machinery in place. The Japanese Army Ministry had issued Order No. 3 as far back as 1931, at the start of the Manchurian Incident, instructing the press not to discuss military matters 'without prior approval'. Notifications 27 and 28 had followed six years later, at the outbreak of the China Incident, prohibiting press accounts of troop movements and army mobilization, respectively. At the same time, the Japanese government moved increasingly to rationalize the media, working with the Newspaper Union to force mergers that benefited the big corporations like Asahi, Mainichi and Yomiuri, while also licensing only those journalists whose stories grasped 'the national spirit'.[7] But in Japan, the media was still a separate entity from the state. The same was not so true in Nazi Germany, where centralization and control were much more advanced. At the start of the war, the Nazi Party dominated radio. It also controlled two-thirds of the country's newspapers, with the rest subjected to close daily supervision. In effect, as one authority observes, the government '"blocked out" troublesome sources of differing views early on; in the Third Reich there was no place for any public divergence from the official line on the war'.[8]

6 P. M. H. Bell, *John Bull and the Bear: British Public Opinion, Foreign Policy, and the Soviet Union, 1941–1945* (London: Edward Arnold, 1990), p. 15.
7 Richard H. Mitchell, *Censorship in Imperial Japan* (Princeton University Press, 1983), pp. 255, 283; Laurie Anne Freeman, *Closing the Shop: Information Cartels and Japan's Mass Media* (Princeton University Press, 2000), pp. 52–4.
8 Aristotle Kallis, *Nazi Propaganda and the Second World War* (Basingstoke: Palgrave Macmillan, 2005), pp. 30–1; Jörg Echternkamp, 'At War, Abroad and at Home: The Essential Features of German Society in the Second World War', in *Germany and the Second World War*, vol. IX: *German Wartime Society, 1939–1945* (10 vols., Oxford: Clarendon Press, 2008), pt. 1, pp. 19–21.

Yet neither the Japanese nor the German government focused purely on suppression. The domestic demand for war news was too intense. Japanese newspapers had been producing special war editions ever since the Manchurian Incident. By the late 1930s, powerful Japanese media organizations like the Asahi were working with the military to get their correspondents to distant parts of the Chinese front, from where they relayed highly laudatory stories about the prowess of Japanese forces.[9] In Germany the situation was more regimented. While Joseph Goebbels' Propaganda Ministry issued regular *Sondermeldungen* (special news bulletins), the Wehrmacht's *Propaganda-Kompanien* (PK) provided battlefield descriptions and images. The PKs were staffed in part by war correspondents, who worked to guidelines established by Goebbels. In 1939, there were seven in the army, four in the Luftwaffe and one in the navy.[10]

Beyond having a clear start, the German government also benefited from holding the initiative on the battlefield. Successful organizations are rarely shy about trumpeting their success. And the Wehrmacht was no different. In September 1939, while Warsaw was rapidly surrounded and effectively cut off from the outside world, German authorities issued communiqués that even critics conceded were more accurate than anything emanating from Poland, Britain or France. In May and June 1940, as German troops scythed through Allied defences and raced for the coast, the Wehrmacht put on an equally impressive show. One lucky group of reporters even experienced the luxury of travelling in 'seven high-powered Mercedes-Benz staff cars', while dining on 'hardtack, canned blood sausage, and champagne'. They were also permitted to write graphic dispatches about events like the evacuation of Dunkirk, recording the 'horrid stench of death' and the rows of Allied trucks that 'stood burned on a dock'.[11]

As well as celebrating military success, the Wehrmacht's media relations benefited from the fact that, like most victorious armies, its operations ran roughly to plan. German authorities could therefore implement media strategies that had been thought through ahead of time. More importantly, they could provide the vital logistical support – especially radio transmitters and couriers – that turned correspondents' front-line observations into publishable dispatches.

9 David C. Earhart, *Certain Victory: Images of World War Two in the Japanese Media* (London: M. E. Sharpe, 2008), p. 71.
10 Daniel Uziel, *The Propaganda Warriors: The Wehrmacht and the Consolidation of the German Home Front* (New York: Peter Lang, 2008).
11 John Fisher, 'I Saw the First Ruins of Dunkerque', in *Reporting World War II, Pt. 1: American Journalism, 1938–1944* (New York: Library of America, 1995), pp. 63–9.

Reeling from defeat, the Allies had no such luxury. Before the German attack, the British had allocated thirty conducting officers and twelve censors to its media unit. Their plan had been to transport reporters to and from what promised to be a fast-moving front, ensuring that they always had facilities to cable their reports. By mid-May, however, this plan was effectively redundant. Communications were often non-existent. Briefers rarely knew what was happening. Struggling either to work out where the front was or get their copy to head office, many correspondents headed to Paris, where they hoped to gain some idea of the catastrophe befalling Allied forces. Those who stayed with the army often found it difficult to cover the fighting. Dunkirk was a case in point. While the Germans were quite open, the British were keen to fudge the gruesome dimension of this disaster. Commanders near the city even turned away a group of accredited reporters, effectively ensuring that the dramatic evacuation was only covered from afar – by reporters based in London or Paris, not war correspondents only a frustrating few miles from the scene. Not until later in the summer, in fact, did British propagandists start to dramatize Dunkirk, glorifying the role that civilians in 'little ships' played in the rescue – an image that chimed neatly with the growing British sense that this was a 'people's war'.[12]

Across the Channel, with a possible German invasion imminent, British censorship remained stringent. This was the backdrop to Casey's mock dispatch suggesting that British censors would only permit the mention of unnamed dead rabbits. But Casey was by no means an isolated voice. Other correspondents privately complained that London censors were stricter than their Berlin counterparts. When it came to reports about British unpreparedness on its south coast, these complaints were fair: Churchill's government was naturally desperate to deny such sensitive intelligence to the enemy. When it came to the air battles fought above southeast England, however, the official British attitude rapidly began to change.

One reason was that the British now had less to hide. In August, not only was the Battle of Britain eminently susceptible to numerical claims of British versus German losses, which allowed the media to turn this battle into a readily understandable pseudo-sporting event; more to the point, it was an attritional fight that the RAF was winning.[13] In September, not only could the

12 Drew Middleton, *Our Share of Night* (New York: Viking Press, 1946), pp. 61, 71–2; Angus Calder, *The Myth of the Blitz* (London: Jonathan Cape, 1991), pp. 96–8.
13 Angus Calder, *The People's War: Britain, 1939–1945* (London: Jonathan Cape, 1969), pp. 140–5, 150–1.

Blitz be portrayed as confirmation that the brutal Nazis were ruthlessly targeting civilians; just as importantly, British officials hoped that radio broadcasts containing vivid sounds of bombs falling in the midst of familiar landmarks would help to generate neutral sympathy for the British war effort, especially in the United States. American reporters working for CBS quickly noticed the difference. While the British allowed Murrow to broadcast live eyewitness accounts from London rooftops, the Germans hustled his colleague William Shirer into a Berlin basement, where he had to use a special microphone that muffled the sound of exploding British bombs. By the end of the year, Murrow had become a major celebrity, feted in both Britain and the United States. Shirer, by contrast, had returned to New York, complaining loudly about the impossibility of reporting the war from Nazi Germany.[14]

The coverage of these air raids marked another new development in war reporting: the smudging of the distinction between front-line reporters and their deskbound colleagues. In earlier wars, editors and bureau chiefs had operated from media hubs like London's Fleet Street. Safe from the distant action, they could focus on the daily tasks of allocating their reporters to cover different stories, getting the official line from government spokesmen, and making up the next day's newspapers. Now they were in the midst of the story, and this soon took its toll. In London, some newspaper office buildings did not survive the bombs. Many employees struggled to sleep at night or get to work in the morning; others suffered from stress and were soon burnt out. Even without the constant daily battles with censors, journalists, bureau chiefs and editors often found it hard simply to get a newspaper out or a broadcast on the air.[15] What they did produce remained light on details: the censors still insisted that places bombed or total casualties from particular raids could not be mentioned. Instead, the media focused on human-interest stories of stoic suffering, designed to underline the message that the British people could 'take it'.[16]

At least these reporters were close to home. As the war continued to expand, so did the opportunity for front-line correspondents to encounter

---

14 A. M. Sperber, *Murrow: His Life and Times* (London: Michael Joseph, 1987), pp. 169–84; William L. Shirer, *The Nightmare Years, 1930–1940* (New York: Bantam Books, 1984), pp. 594–5.

15 See, for instance, William Armstrong (ed.), *With Malice Toward None: A War Diary by Cecil King* (London: Sidgwick & Jackson, 1970), pp. 73–88.

16 Helen Jones, *British Civilians in the Front Line: Air Raids, Productivity and Wartime Culture, 1939–45* (Manchester University Press, 2006), p. 14.

dangers in far more gruelling landscapes even than rubble-strewn London. Many had already frozen in Helsinki in early 1940, when the Finns had welcomed more than 300 reporters from twenty-three countries in a bid to drum up international support for their war against the Soviet Union.[17] Almost as many now headed for the heat of North Africa, as the fighting spread over the winter of 1940–41. In both theatres, the punishing conditions often became an integral part of the story. In North Africa, British and American reporters not only had to endure the sand and the flies; they also felt an acute sense of distance from their home offices. 'It was a strange sensation', recalled Alan Moorehead, who wrote for the *Daily Express*,

> writing dispatches away here in the blue, never knowing whether they would get back to Cairo, let alone London and New York. We had been away now so long without word from the outside world that I, for one, had lost my 'news sense' – that sense of proportion you have that tells you whether a thing is worth writing or not.[18]

A year earlier, some reporters covering the war along the Soviet-Finnish border had felt even more detached from their normal working lives. 'Never before', reported Leland Stowe of the *Chicago Daily News*, after a trip to the Lapland front in January 1940, 'have thousands of men attempted to conquer simultaneously their adversaries and the fierce Arctic winters... Even Jules Verne', he added, 'never dreamed of Arctic winters like this'.[19]

While the Finns had welcomed international reporters during the Winter War of 1939–40, the Soviets had treated them with scorn. Stalin's basic news policy had been both to deny foreign correspondents access to the front and to impose a strict censorship policy on any dispatches they compiled in Moscow. It was a stringent policy that stemmed largely from the Soviet leader's long-standing determination to exert complete control over the news, but it was reinforced by the Red Army's poor performance, when the Finns initially provided unexpectedly stubborn resistance. As such, it provided Stalin with a perfect template when Hitler invaded the Soviet Union in June 1941.

---

17 Jukka Nevakivi, *The Appeal that Was Never Made: The Allies, Scandinavia, and the Finnish Winter War of 1939–1940* (London: Hurst, 1976), pp. 100–1; 'Newspaper correspondents in the Winter War, 1939–40', www.histdoc.net/history/reporters.html (accessed 31 October 2014).

18 Alan Moorehead, *The Desert War* (London: Aurum, 2009), p. 96.

19 Leland Stowe, 'Incredible War Is Being Waged in Arctic Zone', *Chicago Daily News*, 26 January 1940.

As the Soviet disaster on the Eastern Front gathered pace during the summer and autumn of 1941, Stalin's first rule was that nothing could be printed in the press unless the Soviet Information Bureau had already mentioned it. His second banned 'without exception all pieces of information that can call forth a panicky and depressed mood in the army or in the hinterland'. In practice, these strictures immediately translated into by far the most restrictive media policy of the war. The Soviet press was already suffering from severe newspaper shortages, while radio broadcasted to a much smaller proportion of the population than in any other belligerent country. It scarcely mattered given the paucity of war news in either medium.

During the first catastrophic months, many Soviet reports merely stated that 'Our troops continued to engage the opponent in battle all along the front'. Often, Stalin refused to countenance anything more. Indeed, the Soviet leader frequently took a personal interest in the Information Bureau's communiqués, and on some occasions he personally deleted large chunks detailing the extent of retreats or the loss of cities. But not even Stalin could conceal the true magnitude of the defeat. And when the Germans announced that Kiev or Smolensk had fallen, Soviet authorities had little choice other than to concede what had happened – albeit initially only to international reporters, rather than their own people.[20] When the time finally came to divulge the news to the home front, Stalin was careful to play the blame game, deploying *Pravda* to shift responsibility away from his government and party and toward the military commanders, some of whom were duly purged.[21]

There was, however, a major cost associated with this reticence: scarcely anyone believed what they read in the newspapers. Even in a totalitarian regime like the Soviet Union this could be a problem, since rumour and speculation tended to fill any obvious information vacuum.[22] In the democracies, an absence of news or misleading official information could be even more damaging. In the radio age, people could tune in to enemy broadcasts. Newspapers might also use alternative sources of information, including enemy assessments, something that did indeed happen with surprising regularity after the United States entered the war in December 1941.

20 Karel Berkhoff, *Motherland in Danger: Soviet Propaganda During World War II* (Cambridge, Mass.: Harvard University Press, 2012), pp. 35–44.
21 Amir Weiner, *Making Sense of War: The Second World War and the Fate of the Bolshevik Revolution* (Princeton University Press, 2001), pp. 43–4.
22 Berkhoff, *Motherland in Danger*, pp. 37, 41, 66. A similar process operated in Germany; see Kallis, *Nazi Propaganda*, pp. 137–48.

War on the sea and in the air, 1941–1943

America's entrance into the war initially exposed a major tension between the desirability of publicity and the necessity of censorship. On the one hand, wartime censorship measures sat uneasily beside the US Constitution's guarantee of freedom of speech. The American government responded with a dual system. While news stories written inside the United States would be subjected only to a voluntary censorship code, war correspondents who travelled overseas would have to go through the process of accreditation, which entailed agreeing to submit anything they wrote to a military censor before it was transmitted home. Although this promised to eradicate the most blatant security lapses, American war correspondents remained fiercely independent and highly competitive. Even the most patriotic were determined to grab scoops for their demanding editors.[23]

Yet the first battles these American reporters wanted to cover fell under the purview of the US Navy. And like all navies, it had a well-earned reputation for suppression. This was partly because navy commanders generally had more opportunity than the other services for restricting media access to their activities. It was obviously impossible for reporters to cover what went on in the vast spaces of the Atlantic or Pacific without permission to go on board a ship. On the other hand, naval officers only tended to grant this permission grudgingly because they felt they had more reason than any other service to worry about how the enemy could use indiscreet reports. Naval warfare was, after all, a lethal cat-and-mouse game in which intelligence was crucial. If German U-boats patrolling the Atlantic knew which Allied ships were leaving from which port, or which route a particular convoy was taking, then they could lie in wait and cause havoc. Surprise was equally crucial in the Pacific. Here, as well as the importance of holding the initiative, modern technology meant that the two fleets invariably engaged each other at such long distances that neither side had a clear sense of how many losses they had inflicted on the other. Small wonder that the navies were the so-called 'silent service', united in a determination not to give out any information that might give the other side an edge.[24]

The Pearl Harbor attack of 7 December 1941 demonstrated how the logic of naval censorship tended to transcend the political divide. For the Japanese,

23 Michael J. Sweeney, *The Military and the Press: An Uneasy Truce* (Evanston, Ill.: North-western University Press, 2006), pp. 63–77.
24 Elmer Davis, 'War Information and Military Security', 19 November 1942, Subject File: OWI, box 10, Elmer Davis Papers, Library of Congress.

Pearl Harbor was a stunning tactical victory. As David Earhart points out, the Japanese navy was the 'only source of information of the Pearl Harbor attack, but the information was not immediately released, leaving private news organizations in a quandary'. Not until 24 December – two and a half weeks after Japanese forces had sunk or damaged eighteen US naval vessels and destroyed 180 aircraft – did the *Asahigraph* run the first story, entitled 'Annihilation of America and Britain Report 1'.[25] In that time, the US navy was equally reticent. On 7 December it immediately stopped all radio-telephone transmissions from Hawaii, even cutting off one news alert halfway through. When newspapers like the *New York Times* got hold of hard facts that suggested a huge disaster, the US Navy Department quickly prevailed on them not to publish.[26]

The contrasting reactions were significant. While the Japanese enjoyed what one journalist observer dubbed an orgy of 'national intoxication',[27] the Americans launched into a fury of speculation. In the next few months, as the US Navy continued to block news of American losses, the media simply turned to enemy sources. According to one survey, there was 'a marked disposition on the part of the American press and radio' to use official German news agency sources, which in turn 'conveyed to the public the impression that losses far greater than those officially admitted by the United States were sustained in the Pacific'. The Associated Press was a major culprit, printing on one occasion Japanese claims that 93,000 Dutch and 5,000 British and American troops had surrendered on Java.[28]

Before long, some US naval leaders recognized the cost of overzealous suppression. By the time of the American victories at Coral Sea and Midway, they permitted reporters to travel with the fleet. The result was a series of reports by Stanley Johnston, published five weeks after the battle and containing graphic descriptions of a US carrier being 'bombed, machine gunned, and torpedoed'. But herein lay a major irony. Johnston worked for the *Chicago Tribune*, a newspaper so critical of President Franklin D. Roosevelt's war policy that it had committed a number of major security breaches. By the time his story on the Coral Sea battle had appeared, the US Navy believed that Johnston had not only brazenly violated the censorship

25 Earhart, *Certain Victory*, p. 222.
26 Steven Casey, *When Soldiers Fall: How Americans Have Confronted Combat Losses from World War I to Afghanistan* (New York: Oxford University Press, 2013), pp. 46–7.
27 Masuo Kato, *The Lost War: A Japanese Reporter's Inside Story* (New York: A. A. Knopf, 1946), p. 88.
28 Casey, *When Soldiers Fall*, p. 50.

code, but had also been responsible for a story that revealed one of the Allies' biggest secrets: the breaking of the Japanese naval codes. Small wonder that a joke soon circulated around Washington that the naval chief's 'idea of war information was that there should be just *one* communiqué. Some morning we would announce that the war was won and that we had won it'.[29]

While navies continued to prioritize censorship, air forces tended to sit at the other end of the suppression–publicity spectrum. The newest of the three services, they wanted to forge their own identities. Headed by publicity-conscious leaders, they were determined to trumpet how they could make a decisive difference to the war effort. So, in 1939 and 1940, German newsreels flaunted both the actions of Luftwaffe bombers and the wreckage they left behind. 'It is mainly due to the Luftwaffe's contribution', boasted Hermann Göring, 'that we owe this annihilation of the enemy... What the Luftwaffe has shown in Poland it will fulfil in the coming battles in England and France'.[30] When the Luftwaffe duly fulfilled this promise the following summer, the RAF was keen to lavish public praise on its own fliers. As well as allowing the names of ace pilots to be published, it actively worked with film-makers to produce drama-documentaries like *Target for Tonight*, and even invited war correspondents on dangerous bombing missions. Soon, a romantic image of the RAF was firmly fixed in the British public discourse. Its fighter pilots were 'knights of the air' who had won the Battle of Britain. Its bomber boys were from the one service that was carrying the fight to the heart of Hitler's Reich.[31] Less than two years later, these fliers had to share the limelight with American flyboys. The US Eighth Air Force, observed one reporter, 'was a high-octane outfit. It was run by ambitious men and backed by an ambitious command in Washington. It had set up a large public-relations staff – men from newspaper, publicity firms, advertising agencies – and made use of Hollywood celebrities'.[32] It was never shy about seeking headlines, a trait that reached its height with the formation of the 'Writing Sixty-Ninth': a group of correspondents who, after a week's

29 Dina Goren, 'Communication Intelligence and the Freedom of the Press: The *Chicago Tribune*'s Battle of Midway Dispatch and the Breaking of the Japanese Naval Code', *Journal of Contemporary History* 16 (1980), 663–6; Allan M. Winkler, *The Politics of Propaganda: The Office of War Information* (New Haven, Conn.: Yale University Press, 1978), p. 49.
30 David Welch, *The Third Reich: Politics and Propaganda* (London: Routledge, 1993), pp. 95–6.
31 Martin Francis, *The Flyer: British Culture and the Royal Air Force, 1939–1945* (Oxford University Press, 2008), ch. 2.
32 Harrison E. Salisbury, *A Journey for Our Times: A Memoir* (New York: Harper & Row, 1983), p. 195.

training, took off in B-17s and B-24s to cover a bombing mission against the German port of Wilhelmshaven. Their resulting dispatches were particularly vivid. 'American Flying Fortresses', wrote Walter Cronkite, 'have just come back from an assignment to hell – a hell of 26,000 feet above earth, a hell of burning tracer bullets and bursting gunfire, of crippled Fortresses and burning German fighter planes, of parachuting men and others not so lucky'.[33]

Morale and fighting spirit, 1941–1943

The grim tone and realistic imagery of such stories was partly a response to editors' demands. Cronkite, for example, was employed by the United Press, whose boss instructed his reporters 'to get the smell of warm blood in their copy'.[34] Yet such reports still had to pass through censors' hands. It was significant, therefore, that at the mid-stage of the war, governments on all sides also saw much to be gained by refusing either to gloss over the war's grisly side or to paint the fighting in an overly optimistic and sanitized way.

Goebbels was particularly quick to recognize the pitfalls of over-optimism, although he could not always resist the temptation to exacerbate it. During the first months of Germany's invasion of the Soviet Union, his Propaganda Ministry helped to ensure that war reporting clearly contained a 'triumphalist tenor'. As early as August 1941, though, Goebbels started to contemplate whether or not to tone down this overconfident line. The massive victories around Kiev and Smolensk a month later made this task difficult. Caught up in the excitement, the *Völkischer Beobachter* splurged banner headlines announcing 'the greatest battle of annihilation of all time', while a *Sondermeldung* estimated the capture of no less than 665,000 Red Army troops in the Kiev pocket. Goebbels remained somewhat uneasy, especially once the German advance stuttered. Only now he faced a challenge from Otto Dietrich, the *Reichspressechef*, who passed on Hitler's confident attitude to the media. The apogee of optimism came in October 1941, when Dietrich announced that 'the very last remnants of the Red Army were locked in two steel German pockets before Moscow and were undergoing swift, merciless annihilation'. Goebbels thought this went way too far. Such a 'reckless news policy', he complained, would create 'dangerous illusions', especially if the Red Army

---

33 Douglas Brinkley, *Cronkite* (New York: HarperCollins, 2012), pp. 89–103; Timothy M. Gay, *Assignment to Hell: The War Against Nazi Germany with Correspondents Walter Cronkite, Andy Rooney, A. J. Liebling, Homer Bigart, and Hal Boyle* (New York: New American Library, 2012), pp. 121–49.

34 Brinkley, *Cronkite*, p. 99.

did survive. It also threatened to engender a growing public suspicion of government-dominated war news.[35]

As the war dragged on into 1942, Goebbels moved toward a policy of realism and restraint, while continuing to lament Dietrich's optimistic out-bursts, which he regarded 'as extremely dangerous'.[36] With the defeat at Stalingrad in early 1943, he then pushed war reporting in an even gloomier direction. 'Pessimism', as one historian has written, 'became the means of persuading the German nation of the necessity of a more total war effort, of making them accept the harsh measures that now lay in store'. To this end, Goebbels even wistfully contemplated the possibility of recruiting the weather to his cause. 'Every ray of sunlight', he wrote in his diary, 'is an obstacle to the implementation of total war. I would much prefer it if winter would prevail for a few more weeks, albeit in milder form. The worse the image of the war appears, the easier it is to draw the necessarily harsh consequences'. When the weather stubbornly refused to cooperate, British and American bombers exploited the clearer skies to intensify their raids on German cities. As war's harsh consequences hit home, Goebbels' response was a two-pronged policy of both 'realism (in acknowledging the conse-quences on civilian populations and cities) and caution (in avoiding either exaggeration or embellishment of the situation)'.[37]

Among the Allies, senior officials were equally determined to divulge more of the war's grim reality during 1943, although their overriding concern was very different. In the wake of the successful campaigns in North Africa and Sicily, they were keen to dampen the public's excessive complacency about the prospect of an early victory, which they believed stemmed partly from the media's sanitized coverage of the battlefield. So at the end of 1943, the US military permitted the release of much more graphic images. The army chief wrote to subordinates in the field, urging them to pass pictures for publication that would 'vividly portray the dangers, horrors, and grimness of war'.[38] The US Navy also got in on the act, producing *With the Marines at Tarawa*. Based on graphic combat footage, this film went on general release with Roosevelt's expressed approval. 'These are the marine dead', the

35 David Stahel, *Kiev, 1941: Hitler's Battle for Supremacy in the East* (Cambridge University Press, 2012), pp. 191–2, 300–1; Kallis, *Nazi Propaganda*, pp. 111–13.
36 Kallis, *Nazi Propaganda*, pp. 123–6.
37 Gerald Anthony Kirwin, "Nazi Domestic Propaganda and Popular Response, 1943–45" (University of Reading PhD, 1979), p. 47; Kallis, *Nazi Propaganda*, p. 161.
38 George H. Roeder, *The Censored War: American Visual Experience During World War II* (New Haven, Conn.: Yale University Press, 1993), pp. 11–12.

narrator intoned toward the end, over pictures of prostrate American bodies lying on the sand and bobbing in the shallow sea. 'This is the price we have to pay for a war we didn't want. And before it's over, there will be more dead on other battlefields'.[39]

As well as reinforcing domestic morale, military establishments had more positive motives for providing realistic battlefield information. One was to forge some sort of bond between the soldier and the public back home. This was particularly important in the Pacific, where the massive distances between the fighting and home fronts threatened to create a real divide. American leaders, struggling to instil a sense of martial spirit into a nation that had only just discarded its isolationist instincts, certainly fretted that there was 'a growing disposition on the part of our people to set apart the army and the navy from civilian life', to view them 'as a disconnected task force which has been selected to perform a difficult, unpleasant, and dangerous job'. In the opinion of Secretary of War Henry Stimson, this chasm could only be narrowed by the release of more truthful information about conditions at the front.[40] His enemy agreed with the problem, if not always the cure. As the historian Barak Kushner observes, 'Japanese wartime propaganda centred on one major goal: unifying the battlefront with the home front'. Initially, this was to be achieved by trying to ensure that both soldiers and the home front endorsed the nation's war aims. Increasingly, though, the Japanese government and media recognized the need to disseminate news of the military's sacrifices, including the 'military mass suicide' on Attu in May 1943, in order to emphasize and reinforce the nation's fighting 'spirit'.[41]

With governments inclining toward realism, more space opened up for war correspondents to depict life at the front. The most successful were those who were not constrained by providing constant breaking news, for the censors continued to cut numerous details about each day's operations. Rather, they were reporters with the writing skill to convey a sense of the fighting's grimness, while reinforcing key tenets of their home front's view of the war. The American Ernie Pyle was a prime example. Pyle's war career was varied. Starting with the Blitz in 1940, he followed the GIs across North Africa, Sicily

39 Peter Malowski, *Armed with Cameras: The American Military Photographers of World War II* (New York: The Free Press, 1993), pp. 259–60. Michael D. Pearlman, *Warmaking and American Democracy: The Struggle Over Military Strategy, 1700–Present* (Lawrence: University Press of Kansas, 1999), p. 250.

40 Casey, *When Soldiers Fall*, p. 56.

41 Barak Kushner, *The Thought War: Japanese Imperial Propaganda* (Honolulu: University of Hawaii Press, 2006), p. 6; Earhart, *Certain Victory*, p. 380.

and Italy in 1942–43, then into France the day after D-Day, before finally succumbing to a sniper's bullet on Okinawa in April 1945. In that time, he developed an eye for capturing the GIs' daily experience – including the boredom and fatigue, the grim conditions and bloody casualties – without ever crossing a line and providing his readers with images that they could not stomach. Pyle, his biographer concludes, 'gave Americans all the realism they wanted'. He also provided them with a sense of what their citizen soldiers had become: team players, who looked out for each other, but were often cynical about their officers; stoic survivors, whose daily needs were simple, but who pined to return to their homes, families and cities.[42] Vasily Grossman performed a similar role in the Soviet Union. His experiences were, if anything, more intrepid, stretching from the Red Army's demoralizing retreats of 1941, through the searing street battles of Stalingrad, and all the way to Berlin in 1945. Despite Stalin's strict censorship regime – and, indeed, despite Stalin's personal dislike of him – Grossman produced reams of descriptive stories for *Krasnaya Zvezda*, detailing the heroic feats of battle-hardened Soviet soldiers, from the anger of an anti-tank soldier forced to leave his home to kill Germans, to the exploits of snipers in the ruins of Stalingrad.[43]

Stalin doubtless tolerated Grossman because some of his reports reinforced a key theme of Soviet propaganda: the need to hate the German enemy. In this sense, Soviet war reporting was no different from that in other countries. For the most part, however, Stalin adopted a much more restrictive attitude, even after the tide of battle turned. Unlike the Americans, for instance, he refused to countenance a more candid coverage of battlefield death. David Ortenberg, Grossman's editor on *Krasnaya Zvezda*, explained why. 'There are too many losses', he observed. 'We're not going to make Hitler glad'.[44]

Allied victory, 1944–1945

Despite the Soviet Union's massive casualties, the Allies enjoyed all the advantages of being firmly on the offensive by 1944. The Western powers

42 James Tobin, *Ernie Pyle's War: America's Eyewitness to World War II* (New York: Free Press, 2006), pp. 242–3; Andrew J. Huebner, *The Warrior Image: Soldiers in American Culture from the Second World War to the Vietnam Era* (Chapel Hill: University of North Carolina Press, 2008), pp. 37–43.
43 Antony Beevor and Luba Vinogradova (eds.), *A Writer at War: Vasily Grossman with the Red Army, 1941–1945* (London: Pimlico, 2006), pp. 140, 155–9.
44 Berkhoff, *Motherland in Danger*, pp. 54–6.

were in a particularly good position. Holding the initiative, they could plan where to deploy both their forces and the accompanying war correspondents. Equipped with increasingly impressive resources, they could also present these reporters with the means to get their stories quickly back to their editors.

When American forces landed on Luzon in January 1945, the US Army provided its sixty accredited reporters with a floating press headquarters on three small ships, moored just offshore. This contained a high-speed radio teleprinter that enabled them to wire out more than 170,000 words in the first week of the operation alone. The navy was not to be outdone, laying on laboratory and transmission facilities for the photographers who accompanied the Iwo Jima landings a month later, so that images – including the famous one of marines planting an American flag – could be back in the United States within eighteen hours of the start of the attack.[45] Yet even these operations paled next to OVERLORD. As well as employing 200 censors to scour the half a million words of copy that flowed out on D-Day, the Allies initially established three low-powered radio sets on the far end of the invasion beaches, followed weeks later by a 400-watt Press Wireless commercial transmitter that connected the battlefield zone directly to London and New York. Facilities for photographers were equally impressive, enabling Robert Capa to get his pictures from OMAHA beach to London in two days – and in time to make it into *Life* magazine's first post-invasion issue.[46]

The nature of these offensives also made it easier for the Allied military to control and co-opt war reporters. Engaged in 'liberating' territory, the Allies launched a succession of amphibious assaults against Pacific, Mediterranean and Normandy targets. On each occasion, space on the precious landing craft was at a premium. As a result, military public information officers could control how many correspondents – and which ones – would witness the initial fighting. More importantly, they could forge a close bond with those chosen to accompany the first assault waves. Indeed, before each attack, both parties recognized that security was vital. If the enemy got wind of when, where and in what strength the Allies planned to land, they could

45 'Ideal Press Setup for Luzon' and 'Navy Plans Help Cameramen in Speedy Coverage on Iwo', *Editor and Publisher*, 27 January and 24 February 1945.
46 SHAEF, 'Press Policy', Operational Memo 24, 24 April 1944, Policy re Release of Information to the Press File, Chief of Staff, SGS, DF 000.7, box 2, RG331. 'Communication Arrangements for the Press', undated, Press Coverage and Communications in France, Chief of Staff, SGS, DF 000.7/4, box 3, RG331, US National Archives, College Park, Md.

concentrate a reception party to slaughter the men in the boats. Before D-Day, the risks were so high that the army even asked its invasion-bound reporters to write their own obituaries. 'All the time fear lay blackly deep down upon your consciousness', Pyle recalled of this experience a few weeks later. 'It bore down on your heart like an all-consuming weight'. Gripped by such anxiety, war correspondents rarely disputed the military's fierce determination to enforce total operational security. It seemed to them a prudent precaution to protect life and limb.[47]

When D-Day succeeded, the military then put many of the lessons learned into practice. It worked hard to strike the right balance between confident reports that reassured the public and over-optimistic dispatches that misleadingly underplayed the carnage in places like OMAHA beach. It also worked hard to strike the right balance between allowing media depictions of the grinding battles on the Cotentin Peninsula and ensuring that the enemy did not acquire information of the next phase of planned operations.[48] Yet even with lavish support systems, a relatively tame press corps and the benefits of learning, the Allied military still faced a series of difficulties. Many stemmed from one factor: ego.

Journalists' egos were part of the problem. Fiercely competitive, they jostled constantly for a scoop that would please their editors. On a few occasions, this led to embarrassing stories, including suggestions that the French population had been 'unfriendly' toward Allied troops or that the Germans had behaved in a 'chivalrous' manner during the battle for Caen.[49] But more often than not, a desire for professional advantage resulted in distortions based on a desire to be first to get a particular dateline. On D-Day, some reporters were so keen to cable that they had been first to land on a particular beach that they failed to place this landing in any sort of context. In August, many were so desperate to grab one of the first Paris-based stories that they likewise ignored the wider picture – so much so in Ernest Hemingway's case that the main issue became whether he was the first to liberate the Ritz Hotel.[50] The following year, dateline desperation became so

47 Barney Oldfield, *Never a Shot in Anger* (Santa Barbara, Calif.: Capra Press, 1989), pp. 65–6; 'Word from Ernie Pyle', *Boston Globe*, 11 June 1944.
48 Harry C. Butcher, *My Three Years with Eisenhower* (New York: Simon & Schuster, 1946), p. 575.
49 Pierre J. Koenig to W. Bedell Smith, 30 June 1944, and R. Ernest Dupuy to Chief of Staff, 15 August 1944, both in Policy re Release of Information to the Press File, Chief of Staff, SGS, DF 000.7, box 2, RG331.
50 Kenneth S. Lynn, *Hemingway* (Cambridge, Mass.: Harvard University Press, 1987), pp. 513–14.

intense that a lot of correspondents even missed one of the biggest stories of the war. In April, while Allied troops fought to close the Ruhr pocket and captured more than 300,000 German soldiers, journalists' attention was elsewhere. As one military information officer complained, 'no amount of talk about the importance of snapping shut and destroying the Ruhr, taking with it Germany's war-making capacity, ever dented any war correspondents' consciousness. The Berlin dateline was all that mattered'.[51]

Alongside reporters' ambition came the egos of top commanders, who were keen to burnish their own image. In Europe, Field Marshal Sir Bernard L. Montgomery was perhaps the most prominent, although he had to vie for this status with generals such as George S. Patton. Like many officers, 'Monty' had a somewhat schizophrenic attitude toward the media. While he clearly saw the connection between good troop morale and positive news coverage, he remained wary of individual war correspondents on the basis that 'they play for sensation'. Like many successful generals, moreover, he was a charismatic figure who recognized that upbeat stories of his successes would do his career no harm. Yet Monty was also much more vain than most. He could also be spectacularly undiplomatic, especially in press conferences at crucial moments during the summer and winter of 1944 and 1945, when he brazenly underlined that it was he, not an American general, who was in charge of key battles.[52]

Montgomery's periodic outbursts, in turn, exerted a deep impact on the national egos of the Allied powers fighting in Western Europe. The Americans recoiled at Monty's intimations that the British had effectively rescued them. The Canadians, for their part, bristled at hints that they were peripheral members of the alliance. And in the middle sat Dwight Eisenhower, the careworn commanding general, who had the tough task of trying constantly to remind commanders and correspondents alike that this was an Allied war and that the term 'allied' should take precedence over petty national point scoring.[53]

In the Pacific, the senior army commander, Douglas MacArthur, had no rival for the role of chief publicity hound. His stunts therefore gained enormous coverage, not least his famous wading-ashore escapades on the

---

51 Oldfield, *Never a Shot in Anger*, pp. 229–30.
52 Nigel Hamilton, *Monty*, vol. II: *Master of the Battlefield, 1942–1944* (3 vols., London: Hamish Hamilton, 1983), pp. 179–80; and Nigel Hamilton, *Monty*, vol. III: *The Field Marshal, 1944–76* (3 vols., London: Hamish Hamilton, 1986), pp. 300–6.
53 Forrest C. Pogue, *The Supreme Command* (Washington DC: Office of the Chief of Military History, 1954), p. 520.

Philippines. But MacArthur always balanced such PR antics with a fierce determination to control what information flowed from his front, much to the chagrin of many war correspondents, who bristled at his aggressive censorship methods and winced at his communiqués, especially when they lauded MacArthur's military genius or announced victories before they had actually been won.[54]

When it came to slanting the war news, however, even MacArthur was unable to compete with his enemy. As the fighting moved ever closer to the Japanese home islands, the Japanese press described the battles on Saipan, the Philippines and Iwo Jima as 'victories'. Of course, even the most rudimentary knowledge of geography was sufficient to demonstrate the nonsense of such claims. It was scarcely surprising, therefore, that gloomy rumours proliferated in many parts of Japan. The bloody defeat on Saipan in July 1944 marked a watershed. The island's collapse not only precipitated that of the Tojo government that had taken Japan to war two and a half years earlier, but also intensified the joint effort by the government and the media to glorify the increasingly large Japanese sacrifices. Indeed, the press now lavished tributes on the thousands of troops and civilians who had collectively given their lives on Saipan for the war effort. Thereafter, newspapers poured praise on the kamikaze pilots whose ultimate sacrifice took a major toll on American ships moored off the Philippines or Okinawa. As the enemy closed in, the war's grim reality could not be hidden, but it could be sugar-coated. In the spring of 1945, for instance, the government allowed the press to publish the Iwo Jima commander's personal account of his final battle. This contained inflated estimates of enemy dead, but it also revealed that Japan had lost the island. 'The enemy is already beginning to land on the islands southwest of Kyushu', it ended, 'moving forward with their strategy for the home islands. Finally, the time has arrived... The real fight it still to come'.[55]

While Japanese authorities carefully slanted what the press reported, the Allies ended the war surrounded by renewed allegations of overzealous censorship. This was partly because of continued security concerns, for the final march toward victory was far from smooth. Hitler's decision to attack Eisenhower's army through the Ardennes in December 1944 precipitated one major flurry of panic. Determined to protect those troops caught in the 'bulge', Eisenhower's censors reacted – or overreacted, according to many

54 D. Clayton James, *The Years of MacArthur*, vol. II: *1941–1945* (3 vols., Boston, Mass.: Houghton Mifflin, 1975), pp. 89, 164–5, 277–8, 554–5, 708–9.
55 Earhart, *Certain Victory*, pp. 398–9, 403–4, 429–35; Kushner, *Thought War*, pp. 160–7.

journalists – by instituting a brief, but total, news blackout. In the Pacific, meanwhile, the US Navy threatened to end the war as it had begun: embroiled in a major spat with the media over excessive restrictions. In the summer of 1945, as Japanese kamikaze missions took a heavy toll of the task force that was supporting the Okinawa invasion, the navy clamped down hard on the precise number of ships sunk. The censors claimed that they did not want the Japanese to discover from the American press the damage their kamikazes were inflicting. War correspondents, however, began to suspect a more sinister motive. The navy, complained William H. Lawrence of the *New York Times*, had a policy 'of doing things in a way best calculated to bury the bad news by overwhelming amounts of good'. Lawrence's suspicions were confirmed when the navy finally released his major exclusive on kamikaze-caused losses on the very day that Japan sued for peace.[56]

The Allied military, for its part, was far from happy with the way correspondents covered the end of the war. In Europe, Edward Kennedy of the Associated Press generated a major spasm of anger in May 1945, when he prematurely reported Germany's unconditional surrender. By running with the story, Eisenhower complained, the Associated Press had engaged 'in a clear violation of its word of honour to me'.[57] In Japan, Wilfred Burchett of the *Daily Express* sparked an even bigger furore in September, when he reported on the destruction the atomic bomb had wrought on Hiroshima, including what he dubbed an 'atomic plague' that was still killing people. Burchett, a military spokesman responded, had 'fallen victim to Japanese propaganda', a judgement MacArthur fully endorsed when he tried to expel him from the theatre.[58]

Conclusion

That Burchett ended the war as a pariah of the American military was illuminating. During the war itself, Burchett typified the blurring of national and ideological labels, as correspondents from various backgrounds and differing beliefs united behind their side's war effort. Burchett himself was a radical anti-colonial Australian, who worked for Lord Beaverbrook's pro-empire *Express* and spent the last months of the war with the US Navy. While

---

56 Casey, *When Soldiers Fall*, p. 100.

57 Dwight D. Eisenhower, Statement, undated, Kennedy Release File, Chief of Staff, SGS, DF 000.73/6, box 4, RG331; Ed Kennedy, *Ed Kennedy's War: V-E Day, Censorship, and the Associated Press* (Baton Rouge: Louisiana State University Press, 2012), pp. 157–72.

58 Wilfred Burchett, *At the Barricades* (London: Macmillan, 1981), pp. 106–17.

the enemy remained undefeated, these tensions lingered below the surface. Like many correspondents, Burchett certainly chafed at stringent censorship, while privately bemoaning various aspects of the Allied war effort. But he remained basically loyal to the cause, and his biggest concern was invariably how to get stories that would pass muster with the censors back to his editor on Fleet Street.

After the war, however, the situation was quite different. Burchett was unusual in that his Hiroshima experience made him so suspicious of American power that he left the *Express* to cover the Cold War from the Communist side.[59] But even those reporters who remained firmly entrenched in the Western camp found reporting the hot wars that erupted in Korea and Vietnam a very different experience. First, there was the lack of censorship on the American side, which made it possible to write more graphic stories, but at the cost of being denied more candid background briefings. When the military then recoiled at what it considered excessively negative coverage, the media found itself getting blamed for turning the home front against the war.[60]

This was a charge never levelled at war correspondents during the Second World War. They might not all have been team players all of the time, but even when they acquired the space to convey graphic images of the fighting, they invariably used this to reinforce – rather than challenge – their propagandists' depiction of the war. Thus, from Axis reporters who were firmly entrenched in the state structure, to Allied correspondents who were embedded with their militaries, the stories that flowed from the fighting front invariably provided a version of news that was candid enough to satisfy the home front, but neither explicit nor intelligence-sensitive enough to undermine the war effort. Censorship, in short, worked.

59 Steven Casey, 'Wilfred Burchett and the UN Command's Media Relations during the Korean War', *Journal of Military History* 74 (2010), 523–56.
60 Steven Casey, *Selling the Korean War: Propaganda, Politics, and Public Opinion, 1950–53* (New York: Oxford University Press, 2008); William M. Hammond, *Reporting Vietnam: Media and Military at War* (Lawrence: University Press of Kansas, 1998).

6

International organizations

PATRICIA CLAVIN

In September 1939, the nationalism which characterized politics in the 1930s gave way to the internationalism of war. In the realm of international relations, this translated into a renewed enthusiasm for internationalist ideas, and for projects of international organization that were born also of the desire to cement wartime alliances, and to effect reconstruction and international security once the war was won. The project of international organization was primarily, but not exclusively, the concern of the Grand Alliance: Britain, the USA and the USSR. Among the Axis powers, only Germany showed any interest in building institutions that would promote fascism internationally. By the time the Grand Alliance was victorious, the new superstructure for global governance set up during the war was represented by a range of new institutions that radiated from the new United Nations Organization (UNO) based in New York.

Appending the 'O' – for Organization – onto the United Nations was significant. The term 'United Nations' was used first by President Franklin Delano Roosevelt to describe the Allies in December 1941, and the UNO's first step toward institutionalization came at the Arcadia Conference in January 1942, with the Declaration by the United Nations signed by twenty-six governments: the USA, the UK, the USSR and China (the 'Big Four'), nine US allies in Central America and the Caribbean, the White Dominions and India, and eight European governments-in-exile. The USA aside, all the signatories were, or recently had been, members of the League of Nations, and the Declaration was steeped in the language of Wilsonianism.

The drive to forge new organizations was redolent with history. At the same time, for many, institutionalizing the United Nations into an organization was intended to signal a shift away from the habits of great-power politics and the personal diplomacy of national leaders who dominated the international stage. The United Nations Organization and other organizations that were spawned during the war presented a vision of one world made new. The renewed will to 'organize' international relations reflected the aspiration for a new international order and 'one world' that emanated from very different groups, ranging from big business and feminist activists in the West, to nationalist organizations – later called liberation movements – in Asia and Africa. Marxists active in contexts as diverse as Nazi-occupied France and war-torn Asia offered an alternative model of world organization, demonstrating that the ideological battle between Woodrow Wilson and Vladimir Lenin of 1918 lived on, though both men were long dead. The USSR's contribution to the Allied victory had enabled it to regain prestige and ideological influence on the international stage that had been lost by the failure to offer effective support to the Popular Front in Spain, and by the Nazi-Soviet Pact. But Stalin still frowned upon aspirations to the global organization of communism that had become associated with Trotskyist modes of thought. The Soviet leader had fought a nationalist 'patriotic' war against Hitler, not an international socialist one. His preference was not for a unitary world authority, but for a world divided into discrete spheres of influence.[1]

Big ideas helped to shape the new organizations that emerged in the war. These included the UN Food and Agriculture Organization (FAO), the UN Economic and Social Organization and the Bretton Woods institutions. The aspirations often associated with the UNO – world peace, free trade, international solidarity – were only part of the story. As, if not more, important was the power of bureaucracy – international bureaucracies inherited from the League of Nations, as well as inter-state agencies put together to fight the war – and the influence of technocratic and legal ideas which informed it. As a result, scientists, especially economists, and lawyers took on an increasingly prominent role.

Contrary to popular belief, the start of the war did not mark the end of the League of Nations. Local operations in Geneva and the Permanent Court of International Justice at The Hague were suspended, not ended, in 1940, and a core part of the League's operations moved to the United States. This chapter will show how many of the ideas, practices and people who designed and populated the UNO and its related agencies borrowed heavily from the League of Nations. It will explore how and why discrete international organizations were conceived and established to facilitate international financial cooperation and development, trade, health and global security for the

1 See Chapter 3 by Silvio Pons in this volume.

post-war world. The League's hand was also found in international institutions established to oversee reconstruction after the war, and in regional intergovernmental organizations, notably the European Economic Community (EEC), whose origins lay in this period. Indeed, it was to be the drive to organize international relations on a regional, not global, basis that was to become the most prominent legacy of wartime visions in late twentieth- and early twenty-first-century history.

This chapter will underscore the significance and deep engagement of the United States with the project of international organization. In the West, the drive to build new institutions for global governance had its origins in efforts to make good Wilson's botched handling of Congress and public opinion after the First World War. It was coupled with a new view that America's national security was equated with global security, rather than the notion of hemispheric separation embodied in the Monroe Doctrine. The globalizing of American conceptions of its national interest was also related to the tremendous growth in its productive capacity in the war, which reinforced the importance of the second major theme in the new move to institutionalize global relations: the primacy of economic and financial concerns, and the mores of US capitalism that lay behind the understanding of them. In the final two years of the war, the blueprints of organization were gradually realized.

The period between 1944 and 1945 revealed what was new and what was troublingly familiar. One important strand of continuity from the League to the United Nations was that, despite all the talk of new 'rights' being granted to individuals and to subject peoples, the power of the state and the importance of empire continued. Another was that, from the start, the UNO, too, faced a ceaseless quest for legitimacy. Part of the problem was the lofty ideas and rhetoric that swirled around these new institutions. These sat uneasily with the daily grind and minutiae of international negotiation, where every agreement, no matter how small, was hard fought; every disagreement, no matter how insignificant, was amplified by critics.

The will to organize

Alexander Loveday spent twenty-six years in the service of the League of Nations. 'The most important' reason for dedicating the best part of his working life to the organization, he claimed, was the 'belief in the value of the work that has to be done'. A Scotsman from Fife – originating within a stone's throw of the birthplace of Adam Smith (and Gordon Brown) – he cautioned against undue optimism. For him, 'international organization [triggers] exaggerated ideas about the probable results... In times of crisis a sense of history is much more useful than sentimental idealism'.[2]

But idealism lay deep in the bones of international institutions. The ideological roots of the organizations forged in the war reached back to Jeremy Bentham's 1780 notion of the 'international' as a term for laws that extended beyond the state. Important, too, was the answer to Thomas Hobbes's assertion that, without civil power to regulate behaviour, mankind's search for security would result in 'war of every man against every man'.[3] There was also a religious internationalism – a phenomenon that historians have begun to address only recently – evident, in particular, among Catholic, Quaker, Islamic and Jewish communities. As globalization accelerated in the nineteenth century, other potent ideas were added to the mix, including free trade, workers' solidarity, and the move to develop common international standards in fields such as science and communication. There were also international humanitarian movements, such as that dedicated to the abolition of slavery. Here, the language of liberalism was predominant, though the ideological content of the term became increasingly difficult to define as the nineteenth became the twentieth century, and strands of political liberalism moved in different, contradictory directions. Equally potent was the impact of imperialism, which stressed the 'responsibilities' of the West toward the rest of the world, whose access to rights and resources was increasingly curtailed.

It is wrong to think of internationalism as the counterpoint to nationalism. Historians have frequently stressed the role played by non-state actors – missionary groups or peace activists for example – in international activism, and the way they challenged the power and ideas of the establishment.[4] But in practice, the history of internationalism was as much about recognizing and strengthening the power of the state as it was about challenging it to behave in new ways. It was the First World War which reinforced the importance of multilateral, intergovernmental relations to international organization. The organization of wartime assistance for prisoners, for example, caused

2 Alexander Loveday, *Reflections on International Administration* (Oxford: Clarendon Press, 1956), p. 71.
3 Thomas Hobbes, quoted in Kinch Hoekstra, 'Hobbes on the Natural Condition of Mankind', in Patricia Springborg (ed.), *The Cambridge Companion to Hobbes's Leviathan* (Cambridge University Press, 2007), p. 115.
4 See, for example, Ian Tyrrell, *Reforming the World: The Creation of America's Moral Empire* (Princeton University Press, 2010).

belligerent states to enter into new international agreements with one another. More importantly, waging 'total war' promoted a wider framework of cooperation relating to finance, food and transportation among the Allies and the Associated Power of the United States.

These administrative structures of the First World War fed directly into the architecture of the League of Nations established by the Paris Peace Conference in 1919. Although social and political activists petitioned the League and exhorted its claim to be some sort of global democratic government, the composition and purpose of the League designed by the statesmen in Paris was intended to reinforce the authority of member states, not to challenge it. The primacy of state sovereignty was enshrined in the Covenant of the League and in the organizational structures and institutional practice that emerged. The League presented a vision of the world where the unit that counted was the nation state. Indeed, the organization was hidebound by this principle and by the need for unanimity among its members, or at least its most powerful members, as a precondition of action.[5]

The League largely reflected the pattern of great-power politics in the 1920s, which excluded Germany and Russia. In the 1930s, this was evident in the fate which befell smaller states, such as Czechoslovakia, who looked to the League for support against their aggressive neighbours, but were left bereft. This is not to deny that the League had scored some successes in the fields of territorial arbitration, chemical weapons control, health care, and economic and financial cooperation. But understandably foremost in the mind of its critics was its failure to halt the march to war.

On the eve of war, in August 1939, the League of Nations published a special report entitled *The Development of International Co-operation in Economic Affairs*, also known as the Bruce Report, which proposed a radical overhaul of the organization. In part, this call for change illustrated the fact that the League was at breaking point. It had been wrong-footed by Mussolini's claim that he had intervened in Ethiopia in the name of anti-slavery – a cause dear to key League activists – and the League failed to act effectively against this vicious colonial war waged by one member of the League on another. It found itself similarly powerless to offer comment on the Spanish Civil War or at the start of world war in China. But the Bruce Report was also significant because it signalled the distillation of increasingly intense

5 Zara Steiner, *The Lights that Failed: European International History, 1919–1933* (Oxford University Press, 2007), pp. 351–4; Christopher Thorne, *The Limits of Foreign Policy: The West, The League and the Far Eastern Crisis of 1931–1933* (London: Hamilton, 1972).

discussions, under way since the onset of the Great Depression, that the League's role in preventing war 'could perhaps be more readily and effectively served by the consolidation of peace than by the repression of violence'.[6]

The Bruce Report is often seen as the genesis of the functional model of international organization identified with the Romanian-born naturalized British social scientist David Mitrany. Functionalism, which challenged realist assumptions about the primacy of the state, has been associated with the move to depoliticize international relations, particularly in Western Europe, in the wake of the Second World War. (In fact, the ideas of E. H. Carr, the father of 'realism', and those of Mitrany were shaped by their encounters with the League.) But at the time, the report stressed the importance of economic and social cooperation over issues relating to 'hard security' in the League's agenda. This had a clear political purpose: League functionaries saw the promotion of better living standards and economic growth as the basis for reorienting international organization toward concerns that would speak to 'ordinary' men and women around the world. Ideology divided the world, but all could agree on the importance of recovery from the economic depression that had begun in 1929, and which had never quite gone away. These ideas would inform a new approach to colonial development, as well as drive European union after 1945.

The report sought to answer the pressing question for those men and women whose life's work had been the promotion of internationalism: what was the purpose of an organization dedicated to international cooperation and peace at a time of almost universal war? The answers found in the Bruce Report offered a mature appreciation of the limits of state agency when it came to tackling pressing issues relating to society, the economy, health and the environment, in a language of globalization more typically associated with the twenty-first century: 'The world, for all its political severance, is growing daily closer knit; its means of communication daily more rapid; its instruments for the spread of knowledge daily more efficient'.[7]

In 1939, the League's very existence hung in the balance. The key events in international relations, notably the negotiations over the fate of Czechoslovakia, had completely bypassed Geneva. But if the League was confined by

6 William E. Rappard, *The Common Menace of Economic and Military Armaments: The Eighth Richard Cobden Lecture* (London: Cobden-Sanderson, 1936), p. 37.
7 League of Nations, *The Development of International Co-operation in Economic and Social Affairs* (Geneva, 1939), p. 7.

individual great-power politics, dynamics within the organization also reflected the pattern of national politics and great-power relations outside it. This had been illustrated since the early 1920s by the tensions between Italian liberal internationalists, who were hired to work in the League Secretariat – they formed the third largest national group after the British and the French – and the government delegates who were selected by Mussolini. The hostility between the two groups was not confined to verbal exchanges; it occasionally resulted in all-out brawls.

Italy renounced its membership of the League in December 1937. Germany and Japan had left in 1933. Among others who relinquished their membership between 1938 and 1939, Albania, absorbed by Italy, and Austria and Czechoslovakia, annexed by Germany, did so because they ceased to be independent countries. Of all the transgressors of the principles of the League, only the USSR was punished. It was the last major power to be admitted, in 1934, and it was expelled from the organization on 14 December 1939, for invading Finland. These wars of conquest and annexation waged against League members, which in September 1939 came to include Poland, were reflected inside the League. The organization was leaking members and faced a further reduction of already meagre levels of financial support. After 1938, its annual income fell by at least 50 per cent a year. Once war in Europe was under way fully in 1939, tensions also escalated among staff within the organization.

Inside the League, the Irish Deputy Secretary General, Seán Lester, who would become Secretary General in a matter of months, suggested that the League should become 'a rallying point' for anti-Axis forces. The Secretary General, Joseph Avenol, on the other hand, had sensationally sacked his long-time chef de cabinet, the Frenchman Marcel Holden, for suggesting that France needed to prepare rapidly for war against Germany in 1938, and in 1939 and 1940 consistently argued that it was essential that the League remain neutral. To his mind, the organization should 'not be used as an instrument of the belligerents'.[8]

But it was not just states' claims to neutrality that would be compromised by the war. Avenol, in the search to preserve what he asserted was the neutrality of the League, engaged in a series of manoeuvres that increasingly compromised this claim. They culminated in his attempt to move the League to Vichy in the wake of the fall of France in June 1940. The French regime

8 Howard Bucknall to Cordell Hull, 19 April 1939, National Archives II, Washington DC, RG 59, 500.C113/174–5.

based there refused to take the League in because of France's delicate status as a defeated but not yet occupied power.

Avenol's proposal caused uproar within the League Secretariat, and in London and Washington DC. Britain's new premier Winston Churchill had branded Avenol a Pétainist, and the British government worked hard, in tandem with members from Australia, Eire and Norway, to winkle him from his post. It was not easy. The legal advisor to the Foreign Office discovered, 'strange as it may seem in a supposedly democratic institution, the Secretary General in fact exercises powers which are almost dictatorial'.[9] The Swiss government, too, was twitchy, claiming it feared that the Nazis would use the League's headquarters in Switzerland as the pretext for invading the country to launch a new world order from Geneva.

But neither Britain and its allies, nor the USA, wanted to close the organization down. They strongly supported the efforts by other members of the Secretariat – notably Alexander Loveday, head of the League's Economic and Financial Organization, Frank Walters, the British chief of the Political Section, and Lester – to reach out to American internationalists to find a safe haven in the United States. In May 1940, the Institute for Advanced Study in Princeton, home to Albert Einstein and other internationalist luminaries, offered the Economic and Financial Organization (EFO), the Health Organization of the League and the Opium Section a home. (In the end, the latter, long dominated by US interest in curtailing drugs trafficking in the Pacific, moved to Washington DC.) Although Avenol at first refused to let them go, by 31 August he was forced out of his post, and twelve EFO members began a hazardous journey to the USA as Axis forces closed around them.

Only a skeleton crew, led by Lester, who succeeded Avenol, remained in Switzerland. Most of the beautiful rooms of the Palais des Nations, opened only in 1936, were mothballed and turned over to storage for officials to stow personal possessions such as pianos, bone china and even cars. The Swiss continued to grumble, but the British and Lester were unsympathetic, declaring the Swiss government 'none the worse for being a little embarrassed by the presence of the League organization on Swiss soil'.[10] Contrary to popular memory, the Allies believed it was essential that some element of the League remain functioning in Geneva. Preventing Switzerland from

9 William Malkin to Roger Makins, 17 July 1940, The National Archives, Kew (hereafter TNA), PRO FO 371/24441, C 7839/6953/98.
10 Minute by Makins, 19 October 1940, TNA, PRO FO 371/2441, C 11192/6953/98.

falling further into the Nazi sphere of influence was a minor gain. The key objective was to keep the ideals of international cooperation and organization alive for when the war was won.

The primacy of economics

Given that the League of Nations had 'failed', it was in some ways remarkable that the creation of a host of new international organizations was a key preoccupation of international relations in the war, and at the heart of lesson-learning and post-war planning. The explanation, in large part, lay in the recognition of the challenges that were likely to face the world once the Second World War was won. People would be left destitute and uprooted by a war that put men, women and children on the move. Displaced persons and soldiers would need particular help, and as they and their problems crossed borders, these challenges could best be managed by international coordination and cooperation.

In the twenty-first century, the need for global governance to manage common and shared interests, to negotiate unequal power relationships, and to mediate cultural diversity and diverging values, is largely accepted. This is not to say that there are not powerful disagreements about its institutionalized form. But it is important to recognize that, despite the longer genealogy of the rhetoric of internationalism, it was only after the First World War that any sort of agreement had been found for institutionalizing international relations. Moreover, its basis was tightly limited to the preservation of the society of states, the maintenance of the independence of individual states, and the regulation, but not elimination, of violence among states and societies.

Given the economic and social devastation caused by the first 'total war', it was especially striking that there had been no planning for the economic and financial problems that would confront the world. Nor was there any expectation that international organizations would get involved in facilitating international loans or trade. The hyperinflation in Europe in the 1920s, and the global great depression of the 1930s had changed that. Yet the powers of two organizations established to tackle them – the EFO and the Bank of International Settlements, which was a cooperative club for central bankers – were inadequate to deal with the challenges that confronted them. The world economy had never recovered from the effects of the slump between 1929 and 1933 that had left it ensnared in trade and currency restrictions. Indeed, after a weak recovery, in 1937 global output and trade began to fall once more. The world had been spared a new great depression only by a recovery that was driven by rearmament. It was widely, and rightly, feared that once the war was over, the depression would resume its brutal hold unless there was decisive change.

As early as January 1939, the EFO, the largest agency of the League, had begun working on what it believed would be the key economic, financial and social issues facing the world at war. It followed three lines of inquiry: first, on an assessment of past experience (notably the First World War) and immediate changes triggered by the current war; second, determining likely future structural transformations in the world economy; and third, identifying the likely directions of governments' post-war planning and the future role of international organization.

Once in Princeton, the EFO, its staff bolstered by new recruits, took on a more active role in the nexus of post-war organizational planning. (They included a young Kenneth Boulding, whose pioneering work in environmental economics shaped the agenda of the United Nations some three decades later.) At the heart of this web was the United States. It had been the world's premier financial power before the war, and the financial responsibilities this role carried, what the US economist Charles Kindleberger called its 'hegemonic responsibility', was reinforced by its new productive role in the world economy. Not only were the Western European Allies, in particular, profoundly dependent on US exports, but the future prospects of the most dynamic and powerful US businesses and financial corporations were now more overtly reliant on overseas markets than before.

The more global orientation of the US economy was underpinned by the fact that the USA now equated its national security with the security of the world. For Americans, Pearl Harbor had demonstrated the need for US dominance in the Pacific. But for many historians, this transformation had come a year earlier in the North Atlantic. The US occupation of Greenland in 1940 was a landmark. The Monroe Doctrine of hemispheric separation, which had dominated US foreign policy since it was articulated by the fifth President of the United States in 1823, was thereby consigned to history. That national security was equated with global security, however, did not rest easily with the promotion of norms of international organization. Indeed, the dilemmas were even more acute for states that would make up the new Security Council of the United Nations Organization: Britain, with its complex web of security ties to the empire; China, in the throes of war against the Japanese and then civil war; France, under occupation, and an afterthought in US schemes; and the USSR, ideologically committed to promoting international communism, yet bound in alliance to the world's primary capitalist powers.

Focusing on economic and financial issues offered a way of bypassing the USSR and addressing what contemporaries then saw as the fundaments of a stable world order: capitalism's return to health. (There was a delicious irony in the Anglo-American emphasis on new structures of economic and financial governance that was informed by the Marxist dialectic that privileged economics as the force of change.) It also reflected the importance of economics to the outcome of the war itself in ways that gave economists, and economic ideas and tools, an increasingly prominent role in shaping international organizations, as well as states and societies.

In the first three years of the war, the US State Department, Treasury, Federal Reserve Board and a range of think tanks developed plans for new institutions for reconstruction and global governance. From its base in Princeton, the League made a surprisingly significant impact on this kaleidoscope of planning. This was, in part, because the League's Princeton Mission was a unique repository of intelligence (the data it had brought with it on European trade and demography were especially prized), experience and expertise. But it had one clear limit. While the 'technical' services of the League – its work on economics and finance, health, social well-being and drug trafficking – would be incorporated into the new institutions, the League proper would not be revived at the war's end. The brand was tainted with failure and, despite the energetic protests of US League enthusiasts, the League of Nations now became a story of failure against which the history of the 'new' United Nations organizations would be set in successful contrast.

But the League of Nations was not the only international organization set up after the First World War that found a new home in North America. In 1940, the International Labour Organization (ILO) moved from Geneva to Montreal. In the 1920s, the ILO was primarily identified with its founding champion, the French socialist Albert Thomas, and his pursuit of social justice, in particular, for unionized, male, urban workers. In the 1930s, it had diversified its field of interests, following the League into investigating the working conditions of the world's peasants. With new leadership at the helm – Briton Harold Butler – it, too, had floundered in the face of state and business hostility to its agenda. (Representatives from governments and business, alongside trade unionists, made up its unique tripartite membership arrangement.)

But between 1941 and 1943, the ILO re-emerged as a force in international relations, thanks to the growing sensitivity to the social dimension of post-war planning, and the continued movement of the tectonics of world power. Now the USA was in the war, the British government was becoming increasingly alive to the potentially painful implications of the USA's likely dominance of global institutions. Here, negotiations around the terms of the Lend-Lease Agreement were uppermost in the official mind. Ernest Bevin, the life-long trade unionist head of the Ministry of Labour, and soon to be Foreign Secretary, in particular, believed it was worth supporting the ILO as the natural heir of the League, because of 'its great measure of support among organized Labour in Britain and the Dominions'.[11]

At first, elements in FDR's administration appeared sympathetic to the case. A special International Labour Conference in New York City culminated in a concluding session at the White House on 5 November 1941, and brought together 187 representatives from governments, employers and workers, including deputations from governments-in-exile. The meeting drew special attention to the Atlantic Charter's call for international collaboration with the 'object of securing for all improved labour standards, economic advancement and social security'. The aspiration for a more left-leaning agenda for the new institutions of global governance was fed in some quarters by the fact that the USSR rejoined the ILO in 1942 (it had been expelled from here, too, over Finland), and by the 1944 Philadelphia Declaration. It expressed the aspiration that international organizations should be judged by their ability to promote social justice.

But there were other elements of FDR's post-war vision, particularly an emphasis on the primacy of the market and the value of free trade, that pulled in a very different direction. Any role New Deal rhetoric may have played in US policy fell away as early as 1942, and realpolitik intruded as plans were turned into institutional reality. Principles made way for interests. This suited the British, who found it easier to agree with Americans if they focused on shared economic and strategic concerns, rather than the thorny topic of the place of the British Empire in plans for the new world order. Although Americans remained anti-colonial in principle, they were also thinking about access to oil, tin and rubber, which meant that the USA was likely to behave like a colonial power in practice. When the US Office of War Information asked the American public whether the USA should keep bases in territories that it had conquered in the Pacific, as well as their new outposts in Africa, 61 per cent replied 'yes'.

11 Minute by Makins, 17 June 1941, TNA, PRO FO 371/26661, C 6940/3124/98.

The brand of the United Nations

The term was coined by Roosevelt to cover the multilateral alliance that stood in opposition to the Nazis by December 1941. More forceful than the originally proposed sobriquet of 'Associated Nations', it took life in a war-time announcement of shared war aims in much the way that the League had in Wilson's 'Fourteen Points' in January 1918. The United Nations Declaration, issued portentously on New Year's Day 1942, set out eight objectives for world peace in the language of universalism that had become associated with international organization. It was significant, however, that neutral states were not co-signatories at this stage. Roosevelt put the aims of this new grouping more succinctly in his State of the Union Address to Congress a few days later: 'We of the United Nations are. . .fighting today for security, for progress, and for peace, not only for ourselves but for all men'.[12] In practice, until 1945, the United Nations was a multilateral alliance that included powers with starkly different ideologies and resources that would have at its apex the very different perspectives of the USSR, Britain, China and the USA – Roosevelt's first 'Four Policemen'. But the United Nations Declaration was also redolent with the language of 'One World', and one-worldism was all the rage in the Second World War.

One World, for example, was the title of Wendell Willkie's travel diary, which was translated into numerous languages and sold over 3 million copies around the world. The defeated Republican of the 1940 presidential election, Willkie toured the 'United Nations' in the war, proclaiming the need for a world 'Declaration of Interdependence'. This global avowal would reflect the recognized facts of economic interdependence with an international pro-gramme. But in many ways, this yearning for global solidarity reflected a deep awareness of the ways in which the world was divided. W. E. B. Du Bois, the African American sociologist who had first risen to prominence at the Universal Races Congress in 1911, and now in his seventies, cautioned that plans for international organization should not preserve a global colour line that left most of the world's population without representation or rights.

The challenge was profound, as one glance at the war aims of Britain and its White Dominion allies made clear. Any new institutionalized world order needed to recognize that responsibilities as well as rights had to be shared. The Dominion view was articulated in a Foreign Broadcast Information

12 Declaration by the United Nations, 1 January 1942. http://avalon.law.yale.edu/20th_century/decade03.asp (accessed 3 November 2014).

Service broadcast in 1943 by two 'character witnesses' for the Dominions: Richard Gavin Gardiner Casey, a former Australian Minister to the United States of America, and Walter Nash, New Zealand's representative in Washington DC. While Nash insisted that 'nations must be willing to give up some part of their nationalism in the common interest', Casey reminded his audience that Americans 'who demanded independence for India must be willing to assume their share of responsibility for world security if that security was in any way endangered by granting India independence'.[13]

But there was no more poignant illustration of the rhetorical appeal of the call to world government, and the very particular perspectives that informed it, than General Jan Smuts's 'Open Letter' in *Life* magazine. The Afrikaner lawyer, former Boer leader and promoter of the League of Nations, who was now Prime Minister of South Africa, presented the British Commonwealth and Empire as the greatest experiment in organized freedom in the world. It was his 'model' united nations. He made no reference to the African National Congress's *Africans' Claims in South Africa* issued at its 1943 Congress, which cited the Atlantic Charter and called for voting rights, land reform and an end to discriminatory laws. These divergent perspectives reflect but a part of the kaleidoscope of actors who reached to the 'international'. The renewed drive to institutionalize international relations came about partly because it was recognized that without organization, the tension between the United Nations' universalist claims and the reality of their national policies would drive the world apart.

Institutions made

The first organization of the United Nations, the UN Food and Agriculture Organization (FAO), founded in 1943, was illustrative of the ways in which empire played an important part in the framing of world institutions. The British had hoped to develop a 'comprehensive programme of subjects, all of which are inter-related', with the Americans before opening questions of the post-war order to multilateral negotiations.[14] Instead, news of the food conference first surfaced in a speech by Sumner Welles, Assistant Secretary of State and a member of FDR's inner circle, who spoke of 'a machinery

13 Recounted in Susan A. Brewer, *To Win the Peace: British Propaganda in the United States During World War II* (Ithaca, NY: Cornell University Press, 1997), p. 179.
14 John Maynard Keynes to James Meade, cited in Robert Skidelsky, *John Maynard Keynes*, vol. III: *Fighting for Britain, 1937–1946* (3 vols., London: Macmillan, 2000), p. 300.

for the purpose of assembling and studying all international aspects of problems under the general heading of freedom of want'.[15]

The focus on food undoubtedly was intended to have a broad appeal to a general public who had lived through the 'hungry thirties'. Agricultural issues were shared, along with overt concerns for the USSR and China, FDR's putative partners, as well as for farmers in the US Midwest who were historically committed to an economic policy of protection and an isolationist foreign policy. But the timing of the FAO's foundation was also linked to the Bengal famine, which killed at least 3 million people and intruded into global consciousness in 1943. The USA's concern was both humanitarian and political. The famine had the potential to reinsert the troublesome issue of Indian independence into Anglo-American relations, and to undermine the US articulation of its war aims to free the world from want. Although Allied wartime propaganda presented unconditional sacrifice as a mystical and sacred act, public opinion polls brought home all too clearly that members of the public resented giving up daily comforts. They valued the promise of prosperity once the war was over, and the restoration of capitalism, or as the Americans preferred to call it, free enterprise.

The outline of the new organization was established at the UN Conference on Food and Agriculture, held at Hot Springs, Virginia, from 18 May until 3 June 1943. Its roots lay deep in the League. The prime mover was Frank McDougall, Economic Advisor to the Australian High Commission and long-time League food activist, who prepared the UN 'programme for freedom from want of food'. His plans were nourished by twenty years' experience of promoting issues relating to agricultural production and nutrition at the League of Nations. The programme stressed the importance of understanding hunger in quantitative as well as qualitative terms. (In other words, that human health depended as much on good-quality food as on having enough to eat.) McDougall also promoted schemes to effect commodity regulation, increased food production, tariff reduction and, more controversially, the plan to set up a buffer stock agency. This was intended to invest the new international organization with the power to purchase key commodities when prices were in a long downward trend, and to sell them when prices were rising. Its operations would thereby act as a stabilizing influence on world commodity prices. The UN FAO was formally inaugurated on 16 October 1945. It took up home in the offices of the International Institute

---

15 Radio Bulletin No. 49, US Department of State, 26 February 1943, LN S566.

for Agriculture (IIA), an organization founded by the Polish-American citizen David Lubin in Rome in 1905. During the interwar period, the IIA had fallen increasingly into the orbit of the Italian Fascist Party, which had a particular interest in agricultural policy. By moving to Rome, the FAO inherited the IIA's statistical know-how on the global agricultural market, a bank of information on plant disease and its prevention, and a range of connections to farmers' associations and academic institutions that represented their interests. (It also provided a way to reintegrate this erstwhile enemy back into international organization, which reflected Italy's prominent role in internationalism before 1935.) But at the top, the new organization was dominated by key League activists, including McDougall, the nutritionist Wallace Aykroyd (who had also served on the inquiry into the causes of the Bengal famine) and John Boyd Orr, who had advised the League on animal husbandry and nutrition and who was the first Director General of the FAO.

The year 1943 was when the architecture of international relations was set out. Though it claimed to be new, key elements were recycled from the League. Having helped behind the scenes at Hot Springs in May that year, the League's Princeton Mission was invited to the office of Governor Herbert Lehman to discuss what he described as 'tentative plans' for a United Nations Relief and Rehabilitation Administration (UNRRA). The news went some way to easing Keynes's fears that FDR's preoccupation with 'agricultural questions' was disastrous if it meant that issues of wartime relief were ignored.[16]

UNRRA was the first UN organization formally to begin work. It leaned heavily on the League's experience of how to recruit staff and manage relations between the international organization and the intergovernmental representatives who were sent to work with it. The US and British officials who led the new institution understood the question of post-war relief primarily as a matter of procurement: matching raw material supplies to the populations in greatest need. The challenges before them were viewed as logistical and international; nations were urged not to earmark essential items for their own populations or to build up reserves, but to be prepared to pool supplies and deliver them to where the need was greatest. Confirmation of its entangled history with the League was provided when UNRRA

---

16 Keynes to Meade, cited in Skidelsky, *John Maynard Keynes*, vol. III, p. 300; 'Record of Third Treasury–Foreign Office Meeting on March 2nd, 1943', TNA FO 371/35331, 393/147/70: the Treasury argued that food was 'a bone thrown to the United Nations dogs', while the Foreign Office took the view that it was one 'of the general economic questions which would have to be solved by international means'.

set up shop in the Palais des Nations, with Arthur Salter, a former Director of the League's Economic and Financial Organization, as its Deputy Director.

This approach, which was not intended to shape either US or British domestic policies, but to determine the line that UNRRA would take to formerly occupied territories, privileged internationalism over nationalism. It was based on the notion that post-war states and peoples would be subject to international agency, rather than joining as participants, while at the same time relying on post-war states and peoples feeling secure enough to take this larger international view. The League's Princeton Mission and European governments-in-exile took a dim view of this approach. Ludwik Rajchman, the former Director of the League's health organization who drafted plans for UNRRA's medical programme, was in good company when he argued that it was a mistake to limit UNRRA's Council to the 'Big Four'. He complained about great-power dominance, and the fact that Central and Eastern European needs – especially those of his native Poland – featured insufficiently in Anglo-American minds.

The drive to international organization would be no antidote to great-power politics. Indeed, during the Second World War, smaller countries grew increasingly fearful that international relations would be biased against them in favour of the big powers. Neutral states, having been instrumental in the case for the League, were also alarmed at the prospect that there would be no place for them in the new institutions. In short, the problem of representation in international organizations did not receive as much attention as it deserved from Anglo-American post-war planners. Why not? Part of the answer was that it opened up thorny, potentially irreconcilable, political issues. It was also because concerns over money – money to effect reconstruction and to fund these new institutions – put the USA in the driving seat, and put new organizations to support the functioning of capitalism at the top of the agenda.

Capitalism restored

Economics and economic scientists populated the engine rooms of the new and incipient international organizations. They argued that the emerging post-war world should be the beneficiary of hard-won knowledge and experience, and that this time, unlike in 1919, states should not rush to liberate themselves from economic controls. Economists and financiers sought to create a reformed monetary order that would shape the behaviour and expectations of markets, but in the first instance, the re-liberalization of the world economy had to be facilitated more by state and international man-agement than by market forces. Governments should agree in advance some principles to ensure the orderly demilitarization of their economies, and an internationally coordinated approach to the challenges of economic revival. These ideas formed the basis of new institutions of financial and economic cooperation set up at Bretton Woods in July 1944, which dominated inter-national relations until the early 1970s.

In the roll call of wartime conference locations, the sleepy New Hampshire town of Bretton Woods struck a strangely low-key note. Historians generally recount the creation of the International Monetary Fund (IMF) and the International Bank for Reconstruction and Development (IBRD), more usu-ally called the World Bank, through the relationship of the brilliant British economist John Maynard Keynes and his mercurial counterpart in the US Treasury, Harry Dexter White. But the focus on Keynes and White unbal-ances the story in a number of ways. The approach both men took in the negotiations drew on a much wider network of advisors, and a body of international experience. Although Keynes's intellectual reputation was a formidable asset, the USA's evident financial, economic and technological superiority gave it the clear advantage in negotiations. Money talked. And it all too frequently drowned out the views of the other forty-three countries attending the conference. The dominance of the USA had long-term implica-tions for these organizations' claim to legitimacy and their role in inter-national relations.

The IMF, the IBRD and plans for an International Trade Organization (ITO) sprang from three widely held objectives for the post-war organiza-tions. First, the common desire to return to economic growth, stability and high levels of employment; second, the search for capital to facilitate domes-tic financial stability and the return to international financial convertibility; and finally, the need for some sort of international agency to combat the common menace that economic crisis posed. There was also an impulse to reduce unprecedented levels of international protectionism, embodied in plans for an ITO, but these fell foul of US protectionist groups. They were revived in a more limited form in the General Agreement on Tariffs and Trade, which was agreed in 1947.

The novelty of the new financial order was to place the IMF at the centre of the new monetary system. It managed a system of fixed but adjustable exchange rates and lent money on a short-term basis to countries facing 'temporary' balance of payments crises. The World Bank served as a longer-term complement, raising capital in money markets with the intention to lend it to war-torn and developing countries. It is worth noting the emergence of the term 'development', which reflected the interest of Central and South American countries in gaining access to sources of capital that might otherwise be sucked up by Western Europeans. 'Development' had also emerged as an explicit goal in British policy during the war, as it would for other European colonial powers, as a means to sell the colonial project to sceptical Americans. But it had origins, too, in the League's intervention in Central and Eastern Europe, where the dearth of capital and therefore the means to support economic and social security were understood to have facilitated the rise of fascism.

At the time, the Bretton Woods Institutions were regarded as an integral part of institutionalization of the United Nations, but they were distinguished from the start from other UN organizations. Membership of the Fund and the Bank was conditional. Countries had to belong to the IMF in order to be members of the World Bank. In turn, to be members of the IMF, countries had to accept specific terms and responsibilities, including the IMF monitoring their exchange rates. The second key difference was that the organizations were not funded by contributions from member states. Each organization derived its income from lending operations and investments they made with their own capital, seed corn that was first provided in the war. This gave them independence both from member countries and from the UNO. There were other important distinctions. The USA was determined from the outset that the IMF and the World Bank would be located in its capital, Washington DC, and would work exclusively in English.

Together, these institutions added a novel and important wing to the edifice of international organization that emerged during the war. But in the short term, their significance was limited. They did not have enough funds to stave off currency crises, promote convertibility or fund reconstruction. It was only in the 1950s that they developed a discrete and modest role in the world economy. But in 1944 and 1945, their political significance was considerable. They signalled the coordinated and determined will of Western states that capitalism would be restored 'Anglo-Saxon style'. Significantly, the approach also excluded the USSR.

Two worlds, not one

A 'peace built stone by stone' was the way the author of the charter of the United Nations Organization, Leo Pasvolsky, described the place of institutions in the international relations of the Second World War. By the summer of 1944, with plans for the economic and financial institutions set by Bretton Woods, the absence of an organization for the United Nations was glaring. So, too, was the need to re-engage the USSR. Intense Anglo-American diplomacy with the USSR came just a few weeks later, at the Dumbarton Oaks Conference, which opened on 21 August 1944 in Washington DC. In a marked shift from the 'open diplomacy' touted by the League, and the media circus around Bretton Woods, Dumbarton Oaks was characterized by private meetings of small, specialized delegations from the USA, the USSR, Great Britain and China, which were intended to address issues of global security, notably the composition and powers of the organization intended to replace the League of Nations.

By 9 October the deal was done, and it was reaffirmed at the Yalta Conference early in 1945. The new United Nations Organization was inaugurated by the world in conference in San Francisco from April to June that year. The United Nations asserted that the new organization offered 'another, better sustained effort to achieve the objects of international peace and co-operation'.[17] But in many ways, Dumbarton Oaks marked the end of more expansive interpretations of global security centred on notions of collective security, with an independent UNO-run military force. Lost, too, was the aspiration to integrate a strong economic and social dimension into notions of global security, articulated, for example, by the ILO. It lingered on only in the talk of development that was elided all too easily with colonial projects.

Bretton Woods had made the emerging world order explicitly capitalist – and the USSR was the most significant outsider. In 1945, the question of how command and capitalist economies would relate to each other in this new international order remained unclear. More generally, the USSR was presented as a separate world from that of global capitalism. During 1945, this rhetorical device rang increasingly hollow. These separately imagined worlds now threatened to collide in the real one as Soviet troops converged with those of the other United Nations on German soil.

The San Francisco Conference opened in April 1945, with plenary sessions held in the beautiful Beaux Arts War Memorial Opera House, the first public opera house in the USA raised by public subscription. An army of volunteers helped to host the event, including over 2,000 military personnel, 800 boy scouts and 400 members of the Red Cross. The public fanfare that sounded

---

17 Memorandum by Arthur Sweetser, 'Dumbarton Oaks and the Covenant', undated, in Papers of Arthur Sweetser, Manuscripts Division of the Library of Congress, box 40.

this new organization and the world it represented was in sharp contrast to the way League officials had snuck out of Geneva in 1939. Despite the concerted attempt to present one world made new in 1945, there were important continuities with the ideas and practices of international relations before the war began.

Viewed apart from its glitzy launch, the institution that emerged in 1945 was remarkably similar to its 1920 predecessor. The League Assembly was reborn as the General Assembly, and the eleven-nation membership of the Security Council, too, followed the League, although its focus was more clearly on 'hard security', with a voting and veto structure that reflected what was understood as the special responsibility of the major powers to make the world safe. It had five permanent members, the USA, the USSR, Britain, China and, most controversially, France, thereby preserving great-power domination in ways that were troublingly redolent of the world they proclaimed they had left behind. New was the veto over action enjoyed by members of the Security Council. It was intended at the time to facilitate more great-power cooperation, notably between the USA, the UK and the USSR, than had been evident in the League in the interwar period. But the veto became notorious, and resulted in dividing the great powers and the UN in ways that reflected the period before 1939.

There was more talk of 'rights', but their recognition and enforcement proved as troublesome after 1945 as it had been after 1918. A concern for individual rights now took priority over the preoccupation with collective rights, notably those of minority groups, which had shaped the interwar period. There were radical expectations. W. E. B. Du Bois, the US civil rights activist who had been at the First Pan-African Congress in Europe in 1919, was now in San Francisco to explore his international message of racial equality in San Francisco, with sympathetic ears from Ethiopia, Egypt, Liberia and Haiti. But when the Philippine delegate at the conference, General Carlos Romulo, demanded a voice for the millions of unrepresented colonized individuals, the British delegate, Lord Cranborne, spoke of a world separated into 'peoples of different races, peoples of different religions, and peoples at different stages of civilization'.[18]

The endurance in ideas from the interwar to the post-war period was evident, too, in the continuity of personnel in many of the UNO's satellite institutions: staff from the Economic and Financial Organization of the

---

18 Discussed in Glenda Sluga, *Internationalism in the Age of Nationalism* (Philadelphia: University of Pennsylvania Press, 2013), p. 91.

League moved into the IMF, the World Bank, the FAO and the UN World Health Organization, the latter also recruiting staff from the League's Heath Organization. The League, more generally, had helped to socialize into international life many individuals who were to play leading roles in international organizations after 1945, including the future Secretary Dag Hammarskjöld, who had studied business cycles for the League.

Hammarskjöld also represented one of the most enduring developments that had emerged as a result of the working habits of the League: the emphasis on technocracy. The 'expert' had come to play a pivotal role in this wider network of UN organizations. The stress on expertise represented the continued power of the idea that the world could be directed by using figures, numbers and statistical categories. What was new in 1945 was the sense that technocratic, and indeed international, work was best conducted beyond the public's gaze. Gone was the emphasis on 'open' diplomacy promised by Wilson. In some ways, the desire to make the process on which decisions were reached 'scientific' and bureaucratic was a logical outgrowth of experts' deep sense of frustration with what they regarded as the 'reckless' behaviour of statesmen that had led the world into war in 1939.

The lack of transparency that came to characterize the IMF, the World Bank and the EEC, which also leaned heavily on networks forged in the League, risked their claim to legitimacy. (Among the EEC's founding fathers, Jean Monnet, Paul-Henri Spaak and Paul Van Zeeland, to name just a few, had all played key roles in the League.) The increasing specialization and the size of the UN's organizational agency brought new challenges as well as advantages, most immediately in questions of how to coordinate and relate the activities of the different organizations.

But the international world that emerged in 1945 represented a break with the past too. Most obviously it had a new home. There was a brief stay in the former plant of the Sperry Gyroscope Company at Lake Success in New York. Thereafter, the UNO moved to a purpose-made building in Turtle Bay, Manhattan, where the architects had to respond to the rising number of states as a result of both changes to state boundaries triggered by the war and, later than many national aspirants had hoped, decolonization. Fifty-one states signed the founding charter in 1945; by 1955, the number had risen to 75, and to 147 by 1975. The primacy of statehood that was enshrined in both the League and the UNO helped to induce and delineate national aspirations which were the defining element of international relations in the twentieth century.

The years between 1939 and 1945 marked the most energetic period of global institution building in modern history. What was strikingly absent, however, was the popular enthusiasm for it that had shaped internationalist ideas and movements from the nineteenth century onward. In April 1946, the remaining members of the League of Nations gathered in Geneva to consign the organization to history. Here, neutral states, such as Finland, Ireland and Portugal, were welcome, in contrast to New York, where they had still to find a place in the new order. In Geneva, delegates reflected on the disappointments of the League, but voiced an even greater disenchantment with the UNO. As the French Senator and former Prime Minister Joseph Paul-Boncour put it, 'those of us who were at San Francisco...certainly did not find there the atmosphere of enthusiasm and faith we found when the League was being built up in Geneva'.[19] In contrast to the League, the inauguration of the UNO was met with a whimper.

European states sought to recover some of what was lost with the demise of the League through new European organizations. Meanwhile, global grass-roots activism on refugees, rights, development and, later, the environment went on to spawn new types of non-governmental global organization, which came to question the utility of intergovernmental organization in more fundamental ways. Shortly before his death in April 1945, Roosevelt had declared that 'at the heart' of his principles for the future organization of the world was that 'the misuse of power, as implied in the term "power politics", must not be a controlling factor in international relations'.[20] After 1945, the paralysis that frequently gripped the United Nations, and the rise of non-governmental organizations, demonstrated that this lofty aspiration remained unfulfilled.

---

19 'Lack of Enthusiasm for the UNO', *Manchester Guardian*, 11 April 1946, p. 5.
20 Franklin D. Roosevelt, 'Message to Congress', *Congressional Record*, vol. 91, pt. 1, pp. 68–9.

7

Nazi genocides

JÜRGEN MATTHÄUS

The Nazi regime's genocidal policies evolved as a result of the dynamic interaction between racial ideals, societal interests, systemic paroxysms and structured violence. The importance of the Second World War for the Third Reich's extreme destructiveness can hardly be overestimated – mass violence occurred predominantly between 1941 and 1945 in the regions earmarked as future German 'living space'. A clear differentiation between military aggression and the targeted destruction of civilian life remains problematic. The Holocaust, the most extreme manifestation of Nazi genocide,[1] attests to this crucial correlation. At the same time, the way Nazi Germany waged war against its external and internal enemies after 1939 was heavily rooted in earlier developments – in the case of the 'Final Solution of the Jewish question', anti-Semitism transcended Hitler's grasp for European domination, chronologically as well as geographically. This chapter is designed to provide a historical overview of the characteristics of mass violence under Hitler – for the most part excluding the autonomous policies adopted by the Third Reich's allies – that led to the murder of an estimated 13 million civilians, the vast majority killed by Germans and their helpers in Eastern and Southeastern Europe, and almost half of them Jews.

Pre-war determinants and racial policies

The systematic killing of civilians under the Nazi regime involved decisions oriented toward military conquest and a radical restratification of German

---

The arguments made in this chapter are those of the author; they do not reflect the opinions of the US Holocaust Memorial Museum.

1 On the concept of genocide, its applications and limitations, see Donald Bloxham and A. Dirk Moses (eds.), *The Oxford Handbook of Genocide Studies* (Oxford and New York: Oxford University Press, 2010).

society. The Nazi leadership's policy was based on a worldview that sharply differentiated between racially defined ingroups and outgroups, us and them, good and bad. Between the two poles of this antithetical *Weltanschauung*, there could be no compromise, only temporary accommodations for tactical purposes.[2] Rooted in the party's ideology and institutional culture, yet flexible in its implementation, Nazi policy evolved in stages, either as a result of external developments or from internal dynamics fed by specific interests and the interaction between the regime and German society.

Starting in early 1933, nationalist consensus and Nazi objectives determined who was to be persecuted by the new government in its drive to replace Weimar democracy with autocratic rule. In this early phase, violence was primarily used against political opponents, yet the party's ideological thrust, particularly the conviction that communism was a facade to cover the Jewish drive for world domination – a trope closely related to the concept of 'Judeo-Bolshevism' virulent among right-wing circles in Eastern Europe since the Russian Revolution[3] – implied more sweeping measures. Communists, social democrats and others labelled enemies of a Nazi 'new order' fell victim to random, often retaliatory physical abuse and emerging state policy, both merging in the concept of 'protective custody' and the socio-spatial construct of the concentration camps. In the first year of Nazi rule, roughly 100,000 persons were arrested; the number of murder victims is estimated at around 1,000, almost exclusively men, including a disproportionally high figure of Jews. After this early period, the majority of concentration camp inmates were released, the number of political prisoners decreased, and most of the improvised camps were closed.[4] Still, important patterns had been established: the concentration camp system remained in place and underwent significant reorganizations; the political police (Gestapo) and the SS, from mid-1936 under the unified command of Heinrich Himmler, emerged as the key executive force in the fight against internal opponents; and Hitler had become, due to the abdication or consent of Germany's traditional elites, the sole source of political authority in the Reich.

---

2 Claudia Koonz, *The Nazi Conscience* (Cambridge, Mass.: Belknap Press, 2003); Boaz Neumann, *Die Weltanschauung der Nazis* (Göttingen: Wallstein, 2011).
3 André Gerrits, *The Myth of Jewish Communism: A Historical Interpretation* (Brussels: Peter Lang, 2009).
4 Jane Caplan and Nikolaus Wachsmann (eds.), *Concentration Camps in Nazi Germany: The New Histories* (London and New York: Routledge, 2010); Geoffrey Megargee (ed.), *The USHMM Encyclopedia of Camps and Ghettos 1933–1945*, vol. 1: *Early Camps, Youth Camps, and Concentration Camps and Subcamps under the SS-Business Administration Main Office (WVHA)* (Bloomington: Indiana University Press, 2009).

The pursuit of a Nazi racial agenda followed the regime's stabilization as much as it contributed to it. Anti-Semitism was an issue in which Nazi designs dovetailed with traditional goals of the Völkisch right, but it took organized efforts to undo the effects of emancipation. The prevalence of practical problems in the Nazis' early handling of the 'Jewish question' became visible during the regime's first nationwide anti-Jewish initiative, the highly symbolic, yet largely ineffective, boycott of stores owned by Jews on 1 April 1933. Party and state leaders searched for a racial policy that fitted their reading of the domestic and international situation, while activists continued to pursue boycotts and other forms of anti-Jewish violence on a local basis.[5] Subsequently, Hitler's bureaucracy produced a series of laws and regulations that discriminated against 'non-Aryans' (defined as persons descended 'from non-Aryan, especially Jewish, parents or grandparents') in areas of social and economic life that German anti-Semites had long identified as being in need of restrictions.

On racial policy issues where there seemed to be broader consensus on goals and means, the regime proceeded aggressively. Compared to the 1933 Civil Service Law, with its exemptions for First World War veterans, which, until the enactment of the Nuremberg Laws in September 1935, severely reduced the number of Jews affected by lay-offs, the 'Law for the Prevention of Hereditarily Sick Offspring', enacted on 14 July 1933, presented a more radical departure, by allowing the compulsory sterilization of persons suffering from such ill-defined conditions as schizophrenia, feeble-mindedness, epilepsy, alcoholism or hereditary deaf- and blindness. Designed to improve the vitality of the 'people's community', the measure targeted those deemed unable to produce healthy offspring, and required for its implementation close cooperation between state officials, doctors and hospitals. Until the end of the war, the law facilitated the sterilization of an estimated 400,000 persons in Germany and its annexed territories; women were affected in much greater numbers than men, most notably the estimated 6,000 women whose medical procedures had fatal consequences. Furthermore, the law provided the eugenic indication for roughly 30,000 abortions – a number close to that of German women convicted during the Third Reich for illegal abortions. Outside religious, mostly Catholic quarters, the measure created no significant controversy; indeed it seemed to follow an international trend in public health toward 'cleansing the

5 Michael Wildt, *Hitler's Volksgemeinschaft and the Dynamics of Racial Exclusion: Violence Against Jews in Provincial Germany, 1919–1939* (New York: Berghahn, 2012).

nation' of disabled and others deemed unsuitable, thus alleviating the burden of care-giving placed on society.[6]

In contrast to other countries that pursued eugenicist programmes, such as the USA and Scandinavian countries, in the Reich, such programmes tended to escalate over time.[7] Beyond the groups listed in the Hereditary Health Law, categories regarded as outsiders and unwanted, particularly Sinti and Roma ('gypsies'), homeless, homosexuals, former felons or children of colour (mostly the offspring of black Allied soldiers stationed in western Germany after the First World War), became targets of sterilization and other eugenicist measures. The persecution of 'gypsies' until 1939 points to the multi-causal nature of racial persecution in Nazi Germany and its nexus with other ideologically driven programmes. Traditionally stigmatized in many European states, 'gypsies' found themselves the targets of Nazi discrimination for their antecedence as well as for their way of life. As German police criminalized 'gypsy vagrancy' and invoked national security concerns, as municipalities restricted Sinti mobility and created special 'gypsy camps', and as race scientists tried to ascertain the group's racial characteristics, they created the basis for forced sterilizations, racial experimentation and mass murder during the war on a European scale.[8]

Similarly, Nazi anti-Jewish persecution before the Second World War gained in intensity. By mid-1935, frustration at the party base over the unfulfilled promise of removing German Jews from the 'people's community', together with eroding foreign policy concerns among Nazi leaders, increased the momentum toward 'solving the Jewish question'. The Nuremberg Laws combined anti-miscegenation with loss of civil rights, made possible after bureaucrats had devised a workable pseudo-racial formula for differentiating 'Jews' (defined as persons with at least three grandparents of Jewish denomination, or someone with two Jewish grandparents who her/himself practised the Jewish religion or was married to a Jew) from persons of 'German blood', with so-called 'mixed-breeds' (*Mischlinge*) in a precarious and, until the end of the war, undetermined intermediate position. Subsequent restrictions accelerated the 'social death' of German

---

6 Henry Friedlander, *The Origins of Nazi Genocide: From Euthanasia to the Final Solution* (Chapel Hill: University of North Carolina Press, 1995), pp. 246–7, 254; Gisela Bock, *Zwangssterilisation im Nationalsozialismus. Studien zur Rassenpolitik und Frauenpolitik* (Opladen: Westdeutscher Verlag, 1986), pp. 354–67, 462–4.

7 Alison Bashford and Philippa Levine (eds.), *The Oxford Handbook of the History of Eugenics* (Oxford University Press, 2010).

8 Michael Zimmermann, *Rassenutopie und Genozid. Die nationalsozialistische 'Lösung der Zigeunerfrage'* (Hamburg: Christians, 1996).

Jews.[9] Until the beginning of the war, measures aimed at forced emigration drove roughly half of them out, yet did not produce the effect desired by Nazi planners, as foreign countries were loath to accept Jewish immigrants due to the effects of the world economic crisis and the strength of home-grown anti-Semitism. Furthermore, Nazi officials were not content with pushing Jews out, but also wanted to extract as much wealth as possible, leaving would-be emigrants with few material prospects for building a new life abroad. Once the regime started to expand its borders, it added significant numbers of Jews, thus calling for new, more radical measures to alleviate the self-inflicted problem.

For the escalation of pre-war Nazi violence, the annexation of Austria in March 1938 served as a watershed. Street brutality against Jews converged with mass arrests and state-sponsored plunder to produce an exodus of almost 100,000 Jews within one year. In the process, Reinhard Heydrich's Security Police and SD (*Sicherheitsdienst* – Nazi Party security service) apparatus asserted itself as the frontrunner in the competition between state and party agencies over determining anti-Jewish policy. Deportations across the Polish border in late October 1938 of 15,000 to 17,000 Polish citizens residing in Germany preceded the Germany-wide pogrom euphemistically referred to as 'Kristallnacht', which claimed the lives of more than a hundred Jews, led to the arrest of roughly 26,000 Jews, and ratcheted up state-sponsored robbery of Jewish property from a community under constant siege. This development coincided with the intensified persecution of other 'outgroups': in the concentration camps, the Jews arrested during the November pogrom encountered more than 10,000 persons, mostly non-Jews, incarcerated since June 1938 as part of a campaign by police and communal officials throughout the Reich targeting so-called 'asocials' and 'work-shy'.

In preparing for the revision of post-First World War borders by military means, Hitler and his lieutenants not only attempted to close the ranks of the *Volksgemeinschaft* (people's community – Nazi vision of a conflict- and outgroup-free German society), but also claimed that German minorities living across the Reich's borders (ethnic Germans, or *Volksdeutsche*) were facing increasing persecution. This subterfuge figured prominently in the run-up to the dismemberment of Czechoslovakia (succeeded by the

9 Marion A. Kaplan, *Between Dignity and Despair: Jewish Life in Nazi Germany* (New York: Oxford University Press, 1998), p. 5, based on the concept of 'social death' developed by Orlando Patterson, *Slavery and Social Death* (Cambridge, Mass.: Harvard University Press, 1982).

German-controlled 'Protectorate Bohemia-Moravia' and a Slovak puppet state) and foreshadowed Nazi propaganda in the run-up to the Polish campaign. Hitler himself created a powerful link between earlier Nazi policy and racial war goals on the one hand, and military aggression and anti-Bolshevism on the other, when he threatened, during a speech to the Reichstag on 30 January 1939, in conjunction with complaints about Western countries' unwillingness to open their borders for German Jews, that 'if the international Finance-Jewry inside and outside of Europe should succeed in plunging the peoples of the earth once again into a world war, the result will not be the Bolshevization of earth, and thus a Jewish victory, but the annihilation of the Jewish race in Europe'.[10] Once the war had started, Hitler and his spokesmen repeatedly referred to this 'prophecy', but deliberately misdated it to 1 September 1939, the first day of what would become the Second World War.

Military aggression and mass violence, 1939–1941

The most important factor for the expansion of Nazi violence against civilians was the war. For Hitler and his deputies, the military conflict provided crucial opportunities as well as legitimization to deploy massive force in the fight against the regime's internal and external enemies.[11] The first battles in this two-front war were the Polish campaign and the murder of disabled children and hospital patients in the Reich. Disposing of costly and unproductive members of society followed the same logic that since 1933 had prompted forced sterilizations and other eugenicist measures; as they were sending 'the nation's best' to the battlefields, Nazi functionaries saw in the disabled a burden on the nation's war effort and a threat to the post-war *Volksgemeinschaft*. Similar to other areas of Nazi policy-making, the process from plan to implementation was complex, but unfolded with unprecedented speed as ideas discussed at the regime's top dovetailed with initiatives from local health officials, doctors and racial experts. By September 1939, a system had been organized that involved reporting disabled newborn and facilitated their selection prior to their murder. Undertaken in secret to avoid outside propaganda and domestic discontent, the programme grew over time to include adolescents, and during the war claimed more than 5,000 lives.[12]

---

10 Hitler, Reichstag speech, 30 January 1939; trans. from www.ushmm.org/wlc/en/media_fi.php?ModuleId=10005175&MediaId=3108 (accessed 3 November 2014).
11 Richard J. Evans, *The Third Reich at War, 1939–1945* (London: Allen Lane, 2008).
12 Friedlander, *Origins of Nazi Genocide*.

Handicapped adults were next. Under the codename Aktion T4, and with Hitler's explicit approval, from the autumn of 1939 an intricate apparatus was set up, exclusively devoted to the murder of hospital inmates across the Reich. The T4 killing machine took care of the selection of patients, transport to six killing sites, murder by gassing, medication or injection, and the disposal of the bodies. Given the scale of the operation, attempts at keeping it secret had to fail; the growing number of inquiries from within the German public and members of the elite about conspicuous cases of deaths contributed to Hitler's decision in late August 1941 to terminate T4. Until that time, more than 70,000 patients, including an unknown number of Jews, had been murdered. T4 highlights three characteristics of Nazi genocidal policies: their rootedness in pre-war racial planning measures and multi-causal origins; their interconnectedness, despite different target groups and developmental patterns; and their tendency to escalate. Of the more than 300 T4 functionaries, roughly one-third came to be deployed in 1942–43 during the murder of the Polish Jews. After August 1941, T4 doctors were involved in the selection and killing of up to 20,000 concentration camp inmates, under the codename 'Aktion 14f13'.[13]

Once Poland had been overrun and dismembered, the new goal of 'Germanization' perpetuated the Janus-faced model of earlier racial policy in the Reich with its positive and negative components – the former designed to foster the racial health of the *Volk*, the latter aimed at ostracizing out-groups – yet, from the start, it showed a clear propensity for mass violence as part of the drive to 'pacify', exploit and ethnically restratify the conquered territory. Against the background of the prevailing perception of Poles as inferior, Jews as subhuman, and 'the East' as a space destined to come under German domination, during the brief Polish campaign the Wehrmacht, in conjunction with special SS and security police units (*Einsatzgruppen*), adopted measures against the civilian opposition that vaguely foreshadowed the 'war of annihilation' against the Soviet Union. The number of Polish civilians killed between September and the end of 1939 in the western Polish regions annexed to the Reich (thus excluding central Poland, the so-called *Generalgouvernement*) is estimated at 60,000. It was in these same regions earmarked for 'Germanization' that, from early 1940, new annihilation techniques were used first: in western Poland, German security policemen

13 Ulf Schmidt, *Karl Brandt: The Nazi Doctor. Medicine and Power in the Third Reich* (London: Continuum, 2007); Michael Burleigh, *Death and Deliverance: 'Euthanasia' in Germany, c.1900–1945* (Cambridge and New York: Cambridge University Press, 1994).

murdered hospital patients in gas vans – mobile killing installations were deployed in Serbia later during the war, and on an even larger scale in the occupied Soviet Union; in late 1941, the first annihilation camp became operational near Chełmno (German: Kulmhof) in the annexed 'Reichsgau Wartheland', and, until 1944, it claimed the lives of at least 152,000 men, women and children, mostly Jews from the Łódź ghetto, but also several thousand 'gypsies'. The security police units involved in these murders had previously killed hospital patients in the Reich as part of Aktion T4.[14]

The radicalizing dynamics of Nazi occupation policy manifested themselves on the planning as well as on the practical level. On 7 October 1939, Hitler appointed Himmler as Reich Commissioner for the Strengthening of Germandom (*Reichskommissar für die Festigung deutschen Volkstums*), with the following complementary tasks:

> (1) to bring back those German citizens and ethnic Germans abroad who are eligible for permanent return to the Reich; (2) to eliminate the harmful influence of such alien parts of the population as constitute a danger to the Reich and the German community; (3) to create new German colonies by resettlement, and especially by the resettlement of German citizens and ethnic Germans coming back from abroad.[15]

This grand design, influenced by mass resettlements in Europe since the late nineteenth century, was driven by the desire to massively revise the post-First World War order.[16] Himmler's assignment prompted breathtaking ethno-political plans for all of German-dominated Europe, starting with the mass settlement of *Volksdeutsche* on German-annexed Polish territory that was to be facilitated by the deportation of up to 5 million Poles (non-Jews and Jews) to a vaguely sketched out 'dumping ground' in the *Generalgouvernement*. By early 1942, and in line with Nazi expectations vis-à-vis the Soviet Union, a new *Generalplan Ost* showed the ethnic map of Eastern Europe up to the Ural Mountains completely redrawn in favour of Germanic settlers, with 30–50 million Slavs to be removed or otherwise disposed of, and the remaining non-Germans relegated to some form of serfdom. While remaining largely unfulfilled, these plans verbalized the Nazi desire for the physical elimination

14 Volker Riess, *Die Anfänge der Vernichtung 'lebensunwerten Lebens' in den Reichsgauen Danzig-Westpreussen und Wartheland, 1939/40* (Frankfurt am Main and New York: Lang, 1995).
15 Cited in Evans, *Third Reich*, p. 29.
16 Donald Bloxham, *The Final Solution: A Genocide* (Oxford and New York: Oxford University Press, 2009).

of millions of people deemed 'harmful influences' or 'useless eaters', on a historically unprecedented scale.[17]

Radicalization clearly formed a defining feature of Nazi policies during the war, yet this process did not evolve in a predetermined, linear or all-encompassing fashion. Other priorities affected the trajectory of 'Germaniza-tion' policy, either as impediments – in the form of competing military and administrative interests – or as aggravating factors. The ideology-driven determination to exploit resources in the conquered areas for the benefit of the German war economy reflected a destructive rationale that impacted the life of civilians, especially in Eastern Europe. In the German-annexed parts of Poland, more than 1.5 million people, mostly Slavs, had to vacate their homes; an estimated 400,000 Poles, including several tens of thousands of Jews, were deported to the *Generalgouvernement*. Among the latter were those affected, in late 1939, by the short-lived 'Nisko project' organized by Adolf Eichmann, the 'resettlement' expert in the newly created SS Reich Security Main Office (*Reichssicherheitshauptamt*, RSHA) under Heydrich. As a result of German officials' eagerness to report their area of influence as 'free of Jews', the Lublin region became the destination for deportation transports with Jews from the Reich and the 'Protectorate Bohemia-Moravia' until the project was terminated in early 1940, as it confronted insurmountable logis-tical problems.[18] Radicalization also depended on where and against whom the Third Reich was waging war. After the explosion of mass violence in Poland, the 1940 German military campaigns in Western Europe resembled more traditional forms of modern warfare, despite the prejudice-driven mistreatment of coloured POWs captured by the Wehrmacht and forced population movements targeting the Reich's western border regions. At the same time, the French defeat triggered a plan developed by the German Foreign Office, with the support of the RSHA, for the mass removal of European Jews to the ill-suited island of Madagascar, which elevated earlier 'resettlement' fantasies targeting Jews to a new level. In the spring of 1941, German interventions in the Balkans, particularly in Yugoslavia, produced a

---

17 Mechtild Rössler and Sabine Schleiermacher (eds.), *Der 'Generalplan Ost'. Hauptlinien der nationalsozialistischen Planungs-und Vernichtungspolitik* (Berlin: Akademie Verlag, 1993).

18 Christopher Browning, with contributions by Jürgen Matthäus, *The Origins of the Final Solution: The Evolution of Nazi Anti-Jewish Policy, September 1939–March 1942* (Lincoln: Nebraska University Press, 2004); Götz Aly, *'Final Solution': Nazi Population Policy and the Murder of the European Jews* (London and New York: Arnold, 1999). For a group biography of RSHA officers, see Michael Wildt, *An Uncompromising Generation: The Nazi Leadership of the Reich Security Main Office* (Madison: University of Wisconsin Press, 2009).

similarly new departure, as Wehrmacht leaders resorted to the massive use of violence in their attempts to assert control over a restive population.[19]

As much as post-September 1939 military strategies and racial policies portended the consequences of the German attack on the Soviet Union, the explosion of genocidal violence that followed in its wake was unprecedented. Operation BARBAROSSA was designed from the outset as a war of annihilation. Pre-campaign discussions and directives leave no doubt about the broad consensus between the political and military leadership on core issues: the shared determination to crush the Red Army and destroy the 'Judeo-Bolshevist' system, together with its proponents; the unquestioned acceptance of the need for ruthless suppression of actual and potential resistance; and the firm conviction that, as a result of the systematic exploitation of the region's resources for the German war effort, and in line with long-term occupation goals, millions of Soviet civilians would have to perish. The logic of the Blitzkrieg, with its reliance on rapid and flexible deployment of massive force, this time over an enormously extended front line, merged with ideological convictions about the expandability, if not redundancy, of Slavs, the enmity of Jews, and the backwardness of all other peoples in the Soviet Union. So that the occupied regions could be 'pacified' as swiftly and thoroughly as possible, army orders gave German soldiers a pass on established rules of warfare, while *Einsatzgruppen* and other SS and police units equipped with special executive authorities swept through the rear areas. Even before 3 million German troops, followed by forces supplied by the Reich's allies, started invading Soviet territory on 22 June 1941, the stage was set for a new level of mass violence.[20]

The brutality of the battlefield extended to the German treatment of captured Red Army soldiers. Wehrmacht high command directives called for persons suspected of being Soviet commissars to be finished off immediately; from July 1941, Heydrich's *Einsatzgruppen* helped to weed out suspicious elements, including Jews and members of other racial outgroups in the POW camps. There, lack of basic provisions caused a much higher casualty rate than in any other military campaign. Within one year, up to 2 million of the 3.7 million Soviet POWs had died in German custody. The daily death rate

---

19 Ben Shepherd, *Terror in the Balkans: German Armies and Partisan Warfare* (Cambridge, Mass.: Harvard University Press, 2012); Raffael Scheck, *Hitler's African Victims: The German Army Massacres of Black French Soldiers in 1940* (Cambridge and New York: Cambridge University Press, 2006).

20 Geoffrey P. Megargee, *War of Annihilation: Combat and Genocide on the Eastern Front, 1941* (Lanham, Md.: Rowman & Littlefield, 2006). On German anti-partisan warfare on the Eastern Front, see also Chapter 24 by Ben Shepherd, 'Guerrillas and counter-insurgency', in Volume 1 of this work.

reached its height in late 1941/early 1942, following cuts in the already insufficient food rations; until the summer of 1942, no other group, including Jews, faced such a level of German violence. The overall number of Soviet soldiers who died in German captivity is estimated to be in the range of 3 million.[21] To ensure the swift 'pacification' of the conquered regions, from the tracing and arrest of suspects to their execution, Wehrmacht, police and SS units worked much more smoothly together than in Poland. Building on already established patterns of Nazi violence, the eagerness of German functionaries to meet broadly defined and rarely specified goals provided crucial momentum and shaped group behaviour, in an order climate dominated by ideology-driven perceptions of military security and the absence of de-escalating mechanisms. The unanimity between leading members of the German military and police/SS apparatus in this early phase of the war against the Soviet Union is reflected in the fact that even Wehrmacht officers later involved in the anti-Nazi opposition cooperated closely with their *Einsatzgruppen* counterparts.[22]

The crucial role of the Wehrmacht in the murder of Soviet Jews and in creating what, in retrospect, appears as the most important segue from anti-Jewish persecution to genocide can be gathered from the fact that the written directives initially issued by the army were more aggressive and encompassing in their targeting of civilians than those transmitted to the *Einsatzgruppen*. As much as Himmler's forces drove the genocidal process in large parts of the occupied region, it was the Wehrmacht that arrived first on the scene and provided logistical support, with arrests, round-ups and executions behind the front line. The Germans' first mass murder actions targeted Jewish men of military age and were often triggered by rumours about anti-German violence. At the same time, pogroms staged by locals – some motivated by nationalistic fervour, others by the urge to act out their aggression against a convenient scapegoat for Soviet terror, many by material interests – and the brutality of Hitler's Romanian ally at the southern sector of the front contributed to the rapid escalation of anti-Jewish violence.[23] Heydrich's early

21 Christian Streit, *Keine Kameraden. Die Wehrmacht und die sowjetischen Kriegsgefangenen 1941–1945* (2nd edn, Bonn: Dietz, 1997); Reinhard Otto, *Wehrmacht, Gestapo und sowjetische Kriegsgefangene im deutschen Reichsgebiet 1941/42* (Munich: Oldenbourg, 1998).

22 Christian Gerlach, 'Men of 20 July and the War in the Soviet Union', in Hannes Heer and Klaus Naumann (eds.), *War of Extermination: The German Military in World War II, 1941–1944* (New York: Berghahn Books, 2000), pp. 126–45.

23 Jan T. Gross, *Neighbors: The Destruction of the Jewish Community in Jedwabne, Poland* (Princeton University Press, 2001); Jan T. Gross with Irena Grudzińska Gross, *Golden Harvest: Events at the Periphery of the Holocaust* (New York: Oxford University Press, 2012); Radu Ioanid, *The Holocaust in Romania: The Destruction of Jews and Gypsies under the Antonescu Regime, 1940–1944* (Chicago, Ill.: Ivan R. Dee, 2000).

directives to the *Einsatzgruppen* included encouragement of 'self-cleansing measures by anti-communist and anti-Jewish circles', combined with executions of 'Jews in party and state functions, [and] other radical elements (saboteurs, propagandists, snipers, assassins, inciters, etc.)'.[24] Yet Heydrich could be sure that his field officers, given their prior experiences and familiarity with key tenets of Nazi policy, would not need detailed to-do lists, but were independent-minded enough to determine the proper line of action and to make use of new opportunities opening up along the way.

After 1945, the inherently genocidal dimensions of Operation BARBA-ROSSA, together with the key role of the Wehrmacht in the murder of Soviet POWs and civilians, were long ignored. The exigencies of the Cold War in general, and the West German avoidance of confronting the 'war in the East' in particular, cannot fully explain this phenomenon. It seems that the persistence of ethno-political stereotypes in the West contributed to the longevity of established myths about German military campaigning and occupation policy in Europe, extended by the problematic implications of 'pacification' strategies and partisan warfare confronting occupation armies until today. Only recently has scholarship started to pay proper attention to the mass murder of civilians, particularly Jews, in the German-occupied Soviet Union;[25] nevertheless, other forms of Nazi genocidal policies in the region, as well as their context – from the sources of German conduct to patterns of persecution and the role of non-German groups – are awaiting appropriate exploration.

Total war, the Holocaust and other genocides, 1941–1945

Accepted caesural events in the military history of the Second World War match only partly the evolution of Nazi mass violence. Months before the entry of the United States into the war, this violence had reached unprecedented

---

24 Heydrich to *Einsatzgruppen* leaders, 29 June 1941, and to Higher SS and Police Leaders, 2 July 1941, trans. from Andrej Angrick, Klaus-Michael Mallmann, Jürgen Matthäus and Martin Cüppers (eds.), *Deutsche Besatzungsherrschaft in der UdSSR 1941–1945* (Dokumente der Einsatzgruppen in der Sowjetunion, 3 vols., Darmstadt: Wissenschaftliche Buchgesellschaft, 2011–14), pp. 173–5.

25 See, for example, Alex J. Kaye, Jeff Rutherford and David Stahel (eds.), *Nazi Policy on the Eastern Front, 1941: Total War, Genocide, and Radicalization* (Rochester, NY: University of Rochester Press, 2012); Dieter Pohl, *Die Herrschaft der Wehrmacht. Deutsche Militärbesatzung und einheimische Bevölkerung in der Sowjetunion 1941–1944* (Munich: Oldenbourg, 2008); Ben Shepherd, *War in the Wild East: The German Army and Soviet Partisans* (Cambridge, Mass.: Harvard University Press, 2004); Waitman Beorn, *Marching into Darkness: The Wehrmacht and the Holocaust in Belarus* (Cambridge, Mass.: Harvard University Press, 2014).

levels, as the Wehrmacht's advance at the Eastern Front heavily affected civilians – the siege of Leningrad alone in the end claimed the lives of roughly a million.[26] High German casualty rates on the Eastern Front triggered increasingly brutal deportations of foreign labourers into the Reich, and relentless exploitation produced rampant starvation, disease and death, especially in occupied Soviet cities, which increased the pressure on the local population to collaborate with the Germans in the interest of survival. Within weeks of the start of Operation BARBAROSSA, Soviet Jewry had been massacred en masse and concentrated in ghettos that, from the autumn of 1941, also became the destination of deportation transports from the Reich – by the end of 1941 producing a death toll of up to 800,000 men, women and children. Conditions in Southeastern Europe, where destructive German 'pacification' policies dovetailed with attempts by Nazi-allied elites at ethnic cleansing, were hardly better: the number of Serbs murdered in Croatia and Bosnia exceeded 325,000, and by the spring of 1942, after they had killed the remaining Jewish women and children, German authorities declared Serbia as being 'free of Jews'.

In the ongoing attempt to explain the Holocaust, scholars have long stressed the importance of the Nazi leadership's persistent commitment to bring about a 'Final Solution of the Jewish question', based on their racial hatred and a societal tradition of anti-Semitism. In light of the Third Reich's history of mass violence, we can see that this *Weltanschauung* encompassed visions of radical change that were broader than the 'Jewish question', and over time underwent significant transformations. Changing circumstances opened up new opportunities to address core items of the regime's agenda and determined the decision-making process at all levels of the Nazi system. Most scholars would agree that the crucial time period for Nazi Germany passing the threshold from the persecution of Jews to their destruction was the second half of 1941. As the 'Madagascar plan' turned out to be impractical, a 'territorial solution' occurred on the Eastern horizon, the contours of which the *Einsatzgruppen*, and other units responsible for mass executions of Jewish men, women and children, had started to outline in the course of Operation BARBAROSSA. Resettling Jews and confining them to ghettos and labour camps, staple items of Nazi 'Germanization' policy since the defeat of Poland, helped to prepare the ground for their physical extermination.[27]

26 Jörg Ganzenmüller, *Das belagerte Leningrad 1941 bis 1944. Die Stadt in den Strategien von Angreifern und Verteidigern* (Paderborn: Schöningh, 2005), p. 41.
27 For an overview, see Gustavo Corni, *Hitler's Ghettos: Voices from a Beleaguered Society, 1939–1944* (London: Arnold, 2002). Still unsurpassed on the ghettos' internal

Raul Hilberg has described the Holocaust as 'a total process, comparable in its diversity to a modern war, a modernization, or a national reconstruction'.[28] Among the factors that during the second half of 1941 fed this process, impacted its direction and speed, and helped overcome hurdles, the decisiveness and activism of functional elites played a key role, none more so than Himmler's deputies in the East: *Einsatzgruppen* and police officers, as well as the *Reichsführer*'s direct representatives, the Higher SS and Police Leaders (*Höhere SS- und Polizeiführer*, HSSPF).[29] Committed to the 'pacification' of their area of influence and accustomed to operating independently on the basis of broadly defined assignments, these men made the mass annihilation of Jews become a reality, with potential for further expansion. Standing out among the countless mass shootings of Jewish men, women and children were those in Kamenets Podolsky between 26 and 29 August, with more than 26,000 victims; in Babi Yar near Kiev (more than 33,000 on 29 and 30 September); in the Lithuanian city of Kaunas (almost 10,000 in late October); in Minsk (12,000 in early November); and in Riga (26,000 in late November/ early December). From the preparation of the shootings to the alignment of bodies at the mass graves and the disposal of the victims' personal property, the murder squads had adopted a standardized, highly efficient method, yet one that could not be kept secret. Despite orders to the contrary, Wehrmacht soldiers and other German officials took photographs of mass executions or shared stories with people at home. Allied leaders, based on intercepted reports and intelligence reports, were aware of German mass atrocities from the early stages of Operation BARBAROSSA, but failed to grasp their meaning. Jewish activists and organizations received incoherent information from a limited number of often unreliable sources, and struggled to make sense of the course of German conduct.[30]

stratification is Isaiah Trunk, *Judenrat: The Jewish Councils in Eastern Europe under Nazi Occupation* (New York: Macmillan, 1972). Aiming at comprehensiveness is Martin Dean (ed.), *The United States Holocaust Memorial Museum Encyclopedia of Camps and Ghettos, 1933–1945*, vol. II: *Ghettos in German-Occupied Eastern Europe* (Bloomington: Indiana University Press, 2012).

28 Raul Hilberg, *The Destruction of the European Jews* (rev. edn, New Haven, Conn.: Yale University Press, 2003), p. 1060.

29 In the Soviet Union, SS generals Friedrich Jeckeln (1895–1946), Hans Adolf Prützmann (1901–45) and Erich von dem Bach-Zelewski (1899–1972) served as HSSPF; see, in general, Ruth Bettina Birn, *Die Höheren SS- und Polizeiführer. Himmlers Vertreter im Reich und in den besetzten Gebieten* (Düsseldorf: Droste, 1986).

30 Frank Bajohr and Dieter Pohl, *Massenmord und schlechtes Gewissen. Die deutsche Bevölkerung, die NS-Führung und der Holocaust* (Frankfurt am Main: Fischer Taschenbuch Verlag, 2008); Richard Breitman, *Official Secrets: What the Nazis Planned, What the British and Americans Knew* (New York: Hill and Wang, 1998); Jürgen Matthäus, with

Nazi attempts at disguising the murderous reality in the East, the Allied focus on winning the war, and the legacy of anti-German atrocity propaganda during the First World War contributed to the prevailing disbelief among those witnessing the unfolding genocide. More importantly, however, the totality of the destruction process was barely visible at the time, for, while the central planning for the 'Final Solution' implied its Europe-wide dimension, its execution depended on regional, sometimes local factors. In early 1941, Göring had tasked Heydrich with the preparation of a blueprint for 'a solution most attuned to the conditions of the time', an assignment confirmed at the end of July 'in the form of emigration or evacuation'.[31] In the intervening months, the parameters of Heydrich's task had massively shifted, both in terms of the challenges – with roughly 2.5 million Jews in the Soviet Union coming under German domination, while conditions in Polish ghettos continued to deteriorate – and the possibilities, as attested to most graphically in the execution figures that the *Einsatzgruppen* reported to Berlin. Hitler's approval of the deportation of German Jews in September 1941, legitimized with recourse to the classic Nazi trope of 'self-defence' against the arch-enemy and to Stalin's recent decision to deport the Volga Germans to Siberia, gave the signal for a further proliferation of activism. Based on earlier experiences, the ensuing 'solution to the Jewish question' combined 'evacuation' with extermination, and overlapped in many important respects with the persecution of other, primarily racially defined groups.[32]

In the last quarter of 1941 and the first of 1942, German efforts focused on creating the means for systematic mass murder. The result was an uneven pattern of intense violence emanating partly from the periphery where genocide was already happening, and partly from the Berlin centre. Deportations organized by the RSHA between mid-October 1941 and February 1942, to Łódź, Minsk, Kaunas and Riga, which engulfed more than 53,000 Jews and 5,000 'gypsies' living in Germany proper, Austria and the Protectorate, involved a wide spectrum of agencies – state and municipal officials, eager to strip the deportees of their last possessions and vestiges of lawful status, railway planners devising timetables, order police units guarding the trains – and increased the pressure at the receiving end to find ways of dealing with the influx of the unwanted. In doing so, functionaries in the East

---

Emil Kerenji, Jan Lambertz and Leah Wolfson, *Jewish Responses to Persecution, 1941–1942* (Lanham, Md.: AltaMira, 2013).
31 Göring to Heydrich, [31] July 1941, trans. from Angrick et al., *Deutsche Besatzungs-herrschaft*, pp. 269–70.
32 Browning, *Origins of the Final Solution*, pp. 244–423.

showed initiative and creativity, but few, if any, signs of moral inhibitions. In Minsk, Kaunas and Riga, Germans murdered local Jews to 'make room' for deportees from the Greater Reich; in the absence of clear orders from Berlin, some of the arriving Jews were shot immediately (in Kaunas and Riga); others were crowded into the completely under-supplied ghettos. German officials exempted Jews deemed fit to work, sometimes including their families, from immediate destruction, which led to so-called 'selections' in ghettos and camps, based on highly random criteria of economic utility, applied, often in an instant, by minor functionaries.

As efficient as mass shootings had turned out to be, alternative methods in the form of gassing had been successfully applied since the beginning of the war during Aktion T4. Following Hitler's decision in August 1941 to stop the T4 programme, its experts stood ready to advise others, especially Himmler, who was keen to dispose of 'useless eaters' among concentration camp prisoners – prompting Aktion 14f13, which, between 1941 and 1943, claimed the lives of up to 20,000 victims – and to lighten the psychological burden of mass shootings for his men. While the RSHA developed gas vans for use in the occupied Soviet Union,[33] local chiefs made their own plans for stationary killing sites. Some, including death camps with mass gassing installations and crematoria in Mogilew and Riga, remained unrealized; others – especially those built under the authority of the Lublin SS and Police Leader Odilo Globocnik – took months to become operational. After the first death camp (Chełmno) created by the Wartheland's Gauleiter Greiser had started to murder Jews and 'gypsies' from the Łódź ghetto in December 1941, there was a considerable time lag before similar sites went into the production of mass death. In the *Generalgouvernement*, Bełżec, under construction since the autumn, started to murder deported Jews in March 1942, followed by Sobibor (May) and Treblinka (July). In the second half of 1942, these camps became the killing sites of Aktion Reinhard, which, together with gassings in the Majdanek concentration camp and ongoing murder actions throughout the region, reduced the roughly 3.2 million Polish Jews living under German rule to an estimated half-million.[34] Simultaneously, most of the remaining Jews in the Nazi-occupied Soviet Union were murdered in another killing sweep, often in conjunction with

33 See Christian Gerlach, *Kalkulierte Morde. Die deutsche Wirtschafts-und Vernichtungspolitik in Weissrussland 1941 bis 1944* (Hamburg: Hamburger Edition, 1999), pp. 764–73.
34 Bogdan Musial (ed.), *Aktion Reinhardt: Der Völkermord an den Juden im Generalgouvernement 1941–1944* (Osnabrück: Fabre, 2004).

the increasingly violent German anti-partisan warfare, which, until the German retreat, claimed the lives of hundreds of thousands of civilians.

As the 'Final Solution of the Jewish question' became the most destructive Nazi genocidal campaign, it spread to other Axis-controlled regions. Almost a million Jews had already been killed, the vast majority in Eastern Europe, when, on 20 January 1942, state secretaries and other officials from a range of German institutions gathered at what became known as the Wannsee Conference. Convened and chaired by Heydrich, the meeting served two main purposes: first, to prepare a coordinated approach in subjecting an estimated 11 million European Jews to a 'Final Solution' that was to start in the Greater Reich and proceed from West to East. 'Work in the East' served as the euphemism used in the conference protocol, combined with the expectation that '[d]oubtless the large majority will be eliminated by natural causes', while the 'final remnant. . .will have to be dealt with appropriately because otherwise, by natural selection, they would form the germ cell of a new Jewish revival'.[35] Second, Heydrich wanted institutional competitors to acknowledge that his RSHA was in charge of the project, despite the fact that the approach sketched out in the protocol hardly qualified as a workable plan, and that even within Himmler's apparatus there were others violently pursuing the 'Jewish question' in their own realm of influence. It took until the spring of 1942 to specify how the deportations were to be organized and what was to happen to the Jews at their destinations. In addition to the mass killing sites in the East that had already proven their effectiveness, Eichmann and his RSHA colleagues created a new murder facility in Auschwitz that was to become emblematic of the post-war perception of the Holocaust.

Auschwitz, located in the German-annexed part of Polish Upper Silesia, had previously served as forced labour pool for the SS, where inmates suffered the broad range of victimization typical of the concentration camp system. It was expanded in the second half of 1941 by adding a large complex in Birkenau to house more than 50,000 Soviet POWs, of whom only a fraction arrived, as the rest had died in Wehrmacht camps. In early September 1941, experimental gassings of inmates deemed unfit to work marked the site's transformation to a death camp that, until January 1945,

---

35 Quoted in Mark Roseman, *The Wannsee Conference and the Final Solution: A Reconsideration* (London: The Folio Society, 2012), p. 116. See also Norbert Kampe and Peter Klein (eds.), *Die Wannsee-Konferenz am 20. Januar 1942. Dokumente, Forschungsstand, Kontroversen* (Cologne: Böhlau, 2013).

claimed the lives of more than 1.1 million victims, the vast majority Jews, but also Soviet POWs, 'gypsies' and members of other outgroups, asphyxiated in gas chambers by SS men applying the pesticide Zyklon B. From July 1942, most of the RSHA deportations from across German-dominated Europe arrived in Birkenau, where 'selections' left a small percentage of the deportees alive for forced labour in private companies (among them IG Farben), while all others were murdered.[36] From early 1943, the construction of large-scale gas chambers with adjacent crematoria allowed for an accelerated murder pace, which reached its height with the arrival of transports from Hungary in mid-1944: between 15 May and 9 July, most of the more than 420,000 Hungarian Jews arriving in Auschwitz-Birkenau were killed on arrival.[37]

In their efforts to organize the 'Final Solution' on a European scale, Eichmann's men had to take into account the constraints emanating from the war – for example, in the form of transport restrictions and labour needs (especially the Wehrmacht's), but also the level of German influence in each country, the interests prevailing among its elites, and the degree of local assistance. The RSHA experts had a comparatively easy task in the occupied parts of Western and Southeastern Europe, but Jewish death rates differed markedly even between adjacent countries, such as the Netherlands (75 per cent), Belgium (40 per cent) and France (25 per cent).[38] Among the factors determining the deadly speed and efficiency of German eliminationist measures throughout Europe, the degree of local collaboration and societal buy-in played a significant, and in some cases crucial, role. Conversely, the same applies to Jewish resistance and escape attempts, the success of which required not only courage and determination in the face of immense obstacles, but also networks of non-Jewish helpers.[39]

36 For a very concise historical overview, see Sybille Steinbacher, *Auschwitz: A History* (New York: ECCO, 2005); more comprehensive is Wacław Długoborski and Franciszek Piper (eds.), *Auschwitz, 1940–1945: Central Issues in the History of the Camp* (5 vols., Oświęcim: Auschwitz-Birkenau State Museum, 2000).

37 Randolph L. Braham, *The Politics of Genocide: The Holocaust in Hungary* (New York: Columbia University Press, 1981); and, most recently, Zoltan Vagi, Laszlo Csősz and Gabor Kadar, *The Holocaust in Hungary: Evolution of a Genocide* (Lanham, Md.: AltaMira, 2013).

38 Pim Griffioen and Ron Zeller, *Jodenvervolging in Nederland, Frankrijk en België 1940–1945. Overeenkomsten, verschillen, oorzaken* (Amsterdam: Boom, 2011). See also Dan Michman (ed.), *Belgium and the Holocaust: Jews, Belgians, Germans* (Jerusalem: Yad Vashem, 1998); Bob Moore, *Survivors: Jewish Self-Help and Rescue in Nazi Occupied Western Europe* (Oxford University Press, 2009).

39 Nechama Tec, *Resilience and Courage: Women, Men, and the Holocaust* (New Haven, Conn., and London: Yale University Press, 2003); Beate Kosmala and Georgi Verbeeck

Anti-Semitism and material interests made some Axis regimes more amenable to German pressure, as in the case of Slovakia: in March 1942, its government was the first to agree to the deportation of the country's Jews (until October, roughly 58,000, mostly to Auschwitz). Yet even the Romanian regime, responsible for the murder of an estimated 350,000 Jews in Bukovina, Bessarabia and Transnistria, kept an eye on the tide of war and, from mid-1942, resisted German requests to hand over its Jews. As determined as Nazi leaders were to kill Europe's Jews, they did not want to jeopardize existing alliances by forcing the issue. The same applied to Italy and Hungary; deportations from there only started after the German occupation, in October 1943 and March 1944 respectively. Wherever the Wehrmacht still managed to gain control over new territory, deadly anti-Jewish violence followed on the soldiers' heels; even during the summer of 1942, when Rommel's troops advanced through North Africa, Himmler stood ready with a special unit to kill the roughly 500,000 Jews in Palestine.[40]

As the regime intensified its war efforts, massive surges in the level of violence engulfed the regions heavily affected by anti-partisan campaigns undertaken jointly by Wehrmacht, SS and police units. Civilian losses in Poland and the Soviet Union are estimated to exceed 2 million, and several hundred thousand in Yugoslavia. While Nazi propaganda tried to utilize 'fighting Jewish Bolshevism' as a pep slogan with pan-European appeal, existing patterns of persecution gained destructive momentum beyond the 'Jewish question', causing the deaths of more than 100,000 Sinti and Roma, and contributing to the 'scorched earth' tactics deployed during the German retreat from the East. Despite imminent defeat, and in stubborn adherence to Hitler's promise of a last-ditch effort toward 'final victory', Nazi officials used their remaining resources to liquidate not only camp inmates and members of other outgroups, but an expanding circle of 'defeatists' among the German population. Mass violence and military aggression had come home to a 'people's community' in ruins.[41]

(eds.), *Facing the Catastrophe: Jews and Non-Jews in Europe During World War II* (New York: Berg, 2011).

40 See Klaus-Michael Mallmann and Martin Cüppers, *Nazi Palestine: The Plans for the Extermination of the Jews in Palestine* (New York: Enigma Books, 2010).

41 Daniel Blatman, *The Death Marches: The Final Phase of Nazi Genocide* (Cambridge, Mass.: Belknap Press of Harvard University Press, 2011); Nikolaus Wachsmann, *Hitler's Prisons: Legal Terror in Nazi Germany* (New Haven, Conn.: Yale University Press, 2004); Andreas Kunz, *Wehrmacht und Niederlage. Die bewaffnete Macht in der Endphase der nationalsozialistischen Herrschaft 1944 bis 1945* (Munich: Oldenbourg, 2005).

8

War crimes trials

DONALD BLOXHAM AND JONATHAN WATERLOW

This chapter examines how perpetrators of breaches of international law were punished during and after the war. Although 'Nuremberg' is best known, it was one of thousands of trials in the post-war period. At least 96,798 Germans and Austrians were convicted of war crimes, crimes against humanity and other Nazi-related offences. Most were sentenced within ten years of the war's end.[1] More than 5,700 Japanese were also indicted, as well as much smaller numbers of Koreans and Taiwanese. We do not apportion our chapter to reflect absolute or relative numbers of suspects tried, but to indicate key themes of principle, practice and representation across them. Our approach is structured around four questions: Why was there a legal response at all? What were the forms and contents of the trials? Why did the punishment programmes come to an end? And how did trial and punishment shape the meaning and memory of conflict?

The trial programmes under consideration comprise: the International Military Tribunal at Nuremberg (IMT), involving twenty-two leading Germans and six organizations; its sibling, the International Military Tribunal for the Far East at Tokyo (IMTFE), involving twenty-eight Japanese military and civilian leaders ('class A' suspects, as opposed to the class B and C suspects comprising the vast majority of Japanese tried after the war); the twelve Nuremberg successor trials (the Nuremberg Military Tribunals (NMTs)), tried under an inter-Allied statute (Control Council Law no. 10 (CCL10)), but by American personnel only, and concerning 185 German 'major war criminals of the second rank', meaning groups of high-ranking soldiers and SS officers,

The authors thank Jared McBride, Devin Pendas, Kim Priemel, Jacques Schuhmacher, David Crowe, and the volume editors for their feedback on drafts of this chapter.
1 The figure of 96,798 comes from Norbert Frei (ed.), *Transnationale Vergangenheitspolitik: Der Umgaging mit deutschen Kriegsverbrechern in Europa nach dem Zweiten Weltkrieg* (Göttingen: Wallstein, 2006), pp. 31–2. Statistics are not available from all countries.

diplomats, civil servants, industrialists, jurists, doctors and scientists; trial programmes instituted by individual victor, liberated and even conquered states within their own boundaries and according to individual states' civilian or military laws, including trials instituted in German-run courts during the occupation; and those cases in which occupying powers acted as sovereign prosecutors within their respective zones, or as colonial authorities in Germany and Southeast Asia. In the space available, we cannot directly address collaboration trials or political lustration (including 'de-Nazification'), quasi-judicial or otherwise, although these programmes certainly comprise important contexts for our discussion, and in some instances it is impossible to delineate them entirely from criminal trials (notably true of the Czech trials and of Soviet trials in their occupation zone of Germany (SBZ)).

Our parameters are 1943–58, although the gravity of the discussion concerns 1945–48. The first trials in Soviet territory began in 1943, as did the evidence-gathering work of the United Nations Commission for the Investigation of War Crimes (UNCIWC; later the UN War Crimes Commission (UNWCC)) and also the Moscow Declaration (30 October 1943). The Declaration warned that those who had taken 'consenting part' in atrocities would 'be sent back to the countries in which their abominable deeds were done in order that they may be judged and punished according to the laws of those liberated countries and of free governments which will be erected therein', while major 'German criminals whose offenses have no particular geographical localization' would be 'punished' – the language was deliberately vague – 'by joint decision of the government of the Allies'.[2] In 1945, the IMT trial was initiated, as were a range of independent trial programmes by victorious and liberated states, as well as trials within occupation zones conducted sometimes by the occupiers, sometimes by the occupied. The following year saw the beginning of the IMTFE, some other national and occupation trial programmes, and the planning and inception of the NMT proceedings. The onset of the Cold War affected most trial programmes; the few that continued beyond 1948 were over or almost completed by 1950–51 – the time, inter alia, of the Korean War. The next great geopolitical development in Europe came in 1955: the final, sovereign emergence of the Federal Republic of Germany (BRD) and the German Democratic Republic (DDR). The following year – which Tony Judt considered the end of this 'post-war

2 Raymond M. Brown, 'The American Perspective on Nuremberg: A Case of Cascading Ironies', in Herbert R. Reginbogin and Christoph Safferling (eds.), *The Nuremberg Trials: International Criminal Law Since 1945* (Munich: K. G. Saur, 2006), pp. 21–9.

decade' – saw the British release war criminals en masse, and the highly symbolic release of the perpetrators of the Oradour-sur-Glane massacre that had framed the French punishment programme for so many in France (French prisons would be empty by 1957), and of the German POWs dubbed criminal by the USSR. American war crimes jails in Japan and Germany were completely emptied in 1958, after years of heavy inmate reduction.

Why legal responses?

The decision to hold trials at all seems surprising: the attempt to prosecute German war crimes in German courts after the First World War, in Leipzig in 1921–27, had proved a fiasco of patriotically motivated acquittals that no one wished to revisit.[3] On the other hand, during the war itself the trial medium had accrued precedents, and not only on the side of the USSR. The Wehrmacht and SS also conducted war crimes investigations against the Allied forces, in some cases leading to military tribunals which, although conducted under German military law, nevertheless often referred to and attempted to draw legitimacy from the Geneva and Hague Conventions.[4]

That the Americans were the instigators and main proponents of transitional justice in the form of military tribunals has long been accepted in Western historiography.[5] Nevertheless, while a consensus had developed in the course of 1942 among the Allies that German war crimes should be met with judicial redress of some kind (as evidenced by the St James's Palace Declaration of 13 January, Roosevelt's statements of 21 August and 7 October, and the announcement, also on 7 October, of the establishment of the UNCIWC/UNWCC), it was the Soviet Foreign Minister, Molotov, who first publicly promoted the idea of a 'special international tribunal' using 'criminal law'.[6] Molotov's proposal treated the Nazi regime itself as criminal; rather than advocating only the pursuit of individuals guilty of specific crimes, he named leading Nazis, including Hitler, Göring, Hess, Goebbels and Himmler, to stand trial to answer for the regime at large. High-ranking Soviet legal

---

3 Gerd Hankel, *Die Leipziger Prozesse: Deutsche Kriegsverbrechen und ihre strafrechtliche Verfolgung nach dem Ersten Weltkrieg* (Hamburg: Hamburger Edition, 2003).

4 Thanks to Jacques Schuhmacher for this point; see also Alfred de Zayas, *The Wehrmacht War Crimes Bureau, 1939–1945* (Lincoln: University of Nebraska Press, 1989).

5 Hilary Earl, *The Nuremberg SS-Einsatzgruppen Trial, 1945–1958: Atrocity, Law, and History* (Cambridge University Press, 2010), p. 22.

6 *Arkhiv Vneshnei Politiki Rossiiskoi Federatsii* (Russian Federation Foreign Policy Archive), hereafter AVPRF, 6/4/4/35/49 (14 October 1942); published the following day in *Pravda*.

theorists had also for some time been developing ideas about war crimes and how to prosecute them. Indeed, Francine Hirsch has shown that the formulation 'crimes against peace' – a major component of the IMT's Charter – was coined by the Soviet scholar A. N. Trainin.[7]

The aim of deterrence was evident from the first Allied trials, conducted during the war by the Soviets in Krasnodar (14–17 July 1943), against Soviet collaborators, and in Kharkov (15–18 December 1943), against three Germans and one collaborator. Krasnodar sentenced eleven Soviet citizens; eight were hanged publicly before crowds of 30,000.[8] Although labelled 'treason' and 'collaboration', the crimes for which they were sentenced were unambiguously war crimes, namely the mass murder of civilians.[9] In Kharkov, all the defendants were sentenced and hanged, this time explicitly for war crimes. The British also pushed to announce publicly that accused war criminals would be sent back to the place of perpetration, with judgment to be exercised by the relevant local power, hoping this would discourage further atrocities.[10] At the war's end, deterrence remained key and the Allies agreed that trials needed to be immediate and demonstrative.

Punitive justice with the aim of future deterrence ran in parallel with the ambition to 're-educate' Germans, a process complemented by the assumption that a demonstration of due legal process would create fertile ground for democracy, however defined. Trials were also intended to create an indelible record of Axis criminality, thus justifying the Allied war effort and Allied hegemony in post-war Europe. The Nuremberg prosecutor Gordon Dean made this plain in a letter to the US Chief Prosecutor in the IMT, Robert H. Jackson: 'One of the primary purposes of the trial of the major war criminals is to document and dramatize for contemporary consumption and for history the means and methods employed by the leading Nazis in their plan to dominate the world and to wage an aggressive war'.[11]

---

7 Francine Hirsch, 'The Soviets at Nuremberg: International Law, Propaganda, and the Making of the Postwar Order', *American Historical Review* 113 (2008), 706–9; cf. A. N. Trainin, *Ugolovnaia otvetstvennost' gitlerovtsev* (Moscow: Iuridicheskoe izdatel'stvo NKIu SSSR, 1944), ch. 5, esp. p. 41.

8 Ilya Bourtman, '"Blood for Blood, Death for Death!" The Soviet Military Tribunal in Krasnodar, 1943', *Holocaust and Genocide Studies* 22 (2008), 250.

9 *The People's Verdict: A Full Report of the Proceedings at the Krasnodar and Kharkov German Atrocity Trials* (London: Hutchinson, 1944), p. 15.

10 Churchill wrote to Stalin strongly advocating this in an early draft of the Moscow Declaration. *Rossiiskii Gosudarstvennyi Arkhiv Sotsial'no-Politicheskoi Istorii* (Russian State Archive of Socio-Political History), 558/11/264/47–50 (13 October 1943).

11 Gordon Dean to Robert Jackson, 11 August 1945, Papers of Robert H. Jackson, Library of Congress, Washington DC, container 107.

Dean's statement hints at a strategic goal that existed alongside the didactic, retributive, reformative and self-justificatory aims of legal recourse. What makes the IMT and the later IMTFE stand out in this period is the scope of their self-assigned remit, and their intent to give a firm basis in hard case law to hitherto precarious and tentative theoretical legal concepts, most notably the attempt to criminalize wars of aggression – a goal endorsed by the USSR just as much as the USA. The agreement for trial, signed by Allied representatives in London on 8 August 1945, affirmed the intention to try 'war criminals whose offences have no particular geographical location, whether they be accused individually or in their capacity as members of organizations or groups or in both categories'. Each defendant faced one or more of four counts (the six organizations were simply to be judged upon whether they were 'criminal'). The first count concerned participation in 'the formulation or execution of a common plan or conspiracy to commit, or which involved the commission of, crimes against peace, war crimes and crimes against humanity'. The second charged complicity in 'the planning, preparation, initiation and waging of wars of aggression, which were also wars in violation of international treaties, agreements and assurances'. The third involved 'war crimes', and the fourth, 'crimes against humanity'.[12] The US prosecution presided over the first count, and sought to connect all Nazi criminality with one central idea: the plan for continental and world domination. War was the ultimate and all-inclusive crime, facilitating and encouraging further atrocities in conquest and pacification; explaining war required recourse to the conspiracy.[13] Further, in the 'conspiracy–criminal organization plan', which sought to establish complicity across a wide range of economic, administrative, political and military institutions in the Third Reich, evidence against individuals could be held against relevant organizations, and vice versa. A finding of criminality against an organization would thus expedite mass criminal prosecutions or de-Nazification, depending on types and levels of culpability, as guilt would hold for every member and the burden of proving innocence would lie with the defendant. In practice, the results were not always those desired by the theory.

In many ways, the IMTFE and NMTs were shaped to consolidate the IMT's successes and to compensate for some of its failings. 'Crimes against peace'

---

12 Text of London Agreement, appended Charter of the IMT and the indictment are all reproduced in International Military Tribunal, *Trial of the Major War Criminals Before the International Military Tribunal* (42 vols., Nuremberg, 1947–49), vol. 1.

13 On the Bernays plan from which some of this thinking flowed, see Bradley F. Smith, *The Road to Nuremberg* (New York: Basic Books, 1981).

remained vital in the IMTFE, though to a significantly lesser degree before the NMTs. As a British Foreign Office legal advisor warned bluntly, a failure by the IMTFE to convict under this charge 'would inter alia mean...that the Judgment of the Nuremberg Tribunal was based...in part upon bad law'. The Dutch also pressured Judge Bernard Röling to desist from his opposition to this charge.[14] A conspiracy to commit crimes against peace was alleged to have existed among Japan's civilian and military leaders, with the aim, from 1928, of seizing control of East Asia and the Pacific and Indian Oceans, but for this the prosecution had little evidence other than the war itself; by pursuing this line, nonetheless, the prosecution 'pulled the carpet from under the more plausible notion' for which proof could have been presented – that a select few of those defendants (and others not on trial) had held such aims and pursued them.[15] For lack of evidence tying the defendants directly to the substantive crimes, the notion of a 'conspiracy' was repeatedly evoked in order 'to produce guilt by association'.[16] The number of convictions on this shaky ground was but one reason why the IMTFE did not meet the standards of the IMT or NMTs in their attempts to be fair and to be seen to be fair.[17]

The priority attached to outlawing aggressive war/crimes against peace requires explanation, given that this sought to stigmatize one of the instruments by which great powers assert themselves. The goal makes some sense in light of the UN Charter, with its determination to restore respect for, and sovereignty within, state boundaries. It was deemed legitimate to infringe the defendants' state's sovereignty by trial, provided that the defendants had themselves already infringed the sovereignty principle by their warfare. But this could hardly assuage all legal-strategic concerns. Britain correctly anticipated problems analogous with the 1941 Atlantic Charter, insofar as that clarion call for freedom in the face of fascist and communist imperialism touched on sovereign rights of self-determination for peoples under pre-existing colonial occupation. The potential for inadvertent Allied self-constraint by lawmaking, and for hypocrisy, was still further magnified when confronting Japanese colonialism in Southeast Asia, given the backdrop

---

14 Erik Beckett, quoted in Kirsten Sellars, 'Imperfect Justice at Nuremberg and Tokyo', *European Journal of International Law* 21 (2011), 1097–8, quote at 1097.
15 Neil Boister and Robert Cryer, *The Tokyo International Military Tribunal: A Reappraisal* (Oxford University Press, 2008), pp. 73, 141–2, quote at p. 329.
16 Ibid., p. 245.
17 On the NMT programme, see Kevin Jon Heller, *The Nuremberg Military Tribunals and the Origins of International Criminal Law* (Oxford University Press, 2011); Kim Priemel and Alexa Stiller (eds.), *NMT: Die Nürnberger Militärtribunale zwischen Geschichte, Gerechtigkeit und Rechtschöpfung* (Hamburg: Hamburger Edition, 2013).

of American and European imperial ventures in that region, and the context of attempted post-war re-establishment of empire in Indonesia and Indochina (e.g. Dutch resisters to Nazi occupation played an important role – war crimes and all – in the Indonesian War of Independence, 1945–49[18]). It was one thing condemning the sort of expansionism that had shattered the interwar Paris dispensation, but quite another for the victors to create a precedent for the condemnation of their own foreign adventures.

The Allies took the easiest and most realistic, but least externally convincing, solution: they made their own trials ad hoc rather than part of the permanent architecture of the post-war world, establishing in the terms of the international trials that these addressed only Axis criminality. But at the IMT and, especially, the IMTFE, the Americans in particular tried to establish a philosophy to justify this. Jackson was clearly aware of the problem: in his closing speech he reflected that the 'intellectual bankruptcy and moral perversion of the Nazi regime might have been *no concern to international law* had it not been utilized to goosestep the Herrenvolk across international frontiers'. As Kirsten Sellars notes, Jackson oscillated between the philosophies of legal naturalism and realism, but here came down firmly for the latter: 'The law', he said, 'unlike politics, does not concern itself with the good or evil in the *status quo*, nor with the merits of the grievances against it. It merely requires that the *status quo* be not attacked by violent means and that policies be not advanced by war'.[19] Joseph Keenan, American Chief Prosecutor before the IMTFE, was yet blunter. 'If Japan had the right to change its geographical and economic status suddenly by war', he argued, 'then every other nation as badly situated, from the economic standpoint, had the same right'.[20] Keenan's drift was not missed by Radhabinod Pal, the Indian judge who issued the most famous of the three dissenting opinions on the IMTFE's judgment, and the only one insisting that no defendant was guilty. He did not doubt that grievous crimes had been committed during warfare and occupation, but questioned the competence of the IMTFE, criticized the use of *ex post facto* law and the tenuous conspiracy charge, and referred to the Allied area and atomic bombing campaigns to underline his contention of tainted victors' justice. Adverting to the prosecuting powers' record of imperialist violence in Asia, he also observed their interest

---

18 Peter Romijn, 'Learning on "the Job": Dutch War Volunteers Entering the Indonesian War of Independence, 1945–46', *Journal of Genocide Research* 14 (2012), 317–36.
19 Kirsten Sellars, *'Crimes Against Peace' and International Law* (Cambridge University Press, 2013), p. 119; emphasis is Sellars's.
20 Sellars, 'Imperfect Justice', 1095.

in maintaining or restoring 'the very *status quo* which might have been organized and hitherto maintained only by force by pure opportunist "Have and Holders"'. He correctly intuited the unjust logic of Keenan's and Jackson's pronouncements, given that much of humankind 'faced not only the menace of totalitarianism but the *actual plague* of imperialism'.[21]

Trial forms and contents

If some of the intention behind the trials thus fed into the broader desire to create a stable post-war order, albeit with divergent views among the major power brokers as to what constituted the most desirable instantiation of stability, trials were only one part of a much larger complex of political activity. The determinants of stability in Europe were the unconditional victory over Germany and, soon thereafter, the consolidation of transnational state blocs under superpower supervision, which ensured that the hot conflicts of the Cold War would not be conducted in Europe. But we might also think of the flight and expulsion of 12 million ethnic Germans from East Central and Southeastern Europe into a greatly reduced Germany. This was a principal instrument to remove the basis of future German irredentist claims and internal instability in those countries which had had large German minorities. It effectively created a demographic-territorial fait accompli of the sort that other programmes of ethnic cleansing had done over recent generations in Europe. The nationalist agendas of extant or returned exile elites from Poland, Czechoslovakia and Hungary dovetailed with these broader strategic designs of the Big Three Allies.[22]

The expulsions were part of a still more complex phenomenon. Across Europe, the prosecution of genuine war criminals was frequently coupled with a second, more domestic concern: the purge of collaborators and potential political opponents. Ethnic Germans were often seen as both. An early and significant legal reckoning with the ethnic Germans was clearly a part of legitimating expulsions from East Central Europe. Obversely, as Benjamin Frommer has detailed in the Czechoslovak case, trials of ethnic Germans diminished relatively quickly in proportion to trials of titular nationals, because detainment and trial could delay expulsion.[23]

---

21 Sellars, 'Crimes Against Peace', p. 237. Emphasis in original.
22 Donald Bloxham, *The Final Solution: A Genocide* (Oxford University Press, 2009), pp. 105, 303.
23 Benjamin Frommer, *National Cleansing: Retribution Against Nazi Collaborators in Postwar Czechoslovakia* (Cambridge University Press, 2005); chapters by Wlodzimierz Borodziej, Katerina Kocova and Jaroslav Kucera in Frei (ed.), *Transnationale Vergangenheitspolitik*.

As in Czechoslovakia, so in the SBZ/DDR: owing to a lack of concrete figures, as well as significant overlap between prosecutions for war crimes and for 'political crimes', we can only note that, between 1945 and 1955, some 70,000 Germans there were sentenced by Soviet courts, of whom about 34,000 were POWs and the rest civilians.[24] We may assume, then, that these figures include far more purge than war crimes prosecutions.

'Purge' is a term most commonly associated with Stalinist politics, but after 1945, political self-lustration was practised to some degree in almost every European country. Britain and the USA were exceptions, having at no point experienced occupation and hence significant collaboration, beyond the Channel Islands, whose experience is conveniently disregarded in British war memory. Often, the scale of trials for indigenous collaborators in Europe was of a different order to that of war criminals.[25] In much of Northern, Western and Southern Europe, collaboration trials accounted for thousands and tens of thousands, rather than tens or hundreds of war crimes convictions (Belgium, at least eighty-three convictions; Denmark, seventy-seven; Norway, ninety-five; Greece, fourteen; Italy, around thirty-five). Shortly after the liberation of the Netherlands, for instance, up to 150,000 Dutch National Socialists were interned, awaiting possible investigation. Over the next six years, 16,000 were tried for collaboration and most convicted; this stands against 241 convicted for war crimes.[26] And while France tried more war criminals than either Britain or the USA (2,345 convicted within France, and at least 780 in the French zone of Germany), the purge of collaborators was more important symbolically within France, as well as quantitatively greater, touching the lives of many more French people. Thus before the establishment of the post-liberation French government after August 1944, between 9,000 and 15,000 French citizens were executed summarily, or after 'kangaroo' trials. From 1945 onward, properly constituted French courts passed another 1,500 death sentences, and 40,000 prison sentences.[27]

24 Cf. Andreas Hilger and Mike Schmeitzner, 'Einleitung: Deutschlandpolitik und Strafjustiz. Zur Tätigkeit sowjetischer Militärtribunale in Deutschland 1945–1955', in Andreas Hilger, Mike Schmeitzner and Ute Schmidt (eds.), *Sowjetische Militärtribunale* (2 vols., Cologne: Böhlau, 2003), vol. II, pp. 14, 18–19.

25 Adalbert Rückerl, *NS-Verbrechen vor Gericht* (Heidelberg: Müller, 1982), pp. 102–4.

26 See the chapter by Dick de Mildt and Joggli Meihuizen in Frei (ed.), *Transnationale Vergangenheitspolitik*. That chapter suggests 100,000 initial internees, whereas Romijn, 'Learning', 322, cites 120,000–150,000.

27 Henry Rousso, *The Vichy Syndrome: History and Memory in France Since 1944* (Cambridge, Mass.: Harvard University Press, 1991); Philippe Bourdrel, *L'Épuration Sauvage, 1944–1945* (Paris: Perrin, 2002), pp. 533–9.

Some of the explanation for these differentials lies in different timelines of redress. National judiciaries sometimes waited for the IMT's judgment to provide direction and the legitimacy of precedent. Some states also had to wait for the extradition of wanted criminals. But one also suspects that many states were more immediately interested in cleansing their own bodies politic to legitimate new orders than with charting the range of substantive crimes committed in their territory that were sometimes perceived, problematically, to have been the sole preserve of Germany.[28] After all, Poland, which also relied on many extraditions, tried far more war criminals in absolute numbers (between 1944 and 1985, Polish courts tried in excess of 20,000 defendants, including 5,450 German nationals), and in proportion to collaborators, than did most other states. Although Poland certainly also used its legal system to declare entire groups criminal in order to facilitate the expulsion of Ukrainians and ethnic Germans from its territory, Poland's extensive engagement with genocide and other atrocities has never received the historiographical attention it might have done, most likely due to its geopolitical location after 1945.[29]

In its own territory, the USSR punished any citizens deemed to have collaborated (between 1943 and 1953, over 320,000 were arrested on such charges),[30] and did so under some of the same laws used against war criminals.[31] A key piece of legislation employed to prosecute German war crimes was *ukaz* 39, introduced on 19 April 1943, which punished fascist violence and atrocities against Soviet citizens and POWs. But *ukaz* 39 was intended first and foremost to penalize collaboration: of 81,870 cases conducted under this law up to 1952, 'only' 25,209 were directed against non-Soviets.[32] Soviet sentences were usually harsher than Western ones – typically ten or twenty-five years, often with hard labour (*katorga*). Up to 1947, when it temporarily abolished capital punishment, the USSR also sentenced at least 1,161 Germans to death for war and Nazi crimes.[33] To do so, they made use of CCL10, Soviet law (drawn from that of the RSFSR)

28 See István Deák, Jan Gross and Tony Judt (eds.), *The Politics of Retribution in Europe: World War II and its Aftermath* (Princeton University Press, 2000).
29 E.g. Alexander Prusin, 'Poland's Nuremberg: The Seven Court Cases of the Supreme National Tribunal, 1946–1948', *Holocaust and Genocide Studies* 24 (2010), 1–2, 6.
30 O. B. Mozokhin, *Pravo na repressii: Vnesudebnye polnomochiia organov gosudarstvennoi bezopastnosti (1918–1953)* (Moscow: Kuchkovo pole, 2006), pp. 353–462.
31 *Ukaz* 39 and the Soviet/RSFSR Criminal Code; not CCL10.
32 Andreas Hilger, '"Die Gerechtigkeit nehme ihren Lauf"? Die Bestrafung deutscher Kriegs-und Gewaltverbrecher in der Sowjetunion und der SBZ/DDR' (hereafter, 'Sowjetunion'), in Frei (ed.), *Transnationale Vergangenheitspolitik*, pp. 200–1.
33 Ibid., pp. 193–4.

and *ukaz* 39. Along with the continued deportations of 'suspect' nationalities from the newly acquired Soviet territories,[34] the confinement and 'filtration' of returning Soviet POWs in Gulag-like camps on suspicion of collaboration,[35] and countless expulsions from the Communist Party itself,[36] prosecutions under the *ukaz* were just one element of the broader project of 'cleansing' post-war Soviet society.

The importance of the trials' didactic message explains why only eighteen of the thousands of Soviet trials were conducted publicly; straightforward punishments were numerically greater, but control over the message of the trials was accorded a much higher value. In the public Soviet trials, defendants were carefully selected to represent a broad spectrum of German perpetrators, drawn from differing ranks, units and organizations, just as in the American NMTs and in the IMT itself;[37] the National Socialist system was thus indicted at large. Collective guilt was, indeed, central to all Soviet trials; this is unsurprising for two related reasons. First, the Soviets saw the invasion and occupation of the USSR as a crime in which all German military and political organs were complicit. For them, the notion of guilt via association embodied in the 'criminal organizations' statute of the IMT and of CCL10 (Article 2.1(d)) was not so readily disempowered as it was by the Americans in light of the IMT judgment, and by the British in light of both that judgment and their own prior misgivings. Second, as Hirsch has shown, ideas of mass complicity shaded imperceptibly into the amorphous Soviet law on 'counter-revolutionary organizations'; Trainin dedicated a whole chapter of his book on punishing 'the Hitlerites' to this concept, reminding the reader of its importance, as elucidated by Vyshinskii during the Moscow show trials.[38] Indeed, the idea of collective guilt fitted well with existing Soviet ideological (and legal) understandings, in which 'membership' of another large 'organization' – a class – was not only taken to be proof of criminal,

---

34 Ronald Grigor Suny and Terry Martin (eds.), *A State of Nations: Empire and Nation-Making in the Age of Lenin and Stalin* (New York: Oxford University Press, 2001), pp. 14–15.
35 Mark Edele, *Soviet Veterans in the Second World War: A Popular Movement in an Authoritarian Society, 1941–1991* (New York: Oxford University Press, 2008), pp. 103–22.
36 Elena Zubkova, *Russia After the War: Hopes, Illusions, and Disappointments, 1945–1957* (New York: M. E. Sharpe, 1998), pp. 79–82, 133–5.
37 Alexander Prusin, '"Fascist Criminals to the Gallows!" The Holocaust and Soviet War Crimes Trials, December 1945–February 1946', *Holocaust and Genocide Studies* 17 (2003), 1.
38 Hirsch, 'Soviets at Nuremberg', 707–8; Trainin, *Ugolovnaia otvetstvennost'*, ch. 8, and p. 85 on Vyshinskii.

counter-revolutionary intent, but, moreover, was a category that was in practice ascribed, and hence controlled, by the state.[39]

All this raises the question of to what extent Soviet trials were 'show trials'. Before answering that question, the concept 'show trial' requires further consideration, since all trials consist of the execution, but also the 'performance' of justice.[40] Indeed, the Russian term, *pokazatel'nyi protsess*, unlike the English expression, does not carry strong pejorative connotations of falsehood, implying instead an active, educative purpose. This brings us closer to the reality of the Soviet war crimes trials, but also, in fact, to that of counterpart Western initiatives. The question is of the balance between due process and performance: if, where and how far the former was subordinated to the latter; where adherence to the letter of the law might coexist with infringement of its spirit, and where political priorities could coexist harmlessly with the needs of justice.

Certainly, the Soviet trials featured personnel who had been involved in the famous Moscow show trials of 1936–37, yet this in itself is hardly significant; the leading legal professionals of the country would inevitably be involved in such significant, well-publicized trials. More importantly, Soviet law was notoriously 'flexible', and that the elements of it utilized by Soviet prosecutions were the infamous Articles 58 and 59 (counter-revolutionary and anti-state crimes) only re-emphasizes this point.[41] Nevertheless, the Soviet trials were actually a mixture of justice and injustice, of stable and unstable law. A useful analogy can be found in Soviet-made 'documentary' films of Auschwitz: although many of the iconic individual shots were staged and scripted, they were not straightforwardly 'false' in what they sought to portray; likewise, while most of the Soviet war crimes trials (we do not include here the connected yet distinct trials against civilians for political reasons) were staged, the crimes of which defendants were accused were real, and many, if not most, defendants were probably complicit in them. This helps explain why Soviet trial records have not infrequently proven reasonably reliable sources for Holocaust historians.

39 Sheila Fitzpatrick, 'Ascribing Class: The Construction of Social Identity in Soviet Russia', *Journal of Modern History* 65 (1993), 745–70. This is not to say that there was no individuating potential for the treatment of particular offenders.

40 Mark Osiel, *Mass Atrocity, Collective Memory and the Law* (New Brunswick, NJ: Transaction, 1999); Lawrence Douglas, *The Memory of Judgment* (New Haven, Conn.: Yale University Press, 2001).

41 Friedrich-Christian Schroeder, 'Rechtsgrundlagen der Verfolgung deutscher Zivilisten durch Sowjetische Militärtribunale', in Hilger et al. (eds.), *Sowjetische Militärtribunale*, vol. II, pp. 48–53.

A striking distinction between the Soviet and Anglo-American trials is that the former almost always produced a confession, while the latter rarely did. The immediate suspicion is that confessions were obtained under physical threat and torture; there are innumerable accounts of the NKVD (predecessor of the KGB) using such methods, and although this does not prove a rule, it does imply a significantly more frequent practice than, say, the violence and duress deployed by some American military war crimes investigators for the 'Dachau' trials.[42] Whether or not torture was routinely used by the Soviets to extract confessions, the consistency with which confessions were made demonstrates an important ideological element which shaped the nature of the Soviet trials. This was a dedication to an ideologically defined 'truth': whether or not a confession described events that had actually taken place, it was vital in the USSR for the official 'truth' to be performed; the version of events recorded was considered to be truthful once spoken in confession, and the Soviet understanding of 'guilt' was such that it had to be recognized by the perpetrator themselves for the matter to be considered closed.

If the trials were a performance, then the Soviets undeniably wrote the script beforehand. This was far less frequently the case in trials conducted by the Western Allies, though recent scholarship tends toward confirming the view recorded by *Newsweek*'s Robert Shaplen of the controversial Yamashita trial in Manila in late 1945. In 'the opinion of probably every correspondent covering the trial the [American] military commission came into the courtroom the first day with the decision already in its collective pocket'.[43]

Even if the defendants' words were not scripted, one could bar them from broaching certain topics, or at least bar the court from taking judicial notice of those topics. Here, every power had some desire for censorship. The fact that the Allies explicitly could not themselves be placed in the dock meant that the image of the war and of war crimes to emerge from the trials was exclusively one of Axis wrongdoing. The British firebombing of Dresden; the Soviet massacre at Katyn; and the American atomic bombing of Hiroshima and Nagasaki were not to feature. Similarly, the 'common international good' was clearly served in British and American eyes by the careful avoidance in court of any indictment of the Japanese emperor. The Western Allies

---

42 See Tomaz Jardim, *The Mauthausen Trial: American Military Justice in Germany* (Cambridge, Mass.: Harvard University Press, 2012), pp. 82–3.

43 Allan A. Ryan, *Yamashita's Ghost: War Crimes, MacArthur's Justice and Command Accountability* (Lawrence: University Press of Kansas, 2012). Shaplen quote from Peter Maguire, *Law and War: An American Story* (New York: Columbia University Press, 2001), p. 138.

kept the ace of prosecution up their sleeves, but the paramountcy of political stability ultimately overrode the demands of the legal and historical record.[44]

While the British and Americans generally left the script more open-ended, they nevertheless controlled which characters would appear on stage; the exemption of Hirohito was only the most obvious case. We might also refer to the immunity granted to Japanese Unit 731,[45] which had conducted experiments in chemical and biological warfare, in order that the USA might exploit its research expertise, or the 'leniency' shown to the managers and owners of the *zaibatsu*, the industrial and financial conglomerates complicit in both militarism and POW abuse. Or SS chief Karl Wolff, who also evaded Allied prosecution owing to his usefulness to American intelligence; or Field Marshal Erich von Manstein, who would never have been indicted had Britain been left to its own devices. Consider also Greece, where the government and administrative officials who had collaborated with the Nazis were now strongly backed by the British in the desire to prevent the communist resistance gaining power; here, there was practically no interest in holding trials.[46]

If one could decide who appeared on the stage, one could also exercise control over the relative prominence of different players, largely via prioritization. The American promotion of the trial of Nazi doctors and scientists to the opening case of the NMT programme evinced a desire to begin with a likely 'winner', as opposed to a more geopolitically controversial trial of industrialists, whose outcome was less certain.[47] A very different example is the first trial conducted by Britain in Singapore: the January 1946 proceedings against Captain Gozawa Sadaichi and nine others had distinct propaganda value, given that it occurred simultaneously with trials of anti-British Indian National Army members in Delhi (the 'Red Fort trial' and its successors) on charges of murder, torture and, effectively, treason. The Sadaichi trial conveniently revealed the Japanese torture of Indian POWs who refused

---

44 Yuma Totani, *The Tokyo War Crimes Trial: The Pursuit of Justice in the Wake of World War II* (Cambridge, Mass.: Harvard University Asia Center, 2009), pp. 43–62.

45 The USSR, however, tried twelve members of Unit 731 in Khabarovsk during 25–30 December 1949; they received varying labour camp sentences, but were repatriated in 1956. *Materialy sudebnogo protsessa po delu vyshikh voennosluzhashchikh iaponskoi armii, obviniaemykh v podgotovke i premenenii bakteriologicheskogo oruzhiia* (Moscow: Gosudarstvennoe izdatel'stvo politicheskoi literatury, 1950).

46 See Hagen Fleischer's chapter in Frei (ed.), *Transnationale Vergangenheitspolitik*; Tony Judt, *Postwar: A History of Europe Since 1945* (London: William Heinemann, 2005), ch. 2; Mark Mazower, *Inside Hitler's Greece: The Experience of Occupation, 1941–44* (New Haven, Conn.: Yale University Press, 2001), p. 374.

47 Paul Weindling, 'Ärzte als Richter', in C. Wiesemann and A. Frewer (eds.), *Medizin und Ethik im Zeichen von Auschwitz* (Erlangen: Palm Enke, 1985), pp. 31–44.

to join the INA, thus implying that opposition to British rule was neither widespread nor voluntary.[48]

All prosecuting states could also exploit the concepts of 'representative' defendants and 'representative' examples of Axis criminality in order to further their own interpretations of what was most important to say about the sources, manifestations and meaning of that criminality. The notion of 'representative examples' actually emphasized some rather unrepresentative instances of atrocity, as with the American and British focus at the IMT trial on 'orthodox' German concentration camps rather than Polish extermination centres, or the French promotion before the IMT of former resisters and a range of other victim-witnesses, none of whom was Jewish.[49]

Across the post-war world, most trials concerning Axis criminality addressed 'conventional' war crimes, as well as other substantive crimes that might today (and were sometimes then) called crimes against humanity – that is, atrocities committed against servicemen in the field or in incarceration, or against civilians individually or en masse. All of the cases concerning the approximately 5,700 Japanese Class B and C suspects fell into these categories, as did parts of the IMTFE. Alongside the staples of massacre, enslavement, torture and deprivation, gendered criminality was also occasionally revealed. Yuma Totani's scrutiny of the Tokyo trial records has shown that, contrary to previous beliefs, some IMTFE prosecutors, notably the Chinese and Dutch, did try to draw attention to Japanese sexual violence perpetrated in the course of warfare and colonization.[50] Likewise, a French court convicted a Japanese civilian who had forced women on Java into prostitution in the form of sexual slavery for the military.[51] In Europe, the range of atrocities was broader still, reflecting the peculiar extent and character of Nazi criminality. For instance, the American zonal 'Dachau' series, conducted by the US Army, tried 1,030 staff of various concentration camps and the Hadamar 'euthanasia' institution, and 646 defendants accused of war crimes against American aviators and ground troops.[52] Within this

---

48 Colin Sleeman (ed.), *The Trial of Gozawa Sadaichi and Nine Others* (London: William Hodge, 1948); Arujunan Narayanan, 'Japanese Atrocities and British Minor War Crimes Trials After World War II in the East', *Jebat* 33 (2006), 1–28, here 12.

49 Donald Bloxham, *Genocide on Trial: War Crimes Trials in the Formation of Holocaust History and Memory* (Oxford University Press, 2001), chs. 2–3.

50 Totani, *Tokyo*, pp. 120–1, 125–7, 153, 178–86.

51 Robert Barr Smith, 'Japanese War Crimes Trials', *World War II* (September 1996). www.historynet.com/japanese-war-crime-trials.htm (accessed 7 November 2014).

52 Lisa Yavnai, 'Military Justice: The US Army War Crimes Trials in Germany, 1944–1947' (PhD dissertation, London School of Economics, 2007).

vast mass of horror, what were the possibilities for and constraints on the description of the most extreme German crimes?

The prevalent view remains that the Soviet Union ignored or even repressed knowledge of the Holocaust to avoid highlighting the specificity of any one ethnic group within the suffering inflicted upon the USSR. Certainly, the context of increasing state anti-Semitism cannot be dismissed.[53] Nevertheless, the orthodox view is not quite accurate: the Soviet media followed no consistent practice in the reporting of atrocities against Jews. As cuts made from contemporary newsreel and documentary film footage show, while the Jewish identity of Nazi victims might be elided, there was no clear policy dictating this, and state-backed films, such as Mark Donskoi's *The Unvanquished* (*Nepokorennye*, 1945), even specifically highlighted the fate of the Jews.[54]

Since the 1990s, Western scholarship has come to rest on a more Holocaust-oriented view of the war, which is an important corrective to an earlier view in which the Holocaust was largely absent; but we have yet also to come to terms with a Soviet-centred view. Of the Soviet dead (27 million, of whom roughly two-thirds were civilians),[55] about 3 million were Soviet Jews. It should not diminish the fate of those Jewish victims, nor detract from the particularly intensive and fervent Nazi pursuit of Jews among all victim groups, to note the numerical fact that the great majority of Soviet dead were not Jewish. Moreover, Slavs were not much higher than Jews in the Nazis' racial hierarchy, as the Soviet leadership was plainly aware: in drafting the Nuremberg indictment, the Soviets wanted the racial motivation for Nazi mass killing made clear, but, while they accepted reference to Jewish victims of Nazi ideology, they nevertheless wanted Slav (or just Russian) victims noted, too, and expected them to be accorded higher priority.[56]

53 G. V. Kostyrchenko, *Stalin protiv 'kosmopolitov'. Vlast' i evreiskaia intelligentsiia v SSSR* (Moscow: Rosspen, 2009).

54 Jeremy Hicks, *First Films of the Holocaust: Soviet Cinema and the Genocide of the Jews, 1938–1946* (Pittsburgh, Pa.: University of Pittsburgh Press, 2012).

55 Estimates vary; these figures are lower than some. Cf. David R. Stone's chapter in Volume I, and Richard Bessel's in Volume III of this work.

56 Vyshinskii to Molotov on Rudenko's amendments to the indictment, AVPRF, 6/7/20/208/12 (13 October 1945): 'When listing the national and racial groups against which the fascists carried out a policy of mass destruction, Slavs must also be added (so not just Jews, Gypsies)'. For an indication of victim hierarchy, see Molotov, Beria, Malenkov and Mikoian to Stalin: '[The Nazis pursued] the physical destruction of the adult population, of women, the elderly, and children, especially of Russians, Belorussians, Ukrainians and the widespread destruction of Jews'. Ibid., 29 (16 October 1945).

In truth, the extermination of European Jewry was not at the top of any of the victors' agendas (the mass murder of Romani and Sinti did not figure at all); nor would 'the Holocaust' as we now understand it begin to take conceptual form in the West until the late 1950s. In the DDR, as Norbert Frei puts it, 'the murder of European Jews never developed into a topic of itself', in scholarly or popular understanding.[57] In states which had colluded by omission or commission in the 'Final Solution', full confrontation with that crime could fall victim to the logic of state re-formation based on the myth of opposition to Nazism and its crimes. In a related but different sense, there was often a tension between the national cleavage of the various trial programmes in existence and the international nature of Nazi criminality, in terms of the locus and coordination of the crimes and the profile of the victims. (The NMT programme (see below) was something of an exception to this, perhaps precisely because it was not a national programme.) The fate of the Jews as a diaspora community was an emblematic Nazi crime; but as a dispersed minority, who was consistently to take up the cause of Jewish suffering in a world in which the emphasis was on the restoration of state boundaries and sovereignty, and, essentially, on putting one's own affairs in order? This question still remains to be answered in the case of the Romani.

This argument about attention to the Holocaust – or lack thereof – should not be taken to extremes. There were certainly occasions when aspects of it (rarely its full scope) came to the fore in the courtroom, especially in national trial series conducted in areas where the genocide had actually taken place – albeit that many such trials had very little impact outside the country in question. In Poland, for instance, state courts tried Rudolph Höss, former commandant of Auschwitz-Birkenau, and examined the operations of Chełmno in the Warthegau area of western Poland, during the trial of Arthur Greiser, the former governor of that region. Moreover, in 1951, West German courts used the authority devolved to them the previous year to try a case involving the Treblinka extermination centre.[58] For the stimulation of more high-profile international reportage, though, and more attention to the central German authorities responsible for genocide and other crimes with no one geographical location, the NMT programme was obviously important.

---

57 Norbert Frei, 'Auschwitz and the Germans: History, Knowledge, and Memory', in Neil Gregor (ed.), *Nazism, War and Genocide* (University of Exeter Press, 2005), p. 164.
58 Adalbert Rückerl, *NS-Vernichtungslager im Spiegel deutscher Strafprozesse* (Munich: dtv, 1977), pp. 331–46; Prusin, 'Poland's Nuremberg'; Helge Grabitz and Justizbehörde Hamburg, *Täter und Gehilfen des Endlösungswahns: Hamburger Verfahren wegen NS-Gewaltverbrechen 1946–1996* (Hamburg: Ergebnisse, 1999), p. 11.

When considering the representation of atrocities and genocide in the NMT trials, it is important to remember that, to an extent, the Office, Chief of Counsel for War Crimes (OCCWC) reproduced Jackson's view of specific crimes against humanity as an offshoot of crimes against peace and the conspiracy thereto. But there were also important developments toward a different paradigm of prosecution, alongside increasing expertise in analysing the power structures and multifarious activities of the Nazi-German state. Unlike the pursuit of *Tatkomplexe* – clusters of crime, including mass exterminations – by the authorities of the BRD in later years, some of the subsequent trials were concerned with one group or more of related *criminals* (related, that is, within the German power structure), as in the military 'High Command' case and the '*Einsatzgruppen* trial' of SS killing squad leaders.[59] In cases of that sort, the types of criminals identified by the OCCWC, with its determination to indict representatives of the full breadth of the German state, significantly dictated the sorts of crimes that were brought to consideration. Nevertheless, the OCCWC did differentiate with increasing thematic precision between the categories of crime that those defendants had committed. For instance, in the 'RuSHA' case, against leaders of the SS Race and Settlement Office, there were extensive investigations into the intertwined histories of expulsion, forced 'Germanization' and the kidnapping of children. Further, in cases like the 'Medical' trial and the 'Hostages'/'Balkan Generals'/'Southeastern Generals' case, as this was variously dubbed, the crimes considered seemed to have dictated the choice of defendants more than the other way round. The Medical trial concerned much more than just the activities of doctors, and in fact was a composite title for quite distinct investigations into themes like 'euthanasia' and human experimentation. And while the industrialist trials were, by their titles, themed according to the firms in question, the similarity of charges across the trials shows a clear conceptualization of crime 'clusters'. The neologism 'genocide' itself was also invoked more frequently at the NMTs than the IMT; while it was used more as a device for framing Nazi intentions in a historical sense than as an organizing legal concept, its presence nevertheless

---

59 For some similarities, too, in the 'RuSHA' (*Rasse-und Siedlungshauptamt* – SS Race and Settlement Office) case, see Alexa Stiller, 'Die frühe Strafverfolgung der nationalsozialistischen Vertreibungs- und Germanisierungsverbrechen: Der "RuSHA Prozess" in Nürnberg 1947–1948', in Timm C. Richter (ed.), *Krieg und Verbrechen. Situation und Intention: Fallbeispiele* (Munich: Peter Lang, 2006), pp. 231–41, here p. 239. On *Tatkomplexe*, see Erich Haberer, 'History and Justice: Paradigms of the Prosecution of Nazi Crimes', *Holocaust and Genocide Studies* 19 (2005), 487–519.

indicates an increasing macro-level discernment within the broader and less precise category of crimes against humanity.[60]

Ending the punishment programmes

The number of trials and convictions under Soviet courts was far greater than in the West, but in addition to confirming that law was ever an instrument of the revolution, this fact says something about the political decision for effective amnesties in the West. Indeed, once we move from the numbers and nature of prosecution to the rhythms of justice in the post-war period, we encounter significant points of comparison across place and regime. Soviet and East German prisons were entirely or substantially emptied of war criminals at almost exactly the same time in the later 1950s as British, French or American jails, whether in Europe or Southeast Asia. In Japan, all those convicted and held in Sugamo prison were released in 1958 – the last IMTFE convict had been freed in 1956 – principally because the USA sought to develop its occupation into an alliance with Japan. Whatever the significance of the legal developments of 1945–46 for the future of inter-national law and norm articulation, in the political arena these releases signified the prioritization of politics over law, albeit that the convicts of the IMT, uniquely, could not be released without the (unforthcoming) permission of the Soviets.[61]

In brief, the story is this. In 1947, serious schisms developed in the Council of Foreign Ministers of the 'Big Four' powers; the Truman Doctrine was announced; Stalinization intensified in eastern Germany and throughout the Soviet sphere; and communists and socialists were evicted from various coalition governments in the West. If legal and quasi-legal purges had aimed to secure and legitimate new orders, the cause of consolidating national unity increasingly meant that, from 1947, sentences became less severe and increas-ing numbers simply escaped trial or purge. Increasing amnesties or rough equivalents were the order of the day for certain categories of 'collaborator', as, for instance, in Austria and France in 1947. Note also the French Bataillon d'Infanterie Légère d'Outre-Mer, created in 1948 for participation in the 'First Indochina War', which comprised erstwhile collaborators from the Légion

---

60 Heller, *Nuremberg Military Tribunals*; Priemel and Stiller (eds.), *NMT*; Earl, *Einsatz-gruppen Trial*.
61 Norman J. W. Goda, *Tales from Spandau: Nazi Criminals and the Cold War* (Cambridge University Press, 2006).

des volontaires français contre le bolchevisme and the Waffen-SS Division 'Charlemagne' – political prisoners now serving in return for suspensive pardons.[62] In Italy, the process had begun in June 1946 with the Togliatti amnesty.

At the same time, international tensions ended the extradition of war crimes suspects from Germany, which perforce limited the ability of Eastern European states to try Germans who had fled westward, fuelling the propagandist claims of the latter that the West was a haven for Nazis. However, Western countries such as the Netherlands were also adversely affected by the reluctance of the British and American authorities to extradite, as was Australia in the Southeast Asian context. British officials had also decided to wind down their trial programme by the end of 1946, though here, as in other programmes such as East German 'de-Nazification', winding down first entailed speeding up to get through the backlog. In 1946, Britain also found US War and State Department agreement as to the undesirability of a second quadripartite case, thereby thwarting French and Soviet pressure for one.[63] American prosecutors went it alone with the NMT trials, which, along with trials in the USSR and the SBZ/DDR, and French trials in Southeast Asia, comprised significant exceptions to the general trajectory of punishment programmes and revisionist memory politics.

Although 1947 was likewise a turning point in Soviet trial policy, it was not until 1950 that prosecutions for war crimes were concluded in the USSR and SBZ. After the Sachsenhausen prosecutions (October 1947), there would be no further public Soviet trials, as increasing criticism from the West and the waning importance of the war in domestic politics neutralized the usefulness of further demonstrative justice. In August 1947, the Soviet Union transferred the prosecution of numerous war and Nazi criminals to East German courts, with the intention of speeding up the process of de-Nazification (prosecutions in those courts duly increased sixfold in 1948). In the SBZ/DDR, trials from 1947 largely abandoned *ukaz* 39, making far greater use of CCL10 and Article 58-2 to prosecute Germans.[64] This measure reflected the twin policy aims of shrugging off Western accusations of arbitrary justice by reducing dependence on an emergency decree, and consolidating their hold over their zone by arresting potential opponents.

---

62 Robert Forbes, *For Europe: The French Volunteers of the Waffen-SS* (Mechanicsville, Pa.: Stackpole Books, 2010), ch. 18.
63 Bloxham, *Genocide on Trial*, ch. 1.
64 Hilger, 'Sowjetunion', pp. 222, 231–2.

The flurry of Soviet prosecutions in the late 1940s was matched by systematic reappraisals in the early to mid-1950s. Stalin's death in 1953 prompted a review of German prisoners held in the USSR; in October, nearly 5,300 war criminals were repatriated; over the winter of 1953–54, a further 4,800 convicted war criminals and civilians joined them. At the same time, 5,958 convicts received early release from prisons in the DDR. Theoretically, those released were the least grievous offenders. Soviet Military Tribunals (SMTs) were disbanded in 1955, when the state of war with Germany officially ended, removing the legal framework for prosecuting Germans under occupation law. By 1955, the majority of prisoners convicted by SMTs and still held in the DDR were not war criminals, but those convicted of 'counter-revolutionary' offences. Adenauer's visit to the USSR in 1955, and the opening of formal diplomatic relations with the BRD, prompted further amnesties. By spring 1956, all German convicts, regardless of the severity of their crimes, had been repatriated; 8,877 were freed outright, while 749, whose crimes were judged most severe, were handed over to the West and East German authorities. Khrushchev's 'Secret Speech' in 1956 pushed the Socialist Unity Party of East Germany into releasing more of these prisoners, contrary to Ulbricht's wishes. In November 1955, there were 4,355 SMT convicts; just over a year later, there were 498, of whom only six had committed war crimes or crimes against humanity. By 1965, the DDR held only fifteen prisoners sentenced by SMTs, just two of whom, it seems, were convicted war criminals: these were the only ones to serve their full sentences and they were released in the 1970s.[65]

Why did the NMT programme persist into April 1949, when the final judgment of the 'Wilhelmstrasse' trial was made? Part of the explanation is structural. General Telford Taylor's OCCWC was established as a semi-permanent part of the occupation framework, which, in turn, had considerable autonomy from the parent War Department. At the top of the occupation hierarchy, General Lucius Clay was given significant discretion in running the US zone. Here, the structural fuses with a personal explanation. Clay shared the increasingly popular view that Germany had to be resurrected to remove an economic burden upon the Allies and to establish a bulwark against communism, but for him, this did not necessarily entail leniency toward war criminals. Indeed, he put his weight behind the NMT programme, insulating Taylor's staff somewhat from the direct influence of American public and political opinion.

---

65 Ibid., pp. 239, 242–3, 238.

One suspects that the State Department would have been perturbed if it had realized in early 1946 how long the NMTs would go on and under what circumstances. But while pressure built on the OCCWC to bring the NMTs to an end, and the ambition to hold additional trials was thwarted, Taylor's office succeeded in indicting many of its targets, and most of its principal ones.[66]

Given the impressive scale of the NMT legal edifice, its political dismantling under Cold War pressures in the 1950s, alongside the revisiting and reduction of most remaining Dachau trial sentences, was all the more dramatic. The need to cultivate German allegiance pushed the USA to accommodate West German opposition to the trials. Opposition was stoked by German social and functional elites who invoked sovereignty infringement, victors' justice, German war-victimhood and, in general, diminished and obfuscated responsibility for wartime criminality. Renowned (if far from infallible) indicators of the success of this opposition are opinion surveys revealing that among Germans in the American zone and West Berlin, popular belief that the trials were 'fair' plummeted from 78 per cent in October 1946 to 38 per cent by late 1950.[67]

Clay's actions in Germany contrast somewhat with those of MacArthur, the 'American Caesar' in Japan, although because the IMTFE ended much later than the IMT, in autumn 1948, MacArthur was in a very different position than Clay had been in two years before. Those class A Japanese suspects remaining in detention without trial were released on 24 December 1948, the day after the seven death sentences of the IMTFE case had been carried out – other class A suspects had been released earlier, meaning that more avoided than faced trial. Overall, the US prosecutions of Japanese war criminals were of a similar magnitude to those of Germans: the USA tried 1,344 Japanese, with 140 executions and 182 acquittals. (Comparatively, the USSR tried about 3,000 Japanese POWs, but on a range of charges, and it is not clear how many of these were effectively war crimes trials; China tried at least 800 Japanese for war crimes, convicting at least 500.)[68]

66 Bloxham, Genocide on Trial, pp. 26–52.
67 Anna J. Merritt and Richard L. Merritt (eds.), Public Opinion in Semisovereign Germany: The HICOG Surveys, 1949–1955 (Urbana: University of Illinois Press, 1980), p. 101. Generally, on German opposition, see Frei (ed.), Transnationale Vergangenheitspolitik; Frank M. Buscher, The US War Crimes Trial Program in Germany (New York: Greenwood, 1989).
68 Richard B. Finn, Winners in Peace: MacArthur, Yoshida and Postwar Japan (Berkeley: University of California Press, 1992), pp. 184–5. On China statistics, see Smith, 'Japanese War Crimes Trials'.

Much has been written about the difficulties and compromises of purging Germany, but this was not a specifically European problem. Trials may have influenced the meaning of the war itself, but expertise, traditional authority and connections proved more important in defining the nature of the post-war period in the defeated countries. For instance, four years after being paroled from Sugamo, Shigemitsu Mamoru became Japan's Foreign Minister – his sentence in 1948 had been seven years, of which he served two.[69] From 1949 onward, Chiang Kai-shek's nationalists even hired former Japanese officers to train their forces to fight those of the Chinese Communist Party; in limited form, the Imperial Army fought on against communism and for 'world peace and a liberated Asia', as it had claimed to throughout the war.[70] For some, then, the trials did not even end the war. Moreover, several key figures involved with this 'White Group' of Japanese soldiers went on, like Shigemitsu, to hold political office, and were involved in the Association to Help those Sentenced for the War', founded just before the Americans left and dedicated to supporting convicted war criminals and their families, and to 'pray[ing] for the spirits of the martyred'. Just as in West Germany, self-serving rhetoric of the 'war-guilty' or 'war-convicted' (*Kriegsschuldigen, Kriegs-verurteilten*) ultimately superseded talk of moral or criminal culpability; for the Association, 'Due to the circumstances of the defeat these soldiers became victims of sorts'.[71]

Legacies of meaning

By far the most important 'war crimes trial' in Japanese consciousness, the IMTFE case left no singular 'meaning'. In one sense, the absolution granted to the emperor, implicitly heaping the totality of blame upon the twenty-eight defendants in the dock, meant that, for many Japanese, the close of the trial drew a line under the wartime past. At the same time, there was scope for an equally collectivist rejection of the trial *in toto*. The reality of occupation, the fact that the trial was clearly a function of military defeat, and

---

69 Boister and Cryer, *Tokyo International Military Tribunal*, p. 317.
70 Barak Kushner, 'Ghosts of the Japanese Imperial Army: The "White Group" (Baituan) and Early Post-War Sino-Japanese Relations', in Matthew Hilton and Rana Mitter (eds.), *Transnationalism and Contemporary Global History, Past & Present* supplement 8 (2013), 138–41, quotation at 139.
71 Quoted in ibid., 147–8; on Germany, see Heiner Lichtenstein, 'NS-Prozesse', in Andreas Nachama and Julius Schoeps (eds.), *Aufbau nach dem Untergang: Deutsche-Judische Geschichte nach 1945* (Berlin: Argon, 1992), p. 144.

therefore of power relations, kept alive a resentment that it was simply a manifestation of partial, victor's justice.[72] As in post-1945 West Germany, ostensibly contradictory reactions amounted to the same thing: acceptance of trial because it was seen as exculpating the majority, or rejection of trial because it was seen as indicting the political culture in which the majority had acted.

Where the Japanese case differs from the German is in the level of the ongoing struggle with the past, in which the Tokyo trial is more problematic today than Nuremberg is to German memory. Politicized responses have now dichotomized into a leftist sense that the trial did not go far enough in its investigations – into either the actions of the emperor or crimes against Asian civilians under Japanese occupation – and a rightist sense that it distorted history to the detriment of Japan's name.[73] That such ambivalence did not interfere greatly with the internal 'democratization' process from 1945 should not obscure the difficulties that it still produces in Japan's external relations with its neighbours and former victims.[74] In 1978, the executed IMTFE defendants were reburied in Tokyo's Yasukuni Shrine, a place of honour for Japan's war dead. Japanese Prime Minister (2006–7, 2012–) Abe Shinzo has repeatedly relativized, or simply denied, Japanese wartime abuse of Chinese, Korean and other 'comfort women', and even questioned whether the word 'invasion' is applicable to Japan's attack and occupation of China in 1937.[75]

Clearly, contemporary Germany is far more open about its criminal past than Japan, but what does this owe to the post-war trials? And to what extent is the tale of the Allied climbdown in West Germany qualified by the BRD's renewed legal self-purge at almost the same time as the last prisoner left the US prison at Landsberg? There is certainly an interesting symmetry around

72 Madoka Futamura, 'Individual and Collective Guilt: Post-War Japan and the Tokyo War Crimes Tribunal', *European Review* 14 (2006), 471–84; Madoka Futamura, *War Crimes Tribunals and Transitional Justice: The Tokyo Trial and the Nuremberg Legacy* (Abingdon: Routledge, 2008). More generally on the trials and Japanese responses, see John Dower, *Embracing Defeat: Japan in the Aftermath of World War II* (London: Penguin, 2000).
73 Totani, *Tokyo*, p. 250; Futamura, *War Crimes Tribunals*.
74 For an impressionistic account of some such attitudes, see Zhang Wanhong, 'From Nuremberg to Tokyo: Some Reflections on the Tokyo Trial', *Cardozo Law Review* 27 (2006), 1673–82, here 1677–9.
75 Franziska Seraphim, *War Memory and Social Politics in Japan, 1945–2005* (Cambridge, Mass.: Harvard University Press, 2006); Boister and Cryer, *Tokyo International Military Tribunal*, pp. 314–15, 318–19; Rana Mitter, 'The New Remembering', *New Statesman* (26 July – 8 August 2013), pp. 26–31.

our second parameter year of 1958. It witnessed the Ulm trial of members of SS killing squads, which drew significant attention to the inception of the Holocaust by massacres of Jews during the German invasion of the Soviet Union, and saw the establishment of the Ludwigsburg Central Office for the Investigation of National Socialist Crimes, which brought some significant prosecutions in years to come.

Yet the pursuit of Nazi criminals, while partially stimulated by the expiry of the statute of limitations for manslaughter in 1960, owed more to pressure by committed journalists and falsely self-righteous East German propaganda pressure exerted on the government by the scandal of 'rediscovery' of former Nazis in prominent social positions.[76] And the trials that followed only reveal a limited will to confront the past, since prosecutions were still heavily dependent on the zeal of individual prosecutors in a legal-bureaucratic system predictably unprepared to purge itself. The overwhelming majority of Germans indicted in the BRD were direct perpetrators of atrocity, not administrators of genocide. When, say, concentration camp guards were brought to book, it was easy for the public to stigmatize the obvious sadists, while, by default, exculpating the rest, who had 'merely followed orders'.[77]

Though it is beyond the scope of this chapter, we would argue that it was the cultural shift of the 1960s and generational change, not trials of perpetrators, that finally forced a more candid confrontation with the Nazi past, and, with it, a retrospective re-embracing of the metonym 'Nuremberg'. As to the period under consideration hitherto, the ongoing work of Devin O. Pendas points to fascinatingly counter-intuitive conclusions about the relationship between justice, memory, and post-war regime transition and social change. It compares the trials conducted by German authorities under the eyes of the occupying powers in 1945–50 in western and eastern Germany. On the one hand, the more efficient 'anti-fascist' justice in the SBZ, focused as it was on legal 'consequentialism' or 'substantivism' (i.e. a desire for sentences bearing some relation to the gravity of the defendant's crime), served to legitimate communist dictatorship by facilitating extensive purges of Nazi personnel and moral condemnation of the Nazi order. On the other hand, in the west, highly technical debates around legal procedure and *ex post facto* law meant

76 Annette Weinke, *Die Verfolgung von NS-Tätern im geteilten Deutschland. Vergangenheits-bewältigungen 1949–1969 oder: Eine deutsch-deutsche Beziehungsgeschichte im Kalten Krieg* (Paderborn: Ferdinand Schöningh, 2002).
77 Devin O. Pendas, *The Frankfurt Auschwitz Trial, 1963–1965: History, Genocide, and the Limits of the Law* (Cambridge University Press, 2006); Rebecca Wittmann, *Beyond Justice: The Auschwitz Trial* (Cambridge, Mass.: Harvard University Press, 2005).

that criminals often got off the hook, or were given very light punishment. But the jurists who pressed such an approach in the west, albeit often cynically, actually bound themselves and their profession to legal 'procedural-ism' for the future, meaning an adherence to the norms of due process. This is certainly not the orthodoxy propounded by cheerleaders for 'transitional justice'.[78]

In parts of Eastern Europe, the position of war crimes trials in collective memory is especially affected by the memory of Soviet policy. Although the Soviets did far more to pursue and prosecute war criminals than did other European countries, they simultaneously arrested and deported hundreds of thousands of people for alleged connections to nationalist movements who were not guilty of any real crime; the picture, therefore, was and remains ambiguous, and trial narratives are often ignored in favour of a less challenging story of Soviet injustice and oppression. In Ukraine, contests over war memory and memorialization retain significant political charge due to their elision with the earlier mass death caused by the collectivization famine of 1932–33.[79] This is imagined within a continuum of violence which merely culminated during the war; the trials are therefore dismissed for failing to punish the 'true' perpetrators of Ukrainian suffering: the Soviet government or, more simply, 'Russia'. That many proponents seeking recognition of the 'Holodomor' famine as genocide are affiliated with nationalist groups (persecuted by the USSR after the war) which collaborated with the Nazis and murdered Ukrainian Jews complicates this picture still further, with 'victimhood theft',[80] or competitive victimhood, the most baleful result.

Some Eastern European governments have refused to participate in ongoing investigations and prosecutions of war criminals from their respective states since there is no domestic political capital in pursuing this uncomfortable subject: the principal objectives here are not truth and reconciliation, but usable pasts and the consolidation of post-Soviet national identity.[81] After all, in these countries, ideas of restitutional justice for the invasion and

---

78 Devin O. Pendas, 'Transitional Justice and Just Transitions: The German Case, 1945–1950', *European Studies Forum* 38 (2008), 57–64; Devin O. Pendas, 'Retroactive Law and Proactive Justice: Debating Crimes against Humanity in Germany, 1945–1950', *Central European History* 43 (2010), 428–63.

79 Heorhii Kas'ianov, *Danse macabre: Holod 1932–1933 rokiv u polihytsi, masovii svidomosti ta istoriohrafii (1980-ti-pochatok 2000-kh)* (Kiev: Nash chas, 2010).

80 John-Paul Himka, 'Encumbered Memory: The Ukrainian Famine of 1932–33', *Kritika* 14 (2013), 425.

81 Andrej Angrick and Peter Klein, *The 'Final Solution' in Riga: Exploitation and Annihilation, 1941–1944* (New York: Berghahn Books, 2009), esp. ch. 20 and Conclusion.

subjugation of Eastern European peoples were not so easily limited to German invaders and subjugators: in the Baltic states, Soviet control preceding and succeeding the war was readily drawn into the same conceptual framework which underlay the war crimes tribunals. In propagating such notions of justice and redress, if the trials shaped the meaning of war and violent occupation at all, it was not in the restrictive manner intended by the Soviet Union.

Lest pan-regional generalizations degenerate into stereotypes, be it noted that in each state, ambivalence and complexity in attitude interact with historical and contemporary political specificity. In Lithuania, for instance, public space has been given to Holocaust remembrance and debates on collaboration, but in an uneasy simultaneity with anti-Soviet 'partisan' celebrations, which valorize former members of police battalions that were themselves agents of atrocity.[82] Whatever the precise course of memory politics across the former Eastern bloc, it is not at all clear that the general tendencies on display are different in nature from the self-exculpatory self-referentiality displayed for decades in France, for instance, with its 'Vichy syndrome'.

Conclusion

By whomever they were conducted, war crimes trials were very often exercises in *Vergangenheitsbewältigung* – attempts to 'master' or at least cope with the past in the interests of self-justification in the present. This does not mean that legal philosophies or conceptions of the past were simply instrumentalized. Legal:political is no more a polar opposition than due process: show trial. At the same time, memory of the trials does not necessarily equate to memory of justice. Legal and political tributaries both converged and diverged over the course of the 'post-war decade'. Punishment for wartime criminality was ultimately time-limited; the desire of victors and vanquished to move on increased together with the pressures of new political realities and priorities. The continuing conflicts over memory and representation in various countries follow this pattern up to the present day.

82 Thanks to Kim Priemel for this point.

PART II

*

DIPLOMACY AND ALLIANCES

Introduction to Part II

RICHARD J. B. BOSWORTH AND JOSEPH A. MAIOLO

When did the Second World War begin? What seems to be a straightforward question raises fundamental issues about the war's origins.[1] In Europe, the textbook answer to the question of the war's start date is 1 September 1939, the day Germany invaded Poland. Two days later, Britain and France declared war on Germany, in fulfilment of their guarantees to uphold the sovereignty of Poland. Was the European war the work of Adolf Hitler, who mesmerized the Germans into following him down the path of autarchy and aggression? Or does the culpability for the war lie in London and Paris? Did the British and French bid to appease the dictators with diplomatic concessions encourage Hitler to make war? If so, would a show of resolve have prevented the war? By failing to use force to stop Italy's invasion of Ethiopia in 1935, or to block Germany's occupation of the Rhineland in 1936, so runs the old argument, Britain and France only encouraged Hitler to demand more and to gamble in 1939. If the war was preventable by an early display of resolve or force, then perhaps Washington and Moscow share the blame? Did Washington fail to encourage Paris and London to confront Berlin and Rome, or did supine British and French leaders, intent on appeasement, rebuff genuine American offers of support? Did France and Britain spurn Moscow's effort to rally Europe against aggression with a secret hope that German dynamism would find its outlet in a war against the USSR? Was Russia's call for collective security merely cover for the clandestine pursuit of an aggressive alliance with Germany? If Hitler was bent on a great war, whatever the odds stacked against Germany, or if, in 1939, he was

---

1 For an analysis of the Second World War's meaning in national collective memories and historiographies, see Richard J. B. Bosworth, *Explaining Auschwitz and Hiroshima: Historians and the Second World War, 1945–1990* (London: Routledge, 1993); Patrick Finney, *Remembering the Road to World War Two: International History, National Identity, Collective Memory* (London: Routledge, 2010).

desperate to launch a great war *before* the odds against him became too great, then neither firmness nor conciliation, nor a greater effort to pile up arms and form alliances against Berlin would have ultimately averted war.[2]

Perhaps the focus on 1939 is misplaced. Arguably, the first shot of the Second World War was fired in Spain in July 1936. At the time, many Europeans saw the Spanish Civil War as the European epicentre of a civil war between ideological, cultural and social groupings that transcended the national frontiers of the states system.[3] The emphasis in this interpretation on transnational forces such as ideological and cultural conflict raises questions about the origins of the Second World War in the economic, social and political trauma of the First World War. At the time and since, many saw the onset of the Great Depression, which came from the economic chaos and dislocation of 1914–18, as the first stage in the coming of another world war. The crises in the global economic and political systems reinforced each other because both structures had been placed on the same shaky foundations in the early 1920s. This dual crisis intensified tensions between those great powers that benefited from the status quo, and radicalized those that sought to revise the post-1919 order.[4] The further we draw back from interpreting the outbreak of the Second World War narrowly as Hitler's war and consider the much larger systemic shocks and structural forces that made another world war probable, the more important the extended crisis in Asia becomes to an understanding of the 1930s.

The first shot of the Second World War may well have been fired in September 1931 near Mukden (Shenyang), when the Japanese army in Manchuria began its conquest of the region and established the puppet state of Manchukuo. This clash of Japanese imperialism and Chinese nationalism against a backdrop of Russia's fast-growing military revival in Siberia exposed just how precarious the peace in East Asia was. The fighting between Chinese and Japanese armies ended with a truce in 1934, but Japan's challenge to the international status quo had set the stage for the fascist challenge to peace in the wider world. The year 1937 is perhaps the most persuasive alternative to 1939 as a start date for the Second World War because that is

2 Donald Cameron Watt, *How War Came: Immediate Origins of the Second World War, 1938–39* (New York: Pantheon Books, 1989); Joseph A. Maiolo, *Cry Havoc: How the Arms Race Drove the World to War, 1931–1941* (New York: Basic Books, 2011).

3 Donald C. Watt, 'The European Civil War', in Wolfgang J. Mommsen and Lothar Ketternacker, *The Fascist Challenge and the Policy of Appeasement* (London: Allen & Unwin, 1983), pp. 3–21.

4 Robert Boyce, *The Great Interwar Crisis and the Collapse of Globalization* (Basingstoke: Palgrave, 2012).

when the European and Asian conflicts began to converge politically. In July 1937, a skirmish between Chinese and Japanese troops at the Marco Polo Bridge outside Peking escalated into an all-out war that lasted until Japan's surrender in 1945. The Sino-Japanese War was the longest and bloodiest of the interrelated wars of Europe and Asia that coalesced into the Second World War. The war drew in the powers with security, commercial and colonial interests in China. Moscow, London and Washington supplied increasing military and economic aid to China to frustrate Japan's expansion, and Russian and Japanese troops fought several battles along the Siberian-Manchurian frontiers. In an attempt to isolate China and coerce the United States and Britain to allow Japan's penetration into Southeast Asia, Tokyo aligned itself closer to Germany and Italy, the revisionist powers in Europe, by reinforcing the Anti-Comintern Pact of November 1936 with a new agreement, the Tripartite Pact of September 1940.

While scholars may debate the start point of the Second World War and draw different conclusions about its origins, there is a consensus that the war reached a culminating point at the beginning of 1942. By then, Germany was master of Europe and had plunged its armies deep inside the Soviet Union. Japan had struck the US fleet at Pearl Harbor and its armed forces were in control of much of East Asia and marching on the bastion of the British Empire in Asia, Singapore. With the entry of the Soviet Union and the United States into the war, the alignment of the great-power combatants was complete and the European and Asia-Pacific wars had become global. Although few perceived it at the time, the entry of the Soviet Union and the United States into the war made the defeat of Germany, Italy and Japan certain.[5]

Part II of Volume II of *The Cambridge History of the Second World War* explores the origins and alliance politics of the conflict. The first two chapters examine the pre-war period and ask whether diplomacy might have averted war in Europe or Asia-Pacific. Peter Jackson begins by defining diplomacy not simply as the activities of diplomats, but also an institution built on a shared understanding among political elites about the nature and purposes of international politics. Jackson shows that there was no such agreement among the great powers about what a stable and just world order would look like. While the victorious powers of 1919 tried to construct a durable

---

5 Mark Harrison, 'The Economics of World War II: An Overview', in Mark Harrison (ed.), *The Economics of World War II: Six Great Powers in International Comparison* (Cambridge University Press, 2000).

peace based on liberal ideals, the revisionist powers did not regard peace and stability as desirable. For them, diplomacy was a tool for tearing down the old order and creating the conditions for war and revolution. Peter Mauch draws a similar conclusion about the diplomatic origins of the Asia-Pacific conflict. After the Japanese attack in December 1941, the British and American ambassadors to Tokyo argued that had their governments adopted more flexibility in negotiating with the Japanese over trade and China in 1941, then diplomacy would have bought much more time for the Allies to prepare for war against Japan, if not ultimately to prevent the conflict. Mauch, however, argues that the underlying incompatibility of strategic goals on both sides left no scope for even a temporary deal. Once Japan signed the Tripartite Pact, he argues, Washington and Tokyo were on a collision course.

The next two chapters compare the diplomacy of the Axis and the Grand Alliance. As Norman Goda and David Reynolds show, the contrast between the two blocs could not have been greater. The Axis was a collection of predators waging separate regional wars of conquest, whose mutual relations were marred by discord and distrust. In Europe, the Germans tended to treat their Axis allies as contemptible auxiliaries, worthy only insofar as they served the goals of the Nazi New Order. Given the distance and divergent goals between Berlin and Tokyo, coordinating their military strategies and sharing resources would have been difficult even under the best of conditions. By comparison, the Grand Alliance cooperated to a remarkable degree: Britain, the United States and the Soviet Union shared some intelligence, and coordinated strategy through regular conferences and pooled resources. Relations between Washington and London were closest, but were not without friction, especially over grand strategy and a cross-Channel invasion. Distrust was greatest between the Western powers and the Soviet Union over the post-war settlement. German aggression had made the alliance, and Germany's impending defeat in early 1945 weakened its shared sense of purpose. Disagreement about what the post-war order should look like pushed the Allies apart and set the stage for the Cold War. As Jackson and Mauch argued in the first two chapters, diplomacy cannot make a cooperative international order when visions of what that order should look like differ sharply.

The last two chapters compare the experiences of neutral Sweden and non-belligerent Spain, and illustrate just how important the course of the war was to the foreign policies of the non-warring states. As Klas Åmark shows in his analysis of Swedish diplomacy and trade policy, neutrality inevitably involved unpleasant political and moral compromises. Without the military might to impose neutrality, Sweden had to negotiate the terms of its neutrality with the great powers, and those terms changed with the fortunes of war. While the Nazi regime was in the ascendant, Sweden allowed Berlin use of its railways to transport troops on leave from occupied Norway and curbed press freedom to mute criticism of Berlin. Once Germany's defeat neared, Stockholm began to reverse its policies of cooperation with the Third Reich. The fortunes of war likewise shaped Spain's foreign policy during the war. As Paul Preston explains in his chapter, Franco desperately wanted to profit from Hitler's victories of 1940–41, but the Spanish economy was too weak for war. Although Franco's propagandists would later portray his policy of non-belligerence as strategic foresight, in truth, the Germans knew that Spain's entry into the war would only be more of a burden to them. Hitler and his officials received offers to join the Axis war effort with contempt, while the British achieved a measure of success in applying economic and diplomatic pressure to prevent Spain entering the war. In sum, the tentacles of the Second World War reached out even to those who avoided being combatants in it, and also left a legacy to be debated with passion and bias well after the fighting ended.

9

Europe
The failure of diplomacy, 1933–1940

PETER JACKSON

The liberal international order established at the Paris Peace Conference was overthrown between 1933 and 1939. This opened the way for Nazi Germany and Fascist Italy to launch wars of conquest aimed at creating empires in Europe and the Mediterranean. This chapter considers whether the outbreak of war in September 1939 should be understood as a failure of European diplomacy.

To address this question, it is necessary first to derive a working definition of diplomacy, as well as a conceptual framework for understanding its core functions. The influential French diplomat Philippe Berthelot once observed that 'diplomacy was the first inexact science, and it remains the last of the fine arts'.[1] Not surprisingly, there is no universally accepted definition of diplomacy. Yet nearly all existing discussions of its nature and role understand diplomacy as the peaceful management of relations between distinct political actors in the international sphere. Peace is considered to be the ultimate aim of all diplomatic practice, even in wartime. One of the earliest and most influential treatises on the subject, by the French statesman François de Callières, asserted that the overriding functions of diplomacy were to promote moderation, limit conflict and provide order in relations between sovereigns.[2] This conceptualization has been echoed in theoretical discussions of the role of diplomacy ever since. Hedley Bull observed that a core function of the diplomat is 'by means of reason and persuasion, to bring princes to act on a true appreciation of their interests... to recognise common interests'. Martin Wight defined diplomacy as 'the attempt to adjust

---

1 Quoted in Comte de Saint-Aulaire, *Je suis diplomate* (Paris: Éditions du Conquistador, 1954), p. 13.
2 Maurice Keens-Soper, 'François de Callières and Diplomatic Theory', in R. Langhorne and C. Jönsson (eds.), *Diplomacy*, vol. 1: *Theory of Diplomacy* (3 vols., London: Sage, 2004), pp. 14–15.

conflicting interests by negotiation and compromise'.³ This emphasis on moderation, cooperation and conciliation has led many writers to define diplomacy in opposition to war. 'All the efforts of diplomacy', observed the celebrated diplomat Jules Cambon, 'are devoted to finding means by which recourse to arms can be avoided.' The British practitioner and theorist Harold Nicolson went further. 'The aim of sound diplomacy', Nicolson argued, 'is the maintenance of amicable relations between sovereign states. . . Once diplomacy is deployed to provoke animosity, it ceases to be diplomacy and becomes its opposite, namely war by another name.'⁴

The emphasis on peaceful relations in the literature does not rule out the threat of force as a tool of diplomacy. Britain's use of 'gunboat diplomacy' in the nineteenth century, for example, stimulated the first systematic reflections on what is nowadays termed 'coercive diplomacy'.⁵ The political theorist Hans Morganthau insisted that the threat of force must always be present in the diplomacy of a great power. But he also judged that 'a diplomacy that ends in war has failed in its primary objective, the promotion of the national interest by peaceful means'.⁶ Nor does this conception of diplomacy rule out diplomatic exchanges between warring states. It instead underlines the fact that the aim of these exchanges is always to bring an end to hostilities. The distinction between diplomacy and war remains fundamental to virtually all theoretical reflections on the practice of diplomacy.

François de Callières, author of one of the canonical works on diplomatic practice, argued that a preference for peace over war is a precondition for effective diplomacy. He insisted that diplomacy is only possible if the various actors in a given political system recognize the need for peaceful coexistence:

> To understand fully the utility of [diplomacy] we must think of the states of which Europe is composed as joined together by all kinds of necessary relations and commerce in such a way that we can regard them as members of the same Republic and that no considerable change can take place in any one of them without disturbing the peace of all the others.⁷

3 Hedley Bull, *The Anarchical Society: A Study of Order in World Politics* (London: Macmillan, 1977), p. 169; Martin Wight, *Power Politics* (Harmondsworth: Penguin, 1978), p. 89.
4 Jules Cambon, *Le diplomate* (Paris: Hachette, 1926), pp. 23–4; Nicolson quoted in Thomas Otte, 'Harold Nicolson', in G. R. Berridge, Maurice Keens-Soper and Thomas Otte (eds.), *Diplomatic Theory from Machiavelli to Kissinger* (London: Palgrave, 2001), p. 156.
5 Thomas Otte, 'Satow', in Berridge et al. (eds.), *Diplomatic Theory*, pp. 142–3.
6 Hans J. Morgenthau, *Politics Among Nations: The Struggle for Power and Peace* (New York: McGraw-Hill, 1978), pp. 361–2.
7 Monsieur de Callières, *De la manière de négocier avec les souverains* (Amsterdam: La Compagnie, 1716), pp. 57–8.

For de Callières, no durable international order is possible unless *all sovereign members* of a given system acknowledge the common interest in coexistence, unless there is a shared sense of belonging to 'the same Republic'. To perform its function effectively, in other words, diplomacy requires a minimum level of common interest among sovereign actors. Such common interest can centre either on preserving the foundations of the existing order or on ensuring that systemic change is managed peacefully. But it must exist.

Callières' minimum condition for the effective functioning of diplomacy did not prevail in the decade before the outbreak of the Second World War. Three of the five European great powers aimed at the complete overthrow of the existing order. The Soviet Union sought to replace the liberal-capitalist system with a revolutionary socialist alternative that would instal Communism across Europe. The political aims of Fascist Italy and Nazi Germany were equally revolutionary. Both regimes pursued war as a necessary and desirable aim in its own right, one that would revitalize their respective populations and open the way to national greatness through imperial expansion. This state of affairs made it impossible for European diplomacy to preserve peace. The best the diplomacy of the non-revisionist powers could hope to achieve was to deter revisionist aggression in the short term, and, in the longer term, to ensure that a future conflict would take place under the most favourable political and military conditions. The diplomacy of the two principal status quo powers, Britain and France, failed in these tasks. The reasons for this failure can only be understood, however, if they are placed within the specific context of European politics between the two world wars.

Diplomacy and European politics between the two world wars

One of the most important legacies of the First World War was the introduction of new international norms and new standards of international legitimacy. Decision-makers and professional diplomats were forced to adapt to this new international context. The new set of practices that emerged would prove fundamentally unsuitable to meet the challenge posed by Fascist and especially Nazi revisionism. European diplomacy had evolved through a number of key stages from its inception in the fifteenth century. The first was the emergence of a system of resident embassies among the Italian city states. By the end of the sixteenth century, this system had spread throughout most of Europe. Another important stage was the legal recognition of the extraterritoriality of permanent residences during the seventeenth and early eighteenth centuries. Also significant was the gradual professionalization of a recognizably distinct diplomatic corps to serve well-established ministries of foreign affairs among Europe's great powers over the course of the eighteenth century. Another important development was the establishment of the 'Concert' system of regular consultation between high-ranking diplomatic officials from the European powers after 1815. Of more long-term significance, however, was the rise of the idea of the nation state as a political actor, with interests distinct from those of the sovereign ruler. This last development, which was given early expression by the revolutionary regime in France in the 1790s, opened the way for the gradual emergence of a more 'democratic' conception of diplomacy as a tool of government in the interests of 'the people'.[8]

The emergence of nationalism and notions of democratic legitimacy posed a significant challenge to traditional practices at a time when scientific developments such as steam power, railways and telegraphic communications revolutionized existing conceptions of time and space, and transformed the scope and pace of diplomacy and foreign policy-making.[9] These changes created the conditions necessary for the emergence of transnational civil society. Of particular importance was a transatlantic movement for peace through international cooperation and the codification of international public law. The ideology of nineteenth-century 'internationalism' underpinned the two Hague Peace Conferences of 1899 and 1907. The main objectives of both conferences were to establish an international regime of arms limitation and to replace the balance of power with the rule of law as the chief arbiter of international relations.[10]

The internationalist movement remained firmly on the margins of both domestic and international politics. But the unprecedented scale and destructiveness of the Great War created political space for internationalist approaches to peace and international security. Traditional diplomacy was widely condemned either for causing the war or for failing to prevent its outbreak. Expectations for the future behaviour of 'civilized' states were altered in a fundamental sense by four years of industrial slaughter. Socialists began to regroup and to coordinate their campaign for a new international order based on working-class cooperation. Liberal internationalists called for

---

8 H. M. Scott, *The Birth of a Great Power System, 1740–1815* (London: Longman, 2006), pp. 244–359.

9 Kevin O'Rourke and Jeffrey Williamson, *Globalization and History* (Cambridge, Mass.: MIT Press, 2001).

10 Glenda Sluga, *Internationalism in the Age of Nationalism* (Philadelphia: Pennsylvania University Press, 2013).

the democratization of both foreign policy and diplomacy. Increasingly large and influential civil society associations in Britain, France and the USA lobbied for the creation of a 'league' or 'society' of nations. Internationalist campaigning was given inspiration and political legitimacy by the public proclamations of American President Woodrow Wilson. In May 1916, Wilson publicly declared US support for the creation of a 'League of Nations'. The following January, he called for the balance of power to be replaced by a 'community of power' working through this new organization. The American President's programme amounted to a revolution in international politics, aimed specifically at overturning the military alliance building and balance of power thinking that had characterized pre-1914 diplomacy.[11]

Two developments in 1917 shook the foundations of the international system and would have decisive long-term ramifications for the practice of diplomacy. Successive revolutions in February and October resulted in the advent of a revolutionary Bolshevik movement in Russia. One of the first measures taken by the new regime was to publish records of secret negotiations between the Allied powers that included plans for far-reaching annexations of German, Austro-Hungarian and Ottoman territory. This was accompanied by a 'Peace Decree', calling for 'absolutely open' discussions, leading to peace 'without annexations or indemnities'. The underlying aim of this early exercise in Cold War diplomacy by propaganda was to provoke a Europe-wide revolution.[12] The second seismic event was the American entry into the war on the side of the Allies in April 1917. The USA, by this time, was well on its way to becoming the world's most powerful state. The Wilson administration entered the war intent on exercising American power to establish a new basis for world politics. To make this case, the President outlined 'Fourteen Points', which he argued represented 'the only possible program' for the post-war international order. The first point attacked the principle of secret diplomatic negotiations and called for 'open covenants of peace, openly arrived at, after which there shall be no private understandings of any kind but diplomacy shall proceed always frankly and in the public

11 'Peace Without Victory Address', in A. S. Link et al. (eds.), *The Papers of Woodrow Wilson* (69 vols., Princeton University Press, 1966–94), vol. xxxx, pp. 533–9; Thomas Knock, *To End All Wars: Woodrow Wilson and the Quest for a New World Order* (Princeton University Press, 1992), pp. 11–13; Ross Kennedy, *The Will to Believe: Woodrow Wilson, World War I, and America's Strategy for Peace and Security* (Kent, O.: Kent State University Press, 2009), pp. 71–103.

12 Richard Debo, *Revolution and Survival: The Foreign Policy of Soviet Russia, 1917–1918* (Liverpool University Press, 1979), pp. 14–24, 72–88; Michal Carley, *Silent Conflict: Early Soviet-Western Relations* (New York: Rowman & Littlefield, 2014), pp. 5–27.

view'. The fourteenth declared that 'a general association of nations must be formed' to provide a framework for lasting peace. Existing practices of diplomacy must undergo radical reform.[13]

Wilson's Fourteen Points outlined an agenda for what was widely termed the 'New Diplomacy' after 1918. The American President was giving expression to widespread popular pressure for new standards of international behaviour. Three new international norms, in particular, exercised particular legitimacy in the post-war era. The first was the widely held assumption that war was no longer a legitimate tool of foreign policy in Europe. The second was that diplomacy must be accountable to public opinion – or at least accountable to opinion within the victorious powers. The third was that multilateralism, preferably under the auspices of an international organization, should replace exclusive alliances and the balance of power as the organizing framework of international politics. These norms would continue to influence the practice of diplomacy in Britain and France well into the 1930s. They played an important role in shaping British and French responses to the revisionist challenge.

The influence of these norms was reflected in the course of international relations in the post-war decade. The Paris Peace Conference ushered in the practice of 'summitry' that has been fundamental to international relations ever since. The leaders of the most powerful states, Woodrow Wilson (USA), Lloyd George (Great Britain) and Georges Clemenceau (France), were all known for their mistrust of career diplomats. All three justified their decision to conduct negotiations directly with one another in terms of democratic legitimacy and with implicit references to the low standing of traditional diplomacy. While their talks did not take place in public, the terms of the various agreements that made up the settlement were widely publicized even before the treaties were signed. The first fruit of their labours was the creation of a League of Nations.

The League was intended to offer a multilateral alternative to the alliance blocs and joint military planning that had dominated European politics before 1914. Although the US Congress refused to ratify the Treaty of Versailles, and thus American entry into the League, the multilateralism embodied by that organization enjoyed tremendous international legitimacy.

---

13 'President Wilson's Fourteen Points', in R. S. Baker (ed.), *Woodrow Wilson and World Settlement* (3 vols., Garden City, NY: Doubleday, 1923), vol. iii, pp. 42–5, doc. no. 3; see also John Milton Cooper, *Breaking the Heart of the World: Woodrow Wilson and the Fight for the League of Nations* (Cambridge University Press, 2010).

The 1920s were an era of conference diplomacy and multilateral treaties. Virtually all of the great international agreements of the 1920s, from the conferences at Washington (1922) and London (1924), to the Locarno accords (1925) and the financial arrangements agreed at The Hague (1929–1930), were multilateral in character. The League grew steadily in size and influence in these years. A watershed moment for the new institution was the admission of Weimar Germany into both the Council and the Assembly in 1926. Through to the end of the decade, British, French and German foreign ministers attended regular 'Geneva tea parties' to discuss issues and resolve differences. Many European diplomats of this era developed a new political reflex which inclined them toward seeking security and prosperity through complex multilateral arrangements, resting ultimately on the legitimacy of international law. Bilateral alliances, conversely, disappeared almost entirely from the European international landscape in the post-war decade.

The multilateral phase of interwar international relations unravelled only slowly. The world economic crisis had a corrosive effect on the structures of political and economic cooperation put in place after 1918. It contributed decisively to the rise of radical politics across Europe and, in particular, to the advent of the National Socialist regime led by Adolf Hitler in Germany in January 1933. From the early 1930s, the character of international politics underwent dramatic changes, as the leaders of Fascist Italy and Nazi Germany pursued policies based on aggressive nationalism that aimed at overthrowing the international order through wars of conquest. One of the chief tactics employed by both, ironically, was to exploit the normative standards of the post-1918 era.

The revisionist challenge

There was no role for diplomacy in Fascist or Nazi policy beyond buying time for rearmament and establishing suitable conditions for future wars of conquest. But Italy and Germany were not the only European great powers to anticipate the ultimate destruction of the international system. Soviet Russia also saw the European liberal-capitalist order as a threat to its existence. From its inception, the USSR mounted a dual foreign policy. On the one hand, its Commissariat for Foreign Affairs (*Narkomindel*) conducted formal diplomatic relations with capitalist states. On the other hand, the Communist International (Comintern) was charged with promoting revolutionary subversion abroad. The Comintern was founded in March 1919 as the Bolshevik regime was waging a brutal struggle for survival against both internal enemies and an Allied military intervention. It operated primarily through communist parties abroad, and its first chief was the professional revolutionary Grigory Zinoviev. The Commissar for Foreign Affairs for most of the post-war decade, career diplomat Georgii Chicherin, described Soviet foreign policy as 'an experiment in peaceful coexistence with bourgeois states'.[14] This jarred with the overriding aim of the Comintern, which was to export the Bolshevik revolution to every corner of the globe. The unique internal/external challenge posed by Soviet policy would endure through much of the interwar period.

One of the chief legacies of the Comintern for Soviet diplomacy in the 1930s was the enduring hostility and suspicion of those Western European states that were specific targets for revolutionary propaganda and subversion in the 1920s. Comintern operations were conducted primarily from Soviet embassies and legations where its agents enjoyed immunities and protections. Efforts to promote revolution went hand in hand with facilitating Soviet espionage abroad. Comintern activities within France and Britain (and their empires) led to a series of crises in Soviet relations with those states (including a two-year break in Anglo-Soviet relations between 1927 and 1929). The overall result was a general atmosphere of profound mistrust that was to have a crippling effect on all subsequent efforts at rapprochement with the USSR in the face of Nazi revisionism. In this way, the machinations of the Comintern, which themselves cannot be understood without taking into account the legacy of Allied intervention in the Russian Civil War, limited the effectiveness of Soviet diplomacy and undermined the prospects for forging a powerful united front against German and Italian revisionism in the 1930s.

Soviet diplomats found it necessary to adapt to the more traditional practices of international diplomacy. In terms of dress and personal comportment, Soviet diplomats posted abroad generally adopted the practices that prevailed throughout the European diplomatic community. This adaptation was driven by the overriding aim of achieving 'normal' diplomatic relations with the other major powers during the early 1920s. From the outset, however, Soviet diplomats were forced to walk a tightrope as they struggled to secure acceptance in the cosmopolitan society of international diplomacy, while at the same time retaining their Communist credentials at home. After

14 Christopher Read, 'The View from the Kremlin: Soviet Assumptions about the Capitalist World in the 1920s', in S. Casey and J. Wright (eds.), *Mental Maps in the Era of Two World Wars* (London: Palgrave, 2008), pp. 38–57.

1935, this became a matter of life and death for many within *Narkomindel*. This challenge reflected the wider tension between the Soviet state's ideological commitment to overthrowing the liberal-capitalist order, on the one hand, and the need to safeguard its position and interests in that same order, on the other. The latter imperative became particularly acute after the rise to power of Hitler in Germany in 1933. With the advent of an aggressively anti-Bolshevik regime in Germany, pursuit of 'collective security' became a major theme in Soviet foreign policy. The USSR joined the League of Nations in September 1934 (nearly a year after Germany left), and Chicherin's replacement, Maxim Litvinov, became one of the most voluble voices calling for collective resistance to aggressive revisionism in Geneva. Most historians nowadays agree that the majority of Soviet diplomats were genuinely committed to this policy. But it is important to remember that at no point did Litvinov or any other professional diplomat have a decisive voice in the overall direction of the USSR's foreign policy. This was the preserve of the Politburo of the Communist Party and, in particular, General Secretary Joseph Stalin.

A prominent member of the Bolshevik movement from its inception, Stalin had secured a dominant position within the higher echelons of the Soviet regime by the beginning of the 1930s. While he accepted the need to maintain diplomatic relations with the outside world, Stalin continued to view international politics from the perspective of Marxism-Leninism. Historians disagree over the extent to which the Soviet leader was seriously committed to collective security. What is not in doubt, however, is Stalin's conviction that there could be no long-term accommodation between the USSR and liberal-capitalist states. The Soviet Union, for Stalin, remained 'encircled by enemies'. As early as 1930, he observed that

> The bourgeois states are furiously arming and rearming. What for? Not for friendly chats, of course, but for war. And the imperialists need war, for it is the only means by which to re-divide the world, to re-divide markets, sources of raw materials and spheres for the investment of capital.[15]

This ideologically charged understanding of world politics was supported by a system of intelligence gathering and dissemination designed, above all, to produce evidence of threats to the workers' homeland. It did not fail in this

---

15 J. V. Stalin, 'Political Report of the Central Committee to the Sixteenth Congress of the CPSU(B)', 27 June 1930, published in *Pravda* III (29 June 1930); see also James Harris, 'Encircled by Enemies: Stalin's Perceptions of the Capitalist World, 1918–1941', *Journal of Strategic Studies* 30:3 (2007), 513–45.

task. Throughout the 1930s, Soviet intelligence produced a steady stream of reports indicating the existence of a vast (if inchoate) anti-Soviet coalition. This grouping was usually comprised of some combination of Britain, Germany, Poland, Romania and Japan, but occasionally included France, the United States and Fascist Italy. The Anti-Comintern Pact, signed by Germany and Japan in 1936, and then by Italy in 1937, reinforced the Soviet perception of encirclement. From Stalin's perspective, diplomacy could only forestall a war with the capitalist powers that was understood as inevitable, given the world historical processes at work. And diplomats, who lived and worked abroad, and who engaged in private conversations with agents of capitalism, were viewed with suspicion and kept at arm's length from the centre of power.

It was probably inevitable that the Commissariat for Foreign Affairs would become a central target of the Great Terror under Stalin from 1936 onward. Nearly half of all senior Soviet diplomats were removed from their posts between 1936 and 1939. Of these, more than 30 per cent were arrested, and more than 20 per cent were executed.[16] Although *Narkomindel* got off relatively lightly compared to the Red Army high command (which was essentially decapitated), the purges all but destroyed its ability to conduct effective diplomacy. Litvinov observed to Stalin in January 1939 that '[a]t present the post of ambassador is unfilled in nine capitals: Washington, Tokyo, Warsaw, Bucharest, Barcelona, Kaunas, Copenhagen, Budapest and Sofia... In some of the capitals mentioned there has been no ambassador for over a year'. The Commissar for Foreign Affairs went on to complain that officials who were recalled or returned to the USSR on leave were almost never given permission to return. The result was a crippling lack of expertise in virtually all Soviet missions abroad.[17] Replacements were drawn overwhelmingly from outside *Narkomindel*. Litvinov himself was dismissed on 3 May 1939 and replaced by Stalin's confidant, Vyacheslav Molotov. The USSR was, in effect, withdrawing from international society just as the Nazi regime was embarking on the aggressive phase of its foreign policy, and as voices within the British and French policy elite were beginning to call for the creation of a 'grand alliance' with Soviet Russia to meet this threat.

For Stalin and his inner circle, however, such an alliance could never constitute more than a temporary expedient, and certainly not a durable

16 Sabine Dullin, *Des Hommes d'influences. Les ambassadeurs de Staline en Europe* (Paris: Payot, 2001), pp. 334–9.
17 Quoted in Alistair Kocho-Williams, *Russian and Soviet Diplomacy, 1900–1939* (London: Palgrave, 2012), p. 128, but see, more generally, pp. 124–39.

source of security. Mutual assistance pacts signed with France and Czecho-slovakia in 1935 were understood within this conceptual framework. From the perspective of the Soviet leadership, war was an inevitable product of the contradictions and iniquities of the capitalist system. The capitalist powers, whose continued existence depended on fomenting future wars, could never be trusted to accept coexistence with the USSR in the long term. The exclusion of the Soviet Union from the Munich Conference of September 1938 could only have confirmed this conviction. Stalin judged that the agreement constituted tacit encouragement to Germany to direct its aggression eastward. This view of the international situation made the successful negotiation of a grand alliance in the summer of 1939 very unlikely. Anything short of an offer of a full military alliance by France and Britain would be refused out of hand. Soviet decision-makers viewed the Western democracies as a less immediate threat than Nazi Germany. But they were unwilling to commit to fight alongside these powers without full reciprocity. As Stalin observed to the Politburo after the outbreak of war, he could

> see nothing wrong in their [Germany, France and Britain] having a good hard fight and weakening each other. It would be fine if at the hands of Germany, the position of the richest capitalist countries (especially Britain) were shaken. Hitler, without understanding it or desiring it, is shaking and undermining the capitalist system... We can manoeuvre, pit one side against the other to set them fighting as fiercely as possible.[18]

Within this policy conception, the function of diplomacy was not to preserve peace through negotiation and compromise. Diplomacy was instead a tool to help ensure that 'inevitable war' would take place under conditions favourable to the USSR.[19]

War was even more central to the Fascist conception of world politics under the charismatic leadership of Benito Mussolini. The overarching aim of the Fascist regime that came to power in 1923 was to remake Italian society in preparation for wars of conquest. Italy, according the Fascist vision, would provide an aggressively nationalist alternative to both decadent liberal capit-alism and the divisive class warfare of Marxism. The ultimate purpose was to forge a second Roman Empire by imposing Italian hegemony in the Medi-terranean and North Africa.

18 Quoted in Ivo Banac (ed.), *The Diary of Georgi Dimitrov* (New Haven, Conn.: Yale University Press, 2003), pp. 115–16.
19 Sylvio Pons, *Stalin and the Inevitable War, 1936–1941* (London: Frank Cass, 2002).

Fascism, like Nazism, emerged out of the violence of the Great War. It was Mussolini's insistence that Italy must be involved in this conflict that had led to his expulsion from the Italian Socialist Party and his final embrace of violent nationalism. Mussolini repeated, again and again, that the Italian nation could realize its historic mission only through war. At the Fascist Party Congress of 1925, he proclaimed that it would be necessary to create 'a new class of warriors, always willing to die' for the greater good of the nation. A 'new Fascist Man' would emerge out of the 'virile warrior education' imposed on the people and would 'display a sense of virility, of power, of conquest'. Mussolini insisted on Italy's calling to become 'the dominating nation of the Mediterranean and discharge on the African shores of that sea the majority of its population and energies'.[20]

Historians remain divided over the extent to which the Duce's rhetoric was ever translated into a serious foreign policy programme. One school of interpretation characterizes Fascist foreign policy as essentially 'realist' in its pursuit of Italy's national interests. The Fascist leadership, according to this view, understood and accepted that Italy's size and modest levels of industrialization placed limitations on ambitions to create a Mediterranean empire. A contending interpretation argues that the revolutionary dynamism of Fascist ideology drove the Italian state ineluctably toward war.[21] Though the evidence on both sides is mixed, it is hard to dispute the fact that pursuit of war was the unifying concept at the heart of Fascist politics and foreign policy.

For most of the 1930s, Mussolini felt constrained by Italy's relative lack of economic and military power. Italian policy sought to profit from the tensions created by Nazi revisionism in Europe. According to the Fascist diplomat Dino Grandi, Italy's interests were best served by intervening to exercise the *'peso determinante'* (decisive weight) during European crises.[22] Mussolini appeared to follow this course when he proposed a Four-Power Consultative Pact to ease international tensions after the Nazi rise to power in 1933. Italy also opposed the attempted Nazi takeover of Austria in 1934, and hosted a Franco-British-Italian conference in response to German rearmament, at Stresa in 1935. In the aftermath of Stresa, the Italian and French army

20 Quotations from MacGregor Knox, *Common Destiny: Foreign Policy and War in Fascist Italy and Nazi Germany* (Cambridge University Press, 2000), pp. 67, 68, 70.
21 See R. J. B. Bosworth, *The Italian Dictatorship: Problems and Perspectives* (London: Arnold, 1998), pp. 82–105.
22 Renzo De Felice, *Mussolini il duce*, vol. 1: *Gli anni del consenso, 1929–1936* (4 vols., Torino: Einaudi, 2007), p. 206.

and air staffs engaged in detailed joint planning for war against Germany in Europe. Mussolini intervened most famously to facilitate negotiations during the Czechoslovak Crisis in September 1938.

All of these measures could be interpreted as evidence of the Fascist regime's commitment to diplomacy and deterrence as part of a collective effort to contain the Nazi challenge. But they might also have been part of a wider programme of preparing the best possible conditions for wars of imperial expansion. Almost from its inception, the Fascist regime had begun military planning for operations against Yugoslavia in the Mediterranean and Ethiopia in East Africa. In a much-publicized speech on Ascension Day in 1927, Mussolini predicted that Europe would reach 'a crucial point in its history' between 1935 and 1940. Italy must then be prepared to 'make its voice heard and see [its] rights recognised', by placing 5 million men under arms and constructing an air force powerful enough to 'blot out the sun'.[23] The problem was that the poor state of Italy's ground and air forces ruled out war with another European power. Focus therefore shifted to Ethiopia. In 1932, Mussolini approved planning for an offensive campaign against that state, with a target date of 1935.

Nazi foreign policy constituted both a threat and an opportunity for Italian ambitions. German designs on Austria and for economic domination of the Danubian basin posed a threat to Italian interests in Southern Europe. Yet the destabilizing effects of Nazi revisionism also created opportunities for imperial expansion. 'We will be at war between 1935 and 1936', Mussolini predicted; 'Italy must be ready.'[24] In return for Italian cooperation against Germany in Europe, Mussolini demanded French and British acquiescence to the conquest of Ethiopia. Both Britain and France proved willing to bargain. The 'Hoare–Laval Plan' was an old-fashioned imperial/diplomatic arrangement negotiated with the Fascist regime in 1936. It aimed to avoid war by offering Ethiopia to Italy in phases. The problem was that Ethiopia was a member of the League of Nations. The Hoare–Laval project ignored the enduring strength of post-1918 international norms, particularly within British popular opinion. It foundered in the face of popular support for the League of Nations and collective security in Western Europe. In the end, the League imposed sanctions on Italy and Britain threatened war. Mussolini turned to Germany for the oil

23 Quotations from Knox, *Common Destiny*, pp. 125, 123.
24 Quoted in John Gooch, *Mussolini and His Generals: Armed Forces and Fascist Foreign Policy, 1922–1940* (Cambridge University Press, 2007), p. 128.

and coal it needed to keep its economy afloat. From this point forward, Italy moved ever more decisively toward cooperation with the Nazi regime.

The Abyssinian crisis demonstrated Mussolini's determination to pursue his imperial project even at the risk of war. Italy's Mediterranean ambitions made conflict with Britain inevitable at some point. Mussolini repeatedly characterized British power as the chief barrier to Italy's historic mission. 'Gibraltar, Malta, Suez, Cyprus', he claimed, 'represent a chain that permits Britain to encircle, to imprison Italy in the Mediterranean.' Breaking this chain meant war was 'inevitable' at some point with Britain, and probably with France. This outcome was acceptable, and even desirable, given Mussolini's conviction that war was the necessary crucible within which the new Italian character would be forged. Diplomacy, in this context, could serve only as an instrument to ensure that, when war came, it would be fought under the most favourable conditions possible. 'We are now launched', Mussolini observed in April 1936, 'and we shall overthrow anyone who endeavours to stop us, both with force and with diplomacy.'[25]

This approach to foreign policy was predictably not to the taste of most Italian diplomats. Count Sforza, a senior diplomat and former Foreign Minister, dismissed Fascist foreign policy as 'a mere summary of sentiments and resentments'.[26] He resigned when Mussolini was appointed head of government in 1922. To ensure that Italian diplomacy performed its allotted role in the Fascist quest for empire, the Foreign Ministry staff was purged in 1927. When Salvatore Contarini retired as Secretary General of the Ministry, he was not replaced, and the position remained vacant thereafter. Admission requirements for a diplomatic career were altered to permit a 'Fascist call-up'. A cohort of Fascist Party members, the *Ventottisti*, were drafted into the *Palazzo Chigi* in 1928 and the Fascist Dino Grandi was appointed Foreign Minister the following year. When Grandi proved over-cautious in pursuit of Italy's imperial calling, he was replaced by career diplomat Fulvio Suvich. But Suvich also lacked the necessary zeal. He was alarmed by Mussolini's contempt for diplomatic finesse and opposed an ideological alliance with Nazi Germany. Suvich was removed to make way for Galeazzo Ciano, Mussolini's son-in-law and former Propaganda Minister. Ciano would remain as Foreign Minister through to the end of the Fascist regime. Under his

---

25 Quoted in R. J. B. Bosworth, *Mussolini* (London: Arnold, 2002), p. 328.
26 Quoted in Alan Cassels, *Mussolini's Early Diplomacy* (Princeton University Press, 1970), p. 9.

direction, great emphasis was placed on the *tona fascista* of Italian external policy. Foreign Ministry communications could be characterized by heroic rhetoric and suffused with bellicose references to empire. Italian diplomacy ceased almost completely to function as a source of policy advice and a tool for negotiations. For most of the Fascist era, Mussolini instead displayed a marked preference for circumventing professional diplomats, either through the use of unofficial agents or in direct contact with foreign leaders.

The extent to which Fascism pursued war as an aim in and of itself is illustrated by the regime's commitment to massive rearmament. Spending on armaments and other defence-related projects more than doubled by the opening of the 1930s, and rose dramatically thereafter. Between 1935 and 1938, Italian military spending as a proportion of national income was second only to Nazi Germany, and nearly double that of Britain and France.[27] An overriding aim of all Fascist policy was to reorganize Italy's economy and society around preparations for war. The strategy was to create a planned economy using a corporatist model to harness the energies of the nation. League of Nations sanctions only hardened Mussolini's determination to achieve autarchy as a precursor to future wars of conquest. Before the National Assembly of the Fascist Corporations, he stressed the 'inevitability that the nation will be called to the trial of war'. 'In the present historical period', Mussolini argued, 'the fact [of] war is, together with the doctrine of Fascism, a determining element in the position of the State towards the economy'.[28] But there were powerful limits on the extent to which this vision could be realized. Italian society was not modern, and Italy's heavy industry was tiny compared to that of Germany, Britain and even France. Defence output fell continually short of the ambitious targets set by Fascist rearmament programmes. In 1938, the pace of rearmament actually declined as a result of a chronic lack of key raw materials and the financial resources to purchase them abroad.[29] The Fascist regime's expansionist ambitions vastly outstripped the reality of Italy's limited economic and military power.

But the drive for conquest cannot be denied. At Mussolini's insistence, Italy embarked on its Ethiopian adventure despite misgivings throughout the policy establishment. Success in this campaign, obtained in defiance of the liberal democracies and the League of Nations, emboldened the Duce to

---

27 MacGregor Knox, *Mussolini Unleashed: Politics and Strategy in Fascist Italy's Last War* (Cambridge University Press, 1982), pp. 12–36.
28 Quote from Chatham House, *Bulletin of International News* 12:19 (1936), 758.
29 Joe Maiolo, *Cry Havoc: The Arms Race and the Second World War* (London: John Murray, 2010), pp. 198–9.

intervene in support of the nationalist rebellion against the Spanish Popular Front in July 1936. Italian involvement in the conflict outstripped that of other European powers, including Germany, and made a mockery of the international diplomatic regime of non-intervention to which the Fascist regime had signed up in late 1936. Although the Spanish enterprise was ultimately successful, it proved extremely costly in terms of money and material. When the civil war in Spain drew to a close in 1939, Italy's armed forces were significantly weakened. Yet this effort aimed at more than support for the right-wing Franco regime. It was part of the larger project to remake the Italian character. 'When the war in Spain is over', Mussolini advised Ciano, 'I will invent something else, the character of the Italians must be forged in combat'.[30]

Pursuit of war for its own sake inclined Fascist policy increasingly toward ever greater cooperation with Nazi Germany. Like Adolf Hitler, Mussolini was perfectly willing to indulge in what he called 'verbal pacifism'. This entailed frequent public reassurances of Italy's peaceful intentions, aimed at the international community. In private, the Duce characterized this tactic as a 'formula' to 'put the democracies to sleep'.[31] Bypassing the Foreign Ministry in early 1936, he assured an unofficial emissary from Germany that while 'Italy cannot at this point lay its cards on the table', or 'openly show France and Britain our attitude toward Germany', an alignment between Fascism and Nazism 'must happen'. This was because 'between German and Italy there exists a community of destiny. It will become ever stronger. It cannot be denied.'[32] Mussolini demonstrated his commitment to this 'community of destiny', first, by indicating to the German ambassador that Italy would not oppose German domination of Austria, and then by encouraging Hitler to remilitarize the Rhineland. The following November he went further, proclaiming the existence of a 'Rome–Berlin Axis' around which European politics must turn.[33]

The Fascist regime nonetheless feared being drawn into a war for which it was profoundly unprepared. It therefore resisted German pressure for a full-blown military alliance through to the end of 1938. But Mussolini left no

---

30 Quoted in Stanislao Pugliese (ed.), *Galeazzo Ciano: Diary, 1937–1943*, trans. R. L. Miller (London: Enigma, 2002), 13 November 1937, p. 25.
31 Knox, *Common Destiny*, p. 142.
32 Quoted in Robert Whealey, 'Mussolini's Ideological Diplomacy', *Journal of Modern History* 39:4 (1967), 435.
33 Benito Mussolini, *Scritti e Discorsi dell'Impero, 1935–1936* (12 vols., Milan: Hoepli, 1936), vol. x, pp. 199–212.

doubt of his intention to move in this direction as soon as rearmament permitted. When the time was right, the Duce assured Nazi Foreign Minister Joachim von Ribbentrop, 'We must not make a purely defensive alliance... Instead we wish to make an alliance in order to change the map of the world.'[34] The problem was that Mussolini's ambitions far outstripped Italy's national capacities. Nor was the regime ever able to secure the kind of mass popular support necessary to truly harness the energies and enthusiasms of the Italian people for its empire project. Italian Fascism never constituted anything close to the threat posed to the international order by Adolf Hitler and Nazi Germany.

When the National Socialist Party came to power in January 1933, it had already determined a clear direction for German foreign policy. The unifying theme was the need to launch a war of conquest to build a coherent racial empire in Central Europe and European Russia. This would provide the new German Reich with the arable land and raw materials it required to thrive in an international system characterized by an unending and pitiless struggle for domination between 'races'. The Nazi conception of both domestic and international politics was animated by a virulent racism that made its foreign policy far more radical than that of the most determined revisionists among the German military and diplomatic elite. Race, for Hitler, was 'the driving force of world history'. War, meanwhile, was the supreme test of a nation's vitality, the ultimate and inevitable arbiter of all relations between nations and races.

The implementation of Hitler's foreign policy programme required the transformation of German society. Once the Nazi regime had acquired complete control of the machinery of the German state, it implemented a policy of 'coordination' (*Gleichschaltung*) to reorganize German society around the principles of National Socialism. The ultimate aim was the creation of a militarized 'racial community' (*Volksgemeinschaft*), capable of waging the wars of conquest that alone could ensure the survival of the German people. As Richard Bessel has observed, Nazism was 'an ideology of war' in which 'peace was regarded merely as preparation for war'.[35] Race and war provided the central pillars of foreign and domestic policy in Hitler's Germany.

The new regime pursued this nightmare vision with single-minded determination. Only days after his appointment as Chancellor, Hitler outlined his

---

34 Quoted in Maiolo, *Cry Havoc*, p. 267.
35 Richard Bessel, *Nazism and War* (London: Weidenfeld & Nicolson, 2004), p. 1.

core aims to a meeting of senior figures within the army high command. He opened the meeting with the observation that, 'as in the life of individuals, the stronger and better always prevail, so it is in the life of peoples'. He then asked, 'How can Germany be saved?. . . Through a large-scale settlement policy that has as its precondition the expansion of the living space of the German people. . . One can no longer be a citizen of the world. Democracy and pacifism are impossible.' The first priority would be to destroy all internal opposition. Then Germany would rearm so that 'the army will be able to conduct an active foreign policy, and the goal of expanding the living space of the German people will be achieved with arms'.[36]

Hitler, in effect, promised to make rearmament a priority in return for the army's support for his domestic programme. And he proved true to his word. During the first two years of Nazi rule, military spending was relatively modest, as the regime focused on internal consolidation. The purse strings were opened in early 1935 however. On 10 March of that year, Hermann Göring proclaimed the existence of the Luftwaffe to the outside world. One week later, Hitler announced the introduction of conscription and the intention to build up the German army to a strength of thirty-six divisions. The disarmament clauses of the Versailles Treaty were thus consigned to the dustbin, and the era of unlimited rearmament had begun. By 1938, military spending had increased by nearly 500 per cent.[37] The aim was to rearm both in breadth and in depth. Colonel Georg Thomas, head of the *Wehrwirtschaftstab* (Economic Planning Staff) within the Wehrmacht General Staff, observed that 'Modern war is no longer a clash of armies, but a struggle for the existence of the peoples involved. All the resources available to a warring nation must be pressed into service, not just the population, but the industry and the economy.'[38]

The breakneck pace of the armaments build-up imposed massive strains on the economy and society in Germany. Critical shortages of labour, raw materials and, especially, foreign exchange threatened to hamstring the rearmament and leave Germany with an acute balance of payments crisis. Prominent voices within the Nazi government argued for slowing the pace of armaments production and prioritizing exports. Hitler's response was to accelerate rearmament, regardless of the financial consequences. In August

---

36 Reinhard Müller, 'Hitlers Rede vor der Reichswehrführung 1933. Eine neue Moskauer Überlieferung', *Mittelweg 36*:1 (2001), 81–3.
37 Zara Steiner, *The Triumph of the Dark: European International History, 1933–1939* (Oxford University Press, 2011), p. 331.
38 Quoted in Maiolo, *Cry Havoc*, p. 45.

1936, he personally drafted instructions for the introduction of a 'Four-Year Plan' in a memorandum for Defence Minister Werner von Blomberg and Air Minister Hermann Göring. The memorandum began with the observation that 'Politics are the conduct and the course of the historical struggle of nations for life. The aim of these struggles is survival'. The world was faced with a millenarian threat in the form of Bolshevism and Judaism. Germany's role was to serve as the bulwark against this threat. 'A victory of Bolshevism over Germany', Hitler warned, 'would lead not to a Versailles Treaty, but to the final destruction, indeed the annihilation, of the German people.'[39] This conception of international life left little room for classical diplomacy.

The central theme of the Four-Year Plan was that preparation for the coming struggle must shape all aspects of political and economic life in Germany. To achieve this, the economic energies of the entire nation must be harnessed. The Führer insisted that overcoming the financial and industrial challenges thrown up by massive rearmament was 'solely a question of will'. He warned that

> The nation does not live for the economy, for economic leaders or for economic or financial theories; on the contrary, it is finance and the economy, economic leaders and theories, which all owe unqualified service in this struggle for the self-assertion of our nation... There is, however, no point in endless repetition of the fact that we lack foodstuffs and raw materials, what matters is the taking of those measures which can bring about a *final* solution for the *future* and a *temporary* easing of conditions during the *transition* period.[40]

The 'transition period' would be characterized above all by war preparations. 'The extent of the military development of our resources cannot be too large, nor its pace too swift', Hitler insisted. The 'final solution', he went on, 'lies in extending our living space'. For this, he concluded, 'I set the following tasks:

1. The German armed forces must be operational within four years.
2. The German economy must be fit for war within four years.'[41]

Göring was named Minister in Charge of the Four-Year Plan and would eventually take over as Minister of Economics. With the introduction of the Plan, Germany had embarked irreversibly down a road that must end in war.

---

39 'The Four Year Plan', in J. Noakes and G. Pridham (eds.), Nazism, *1919–1945: A Documentary Reader*, vol. II: *State, Economy and Society, 1933–1939* (Exeter University Press, 1984), p. 281, doc. no. 185.
40 Ibid., emphasis in original.
41 Ibid.

The Reich was to be transformed into a vast armed camp. By 1939, more than one-quarter of Germany's entire labour force was employed in the rearmament of the Wehrmacht. Even more were working on defence-related infrastructure projects.[42] Such an economic programme was not sustainable. The military machine under construction would have to be used before it destroyed the German economy. 'No end of the rearmament is in sight,' Göring advised a gathering of leading German industrialists.

> The struggle which we are approaching demands a colossal measure of productive ability... The only deciding point in this case is victory or destruction. If we win, then business will be sufficiently compensated... Our whole nation is at stake. We live in a time when the final battles are in sight. We are already on the threshold of mobilization and are at war, only the guns are not firing.[43]

The chief task of German diplomacy was therefore to prepare the way for the coming race war.

This reality had not been clear at the outset. The decision to retain the respected career diplomat Konstantin von Neurath as Foreign Minister suggested that there would be no radical break with the foreign policy of the Weimar Republic. Without exception, Germany's professional diplomats supported the revisionist aims of Nazi foreign policy. Return of the 'Polish Corridor', union with Austria and a reimposition of German economic and political dominance in East Central Europe were long-term objectives of German foreign policy before and after Hitler's rise to power. But this did not mean that German diplomats shared Hitler's apocalyptic vision of an inevitable race war. The diplomatic corps was comprised overwhelmingly of conservative elites with little sympathy for Nazi ideology. Only one senior diplomat joined the Nazi Party in 1933 and he was promptly removed from his post.[44] Wilhelmstrasse officials initially believed that Nazi ideology could be moderated and harnessed to serve the enduring interests of the Reich. This belief was entirely unfounded.

From the perspective of German professional diplomats, there was, in any case, much to support in the Nazi programme. Nearly all approved of Hitler's determination to rearm and backed his efforts to sabotage the

---

42 Richard Overy, *War and Economy in the Third Reich* (Oxford University Press, 1995), pp. 20–1.

43 Quoted in Adam Tooze, *The Wages of Destruction: The Making and Breaking of the Nazi Economy* (London: Penguin, 2007), p. 224.

44 D. C. Watt, 'Diplomacy and Diplomatists', in R. Boyce and J. Maiolo (eds.), *The Origins of World War Two: The Debate Continues* (London: Palgrave, 2003), pp. 335–6.

World Disarmament Conference. The vast majority also endorsed the decision to leave the League of Nations in October 1933. There were some misgivings about the Führer's determination to remilitarize the Rhineland in March 1936. By the time Nazi foreign policy entered its radical phase in early 1938, one-third of the ninety-two senior diplomats had joined the Nazi Party. Only a small number were relieved of their posts for opposing Nazi policy. Fewer still left the service for reasons of conscience. Some senior officials did become alarmed at the risks Hitler was willing to take. Several, including Erich Kordt, Ernst von Weizsäcker, Ulrich von Hassell and Hans (Johnny) von Herwath, opened back-channel communications to their British, French and American diplomatic colleagues in an attempt to avert war. But their efforts were too cautious and too late to make any difference to the course of events.[45]

Hitler, for his part, dismissed the Wilhelmstrasse as 'an intellectual garbage dump' and characterized its diplomats as 'Santa Claus types' who were best suited for 'quiet times'.[46] His strong preference was to circumvent the official channels of European diplomacy wherever possible, either through direct communications with other heads of government or through his own hand-picked representatives. A number of rival institutions emerged to challenge the prerogatives of the Foreign Ministry. One was the Nazi Party's own Foreign Office, the *Aussenpolititische Amt*, under the direction of chief racial theorist Alfred Rosenberg. Although Rosenberg aspired to gain control of external policy, his office was almost entirely lacking in either experience or foreign contacts. A more serious threat was posed by the *Ausland-Organization* (AO) run by Ernst Bohle, under the patronage of Deputy Führer Rudolf Hess. The AO was charged initially with conducting relations with Germans and Nazi sympathizers overseas. But its remit expanded to serve as the key conduit between Spanish nationalist General Francisco Franco and the Nazi regime. Neurath and the Foreign Ministry were bypassed entirely because of their opposition to Germany's intervention in that conflict. In January 1937, Bohle secured an official appointment to the Foreign Ministry with the rank of State Secretary, and the AO claimed the right of veto over foreign service appointments.[47]

---

45 See, above all, Gerhard Weinberg, *The Foreign Policy of Hitler's Germany*, vol. I: *A Diplomatic Revolution in Europe*, and vol. II: *Starting World War II* (2 vols., University of Chicago Press, 1970, 1980).

46 Quoted in Keith Hamilton and Richard Langhorne, *The Practice of Diplomacy* (2nd edn, London: Routledge, 2012), p. 181.

47 Ernst Freiherr von Weizsäcker, *Memoirs of Ernst von Weizsäcker*, trans. J. Andrews (London: Gollancz, 1951), pp. 88–109.

Joachim von Ribbentrop was the most formidable rival to the Foreign Ministry. A businessman with wide-ranging international contacts, Ribbentrop fascinated Hitler from the moment the two first met in the late 1920s. Ribbentrop's first appointment was to serve as the Führer's 'special commissioner' to the disarmament conference. By 1934, he had set up the *Dienstelle Ribbentrop* as an alternative foreign service, located directly across the street from the Foreign Ministry building on the Wilhelmstrasse. In June 1935, Hitler charged Ribbentrop with negotiating a naval treaty with Great Britain. The resulting Anglo-German Naval Agreement was achieved despite Ribbentrop's contempt for basic diplomatic practice. At the first meeting in London, he demanded that Britain recognize Germany's right to build a fleet 35 per cent the size of the Royal Navy as a precondition to further discussions. The lead negotiator on the British side, Sir John Simon, responded that it was highly unusual to make such conditions at the very beginning of negotiations. Paul Schmidt, the German Foreign Ministry interpreter and an experienced diplomat, was shocked at Ribbentrop's mockery of diplomatic convention:

> I wondered why Ribbentrop had brought up the most difficult question of all so undiplomatically right at the start... Was it lack of experience of international conferences? Was it a typical National Socialist attempt to be unconventional?... I was already wondering what the weather would be like on the flight home.

To Schmidt's astonishment, however, the British accepted Ribbentrop's demand and negotiations proceeded. The result was the Anglo-German Naval Agreement, which placed another nail in the coffin of the Versailles Treaty.[48]

The episode of the Anglo-German Naval Agreement was a classic example of Hitler's preference to avoid traditional diplomacy wherever possible in pursuit of his key foreign policy objectives. Ribbentrop was later appointed ambassador in London, in the hope that he could secure an alliance with Great Britain. His abject failure in this undertaking was offset by his later success in leading the negotiations that resulted in the Anti-Comintern Pact. A demoralized von Neurath was coaxed into retirement in a major shake-up of the Wilhelmstrasse in February 1938. He was replaced by Ribbentrop. This change at the top opened the way for the 'Nazification' of the Foreign Ministry, the purpose of which was to provide the regime with a willing

48 Quoted in Michael Bloch, *Ribbentrop* (London: Bantam, 1992), pp. 72–3.

tool as it embarked on foreign aggression.[49] Ribbentrop, for his part, was just as committed to a future European war as his Führer. '[Ribbentrop] wants war, his war', a bemused Ciano observed after one meeting in late 1938. 'He doesn't have, or doesn't say, what his general marching plan is. He doesn't single out his enemies, nor does he indicate his objectives. But he wants war.'[50]

Hitler had made his intention to embark on war clear in a meeting with high-level soldiers and diplomats during the infamous 'Hossbach Conference' of 5 November 1937. Here, the Führer observed that the primordial task of German policy was 'the safeguarding of the racial group. . . Germany's future was therefore wholly conditional upon solving the need for space'. This problem 'could be solved only by the use of force', which was 'never without attendant risk'. Rather than seek far-flung colonies, Hitler argued, Germany would be best served building its empire 'in the heart of Europe'. The first stage must see Austria and Czechoslovakia attacked and absorbed by 1943–45. But the Nazi leader also observed that 'certain contingencies' might require the acceleration of this programme. The first was the possibility of France being torn apart by internal strife. The second was a Mediterranean conflict involving Italy, Britain and France. Hitler noted that he saw this latter contingency 'coming definitely nearer'.[51]

The extent to which Hitler intended to force the pace was evident in March 1938, when Germany intervened to annex Austria without any diplomatic consultation whatsoever. Europe was presented with a fait accompli that provided yet another illustration of Hitler's contempt for the machinery and methods of diplomacy. Little more than two months later, he declared his 'unalterable decision to smash Czechoslovakia by military action in the near future'. The German high command was instructed to accelerate planning for an invasion of Czechoslovakia, with the target date set for 28 September. There was no mention of diplomacy in Hitler's directive, which observed merely that 'it is the business of the political leadership to bring about the suitable moment [for an attack] from a political and military point of view'.[52] The Führer was deeply chagrined that the ensuing crisis over Czechoslovakia did not result in war. The Munich Conference of 29–30

49 Steiner, *Triumph of the Dark*, pp. 91–2, 254–64, 317–18, 332–5.
50 Pugliese (ed.), *Ciano: Diary*, 28 October 1938, p. 149.
51 The 'Hossbach Memorandum', in J. Noakes and G. Pridham (eds.), *Nazism, 1919–1945: A Documentary Reader*, vol. III: *Foreign Policy, War and Racial Extermination* (3 vols., Exeter University Press, 1988), pp. 680–7, doc. no. 503.
52 Order for 'Operation Green' (*Fall Grün*), 28 May 1939, in ibid., p. 712, doc. no. 523.

September 1938 gave Germany possession of large swathes of formerly Czechoslovak territory, without the invasion and conquest that was his true aim.

Three weeks later, Hitler ordered the 'liquidation' of the remainder of Czechoslovakia. Henceforward he resolved to eschew even the pretence of a commitment to peaceful diplomacy. 'For years circumstances have compelled me to talk about almost nothing but peace', he revealed to a gathering of journalists in late 1938:

> Only by continually stressing Germany's desire for peace and her peaceful intentions could I achieve freedom for the German people bit by bit and provide the armaments which were always necessary before the next step could be taken. . . It was only out of necessity that for years I talked of peace. But it is now necessary gradually to re-educate the German people psychologically and to make it clear that there are things which must be achieved by force.[53]

Speaking to a group of senior military officials the following February, Hitler advised that:

> I have taken it upon myself to solve the German question, i.e. to solve the German problem of space. . . Be convinced that, when I think it possible to advance a step at some moment, I will take action at once and never draw back from the most extreme measures.[54]

Shortly after occupying the remainder of Czechoslovakia on 15 March 1939, Hitler approved the order to finalize plans for an attack on Poland. Diplomacy was to be used to ramp up pressure over the question of Danzig and the Polish Corridor. But the real purpose, as the Nazi leader revealed on 23 May, was 'to attack Poland at the first suitable opportunity'. He added: 'It is not Danzig that is at stake. For us it is a matter of the expansion of living space in the east.' By this time, Hitler had also begun to see war with Britain as inevitable. 'England is our enemy', he warned, 'and the showdown with England is a matter of life and death.'[55]

All diplomacy under the Nazi regime was, by definition, no more than a prelude for war. This is the framework within which Nazi diplomatic initiatives leading to the Anti-Comintern Pact, the Pact of Steel and, finally,

---

53 Hitler address, 10 November 1938, in ibid., p. 721, doc. no. 529.
54 Quoted in Ian Kershaw, *Hitler, 1936–1945: Nemesis* (London: Allen Lane, 2001), p. 168.
55 Record of a meeting between Hitler and the German high command, 23 May 1939, in Noakes and Pridham (eds.), *Foreign Policy, War and Racial Extermination*, pp. 736–8, doc. no. 539.

the Nazi-Soviet Pact must be understood. War was always the ultimate aim of Nazi foreign policy. It was the supreme test, the revitalizing and purifying process through which the German people must pass to realize their destiny. As Hamilton and Langhorne note, with its systematic and relentless pursuit of war, Nazi diplomacy was 'a gross perversion' of diplomatic practice.[56] The very existence of Nazism in Germany removed all possibility of finding diplomatic solutions to the great problems of European peace.

It is worth pausing at this point to consider briefly the role of the four core functions of diplomacy in the policies of the revisionist great powers. Diplomacy functioned as a means of *communication* with other actors in all three cases. But at no point did it succeed in the crucial role of *generating confidence* among the great powers. Indeed the dominant narrative of the 1930s is one instead of a steady collapse of confidence and the fragmentation of the international community that had begun to emerge in Europe in the 1920s. Such a collapse was a central foreign policy objective for all three revisionist powers. Turning to the second core function of negotiation: of the three revisionist states, only the Soviet Union relied on its diplomatic machine in the conduct of *negotiations*. Both Mussolini and Hitler demonstrated a marked preference for using either unofficial representatives or negotiating face-to-face with other heads of government. Nor were Soviet, Italian or German diplomats able to perform effectively the third key task of providing *accurate information on the outside world*. They served political masters with such firmly fixed ideas that diplomatic reporting made little or no difference to the policy process. The same is true of the final function of *giving policy advice*. The classic responsibility of diplomats to identify common interests and common ground for negotiation and compromise could play little role in a policy context dominated by ideological assumptions about the inevitability of war.

In sum, all three revisionist powers aimed at overthrowing the liberal international order established in Paris in 1919. It is true that Soviet policy, unlike that of Fascist Italy and Nazi Germany, did not pursue war for its own sake. But neither was it committed to upholding peace.

The status quo powers: Britain and France

Britain and France sought throughout the 1930s to preserve the liberal-capitalist order entrenched at the Paris Peace Conference. This fact attributed

---

56 Hamilton and Langhorne, *Practice of Diplomacy*, p. 184.

a central role for diplomacy in French and British foreign policy. Ultimately, however, Fascist and Nazi pursuit of war imposed powerful limits on what diplomacy could accomplish. Because neither regime viewed peace as a desirable state of affairs for its own sake, the most that could be expected of French and British diplomacy was to construct a powerful coalition capable either of deterring the revisionist states or ensuring their ultimate destruction. This imposed three overriding priorities on French and British diplomacy. The first was to develop an accurate assessment of the long-term intentions of the revisionist powers. The second was to formulate a coherent strategy for coalition-building. The third task was to convince political leaders in both states to accept the risk of war. In other words, it was necessary to both understand and adapt to the new international environment created by the rise of aggressive revisionism in Italy and Germany.

Professional diplomats in France and Britain were slow to meet these challenges. Sharp divisions over the correct interpretation of the long-term policy orientations of the USSR, Italy and Germany endured in both Paris and London well into the late 1930s. In fact, it was not until spring 1939 that negotiations for a Franco-British military alliance began in earnest. The argument that the USSR should be included to form a 'grand alliance' against the Axis powers, meanwhile, did not gain wide acceptance until the very eve of war.

There were formidable obstacles in the way of any attempt to fashion an effective diplomatic response to the revisionist challenge. The immediate challenge was to assess the intentions of the other powers. Estimating intentions entails predicting how foreign decision-makers will respond to future events. It is fraught with uncertainty at the best of times. The problem was compounded by the fact that Soviet Russia, Fascist Italy and Nazi Germany all presented unique and unprecedented challenges to outside observers. None was a traditional great power. Their external policies were shaped by ideological assumptions that were alien to most diplomats from liberal democracies. Another challenge was that Fascist and Nazi policy were impervious to the 'normative pull' of the 'New Diplomacy'. Both viewed 'world opinion' as something to be manipulated rather than a factor that must always be taken into account in policy calculations. Their aim was to destroy the post-1918 normative order. This fact had profound consequences for the practice of diplomacy. French and British diplomats needed to abandon the operating assumptions and policy reflexes that they had acquired over the course of the previous decade. The fact that this took time should not surprise students of international relations. The process was further complicated by the ability of both Hitler and Mussolini to manipulate international perceptions by speaking continually of peace while rearming and preparing for war.

A third impediment to effective diplomatic responses to the revisionist challenge was the domestic political context in both Britain and France. The 'long shadow' of the First World War still loomed over all discussions of peace and security in both countries. Through to the end of the 1930s, elite and popular opinion in the two nations remained reluctant to accept the possibility of another great war. A powerful attachment to peace combined with the debilitating effects of the Great Depression to undermine popular support for policies of resistance based on rearmament and alliance-building for most of the pre-war decade. Girding for war was a psychological and a material process that began later and proceeded more slowly in status quo powers than it did in the revisionist states. British and French political leaders proved consistently reluctant to embrace diplomatic advice based on pessimistic readings of the international situation. A final obstacle was a predilection for conducting personal diplomacy on the part of strong-minded heads of government, such as Pierre Laval and Neville Chamberlain. While French and British diplomats typically exercised greater influence than their Soviet, Italian or German counterparts, they did not decide policy and could also be marginalized or circumvented.

The dominant preoccupation for interwar French foreign policy was security from a resurgent Germany. The collective security provisions elaborated in the League of Nations Covenant were never considered strong enough to provide true security for France. In the aftermath of the Peace Conference, France signed traditional military alliances with Belgium and Poland. In the mid-1920s, these arrangements were supplemented by less binding political treaties with Czechoslovakia, Yugoslavia and Romania. Together, these agreements are often referred to, somewhat misleadingly, as France's 'eastern alliance system'. In truth, these various arrangements never constituted anything close to a 'system', because Poland and Czechoslovakia, the two strongest 'successor states' in Eastern Europe, refused to cooperate with one another. The eastern allies were, in any case, never sufficiently powerful to constitute an 'eastern counter-weight' comparable to Imperial Russia before 1914.

The chief priority for French policy was instead a strategic commitment of some kind from Great Britain. Such a commitment, it was hoped, would, in effect, guarantee the European status quo. Through to late 1924, French diplomats strove to resurrect the wartime military *entente*. Britain proved consistently unwilling to negotiate a traditional alliance of this kind however.

French policy elites therefore adapted their strategy by seeking to integrate both Britain and Germany in a multilateral mutual assistance regime that would bring with it a clear British commitment to defend France and its allies to the East. But successive British governments refused to make a Europe-wide commitment of this kind. In 1925, Britain did agree to participate in a five-power mutual assistance arrangement that included France, Belgium, Italy and Germany, in the Locarno accords. The problem was that the Locarno system was limited to Western Europe. Its very existence implied a distinction between West and East European security.

Locarno nonetheless provided the conceptual framework for French diplomatic strategy over the next decade. Through to the mid-1930s, the central thrust of all French diplomacy was to extend the Locarno system of interlocking mutual assistance pacts eastward, to include the successor states Poland, Czechoslovakia, Romania, Yugoslavia and, if possible, Austria, Hungary and the Soviet Union. The aim was not to prevent all revision of the Versailles Treaty. Rather it was to ensure that any revision that took place was peaceful and a product of diplomatic negotiations. The result was a series of projects for an 'eastern Locarno', a 'Mediterranean Pact' and a 'Danubian Pact', championed by France over the next ten years. The strategy was to enmesh Germany in a Europe-wide security system underwritten by Britain and France. Britain was therefore vital to all of these French schemes. Foreign Ministry officials at the Quai d'Orsay argued consistently that only British participation in the envisaged pacts would provide them with the credibility necessary to ensure their effectiveness.[57] But Britain remained emphatically opposed to any commitments beyond Locarno.

France's diplomatic strategy has been criticized, with some justification, for having been dominated by 'illusions of pactomania'.[58] French Foreign Ministry officials essentially failed to adapt their strategy to the new conditions created by the advent of National Socialism in Germany. Through mid- to late 1936, French diplomacy was based on a misreading of Nazi radicalism. The majority of officials within the Quai d'Orsay accepted the judgement of André François-Poncet, France's ambassador in Berlin, that Hitler's long-term objectives were essentially the same as those of previous German statesmen:

57 See France, Ministère des Affaires Etrangères (hereafter MAE), Série Papiers d'Agents – Archives Privées (hereafter PA-AP) 217, *Papiers René Massigli*, vol. 9, 'Conférence pour la réduction des armements'; vol. 10, 'Limitation des armements et projet de pacte aérien'; vol. 11, 'Sécurité en Méditerranée'; and vol. 15, 'Europe Centrale'.
58 Jean-Baptiste Duroselle, 'The Spirit of Locarno: Illusions of Pactomania', *Foreign Affairs* 50 (1972), 752–64.

Like the Chancellors who preceded him, Hitler wishes to secure for Germany the means with which to speak the language of a Great Power, both in Europe and in the rest of the world; and he wishes to undertake, under more favourable conditions, problems (such as treaty revisionism and the Corridor) to which Germany has no chance of obtaining a satisfactory resolution today.

Significantly, François-Poncet underlined the restraints on Hitler's freedom of action and stressed that fear of isolation would combine with the threat of general social unrest to force Hitler to adopt a more reasonable external policy. He judged that 'the Nazi programme, insofar as it merits such a description, in no way precludes an understanding with France'.[59]

François-Poncet's assessment reflected, but also crucially reinforced the ongoing commitment to multilateralism in French diplomacy. A Foreign Ministry memorandum on Nazi violations of the Treaty of Versailles in 1934 concluded that 'all military action must be ruled out'.[60] Neither Germany's exit from the League, nor mounting evidence of accelerating German rearmament caused the Quai d'Orsay to reassess its overall strategy. In April 1934, a conservative French government decided to respond to these developments with the traditional policies of rearmament and a military alliance with Russia. Significantly, the strategy of a Franco-Soviet alliance was resisted by senior diplomats, who argued for a multilateral approach. Secretary General Alexis Léger argued that any arrangement with the USSR must function as a cornerstone of another 'eastern Locarno' that would include Germany and the smaller states of East Central Europe. 'A regime of mutual obligations that includes Germany', Léger advised, 'holds out the promise of the eventual participation of Britain that alone will give it both moral and practical value for our security.'[61] Foreign Minister Louis Barthou was persuaded by this argument. The overarching aim of French policy remained an East–West security regime sponsored by France and Britain. This system, it is worth emphasizing, was designed to enmesh and contain *both* Germany and the USSR.[62] French diplomats were loath to abandon the multilateralist

---

59 France, Imprimerie Nationale, *Documents Diplomatiques Français* (hereafter DDF), 1ère série, vol. iii, André François-Poncet to Paris, 22 June, 9 and 30 March 1933, doc. nos. 419, 259, 70.

60 *DDF*, 1ère série, vol. iii, 4 July 1934, doc. no. 448.

61 MAE, Série Z (Europe 1918–1940), *URSS*, vol. 965, 'Note pour le ministre', 30 March 1934; ibid., vol. 970, 'Pacte de l'est', 1 October 1934.

62 MAE, PA-AP 217, *Papiers Massigli*, vol. 7, 'Pacte de l'est', 30 October 1934; MAE, Série Z (Europe), *URSS*, vol. 971, 'Genèse et étapes du projet de pacte régional de l'Est', 8 January 1935.

reflexes that they had acquired over the course of the 1920s. There was no hope that Britain, let alone Germany, would participate in any such pact. And yet, as late as autumn 1937, the Foreign Ministry was drafting plans to revive Locarno with a 'Western pact', based on reciprocal mutual assistance agreements.[63]

Relations with Italy were an issue that caused deep divisions within France's diplomatic establishment. The ambiguities in Fascist policy made it particularly difficult to assess Italian medium- and long-term intentions. A minority of Foreign Ministry officials argued for rapprochement with Italy. This line of policy was opposed by Secretary General Léger and majority opinion within the Quai d'Orsay. 'The government of the Duce', advised the Ministry's Political Directorate, 'is an element of perpetual instability in European affairs and this state of affairs is unlikely to change. All evidence indicates that Italy's chief aim is to drive a wedge between France and Britain'.[64] During the Abyssinian crisis, the premier and Foreign Minister Pierre Laval resolved to ignore this advice. He favoured appeasing Italy in cooperation with the British. The resulting Hoare–Laval Pact was undermined, however, when Quai d'Orsay officials leaked details of the agreement to the French and British press.

Discord between the Foreign Minister and career diplomats surfaced again during and after the Czechoslovak Crisis of 1938. The question of whether France should go to war in support of its ally divided both diplomatic personnel and the government of premier Edouard Daladier. Foreign Minister Georges Bonnet consistently favoured accommodating German demands for Czechoslovak territory. He hoped that this concession would serve as a prelude to a Franco-German understanding that would remove the prospect of war. This policy was opposed by the Foreign Ministry's Political Director, René Massigli. 'Far from convincing Germany to adopt a policy of cooperation', Massigli warned, 'success [over Czechoslovakia] will only encourage it to persevere with its methods.' Acquiescing in the dismemberment of Czechoslovakia, he added, would be 'to reduce our policy to an act of faith in the pacific evolution of this new Pan-Germanism'. The damage to France's prestige would be devastating.[65] The majority of senior diplomats agreed with Léger, who, despite sharing Massigli's analysis of the motivations of

63 MAE, PA-AP 217, *Papiers Massigli*, vol. 7, 'Problèmes posés par la négociation du pacte occidental', 26 November 1937.
64 MAE, *Papiers 1940: Laval*, 'Note pour le ministre', 30 November 1935.
65 MAE, PA-AP 217, *Papiers Massigli*, vol. 19, 'Note sur les conséquences pour la France de l'affaiblissement de la Tchécoslovaquie', 19 September 1938.

Nazi foreign policy, argued that France could not contemplate war over Czechoslovakia without iron-clad assurance of British military support. This was the position eventually adopted by premier Daladier, with the support of the majority of his Cabinet. When Hitler refused to negotiate on a reasonable basis, and Britain refused to commit to marching beside France, the betrayal of Czechoslovakia became all but inevitable.

The question of an alliance with the USSR was also divisive. The operation of the Franco-Soviet mutual assistance pact of 1935 had always been intended to form part of a wider security regime. There was no enthusiasm among French diplomats for going further to negotiate a full military alliance. The great purges of 1936–37 only confirmed pre-existing assumptions that the USSR could not be counted upon to be a pillar in an anti-German coalition. With the important exceptions of Massigli and Robert Coulondre, the French ambassador in Moscow, there was little support among senior French diplomats for including Russia in a broad anti-German front. Historians debate whether this assessment was a product of clear-headed calculation or ideological bias. What is not in doubt is that mistrust of Soviet motives was behind the decision to exclude the USSR from the Munich Conference and, ultimately, undermined all hope for a 'grand alliance'.

The lone power considered indispensable to an anti-revisionist coalition was Great Britain. This was a principle on which virtually all French diplomats, politicians and military personnel agreed. But in 1938 British policy elites remained as reluctant as ever to make a substantial military commitment to France. From June 1936, the Popular Front government of Léon Blum tried to redress the situation by rallying France's allies in Eastern Europe and introducing an ambitious rearmament programme. Neither initiative bore fruit in the short term, however, and French strategic dependence on Britain only increased.

Britain's interwar European foreign policy was dominated by two principles. The first was that European security could be divided along East–West lines. While there was broad agreement that affairs in the West concerned Britain closely, Eastern Europe was not deemed a vital region for British security. The second principle was that it was both possible and desirable to reach a durable agreement that would bind Germany into a peaceful revision of the political status quo in Europe. Although a growing number of diplomats came to reject both principles, they remained at the heart of British foreign policy until early 1939.

In the aftermath of Hitler's accession to power, the British Embassy in Berlin provided a series of alarming assessments of Nazi foreign policy.

Among the most astute were the judgements of outgoing ambassador Sir Horace Rumbold in May 1933. Rumbold emphasized the swiftness with which the National Socialists had seized political control and destroyed the workings of Weimar democracy. He then provided a succinct analysis of the intellectual underpinnings of the Nazi approach to international relations:

> Hitler's thesis is simple. He starts with the assertions that man is a fighting animal; therefore the nation is, he concludes, a fighting unit, being a community of fighters. Any living organism which ceases to fight for its existence is, he asserts, doomed to extinction. A country or a race which ceases to fight, is equally doomed... Pacifism is the deadliest sin, for pacifism means surrender of the race in the fight for existence.

Rumbold warned that these ideas must be taken seriously as a source of future German policy. He judged that the chief goal of Nazi policy was eastward expansion into the Baltic region and European Russia. And he dismissed the idea that engagement with international society would cause Hitler to moderate his views. Hitler, Rumbold argued, 'cannot abandon the cardinal points of his programme any more than Lenin or Mussolini... it would be misleading to base any hopes on a return to sanity or a serious modification of the views of the Chancellor and his entourage'.[66] This view was echoed by Britain's senior diplomat, Sir Robert Vansittart, who, in a memorandum circulated to the British Cabinet in August 1933, insisted that 'there is no doubt whatsoever about the ultimate intentions of the Nazis'. Germany would rearm in preparation for war. It was an 'open secret' that 'anything peaceful said by Hitler is merely for foreign consumption and designed to gain time'. The true intention was 'to strike when ready'. Vansittart warned that German aggression must be expected in less than a decade.[67]

The great problem was that there was no obvious policy response to these and other highly pessimistic assessments of Nazi intentions. As Rumbold's successor, Sir Eric Phipps, observed, taking Hitler's policy pronouncements literally meant assuming that the German Chancellor could not be trusted. This would 'undermine all prospects for diplomatic solutions' and 'condemn us to a policy of sterility'. Phipps suggested, instead, a strategy of obtaining clear legal commitments from Germany. Hitler, he argued, would find it

---

66 Britain, The National Archives – Public Record Office (hereafter TNA–PRO), CAB 24/259, CP 13 (36), 'The German Danger', enclosing Sir Horace Rumbold to Sir John Simon, 3 May 1933.
67 TNA–PRO, CAB 24/243, CP 212 (33), 'A Memorandum on the Present and Future Position of Europe', 23 August 1933, circulated to Cabinet by Foreign Secretary Sir John Simon, 30 August 1933.

difficult to break such commitments. 'His signature, once given, will bind his people as no other could'.[68] This was the logic underpinning the Anglo-German Naval Agreement and all subsequent attempts to appease Nazi Germany. The goal of limiting German rearmament and constraining German policy though bilateral negotiations remained central to British policy through to the end of 1938. It achieved nothing beyond legitimating the gradual destruction of the European international order. The alternative, however, was a return to pre-1914 practices of power-balancing and exclusive alliances. This was something which the majority of British diplomats and policy elites remained unwilling to accept.

The views of the Assistant Under-Secretary at the Foreign Office, Orme Sargent, illustrate the enduring influence of post-1918 international norms, even within the Foreign Office. Sargent argued that 'the establishment of a feeling of security is an end in itself, and like virtue is its own reward'. He therefore consistently opposed abandoning collective security in favour of a British military alliance with France or any other European state, arguing that 'we have consistently endeavoured to prevent such a return to the old habits of the pre-war period'.[69] Sargent's preferred strategy was to obtain a German commitment to limit rearmament and renounce aggression that would be embedded in a multilateral agreement involving the other Western European great powers. He remained sceptical of any commitment to Eastern Europe and utterly opposed to involving the USSR in any collective arrangements. Only in late 1937, when it became clear that a multilateral settlement was impossible, did Sargent come to oppose appeasement.

Other voices within the Foreign Office and the rest of Whitehall pushed for an agreement with Germany, even to the exclusion of interested third parties. Phipps, as we have seen, stressed the benefits of forcing the Nazi leader to state his price for a general settlement and pledge his word. Both Phipps's replacement, Nevile Henderson, and the future Permanent Under-Secretary Alexander Cadogan, went further to argue that German domin-ation of East Central Europe was inevitable, and not necessarily harmful to Britain's vital interests. This view complemented those of Robert Craigie, head of the American Department at the Foreign Office and then ambassador to Japan, and the Chiefs of Staff of the armed services. All argued that Britain

---

68 TNA–PRO, CAB 24/259, CP 13 (36), 'The German Danger', enclosing Sir Eric Phipps to Samuel Hoare, 12 June 1935.
69 Quotations from Keith Neilson, 'Orme Sargent, Appeasement and British Policy in Europe, 1933–1939', *Twentieth Century British History* 21:1 (2010), 26, 21.

must reduce its potential enemies in order to meet its global security requirements. This meant some kind of agreement with Germany – preferably a multilateral accord, but, if necessary, a bilateral treaty along the lines of the 1935 Anglo-German Naval Agreement. Advocates of this policy were willing to support German claims for treaty revision in Eastern Europe in order to secure a durable understanding with the Nazi regime.

This line of policy was opposed vigorously by Vansittart, who had long warned that international politics had changed since the 1920s. He argued that Britain must respond with a traditional balance-of-power strategy. Vansittart insisted that Nazi Germany constituted Britain's 'ultimate potential enemy', and advocated support for France as an essential precondition of European security. Such a strategy would require large-scale rearmament and, more controversially, the construction of a land army capable of intervening once again on the Continent. Vansittart similarly rejected any attempt to coerce Eastern European states into making territorial concessions to Germany. Such 'appeasement' of German grievances, he insisted, would only strengthen the Nazi regime and make future aggression more likely. 'The Germany of today', he cautioned, 'has no intention of remaining within her present boundaries or of respecting the integrity of her smaller neighbours...no matter what papers she may sign'.[70] Along with Lawrence Collier, head of the Foreign Office's Northern Department, Vansittart argued that Britain must take the lead in building a coalition against German aggression. Both insisted, moreover, that Soviet Russia be included in this coalition. This was a highly divisive position. Much of the British policy elite remained reluctant to negotiate an alliance with France. The vast majority had no faith in Soviet motives and opposed integrating the USSR into the wider effort to contain the revisionist powers.

The one strategy about which there was near consensus in Whitehall was the need to rearm in order to deal with the dictators from a position of strength. The most determined and influential advocate of this strategy was Neville Chamberlain, Chancellor of the Exchequer until he became Prime Minister in November 1937. 'Our best defence', Chamberlain argued consistently, 'would be the existence of a deterrent force so powerful as to render success in attack too doubtful to be worthwhile'. The most effective way to construct such a deterrent, he submitted, was to focus on air power. Joe Maiolo has persuasively argued that air rearmament was pivotal to what was

---

70 TNA–PRO, FO 371, 19902, C2842/4/18, Sir Robert Vansittart to Maurice Hankey (Cabinet Secretary), 16 April 1936.

essentially a 'go-it-alone strategy' followed by Chamberlain. A powerful air force would allow Britain to negotiate a European settlement directly with Germany, without the need to involve itself in entangling alliances of the kind that had dragged it into war in 1914.[71] For most of the 1930s, Chamberlain remained steadfastly opposed to making a strategic commitment to any part of Europe.

Chamberlain's policy conception left little room for traditional diplomacy. It assumed, instead, that the core issues threatening the peace of Europe could be settled in direct negotiations between heads of government. Divisions within the diplomatic establishment made it easy for Chamberlain to ignore opposition to his strategy. Critics of appeasement were either circumvented or marginalized. To get around growing scepticism from within the Foreign Office, Chamberlain used the familiar tactic of sending personal emissaries to pave the way for future negotiation. Lord Halifax, then leader of the House of Lords, was dispatched to Germany, to give Hitler private assurances that Britain did not, in principle, oppose frontier revisions in Eastern Europe. Chamberlain similarly used his parliamentary ally Joseph Ball to conduct secret communications with Mussolini, without the knowledge of Foreign Secretary Eden (who opposed a policy of rapprochement with Italy). Vansittart, meanwhile, was removed from his post as Permanent Under-Secretary and named Chief Diplomatic Advisor, a position from which he could safely be ignored. His replacement, Alexander Cadogan, was more amenable to pursuing a comprehensive agreement with Germany at the expense of third parties.

Traditional diplomacy was marginalized altogether when Chamberlain flew three times to meet directly with the German Chancellor during the Czechoslovak crisis of September 1938. In these meetings, the British Prime Minister took it upon himself to negotiate on behalf of France and Czechoslovakia. Asked by Hitler at Berchtesgaden on 15 September to guarantee the self-determination of Germans living inside Czechoslovakia, Chamberlain replied that he could not do so without consulting his Cabinet. He made no mention of consultations with either the French or the Czechoslovaks. Chamberlain's myopic focus on the quest for a durable agreement with Germany was ill-conceived and futile. It was also the antithesis of classic diplomacy.

During the 1930s, professional diplomats in Britain and France failed to provide clear and effective policy guidance to their respective governments.

---

71 Maiolo, *Cry Havoc*, pp. 227–9.

The foreign policies of both states were slow to adapt to the changed international circumstances of the 1930s. What was needed, as Vansittart warned at an early stage, was a return to more traditional practices of power-balancing and alliance-building. The entrenched opposition to integrating the Soviet Union into an anti-revisionist coalition was another failing. Whether the USSR would have participated in such a front is an open question. What is not in doubt is that Franco-British efforts to incorporate the Soviets were too late and almost certainly doomed to fail during the summer of 1939.

These failures must be situated in their proper context, however. In both France and Britain, foreign policy was made in political contexts that did not favour a return to those same traditional strategies that were widely blamed for having caused the Great War. Both societies recoiled from the prospect of another world war. Political leaders in both states understood this fact and resolved to avoid war until it became evident to all but the most die-hard appeasers that no durable understanding with the revisionist powers was possible. When the advice of diplomats did not complement this policy orientation, it was ignored.

Conclusion

The outbreak of the Second World War in 1939 cannot be attributed to a failure of great-power diplomacy. The diplomatic shortcomings of French and British policy are undeniable. Diplomats from both status quo powers adapted too slowly, and their policy prescriptions were undermined by internal discord. The result was a comprehensive failure to create a broad anti-revisionist front that might have deterred Nazi Germany and Fascist Italy in the short term, and, in the longer term, established better conditions for waging war when it came.

But war would certainly have come. Two of the five European great powers pursued war as a political objective in its own right. Fascism and Nazism rejected utterly any sense of belonging to a wider European society of the kind posited by de Callières as constituting the necessary precondition for effective diplomacy. Both, instead, aimed to use violence to destroy the existing political order. Nor was the Soviet Union committed to upholding the liberal-capitalist international system. It looked abroad and saw only imminent and longer-term enemies that desired its destruction. Given the ideological fissures in the European political order, there was no international society left to preserve.

10

Asia-Pacific

The failure of diplomacy, 1931–1941

PETER MAUCH

Joseph C. Grew, one of America's most venerable mid-twentieth-century professional diplomats, returned to the United States in August 1942, some eight months after the Pearl Harbor attack had brought a dramatic end to his ambassadorial mission to Japan. He carried with him a report which he had prepared during his post-Pearl Harbor internment. It was animated by the question as to whether the United States might profitably have avoided war with Japan. Grew's answer was unequivocally affirmative. His report overtly criticized policy-makers in Washington for having adopted an unnecessarily inflexible diplomatic posture in the weeks and months before the Pearl Harbor attack. He was particularly concerned that a Japanese proposal in August–September 1941 for a presidential-prime ministerial summit had provoked not enthusiasm, but scepticism among his colleagues in the State Department. Grew argued that, instead of stonewalling the Japanese proposal, his government should have accepted the risk of a failed summit. Grew was, in a word, charging his own government with critical failings in diplomacy.[1]

He met with a stinging rebuke. Secretary of State Cordell Hull – confirming his reputation for both a short temper and an acid tongue – challenged Grew's findings so vigorously that the 'rising tones of...profanity' were clearly audible from outside the Secretary's office. Less heated, but perhaps more considered, was the judgement offered some decades later by Grew's perceptive biographer, Waldo Heinrichs. He suggested that Grew's arguments were 'retrospectively...more convincing' than they could ever have been before the Pearl Harbor attack. Whatever the case, Grew shelved his

---

1 An edited version of Grew's report can be found in Joseph C. Grew, *Turbulent Era: A Diplomatic Record of Forty Years, 1904–1945* (2 vols., Freeport, NY: Books for Libraries Press, 1952), vol. II, pp. 1244–375.

report. In so doing, he declined to challenge the wartime American consensus, which maintained that the Japanese had 'deceitfully negotiate[d] for peace while preparing a surprise war'. This notion of Japanese perfidy contrasted sharply with widespread notions of America's diplomatic sincerity; as President Franklin D. Roosevelt himself once defiantly put it, his administration had compiled a 'good record' in its diplomatic dealings with the Japanese.[2]

Grew was not the only diplomat who retroactively pinpointed failings in the lead-up to Pearl Harbor. His long-time British counterpart in Tokyo, Sir Robert Craigie, was no less critical than Grew of diplomacy vis-à-vis Japan. In mid-1942, Craigie returned to London from his own post-Pearl Harbor internment, and submitted a report which lambasted not only the United States, but also Britain for diplomatic failings in the final days before war. The Anglo-American response to Japan's final diplomatic proposal of late November 1941, in particular, drew from Craigie a 'blistering attack...for not having taken the opportunity to avoid war' with Japan.[3]

Craigie's report left little more impression in London than Grew's report had in Washington. Prime Minister Winston Churchill dismissed it summarily as a 'very strange document'. Well he might have. Long before Pearl Harbor, Churchill had assiduously courted the United States, in the belief that American participation in the war against Germany was a necessary prerequisite of victory. The Pearl Harbor attack delivered US belligerence. It also, admittedly, protected Japanese forces' flank as they removed the British from the Far East. Hong Kong, Malaya, Burma and even Singapore fell with dizzying and humiliating rapidity. Churchill – if not Craigie – deemed that a price worth paying. He later recalled having learned of the Pearl Harbor attack casually from BBC radio, and noted that he 'went to bed and slept the sleep of the saved and thankful'.[4] Not to belabour the point, but Churchill

2 For a colourful retelling of Grew's meeting with Secretary of State Hull, see John K. Emmerson, *The Japanese Thread: A Life in the US Foreign Service* (New York: Holt, Rinehart, and Winston, 1978), p. 123. For Heinrichs' assessment of Grew's report, see Waldo H. Heinrichs, Jr., *American Ambassador: Joseph C. Grew and the Development of the United States Diplomatic Tradition* (New York: Oxford University Press, 1986), p. 360. Regarding wartime American notions of diplomatic treachery and deceit, see Emily S. Rosenberg, *A Date which Will Live: Pearl Harbor in American Memory* (Durham, NC: Duke University Press, 2004), p. 12. For the Roosevelt quotation, see Robert E. Sherwood, *Roosevelt and Hopkins: An Intimate History* (New York: Harper and Brothers, 1948), p. 427.
3 Antony Best, *Britain, Japan, and Pearl Harbor: Avoiding War in East Asia, 1936–1941* (London: Routledge/LSE, 1995), p. 197.
4 For Churchill's reaction to Craigie's report, see Christopher Thorne, *Allies of a Kind: The United States, Britain and the War Against Japan, 1941–1945* (London: Hamish Hamilton,

did not regard the opening shot of war in Asia and the Pacific as a diplomatic failure. It was, for him, vindication of many months of diplomatic effort.

In the spirit of ambassadors Grew and Craigie, this chapter searches for diplomatic failings between 1931 and 1941 that contributed to the outbreak of war in Asia and the Pacific. It finds few of consequence. In this sense, this chapter takes its cue from Hull and Churchill. Or, to be more precise, this chapter echoes Hull's and Churchill's above-mentioned responses to charges of diplomatic failings. It not only locates numerous diplomatic success stories; it examines those national policies which set the confines within which the diplomats operated. Those confines were often antithetical to negotiation, and quite often precluded diplomatic agreement. In a nutshell, this chapter proceeds from the assumption that diplomacy does not exist merely to prevent war, and that it would therefore be ahistorical simply to tell the story of a litany of diplomatic failures that led to war in Asia and the Pacific.

The Manchurian Incident

The United States Department of State, in 1943, fast-forwarded its usual declassification process and published – some three decades earlier than might otherwise have been expected – a collection of archival documents concerning the causes of the Second World War in Asia and the Pacific. The two-volume account opened with a telegram which the State Department received on 19 September 1931 from its minister in Peking, Nelson Trusler Johnson. 'Japanese soldiers', he wrote, 'had apparently run amuck' around the Manchurian city of Mukden. Only two days later, Johnson was reporting that 'all of Manchuria south of Changchun and east of the Peking–Mukden Railway line [was] under Japanese military control'.[5] Thus began the so-called Manchurian Incident, which involved not only territorial conquest, but ultimately also the creation of the puppet state of Manchukuo and Japan's withdrawal from the League of Nations. Whatever the case, readers of this

---

1978), p. 75. For Churchill's reaction to news of Pearl Harbor, see Winston Churchill, *The Second World War*, vol. III: *The Grand Alliance* (6 vols., London: Cassell, 1950), p. 540. An earlier draft of this passage made clear how well Churchill slept that night. 'One hopes', he wrote, 'that eternal sleep will be like that.' Quoted in David Reynolds, *In Command of History: Churchill Fighting and Writing the Second World War* (New York: Random House, 2005), p. 264.

5 US Department of State, *Foreign Relations of the United States: Japan, 1931–1941* (2 vols., Washington DC: US Government Printing Office, 1943), vol. I, pp. 1–2.

collection of State Department documents could be forgiven for inferring that herein resided the genesis of the Second World War in Asia and the Pacific. Even today, most scholars – not only Western, but also Japanese and Chinese – agree that the Manchurian Incident looms large as a verifiable entry point on the road to war.

In the context of this chapter, it is necessary to ask whether diplomatic failure preceded this important early stepping stone on the road to war. The answer is, at best, a qualified yes. Admittedly, the Imperial Japanese Army officers who planned and then launched the conquest of Manchuria were fiercely critical of what they derisively called (in reference to Foreign Minister Shidehara Kijuro) 'Shidehara diplomacy'. The failings with which they charged Shidehara, however, had less to do with diplomacy – Shidehara was, after all, an extremely skilful negotiator – than with overall policy. In their reckoning, Shidehara's twofold emphasis on commercial penetration of China and amicable relations with the Anglo-American powers neither protected Japan's extensive interests on the Asian continent nor prepared Japan for the likelihood of another world war. That Shidehara served in a political party cabinet merely added grist to the uniformed army officers' mill, for they were convinced that politicians were contemptible, corruptible and cravenly beholden to narrow, partisan interests. Such thinking was particularly prevalent in that infamous Japanese garrison force in Manchuria known as the Kwantung Army.[6]

Operating within this intellectual milieu, field-grade officers of the Kwantung Army hatched an audacious plot for the conquest of Manchuria. Lieutenant Colonels Ishiwara Kanji and Itagaki Seishiro, whom one authority has labelled 'the perfect combination of brilliant planner and man of action', were the conspiratorial ringleaders. They staged an explosion of Japanese-owned railway track just outside the city of Mukden and blamed soldiers from a nearby Chinese military base. In so doing, they created for the Kwantung Army its *casus belli*. Some officers in the War Ministry and Army General Staff were in active connivance with this plot; the Kwantung Army otherwise left policy-makers in Tokyo deliberately uninformed. This was a

---

6 Regarding Shidehara's foreign policies, see Barbara J. Brooks, *Japan's Imperial Diplomacy: Consuls, Treaty Ports, and War in China, 1895–1938* (Honolulu: University of Hawaii Press, 2000). For an overview of Japanese and US policies throughout the 1920s, see Akira Iriye, *After Imperialism: The Search for a New Order in the Far East, 1921–1931* (Cambridge, Mass.: Harvard University Press, 1965). Regarding the army officers' disenchantment with Shidehara's approach to foreign affairs, see Mark R. Peattie, *Ishiwara Kanji and Japan's Confrontation with the West* (Princeton University Press, 1975), pp. 88–9.

breathtaking act of insubordination. 'Today the state is dragged on by the army', wrote a junior staff officer of the Kwantung Army, 'and the army [is dragged on] by us, the Kwantung Army'.[7]

Japanese diplomats tried to delimit the fighting in Manchuria. Two examples of the diplomats' early efforts – and the results – are instructive. In the first example, Shidehara made an urgent phone call soon after the outbreak of fighting to General Kanaya Hanzo, who, as Chief of the Army General Staff, had the authority to call off the operations in Manchuria. (He was, parenthetically, little better informed than was Shidehara about the Manchurian conspiracy.) Yet the phone call focused less on the Kwantung Army's actions than it did on the propriety of the Foreign Minister's actions in summoning the Army Chief of Staff to the telephone. This, doubtless, provoked Shidehara's exasperation. Perhaps more importantly, it also exemplified the army authorities' subsequent and repeated refusal to reject what quickly became a fait accompli in Manchuria. In the second example, acting Japanese Consul General Morishima Morito rushed to Lieutenant Colonel Itagaki's residence soon after the outbreak of hostilities and counselled a diplomatic settlement. Conspirator-in-chief Itagaki shouted Morishima down; Major Hanaya Tadashi drew his sword and threatened to 'kill anybody that interferes'. This episode is not only colourful. It is wonderfully illustrative of the Kwantung Army's utter imperviousness to the persuasive talents of Japan's diplomats.[8]

If Japan's diplomats were powerless to slow the Kwantung Army in its relentless pursuit of Manchurian empire, it makes sense to ask whether Chinese diplomacy contributed in some way to this act of aggression. Certainly, the Kwantung Army feared that Chinese nationalist leader Chiang Kai-shek's anti-imperialist diplomacy threatened Japan's privileged position in Manchuria. Kwantung Army officers regarded the Sino-British negotiations

---

7 For the characterization of Ishiwara and Itagaki, see Edward J. Drea, *Japan's Imperial Army: Its Rise and Fall, 1853–1945* (Lawrence: University Press of Kansas, 2009), p. 166. For the diary excerpt, see Sadako N. Ogata, *Defiance in Manchuria: The Making of Japanese Foreign Policy, 1931–1932* (Berkeley: University of California Press, 1964), p. 103.

8 Regarding Shidehara's phone call to General Kanaya, see Shigemitsu Mamoru, *Japan and her Destiny: My Struggle for Peace* (New York: E. P. Dutton, 1958), pp. 81–2. As for the Kwantung Army's reception of Morishima, see Seki Hiroharu, 'The Manchurian Incident, 1931', in James W. Morley (ed.), *Japan Erupts: The London Naval Conference and the Manchurian Incident, 1928–1932. Selected Translations from Taiheiyō Sensō e no Michi* (New York: Columbia University Press, 1984), p. 229. It might be noted that a number of Japanese consular officials in Manchuria were critical of Foreign Minister Shidehara for having been too weak in his dealings with the army. See Brooks, *Japan's Imperial Diplomacy*, pp. 142–7.

of 1929 and, in particular, British diplomats' concession of what the British regarded as 'non-essential rights and privileges' in Chinkiang, Amoy and Weihaiwei as a most disturbing precedent. The Manchurian Incident was, in this sense, a pre-emptive strike against any further successes – not failures – in Chinese diplomacy, particularly as it related to Manchuria.[9]

What of the Chinese response to the Kwantung Army's actions? Militarily, the Chinese chose the path of non-resistance. This was due, in no small part, to the virtually non-existent chances of military success: Manchurian warlord Chang Hseuh-liang's forces, which would have borne the brunt of the fighting, were no match for the outnumbered, but infinitely better-trained and -equipped Japanese. China's Nationalist government in Nanjing, which could claim authority in Manchuria only because warlord Chang (the so-called Young Marshal of Manchuria) had declared his allegiance, fully supported the policy of non-resistance. Indeed, Chiang Kai-shek worried that war with Japan might cause his nation to 'perish'. Rather than court that disastrous possibility, he hoped to convince the great powers to restrain Japan. Chiang, in other words, sought to achieve diplomatically what was otherwise impossible.[10]

It was a strategy doomed from the outset. Domestically, military non-resistance looked suspiciously like inaction and sparked outrage. To cite but one example: barely a week after the Kwantung Army launched its Manchurian invasion, a party of students assaulted Foreign Minister C. T. Wang and destroyed his house. He resigned his ministerial post within days. Chiang Kai-shek avoided attacks on his person; he did, however, resign all his government posts amidst a storm of criticism in mid-December 1931. Almost immediately thereafter, Chiang's successors instructed warlord Chang to take the fight to the Japanese. The Young Marshal ignored them.[11]

The international response offered little hope to the beleaguered Chinese. As early as 21 September, China appealed to both the League of Nations and the United States for support. The League responded – with deceptive

9 Regarding the Sino-British negotiations of 1929, see Edmund S. K. Fung, *The Diplomacy of Imperial Retreat: Britain's South China Policy, 1924–1931* (Oxford University Press, 1991), pp. 175–80, quotation at p. 179.

10 Regarding the military policy of non-resistance, see Parks M. Coble, *Facing Japan: Chinese Politics and Japanese Imperialism, 1931–1937* (Cambridge, Mass.: Harvard University Asia Center, 1991), pp. 27–31. Regarding Chiang's stance on this issue, see Jay Taylor, *The Generalissimo: Chiang Kai-shek and the Struggle for Modern China* (Cambridge, Mass.: Harvard University Press, 2009), pp. 94–5, quotation at p. 95.

11 Regarding C. T. Wang, see Fung, *Diplomacy of Imperial Retreat*, p. 237. Regarding Chiang, see Taylor, *The Generalissimo*, p. 96. As for the instructions to Chang, see Coble, *Facing Japan*, p. 38.

alacrity – on 24 October, when it called on Japan to withdraw its troops by mid-November. The League then (to borrow the words of British Foreign Secretary Sir John Simon) 'look[ed] on while its own summons [was] ignored'.[12] The League in December established the so-called Lytton Commission. The Commission deliberated and Japan acted. The supposedly independent state of Manchukuo (which, in reality, was utterly reliant for its existence on the Kwantung Army) came into being in March 1932. The Lytton Commission produced its report some seven months later. It sought the withdrawal of Chinese and Japanese troops from Manchuria. It suggested a series of Sino-Japanese treaties that would safeguard Japanese interests in Manchuria and would preclude any future recourse to arms. It also proposed a largely autonomous Manchurian administration, albeit under Chinese sovereignty. At least partly because the Lytton Commission gave due consideration to Japan's extensive interests in Manchuria, the Japanese emperor held its suggestions in high regard. He was, however, out of step with his army and his government. Japan withdrew from the League, but not before an intemperate Matsuoka Yosuke stunned delegates in Geneva by likening Japan in its international opprobrium to a latter-day Jesus Christ. 'Some of the people in Europe and America may wish to crucify Japan in the twentieth century', he railed. Assuring his audience that Japan stood 'ready to be crucified', Matsuoka made clear that 'world opinion' would change and that Japan would then return to its rightful position in international society.[13]

US diplomacy was no more effective than that of the League. Secretary of State Henry Stimson, on 7 January 1932, set forth what became known as the Stimson Doctrine. The doctrine bluntly censured Japan, and made clear the US refusal to recognize any changes to China's territorial and administrative integrity. Stimson's moral principles were unimpeachable; his diplomacy has nonetheless been criticized for two critical sins of omission. First, he failed to line up international support for his policy of non-recognition (even the British distanced themselves from his principled stand). Second,

---

12 See Ian Nish, *Japan's Struggle with Internationalism: Japan, China, and the League of Nations, 1931–3* (London: Kegan Paul International, 1993), pp. 34, 45.

13 The Lytton Commission and its report receive judicious treatment in Christopher Thorne, *The Limits of Foreign Policy: The West, the League and the Far Eastern Crisis of 1931–1933* (New York: G. P. Putnam's Sons, 1972), pp. 277–84. Regarding Japan's withdrawal from the League, see Rustin Gates, 'Meiji Diplomacy in the Early 1930s: Uchida Kōsai, Manchuria, and Post-Withdrawal Foreign Policy', in Masato Kimura and Tosh Minohara (eds.), *Tumultuous Decade: Empire, Society, and Diplomacy in 1930s Japan* (University of Toronto Press, 2013), pp. 197–200. Matsuoka's speech is quoted at length in Louise Young, *Japan's Total Empire: Manchuria and the Culture of Wartime Imperialism* (Berkeley: University of California Press, 1998), p. 154.

non-recognition provoked Japan, even though there was nothing that America's emaciated armed forces could do to counter Japanese aggression. It was, to borrow the words of historian Armin Rappaport, 'dangerous enough to risk Japanese ire without the means for military implementation, but to do it alone was double jeopardy'.[14] Needless to say, Stimson's diplomacy did nothing to help the beleaguered Chinese.

The Shanghai Incident and fighting in northern China

Shanghai in late January 1932 became the scene of Sino-Japanese hostilities. The so-called Shanghai Incident owed its origins not to any failures in diplomacy, but instead to an attack against Japanese monks in Shanghai. Rear Admiral Shiozawa Koichi, who was in Shanghai as Commander of the Imperial Japanese Navy's First Overseas Service Fleet, devised an iron-fisted response, in the confident expectation that China's 19th Route Army would not resist. Shiozawa's expectation proved hopelessly mistaken, and Japan's badly outnumbered marines found themselves engaged in a pitched battle on the streets of Shanghai. This was all the more troubling because Shanghai, with its International Settlement and French Concession, was the nerve centre of the great powers' position in China. To some, Japan seemed to be courting war with the Anglo-American powers; it was, at the very least, flirting with ever-greater levels of diplomatic confrontation.

That Japan did not pit itself – diplomatically or militarily – against the Anglo-American powers as a result of the Shanghai Incident was attributable to some nimble naval diplomacy. It should be noted that this proved possible because Japan carefully and deliberately delimited its objectives: it sought neither territory nor indemnities, and considered only the lives and property of Japanese in Shanghai as non-negotiable. Commander of the Japanese navy's hastily organized Third Fleet, Vice Admiral Nomura Kichisaburo pursued hostilities against the 19th Route Army, and all the while engaged in effective and substantive on-the-spot diplomacy with Commander-in-Chief of the Royal Navy's China Station, Admiral Sir Howard Kelly. When Nomura unilaterally declared a ceasefire in early March, he not only paved the way for a Sino-Japanese truce agreement (eventually concluded in Geneva on

---

14 Armin Rappaport, *Henry L. Stimson and Japan, 1931–33* (University of Chicago Press, 1963), p. 102. Regarding Britain's refusal to cooperate more closely with Stimson, see Robert H. Ferrell, *American Diplomacy in the Great Depression: Hoover–Stimson Foreign Policy, 1929–1933* (New Haven, Conn.: Yale University Press, 1957), pp. 158–62, 178–83.

5 May 1932), he chipped away at the otherwise fast-solidifying image of an aggressive Japan ruthlessly on the march.[15]

The Japanese army, however, proved itself intractably expansionist. Field officers in early 1933, acting once again independently of Tokyo, launched operations that resulted in the annexation of China's Jehol province to Manchukuo. In so doing, Japanese troops took the fight so far south of the Great Wall that they threatened Peking and Tientsin. Fearful for its survival – and bitter experience having taught it that it could not rely on the outside world for support – the Chinese Nationalist government sued for peace. It came in the form of the Tangku Truce. Concluded on 31 May 1933, it created a demilitarized zone south of the Great Wall.

Whether the Tangku Truce should be considered a diplomatic success or a diplomatic failure is very much a matter of perspective. Chiang Kai-shek, who was back in charge of the Chinese military, regarded the truce as successful – if doubtlessly distasteful – because it bought some much-needed time to build China's national strength. Ultimately, however, the truce drew 'spirited fire' throughout China, where 'pro-resistance elements' regarded it as 'defeatist and traitorous'. Those in the Japanese army who sought to devote their energies and attentions to the nation-building project in Manchukuo welcomed the truce, for they now had some time to consolidate their gains. Ominously, those belligerent officers who sought to extend Japanese influence beyond Manchukuo and into northern China also regarded the truce highly, for it provided them a foothold for ever-widening operations. International reactions to the Tangku Truce were largely muted, although it is notable that the administration of US President Franklin D. Roosevelt quietly extended diplomatic recognition to the Soviet Union in November 1933. This realized very little in the short term, although Roosevelt doubtless saw it as a diplomatic success story. After all, it raised the prospect of the United States and the Soviet Union acting in concert to deter further Japanese aggression.[16]

---

15 Peter Mauch, *Sailor Diplomat: Nomura Kichisaburō and the Japanese-American War* (Cambridge, Mass.: Harvard University Asia Center, 2011), pp. 80–7.
16 Regarding the Kwantung Army's actions in early 1933, see Shimada Toshihiko, 'Designs on North China, 1933–1937', in James W. Morley (ed.), *The China Quagmire: Japan's Expansion on the Asian Continent, 1933–1941. Selected Translations from Taiheiyō Sensō e no Michi* (New York: Columbia University Press, 1983), pp. 11–230. For Chiang's reaction to the Tangku Truce, see Taylor, *The Generalissimo*, pp. 99–100. For wider reactions throughout China, see Coble, *Facing Japan*, pp. 114, 119.

The end of the era of naval limitation
and the Anti-Comintern Pact

Then came announcement of the so-called Amo Doctrine. Foreign Ministry official Amau (or Amo) Eiji told a press conference on 17 April 1934 that Japan alone had the duty 'to keep peace and order in East Asia', and that Japan objected to foreign nations offering so much as 'technical or financial assistance' to China. This brazen assertion of Japan's autarchic aspirations was not only unauthorized, it was an act of extreme diplomatic clumsiness. The Japanese Foreign Ministry sought over the ensuing days to soften the message, yet it should hardly be surprising that the Amo Doctrine prodded the Anglo-American powers into stepping up their diplomatic cooperation. Most immediately, it convinced the Americans and the British to stand firm – and to stand together – behind the naval arms limitation ratios that had long since provided a pillar of Anglo-American-Japanese relations.

The Second London Naval Conference was scheduled to meet in 1935. At issue was the ratio of 5:5:3 for the US, British and Japanese fleets. The ratio, which first emerged at the Washington Conference of 1921–22, had prevented a naval arms race among the world's great naval powers. It had also practically eliminated war as a rational option in the western Pacific, because none of the three powers could initiate hostilities against either (or both) of the others in the confident expectation of victory. Whatever its efficacy, the ratio had been the subject of white-hot controversy (particularly) in the Japanese navy. In 1934, Japan's uniformed naval officers publicly demanded a radical revision of the existing naval arms limitation formula: they made clear that their Anglo-American counterparts could either acquiesce in parity (a ratio of 5:5:5) or accept an end to the era of naval limitation. Preliminary talks in London in 1934 revealed that neither the United States nor Britain was responsive to the Japanese insistence on naval parity.[17]

When the Second London Naval Conference convened on 7 December 1935, the Japanese delegation continued to insist on parity. The British and American response was predictably negative, and the era of tripartite Anglo-American-Japanese naval limitation came to an end. To borrow the words of

---

17 See Joseph Maiolo, *Cry Havoc: The Arms Race and the Second World War, 1931–1941* (London: John Murray, 2010). See also Stephen E. Pelz, *Race to Pearl Harbor: The Failure of the Second London Naval Conference and the Onset of World War II* (Cambridge, Mass.: Harvard University Press, 1974); and Sadao Asada, *From Mahan to Pearl Harbor: The Imperial Japanese Navy and the United States* (Annapolis, Md.: Naval Institute Press, 2006), pp. 198–205.

historian Stephen Pelz, this result was not only 'expected and inevitable', it also set off a 'race to Pearl Harbor'. Should the Second London Naval Conference, then, be considered a diplomatic failure? Perhaps. Still, it is instructive to consider the strictures within which delegates in London operated. Japan's head delegate – the 'blunt and forceful' Admiral Nagano Osami – well understood that he was 'bound by government instructions' to settle for nothing less than Anglo-American-Japanese naval parity.[18] Were diplomatic agreement the sole motivation of Admiral Nagano's British and American counterparts, they might well have granted Japan's demand, and in so doing ceded to Japan absolute and unassailable maritime supremacy in the western Pacific. This, however, would have been tantamount to acceding to the above-mentioned Amo Doctrine. That was unacceptable. At the same time, the prospect of leaving the Second London Naval Conference empty-handed was undesirable. Franklin D. Roosevelt hoped that the three great naval powers might agree at least to 'notify every other nation of all ships authorized or laid down for construction'. He got instead a meaningless treaty which the Japanese refused to sign and which collapsed quickly.[19]

Even as the admirals declined to come to terms in London, Japan's generals continued to engage in their own aggressive diplomatic pursuits in China. Field officers in June 1935 yet again acted independently of their superiors in Tokyo and foisted on the dispirited Chinese the so-called Umezu–Ho Agreement. The Chinese found the terms so distressing – and the Japanese negotiators so irrepressibly insistent – that it was difficult to convince any official of suitable authority and courage to enter the negotiations. The agreement practically removed China's Nationalist government, both militarily and politically, from north China. Not unexpectedly, the Kwantung Army (as well as the Tientsin Garrison) regarded the Umezu–Ho Agreement as a resounding success. The north China foothold gained by the earlier Tangku Truce now seemed tantalizingly close to independence from Nanjing.[20]

Conclusion of the Japanese-German Anti-Comintern Pact in November 1936 revealed, if nothing else, that the Japanese army's strategic focus and diplomatic initiatives went wider than China. Indeed, when Major General Oshima

18 Pelz, *Race to Pearl Harbor*, p. 152. For the characterization of Nagano, see Asada, *From Mahan to Pearl Harbor*, p. 203.
19 Roosevelt to Secretary of the Navy, 20 July 1935. Subject File: London Naval Conference 1935, box 142, President's Secretary's File, Franklin D. Roosevelt Presidential Library, Hyde Park, New York.
20 Youli Sun, *China and the Origins of the Pacific War, 1931–1941* (New York: St Martin's Press, 1993), p. 55.

Hiroshi broached with Joachim von Ribbentrop in October 1935 the possibility of a Japanese-German alliance, China received not a mention. Oshima, who was serving as military attaché to the Japanese Embassy in Berlin, sought instead an alliance that would target the Soviet Union. He was acting not on specific instructions, but on his service's long-held antipathy toward the Soviet Union, as well as its long-standing empathy for the German army. Ideologically, Oshima outstripped his service's admiration for Nazi Germany's extreme right-wing ideology and its hatred of Soviet Communism. Most immediately, Oshima hoped that a Japanese-German alliance would confront the Soviet Union with a diplomatic pincer movement and thereby restrain Soviet activities beyond its borders. Ribbentrop, an ex-champagne salesman who had shot to prominence as Hitler's diplomatic troubleshooter, reciprocated these sentiments in more or less equal dose. Oshima and Ribbentrop shared one further trait: both men disdained their nation's diplomats and neither used established diplomatic channels. In this way, the Anti-Comintern Pact presents the curious case of a treaty of alliance which had only the barest of input from either of the signatories' foreign ministries.[21]

Was the pact a diplomatic success? Oshima and Ribbentrop certainly thought so. The Japanese army, on the whole, also regarded the pact as a success. So, too, did Japanese Prime Minister Hirota Koki. In Tokyo, the principal dissenting voice was that of Japan's last *genro* (elder statesman), Saionji Kimmochi. 'It...contains nothing of advantage to us', he complained. Advantageous or otherwise, the Anti-Comintern Pact had the effect of distancing Japan ever further from the Western liberal democracies. It also meant, in the estimation of historian Carl Boyd, that Japan was now participating, alongside Germany, in 'totalitarian diplomacy'. Whatever else one might make of that term, it is clear that Japan had distanced itself from the Anglo-American powers.[22]

The Sino-Japanese War

The Marco Polo Bridge Incident of 7 July 1937 provides the next major milestone along the path to the Second World War in Asia and the Pacific.

21 See Ohata Tokushiro, 'The Anti-Comintern Pact, 1935–1939', in James W. Morley (ed.), *Deterrent Diplomacy: Japan, Germany, and the U.S.S.R., 1935–1940. Selected Translations from Taiheiyō Sensō e no Michi* (New York: Columbia University Press, 1976), pp. 9–37.
22 For the Saionji quotation, see ibid., p. 35. For reference to 'totalitarian diplomacy', see Carl Boyd, 'The Berlin–Tokyo Axis and Japanese Military Initiative', *Modern Asian Studies* 15:2 (1981), 320.

The essentials of the incident can be summarized briefly: a Japanese soldier went missing during night exercises conducted west of Peking; his commanding officer demanded the right to conduct a search; the mayor of Peking suggested a joint Sino-Japanese search and ordered Chinese forces to resist if the Japanese acted unilaterally. By the time the missing soldier was again accounted for, it was evident he had not fallen prey to any nefarious Chinese plot, but had merely fallen out of formation to relieve his overfull bladder (the question as to why it took so long to find the missing soldier remains unanswered). Whatever the case, Japanese and Chinese forces quickly began firing on each other. Within hours, each side had rushed a battalion to the scene, and thus began eight unrelenting years of Sino-Japanese warfare. Throughout the Marco Polo Bridge Incident, diplomacy was conspicuous not for its success or failure, but rather for its absence.

The immediate aftermath of the incident was witness to some genuine, on-the-spot diplomacy. Indeed, Japanese and Chinese representatives on 11 July signed a local agreement that promised to end the fighting. That it did not last was due less to diplomatic failures than it was to dynamics beyond the power of diplomacy to control: in Tokyo, most policy-makers remained wedded to the notion that a show of overwhelming force would bring Chiang Kai-shek to his knees, while in Nanjing, Chiang had finally determined to resist Japanese expansionism. War was the only plausible outcome.[23]

The spread of fighting beyond Peking's vicinity did not spell the end of diplomacy. Indeed, it led to some interesting diplomatic encounters. The Soviets and the Chinese in August concluded a Treaty of Non-Aggression by which they agreed not to make separate deals with Japan. Chinese negotiators, moreover, asked for aid in the form of war materiel. The Soviets presumably felt little love for the violently anti-communist Chiang Kai-shek, yet they evidently reasoned that he was preoccupying the Japanese army – and thereby keeping its attention away from the Manchurian-Soviet border. Planes, tanks and guns seemed but a small price to pay. This diplomatic episode was stripped of all niceties, completely void of ideological considerations, and based squarely on both parties' needs, capacities and interests. And, insofar as both parties got precisely what they wanted, it was very much a diplomatic success story.

---

23 See, for example, Mark R. Peattie, 'The Dragon's Seed: Origins of the War', in Mark R. Peattie, Edward Drea and Hans van de Ven (eds.), *The Battle for China: Essays on the Military History of the Sino-Japanese War* (Stanford University Press, 2011), esp. pp. 77–8.

The Western powers were initially less inclined than were the Soviets to aid China materially. The League of Nations, to be sure, offered China its moral support, and on 6 October publicly denounced Japan for its aggression. Few noticed; fewer still cared. The United States, which remained outside the League, offered little. Americans had reacted to the above-mentioned end of the era of naval disarmament, as well as Japan's unceasing aggression in China (not to mention the Italian invasion of Ethiopia and Nazi German rearmament), by seeking a way to insulate themselves and their nation from what they saw as the inevitability of foreign wars. In this spirit, US Congress, in 1935, 1936 and 1937, legislated neutrality and thereby forbade trade with nations at war. (Parenthetically, the Neutrality Acts provided Japan and China with at least one point on which they could agree: neither side could afford to risk its trade with the United States, so both sides agreed to use the euphemism 'incident' for what was, in reality, large-scale warfare.)

Precisely because his nation was in the grip of isolationist sentiment, on 5 October 1937, President Roosevelt garnered considerable attention with his so-called quarantine speech. Delivered in the isolationist stronghold of Chicago, Roosevelt's speech held out the prospect whereby the 'peace-loving nations' might 'quarantine' those aggressive nations which were enamoured with 'greed for power and supremacy'. Roosevelt declined to pursue this idea any further, so it is difficult to discern precisely what he hoped to achieve with this speech. Still, it is undeniable that Roosevelt had publicly and frontally confronted the basic isolationist idea that the United States could avoid war simply by shunning international contacts. Roosevelt's target audience was nonetheless domestic, and his quarantine speech achieved little on the international stage. Indeed, according to historian D. C. Watt, British Prime Minister Neville Chamberlain regarded Roosevelt as an 'unreliable windbag'. Isolationism had hobbled American diplomacy.[24]

Japanese diplomacy fared poorly in the wake of the Marco Polo Bridge Incident. The most intriguing – if hopelessly naive – diplomatic effort ended with an unseemly arrest. Prime Minister Konoe Fumimaro dreamed up a summit meeting at which he and Chiang Kai-shek might negotiate all outstanding Sino-Japanese issues. Konoe's personal choice as go-between was China expert Miyazaki Ryusuke (whose father had been Sun Yat-sen's

---

24 For the text of Roosevelt's quarantine speech, see US Department of State, *Foreign Relations of the United States: Japan, 1931–1941* (2 vols., Washington DC: US Government Printing Office, 1943), vol. I, pp. 379–83. For the 'unreliable windbag' quotation, see Donald Cameron Watt, 'Roosevelt and Neville Chamberlain: Two Appeasers', *International Journal* 28:2 (spring 1973), 185.

leading Japanese supporter). Miyazaki never made it to China. Japan's notorious military police arrested him as he boarded a vessel in the western port city of Kobe. A more promising diplomatic avenue presented itself when Oshima Hiroshi asked his National Socialist friends in Berlin whether they might consider mediating the conflict. Hitler readily agreed (and became the most unlikely of peacemakers). By 3 December, ambassador Oskar Traut-mann in Nanjing had convinced Chiang Kai-shek to accept German medi-ation. Japan had already tabled a set of stiff terms for peace, and might reasonably have expected to foist most of them on Chiang. The imminent fall of the Chinese capital in Nanjing, however, raised Japanese expectations and policy-makers began to regard a negotiated settlement as undesirable. German mediation fell by the wayside. Against this backdrop, on 16 January 1938, Prime Minister Konoe issued his notorious *aite to sezu* declaration, which clarified Japan's refusal to meet Chiang's Guomindang government anywhere but the battlefield.[25]

Whatever else it achieved, Konoe's refusal to negotiate with Chiang left the Japanese army with no discernible exit from the fighting in China. When Nanjing fell, Chiang moved his capital to Hankow. The Japanese army took it too, but Chiang pushed even further west, this time to Chongqing. That city, deep in China's interior, became the target of a furious aerial bombard-ment campaign, but was otherwise beyond the reach of Japan's overextended military. There would be no knockout blow. As if to complicate matters, in July 1938, the Japanese army took the fight to the Soviets along the Manchurian-Soviet border. The fighting lasted only a few weeks before a ceasefire was concluded. Still, the so-called Changkufeng Incident seemed to confirm the unlikelihood of any substantive Japanese diplomatic effort aimed at halting Soviet material assistance to Chongqing. This, in turn, did nothing for the prospect of crushing Chinese morale. In belated recognition of the corner Japan was in, in November 1938, Konoe publicly reversed his *aite to sezu* declaration and announced his hopes for a 'new order' in East Asia, centring on Japan, a reborn China and Manchuria. Konoe argued that the new order was readily achievable, if only Chiang would drop his 'anti-Japanese' attitude and cooperate with Japan.

Konoe probably did not foresee the response. Chiang heaped ridicule on Konoe's efforts at appearing magnanimous, and declared that Japan was

---

25 For an extremely critical view of Japan's war in China, and of Konoe's *aite to sezu* declaration, see Marius B. Jansen, *The Making of Modern Japan* (Cambridge, Mass.: Belknap Press, 2000), pp. 620ff.

fighting for nothing less than 'an enslaved China...which would abide by Japan's word from generation to generation'.[26] The Anglo-American powers were no less leery of Konoe's new order declaration. To them, the presumption of a new order seemed to embody or codify everything the Japanese army had done since the outbreak of hostilities to the detriment of Anglo-American interests in China: it had squeezed out American and British interests; it had manipulated currency and exchange rates; it had established (or facilitated the establishment of) monopolies; it had closed the Yangzi River to international navigation; and it had brazenly interfered with international port facilities. In Washington, the Roosevelt administration announced its refusal to recognize a unilaterally imposed new order. More significantly, it extended a $25 million loan to China. In London, Neville Chamberlain's Cabinet extended a £10 million loan to Chongqing. The other powers with a stake in the fighting in China had all lined up behind Chiang and against Japan.

Japan's diplomatic isolation deepened in 1939. In February, the Japanese navy occupied Hainan, which raised questions as to Japanese intentions in Southeast Asia. Colonial authorities in the Dutch East Indies responded by drastically reducing imports from Japan. The Japanese army, in June, tested British resolve by blockading the British concession in Tientsin. The British were preoccupied with the ever-worsening situation in Europe and were in no position to stand up to the Japanese. Ambassador Craigie in Tokyo signed off on what one commentator has described as 'a Far Eastern version of the Munich concessions'. The British, in other words, agreed to all of Japan's demands concerning its special needs in China. Lest Tokyo regard this as a diplomatic success, US Secretary of State Cordell Hull announced, in July, America's intention to abrogate its treaty of commerce with Japan. Once the treaty expired in January 1940, the Roosevelt administration would be in a position to halt Japanese-US trade. This was a strong diplomatic warning against any notions of closing Britain – and, more broadly, the West – out of China. Recognizing the devastating effect this would have on the war-weary Japanese economy, in late 1939 to early 1940, the Cabinet of Prime Minister Abe Nobuyuki sought to ameliorate US concerns and to negotiate the terms of a new treaty. This proved a tall order. On the eve of the treaty's expiration, American ambassador Joseph Grew announced that there would be no automatic imposition of commercial penalties and that trade would

---

26 Chiang, quoted in Pei-kai Cheng and Michael Lestz (eds.), *The Search for Modern China: A Documentary Collection* (New York: W. W. Norton, 1999), pp. 319–24.

continue for the meantime. In the circumstances, this was probably the best diplomatic outcome for which Japan could have hoped, even if it barely papered over the widening Japanese-US divide.[27]

Hitler, in the meantime, had plunged Europe into war and Japan ever deeper into diplomatic isolation. The Nazis, throughout 1938 and the first half of 1939, had pursued a Japanese-German-Italian military alliance. The Japanese army had enthusiastically embraced the Germans' insistence on a treaty that targeted not only the Soviet Union, but also Britain; Navy Minister Yonai Mitsumasa stood unalterably opposed. The Japanese decision-making process required complete ministerial unanimity, so Yonai's stubborn opposition ensured against any alliance. By August 1939, Hitler lost patience with Japan and concluded instead a Non-Aggression Pact with the Soviet Union, and agreed to divide Poland. German forces marched into Poland on 1 September; Britain and France declared war on Germany the following day. Japanese policy-makers' shock at Hitler's cynical about-face was palpable. For one thing, Germany had come to terms with the very nation that was (supposedly) the common Japanese-German enemy. Even more stunning, Hitler had done this even as the Kwantung Army was fighting a disastrous border war against the Soviet Red Army at Nomonhan. As if to further its isolation, throughout 1938 and 1939 – and, indeed, much of 1940 – Japan declined to extend formal recognition to the collaborationist Wang Ching-wei regime in Nanjing.[28]

The Tripartite Pact and the pre-Pearl Harbor Japanese-US negotiations

The year 1940 was witness to a monumental Japanese diplomatic blunder. Conclusion of the Japanese-German-Italian Tripartite Pact on 27 September 1940 put Japan on a collision course with the United States and Britain. The

---

27 For the characterization of the Arita–Craigie Agreement, see Leonid Nikolaevich Kutakov, *Japanese Foreign Policy on the Eve of the Pacific War: A Soviet View* (Tallahassee, Fla.: Diplomatic Press, 1972), p. 126. For the US decision to abrogate the commercial treaty, see Edward S. Miller, *Bankrupting the Enemy: The US Financial Siege of Japan before Pearl Harbor* (Annapolis, Md.: Naval Institute Press, 2007), pp. 48–74. For the Japanese reaction, see Mauch, *Sailor Diplomat*, pp. 94–113.

28 For the best discussion of the army–navy debates concerning an alliance with Germany, see Asada, *From Mahan to Pearl Harbor*, pp. 212–29. Regarding Nomonhan, see the masterful Alvin D. Coox, *Nomonhan: Japan Against Russia, 1939* (Stanford University Press, 1990). As for Wang's travails, see John Hunter Boyle, *China and Japan at War, 1937–1945: The Politics of Collaboration* (Stanford University Press, 1972), pp. 167ff.

pact conclusively connected the China Incident to the war in Europe, so that what had been a regional Asian conflict now became a theatre of a wider global war. It signalled Japan's aggressive intentions toward the resource-rich colonial regions of Southeast Asia. And, at least so far as Franklin D. Roosevelt was concerned, it confirmed Japan's place alongside Germany as 'the Prussians of the Far East...drunk with their dreams of dominion'.[29]

Japanese thinking on the eve of the pact's conclusion merits attention. Policy-makers in Tokyo had overcome their revulsion toward the German-Soviet Non-Aggression Pact, primarily because of the stunning success with which the German army had met in the meantime. In the spring and summer of 1940, Hitler's forces overran, in dizzying succession, Denmark, Norway, the Netherlands, Belgium and France. Even Britain looked to be on its last legs. This had enormous implications for the Japanese: Southeast Asia was now defenceless and seemingly ripe for the picking. Characterizing the mood then prevailing, historians Sumio Hatano and Sadao Asada wrote: 'German successes...had so dazzled Japanese officials as to generate a feverish clamor for an opportunistic southern advance that would take advantage of an apparently imminent German victory'.[30]

The only real doubt in Tokyo rested with the United States. Nobody questioned the Americans' unrivalled capacity to make war, but question marks remained over American intentions. Would it intervene in Europe and save the British from their fate? Would it intervene if Japan began dislodging the European colonial powers from Southeast Asia? Or would it retreat into its isolationist shell? Japanese Foreign Minister Matsuoka Yosuke argued that it was possible to frighten the United States so that it remained aloof from both Europe and Asia. According to Matsuoka, this required not only a German-Japanese-Italian military alliance, but also a 'firm stand' on the part of the three partners. In his diplomatic negotiations with German emissaries Heinrich Stahmer and Eugen Ott, Matsuoka got exactly what he wanted. The Tripartite Pact included an ominously phrased commitment on the part of Japan, Germany and Italy, to 'assist one another with all political, economic, and military means when one of the three contracting parties is attacked by a power at present not involved in the European War or the Sino-Japanese conflict'. Few (except perhaps the vainglorious and unstable

29 Roosevelt is quoted in Daniel M. Smith, 'Authoritarianism and American Policy Makers in Two World Wars', *Pacific Historical Review* 43:3 (August 1974), 314.
30 Sumio Hatano and Sadao Asada, 'The Japanese Decision to Move South', in Robert Boyce and Esmonde Robertson (eds.), *Paths to War: New Essays on the Origins of the Second World War* (London: Macmillan, 1989), pp. 386–7.

Matsuoka) could doubt the gravity of this commitment; the Tripartite Pact was, as one contemporary apprehensively noted, 'a treaty of alliance with the United States as its target'.[31]

The Tripartite Pact backfired spectacularly. Far from pushing the United States back into its isolationist shell, it steeled American resolve to resist what one State Department official called an 'organized and ruthless movement of conquest'. The Roosevelt administration quickly identified Britain – and, in particular, the Royal Navy – as its first line of national defence. This, of course, meant that the United States prioritized Europe over Asia and the Pacific. Still, Washington regarded the colonial regions of Southeast Asia as off-limits to Japanese expansion. Japan tested the United States on this point even as diplomat Kurusu Saburo was signing off on the Tripartite Pact in Berlin, for Japanese troops began advancing into the northern half of French Indochina in late September 1940. The Roosevelt administration responded by slapping a total embargo on aviation gasoline, high-grade iron and scrap steel.[32]

In February 1941, Roosevelt invited the newly arrived Japanese ambassador, Admiral Nomura Kichisaburo, to 'sit down with the Secretary of State...to see if...relations could not be improved'. The invitation was genuine. So, too, was the ambassador in his desire for peace. Ultimately, of course, these good intentions counted for little: the Japanese-US negotiations ended with the Pearl Harbor attack. Whether that was attributable to failures in diplomacy is, nonetheless, open to question. Two diplomatic episodes from early 1941 should serve to illustrate this point.

The first episode dates back to late January 1941, when Grew conveyed to Hull information he had picked up on the diplomatic rumour mill in Tokyo. It involved a 'fantastic' Japanese plan. In the event of 'trouble' between Japan and the United States, Grew reported, Japan planned to launch a 'mass surprise attack on Pearl Harbor'. Grew's report found its way within days to Pearl Harbor – specifically, to the desk of Pacific Fleet Commander

---

31 The Tripartite Pact is reproduced in US Department of State, *Japan, 1931–1941*, vol. II, pp. 165–6. The 'firm stand' and 'United States as its target' quotations can be found in Nobutaka Ike (ed.), *Japan's Decision for War: Records of the 1941 Policy Conferences* (Stanford University Press, 1967), pp. 9–10.

32 For the quotation concerning the 'organized and ruthless movement of conquest', see Peter Mauch, 'Revisiting Nomura's Diplomacy: Reconsidering Ambassador Nomura's Role in the Japanese-American Negotiations, 1941', *Diplomatic History* 28:3 (June 2004), 360. For the US reaction to the Tripartite Pact, see Peter Mauch, 'Dissembling Diplomatist: Admiral Toyoda Teijirō and the Politics of Japanese Security', in Kimura and Minohara (eds.), *Tumultuous Decade*, pp. 237–40.

Husband Kimmel – although the Office of Naval Intelligence was careful to inform Admiral Kimmel that it placed 'no credence in these rumors'. The failure in this instance was not one of diplomacy, but instead of imagination: most in Washington summarily dismissed the possibility of Japan actively engaging the United States in hostilities, if only because they regarded as self-evident the certainty of Japan's subsequent defeat.[33]

The second diplomatic episode which deserves attention centres on the abortive Draft Understanding between Japan and the United States. The Draft Understanding's obscure genesis need not detain us here; suffice to note that it elicited at least mild enthusiasm in both Washington and Tokyo before ambassador Nomura presented it to Secretary Hull in mid-April 1941. Ultimately, the Draft Understanding failed largely because Japanese Foreign Minister Matsuoka Yosuke refused to countenance rapprochement with the Americans on anything but the stiffest of terms. Reaffirming his above-mentioned 'firm stand' toward the United States as only he could, Matsuoka harangued Grew in mid-May, and charged the United States with unmanly and cowardly diplomatic conduct. Because Japan's inability to defeat the United States in war placed very real limits on what Japan might reasonably expect the United States to concede in diplomatic negotiations, Matsuoka's churlish reassertion of his 'firm stand' could most certainly be regarded as a diplomatic failure on Japan's part. It could, equally convincingly, be seen as the outcome of a collective failure on the part of Prime Minister Konoe, Navy Minister Oikawa Koshiro and War Minister Tojo Hideki to rein in the increasingly wayward Matsuoka. All three men, after all, saw merit in pursuing the Draft Understanding; none, however, sought to muzzle Matsuoka. Konoe himself saw the situation as one in which Nomura had 'broken his bones' to produce a 'suitably concrete proposal' for Japanese-US rapprochement, only to have Matsuoka wreck it out of 'jealousy'.[34]

The opening shots of the German-Soviet war in late June 1941 provided one of the major turning points of the Second World War. It should hardly be surprising that it had an enormous impact on diplomacy in Asia and the

33 Heinrichs, *American Ambassador*, p. 326. For the Chief Naval Officer's reaction to the rumour, see Edwin T. Layton, *And I Was There: Pearl Harbor and Midway – Breaking the Secrets* (New York: Quill William Morrow, 1985), pp. 73–4.
34 The Konoe quotation can be found in Ito Takashi, Nomura Minoru, Uchida Kazuomi, Terunuma Yasutaka, Fujioka Taishu, Kudo Michihiro, Sasaki Takashi, Moriyama Atsushi, Hatano Sumio and Kato Yoko (eds.), *Takagi Sokichi Nikki to Jōhō* (2 vols., Tokyo: Misuzu Shobo, 2000), vol. II, p. 532. Regarding the ill-fated Draft Understanding and the Japanese government's failure to rein in Matsuoka, see Mauch, *Sailor Diplomat*, pp. 136–81.

Pacific. American policy-makers – almost to a man – quickly concluded that the Soviets could not withstand the German onslaught for any longer than a few weeks. Roosevelt ignored this advice, and instead acted on the hunch that Hitler had overplayed his hand and that the Soviets would at the very least provide the British with some much-needed breathing space. This presidential gut reaction resulted in a high-level and highly successful diplomatic mission to Moscow, led by Roosevelt's alter ego, Harry Hopkins. The outcome was portentous: Roosevelt extended all possible material aid to the besieged Soviets.[35]

The Japanese reached no less portentous a decision in response to the opening of the German-Soviet war: they decided to advance into the southern half of French Indochina. From Washington, Nomura warned repeatedly that such a move would end all hope for Japanese-US diplomacy. He was duly ignored. In Tokyo, the inscrutable Matsuoka fought a furious rearguard action against the Indochinese advance. He argued instead that it was 'best to shed blood' in an assault on the Soviet Union. Matsuoka's spirited arguments were all the more perplexing because, only a few weeks earlier, he had personally negotiated a neutrality treaty with the Soviet leadership. By mid-July, he was relieved of his ministerial responsibilities. This being the case, it would be mistaken to assert that the Indochinese advance was the result of diplomatic failure. The advance might better be understood as directly contravening the diplomats' counsel.[36]

The US response to Japan's Indochinese advance was swift and severe. By early August, it had frozen all Japanese assets in the United States and imposed a complete trade embargo. The British and the Dutch took similar action. This cut Japan off from its most important markets and sources of raw materials, and Japan could not continue in this way indefinitely without inviting national ruin. Konoe tried to break the impasse by means of a summit meeting. By this proposal, the hapless Konoe convinced himself of his own statesmanlike qualities; the State Department in Washington held him to a higher standard. It demanded to know, in advance, the concessions Konoe might make at the proposed summit meeting. Konoe declined to oblige the State Department and clung to the excruciatingly naive hope that Roosevelt might meet him halfway, both geographically and, perhaps, at the

---

35 See, especially, Waldo H. Heinrichs, *Threshold of War: Franklin D. Roosevelt and American Entry into World War II* (New York: Oxford University Press, 1988), pp. 118–46.

36 Mauch, *Sailor Diplomat*, pp. 167–203.

negotiating table. Not surprisingly, the summit never happened. Thus passed what Grew saw as the last, best chance to avert war in the Pacific.[37]

By late 1941, diplomacy stood little chance of preventing war in the Pacific. Even so, in late November, the Japanese suggested a limited agreement which sought to return the situation to what it had been before the fateful Indochinese advance of late July. This created a flurry of diplomatic activity. Even Roosevelt tried his hand at penning a counter-proposal. Ultimately, however, the dire implications that a limited Japanese-US agreement had for Chinese morale – not to mention that of the British and, perhaps, the Soviets – overrode the otherwise understandable American desire to stave off war. So, it was for diplomatic reasons that the Roosevelt administration decided against efforts at a diplomatic resolution of Japanese-US differences. On 26 November, Hull handed ambassador Nomura what Japanese scholars refer to as the 'Hull note'. It included the demands that Japan disavow the Tripartite Pact and immediately withdraw all troops from Indochina and China. For the Japanese, this price of peace was unacceptably high. Hull knew as well as anybody that it meant war. He told Secretary of War Henry Stimson on 27 November that he had 'washed his hands' of the Japanese-US negotiations, and that the situation was 'now in the hands of you and [Secretary of the Navy Frank] Knox – the Army and the Navy'. Days later, Knox told the Australian Minister in Washington, Richard Casey, that although 'the U.S. Army wanted more time to prepare themselves in the Far East, the U.S. Navy was ready'. Beating the war drums, Knox pronounced that 'the sooner the break came, the better'. At practically the same time, in Tokyo, Navy Minister Shimada Shigetaro and Navy Chief of Staff Nagano Osami were arguing that 'diplomacy should be sacrificed in order to win the war'.[38] The Pearl Harbor attack was but days away, and the diplomats were powerless to stop it.

Conclusion

This chapter has taken strong exception to the notion that the outbreak of the Second World War in Asia and the Pacific constituted a failure of diplomacy. The war owed its origins to a multiplicity of causes, not least

37 Ibid.
38 See Peter Mauch, 'A Completely Star Performance? Australian Minister Richard Gardiner Casey in Washington, March 1940–March 1942', *Journal of American-East Asian Relations* 21:2 (2014), 109–33. For the Shimada and Nagano quotation, see Mauch, *Sailor Diplomat*, p. 213.

of which was Japan's aggressive course. Culpability, in this sense, rests principally with the Imperial Japanese Army and its incurably belligerent field officers in China, as well as its institution-wide enthusiasm for an alliance with Nazi Germany. Japan's Imperial Navy agreed on very little with its sister service, but its prerogatives allowed little room for diplomacy: it not only ended the era of naval limitation, it later forsook its significant misgivings concerning an alliance with Germany, not least because it had set its sights on the resource-rich colonial regions of Southeast Asia. Unless and until the Japanese navy forswore such aggressive intentions, it almost invariably raised the overwhelming likelihood of a world war stretching across the Eurasian continent, and also incorporating the Pacific and the United States. In this regard, it is interesting to note Admiral Nomura's reaction to the outbreak of war in the Pacific. In neat contrast to Grew and Craigie in Tokyo (whose criticisms of their governments' handling of diplomacy received treatment at the outset of this chapter), Nomura likened his ambassadorial mission to that of a 'doctor [who] does everything he can for a patient whose fate is already determined'. Hindsight, of course, played a role in this prognosis, but it nonetheless speaks to this chapter's central theme concerning diplomacy and the limited role it played in the road to war.

This is not to say that diplomatic failures did not occur. Very often, these were attributable to a reluctance – or inability – to couple force with diplomacy. As we have seen, Stimson's moral rectitude in the early 1930s did not dislodge the Japanese army from Manchuria. In this and other cases, it is difficult to escape the conclusion that Japan's generals were impervious to anything but the logic of force. For this very reason, the diplomatic success stories which this chapter has located almost invariably reflected powerful political realities. Interestingly, diplomats were at their best when they stood opposed to Japanese aggression. The Sino-Soviet Non-Aggression Treaty of August 1937 provided one example. So, too, did Roosevelt's decision in late 1941 to forsake a temporary agreement with the Japanese. These and other such diplomatic episodes arguably brought forward the day that world war arrived in Asia and the Pacific. At the same time, they helped to forge a wartime alliance which opposed – and eventually defeated – an aggressive and uncompromising Japan (as well as its alliance partners in Germany and Italy). This was no mean feat, and, ultimately, begs the question as to whether US, British, Chinese and Soviet diplomacy in the 1930s and early 1940s should ultimately be seen not as a failure, but as a success.

11

The diplomacy of the Axis, 1940–1945

NORMAN J. W. GODA

In *Mein Kampf* and in his 'Second Book', Adolf Hitler argued that in its next war, Germany would need fewer enemies and more allies. Over the course of the Second World War, Germany stitched together allies and aligned states stretching from Spain in the West to Japan in the Far East. But the Axis, as it was called, was a dysfunctional alliance – far less coordinated than the Grand Alliance that Germany and its allies faced after 1941. It lacked common statements of purpose, common grand strategic conceptions and planning, and even, in some cases, common enemies. Rather it was a collection of predators, none of which trusted one another.

Based on the Rome–Berlin Axis of 1936 and the more formal 1939 military alliance between Germany and Italy, the Axis included Japan when the three powers signed the Tripartite Pact in September 1940. Additional states in Southeast Europe subsequently joined the Tripartite Pact. Other states were aligned, though not allied, with the Axis through their adherence to the Anti-Comintern Pact, a less formal arrangement against communist agitation first signed by Germany and Japan in 1936, and seen later by Berlin as a litmus test of loyalty.[1] From 1939 to 1941, the Soviet Union, though not a signatory to either agreement, was essentially allied to Germany owing to the Non-Aggression Pact of August 1939 and subsequent territorial and economic agreements.

The driving force was Germany. Hitler launched policies independently of his partners, who followed their own aims in the wake of German victories and defeats, and he did so within the context of asymmetrical bilateral relationships that Berlin preferred, rather than through multilateral diplomacy. This chapter is thus organized by the phases of Germany's war

---

1 Gerhard L. Weinberg. *The Foreign Policy of Hitler's Germany*, vol. ii: *Starting World War II, 1937–1939* (2 vols., University of Chicago Press, 1980), pp. 503–4.

between 1940 and 1945. The first is the defeat of France in 1940, which opened the possibility of reshaping the European and overseas colonial maps. The second is Germany's attack on the USSR, the preparations for which demanded the remapping of Eastern Europe and a closer relationship with Japan, which resulted in global war. A third is the German murder of all Jews within reach, a project in which Germany's European allies were expected to help. The fourth is Germany's defeats in the Soviet Union, North Africa and Western Europe, combined with Japan's defeats in the Pacific, during which the Axis eroded.

Remapping the world, 1940–1941

If Germany's attack on Poland in September 1939 opened the door to the German-Soviet partition of Poland, then the overrunning of Denmark, Norway, Belgium, the Netherlands and France in 1940, plus the expulsion of British forces from Europe, opened the continent and even overseas empires to change. Benito Mussolini's Italy moved first to claim spoils. Hitler had not informed Mussolini of his timetable for war in 1939 – he never shared timetables with his allies – and the ill-prepared Italians stayed out of the conflict, claiming 'non-belligerent' rather than neutral status. Even as Germany prepared to attack in the West in March 1940, Mussolini told Hitler that Italy needed a three- to four-month delay. German success altered his thinking, and Italy entered the war during what Mussolini hoped was its final phase on 10 June 1940. Italian forces unsuccessfully attacked the fortified French Alpine front.

Mussolini imagined a 'parallel war', whereby Italy would fight on the German side, but not *with* Germany, to wrest dominance of the Mediterranean from France and Great Britain. Hitler recognized the Mediterranean as Italy's area of expansion. But Berlin would not allow Rome's demands to wreck ceasefire negotiations with France, since they could prompt the French to fight from North Africa with the still intact French fleet. It was preferable for the new French government under Marshal Henri-Philippe Pétain, soon to be located at Vichy, to accept terms that would allow the Germans to continue the war against Great Britain.

The Germans and Italians negotiated completely separate ceasefire agreements with the French. German terms for the *Metropole* were strict. France's northern three-fifths were occupied, the French military was demobilized, and France bore heavy occupation costs. The Germans violated the terms when it suited them – for instance, with the expulsion of non-Germans from

Alsace-Lorraine. But Italy's initial terms – an occupation zone reaching to the Rhône River, the occupation of Corsica, Tunisia, Djibouti and French bases in North Africa, plus the handover of the French fleet – vanished, to the embarrassment of Italian negotiators. Italy occupied virtually no territory, and the French were vaguely allowed enough forces in Africa to maintain order. Mussolini hoped to win greater German support at the peace settlement with France and Great Britain.[2]

In the meantime, Spain, an Anti-Comintern Pact signatory, moved closer to the Axis. Hitler and Mussolini provided critical aid to Francisco Franco in Spain's Civil War. Franco resented subsequent incursions, particularly in the form of German mining concessions.[3] But his coalition of officers and political rightists had territorial designs, featuring Britain's base at Gibraltar and French Morocco, but also the Oran district of Algeria and parts of sub-Saharan Africa. The Spaniards preferred to act alone, occupying the French-administered international Moroccan zone of Tangier on 14 June, and preparing to attack French Morocco. But the movement of French troops to the Spanish Moroccan border gave Madrid pause. On 19 June, Spain offered to enter the war against Britain in return for its list of demands.[4] Berlin ignored the offer. Spain's motley armed forces seemed unnecessary.

The Germans came back to it in September, owing to several developments. Britain's unexpected continuation of the war was one. Another concerned incursions by General Charles de Gaulle's Free French forces in Africa – both the coup against Vichy in French Equatorial Africa in late August, and the failed attempt by British forces to land de Gaulle in the West African port of Dakar in late September. A third was Hitler's desire for strategic bases in northwest Africa, to be developed and used eventually against the United States. Hitler had believed since 1928 that Germany would eventually have to fight the USA, and his more recent conviction that Jews dominated Washington strengthened this belief.[5] The Destroyer-Base deal between Washington and London on 2 September 1940, in which the USA leased eight bases in the West Atlantic, sounded an alarm in Berlin that the USA was interested in bases in the East Atlantic as well.

2 Hermann Boehme, *Der deutsch-französische Waffenstillstand im Zweiten Weltkrieg* (Stuttgart: Deutsche Verlags-Anstalt, 1966).
3 Christian Leitz, *Economic Relations Between Nazi Germany and Franco's Spain, 1936–1945* (New York: Oxford University Press, 1996), pp. 8–125.
4 In general, see Stanley G. Payne, *Franco and Hitler: Spain, Germany, and World War II* (New Haven, Conn.: Yale University Press, 2008), pp. 61–86.
5 Jeffrey Herf, *The Jewish Enemy: Nazi Propaganda During World War II and the Holocaust* (Cambridge, Mass.: Harvard University Press, 2006), pp. 50–137.

In October 1940, Hitler made a grand tour of Western Europe to forge what he called a 'European coalition' to defeat Great Britain. He and Foreign Minister Joachim von Ribbentrop met with Mussolini, Pétain and Franco individually, to secure German strategic aims while providing vague statements concerning each prospective ally's rewards. The Italians, Hitler thought, could still receive their desired prizes – Germany had no interest in these. Spain would get but a slice of French Morocco and the Germans would have bases there. The French would protect the remainder of French Africa and be compensated for their losses from British African holdings. The project failed. Franco insisted on French Morocco. The French were willing to defend their empire against the British and Americans, and indeed did so in 1942, but they expected to keep their territories. Hitler, meanwhile, never trusted the French enough to allow them the means to repel Allied attacks. The West remained stagnant. Gibraltar remained in British hands, and northwest Africa remained vulnerable when the Allies landed in 1942.[6]

Germany's Western campaign also triggered changes in Eastern Europe. The German-Soviet Non-Aggression Pact of 23 August 1939 and subsequent agreements on trade and East European spheres of interest made Joseph Stalin a partner in aggression.[7] The looming German attack in the West drew Berlin and Moscow closer still. A trade treaty of 11 February 1940 provided Germany with raw materials (oil, manganese, grain) in return for an array of products that included industrial machinery, heavy weaponry and even battleship blueprints.[8] Hitler would do nothing at this point to jeopardize the arrangement. Thus when the Soviets attacked Finland in November 1939, starting the so-called Winter War, Berlin provided no help to Helsinki, despite its appeals (though the Italians considered sending aid). The Finns made peace in March 1940, surrendering territories in the Karelian region west of Lake Ladoga, which also held most Finnish industry.[9]

The conclusion of the Winter War, together with Germany's spring offensives, brought additional Soviet revision of the post-First World War settlement. The Baltic states, recognized by Berlin as a Soviet sphere of

6 Norman J. W. Goda, *Tomorrow the World: Hitler, Northwest Africa, and the Path Towards America* (College Station: Texas A&M University Press, 1998).
7 Printed in Germany, Auswärtiges Amt, *Akten zur deutschen auswärtigen Politik 1918–1945*, Serie D: 1937–1941 (Baden-Baden: Imprimerie Nationale, 1951–87) (hereafter *ADAP*), vol. 7, docs. 228, 229, 340; vol. 8, docs. 157, 159, 193.
8 Printed in *ADAP*, D, vol. 8; analysis in *Germany and the Second World War*, vol. IV: *The Attack on the Soviet Union* (10 vols., Oxford: Clarendon Press, 1998), pp. 118–36.
9 Robert Edwards, *White Death: Russia's War on Finland, 1939–1940* (London: Weidenfeld & Nicolson, 2006).

influence, were occupied and incorporated between June and August. Moscow also targeted Romania, which stood between the USSR and the Turkish Straits, and whose interwar guarantors, France and Great Britain, could not help. On 26 June 1940, Moscow demanded Romania's evacuation of Bessarabia (which the Romanians gained from the Russians in 1919) and of northern Bukovina (which Romania got from the destruction of Austria-Hungary). The Germans depended heavily on Romanian oil; in May 1940 they concluded extensive agreements for Romanian crude. They urged the Romanian government to concede, lest a Soviet attack jeopardize Romania's oilfields.[10]

Repercussions from France's defeat were also felt in Asia. By now, Japan's war with China, which began in earnest in 1937, had reached stalemate, despite Japanese control of north China, Peking, Shanghai, Nanjing and Guangdong. Chiang Kai-shek's nationalist government, in Chongqing after October 1938, refused to surrender, thanks partly to backing from the USA, Britain, France, the Netherlands and the USSR, all of which had Far Eastern holdings and all of which watched Japan's aggression with concern. As late as August 1939, Japan's chief ideological and geopolitical enemy was the USSR. Japan's Kwantung Army in Manchuria got the worst of border clashes with the Soviets in Mongolia in that month. But in 1940, with the French, Dutch and British weakened and the Soviets aligned with the Germans, the USA emerged as Japan's primary enemy.

Washington insisted that Japanese forces vacate China. It tightened oil and scrap metal sales to Japan – a critical issue, since the USA was Japan's chief supplier – and provided loans to Chiang's government. Tokyo's emerging policy was never fully coherent.[11] Prince Konoe Fumimaro, Prime Minister from July 1940 to October 1941, hoped to avoid a clash with the USA, but was unwilling to renounce Japan's gains just as the world was being reordered. Japan's military, meanwhile, increasingly adopted a southern strategy that encompassed the oil- and mineral-rich Dutch East Indies and French Indochina. For this vision, a more serious US reaction might be risked. The first step was Japan's occupation of Tonkin, the northern province of French Indochina through which half of Western aid to China moved. The Vichy government tried to enlist German aid in restraining Japan, but, receiving

10 *ADAP*, D, vol. 9, doc. 338; vol. 11, docs. 1, 7, 404. In general, see *Germany and the Second World War*, vol. IV, pp. 386–93.
11 This point is made in Akira Iriye, *The Origins of the Second World War in Asia and the Pacific* (London: Longman, 1987).

none, agreed to the occupation on 23 September 1940.[12] The USA cut scrap iron sales to Japan and augmented its aid to China via Burma.

The answer for Japanese Foreign Minister Yosuke Matsuoka lay in the intimidation of the USA through closer alignment with Germany, a solution that also suited the Germans, who, now preparing for war against the Soviets, worried about US meddling in the Atlantic and hoped to use Japan's surface fleet as a deterrent. Talks began in August, and on 27 September, Matsuoka signed the Tripartite Pact with the Germans and Italians in Berlin. The ten-year agreement recognized each power's sphere of interest and promised mutual economic and military assistance, should one be attacked 'by a power at present not involved in the European war or in the Sino-Japanese conflict', with the terms explicitly not affecting any signatory's relations with the Soviet Union.[13] It was the closest thing the Axis had to a treaty of alliance.

Toward global war, 1941

Hitler announced to his service chiefs on 31 July 1940 that Germany would destroy the Soviet Union the following spring. The campaign in the East was the centrepiece of Hitler's war. Germany's *Lebensraum* lay in the East, and the USSR, Hitler insisted, was the centre of Jewish-inspired Bolshevism. Hitler further believed that the British remained at war owing to London's hope for Soviet and American military aid. The USSR's destruction thus carried a global element. It would free Japan's flank in Manchuria so that Japan could apply pressure to British and US interests in the Pacific. Hitler signed the military directive for Operation BARBAROSSA in December 1940.[14]

Owing to its strategic resources and geopolitical significance on Germany's flank, Eastern Europe had to be calmed. Initially, the problem concerned irredentist claims on Romania by its neighbours, following the Soviet occupation of Bessarabia and northern Bukovina. Hungary insisted that Romania

---

12 Hata Ikuhiko, 'The Army's Move into Northern Indochina', in James William Morley (ed.), *The Fateful Choice: Japan's Advance into Southeast Asia, 1939–1941* (New York: Columbia University Press, 1980), pp. 155–208; *ADAP*, D, vol. 11, docs. 83, 89.

13 Text in *ADAP*, D, vol. 11, doc. 118; Chihiro Hosoya, 'The Tripartite Pact, 1939–1940', in James William Morley (ed.), *Deterrent Diplomacy: Japan, Germany, and the USSR, 1935–1940* (New York: Columbia University Press, 1976), pp. 179–257.

14 Walther Hubatsch (ed.), *Hitlers Weisungen für die Kriegführung, 1939–1945: Dokumente des Oberkommandos der Wehrmacht* (2nd edn, Frankfurt am Main: Bernard & Graefe, 1965), pp. 84–7.

return Transylvania; Bulgaria insisted that it return Dobrudja – both prizes awarded to Romania following the First World War. In September 1940, after bilateral negotiations with Bulgaria, Romania surrendered southern Dobrudja. But the bitter conflict with Hungary over Transylvania threatened war, possible Soviet intervention and danger to Romanian oil, right when Italy, and possibly Spain, would need it.

Berlin and Rome thus intervened, brokering the Second Vienna Award of 30 August 1940, which awarded northern Transylvania to Hungary, while leaving southern Transylvania with Romania. Berlin and Rome guaranteed Romania's new borders as a warning to the Hungarians, who had wanted more of Transylvania, and even to the Soviets, who in June had demanded all of Bukovina.[15] All three southeastern states gravitated toward Germany for protection from the Soviets, to keep their gains or to recoup their losses. In September 1940, German army and air force missions were dispatched to Romania at the request of the new strongman, Lieutenant General (and after August 1941, Marshal) Ion Antonescu. There they helped to create air defences for the oilfields and installations around Ploesti, while retraining the Romanian armed forces.[16] In November, Romania and Hungary, though bitter enemies, both joined the Tripartite Pact.

True to the Axis's character, Mussolini became suspicious of Berlin. In the summer of 1940, Italian Foreign Minister Galeazzo Ciano raised with Hitler the idea of invading Yugoslavia and Greece, both of which held territories dear to Italian irredentists. Hitler vetoed the idea. If Italy attacked Yugoslavia, he said, the Balkan equilibrium would be upset. He suggested, instead, that Italian forces then in Egypt, which had not moved past Sidi el-Barrani, should press further east; he even offered long-range aircraft to mine the Suez Canal from Italian bases in Rhodes.[17] By the autumn, Mussolini believed that the Germans had their own aims in the Balkans and decided to counteract them, this time without asking. 'Hitler', he said, 'always presents me with *faits accomplis*. This time I will pay him back in his own coin. He will discover from the newspapers that I have occupied Greece.'[18]

---

15 The First Vienna Award in November 1938 gave Hungary southern Slovakia and the Carpatho-Ukraine from the remains of Czechoslovakia. The Second Vienna Award negotiations are in *ADAP*, D, vol. 10, docs. 408–13.

16 *ADAP*, D, vol. 11, docs. 380, 381; Rebecca Haynes, *Romanian Policy Toward Germany, 1936–1940* (New York: Palgrave, 2000), pp. 99–166.

17 *ADAP*, D, vol. 10, docs. 129, 166.

18 Quoted in MacGregor Knox, *Mussolini Unleashed, 1939–1941: Politics and Strategy in Fascist Italy's Last War* (New York: Cambridge University Press, 1982), p. 208.

On 26 October, Italian forces, despite woeful unpreparedness, attacked Greece from Italy's protectorate in Albania. Repeated disasters followed in November and December, including the British attack on Italy's naval base Taranto; the Greek counter-attack that pushed Italian troops back into Albania; and the British offensive into Libya that took the Cyrenaica. Hitler had to help Mussolini. Partly owing to Italy's decision to change sides in the First World War, he trusted neither the Italian military nor the monarchy. 'The *Duce*', he would remark in 1943, 'is still the only *man* in Italy.'[19] Worse, Romania's oilfields were now within range of British bases in Crete, and, as Hitler put it to Mussolini, 'I hardly dare think of the consequences, [for] one thing must be realized: there is no effective defence for oil fields.'[20]

The price was the end of Italy's parallel war in the Mediterranean. In February 1941, a German armoured division arrived in Libya under the command of Erwin Rommel, who, though nominally under Italian command, ignored Italian caution and attacked the British on 31 March, driving them back into Egypt. German intervention in Greece was complicated by initial uncertainty over prospective allies in the region, which hinged, as usual, on resentments from the First World War. Bulgaria and Yugoslavia agreed to allow the passage of German troops in return for territorial rewards, both joining the Tripartite Pact in March. Yet a coup in Belgrade overthrew the Yugoslav government on 27 March, two days after it signed. Thus on 6 April, Germany attacked both Yugoslavia and Greece, reordering the Balkans as a whole.

Yugoslavia was dismantled. Italy received southern Slovenia and parts of the Dalmatian coast; Germany occupied northern Slovenia and Serbia; Bulgaria occupied Macedonia; and Hungary, which joined the attack to recover territories lost after the First World War, received Vojvodina. The Ustaša, a Croatian terrorist organization, ruled the new Independent State of Croatia, including much of pre-war Croatia, plus Bosnia and Herzegovina, with Italy and Germany receiving generous zones of influence. Yugoslavia never regained stability, thanks largely to Hitler's indulgence of Ustaša leader Ante Pavelić's ghastly cleansing operations against Serbs.[21] Greece was

---

19 Quoted in Frederick W. Deakin, *The Brutal Friendship: Mussolini, Hitler and the Fall of Italian Fascism* (London: Weidenfeld & Nicolson, 1962), p. 231.

20 *ADAP*, D, vol. 11, doc. 369.

21 Overviews are in Jozo Tomasevich, *War and Revolution in Yugoslavia, 1941–1945: Occupation and Collaboration* (Stanford University Press, 2001); Stevan K. Pavlowitch, *Hitler's New Disorder: The Second World War in Yugoslavia* (New York: Columbia University Press, 2008).

partitioned into occupation zones. The Germans held the port of Salonika. Bulgaria received most of Thrace. Italy occupied the Greek peninsula and most of the Greek islands. Airborne German forces landed in Crete on 20 May 1941, and, despite heavy losses, secured the island, putting Romania's oil out of easy British reach.

Moscow watched apprehensively. In November 1940, Foreign Minister V. I. Molotov travelled to Berlin to complain about Germany's presence in Romania, and to demand greater Soviet influence in Bulgaria, Romania and Turkey. Hitler assured him that Germany 'had been forced by wartime developments to become active in areas in which it was politically disinterested', and that 'as soon as peace prevailed...German troops would immediately leave Romania'.[22] In fact, Moscow still preferred to work against Britain. Molotov offered to join the Tripartite Pact; Stalin accepted Germany's conquests in the Balkans in 1941; and the USSR continued massive deliveries of oil, iron ore, metals, rubber and grain, promising even more for 1942.[23] As Ribbentrop put it to Molotov, 'Both partners of the German-Russian Pact had done good business.'[24]

In March and April 1941, Matsuoka visited Berlin, Rome and Moscow to gain diplomatic cover for Japan's expansion south. Believing that Germany did not need Japan's help against the Soviets, Hitler and Ribbentrop only hinted at the deterioration in relations with Moscow. But they strongly advocated Japanese pressure on the USA, and were worried about talks in Washington involving Kichisaburo Nomura, Japan's new ambassador there, which moderates in Tokyo hoped might avoid war.[25] Hitler urged Matsuoka to act on his own suggestion that Japan attack Britain's base at Singapore while the British were weakened and the USA unprepared. 'Seldom in history', Hitler insisted, 'had a risk been smaller... Such a moment would never return'. To assuage Tokyo's worries, Hitler assured Matsuoka on 4 April that, if an attack on Singapore led to war with the USA, 'Germany would...promptly take part...for the strength of the allies in the Tripartite Pact lay in their acting in common'.[26]

Matsuoka next travelled to Moscow, in order to normalize relations with the Soviets. These negotiations, begun in October 1940, had stalled over the

---

22 *ADAP*, D, vol. 11, doc. 326.
23 *Germany and the Second World War*, vol. iv, pp. 118–36.
24 *ADAP*, D, vol. 11, doc. 325.
25 On Nomura, see Peter Mauch, *Sailor Diplomat: Nomura Kichisaburō and the Japanese American War* (Cambridge, Mass.: Harvard University Press, 2008), pp. 114–225.
26 *ADAP*, D, vol. 12, docs. 222, 266.

issue of south Sakhalin, which Imperial Russia lost to Japan in 1905, and over the 1925 agreement that required Soviet oil deliveries from north Sakhalin. Now, however, owing to concerns regarding Germany's Balkan campaign, Stalin simply wanted an agreement. Both sides signed a five-year neutrality treaty on 13 April. Soviet aid to Chiang ended and Japan, though maintaining its army in Manchuria, could now look south. Stalin's benefits lay ahead after Germany attacked and were far more significant.[27]

On 22 June 1941, 3 million German troops attacked the Soviet Union. They were aided by a collection of European allies that eventually provided over half a million men.[28] All expected territorial gains and assurance of their place in Hitler's New Order. Finland and Romania were the most important allies, allowing Germany to station forces before the offensive and joining the attack almost immediately to recover recently lost lands. Finland's place was anomalous.[29] A parliamentary democracy that abstained from signing the Tripartite Pact, its troops remained under separate command. They retook lost Karelian territory, but refused German requests to cut the railroad to Murmansk or aid in the siege of Leningrad. Romanian forces advanced into northern Bukovina and Bessarabia. But Antonescu then pressed further, over the Dniester River, hoping that by supporting the German drive east he would win Hitler's agreement to return northern Transylvania. Hitler admired Antonescu and awarded Romania administrative authority over Transnistria – the region between the Dniester and Bug Rivers. But he never undid the Second Vienna Award.[30]

Other European Tripartite allies joined in with limited contingents, days after the attack. Slovakia declared war, hoping that Berlin might restore the territories lost to Hungary in 1938 and 1939.[31] Hungary followed suit, hoping to restore in full its pre-First World War borders and fearing that neutrality could cost the recently gained territories. Mussolini deployed an expeditionary force, hoping to redeem earlier misadventures while augmenting Italy's role at the peace table. 'We cannot allow ourselves', he told his generals,

27 Boris Slavinsky, *The Japanese-Soviet Neutrality Pact: A Diplomatic History, 1941–1945* (London: Routledge, 2004), chs. 2, 3.
28 Overview in Rolf-Dieter Müller, *The Unknown Eastern Front: The Wehrmacht and Hitler's Foreign Soldiers* (London: I. B. Tauris, 2007).
29 On Finland, see Olli Vehviläinen, *Finland and the Second World War: Between Germany and Russia* (New York: Palgrave, 2002).
30 On the relationship, see Dennis J. Deletant, *Hitler's Forgotten Ally: Ion Antonescu and His Regime – Romania, 1940–1945* (New York: Palgrave Macmillan, 2006), pp. 69–136.
31 Tatjana Tönsmeyer, *Das Dritte Reich und die Slowakei, 1939–1945: Politischer Alltag zwischen Kooperation und Eigensinn* (Paderborn: Schöningh, 2003).

'to be put in the shadows by Slovakia'.[32] Other states sent volunteer contingents. Franco, for example, saw a crusade against communism and hoped that Spain's so-called Blue Division would improve chilled relations with Berlin. Croatia also assembled a volunteer regiment, expecting that participation would provide leverage against Italian claims on the Adriatic. Only Bulgaria remained neutral, owing to its cultural kinship with Russia and its usefulness in combating Balkan partisans.

Hitler was pleased, as he told Croatian War Minister Slavko Kvaternik in July 1941, that 'the struggle against Bolshevism has united all of Europe'.[33] But the coalition was abnormal, and not simply because the allied forces were undermanned and under-equipped. The entire structure was flawed. Because Hitler wished to keep Operation BARBAROSSA secret, there were no preliminary treaties explaining commitments, rewards or general principles. Most of Hitler's allies had territorial claims on one another. Indeed, keeping the Romanians and Hungarians from fighting over Transylvania was a constant challenge. Nor were there meaningful staff talks between the Germans and their allies. Tripartite units fought within German army groups, hoping for the best. And thanks to German losses in 1941, the Germans insisted in early 1942 that the allies deliver more men and resources, while providing neither the operational details nor oft-promised heavy weapons. Mussolini, on his own insistence, committed 229,000 men for the disastrous 1942 campaign in the Caucasus. Italy's 85,000 men lost in the USSR account for a third of its military losses during the war.[34]

Germany's strongest ally, Japan, did not attack the USSR at all. Despite Matsuoka's urging to the contrary, Japan's military leaders understood that German successes freed Japan to create a 'Greater East Asian Co-Prosperity Sphere' from European holdings in Southeast Asia. The advance began with Japan's occupation of southern Indochina on 28 July. Unlike the Tonkin occupation, which was logistical in nature, the occupation of the south was offensive in character. As Japanese military officials told the Germans in June, it created 'a favorable strategic position with respect to Singapore'.[35] But the occupation of southern Indochina also triggered a freezing of Japanese

32 *Germany and the Second World War*, vol. IV, p. 1038.
33 Andreas Hillgruber (ed.), *Staatsmänner und Diplomaten bei Hitler: Vertrauliche Aufzeichnungen* (2 vols., Frankfurt am Main: Bernard & Graefe, 1967–70), vol. II, p. 553.
34 Coalition warfare issues are described in Richard L. DiNardo, *Germany and the Axis Powers: From Coalition to Collapse* (Lawrence: University Press of Kansas, 2005).
35 *ADAP*, D, vol. 12, doc. 612.

assets in the USA and thus a full embargo of strategic materials. Tokyo worked itself into a diplomatic corner.[36]

Japan's leaders understood the latent power of the USA. But since Washington would not resume normal relations until Japan disgorged its gains, and since Tokyo insisted that Washington acknowledge these same gains, war became increasingly likely. Japan could wilt under US sanctions or take its chances on a general offensive that would include US holdings in the Pacific. Following extensive discussions, military deployment commenced in September, and, by 2 November, the Cabinet decided on hostilities. Naval forces would attack the US base in Hawaii and cripple the US fleet, while Japan grabbed all it could in the so-called prosperity sphere. Fortification of strategic points on the southern perimeter would make a US attempt to undo the conquests so unpleasant that Washington would hopefully accept the new reality in the Pacific. The surprise 7 December attack on Pearl Harbor was thus accompanied by the Japanese invasion and conquest of the Philippines, Malaya (including Britain's base in Singapore), Hong Kong, the Gilbert Islands, Guam, the Solomon Islands, Tarakan, Celebes, Borneo, New Guinea and Java.[37]

In keeping with the tenor of Axis diplomacy, Tokyo did not inform Berlin of its impending offensive. Still, Hitler was elated once it began.[38] Britain and the USA were staggered, and despite the Red Army's decisive counter-offensive against exhausted German forces west of Moscow on 5 December, Hitler was sure that the following year would bring victory. 'The essential thing', Ribbentrop said on 9 December, 'was that Japan now was in the fighting on the side of the Axis'. He described Japan's offensive as 'the most important event to develop since the beginning of the war'.[39] True to the Tripartite Pact, Germany and Italy declared war on the United States on 11 December, and signed a new agreement with Japan not to conclude a separate armistice or peace with the Western Allies. German submarines quickly began sinking US merchant ships off the Atlantic coast.[40] On Berlin's

---

36 Nagaoka Shinjiro, 'The Drive into Southern Indochina and Thailand', in Morley (ed.), *The Fateful Choice*, pp. 209–40.

37 On the decisions, see the essays in John William Morley (ed.), *The Final Confrontation: Japan's Negotiations with the United States, 1941* (New York: Columbia University Press, 1994).

38 On the critical days, see Evan Mawdsley, *December 1941: Twelve Days that Began a World War* (New Haven, Conn.: Yale University Press, 2011).

39 *ADAP*, D, vol. 13, doc. 569.

40 Reference in Jürgen Röhwer and Gerhard Hümmelchen, *Chronik des Seekrieges 1939–1945* (Munich: Oldenbourg, 1968).

insistence – and against Washington's considerably more friendly advice – Slovakia, Hungary, Romania, Bulgaria and Croatia also declared war on the USA, as Ribbentrop said, to demonstrate Axis solidarity. The war was now global.

The diplomacy of the Final Solution, 1942–1943

Germany's attack on the USSR triggered decisions leading to the 'Final Solution of the Jewish question' – the murder of all Jews in Europe, which began in the occupied USSR in June 1941 and spread to German-occupied Poland in December. On 20 January 1942, Security Police Chief Reinhard Heydrich hosted the Wannsee Conference outside Berlin, where he discussed administrative procedures with other agency representatives. This discussion partly concerned the cooperation of governments allied with Germany. Hans Luther, who represented the Foreign Ministry, wrote three days before the meeting that 'The opportunity of this war must be used to settle the Jewish question in Europe once and for all'.[41] But international cooperation remained an open question. While Luther thought that Germany's southeastern allies would pose no problems, Hitler worried that Hungary would be the last country to hand over its Jews.[42]

Indeed it was with Germany's allies that the 'Final Solution' became most frustrating, partly owing to the number of Jews involved – 1.1 million in Hungary and Romania alone. The regimes were anti-Semitic. They imposed anti-Jewish legal disabilities and confiscatory economic policies before the war, and during the war they worked to cleanse their newly acquired lands of foreign Jews. On Antonescu's orders, Romanian forces in Bessarabia and Transnistria killed between 280,000 and 380,000 Jews, most in 1941.[43] Hungarian authorities dumped Jews from the newly acquired eastern regions into Ukraine, where they were massacred in August 1941, and placed some 50,000 Hungarian Jewish men in labour battalions in Ukraine, where most died.[44]

41 Eckart Conze, Norbert Frei, Peter Hayes and Moshe Zimmermann, *Das Amt und die Vergangenheit: Deutsche Diplomaten im Dritten Reich und in der Bundesrepublik* (Berlin: Blessing, 2009), p. 186.
42 Mark Roseman, *The Wannsee Conference and the Final Solution: A Reconsideration* (New York: Picador, 2002), pp. 157–72; Andreas Hillgruber (ed.), *Staatsmänner*, vol. II, p. 553.
43 Figures from the International Commission on the Holocaust in Romania, *Final Report of the International Commission on the Holocaust in Romania* (Bucharest: Polirum, 2005), pp. 175–9.
44 Randolph L. Braham, *The Politics of Genocide: The Holocaust in Hungary* (2 vols., New York: Columbia University Press, 1981), vol. I, pp. 199–207, 285–361.

Bulgarian police arrested and handed over 96 per cent of the Jews in occupied Macedonia and Thrace in March 1943, whereupon the Germans took them to Treblinka.[45]

All became more cautious, however, with German requests that local Jews be handed over. Only Jozef Tiso's government in Slovakia agreed from the start, allowing the Germans to deport 58,000 Jews, beginning in March 1942, and even here, government and church objections triggered a halt in October.[46] Antonescu's refusal, in 1942, to deport Romania's roughly 300,000 Jews is especially puzzling. Historians point to his anger with Germany's endless delays in providing heavy weaponry to his armies in Ukraine, his irritation with Berlin's high-handedness on the Jewish question, and his refusal to agree to such a thing before the hated Hungarians did the same. In any event, he postponed planned deportations in October 1942 and never returned to it.[47] Instead, he adopted a fantastic idea to send – in return for heavy Allied payments – the remaining 70,000 Jews in Transnistria to Palestine, a scheme that made Berlin apoplectic.[48]

The military disaster outside Stalingrad in late 1942 and early 1943, where Hitler's allies held the flanks, shook the alliance badly. In November and December 1942, the Soviets crushed the Romanian Third and Fourth Armies, along with the Italian Eighth Army on the Don. The Hungarian Second Army was destroyed at Voronezh in January. Marshal Antonescu's Foreign Minister, Mihai Antonescu, made soundings to the Allies, as did the conservative Hungarian Prime Minister Miklós Kállay, who had thought Hungary's participation ill-advised to start with. The mass murder of Jews would not make peace efforts easier. Even Bulgaria, surely relieved not to have fought the Soviets, was concerned with what the Allies thought.

In April 1943, Hitler summoned his allies to a series of bilateral meetings at Schloss Klessheim near Salzburg. One by one, he informed them that there would be no compromise with Bolshevism. Germany would launch counter-offensives in the East. But the Jewish question also formed part of these

45 Frederick B. Chary, *The Bulgarian Jews and the Final Solution, 1940–1944* (Pittsburgh, Pa.: University of Pittsburgh Press, 1972), pp. 101–28.
46 Ivan Kamenec, *On the Trail of Tragedy: The Holocaust in Slovakia* (Bratislava: Hajko & Hajkova, 2007), pp. 218–80.
47 Jean Ancel, *The History of the Holocaust in Romania* (Lincoln: University of Nebraska Press, 2011); Radu Ioanid, *The Holocaust in Romania: The Destruction of Jews and Gypsies under the Antonescu Regime, 1940–1944* (Chicago, Ill.: Ivan Dee, 2000).
48 See *ADAP*, E, vol. 5, doc. 28. On the scheme, see Tuvia Friling, *Arrows in the Dark: David Ben-Gurion, the Yishuv Leadership, and Rescue Attempts During the Holocaust* (2 vols., Madison: University of Wisconsin Press, 2005), vol. 1, pp. 145–94.

discussions. The Germans indulged Antonescu. Hitler trusted him to keep Romania in the war, and Germany depended on Romanian oil. Hitler thus emphasized the need to scotch Mihai Antonescu's initiatives, and Ribbentrop pressed for increased oil deliveries. The Jewish question came up in passing, with Antonescu asking Ribbentrop to facilitate the shipping of Romanian Jews to Palestine, and Ribbentrop wondering aloud if they could not be sent to Russia. Ribbentrop was less patient with King Boris of Bulgaria. 'Our opinion on the Jewish question', Ribbentrop insisted, is that 'the most radical solution is the only correct one'. Hitler applied the greatest pressure to the Hungarian Regent, Admiral Miklós Horthy, who allowed Kállay to inaugurate peace feelers while protecting some 800,000 Jews, by then the largest concentration left in Europe. The 'pro-Jewish attitude in Hungary', he said, was 'incomprehensible. . . Whoever believes in compromise on this question is fundamentally mistaken'. Even in his meeting with Tiso, wherein Hitler hinted toward a resumption of deportations from Slovakia, Hitler complained primarily about the Hungarians.[49]

Hitler's allies remained in the war. But there was no movement on the Jewish question. Hungary remained the greatest irritant. Edmund Veesenmayer, Ribbentrop's expert for Eastern Europe, insisted, in April 1943, that Hungary was dominated by 'a refined Jewish plutocratic system. . .which through sabotage, espionage, and the spread of defeatism can become a serious danger for Axis policy'.[50] Bulgaria's government expelled Sofia's Jews to the countryside in May 1943, but as ambassador Adolf-Heinz Beckerle reported in August, 'it is absolutely senseless to insist on deportation. . . [We] shall be able to solve the Jewish problem completely when German successes again come to the fore'.[51] In Bucharest, German minister Manfred von Killinger reported, in February 1944, that Antonescu 'dismisses radical measures because of the unfavourable propagandistic effect in enemy states'.[52]

Germany's closest ally, meanwhile, was an impediment. Owing to Hitler's concerns for Mussolini's prestige, the Italians received occupation zones in Croatia and Greece in 1941. When the Allies invaded North Africa in November 1942, the Germans occupied the remainder of France, wherein the Italians gained an additional occupation zone east of the Rhône River. Mussolini had few qualms about the 'Final Solution', but Italian military

49 *ADAP*, E, vol. 5, docs. 273, 300, 306, 315, 338.
50 Ibid., vol. 7, doc. 43.
51 Haim Oliver, *We Were Saved: How the Jews of Bulgaria Were Kept from the Death Camps* (Sofia: Sofia Press, 1978), pp. 207–8.
52 *ADAP*, E, vol. 4, doc. 279; vol. 7, doc. 220.

and diplomatic authorities rejected German criminality. Thus, as the Ustaša killed some 20,000 of Croatia's Jews while allowing the Germans to deport another 9,000, some 4,000 fled for Italian-controlled territory. As the Germans deported Salonika's Jews in the spring of 1943, the Italians protected Jews in peninsular Greece, perhaps 23,000 in all. And Italian authorities in Nice refused to allow the Vichy police, who had cooperated with the Germans since 1942, to arrest the 30,000 Jews who lived in their zone.

Berlin was furious. *Reichsführer-SS* Heinrich Himmler worried how other governments would respond when 'even our Italian Axis partner is not prepared to follow our lead in the Jewish question'. Ribbentrop viewed Giuseppe Bastianini, Italy's de facto Foreign Minister after February 1943, as 'an honorary Jew', and in March directed ambassador Hans-Georg von Mackensen to pressure Mussolini directly. Mussolini could only complain that his officers followed 'a misguided humanitarian sentimentality. . .inappropriate to our harsh epoch'.[53] Ironically, it was the erosion of the Axis alliance itself under Allied and Soviet blows that helped to solve these problems.

From triumph to defeat, 1942–1945

After Pearl Harbor, ambassador Hiroshi Oshima in Berlin urged the creation of a Tripartite Council to coordinate Axis operations, plus a 'Mutual Aid Economic Pact for Winning the War', to facilitate trade in strategic materials. Berlin agreed, but these efforts amounted to nothing immediate beyond an agreement, in January 1942, to divide the world through eastern India.[54] Both states jealously guarded their economic interests and strategic prerogatives. Worse, the problem of distance confounded even basic communication.

The two sides exchanged trade delegations, but neither was ready to become a raw materials supplier. The Japanese carefully guarded their conquests from German penetration, refusing permanent contracts even for specific commodities. By September 1942, German officials complained that Japan's conquests should have made trade for badly needed rubber and fats easy, and that Tokyo's behaviour ran counter to the Tripartite Pact.

---

53 Daniel Carpi, *Between Mussolini and Hitler: The Jews and the Italian Authorities in France and Tunisia* (Hanover, NH: University Press of New England, 1994), pp. 105, 128; Jonathan Steinberg, *All or Nothing: The Axis and the Holocaust, 1941–1943* (London: Routledge, 1990), p. 118; *ADAP*, E, vol. 5, doc. 189.

54 Bernd Martin, *Deutschland und Japan im Zweiten Weltkrieg: Vom Angriff auf Pearl Harbor bis zur deutschen Kapitulation* (new edn, Hamburg: Nikol Verlag, 2001), pp. 46–80.

Ribbentrop, meanwhile, asked Oshima if Japan's request for 1 million tons of steel was a misprint. The lack of safe routes between Japan and Germany stifled trade anyway. It was reduced to limited deliveries on blockade-running ships and, after March 1943, on submarines. The ships sometimes carried more ballast than cargo, owing to continued disagreements. The so-called Treaty on Economic Cooperation, signed on 20 January 1943, was too little and too late.[55]

The primary disagreement, however, concerned grand strategy. For Hitler, the Soviet Union was the primary enemy; for Japan, the USA was the main foe. The difference resulted in crucial missed opportunities in 1941 and 1942. When Operation BARBAROSSA commenced, Ribbentrop and Hitler pressed the Japanese to attack the USSR from the east, even to the exclusion of a Japanese thrust south, which they now argued could come after the USSR's destruction. Ribbentrop pressed again, in July 1942, as German troops marched to the Don. 'Japan', he told Oshima, 'would never again be offered such a favourable opportunity to remove the Russian colossus for all time [from] East Asia'. And in February 1943, after the Stalingrad debacle, Ribbentrop said that Japanese intervention was 'a necessity of decisive importance for the war' and had to be launched that year.[56]

These issues were partly operational. Thanks to Japan's neutrality, in October 1941, Stalin transferred eighteen battle-hardened divisions, plus tanks and aircraft, from the Siberian and Far Eastern military districts. These forces were critical in the Soviet counter-offensive outside Moscow.[57] But logistical issues were also key. The USA included the Soviets in the Lend-Lease programme in November 1941, and roughly half of all deliveries went from Alaska to Vladivostok. The Soviet-Japanese neutrality treaty protected US ships sailing under Soviet flags. Tokyo insisted to Moscow that no finished military supplies travel via this route – only food, fuel and raw materials. But Oshima admitted to the Germans that, in 1942 alone, 400,000 tons of food reached Vladivostok.[58]

55 On trade issues, see *ADAP*, E, vol. 3, doc. 254, vol. 6, doc. 316. In general, see Martin, *Deutschland und Japan*, pp. 152–71, 210–13.
56 *ADAP*, D, vol. 13, docs. 33, 35, 76; vol. 5, doc. 145. In general, see Martin, *Deutschland und Japan*, pp. 94–109.
57 The role of the Soviet agent in Germany's Tokyo Embassy was critical. See Robert Whymant, *Stalin's Spy: Richard Sorge and the Tokyo Espionage Ring* (New York: St Martin's Press, 1996), chs. 10–13.
58 *ADAP*, E, vol. 5, docs. 105, 145. See also Hubert P. van Tuyll, *Feeding the Bear: American Aid to the Soviet Union, 1941–1945* (Westport, Conn.: Greenwood Press, 1989), pp. 27, 55, 164.

The Japanese argued to Berlin that their entry into the war with the Soviets would enable the USA to use Soviet bases to bomb Japan. In this connection, the April 1942 Doolittle raid on Honshu carried an impact beyond the slight damage that it caused.[59] Tokyo subsequently complained to Moscow about stray US bombers that made emergency landings on Soviet territory, but Tokyo did not want to exacerbate the problem, especially since Stalin, to appease Tokyo, interned US fliers.[60] Japan's pivotal defeat at Midway in June 1942 strengthened this trend. A Japanese statement to the Germans in late July noted that 'the resistance of the USA remains so stubborn that Japan must continue to marshal its forces for future operations against this enemy. . . An action against the Soviet Union would bring about too great a splitting of Japanese forces. . .and furthermore could give the Americans favorable bases for attacks on Japan'.[61] As the war continued, Tokyo worked harder to maintain Moscow's neutrality, sending congratulations to Moscow for the momentous victory over the Germans at Kursk in July 1943, and conceding an end to Soviet oil concessions from north Sakhalin in March 1944. Moscow's apparent goodwill allowed Japan to move twelve divisions from Manchuria that year to deploy against the Americans.[62]

After Pearl Harbor, the Germans also called for a Japanese offensive in the Indian Ocean. A quarter of Allied deliveries to the USSR – including half of all trucks and most aircraft – reached the Soviet Union via the Persian Gulf. British and US deliveries to the British Eighth Army in Egypt – which included badly needed tanks – also travelled via the African east coast. The shipments were of paramount importance after Rommel's triumph at Tobruk in June 1942, which seemed to open the road to Suez. A German-Japanese link-up through the Caucasus and Near East to the Indian Ocean, Berlin thought, would choke the Soviets and British, while leaving the USA isolated. As Ribbentrop said in July, 'it is of the greatest importance for our joint conduct of the war, for the Japanese navy to strengthen its activity in the Indian Ocean, and not just to send more submarines. . .but also cruisers and other large units'.[63]

59 This point is made in Gerhard L. Weinberg, *A World at Arms: A Global History of World War II* (2nd edn, New York: Cambridge University Press, 2005), pp. 332, 346.
60 George Alexander Lensen, *The Strange Neutrality: Soviet-Japanese Relations During the Second World War, 1941–1945* (Tallahassee, Fla.: Diplomatic Press, 1972), pp. 39–52.
61 *ADAP*, E, vol. 3, doc. 142; Lensen, *Strange Neutrality*, pp. 255–7.
62 Weinberg, *World at Arms*, pp. 634–5.
63 *ADAP*, E, vol. 3, doc. 76.

In May 1942, the Japanese closed the Burmese supply route to Chiang's forces. To support this operation, six Japanese carriers ventured westward in March and April, launching attacks on British ships in the Bay of Bengal and on the Colombo naval base in Ceylon. But this was the extent of Japanese surface operations in the region. The Battle of Midway in June and the landing of US forces in the Solomons in August prompted the Japanese to pull their surface fleet back. Japanese submarines continued to operate off the East African coast, but Ribbentrop's complaint that submarines alone were insufficient brought Tokyo's reply that surface operations in the western Indian Ocean would leave Japan 'in a dangerous situation with regard to the US fleet'.[64]

Meanwhile, from November 1941 to February 1945, Tokyo pushed for a separate peace between the Germans and Soviets, so that the Axis could concentrate on the Western Allies. Driven by ideology rather than realpolitik, Hitler never budged. In 1942, Ribbentrop admonished Oshima that even rumours of peace with Bolshevism indicated 'strong support of Stalinist propaganda. . .extremely harmful to our joint interests', and this stance never changed.[65] Meanwhile, there was little hope that Tokyo could convince Stalin to make peace. He did not even receive the new Japanese ambassador Sato Naotake when he arrived in April 1942, and in September 1944, Sato cautioned Tokyo that 'for the sake of our prestige we do not want to ask too often [to mediate] and get a refusal every time'.[66]

In the shadow of Stalingrad and the deteriorating North African position in late 1942 and early 1943, a similar rift opened between Berlin and Rome. After December 1942, Mussolini and his diplomats tried to convince Hitler either to adopt a defensive posture in the East or to find a compromise solution with Moscow. 'You have succeeded', Mussolini wrote to Hitler on 26 March 1943, 'in weakening Russia to such an extent that it cannot. . .constitute any real threat for a long time. . . The Russian chapter must therefore be closed somehow or another'. Thereafter, he insisted, the Axis could 'again seize the strategic initiative in the West'. But as Hitler wrote to Mussolini on 16 February, 'I will. . .continue to fight in the East until this colossus finally collapses. . . For

---

64 Ibid., vol. 3, doc. 142.
65 Ibid., vol. 3, docs. 255, 295; vol. 7, doc. 13.
66 Carl Boyd, *Hitler's Japanese Confidante: General Oshima Hiroshi and MAGIC Intelligence, 1941–1945* (Lawrence: University Press of Kansas, 1993), pp. 149–59. In general, see Gerhard Krebs, 'Japanische Vermittlungsversuche im deutsch-sowjetischen Krieg, 1941–1945', in Josef Kreiner and Regine Mathias (eds.), *Deutschland-Japan in der Zwischenkriegszeit* (Bonn: Bouvier, 1990), pp. 239–88.

I regard the mere existence of this peril as so enormous that Europe cannot have an hour of calm [if it] forgets or simply will not see the truth'.[67]

By March 1943, Axis forces in North Africa had lost Libya and were confined to a bridgehead in Tunisia. Supply, the main problem of the North African campaign, was mostly Italy's responsibility. Germany's refusal to commit to the capture of Malta, from which the British attacked Italian shipping, irritated the Italians, who thought it a priority. Irrespective of British efforts, Italy lacked sufficient cargo space and fuel for their escort vessels, and repeated calls for German logistical support left Rome embittered.[68] As Bastianini complained on 17 March, 'scarcely any of the war materials we have asked for have been sent'.[69] Mussolini grabbed at straws. Perhaps Spain, he thought, would enter the war so that the Germans could outflank the Allies by pushing into Morocco. Franco insisted that his 'heart was with the Axis', but he declined even to see Mussolini in 1943 for fear of Allied trade repercussions.[70] Hitler, meanwhile, prioritized the Eastern Front. Tunisia, he told Mussolini at Klessheim in April 1943, might become a defensive fortress – 'the Verdun of the Mediterranean'.[71]

Tunisia was lost in May. Italy's heightened vulnerability led to efforts by Bastianini to create, under Italian leadership, a coalition of smaller Axis states that might intercede with Hitler to negotiate a settlement, or, should this fail, to conduct secret negotiations with the Allies. Hungarian Prime Minister Kállay raised the idea when he visited Rome in early April. Romanian Foreign Minister Mihai Antonescu pressed it further with Mussolini when they met on 1 July. The scheme played on Mussolini's vanity, but it ran aground on his reluctance to confront Hitler. Mussolini well knew how the Axis worked. He thus proposed to Antonescu that a Tripartite Conference – such a thing had never been called – might discuss matters further, and that he would raise the issue with Hitler in two months.[72] If Mussolini ever intended to follow up, he was quickly out of time. The Allies invaded Sicily on 10 July.

67 *ADAP*, E, vol. 5, docs. 135, 252.
68 On the supply of Tunisia and the planning for Malta, see *Germany and the Second World War*, vol. VI: *The Global War* (10 vols., Oxford: Clarendon Press, 2001), pp. 654–60, 828–40; DiNardo, *Germany and the Axis Powers*, pp. 158–79.
69 Deakin, *Brutal Friendship*, p. 207.
70 Javier Tussell and Genoveva García Queipo de Llano, *Franco y Mussolini: La política española durante la segunda guerra mundial* (Barcelona: Planeta, 1985), pp. 188–93.
71 DiNardo, *Germany and the Axis Powers*, p. 171.
72 Deakin, *Brutal Friendship*, pp. 257–8, 303–13.

The Germans had six divisions in Sicily and southern Italy, and Hitler was loath to send more troops. He was consumed with the German offensive at Kursk in July 1943, which he hoped would turn the tide in the East, and the Soviet counter-offensive that followed. The two dictators, with their military entourages, met at Feltre in Northern Italy on 19 July, even as Allied bombs fell on Rome. Hitler insisted that additional German airpower could not be sent to the Mediterranean, looked to a defence of the Italian mainland, and told the Italians to organize their air forces better.[73] But now, all Italian confidence in Mussolini had vanished. On the night of 24 July, the Fascist Grand Council voted to return the Duce's state functions to King Victor Emmanuel III, who, the next day, removed Mussolini as Prime Minister and had him arrested. The new head of state was Marshal Pietro Badoglio, former Chief of the Italian General Staff, who had been sceptical of the alliance with Germany in 1939. He played for time, repeatedly assuring Berlin that he would remain in the Axis, while conducting secret negotiations with the Allies, hoping that they might land near Rome to protect the capital.[74]

Hitler trusted neither Badoglio nor the king. By the second week of August, seven additional German divisions moved into northern Italy. Badoglio's double game ended quickly. The Allies announced the armistice on 8 September and the next day landed at Salerno. In accordance with long-standing plans, the Germans moved into Rome on 10 September, while cutting off Italian units in France and the Balkans. Badoglio's declaration of war on Germany on 13 October was of no consequence to Berlin. German commandos had rescued Mussolini on 12 September, and Hitler had set him up as the head of the Republic of Salò, in northern Italy. The Tripartite Pact was thereby theoretically restored, and Hitler insisted that his other allies recognize the new republic.[75]

Germany's practical treatment of its oldest ally was less friendly. German units disarmed Italian occupation forces in Italy, France and the Balkans, and more than 600,000 Italian POWs were moved to Germany, where Himmler used most for forced labour. In November 1943, Mussolini intervened to secure better treatment for them, hoping to build Italian loyalty, and an army, for his new republic. He managed to have several transports of sick

73 *ADAP*, E, vol. 6, doc. 159.
74 For Badoglio's diplomacy, see Elena Agarossi, *A Nation Collapses: The Italian Surrender of September 1943* (New York: Cambridge, 2000).
75 *ADAP*, E, vol. 6, doc. 349. In general, see Lutz Klinkhammer, *Zwischen Bündnis und Besatzung: Das Nationalsozialistische Deutschland und die Republik von Sàlo 1943–1945* (Tübingen: Niemayer, 1993).

prisoners sent home in 1944, but these were suspended when the Italian populace blamed Mussolini and the Germans for the returnees' condition. Some 40,000 Italian soldiers died in German captivity.[76] There was a further account to settle regarding the Habsburg territories awarded to Italy in 1919. The Germans conquered the ethnically mixed Istrian peninsula, thus pre-empting the Croatian government, which had renounced earlier agreements with Italy and announced its claim to the Dalmatian coast.[77] German troops also seized the South Tyrol, which Hitler, despite the presence of 250,000 ethnic Germans, had left with Italy as the price of the Italian alliance. Both regions were Germanized, down to the demolition of Italian First World War memorials. As late as December 1944, Mussolini tried, unsuccessfully, to gain assurances from Berlin that the provinces would remain Italian.[78]

By this time, Soviet drives into Eastern Europe triggered additional defections and reprisals. Romania went first, after the Soviets crossed into the country and captured the city of Iaşi on 22 August 1944. The following day, King Michael removed and arrested Marshal Antonescu and members of his Cabinet. He announced to the German minister von Killinger that the new government would sue for an armistice, requesting further that German troops leave Romanian soil. Killinger replied that Germany would accept no changes in Romania's foreign policy. On Hitler's orders, Bucharest was attacked, while in Berlin, a Romanian 'National Government' was formed under Horia Sima, the leader of Romania's fanatically fascist, and heretofore counterproductive, Iron Guard. Bucharest remained under government control, German diplomatic personnel were arrested, and on 25 August, Romania declared war on Germany. The turnabout did not save Romania from Soviet occupation, but it allowed seven Romanian divisions to join in the assault on Hungary, whereby northern Transylvania was reclaimed.[79]

Subsequent defectors experienced different results. Finland concluded a ceasefire with Moscow on 4 September, again losing Karelia and, this time, Petsamo and its nickel mines. Wipert von Blücher, the German minister in

---

76 Gerhard Schreiber, *Die italienischen Militärinternierten im deutschen Machtbereich 1943–1945* (Munich: Oldenbourg, 1990).

77 *ADAP*, E, vol. 6, doc. 295; vol. 7, doc. 87.

78 Ibid., vol. 8, doc. 310. In general, see Michael Wedekind, *Nationalsozialistische Besatzungs-und Annexionspolitik in Norditalien, 1943 bis 1945. Die Operationszonen 'Alpenvorland' und 'Adriatisches Küstenland'* (Munich: Oldenbourg, 2003).

79 The final phase of Romania's war is discussed in *Das Deutsche Reich und der Zweite Weltkrieg*, vol. VIII: *Die Ostfront 1943/44* (Munich: Deutsche Verlags-Anstalt, 2007), pp. 731–805. See also Deletant, *Hitler's Forgotten Ally*, pp. 230–44; *ADAP*, E, vol. 8, doc. 195.

Helsinki, rejected Ribbentrop's idea to organize a pro-Nazi underground movement. There was, he said, no local sympathy for such a thing. Bulgaria slipped out of the war on 26 August, despite Hitler's threats. Ribbentrop hoped to establish a new government in Sofia, but the embassy there advised waiting until the Soviets entered the country, so as to gain popular support, by which time it was too late. Slovakia, located on the German border, was less fortunate. Dissident army factions and communists rebelled on 29 August. German army and police units crushed the revolt by late October, a favour for which Tiso thanked Hitler personally. One small German ally, Croatia, remained true to the end. In mid-September 1944, Hitler commiserated with Pavelić over the Finns, the Bulgarians and the Romanians, who, he said, jumped into the water to save themselves from drowning. Pavelić did not disappoint. Croatia, he said, still believed in victory. He demanded more weapons to fight the communist partisans.[80]

All of this made Hungary's fate unique. In March 1944, with Soviet troops a hundred miles from Hungary, the Kállay government pulled Hungarian troops back to the border. Having learned from his experience with Italy the previous autumn, Hitler pre-emptively ordered Hungary to be occupied. Berlin replaced the Kállay Cabinet with one more to its liking under Döme Sztójay, the former Minister to Germany. The new Cabinet cooperated in two long-demanded projects – full Hungarian mobilization, beginning in March, and the deportation of some 437,000 Jews, beginning in May. It also angrily swallowed instances of German plunder, most notably the SS purchase of the Manfred Weiss Works, Hungary's most important heavy industrial and weapons producer, from Jewish shareholders.[81]

In September and October, with the Soviets pressing toward Budapest, and with other allies having defected, the Regent Miklós Horthy secretly negotiated a ceasefire with Moscow and the Western Allies, which he announced on 15 October. 'It is obvious to any sober person', he proclaimed in a crown council meeting that day, 'that the German Reich has lost the war'.[82] Horthy had already infuriated Berlin by halting Jewish deportations in July and replacing Sztójay with Géza Lakatos in August. On the announcement of the ceasefire, an SS detachment stormed the royal palace, captured Horthy, held his son for ransom, and ordered the Regent to instal a new Cabinet under Ferenc Szálasi, the head of the fanatical right-wing Arrow

---

80 *ADAP*, E, vol. 8, docs. 187, 192, 221, 246, 516.
81 Details in Braham, *The Politics of Genocide*, vol. I, pp. 512–24.
82 Miklós Horthy, *Memoirs* (New York: Speller, 1957), p. 259.

Cross, which Berlin had hitherto avoided. Horthy was in German custody thereafter. Hitler's determination to hold Budapest to the last brick ensured the destruction of the city, which was captured in January 1945. Hitler assured Szálasi in the meantime that he would reconquer Hungary.[83]

But in the end, it was Germany that deserted what remained of the Axis. In March and April 1945, with the Reich invaded from east and west, senior officials from Ribbentrop to Himmler tried – without Hitler's knowledge – to negotiate a separate peace with the Western Allies. Hitler committed suicide in his Berlin bunker on 30 April, and the successor government, under Grand Admiral Karl Dönitz, capitulated on 8 May. The Japanese, who learned of the separate peace efforts on British radio, were bitter. The navy, in particular, hoped that the Germans would send 350 still active submarines to the Pacific. In Tokyo, Japanese Foreign Minister Togo Shigenori met with ambassador Heinrich Stahmer shortly before the surrender. He pressed Stahmer to remind the new government of its duties under the Tripartite Pact and the December 1941 agreement not to conclude a separate peace with the Western Allies.[84] Togo was desperate. The Americans began bombing Japan heavily in March, and started the conquest of Okinawa on 1 April. Worse, the Soviets informed Tokyo on 5 April that they would allow the neutrality treaty to lapse. On 6 May, Togo announced that Japan would fight alone. This it did until 2 September 1945, suffering bloody defeats, mass hunger in the home islands, and the only atomic bomb strikes in world history.

From the victories in 1940 to its final defeats in 1945, Axis diplomacy was defined by corrosive self-interest, to the point where one can hardly speak of an alliance at all. The Axis had no common policies on grand strategy, military operations, logistical coordination or even the distribution of raw materials. Rather, each Axis member, having entered the war to plunder its neighbours quickly as the world order was in flux, ultimately stood alone, limited by its individual weaknesses rather than bolstered by the collective strength of its allies. How the Axis might have functioned had it been victorious is a matter of speculation. Surely, as in 1940, the strongest members would have dominated the weaker ones, as they continued to follow self-interested aims, which in the case of Germany involved the mass murder of each of its allies' Jewish citizens. Under the relentless blows of

---

83 The details are in C. A. McCartney, *October Fifteenth: A History of Modern Hungary, 1929–1945* (2 vols., Edinburgh University Press, 1956–57), vol. II.
84 Martin, *Deutschland und Japan*, pp. 218–20; Weinberg, *World at Arms*, pp. 385–6.

their enemies, however, the Axis allies abandoned one another, then devoured one another, as each hoped to survive another day.

Owing to its relative shortage of resources compared to the Grand Alliance, the Axis perhaps could not have won the war in the long term. On the other hand, the diplomatic structure of the Axis, or, better said, its lack of structure, belied all common talk of fascism, anti-communism and vigorous global revisionism. The elements that made the Grand Alliance successful, from its common aims to its joint planning, to the sharing of resources and secrets, to its determination to overcome difficulties between Allies, were all lacking in the Axis. And if the primary Axis leaders in Germany, Italy and Japan led their states to ruin in the hope that their individually held aims could somehow divide the world, then at least their countries could take some solace in the Cold War that followed. The alliances to which they now belonged as junior partners worked far better than the one they had led during history's greatest conflict.

12

The diplomacy of the Grand Alliance

DAVID REYNOLDS

The 'Grand Alliance' was Winston Churchill's name for one of the most remarkable coalitions in history. Remarkable because of the extent of the collaboration between Great Britain, the United States and the Soviet Union, which was vital for winning the Second World War against an Axis that was far less concerted. Remarkable, too, because the collaboration went against the grain of history and ideology, not just in East–West relations, but also across the Atlantic. This chapter will explore the strength and the limits of the Grand Alliance – the combination that won the war, but could not secure a stable peace.

Alliance emerging, 1939–1941

Of these three powers, only Great Britain went to war against Germany in September 1939. The United States remained neutral, while the Nazi-Soviet Pact aligned Moscow clearly with Berlin. The focus of British diplomacy during the so-called 'Twilight War' in the winter of 1939–40 was not America or Russia, but France, with which Britain had become allied for the second time in a quarter-century.

This policy went up in smoke in May 1940. In four crazy weeks, a jumped-up Austrian corporal did what the Kaiser's best generals had failed to do in four years of bloody attrition, and knocked France out of the war. The spectacular German victory owed much to luck, particularly the reorientation of the Wehrmacht's main thrust from Belgium to the Ardennes, but Hitler's overwhelming victory transformed the map of Europe, and also the shape of the Second World War. Throughout the Great War there had always been a Western Front; it was the Eastern Front that crumbled in 1917–18. But after the fall of France it took Britain four years to re-establish a

front in France. In the meantime, Hitler was free, much earlier than anticipated, to turn east in search of *Lebensraum* – outline planning for the invasion
of the Soviet Union began in July 1940. Mussolini, hitherto restrained by his
generals, now jumped into the war to gain his share of the spoils, starting
a conflict in North Africa that would ensnare Anglo-American strategy. And
Japan seized on the weakness of the European colonial powers – the French,
Dutch and British – to accelerate its expansion in Southeast Asia. The fall of
France was, in short, a vital turning point in the war, arguably the fulcrum
of the whole twentieth century.[1]

British diplomacy was also transformed in the summer of 1940. In part, this
followed from the change of Prime Minister: Neville Chamberlain was
replaced by Churchill, half-American by birth and an enthusiast for transatlantic cooperation. But it was also the inevitable consequence of Britain's
predicament after France's collapse. On 25 May, the Chiefs of Staff's outline
of future strategy was predicated on the assumption that the United States
would be 'willing to give us full economic and financial support, *without
which we do not think we could continue this war with any chance of success*'. This
became the basic axiom of British policy for the rest of the war, and indeed
beyond. Churchill would later popularize the notion of a 'special relationship' with America, but as early as July 1940, Lord Halifax, the Foreign
Secretary, noted: 'It may well be that instead of studying closer union with
France, we shall find ourselves contemplating some sort of special association
with the U.S.A.'[2]

Across the Atlantic, however, the mood was much more hesitant. During
the 1930s, politicians and the public had soured about American involvement
in the previous war, Woodrow Wilson's crusade to 'make the world safe for
democracy' having so clearly failed. In 1935–37, Congress passed a series
of Neutrality Acts, intended to insulate America from the economic and
emotional entanglements that, it was believed, had dragged the country into
war in 1917. When Britain went to war against Germany again in 1939,
President Franklin D. Roosevelt managed to persuade Congress to place all
trade with belligerent countries on a 'cash and carry' basis, which meant
no credits and no use of American ships. This maintained the principle of

1 David Reynolds, '1940: Fulcrum of the Twentieth Century', *International Affairs* 66:2
(1990), 325–50.
2 Memo, 25 May 1940, The National Archives, Kew (hereafter TNA), CAB 66/7, WP (40)
168, emphasis in original; Lord Halifax to Sir Maurice Hankey, 15 July 1940, TNA, FO
371/25206, W8602/8602/49.

insulation, while in practice aiding the Allies because of Britain's imperial wealth and large merchant navy.

As for Britain, American policy was totally upset by the fall of France. Convinced that Hitler's domination of the continent of Europe posed a genuine threat to American security, especially if Germany gained control of the British fleet, Roosevelt provided the British with fifty old destroyers in September 1940, acting by Executive Order to circumvent Congress. After his re-election in November, FDR responded to the imminent exhaustion of Britain's American assets with Lend-Lease, which allowed him to transfer weapons and materiel to countries whose survival he deemed 'vital to the defense of the United States'. The question of repayment would be decided after the war, to avoid a repeat of the post-1918 tangle of war debts. Unlike the destroyers-for-bases deal, Lend-Lease was an act of Congress, pushed through in March 1941, after two months of bitter debate. FDR then used it as a mandate for gradually extending US naval patrolling in the Atlantic, acting under his own powers as Commander-in-Chief.

While talking the realist language of American self-interest, Roosevelt – like Wilson before him – also promulgated clear ideological principles. In January 1941, he enunciated 'four essential human freedoms' as 'a definite basis for a kind of world attainable in our own time and generation'. These were freedom of speech and worship, and freedom from want and fear. Roosevelt intended these to apply to America's allies as well as to its enemies. At his first wartime meeting with Churchill, off Newfoundland in August 1941, the so-called 'Atlantic Charter' that FDR foisted on the British not only incorporated the Four Freedoms, but also more specific principles for the post-war world, such as 'the right of all peoples to choose the form of government under which they live'. Ostensibly aimed at Nazi-occupied Europe, this had implications for the British Empire as well. The Atlantic Charter, promulgated while the United States was still neutral, set down ideological markers that would prove central to the subsequent Grand Alliance.[3]

Just at this moment, however, the Anglo-American relationship turned into a *ménage à trois*. Hitler's invasion of the Soviet Union on 22 June 1941 (Operation BARBAROSSA) forced a total reversal of Soviet, British and

---

3 Elizabeth Borgwardt, *A New Deal for the World: America's Vision for Human Rights* (Cambridge, Mass.: Harvard University Press, 2005), pp. 20–1; Theodore A. Wilson, *The First Summit: Roosevelt and Churchill at Placentia Bay, 1941* (2nd edn, Lawrence: University of Kansas Press, 1991), pp. 178–9.

American policies. Hitherto, Stalin had stood on the sidelines of the war; more than that, the Nazi-Soviet Pact of August 1939 had carved up Poland and the Baltic states between them, and had also committed the Soviets to providing massive aid to Germany, including raw materials and forced labour. But in June 1941, the situation changed dramatically. Hitler's preoccupation with his Eastern Front provided much-needed relief for Britain, so both Churchill and Roosevelt pledged all possible help to the Soviet Union. After the 1917 revolution, Churchill had been a notorious opponent of 'the foul baboonery of Bolshevism', but on the evening of BARBAROSSA, he told the world that 'any man or state who fights on against Nazidom will have our aid'. Or, as he put it to his Private Secretary: 'If Hitler invaded Hell, I would at least make a favourable reference to the Devil in the House of Commons.'[4]

Rhetoric aside, however, neither Britain nor America could do much to help the Soviet Union as the Nazi juggernaut rolled on toward Leningrad and Moscow. Nor were they sure that the Red Army could hold out: when BARBAROSSA opened, British intelligence gave the Russians three to six weeks against the army that had smashed France in a month. During the autumn of 1941, the triangular relationship hung in suspense. Stalin had to recognize that the battle for Moscow would be decided by the Soviet Union's own efforts, while, to Churchill's dismay, FDR's support in the Battle of the Atlantic – vital to Britain's supply lifelines – was not translated into full belligerency because of his wariness about Congress. The logjam was broken not in Russia or the Atlantic, but in the Pacific, where Hitler's victories had left the French, Dutch and British empires in the Far East gravely exposed, and Russia fighting for its life on its western front. Only the US Fleet, by then based at Pearl Harbor in the Hawaiian Islands, blocked Japan's ambitions in Asia. Roosevelt intended the fleet to act as a deterrent: instead, it became the bullseye of a remarkable series of assaults mounted by the Japanese across Southeast Asia in December 1941. The attack on Pearl Harbor, in which 2,000 Americans died, prompted a US declaration of war against Japan, but not until Hitler declared war on America did Roosevelt, still anxious about Congress, follow suit. 'Today all of us are in the same boat with you and the people of the Empire', FDR cabled Churchill, 'and it is a ship which will not and cannot be sunk.'[5]

4 Martin Gilbert, *Winston S. Churchill* (8 vols., London: Heinemann, 1975), vol. IV, p. 275; Winston S. Churchill, *The Second World War* (6 vols., London: Cassell, 1950), vol. III, pp. 331–2.
5 R-72x, 8 December 1941, in Warren F. Kimball (ed.), *Churchill and Roosevelt: Their Complete Correspondence* (3 vols., Princeton University Press, 1984), vol. I, p. 283.

In terms of sheer economic power, the President's confidence was justified: the combined resources of America, Britain and Russia far outstripped
those of the Axis. But in early 1942, Hitler's conquests in the Soviet Union
and Japan's acquisition of Malaya, the Philippines, French Indochina and the
Dutch East Indies meant that roughly a third of the world's people and
resources had fallen under Axis control. Given the events of the previous six
months, historian Richard Overy has observed, 'no rational man in early
1942 would have guessed at the eventual outcome of the war'. In due course,
Germany, Italy and Japan would squander their advantages through individual strategic errors and an overall failure to cooperate. But in 1942–43, the
Grand Alliance did not seem much more effective.[6]

Alliance diverging, 1942–1943

Within days of Pearl Harbor, Churchill set out for Washington, where the
Roosevelt administration was desperately trying to mobilize manpower and
resources for global war. Armed with plans already hammered out with his
Chiefs of Staff, Churchill was able to get his way on the principles of grand
strategy, in particular the doctrine of 'Germany first'. This designated Hitler
as the main enemy: once Nazi Germany was defeated, it was assumed, the
other Axis powers would soon crumble. The British and Americans also
created the Combined Chiefs of Staff to oversee grand strategy, and established a series of combined boards to coordinate key aspects of the war effort,
such as shipping, food and raw materials. And they agreed on the principle of
'unity of command' in regional theatres of operations. This would entail not
only a British general serving under an American, and vice versa, but also
generals overseeing admirals or admirals directing generals. In fact, getting
the US Army and Navy to work together was almost more of a challenge
than cooperating with the British. Unity of command was pushed by General
George C. Marshall, the US Army Chief of Staff, who, as a young staff officer
in France in 1918, had recognized its importance for Allied victory in the
Great War.

These agreements in Washington on the strategy and management of the
war were of far-reaching importance. Behind the scenes, Britain and America
were sharing secret intelligence and also cooperating on the development of

6 Mark Harrison (ed.), *The Economics of World War II: Six Great Powers in International
Comparison* (Cambridge University Press, 1998), ch. 1; Richard Overy, *Why the Allies
Won* (London: Pimlico, 1996), p. 15.

the atomic bomb. Never before had two great powers fused their war efforts to such an extent: the contrast with the lack of cooperation between Germany and Japan is profound. But it was easier to agree on paper than in practice. The 'Germany first' policy did not reflect the realities of global war in 1942, as the Japanese exploded across the Pacific to threaten India and Australia by the spring. The US Navy, whose leaders were corrosively suspicious of the British, favoured a 'Pacific first' strategy, but that was anathema to the Army. 'We've got to get to Europe and fight', exclaimed the War Department Director of Plans, Dwight Eisenhower, and 'we've got to quit wasting resources all over the world – and still worse – wasting time'. For Eisenhower and Marshall, the shortest route to Berlin was across the Channel from Britain to France. Yet the US military's preference for an attack across the Channel, certainly in 1943, but ideally in 1942, was blocked by Churchill: given America's Pacific commitments, any landing in France in 1942 would be a largely British and Canadian operation. Haunted by memories of the Somme and mindful of Dunkirk, Greece, Singapore and other disasters in 1940–42, the British were in no mood for what they believed would be virtually a suicide mission.[7]

American and British preferences were not the only considerations in the debate about grand strategy. The Soviet Union also mattered. In early 1942, its crisis seemed to have eased. Japan's preoccupation with the Pacific enabled Stalin to move troops from Siberia to his western front, where they pushed the Wehrmacht back from Moscow in December 1941. Both the Soviets and the Japanese adhered to their 1941 treaty of neutrality until the dying days of the Pacific War, which meant that Stalin was fighting on only one front (admittedly vast), whereas the British and Americans were waging global war, which posed huge logistic challenges for shipping and supply. This contrast would define the Grand Alliance.

Even in 1941–42, Stalin was looking ahead to the eventual peace settlement. He wanted a secret treaty in which his new allies recognized 'the interests of the USSR in restoring its frontiers violated by Hitlerite aggression'. But those were the frontiers agreed in the secret protocol of the Nazi-Soviet Pact of August 1939, by which Hitler conceded the Baltic states of Estonia, Latvia and Lithuania to the Soviet sphere, as well as much of eastern Poland, on whose behalf Great Britain had officially gone to war and whose government-in-exile was resident in London. The idea of ratifying

---

7 Mark A. Stoler, *Allies and Adversaries: The Joint Chiefs of Staff, the Grand Alliance, and US Strategy in World War II* (Chapel Hill: University of North Carolina Press, 2000), p. 71.

Stalin's dirty deal with Hitler appalled many in London and Washington. Although Anthony Eden, the Foreign Secretary, and eventually Churchill reluctantly concluded that Britain must accept Stalin's conditions in order to build trust with Moscow, the US State Department dug in its heels, having (unlike Britain) withheld *de jure* recognition of the Soviet annexation of the Baltic states in 1940. 'Let us stick to the Atlantic Charter', argued Under-Secretary Sumner Welles; giving way on principles now, he asserted, would only lead to 'an indefinite sequence of further Russian blackmail later'. Roosevelt's objections were more pragmatic: he wanted to defer such questions until the war situation was clearer and also to deal with them himself. 'I think I can personally handle Stalin better than either your Foreign Office or my State Department', he told Churchill. 'Stalin hates the guts of all your top people. He thinks he likes me better, and I hope he will continue to do so.' FDR had never met the Soviet leader, so his breezy confidence was utterly without foundation, but it signalled Roosevelt's approach for the rest of the war.[8]

Fortunately for alliance solidarity, in late May 1942, Stalin decided to drop his demand for a treaty about future frontiers. These, he brusquely told Foreign Minister Vyacheslav Molotov, would 'be decided by force'. The reasons for the Soviet leader's U-turn are unclear, but American and British opposition, plus the success of the new German spring offensive, were probably decisive. Stalin now focused on the more urgent issue of the Second Front, as the Germans drove inexorably toward the Don Basin and the oilfields of the Caucasus – to growing alarm in London and Washington. 'I would rather lose New Zealand or Australia or anything else', FDR remarked privately, 'than have the Russians collapse'. In June, FDR made clear to Molotov his desire to land in France that summer, even if the result was 'another Dunkirk', with a death toll of at least 100,000. The communiqué of their talks stated that 'full understanding was reached with regard to the urgent tasks of creating a second front in Europe in 1942' – these words were inserted at Stalin's insistence, though it was, in fact, ambiguous. Molotov was consistently cynical about American sincerity, whereas Stalin seemed more optimistic at this stage, agreeing to a reduction in Allied supply

---

8 Draft treaty, 18 December 1941, in Oleg Rzheshevsky (ed.), *War and Diplomacy: The Making of the Grand Alliance. Documents from Stalin's Archives* (Amsterdam: Harwood Academic, 1996), p. 41; Steven M. Miner, *Between Churchill and Stalin: The Soviet Union, Great Britain, and the Origins of the Grand Alliance* (Chapel Hill: University of North Carolina Press, 1988), pp. 207–8; R-123/1, 18 March 1942, in Kimball (ed.), *Churchill and Roosevelt*, vol. 1, p. 421.

convoys to the USSR, in the hope that this would expedite the cross-Channel operation. In London, Churchill was at pains to suppress any hopes about a landing in 1942, stating to Molotov that the British could 'give no promise in the matter'. But, to compensate, he talked up, without qualification, Allied plans to land 'over a million' troops on the Continent in 1943. Both Western leaders had offered hostages to fortune, which would come back to haunt them later in the war.[9]

In mid-1942, the British still held the whip hand in Anglo-American strategic debate, and they remained opposed to any cross-Channel attack that year. Churchill wanted landings in French northwest Africa, to complement the British forces in Egypt and force the Axis out of North Africa. Marshall and the Pentagon viewed this as yet another diversion from the real strategic issue, but Roosevelt had political imperatives in mind. He was determined to get US troops into action against the Germans that year, not only to propitiate Stalin, but also to mobilize his own public – understandably intent on revenge for Pearl Harbor and often indifferent to the war in Europe. Polls suggested that about 30 per cent of the public favoured a negotiated peace if the German army could topple the Nazis. 'I can see why we are fighting the Japanese', was a familiar refrain, 'but I can't see why we are fighting the Germans.' In order to get American troops into action against the Wehrmacht and fire up his people against Hitler, Roosevelt agreed to Churchill's North African strategy and overruled his generals. Anxious to propitiate Stalin, Churchill flew to Moscow. Sketching a crocodile, he claimed that France was the 'hard snout' of the Axis, whereas the Mediterranean was its 'soft underbelly': here was the true second front for 1942. With the German forces converging on Stalingrad, the Soviet leader was not persuaded by Churchill's rhetoric, but there was nothing he could do.[10]

The landings in French Northwest Africa in November 1942, codenamed TORCH, were a decisive moment in the history of the Grand Alliance, serving to entrench the British and Americans in the Mediterranean. That was not the intention: both Churchill and Roosevelt expected that the Germans would cut their losses in North Africa, paving the way for a serious cross-Channel attack in 1943. On 9 November, the Prime Minister said that the success of TORCH was 'now plainly in sight after one day's campaign',

9 Stoler, *Allies and Adversaries*, p. 72; Rzheshevsky (ed.), *War and Diplomacy*, pp. 138, 177, 210–11, 220–1, 228, 266, 298–9.
10 Richard W. Steele, 'American Popular Opinion and the War Against Germany: The Issue of Negotiated Peace, 1942', *Journal of American History* 65 (1978), esp. 704–5, 708.

and predicted that 'in a month French North Africa should be comfortably and securely in Allied hands'. But things turned out very differently. In deference to Pentagon anxieties about being trapped in the Mediterranean, the initial landings were mounted too far west; Allied commanders failed to push fast and hard for Tunis; and, against all the intelligence reports, Hitler decided to make a fight for North Africa, throwing in troops earmarked for Stalingrad. In a sense, therefore, TORCH *did* help the Russians, but not as Churchill had intended, nor as Stalin had wished. The Germans were able to hang on in Tunisia until the rains came and the sandy roads and airfields turned to mud. Tunis did not fall until May 1943 – too late to move troops and supplies back to Britain for an invasion of France before the Channel turned treacherous in the autumn.[11]

At their Casablanca Conference in January 1943, the British and Americans tried to work out what to do instead. With the US delegation still fatally divided between the Army's focus on Europe and the Navy's preoccupation with Japan, its preparations for the conference were sloppy, and British planners, armed with a mass of papers, maps and statistics, ran rings around them. 'We came, we listened, and we were conquered', General Albert Wedemeyer reflected ruefully. It was agreed that after North Africa was cleared, the British and Americans would land in Sicily (Operation HUSKY), hopefully in July 1943. In the meantime, the Allies talked up the bombing of Germany as their main way of striking at Hitler's heartland.[12]

On the Eastern Front, the Soviets had now finally turned the corner, with the surrender of the German Sixth Army at Stalingrad on 31 January 1943. For the Nazis, this was a disaster of the first magnitude, which could not be concealed from the German people. By comparison, the Anglo-American campaign in North Africa seemed not only small, but also ineffectual. In the early months of 1943, Roosevelt and Churchill sent several messages to Stalin, implying – contrary to the consensus at Casablanca – that invading France was still a possibility for the late summer. But eventually, they came clean, informing Stalin on 4 June that for the rest of the year they would concentrate on knocking Italy out of the war, before building up their forces in Britain for a cross-Channel attack in the spring of 1944. Stalin responded with a clinical summary of their previous nods, winks and half-promises, warning that this decision left the Soviet Army, which was 'fighting not only for its

---

11 David Reynolds, *In Command of History: Churchill Fighting and Writing the Second World War* (London: Penguin, 2004), p. 317.
12 Albert C. Wedemeyer, *Wedemeyer Reports!* (New York: Henry Holt, 1958), p. 192.

country, but also for the Allies, to do the job alone, almost single-handed, against an enemy that is still very strong and formidable'. Churchill's response, mocked by Stalin, that he could not justify to Parliament the loss of 100,000 men on the French coast in what he called a 'useless massacre', underlined the ideological divide between the two Western democracies, on the one hand, and the brutal Soviet dictator, on the other.[13]

This divide was particularly evident in their reactions to the Katyn revelations. On 12 April 1943, the Germans announced that their troops had found in forests near Smolensk the graves of some 10,000 Polish officers, who, it was claimed, had been shot by the Soviets in the spring of 1940. Both the German government and the Polish government-in-exile called on the International Red Cross to investigate, whereupon Stalin accused the London Poles of collusion with the Nazis, and used their 'ingratitude and treachery' to justify breaking off diplomatic relations. As we now know, the German accusations were true – Stalin had personally authorized the executions in March 1940 – and this was also the conclusion drawn privately by Churchill, Roosevelt and their senior officials in the spring of 1943. But their overriding concern, faced with Stalin's calculated public outrage, was to try to minimize any damage to the alliance. 'The winning of the war', FDR observed, 'is the paramount objective for all of us'.[14]

The arguments over Katyn and the Second Front highlighted the need for the Big Three to meet. Churchill had visited Moscow in August 1942, but Stalin had declined to attend the Casablanca Conference, citing his preoccupation with the struggle at Stalingrad. In May 1943, Roosevelt – confident, as we saw in 1942, of his finesse in personal diplomacy – proposed that he and Stalin confer à deux, without staffs and indeed without Churchill, to achieve 'a meeting of minds'. Stalin procrastinated, again citing the situation at the front, and meanwhile Churchill got wind of the President's proposal, complaining bitterly about British exclusion. Roosevelt replied that the whole idea had emanated from Stalin, which was a complete lie, as Churchill knew. The matter was dropped, but it was a sign of changing times. FDR's diplomatic priority was now to build a relationship with Stalin,

---

13 Stalin to Churchill, 27 January, 11 June and 24 June 1943, and Churchill to Stalin, 19 June 1943, in Ministry of Foreign Affairs of the USSR, *Correspondence Between the Chairman of the Council of Ministers of the USSR and the Presidents of the USA and the Prime Ministers of Great Britain During the Great Patriotic War of 1941–1945* (2 vols., Moscow: Foreign Languages Publishing House, 1957), vol. I, pp. 89, 132, 133, 138 (henceforth Stalin, *Correspondence*).

14 Kimball (ed.), *Churchill and Roosevelt*, vol. II, pp. 195, 204.

as the cornerstone of the post-war world. Churchill, though still valued, was becoming the junior partner in the alliance.[15]

Alliance converging, 1943–1944

In July 1943, the Wehrmacht unleashed its third great summer offensive against Russia in as many years, but this time the outcome was very different. The Red Army, at last not taken by surprise, absorbed the shock at Kursk – probably the biggest tank battle in history – and then moved onto the offensive. By December 1943, most of Ukraine had been regained and the Soviets were rolling inexorably toward Berlin.

In the Mediterranean, the British and Americans also achieved striking success, albeit on a smaller scale. Their invasion of Sicily in July prompted the overthrow of Mussolini; the new Italian government signed an armistice with the Allies and sought the status of 'co-belligerent' against Nazi Germany. When the Allies invaded mainland Italy in September, they expected soon to control most of the peninsula, acquiring airfields from which to bomb the industrial cities of southern Germany. Churchill also wanted to pick up the Italian islands in the Aegean before the Germans moved in. These dramatic developments seemed to provide renewed justification for the Mediterranean campaign. The Prime Minister told his advisors in mid-October that 'if we were in a position to decide the future strategy of the war', he would put the invasion of France (codenamed OVERLORD) bottom of his list of priorities, in order to concentrate on Italy, the Balkans and the Aegean. Churchill was not alone. Given the prospects in Italy, wrote Sir Alexander Cadogan, Permanent Under-Secretary at the Foreign Office, 'all this "Overlord" folly must be thrown "Overboard"'.[16]

British hopes were illusory, however: Hitler was determined to fight for Italy, as he had for Tunisia, and the mountainous Apennine terrain offered superb defensive positions. The Italian campaign soon bogged down in mud and snow. Moreover, Churchill's private musings about strategic priorities got back to Washington, where they aroused intense anger in the Pentagon. For Henry Stimson, the US Secretary of War, this showed how determined Churchill was, despite all his 'lip service', to 'stick a knife in the back of

---

15 Stalin, *Correspondence*, vol. II, pp. 63, 66; Kimball (ed.), *Churchill and Roosevelt*, vol. II, pp. 278–9, 283.
16 TNA, CAB 79/66, folios 151–4, COS 254 (43) 4; David Dilks (ed.), *The Diaries of Sir Alexander Cadogan, 1938–1945* (London: Cassell, 1971), p. 570.

Overlord'. Fuming about Churchill's 'halfhearted and doubtful adherence to the agreed European strategy', Marshall told Roosevelt that 'the time has now arrived when further indecision, evasion, and undermining of agreements cannot be borne'. OVERLORD was no longer merely a strategy: it had become a metaphor for who was on top in the Anglo-American alliance.[17]

OVERLORD was first on the agenda when the Big Three finally met at Tehran at the end of November 1943. With American mobilization nearing its peak, Roosevelt was no longer willing to let Churchill exert a veto power over Allied strategy. And Stalin was now ready to deal face to face with his allies, conscious that the tide of war placed him in a strong bargaining position. He stated that the Soviets would enter the war against Japan once Germany was defeated – his clearest commitment to date on a matter of vital concern to the United States – and also said bluntly that Soviet military leaders believed that 'Hitler was endeavoring to retain as many allied Divisions as possible in Italy, where no decision could be reached', unlike France, which was the best place for 'getting at the heart of Germany'. Stalin therefore thought it 'better to take OVERLORD as the basis for all 1944 operations'. Desperately, Churchill kept talking about the value of Mediterranean operations, the significance of Turkey and the importance of capturing Rome, but he was clearly outnumbered two to one. Within an hour of the opening of the Tehran Conference, Roosevelt and Stalin had hammered out the framework of a strategic bargain that would define the rest of the war.[18]

When Eastern Europe was discussed, Roosevelt told Stalin privately that he was not going to make a fuss about either Poland or the Baltic states, suggesting a token plebiscite in the latter to give a patina of consent to Soviet reoccupation. Unlike 1942, neither he nor Churchill now seriously disputed Soviet demands for regaining their 1941 border with Poland (though Eden tartly described it at one point to Stalin as the 'Molotov–Ribbentrop Line'). As compensation for the Poles losing part of Ukraine, there was tentative agreement at Tehran on 'moving Poland westward' into Pomerania and Silesia – heartland of the old Prussia.[19]

---

17 Henry L. Stimson, diary, 28–29 October 1943, Sterling Library, Yale, New Haven, Conn.; George C. Marshall, memos, 29 October and 8 November 1943, Marshall papers, Verifax 189, Marshall Library, Lexington, Va.

18 First plenary meeting, 28 November 1943, in US Department of State, *Foreign Relations of the United States* [hereafter *FRUS*]: *The Conferences at Cairo and Teheran, 1943* (Washington DC: Government Printing Office, 1961), pp. 487–97; Stoler, *Allies and Adversaries*, pp. 167–8.

19 Meetings of 1 December 1943, in *FRUS Teheran*, pp. 594–9.

Underlying Anglo-American policy lay the idea that the wartime alliance was generating a completely new relationship between the Western powers and the Soviet Union. Today, that may seem astonishingly naïve, but we need to put the Cold War on one side and appreciate the perspective of American and British policy-makers in 1943. By then, the Bolshevik revolution was a quarter-century old: under Stalin, the Soviet Union had concentrated on building socialism in one country rather than fomenting world revolution. In 1943, he officially abolished the Communist International and gave unprecedented freedoms to the Orthodox Church – allowing it to hold a synod, elect a patriarch and open new seminaries. These changes were cosmetic, but they strengthened impressions in the West that the Soviet Union was losing its ideological edge and becoming a 'normal' great power, animated mainly by concerns about security and national interest. Conservatives still saw the USSR as a 'totalitarian' state, but there was a consensus that the Soviet Union was not bent on expansion and that its post-war foreign policy would centre on reconstruction and security. Roosevelt was certainly optimistic. In April 1943, he told a journalist, on the record, that he believed 'the revolutionary currents of 1917 may be spent in this war. . .with progress following evolutionary constitutional lines' in future – toward what he called 'a modified form of state socialism'.[20]

If the Soviets were gradually converging toward Western norms, then it was crucial to bring them in from the cold, into what Roosevelt at Tehran called the 'family circle'. His grand design was a great-power concert to keep the peace – America, Britain, Russia and nationalist China – what FDR called the 'Four Policemen'. China's inclusion was a bone of contention with Churchill, who regarded China – wracked by civil war between nationalists and communists, and ravaged by Japan – as of little significance. Its inclusion among the great powers was intended, he claimed, only to ensure a 'faggot vote' for the United States. But FDR was adamant, and Chiang Kai-shek, the nationalist leader, was included in the pre-Tehran Cairo Conference, much to Churchill's fury. FDR put his money on the wrong Chinese horse – Mao and the communists had swept away Chiang's corrupt nationalist regime by 1949 – but he had a shrewder sense than Churchill of China's long-term importance in world affairs.

20 Forrest Davis, 'Roosevelt's World Blueprint', *Saturday Evening Post*, 10 April 1943, p. 21; John Lewis Gaddis, *The United States and the Origins of the Cold War, 1941–1947* (New York: Columbia University Press, 1972), p. 41.

FDR intended that the Big Four would be institutionalized as the corner-stone of the United Nations Organization, the creation of which had become the key goal of the State Department. Ensuring Soviet cooperation in that post-war structure was fundamental for Roosevelt and Hull – hence their indifference to the precise borders of post-Nazi Europe. The President said he 'considered the European questions were so impossible that he wanted to stay out of them as far as practicable except for the problems involving Germany'.[21]

Churchill and the Foreign Office could not afford to be so indifferent to the reconfiguration of the Continent, but they shared the American consensus about the essentially defensive nature of Soviet policy. British diplomats believed that the Soviet desire for security was psychological as much as territorial, reflecting their international pariah status since 1917. The Russians, wrote the British ambassador in Moscow, Sir Archibald Clark Kerr, were 'as sensitive of their reputation as is a prostitute who has married into the peerage', and they now expected to be treated with 'deference' because of their 'military victories and newly found prestige and respectability'.[22] Churchill was less sure that the leopard had changed its spots, but he, like Roosevelt, had no doubt that the key to good relations with the USSR was Stalin himself. The Soviet leader exerted almost a seductive charm over both his Western counterparts. Terse but always to the point, with flashes of dry humour, he was a far cry from the ranting dictators in Berlin and Rome. Churchill was convinced that this was a man with whom he could do business, often contrasting Stalin with the shadowy hardliners who sup-posedly lurked in the dark crevices of the Kremlin. He remarked in January 1944 that 'if only I could dine with Stalin once a week, there would be no trouble at all'. This image of Stalin as a relative moderate became a recurrent motif in Washington as well as London. Both Roosevelt and Averell Harriman, his ambassador in Moscow, were prone to blame displays of truculence on unfriendly factions in the Politburo, or on the failures of Molotov to provide Stalin with accurate information.[23]

21 Memo of conversations with the President, 21 October – 19 November 1944, in W. Averell Harriman papers, Library of Congress, Manuscript Division, box 175, pp. 1–2.
22 Martin H. Folly, *Churchill, Whitehall and the Soviet Union, 1940–45* (Basingstoke: Macmillan, 2000), pp. 98–9.
23 Gilbert, *Churchill*, vol. VII, p. 664; Dennis J. Dunn, *Caught Between Roosevelt and Stalin: America's Ambassadors to Moscow* (Lexington: University Press of Kentucky, 1998), p. 139.

Mid-1944 marked the high point of the Grand Alliance, as the three powers finally converged on Hitler's Reich. American, British and Canadian troops landed on the beaches of Normandy on 6 June. Despite Churchill's fears, they were not driven back into the sea (thanks, in considerable measure, to the deception campaign), but they got bogged down for most of June and July in the bocage country of Normandy. Meanwhile, on 21 June, the third anniversary of BARBAROSSA, the Red Army launched its massive summer offensive in Belorussia (BAGRATION), timed to assist the Allies in France. This was a total success, destroying twenty divisions of Hitler's Army Group Centre (more divisions than the Allies were fighting against in Italy) and driving 450 miles in five weeks, to reach the edge of Warsaw by the end of July. At this point, the Western Allies finally broke out of Normandy and their advance was then equally spectacular, entering Paris on 24 August and liberating Brussels on 3 September – the fifth anniversary of the beginning of the war. Such was the speed of the offensive that, a hundred days into the campaign (D + 100), Allied troops were in positions that military planners had not expected to reach until late May 1945 (D + 350).[24] The attempt by dissident officers to assassinate Hitler on 20 July, though abortive, showed the world that the Third Reich was tottering.

Alliance fragmenting, 1944–1945

Yet as the Axis crumbled, the Grand Alliance was also showing signs of strain – across the Atlantic as well as with the Soviets. The biggest row of the whole war between Churchill and the Americans came to a head just as the invasion of Normandy began. The Prime Minister wanted to keep troops and supplies in Italy rather than having them diverted to southern France, where the Americans wished to mount an operation in support of OVERLORD. Churchill offered strategic rationales, such as a drive northeast to Vienna and Central Europe, but his real motive was diplomatic: Italy, unlike France, was a theatre in which the British still had overall command and troop predominance. This 'element of sheer chauvinism', observes historian Sir Michael Howard, became 'an ever stronger factor in his strategic thinking as time went on'.[25]

---

24 Roland G. Ruppenthal, *Logistical Support of the Armies* (2 vols., Washington DC: Government Printing Office, 1953–59), vol. I, pp. 476, 488.
25 Michael Howard, *The Mediterranean Strategy in the Second World War* (London: Weidenfeld & Nicolson, 1968), p. 57.

With the Combined Chiefs of Staff split along national lines about invading southern France, grand strategy had to be decided by the two leaders – as had happened over North Africa two summers before. But in 1944, unlike 1942, Roosevelt sided firmly with Marshall and the Joint Chiefs, even strengthening some of their tough messages to Churchill. The Prime Minister complained about casting aside 'dazzling possibilities' in Italy for what he predicted would be a 'costly stalemate' in southern France – even preparing a telegram threatening to resign over 'this absolutely perverse strategy'. But the message was not sent and Churchill acquiesced. In fact, it was the drive up the Rhône Valley that proved a dazzling success, while the campaign in Italy degenerated into a costly stalemate. As the Allied armies pushed into Germany, Churchill privately admitted the limits of British power: 'our armies are only about one-half the size of the American and will soon be little more than one-third', so 'it is not so easy as it used to be for me to get things done'.[26]

These strains in the Anglo-American alliance developed amid new tension with Moscow over Poland. The Soviet summer offensive sparked a rising by the Polish Home Army on 1 August, intended to drive the Germans out of Warsaw. Although Soviet troops were just across the Vistula River, Stalin did virtually nothing to help the Poles. He pleaded, with some justice, that the Red Army needed to regroup after the exertions of the previous month, but his callous refusal to provide any aid or even, for some weeks, to allow Western supply planes to use Soviet-controlled airfields, chilled London and Washington. The underlying issue was control of post-war Poland: the Warsaw Rising was intended to pre-empt the Red Army, as Stalin well knew – hence his refusal to help what he called 'the handful of power-seeking criminals'.[27] As with Katyn, so with Warsaw, the British and US governments swallowed their revulsion because of the larger imperatives of the alliance.

The Warsaw Rising was crushed by the SS in early October 1944. By then, the Anglo-American armies had stalled on the borders of Germany, having failed to cross the Rhine at Arnhem, while a new Red Army offensive surged into the Balkans. Determined to seek an understanding with Stalin, Churchill flew to Moscow for a second time. Quite what his now notorious 'percentages agreement' of 9 October was intended to signify remains

---

26 C-721, draft, 30 June 1944, and R-577, 1 July, in Kimball (ed.), *Churchill and Roosevelt*, vol. III, pp. 225–6, 232; Churchill to Jan Smuts, T/2235, 3 December 1944, Chartwell papers, Churchill College Archives Centre (hereafter CHAR), CHAR 20/176.
27 S-C/R, 22 August 1944, in Stalin, *Correspondence*, vol. I, p. 255.

unclear: Churchill sprang the idea not only on Stalin, but on Eden as well, who had to puzzle over it with Molotov. Probably this was an attempt to define 'spheres of interest', without using a term that was anathema in the State Department; perhaps Churchill imagined that quantification would appeal to 'scientific' Marxist-Leninists. At any event, the heart of the deal was a trade-off between Romania, where the Soviets were allotted 90 per cent, and a similar percentage in Greece for Britain – 'in accord with USA', Churchill tactfully added. He also secured a 50:50 split in Yugoslavia, but not in Hungary, where, like Bulgaria, the Soviets were to be predominant.[28]

What were Stalin's objectives as the war neared its end? He clearly did not want a cold war: 'second only to a hot war between the former allies, that was his last choice', observes historian William Taubman. 'What Stalin wanted was nothing less than continued entente' – albeit 'entente Stalinist-style', on his own terms. The Western Allies were right that the Soviet leader's main concerns for the post-war period were security and reconstruction. Although not abandoning hopes of world revolution, he recognized that this was unlikely in the foreseeable future: indeed he gave strict instructions to Italian and French communists not to make a bid for outright power, even in the chaos of 1944–45. Their only route to power, he insisted, must be via popular front coalitions. Stalin was partly responding to the remarkable swing to the left in wartime Europe, observing privately in January 1945, 'perhaps we are mistaken when we suppose that the Soviet form is the only one that leads to socialism'. But his caution in Italy and France also reflected his recognition that these countries were of real interest to America and Britain; likewise Greece, once Churchill had made this clear in Moscow in October 1944. The key issues for Stalin were control over Poland – Russia's buffer against a resurgent Germany – and a German settlement that kept the old enemy weak. As to exactly what that meant, Stalin was less clear, but territorial dismemberment and substantial reparations were the main options being discussed in Moscow. Much depended on what his allies would accept. Stalin believed, in line with Marxist-Leninist ideology, that after the war the imperialist powers would fall out among themselves – hints of which seemed evident in Roosevelt's baiting of Churchill at Tehran – and that they would face a capitalist slump, which would oblige them to offer goods and aid to the USSR.[29]

28 Reynolds, *In Command*, pp. 458–60.
29 William Taubman, *Stalin's Foreign Policy: From Entente to Détente to Cold War* (New York: W. W. Norton, 1982), p. 74; Ivo Banac (ed.), *The Diary of Georgi Dimitrov, 1941–1949* (New Haven, Conn.: Yale University Press, 2003), p. 358.

When Roosevelt, Churchill and Stalin convened at Yalta in Crimea for their second meeting, their mood was therefore cautiously hopeful. After the war, Republicans in America made 'Yalta' into a synonym for the 'betrayal' of Eastern Europe to the Soviets – a 1945 equivalent of Munich – but this was political propaganda rather than historical analysis. The essential decisions about Poland and Eastern Europe had been taken by default in 1942–43, stemming from the Anglo-American failure to mount an early Second Front and the dramatic Soviet drive west from Stalingrad. Before leaving Washington for Yalta, Roosevelt told leading senators 'that the Russians had the power in Eastern Europe, that it was obviously impossible to have a break with them and that, therefore, the only practicable course was to use what influence we had to ameliorate the situation'.[30]

With Poland's eastern border already settled in principle at Tehran, Roosevelt and, particularly, Churchill concentrated on the composition of the Polish government, but this was a gut issue for the Soviet leader. In the end, his allies secured only a promise that the existing communist government would be 'reorganized on a broader democratic basis', that 'free and unfettered elections' would be held 'as soon as possible', and that London and Washington would be 'kept informed about the situation in Poland' by their ambassadors in Moscow. These phrases, Churchill wrote later in his memoirs, were 'the best I could get'. In a similar vein, when chastised by White House Chief of Staff Admiral William Leahy about the 'elastic' nature of the agreements, Roosevelt replied, 'It's the best I can do for Poland at this time'. The Americans hoped that the Declaration on Liberated Europe, a general statement of democratic principles, would act as some kind of constraint on Soviet actions.[31]

For the Americans, two issues were salient at Yalta, and on both they secured essentially their goals. Stalin confirmed Soviet membership of the United Nations Organization and participation in its founding conference, to be held in San Francisco at the end of April. Leahy judged this 'a major victory for the President', ensuring that the new UN, unlike the League of Nations, would include the major world powers.[32] Second, Stalin made a firm commitment to enter the war against Japan once Germany had been defeated. With the atomic bomb still untested and the US Army fearful of

30 Thomas M. Campbell and Edward R. Stettinius (eds.), *The Diaries of Edward R. Stettinius, Jr., 1943–1946* (New York: New Viewpoints, 1975), 11 January 1945, p. 214.
31 David Reynolds, *Summits: Six Meetings that Shaped the Twentieth Century* (London: Penguin, 2007), p. 128.
32 William D. Leahy diary, 7 February 1945, Library of Congress, Manuscript Division.

heavy casualties in any invasion of Japan, this was hugely important. The Americans felt that the week had gone really well. 'For what we have gained here', Marshall remarked, 'I would gladly have stayed a whole month'.[33] Churchill was also delighted with the Soviet pledge on Japan and had no problem with the sweeteners FDR had promised, including offshore islands once under Tsarist control. 'A speedy termination of the Japanese war', he noted, 'would undoubtedly save us many thousands of millions of pounds', and he saw 'no particular harm in the presence of Russia as a Pacific Power'.[34]

On Germany, however, Churchill dug in, and here he was particularly successful, to the evident irritation, at times, of Stalin. On the issue of reparations, for instance, Stalin came to Yalta with a detailed proposal for a total bill of $20 billion – to be paid in kind, not cash – half for the USSR. But Churchill and Eden blocked any mention of figures, anxious to avoid the financial tangle over reparations that had bedevilled Europe in the 1920s. Churchill and Eden also ensured that the French would be given one of the zones of occupation in Germany and a seat on its Control Commission, overcoming the reservations of Roosevelt and Stalin. Mindful of FDR's warnings that Congress would not let him keep an army in Europe for more than a couple of years after the war, they sought another partner to help keep Germany down. Here is a further reminder of how far things still were, in 1945, from the era of NATO.[35]

Seen as a whole, therefore, Yalta was not a simple Western sell-out of Poland, but a set of interlocking deals in which all three powers won on some issues and gave ground on others. Yalta was also intended to be just a holding action, to keep the alliance on course for a final peace conference. Western leaders returned home in optimistic mood. Churchill told sceptics in Parliament that 'Marshal Stalin and the Soviet leaders wish to live in honourable friendship and equality with the Western democracies. I feel also that their word is their bond'.[36] And FDR hyped the conference to Congress as 'a turning point' in 'the history of the world', which should spell the end of spheres of influence, balance of power and other failed expedients of the past.

---

33 Michael Charlton, *The Eagle and the Small Birds: Crisis in the Soviet Empire from Yalta to Solidarity* (London: BBC, 1984), p. 46.
34 Churchill to Anthony Eden, 28 January 1945, CHAR 20/209 (CAC).
35 Reynolds, *Summits*, pp. 119–24.
36 Hugh Dalton, *The Second World War Diary of Hugh Dalton, 1940–1945*, ed. Ben Pimlott (London: Jonathan Cape, 1986), p. 836; House of Commons, *Debates*, 27 February 1945, vol. 408, col. 1284.

'We propose to substitute for all these, a universal organization in which all peace-loving nations will finally have a chance to join'.[37] In a rare display of his infirmity, the President delivered the speech sitting down. This and the pictures of his haggard face at Yalta have raised questions of whether Roosevelt was a 'dying President' who had lost his grip on affairs.[38] But although FDR was clearly ailing, his conduct at Yalta reflected his consistent policy, since 1941, of trying to draw the Soviets into the community of nations.

Over the next few weeks, however, the letter and spirit of Yalta were severely strained. In Romania, the Soviets forced the king to appoint a new government dominated by communists. In Poland, they allowed the communist provisional government to veto candidates for its own 'reconstruction' and to exclude Western observers, while potential rivals in Poland were liquidated. Eventually, at the end of March, FDR acceded to Churchill's pressure and made a joint protest over Soviet conduct in Poland, whereupon Stalin accused them of sounding out the chances of a separate German surrender in the West. He also announced that Molotov was too busy to come to San Francisco and that the Soviet delegation to the UN's founding conference would be led by Andrei Gromyko, then a middle-level diplomat. This was taken not only as a blatant snub, but also as a real threat to the whole structure of post-war cooperation.

Western leaders were hard-pressed to explain the Soviet Union's apparent change of course, but, as usual, they shied away from blaming Stalin himself. State Department officials thought the foot-dragging over the Yalta agreements reflected 'opposition inside the Soviet government which Stalin encountered on his return'. Churchill wrote darkly to Roosevelt about 'the Soviet leaders, whoever they may be'.[39] In fact, as usual, the decisions were made by Stalin himself, who, in March, rather like Churchill, appears to have had a crisis of confidence about the alliance. The amazing Anglo-American surge, once over the Rhine on 23 March – reaching the Elbe, only seventy miles from Berlin, on 12 April – seems to have revived Stalin's fears that Britain and America might do a deal with the Nazis behind his back. So he clamped the Soviet grip on Poland and Romania as quickly as possible, lest

37 George McJimsey (ed.), *Documentary History of the Franklin D. Roosevelt Presidency*, vol. XIV: *The Yalta Conference, October 1944–March 1945* (15 vols., New York: Congressional Information Service, 2003), esp. pp. 638–9.
38 Robert H. Ferrell, *The Dying President: Franklin D. Roosevelt, 1944–1945* (Columbia: University of Missouri Press, 1998).
39 Charles E. Bohlen, *Witness to History, 1929–1969* (New York: W. W. Norton, 1973), p. 217; C-934 in Kimball (ed.), *Churchill and Roosevelt*, vol. III, p. 613.

further gains be denied him. But then the renewed Red Army advance on Berlin, along with FDR's sudden death from a massive stroke on 12 April, helped to change the mood in Moscow. Stalin agreed to send Molotov to America for the founding conference of the United Nations – a public tribute to the dead President and also a sign that the Grand Alliance was still intact.

Roosevelt's successor, Harry Truman, met Molotov in the White House on 23 April. The new President's blunt demand that the Russians honour the Yalta agreements on Poland has sometimes been interpreted as the opening shot in the Cold War. But the talk did not indicate a fundamental change in US policy. Truman, feeling out of his depth in foreign affairs, was trying to show he could not be pushed around by the Soviets. Once he had had time to read the record of Yalta a few weeks later, he realized that the agreements were as elastic as Leahy had warned. Fearful now of being manipulated by Churchill, he kept his distance from the insistent British leader, while concluding a deal with Stalin over Poland that recognized the existing Moscow-imposed government plus a few non-communists for cosmetic purposes.[40] After the crisis in April, American and Soviet policies were back on course – Washington conceding a Soviet sphere of influence in Eastern Europe to advance the larger interests of alliance solidarity, while seeking to cover it with a veneer of democracy, and the Soviet leader pressing as far as seemed prudent without breaking the alliance.

The most erratic member of the Big Three in the spring of 1945 was Churchill. After Yalta, he had made Chamberlainesque professions of faith in Stalin, but then panicked about the situation in Poland. On 12 May, he used the phrase 'iron curtain' for the first time in a telegram to Truman, and a week later he asked the military to draw up a contingency plan for 'Operation UNTHINK-ABLE' – an offensive against the Soviet Union by Anglo-American forces, supplemented by German manpower, in order to get 'a square deal for Poland'. The hypothetical starting date was 1 July 1945. His planners considered the idea 'fantastic and the chances of success quite impossible' – pointing out that it would precipitate a 'total war' against the Soviet Union, in which the chances of victory, judging by Hitler's recent experience, were hardly encouraging.[41]

40 Geoffrey Roberts, 'Sexing up the Cold War: New Evidence on the Molotov–Truman Talks of April 1945', *Cold War History* 4:3 (2004), 105–25; Robert L. Messer, *The End of the Alliance: James F. Byrnes, Roosevelt, Truman, and the Origins of the Cold War* (Chapel Hill: University of North Carolina Press, 1982), pp. 71–84.
41 Lord Alanbrooke, *War Diaries, 1939–1945*, ed. Alex Danchev and Daniel Todman (London: Weidenfeld & Nicolson, 2001), p. 693; Joint Planning Staff report, 'Operation "UNTHINKABLE"', 22 May 1945, TNA, CAB 120/691.

Churchill immediately dropped the whole idea, but even to propose it, only two weeks after the Allied victory over Germany, suggests how unbalanced he had become after the exhaustion of five years of war leadership. Lurching back into more familiar grooves, he insisted that the West must take a firm diplomatic line with the Soviets and save up all the problems for another meeting with Stalin, the man with whom he still believed he could do business.

Churchill, Truman and Stalin finally met at Potsdam at the end of July. Britain's junior position in the alliance – one British diplomat talked sourly about the 'Big 2½ – was accentuated by the surprise defeat of Churchill in the British election. Agreements stitched up between the Americans and the Russians over Poland and Germany did pave the way for the division of Germany into separate blocs, but that denouement was still a long way in the future. Perhaps the most significant moment at Potsdam was when Truman, with studied casualness, mentioned to Stalin that the Americans had tested a new weapon of extraordinary power and that they intended to use it against Japan. Stalin accelerated plans to enter the Pacific War before America grabbed all the spoils, and put the Soviets' own atomic programme into top gear. When Japan surrendered in August 1945, a bipolar global order was still a long way off, but the dropping of the atomic bomb was a major turning point. 'Hiroshima has shaken the world', Stalin reportedly exclaimed. 'The balance has been destroyed.'[42] The Soviet Union's quest for a new balance, what became a balance of terror, would define global history for the next half-century.

Conclusion

What should be emphasized in conclusion is the effectiveness of the Grand Alliance when compared with the Rome-Berlin-Tokyo Axis. Of course, the Big Three had superior resources, compared with their adversaries, once fully mobilized, but, as we have seen, by early 1942, the Axis had carved out strong positions in both Europe and Southeast Asia. Had Germany and Japan concerted their strategies, particularly in the Middle East and the Indian Ocean, even greater gains were within their grasp. Yet the Axis proved to be only a paper alliance, whereas Britain, America and Russia did make a real attempt to concert their war efforts. The Anglo-American side of the triangle was much the strongest – though even here there were serious strains over

---

42 David Holloway, *Stalin and the Bomb: The Soviet Union and Atomic Energy, 1939–1946* (New Haven, Conn.: Yale University Press, 1994), p. 132.

strategy – but by the summer of 1944, cooperation between all three powers was both significant and fruitful. Each contributed to the eventual victory. Britain's survival in 1940 was vital in slowing the Nazi juggernaut. The Red Army's costly resistance in 1941–42 turned the tide of the land war in Europe. And American resources underpinned the whole alliance: Lend-Lease, for instance, covered half of Britain's payments deficit, while foreign aid amounted to 10 per cent of Soviet wartime GDP.[43] Churchill may have romanticized the 'special relationship'; he and Roosevelt deluded themselves about doing business with Stalin; and their attempts to cover the iron curtain with a democratic veil came to nothing – but all these are secondary issues. Measured against the always flawed standards of international cooperation, the Grand Alliance worked and the Axis did not. That simple contrast helps to explain the outcome of the Second World War.

43 Harrison (ed.), *Economics*, pp. 52, 286.

13

Spain

Betting on a Nazi victory

PAUL PRESTON

Introduction

In the wake of a civil war fought against liberal democracy and bolshevism, there was no doubt where General Franco's sympathies lay when his ally Hitler unleashed his own war to exterminate both. In fact, even before the outbreak of war, in August 1939, Franco, entirely on his own initiative, had made preparations for an attack on Gibraltar. He held negotiations with Portugal in August 1940 to secure a free hand for the attack, and boasted to Hitler of his preparations in a letter of 22 September 1940.[1] Barely two months after the German invasion of Poland, the Generalísimo chaired a meeting of the *Junta de Defensa Nacional*, a body consisting of the Chief of the General Staff and the three Army, Navy and Air Force Ministers. The assembled officers agreed on an ambitious rearmament plan, a projected mobilization of 2 million men, and preparations to close the Straits of Gibraltar as part of an assault on British and French maritime trade. This would be the preamble to an attack on French Morocco.[2] The working hypothesis of the high command was that Spain's principal enemies were Britain and France, and that the main objective was to expand the North African empire at the expense of the French.[3]

---

1 *Documents on German Foreign Policy*, series D (hereafter *DGFP*), vol. x (13 vols., London: HMSO, 1957), p. 515; *DGFP*, vol. xi (13 vols., London: HMSO, 1961), p. 154; Report of General Staff to Franco, October 1940, *Documentos inéditos para la historia del Generalísimo Franco* (4 vols., Madrid: Fundación Nacional Francisco Franco, 1992), vol. 2, pt. 1, pp. 371–4.
2 Gustau Nerín and Alfred Bosch, *El imperio que nunca existió: La aventura colonial discutida en Hendaya* (Barcelona: Plaza y Janés, 2001), pp. 19–35; Manuel Ros Agudo, *La guerra secreta de Franco, 1939–1945* (Barcelona: Editorial Crítica, 2002), pp. xxiii–xxvi, 35–51, 56–7, 66–71.
3 Manuel Ros Agudo, *La gran tentación: Franco, el imperio colonial y los planes de intervención en la Segunda Guerra Mundial* (Barcelona: Styria de Ediciones, 2008).

Accordingly, Franco was near to taking Spain into war on the Axis side in the summer of 1940 and on several subsequent occasions. Even after the most acute likelihood of Spanish belligerence had passed by the end of 1940, Franco continued to experience what might be called the Axis temptation, most intensely after the German invasion of Russia in the summer of 1941. In the final analysis, however, the Caudillo's ambitions in foreign policy were restrained by two overriding considerations: his own domestic survival and Spain's economic and military capacity for war. The fact that Franco was unable to participate in what he fervently hoped would be an Axis victory was later recast by his propaganda apparatus into the myth that, with astute caution (*hábil prudencia*), he hoodwinked Hitler and bravely kept Spain out of the Second World War. That, together with the claim that his regime had saved many Jews from extermination, helped to cleanse what has been called 'the Axis stigma'. Both notions have remained dear to the Caudillo's admirers.[4]

Internationally, this propaganda helped to keep him in power, providing a flimsy justification for the Western powers, anxious to incorporate Franco into the anti-Communist front of the Cold War, to forget about his innumerable hostile acts of word and deed during the war. Those acts – the devotion of the Spanish press to the Axis cause, the refuelling and supplying of U-boats, the provision of radar, air reconnaissance and espionage facilities within Spain, the export of valuable raw materials to the Third Reich – although diminished by the spring of 1944, continued until 1945. Nevertheless, the importance of Spanish neutrality to the eventual outcome of the Second World War should not be underestimated. Gibraltar was crucial to British naval control of the Eastern Atlantic. Churchill was sufficiently aware of the danger of losing the Rock that for two years he held in readiness an expeditionary force of a brigade and four fast transports to seize the Canary Islands in response.[5]

4 David Wingeate Pike, 'Franco and the Axis Stigma', *Journal of Contemporary History* 17:3 (1982), 369–407. For the myth, see, inter alios, José María Sánchez Silva and José Luis Saenz de Heredia, *Franco. . . ese hombre* (Madrid: Difusión Libera, 1975), p. 139; José María de Areilza, *Embajadores sobre España* (Madrid: Instituto de Estudios Políticos, 1947), pp. 4–5, 57–8; George Hills, *Rock of Contention: A History of Gibraltar* (London: Robert Hale, 1974), pp. 436–8; José María Doussinague, *España tenía razón* (Madrid: Espasa Calpe, 1949); Brian Crozier, *Franco: A Biographical History* (London: Eyre and Spottiswoode, 1967), pp. 313–75.

5 Winston S. Churchill, *The Second World War*, vol. II: *Their Finest Hour* (6 vols., London: Cassell, 1949), pp. 460, 552, 562. For earlier perceptions of Spain's strategic importance, see Denis Smyth, *Diplomacy and Strategy of Survival: British Policy and Franco's Spain, 1940–1941* (Cambridge University Press, 1986), pp. 1–4; Alexander Cadogan, *The Diaries of*

Inevitably, in 1940, the strategic importance of Spain to the Axis cause made Franco the object of courtship by both sides: the Germans to bring him into the war and the British to keep him out. Despite some internal dispute as to the wisdom of such a policy, the British used the carrot and stick made available to them by the naval dominance which enabled them to control Spanish supplies of food and fuel and to give desperately needed credit. The Germans, on the other hand, took it for granted that Franco would do what they wanted without special wooing. Indeed the Germans ruthlessly insisted on recovering their civil war loans through the export of Spanish foodstuffs.[6] Such rigour did not divert Franco from secret hopes, in 1945, that wonder weapons would turn the tide in favour of the Third Reich, believing that Nazi scientists had harnessed the power of cosmic rays.[7] Even when Berlin fell, the regime's tightly controlled press printed tributes to the inspirational presence of Hitler in the city's defence and to the epoch-making fighting qualities of the Wehrmacht. *Informaciones* declared that Hitler had preferred to sacrifice himself for Europe rather than unleash his secret weapons. On 2 May 1945, *Arriba* reported that Hitler had died as a soldier, whose death, 'unblemished under the terrible German tragedy, deserves twice the respect, since it was communist shrapnel that has taken his life'. Allied victory was seen as the triumph of materialism over heroism. Franco did not break off diplomatic relations with the Third Reich until 8 May, VE Day. Only then were the swastikas removed from the German Embassy building.[8]

Franco's alleged services to Spain and the Allies as the man who heroically held back the Nazi hordes were to be a central theme of his propaganda until his death. The myth bore little relationship to the reality. In the spring of 1940, Franco had been confident of an early German victory.[9] With the Germans at Ostend and the retreat at Dunkirk under way, the Caudillo watched excitedly. He sent his Chief of the General Staff, General Juan Vigón, to Berlin on 10 June, with an effusive letter of congratulation for

Sir Alexander Cadogan, 1938–1945 (London: Cassell, 1971), p. 117; *Documents on British Foreign Policy, 1919–1939* (2nd series, 19 vols., London: HMSO, 1979), vol. XVII, pp. 151–2.

6 David Wingeate Pike, *Franco and the Axis Stigma* (Houndmills: Palgrave Macmillan, 2008), pp. 11–15.

7 Ramón Serrano Suñer, *Entre el silencio y la historia: la historia como fue. Memorias* (Barcelona: Editorial Planeta, 1977), p. 358. Serrano Suñer himself admitted to having been impressed by what he had heard about the V-1 and V-2 and the work of German nuclear scientists: interview with Charles Favrel, The National Archives, Kew, FO 371/ 49663, FO 371/59802.

8 *Arriba*, 2, 3, 5, 10 May 1945; *ABC*, 3, 11 May 1945; *Informaciones*, 3, 7 May 1945; *The Times*, 11 May 1945.

9 *DGFP*, vol. IX (13 vols., London: HMSO, 1956), p. 396.

Hitler.[10] In fact, Hitler kept Spain at arm's length, rebuffing Vigón when he saw him at the Castle of Acoz on 16 June 1940, merely acknowledging Spain's Moroccan ambitions. At that stage, Hitler had no intention of paying a high price for services which he believed could be no more than symbolic, since he expected the British to surrender at any moment.

Franco's price was effectively the reconstruction of Spain's economy and armed forces. He knew that an economically prostrate Spain could not sustain a long war effort, but he could not bear the thought that France and Britain might be annihilated by a new German world order and Spain still not get any of the spoils. Accordingly, fully convinced in 1940 that Hitler's victory was inevitable, he hoped to make a last-minute entry in order to gain a ticket for the distribution of the booty. Hitler was only too aware of the crippling economic cost of turning Spain into a useful ally. Moreover, he came to be ever more irritated by Franco's dogged meanness and inflated sense of destiny. Increasingly, he was looking for no more than passage through Spain for an attack on Gibraltar.

Franco tempted, 1940

Franco first offered Spanish entry into the war shortly after the fall of France, when Britain also seemed on the verge of surrender. He repeated the offer in the autumn of 1940, when he believed that Operation SEALION was about to be launched and British collapse was imminent. The Germans brushed off the first Spanish offer with cavalier disdain, convinced that they did not need it. On the second, when they did need it, they were unable to meet the economic costs of turning Spain into an effective military ally and to satisfy its African ambitions. Nonetheless, Germany enjoyed the benefits of wideranging Spanish benevolence. The German war effort in the Atlantic was favoured as submarines were provisioned in Spanish ports; German reconnaissance aircraft flew with Spanish markings; there were navigation stations at the service of the Luftwaffe at Lugo in the northwest and Seville in the southwest; and German destroyers were secretly refuelled at night in bays on Spain's northern coast. The Spanish merchant fleet was used to carry supplies to German forces in North Africa, and the Spanish navy to escort German convoys in the Mediterranean. The *Abwehr*, German military intelligence,

---

10 Ibid., pp. 509–10; Xavier Moreno Julià, *Hitler y Franco: Diplomacia en tiempos de guerra (1936–1945)* (Barcelona: Editorial Planeta, 2007), pp. 135–47.

was allowed free rein to establish a substantial operation on Spanish soil, both for information gathering and for sabotage activities against Gibraltar.[11]

The scale of Franco's emotional commitment to the Axis can be gauged from the following incident. On 8 June 1940, two days before Italy entered the war, Galeazzo Ciano wrote to Franco's brother-in-law, Ramón Serrano Suñer, at the time Minister of the Interior. He made the astonishing request for Italian bombers to make a long-range attack on Gibraltar and be given refuelling facilities for their return to Italy. Serrano Suñer discussed this with Franco, along with Mussolini's call for Spain to declare itself non-belligerent. Franco agreed to both requests. Serrano Suñer replied that Spain was entirely happy for the Italians to use Spanish territory for this military operation and for any others that Rome might initiate.[12]

With France on its knees and Britain with its back to the wall, Franco felt all the temptations of a cowardly and rapacious vulture. After a Cabinet meeting on 12 June, in accordance with Mussolini's request, Franco changed Spain's official neutrality to the much more pro-Axis position of non-belligerence. Franco told the Italian Chargé d'Affaires in Madrid that 'the present state of the Spanish armed forces prevented the adoption of a more resolute stance but that he was nonetheless proceeding to accelerate as much as possible the preparation of the army for any eventuality'.[13] On 14 June, as the Germans poured into Paris, Franco's forces occupied Tangier, having assured the French that this action was necessary to guarantee its security. In fact, the move was seen by the Falange as the first step to imperial expansion in the region and an aggressive policy of 'españolización' was initiated in the city. Hitler was delighted, all the more because Franco 'had acted without talking'. The Spanish initiative provided the Axis with a major logistical base in the Maghreb.[14] On the day after the French plea for an

11 *DGFP*, vol. IX, pp. 449–53, vol. XI, p. 445; Ros Agudo, *La guerra secreta*, pp. 72–85, 96–132, 205–17, 231–9, 248–51.
12 Mussolini to Franco, 9 June 1940, *I Documenti Diplomatici Italiani*, 9th series (hereafter *DDI*), vol. IV: *9 aprile – 10 giugno 1940* (Rome: Ministero degli affari esteri, 1960), p. 60; Galeazzo Ciano, *L'Europa verso la catastrofe* (Milan: Mondadori, 1948), pp. 559–60; Javier Tusell, *Franco, España y la II guerra mundial: entre el Eje y la neutralidad* (Madrid: Temas de Hoy, 1995), pp. 75–8; Miguel Platón, *Hablan los militares: testimonios para la historia (1939–1996)* (Barcelona: Editorial Planeta, 2001), pp. 32–4; J. A. Giménez Arnau, *Memorias de memoria: descifre vuecencia personalmente* (Barcelona: Destino, 1978), pp. 117–18.
13 Vittorio Zoppi to Galeazzo Ciano, 13, 15 June 1940, *DDI*, vol. IV, pp. 14, 23–4; *ABC*, 13 June 1940; Xavier Tusell and Genoveva García Queipo de Llano, *Franco y Mussolini: la política española durante la segunda guerra mundial* (Barcelona: Editorial Planeta, 1985), p. 79; *DGFP*, vol. IX, p. 560.
14 *DGFP*, vol. IX, pp. 585–8; Paul Reynaud, *Au cœur de la mêlée, 1930–1945* (Paris: Flammarion, 1951), pp. 855–6; Nerín and Bosch, *El imperio que nunca existió*, pp. 82–9, 102–8.

armistice, Franco asserted that, since the further existence of the French empire in North Africa was impossible, Spain demanded French Morocco, the Oran region of Algeria, and the expansion of Spanish Sahara and Spanish Guinea. In the event of England continuing hostilities after the surrender of France, the Caudillo offered to enter the war on the Axis side, in return for 'war materials, heavy artillery, aircraft for the attack on Gibraltar, and perhaps the cooperation of German submarines in the defence of the Canary Islands'. He also requested foodstuffs, ammunition, motor fuel and equipment from French arsenals.[15]

Hitler had brushed aside the offer carried by Vigón, suspicious, in the aftermath of Mussolini's last-minute attack on France, of more surplus last-minute volunteers for a war which he was convinced was already won. He was not about to prejudice the armistice negotiations with France in order to give gratuitous satisfaction to Spain. In contrast to the Spanish efforts at ingratiating themselves with the Third Reich, the Germans were arrogant and dismissive toward the Spaniards. Franco's urgent requests for food were dismissed out of hand on the grounds of the greater needs of Germany and Italy. Although Franco was upset by the Führer's offhand response to his offer, he remained anxious to negotiate Spanish entry into the war. His confidence in Axis triumph increased throughout the summer. In the course of the fourth anniversary celebrations of the military coup of 17 July 1940, he spoke to the National Council of the Falange. He praised Hitler's 'fantastic victories on the fields of Europe'. 'We have shed the blood of our dead to make a nation and to create an empire... We offered five hundred thousand dead for the salvation and unity of Spain in the first European battle of the new order... Spain has two million warriors'.[16]

The unexpected obstinacy of British resistance, and the defeat of the Luftwaffe in the Battle of Britain, led Hitler to abandon his invasion plan. In fact, even before then, German thoughts had turned to the idea of bringing down Britain by means other than frontal attack. On 15 August, General Jodl had already suggested the intensification of U-boat warfare and the seizure of the nerve centres of the British Empire, Gibraltar and Suez, in a bid to give the Axis control of the Mediterranean and the Middle East. Even before then, on 2 August, Ribbentrop had informed the German

15 *DGFP*, vol. ix, pp. 620–1.
16 *The Times*, 18 July 1940; *La Vanguardia Española*, 18 July 1940; *Arriba*, 18 July 1940; Samuel Hoare, *Ambassador on Special Mission* (London: Collins, 1946), pp. 48–9.

ambassador to Spain, Eberhard von Stohrer, that 'what we want to achieve now is Spain's early entry into the war'.[17]

In response, Stohrer drew up a long memorandum on the costs and benefits of a Spanish entry. He quoted a claim by the Spanish Foreign Minister Colonel Juan Beigbeder that, without German assistance, fuel shortages would limit a Spanish war effort to one and a half months. Even this was an absurdly optimistic prediction. Stohrer highlighted such advantages of Spanish belligerency as the blow to English prestige, the curtailing of exports to England of Spanish ores and pyrites, the German acquisition of English-owned ore and copper mines and, above all, control of the Straits. The major disadvantages were seen as possible English counter-seizures of the Canary Islands, Tangier and the Balearic Islands and an extension of the Gibraltar zone, English landings in Portugal or Morocco, and the enormous drain on Axis supplies of food and fuel. Stohrer also drew attention to the logistical difficulties posed by Spain's narrow roads and different railway gauge. He concluded that too early a Spanish entry into the war would be unendurable for Spain and thus dangerous for Germany.[18]

Equally pessimistic conclusions were reached by a report on Spanish military strength compiled by the German high command. It concluded that 'without foreign help Spain can wage a war of only very short duration', given the paucity of its artillery and with enough ammunition for only a few days of hostilities. The Spanish high command was judged 'sluggish and doctrinaire'.[19] German officials began the process of quantifying Spain's essential civilian and military needs in terms of fuel, grain and other vital goods. The figures for civilian needs alone, as presented by Madrid, were colossal, but realistic – that is to say, not an invention to frighten off the Germans: 400,000 tons of gasoline, 600,000–700,000 tons of wheat, 200,000 tons of coal, 100,000 tons of diesel oil, 200,000 tons of fuel oil, as well as large quantities of other raw materials, including cotton, rubber, wood pulp, hemp and jute.[20]

These problems were dismissed by Franco because of his conviction that the conflict would be short and the Third Reich swiftly victorious.[21]

---

17 *DGFP*, vol. x, p. 396; Hoare, *Ambassador*, p. 44; Ramón Serrano Suñer, *Entre Hendaya y Gibraltar* (Madrid: Ediciones y Publicaciones Españolas, 1947), p. 65; Churchill, *Finest Hour*, p. 463.

18 Memorandum by Stohrer, 8 August 1940, *DGFP*, vol. x, pp. 442–5.

19 Note of the high command, 10 August 1940, *DGFP*, vol. x, pp. 461–4.

20 *DGFP*, vol. x, pp. 466–7, 499–500, 521; André Brissaud, *Canaris* (London: Grosset and Dunlap, 1973), pp. 191–4; MacGregor Knox, *Mussolini Unleashed, 1939–1941: Politics and Strategy in Fascist Italy's Last War* (Cambridge University Press, 1982), p. 184.

21 *DGFP*, vol. x, pp. 514–15, 521.

Apprehensive lest Berlin's silence toward his overtures meant Spain would be excluded from a share of the spoils, Franco wrote a buoyant letter on 15 August to Mussolini reminding him of Spanish claims in North Africa, declaring that Spain was 'preparing to take her place in the struggle against our common enemies'.[22]

By the winter of 1940, the strength of British resistance and the deterioration of Spain's economic position made Franco more vulnerable to Anglo-American pressures and blandishments. As the emissary of the British Ministry of Economic Warfare, David Eccles, wrote to his wife on 1 November 1940, 'The Spaniards are up for sale and it is our job to see that the auctioneer knocks them down to our bid'.[23] At the end of the summer, however, Franco remained sanguine about Spain's possible contribution to the Axis war effort. His optimism was still not shared by the Germans.[24]

That was to be starkly clear when Franco's right-hand man, Ramón Serrano Suñer, arrived in Berlin in mid-September to reiterate Franco's earlier offers. Ribbentrop informed him curtly that, in return for German military equipment and foodstuffs, Spain would recognize her Civil War debts to Germany and pay them off through future deliveries of raw materials. French and English mining properties in Spain and Spanish Morocco would be conceded to Germany. Spanish territory on the Gulf of Guinea was to be transferred to Germany. Spain would be integrated into a German-dominated European economy, with a subordinate role, limited to agriculture, the production of raw materials and industries 'indigenous to Spain'.[25]

Serrano Suñer arrived in Berlin just as Operation SEALION was postponed. Reiterating the list of materials necessary for Spain's war effort, he told Ribbentrop that 'Spain's Lebensraum' required all of French Morocco and Oran. Serrano Suñer and Ribbentrop did not take to each other, and this was to have great significance in terms of Spain's ultimate neutrality. The harsh affectation of the German minister put a brake on the Spaniard's fervour for the Axis cause.[26]

---

22 Franco to Mussolini, 15 August 1940, *DDI*, vol. v: *1 settembre – 31 dicembre 1936* (Rome: Istituto Poligrafico e Zecca dello Stato/Libreria dello Stato, 1994), pp. 403–5; *DGFP*, vol. x, pp. 484–6; Serrano Suñer, *Entre Hendaya y Gibraltar*, pp. 103–4.

23 David Eccles (ed.), *By Safe Hand: Letters of Sybil and David Eccles, 1939–42* (London: Bodley Head, 1983), p. 180.

24 *DGFP*, vol. x, p. 561.

25 Ibid., pp. 561–5, vol. xi, pp. 37–40, 81–2.

26 Walter Schellenberg, *The Schellenberg Memoirs: A Record of the Nazi Secret Service* (London: A. Deutsch, 1956), pp. 135, 143.

Ribbentrop quibbled over the material requested by Spain, but finally agreed that it should receive what was absolutely necessary. In return, he brutally demanded one of the Canary Islands for a German base, and further bases at Agadir and Mogador, with 'appropriate hinterland'. Serrano Suñer regarded this as intolerable impertinence.[27] On the following day, Serrano Suñer told Hitler unequivocally that Spain was ready to enter the war as soon as the necessary foodstuffs and war material arrived. Hitler declared enthusiastically how important and easy the capture of Gibraltar would be. The Führer repeated his desire for a base on the Canaries and suggested a meeting with the Caudillo on the Franco-Spanish border.

Hitler wrote to Franco on 18 September, suggesting that the British blockade of Spain could be broken only by the expulsion of the English from the Mediterranean. This, he claimed, would 'be attained rapidly and with certainty through Spain's entry into the war'.[28] Serrano Suñer tried to persuade Franco that Spain's place in the new order would be 'that of an insignificant and exploited satellite'.[29] Given his own plans for an attack on Gibraltar, Franco was never likely to permit the exclusively German operation desired by Hitler, and wrote to Serrano on 21 September that the German claims were more appropriate for the treatment of a defeated enemy, and were 'incompatible with the grandeur and independence of a nation'.[30] Nevertheless, he did not waver in his determination to clinch Spanish participation in the spoils. Far from astutely holding the Germans at bay, while the conversations between Serrano and Ribbentrop were not going well, Franco was anxious to convince them that he was an ally to be trusted.[31]

The idea that it was Serrano Suñer who was the pro-Axis warmonger and Franco the careful pacifist is demolished by the letters that he sent to his brother-in-law during his stay in Berlin. There could be no doubt that, at the time, Franco not only believed blindly in the victory of the Axis, but was fully decided to join in the war at its side. Any doubts concerned only the material conditions for Spanish preparation and future prizes. His tone was of wide-eyed adulation of Hitler. 'One appreciates as always the lofty vision and the good sense of the Führer'. The disagreeable demands made on Serrano were

27 *DGFP*, vol. XI, pp. 83–91; Serrano Suñer, *Entre Hendaya y Gibraltar*, pp. 165–71.
28 *DGFP*, vol. XI, pp. 106–8.
29 Norman J. W. Goda, *Tomorrow the World: Hitler, Northwest Africa, and the Path toward America* (College Station: Texas A&M University Press, 1998), pp. 71–8.
30 Gerhard L. Weinberg, *World in the Balance: Behind the Scenes of World War II* (Hanover, NH: Brandeis University Press, 1981), p. 122; Serrano Suñer, *Entre Hendaya y Gibraltar*, p. 183; Serrano Suñer, *Memorias*, pp. 335–7.
31 *DGFP*, vol. XI, pp. 166–74.

put down to 'the selfishness and inflated self-regard of the Führer's underlings', and to the fact that Ribbentrop and Hitler's economic advisors failed to see how the Spanish Civil War had facilitated Germany's victory over France.[32]

However, continued British resistance saw opposition to entry into the war building within the higher reaches of the Spanish army. The General Staff reported that the navy had no fuel; there was neither a functioning air force nor effective mechanized units; and, after the Civil War, the population could not sustain more sacrifices. Moreover, tensions were brewing between monarchists and Falangists, but Franco was more confident than the Germans themselves that the end of the war was near.[33]

On 28 September, Hitler spoke with Ciano in Berlin, and he made no secret of his impatience with Franco, who promised a friendship that would be implemented only if Germany provided massive deliveries of grain, fuel and military equipment and granted Morocco and Oran. He preferred to leave the Vichy French to defend Morocco against the British. Hitler told Ciano that he opposed Spanish intervention 'because it would cost more than it is worth'. Hitler had to balance the conflicting demands of Franco, Pétain and Mussolini, something which he conceded was possible only through 'a grandiose fraud'.[34] Franco himself was not above a bit of fraud. Without relinquishing his pro-Axis views, Spain's intensifying food shortage forced him to make overtures to the British and Americans. On 7 October, he sent a telegram to Roosevelt saying that Spain would stay neutral if only the USA would send wheat.[35]

Delays and new temptations, 1940–1941

On 18 October 1940, Colonel Beigbeder was replaced as Minister of Foreign Affairs by Serrano Suñer. Mussolini wrote to Hitler on the following day that

32 Franco to Serrano Suñer, 21, 23 September 1940, Serrano Suñer, *Memorias*, pp. 331–42; Serrano Suñer, *Entre Hendaya y Gibraltar*, p. 183.
33 Denis Smyth, 'The Moor and the Money-lender: Politics and Profits in Anglo-German Relations with Francoist Spain', in Marie-Luise Recker (ed.), *Von der Konkurrenz zur Rivalität: Das Britische-Deutsche Verhältnis in den Länden der Europäischen Peripherie* (Stuttgart: Steiner Verlag, 1986), pp. 171–4.
34 *DGFP*, vol. xi, pp. 211–14; Galeazzo Ciano, *Diario 1939–1940* (Milan: Rizzoli, 1950), pp. 310–13; Colloquio Mussolini-Serrano Suñer, 1 October 1940, Colloquio Mussolini-Hitler, 4 October 1940, *DDI*, vol. v, pp. 639–40, 655–8; Knox, *Mussolini Unleashed*, pp. 189, 196.
35 Hugh Dalton, *The Second World War Diary of Hugh Dalton, 1940–1945*, ed. Ben Pimlott (London: Jonathan Cape, 1986), 7 October 1940, p. 89; US Department of State, *Foreign Relations of the United States* [hereafter *FRUS*]: *1940* (5 vols., Washington DC: US Government Printing Office, 1957), vol. ii, pp. 812–17.

Franco's Cabinet re-shuffle 'affords us assurance that the tendencies hostile to the Axis are eliminated or at least neutralized'.[36] However, Spanish promises to join the Axis were reiterated, but not converted into binding contractual commitments, at the historic meeting between Hitler and Franco at Hendaye on 23 October 1940. Despite the myth of Franco gallantly holding out against the threats of the Führer, Hitler had not in fact come to demand that Spain go to war immediately. Rather he was engaged on a reconnaissance mission, seeing Pierre Laval on 22 October at Montoire-sur-Loire near Tours, Franco at Hendaye, and then Pétain on 24 October, again at Montoire, on his way back. Concerned that Mussolini was about to get involved in a costly Balkan war by attacking Greece, Hitler was starting to think that to hand French Morocco over to the Spaniards was to make them vulnerable to British attack. As he told Mussolini in Florence on 28 October, the best solution was to leave the French to defend their own colonies.[37] In any case, the Führer was no doubt aware of the views of his Commander-in-Chief Brauchitsch and his Chief of Staff Halder, that 'Spain's domestic situation is so rotten as to make her useless as a political partner. We shall have to achieve the objectives essential to us (Gibraltar) without her active participation'.[38]

That one direct encounter between the two dictators was to be a central plank in the construction of the image of Franco as the brilliant architect of Spanish neutrality who kept a threatening Hitler at bay. In the words of his hagiographers, 'the skill of one man held back what all the armies of Europe, including the French, had been unable to do'.[39] Yet there was little pressure for Spanish belligerence on the part of Hitler, and Franco remained as anxious as ever, in the autumn of 1940, to be part of a future Axis world order. Franco went to Hendaye seeking profit from what he saw as the demise of the Anglo-French hegemony which had kept Spain in a subordinate position for over two centuries. He failed because Hitler believed that Vichy offered the better deal.

Even if, by this time, Franco perceived that a long struggle might be in the offing, he was still anxious to be in at the death. Always keen to profit from Hitler's successes, but determined not to have to pay for the privilege, Franco had opened the Hendaye meeting with rhetorical assurances – 'Spain would

36 DDI, vol. v, pp. 720–2; DGFP, vol. xi, pp. 331–4.
37 Norman Rich, Hitler's War Aims, vol. i: Ideology, the Nazi State, and the Course of Expansion (2 vols., New York: W. W. Norton, 1973–74), pp. 169–70.
38 Franz Halder, The Halder War Diary, 1939–1942, ed. Charles Burdick and Hans-Adolf Jacobsen (Novato, Calif.: Presidio Press, 1988), p. 262.
39 Sánchez Silva and Saenz de Heredia, Franco, p. 139.

gladly fight at Germany's side', but because of difficulties being made by the USA and Britain, 'Spain must mark time and often look kindly toward things of which she thoroughly disapproved'. The bitter pill for Franco was Hitler's statement that 'If cooperation with France proved possible, then the territorial results of the war might perhaps not be so great'. Franco can hardly have failed to notice that his hopes of massive territorial gain at virtually no cost were being slashed before his eyes. It is not surprising, therefore, that he replied, to Hitler's unconcealed annoyance, with a recital of the appalling conditions in Spain, a list of supplies required to facilitate military preparations and a pompous assertion that Spain could take Gibraltar alone.[40] After being in Franco's company for nearly nine hours, Hitler told Mussolini later that 'Rather than go through that again, I would prefer to have three or four teeth taken out'.[41] In fact, Hitler had thought to deceive the Spaniards over French Morocco by the seemingly frank admission that he could not give what was not yet his, implying that he would indeed give it when it was in his power to do so. He was, of course, confident of being able to dispose of the French colonial empire as he wished, but had no intention of giving it to Franco. That was his 'grandiose fraud'. Serrano Suñer suggested years later that Hitler had not told a sufficiently big lie, because Franco's Africanista obsession was such that, if Hitler had offered Morocco, he would have entered the war.[42]

It was fortunate for Franco that Hitler remained unwilling and indeed unable to pay his price. That price, the cession of French colonies, would almost certainly have precipitated an anti-German movement under de Gaulle that would pave the way for Allied landings. The Hendaye meeting came to a stalemate precisely on this problem. A protocol was signed, committing Spain to join the Axis cause at a date to be decided by 'common agreement of the three Powers', but only after military preparations were complete. This effectively left the decision with Franco. Serrano Suñer informed the American ambassador on 31 October 1940, and repeated it three times, that 'there had been no pressure, not even an insinuation by Hitler or Mussolini that Spain should enter the war'.[43]

40 Serrano Suñer, *Memorias*, pp. 283–301; Paul Schmidt, *Hitler's Interpreter: The Secret History of German Diplomacy, 1935–1945* (London: Heinemann, 1951), p. 196; Brissaud, *Canaris*, pp. 204–9; DGFP, vol. xi, pp. 371–9.
41 Ciano, *L'Europa verso la catastrofe*, pp. 603–4.
42 Heleno Saña, *El franquismo sin mitos: conversaciones con Serrano Suñer* (Barcelona: Ediciones Grijalbo, 1982), p. 193. See also the polemic between Serrano Suñer and Antonio Marquina in *El País*, 19, 21, 22, 26, 28, 29 November 1978.
43 *FRUS: 1940*, vol. ii, p. 824.

Certainly there was no question of hostile German action against Spain. At a meeting with his service chiefs on 31 July 1940, Hitler had already made it clear that his central obsession was the destruction of the Soviet Union. He regarded this as a better strategy for defeating Britain than any action in the Mediterranean. With planning for the attack on Russia already beginning in the summer of 1940, the Wehrmacht had little spare capacity for an assault on Spain. And given the cooperation from Franco, Hitler had no need to contemplate one.[44]

Thereafter, Spain came no nearer than it had in 1940 to joining the Axis. That does not mean that Franco was working hard to keep out of Hitler's clutches. The Caudillo's sympathies continued to lie with Germany and Italy. If Hitler had met the asking price, Franco would almost certainly have joined him. Nevertheless, his own survival was always Franco's paramount ambition. The cancellation of Operation SEALION suggested that the Axis victory that he still thought inevitable might be delayed. This, plus the tensions between the army and the Falange over whether or not to go to war, also gave him pause. The most obvious example of his circumspection and its link to domestic issues was his non-interference during Operation TORCH. Yet between Hendaye and TORCH, there was ample evidence that Franco still hankered after being part of a victorious Axis coalition.

In early November 1940, for instance, it looked as if the disappointments of Hendaye had been overcome. Franco took several initiatives which can only be interpreted as a readiness to fight. On 1 November, he wrote to Hitler promising to carry out his verbal undertaking to enter the war.[45] On 9 November, three copies of the secret German-Italian-Spanish protocol arrived in Madrid and were duly signed by Serrano Suñer and the German and Italian copies sent back by special courier.[46] However, circumstances were changing rapidly in such a way as to curtail Franco's enthusiasm. The economic crisis inside Spain was deepening dramatically, and there were ever more frequent signs that the inexorable conveyor belt of Axis triumphs was slowing down. Hitler in contrast, shaken by the British naval victory over the Italians at Taranto, was becoming keener to force the pace, convinced now of the need for an attack on Gibraltar.

44 Halder, *Diary*, 31 July 1940, pp. 244–6; Alan Bullock, *Hitler and Stalin: Parallel Lives* (New York: A. A. Knopf, 1991), pp. 754–5; Alan Clark, *Barbarossa: The Russian-German Conflict, 1941–1945* (London: HarperCollins, 1965), pp. 17–26. I am grateful to Professor Brian Bond for clarifying this point.
45 *DGFP*, vol. XI, p. 452.
46 Ibid., pp. 478–9.

On 4 November, Hitler told Generals Brauchitsch, Halder, Keitel and Jodl that, having Franco's assurance that Spain was about to join Germany, it would be possible to seize Gibraltar. Detailed plans were drawn up in mid-November for what was to be called Operation FELIX, whereby German troops would enter Spain on 10 January 1941, prior to an assault on Gibraltar on 4 February.[47] Rehearsals for the assault began near Besançon. However, as Hitler's planners quickly discovered, Franco had not exaggerated the feeble condition of the Spanish economy. The different rail gauges on either side of the Franco-Spanish border and the disrepair of Spanish track and rolling stock were notorious. Moreover, a disastrous harvest meant that Spain needed even more grain than specified in her earlier requests to the Germans. With famine in many parts of the country, Franco had no choice but to seek to buy food in the United States, and that necessarily involved postponing a declaration of war.[48]

Nevertheless, Serrano Suñer informed Stohrer that the Spanish government had agreed to German tankers being stationed in remote bays on the northern coast for the refuelling of Kriegsmarine destroyers.[49] Convinced, briefly at least, that Spain was about to declare war, Hitler sent Admiral Canaris to Madrid to discuss the details. However, Franco told him that Spain was simply not sufficiently prepared, particularly in terms of food supplies, to meet Hitler's deadline for an attack on Gibraltar. The deficit in foodstuffs was now estimated at 1 million tons. Franco also expressed his fears that the seizure of Gibraltar would see Spain lose the Canary Islands and its other overseas possessions, and made clear that Spain could enter the war only when England was ready to collapse. On receiving Canaris's depressing report, Hitler decided that Operation FELIX should be discontinued.[50]

The famine, combined with worries over the ongoing hostility between the Falange and his generals, had caused Franco to pull back at the crucial moment. Nevertheless, his regret seemed to be genuine. He declared vehemently to Stohrer on 20 January 1941, that 'his faith in the victory of

---

47 Directive 18, 12 November 1940, in H. R. Trevor-Roper (ed.), *Hitler's War Directives, 1939–1945* (London: Pan, 1964), pp. 39–42.

48 *DGFP*, vol. XI, pp. 528–30, 574–6, 581–2; *FRUS: 1940*, vol. II, pp. 829–38; Charles B. Burdick, *Germany's Military Strategy and Spain in World War II* (Syracuse University Press, 1968), pp. 77ff.

49 *DGFP*, vol. XI, pp. 787–8.

50 Ibid., pp. 812, 816–17, 852–3, 990–4; Heinz Höhne, *Canaris* (London: Secker & Warburg, 1979), pp. 440–1; Brissaud, *Canaris*, pp. 224–6; Serrano Suñer, *Entre Hendaya y Gibraltar*, pp. 258–9.

Germany was still the same', and insisted that 'it was not a question at all of whether Spain would enter the war; that had been decided at Hendaye. It was merely a question of when.'[51] On 5 February 1941, Hitler wrote to Mussolini, asking him to persuade Franco to change his mind.[52] In fact, with the economic situation in Spain deteriorating daily, there was little possibility of that happening. German consuls were reporting that there was no bread at all in part of the country and there were cases of highway robbery and banditry. The Director of the Economic Policy Department in Berlin regarded Spain's consequent requests for economic support as utterly unrealizable.[53]

Franco's meeting with Mussolini took place on 12 and 13 February at Bordighera.[54] Shortly before, Franco had received news of the annihilation of Marshal Graziani's army by the British at Bengazi, and public opinion in Spain was moving strongly against any intervention in the war. The Italian rout in Cyrenaica by a much smaller British force and the British naval bombardment of Genoa on 8 February had a significant impact on opinion within the Francoist establishment.[55] At Bordighera, Franco boasted to Mussolini of his plans to take Gibraltar with his own resources. He also told the Duce of his continued conviction of an ultimate Axis victory. He admitted candidly, 'Spain wishes to enter the war; her fear is to enter too late.' He complained of German reluctance to give explicit assurance that all Spain's territorial ambitions in Africa would be fulfilled. Franco was clearly furious about Hitler's concern to draw France into the Axis orbit. He also stated that the attack on Gibraltar should be carried out solely as a Spanish operation. Mussolini was extremely understanding about Franco's difficulties and the enormous responsibility of entering the war. The Duce asked Franco if he would declare war if given sufficient supplies and binding promises about his colonial ambitions. The Caudillo replied that, even if all the supplies were delivered, which was impossible, given Hitler's other commitments, then Spain's military unpreparedness and famine conditions would still mean several months before it could join in the war. Mussolini was inclined, in consequence, to stop trying to persuade Franco to join the Axis war effort

51 DGFP, vol. XI (London: HMSO, 1964), pp. 1140–3, 1157–8, 1171–5.
52 DGFP, vol. XII (13 vols., London: HMSO, 1964), p. 30.
53 Ibid., pp. 37–42, 51–3, 58, 78–9.
54 Ciano to Serrano Suñer, 22 January 1941, DDI, vol. VI: 29 ottobre 1940 – 23 aprile 1941 (Rome: Ministero degli affari esteri, 1986); Serrano Suñer, Entre Hendaya y Gibraltar, pp. 262–3; Roberto Cantalupo, Fu la Spagna. Ambasciata presso Franco. Febbraio–Aprile 1937 (Milan: Mondadori, 1948), pp. 288–9.
55 Hoare, Ambassador, pp. 95, 104.

in the short term.[56] The Duce informed Hitler about the Bordighera meeting just as the German Department of Economic Planning was reporting that Spanish demands could not be met without endangering the Reich's military capacity. Ribbentrop took the conversations at Bordighera as signifying Franco's definitive refusal to enter battle. On the assumption that Franco had to know, despite his defective military thinking, that Spanish troops alone could never capture Gibraltar, Ribbentrop instructed Stohrer to take no further steps to secure Spanish belligerence.[57]

There was no question of Hitler forcing the issue, since he had already committed his military machine to rescuing Italy from its disastrous involvement in the Balkans.[58] Nevertheless, the changed tone of Hispano-German relations was marked, at the end of February, by German insistence on the repayment of Spain's Civil War debts, which were agreed at 372 million Reichsmarks.[59] This was to be in marked contrast with the attitude of the Anglo-Saxon powers. The British government was exploring Anglo-American economic help for Spain in order to isolate Serrano Suñer. On 7 April 1941, Britain granted Spain credits of £2,500,000.[60]

Operation BARBAROSSA: Spain tempted again?

German victories in the spring of 1941 in North Africa, Yugoslavia and Greece rekindled Franco's pro-Axis fervour. After the British evacuation of Crete in the last week of May, Franco believed that Suez would soon be in Axis hands.[61] The Caudillo's belief in the ultimate victory of the Axis was inflamed by the Nazi invasion of the Soviet Union on 22 June 1941. Serrano Suñer informed Stohrer that, after consultation with Franco, they wished to send volunteer units of Falangists to fight, 'independently of the full and complete entry of Spain into the war beside the Axis, which would take place at the appropriate moment'.[62] The controlled press rejoiced and the British Embassy was stormed by Falangists on 24 June, after Serrano Suñer harangued them at the Falange headquarters in Alcalá, declaring that 'history demanded the

56 Colloquio Mussolini-Franco, 12 February 1941, *DDI*, vol. VI, pp. 568–76; Serrano Suñer, *Entre Hendaya y Gibraltar*, pp. 261–4; Cantalupo, *Fu la Spagna*, pp. 291–3.
57 *DGFP*, vol. XII, pp. 96–7, 131–2.
58 Burdick, *Germany's Military Strategy*, pp. 103ff.
59 *DGFP*, vol. XII, pp. 194–5.
60 *FRUS: 1941* (7 vols., Washington DC: US Government Printing Office, 1959), vol. II, pp. 886–7.
61 Ibid., pp. 891–903; *Arriba*, 31 May 1941; *ABC*, 31 May, 6, 9 June 1941.
62 *DGFP*, vol. XII, pp. 1080–1.

extermination of Russia'. The assault on the British Embassy was facilitated by a truck-load of stones thoughtfully provided by the authorities.

Three days later, Spain moved from non-belligerency to what was described by Serrano Suñer as 'moral belligerency', and preparations began for the creation of the Blue Division of nearly 50,000 Falangist volunteers to fight on the Russian front. This was in addition to the agreement made on 21 August 1941 between the *Deutsche Arbeitsfront* and the *Delegación Nacional de Sindicatos* for 100,000 Spanish workers to go to Germany. Theoretically 'volunteers', but more often levies chosen by the Falange to fit Germany's industrial needs, between 15,000 and 20,000 were eventually sent.[63] In the event, the dispatch of the Blue Division was not a prelude to a declaration of war on Britain. It was a gesture to keep an iron in the fire, showing enough commitment to the Axis cause to merit a say in the future spoils.

As Serrano Suñer described the sending of the Blue Division, 'Their sacrifice would give us a legitimate claim to participate one day in the dreamed of victory and exempt us from the general and terrible sacrifices of the war.' Franco was heard frequently asserting that the Allies had lost the war. On the fifth anniversary of the outbreak of the Spanish Civil War, 17 July 1941, he addressed the National Council of the Falange and expressed his enthusiasm for Hitler's Russian venture, at 'this moment when the German armies lead the battle for which Europe and Christianity have for so many years longed, and in which the blood of our youth is to mingle with that of our comrades of the Axis'. 'I do not harbour any doubt about the result of the war. The die is cast and the first battle was won here in Spain. The war is lost for the Allies.' He spoke of his contempt for 'plutocratic democracies', of his conviction that Germany had already won and that American intervention would be a 'criminal madness', leading only to useless prolongation of the conflict and catastrophe for the USA.[64]

During the summer of 1941, Franco's controlled press frequently attacked England and the USA and glorified the achievements of German arms. In consequence, imports of essential goods dried up, as Spain found it harder to get American export licences and British navicerts.[65] Shortages of coal, copper, tin, rubber and textile fibres presaged an imminent economic breakdown. However, since the requested supplies from Germany did not

63 Hoare, *Ambassador*, p. 140; Manuel Espadas Burgos, *Franquismo y política exterior* (Madrid: Ediciones Rialp, 1988), p. 123; José Luis Rodríguez Jiménez, *Los esclavos españoles de Hitler* (Barcelona: Editorial Planeta, 2002).
64 *FRUS: 1941*, vol. II, pp. 908–11; Serrano Suñer, *Memorias*, pp. 348–9.
65 *FRUS: 1941*, vol. II, pp. 913–25.

materialize, by 6 October 1941, Franco told the US ambassador Alexander Weddell of Spain's difficulties in obtaining wheat, cotton and gasoline, and made clear his desire to see an improvement of economic relations with the USA.[66] The most senior generals, and even Franco himself, could not avoid the alarming conclusion that Hitler had got himself into serious trouble in Russia.

Franco's initial delight at the Japanese attack on Pearl Harbor on 7 December 1941 was cut short when the Japanese invaded the Philippines.[67] Moreover, the second flowering of his pro-Axis enthusiasm would eventually wither, along with the fortunes of the German armies in Russia. Nevertheless, it took him a long time to accept that American involvement meant that the war would be a long and titanic struggle, and thus postpone Spanish entry indefinitely. The precise moment of his so-called *chaqueteo* (or change of coat) is difficult to locate, for the simple reason that it was never definitive. On 13 February 1942, Franco met the Portuguese premier, Antonio Oliveira Salazar, in Seville and declared that an Allied victory was absolutely impossible. He added that, if there were ever a danger of the Bolsheviks overrunning Germany, he would send a million Spanish troops.[68] On the next day, the Generalísimo addressed high-ranking army officers in Seville. Thrilled by the British disaster at Singapore on the previous day, he spoke in the eager voice of a friend of the certain victors. He seemed not have read the many reports from the Spanish Embassy in Berlin about the catastrophic situation of the German forces in Russia. Praising Germany as 'the bulwark that holds back the Russian hordes and defends western civilization', he declared his 'absolute certainty' that the Reich would not be destroyed. Fired with that confidence – and no doubt in the hope that his promise would never be put to the test – he publicly repeated what he had told Salazar: 'if the road to Berlin were open, then it would not merely be one division of Spanish volunteers but a million Spaniards who would be offered to help'.[69]

---

66 Ibid., pp. 924–9.
67 Espadas Burgos, *Franquismo*, p. 124.
68 *DDI*, vol. VIII: *12 dicembre 1941 – 20 luglio 1942* (Rome: Ministero degli affari esteri, 1988), pp. 322–3, 335–8; *Documents secrets du Ministère des Affaires Etrangères d'Allemagne: Espagne* (Paris: Éditions Paul Dupont, 1946), pp. 86–95; *FRUS: 1942* (6 vols., Washington DC: US Government Printing Office, 1961), vol. III, pp. 281–3; *The Times*, 13 February 1942; *ABC*, 13 February 1942; testimony of Serrano Suñer to the author.
69 Ramón Garriga, *La España de Franco*, vol. I: *Las relaciones con Hitler* (2nd edn, 2 vols., Puebla, Mexico: Editorial Cajica, 1970), pp. 345–6; Francisco Franco Bahamonde, *Palabras del Caudillo, 19 abril 1937 – 7 diciembre 1942* (Madrid: Vicesecretaria de Educación Popular, 1943), pp. 203–5.

In late 1941, British intelligence intercepted and decoded German radio messages arising from an ambitious *Abwehr* operation, *Unternehmen Bodden*, personally approved by Franco. The *Abwehr* was constructing, with the aid of the Spanish navy, a seabed sonic detection system across the Straits of Gibraltar, and a chain of fourteen infrared ship surveillance stations. With nine stations on the Spanish coast and a further five in Morocco, the system became fully operational on 15 April 1942. Information on Allied shipping thus gathered was transmitted to U-boats in the Mediterranean and in the Atlantic within range of the Straits. Enormous diplomatic pressure and the threat of curtailing Allied oil shipments obliged Franco, reluctantly, to promise to investigate. On 3 June, his staff admitted that the equipment was being installed by German technicians, but claimed that it was for 'the defence of the coasts of Spain'. Typically, Franco stonewalled for months, ignoring British pressure through the summer. It was not until after the success of Operation TORCH that he asked Admiral Canaris to have his sonar and infrared detection equipment dismantled.[70]

Neutrality, far from being the result of brilliant statecraft or foresight, was the fruit of a narrow pragmatism, and what Serrano Suñer called the 'good fortune' that Germany would not or could not pay the price demanded for entry into the war. The internal political situation in Spain had also played its part. Military hostility to Serrano Suñer was reaching boiling point.[71] Moreover, after Franco's initial enthusiasm for the Japanese assault on the United States, economic and political realism had prevailed and relations had improved with Washington. Less anti-American material was appearing in the press. Nevertheless, Franco's real sympathies often gleamed through the fog of his rhetoric. On 29 May 1942, addressing the Women's Section of the Falange, he compared his regime with that of Isabel la Católica, praising her expulsion of the Jews, her totalitarian racial policy and her awareness of Spain's need for *Lebensraum* (*espacio vital*).[72]

The Caudillo's great political talent was his ability to balance the internal forces of the regime coalition. Under Serrano Suñer, the Falange seemed to

70 Denis Smyth, 'Screening "Torch": Allied Counter-Intelligence and the Spanish Threat to the Secrecy of the Allied Invasion of French North Africa in November 1942', *Intelligence and National Security* 4:2 (April 1989), pp. 339–44; F. H. Hinsley et al., *British Intelligence in the Second World War: Its Influence on Strategy and Operations* (4 vols., New York: Cambridge University Press, 1981), vol. II, pp. 719–21; Ros Agudo, *La guerra secreta*, pp. 218–31; Denis Smyth, *Deathly Deception: The Real Story of Operation Mincemeat* (Oxford University Press, 2010), pp. 15–21, 242–3.
71 *DDI*, vol. VIII, pp. 113, 116–17, 123–4; *Arriba*, 13 January 1942.
72 Franco Bahamonde, *Palabras del Caudillo*, pp. 211–16; *FRUS: 1942*, vol. III, pp. 288–9.

be growing too powerful, and Franco could not risk losing army loyalty. Accordingly, on 3 September 1942, he replaced Serrano Suñer as Foreign Minister with General Francisco Jordana.[73] The broad direction of Spanish policy did not change appreciably. Franco wrote to Mussolini on 18 September 1942, asserting that the decision was motivated by domestic politics and 'did not in the least affect our position in foreign affairs'.[74]

Caution (for the short term), 1942–1943

In the autumn of 1942, when the preparations for Operation TORCH showed that an eventual Axis triumph was far from assured, Franco reacted, not with prophetic awareness of ultimate Allied victory, but rather with an entirely reasonable short-term caution. The massing of force on his borders was hardly the best moment to cross swords with the Allies, particularly in the wake of Rommel's failure to conquer Egypt. In any case, Allied successes in North Africa were so spectacular as to inhibit any Spanish thoughts of hostile action. When Anglo-American forces entered the French Moroccan and Algerian territories which he coveted, Franco was enough of a realist to instruct his ambassador in London to start a rapprochement with the Western Allies. That did not mean that he had lost his belief in an ultimate Axis victory. However, it presaged a typical attempt to exploit German difficulties.

His strategy now was to persuade Berlin that he must be given military help to permit him to stand up to the Allies. The Spanish Foreign Ministry, on 24 November 1942, issued a document stressing that Franco expected German weaponry, without conditions, payment, supervising officers or technicians.[75] It was a characteristic initiative: at face value, a genuine appeal to the Axis for help as the Allies massed near its frontiers. For all his unquestionable sympathy with the Third Reich, Franco was trying to exploit Axis difficulties exactly as he was exaggerating German threats in order to squeeze benefits from the Allies.

---

73 For detailed accounts of the complex machinations that led to Serrano Suñer's replacement, see Paul Preston, *Franco: A Biography* (London: HarperCollins, 1993), pp. 464–9; and Sheelagh Ellwood, *Spanish Fascism in the Franco Era* (Houndmills: Palgrave Macmillan, 1987), pp. 84–90. Serrano Suñer's version is in Saña, *El franquismo*, pp. 271–6. See also Hoare, *Ambassador*, pp. 140, 164–71; Doussinague, *España tenía razón*, pp. 130–1; and Antonio Marquina Barrio, 'El atentado de Begoña', *Historia* 16:76 (August 1982), 11–19.

74 *DDI*, vol. IX: *21 luglio 1942 – 6 febbraio 1943* (Rome: Ministero degli affari esteri, 1989), pp. 138–9; Serrano Suñer, *Entre Hendaya y Gibraltar*, pp. 211–18.

75 Doussinague, *España tenía razón*, p. 205.

The beginnings of a possible slow return to neutrality were visible in the signing, in December 1942, of the Bloque Ibérico agreement with Portugal.[76] Nevertheless, Franco revealed where his heart really lay when the new German ambassador, Hans Adolf von Moltke, arrived in late January 1943.[77] Moltke was surprised when the Caudillo talked to him affably for an hour, rather than the bare fifteen minutes demanded by protocol. Declaring that Germany was his friend, and Britain, America and the 'Bolsheviks' his enemies, Franco swore that, within the limits of the possible, he would 'support Germany in the struggle imposed upon her by destiny'. However, he also expressed concerns about the situation in Italy, and even spoke of the possibility of a negotiated peace.[78]

By spring 1943, it was obvious that the international panorama in which Franco operated had changed dramatically. TORCH had shifted the strategic balance, but until the fall of Mussolini in the summer, Franco remained convinced that the Allies could not win, and that their successes in Africa were of marginal importance. In March 1943, he sent a Spanish armaments commission to Berlin to arrange the details of the weapons agreed in the Secret Hispano-German Protocol. It was headed by General Carlos Martínez Campos, who was also ordered to assess German military capacity in the wake of the defeat at Stalingrad in February. Armed with a list of Spanish aircraft and artillery needs, Martínez Campos was received on 16 March by Marshal Keitel, who was at pains to conceal the fact that Germany could not spare such materiel. Two days later, at the Wolf's Lair, Hitler tried to convince him that it would be better to begin with some small deliveries of less sophisticated weapons. Taken on a ten-day tour of the Nazi war industries, Martínez Campos was seduced by tales about the new wonder weapons with which the Third Reich would destroy Allied cities and armies and easily win the war. On his return to Madrid, he informed a clearly impressed Caudillo that the German war machine remained invincible.[79]

76 Hoare, *Ambassador*, pp. 184–96.
77 Pedro Teotónio Pereira, *Correspondência de Pedro Teotónio Pereira para Oliveira Salazar*, vol. III: *1942* (4 vols., Lisbon: CLNRF, 1990), pp. 280–1; François Piétri, *Mes années d'Espagne, 1940–1948* (Paris: Plon, 1954), p. 86; Klaus-Jörg Ruhl, *Franco, Falange y III Reich* (Madrid: Akal, 1986), pp. 49–50; Doussinague, *España tenía razón*, pp. 131–3; Moltke to Wilhelmstrasse, 13 January 1943, *Documents secrets*, pp. 127–30; Ramón Garriga, *La España de Franco*, vol. II: *De la División Azul al pacto con los Estados Unidos (1943 a 1951)* (2 vols., Puebla, Mexico: Editorial Cajica, 1971), p. 30.
78 Moltke to Wilhelmstrasse, 24 January 1943, *Documents secrets*, pp. 131–4.
79 Carlos Martínez de Campos, *Ayer, 1931–1953* (Madrid: Instituto de Estudios Políticos, 1970), pp. 213–52; Gerald R. Kleinfeld and Lewis A. Tambs, *Hitler's Spanish Legion: The Blue Division in Russia* (Carbondale: Southern Illinois University Press, 1979), pp. 310–13.

Nevertheless, as part of his own precautions against a possible Axis defeat, with what British ambassador Samuel Hoare saw as 'impenetrable complacency', Franco began to present himself as the peacemaker, whose intervention could save the West from the consequences of the destruction of the German bulwark against communism.[80] In early May, he toured Andalusia, making speeches on this theme in Córdoba, Huelva, Seville, Malaga and Almería.[81] In the wake of the fall of Mussolini at the beginning of September, and faced with discontent from his own high command, Franco announced the withdrawal of the Blue Division, although volunteers were to be permitted to stay on in German units. On 1 October 1943, in a speech to the Falange, Franco now described Spain's position as one of 'vigilant neutrality'. That did nothing to prevent incidents such as Falangist attacks on the British Vice-Consulate in Zaragoza and the American Consulate in Valencia.[82] Nor did it inhibit Spanish exports of vital wolfram to the Third Reich.

Wolfram was a crucial ingredient in the manufacture of high-quality steel for armaments in general, and particularly for machine tools and armour-piercing shells. American policy had been to persuade Spain to limit exports to Germany by supplying petroleum and buying Spanish wolfram. On 3 December 1943, Franco told the new German ambassador, Hans Heinrich Dieckhoff, who had arrived after the sudden death in March of von Moltke, that his own survival depended on Axis victory, and an Allied triumph 'would mean his own annihilation'. The crucial issue was that 'a neutral Spain which was furnishing Germany with wolfram and other products is at this moment of greater value to Germany than a Spain which would be drawn into the war'. The Germans had reason to feel some satisfaction with their Spanish policy because Franco was paying off his Civil War debts with wolfram.[83]

By the beginning of 1944, with the tide of war clearly turning, North Africa secure and Italy out of the war, the USA was altogether less inclined to be patient with Franco. The American military staff was furious about continued Spanish wolfram exports to Germany, which were increasingly paid

---

80 On the Bloque Ibérico, see *Dez anos de política externa (1936–1947) a nação portuguesa e a segunda guerra mundial* (14 vols., Lisbon: Imprensa Nacional/Casa da Moeda, 1961–91), vol. XII, pp. 85–96; *The Times*, 23 December 1942; Doussinague, *España tenía razón*, pp. 116–26.

81 *Arriba*, 18, 19, 20, 21 March, 2, 5, 12 May 1943; *The Times*, 18 March 1943; *ABC*, 2, 5, 7, 8, 9 May 1943; Doussinague, *España tenía razón*, pp. 207–9.

82 Franco, speech of 1 October 1943, *Bulletin of Spanish Studies* 21:82 (April 1944), 85; Hoare, *Ambassador*, pp. 239–40.

83 US Department of State, *The Spanish Government and the Axis* (Washington DC: US Government Printing Office, 1946), pp. 34–7; Hoare, *Ambassador*, p. 258.

with gold looted from prisoners in extermination camps.[84] There was uproar in the United States when Franco sent congratulations to José P. Laurel, on his installation by the Japanese as puppet governor of the Philippines. On 27 January 1944, the British ambassador visited the Caudillo with three outraged complaints. The Spanish government was providing new and extensive facilities for German purchases of wolfram; despite the formal withdrawal of the Blue Division, the Falange was still recruiting for the small Spanish legion still in Russia, with a unit of the Spanish air force active alongside it; and finally, extensive anti-Allied espionage and sabotage activities were still being carried out by German agents, with the help of Spanish military personnel.[85]

The Americans then precipitately curtailed petroleum exports to Spain.[86] In the last resort, the Spaniards were forced to accept a dramatic restriction of their monthly exports to a near token amount. When the Germans offered oil in return for wolfram, Churchill persuaded Roosevelt to accept a compromise. The eventual agreement with Franco, signed on 2 May 1944, encompassed the closing down of the German Consulate in Tangier, the withdrawal of all Spanish units from Russia, and the expulsion of German spies and saboteurs from Spain. Needless to say, throughout the rest of 1944, Hoare protested almost daily at the failure of the Spaniards to proceed with the expulsion of the German agents. German observation posts and radio interception stations were maintained in Spain until the end of the war.[87]

Franco also ignored an opportunity to diminish the hostility felt toward him in Allied circles. The death of Jordana on 3 August 1944, and the need to appoint a new Foreign Minister, made possible a clean break with the pro-Axis past. Instead, Franco replaced Jordana with the ultra-rightist José Félix Lequerica, the fiercely pro-Nazi ambassador to Vichy. Nevertheless, from October 1944, a half-hearted diplomatic initiative was begun to convince the Allies that Franco had never meant them any harm, and that his Axis links had been aimed at the Soviet Union. On 18 October 1944, he proposed a

84 Ramón J. Campo, *El oro de Canfranc* (Zaragoza: Mira Editores, 2002), pp. 65–9, 79–85.
85 *FRUS: 1943* (6 vols., Washington DC: US Government Printing Office, 1964), vol. II, pp. 631–2, 722–38; Doussinague, *España tenía razón*, pp. 88–9, 280–90; Hoare, *Ambassador*, pp. 249–56.
86 Warren F. Kimball (ed.), *Churchill and Roosevelt: The Complete Correspondence* (3 vols., Princeton University Press, 1984), vol. II, pp. 725–6, 728, 751; Cadogan, *Diaries*, pp. 602–3; Edward R. Stettinius, Jr., *The Diaries of Edward R. Stettinius Jr., 1943–1946* (New York: New Viewpoints, 1975), pp. 28–9; Hoare, *Ambassador*, pp. 257–62.
87 Kimball (ed.), *Churchill and Roosevelt*, vol. III, pp. 66–8, 99, 106–8, 114; Cadogan, *Diaries*, pp. 622–3; Hoare, *Ambassador*, pp. 262–8; Joan Maria Thomàs, *Roosevelt, Franco and the End of the Second World War* (Houndmills: Palgrave Macmillan, 2011), pp. 67–125.

future Anglo-Spanish anti-Bolshevik alliance to destroy communism. He dismissed his own pro-Axis activities as 'a series of small incidents'. In a startling display of amnesia, he claimed that the only obstacle to better Anglo-Spanish relations in previous years had been British interference in Spain's internal affairs, in particular, the activities of the British Secret Service.[88]

Conclusion

Franco ultimately avoided war not because of immense skill or vision, but rather by a fortuitous combination of circumstances to which he was largely a passive bystander: the skill of British diplomacy; the crude way in which Hitler revealed his contempt for Franco; the disaster of Mussolini's entry into the war, which both made the Führer wary of another impecunious ally, and committed enormous German resources to a rescue operation; and, above all, Spain's economic and military prostration after the Civil War. After 1945, Serrano Suñer wrote, 'Franco and I, and behind us Nationalist Spain, not only placed our bets on a Nazi victory but we desired it with all our hearts'. Posthumously published letters by Franco show that he shared that view.[89] As the Under-Secretary at the Ministry of Foreign Affairs, Juan Peche, told the Anglophile General José Varela, 'our reason for not entering the war was not because Franco resisted German pressure to do so, but rather because Hitler actively did not want us to or because it was not even part of his plans'.[90]

It was hardly surprising, as the German ambassador Eberhard von Stohrer remarked to General Krappe in October 1941, that the Führer should conclude that Spain was more useful to Germany under the mask of neutrality, as its only outlet from the British blockade. This was confirmed by Hitler himself on 10 February 1945, when he told his secretary, Martin Bormann:

> Spain was burning to follow Italy's example and become a member of the Victor's Club. Franco, of course, had very exaggerated ideas on the value of Spanish intervention. Nevertheless, I believe that, in spite of the systematic sabotage perpetrated by his Jesuit brother-in-law, he would have agreed to make common cause with us on quite reasonable conditions – the promise of a little bit of France as a sop to his pride and a substantial slice of Algeria as

88 Hoare, *Ambassador*, pp. 283, 300–4.
89 Serrano Suñer, *Memorias*, pp. 331–48.
90 Tusell, *Franco, España y la II guerra mundial*, p. 200.

a real, material asset. But as Spain had really nothing tangible to contribute, I came to the conclusion that her direct intervention was not desirable. It is true that it would have allowed us to occupy Gibraltar. On the other hand, Spain's entry into the war would certainly have added many kilometres to the Atlantic coast-line which we would have had to defend – from San Sebastian to Cadiz... By ensuring that the Iberian peninsula remained neutral, Spain has already rendered us the one service in this conflict which she had in her power to render. Having Italy on our backs is a sufficient burden in all conscience; and whatever may be the qualities of the Spanish soldier, Spain herself, in her state of poverty and unpreparedness, would have been a heavy liability rather than an asset.[91]

91 François Genoud (ed.), *The Testament of Adolf Hitler: The Hitler-Bormann Documents, February–April 1945* (London: Cassell, 1961), trans. H. Stevens, introd. H. R. Trevor-Roper, pp. 47–9.

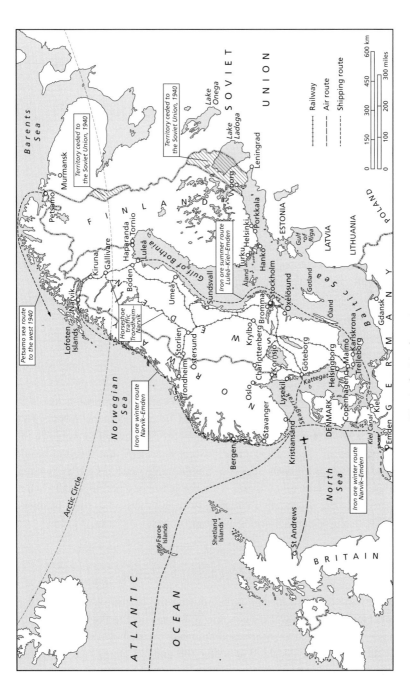

14.1 War in the Nordic region, 1939–40

14

Sweden

Negotiated neutrality

KLAS ÅMARK

When the Second World War started on 1 September 1939, neutrality was the obvious choice for Sweden. Sweden had not been to war since 1814. During the First World War, Sweden was neutral. Historical experience made no other choice than neutrality possible. It was not only the choice of the government, but also the choice of the Swedish electorate. Sweden's government was a coalition comprised of the Social Democratic Party and the smaller Farmers' Party. The Chairperson of the Social Democrats, Per Albin Hansson, was Prime Minister. Hansson reassured the public that Sweden could defend itself if attacked, but in fact, Sweden was not ready for war. Many conscripts lacked basic military training and the army was not ready for winter operations.

The government realized that it could not rely on the armed forces to enforce Sweden's neutrality; instead, it had to negotiate the terms of its neutrality with the belligerents. For example, Stockholm had to convince the representatives of the warring great powers to accept that Sweden would continue to trade with both sides. For a vulnerable neutral such as Sweden, negotiating trade and other issues with the great powers, especially when Germany was the ascendant military power, was always a risky business, fraught with unpleasant choices and compromises.

The Swedish political landscape

To understand Swedish foreign policy during the Second World War, it is first necessary to survey the domestic political and ideological landscape of Sweden. The Social Democrats dominated Swedish politics during the 1930s and the Second World War. After the general election in 1932, they became the dominant governing party, in part, because of the general perception that their economic policies had been a success in coping with the onset of the Great Depression. In the parliamentary election of 1940, the Social Democrats achieved their best result, with 53.8 per cent of the votes.

Of the three non-socialist parties in the Swedish parliament, the conservative Right Party was the largest. Some party members were pro-German. The Right Party also had a positive attitude toward Finland, which had been part of the Swedish realm from the twelfth century to 1809, when Sweden lost Finland to Russia. Many conservatives were, by tradition, hostile to Russia, an attitude that was strengthened when Russia became the Soviet Union. The Farmers' Party was, in some respects, a conservative party, but with very pronounced xenophobic ideas, an everyday racism and sometimes open anti-Semitism. The Farmers' Party was, in fact, a 'blood-and-soil' movement, in some respects similar to that of the German National Socialist Party. Although the Farmers' Party and the Social Democrats appeared to be ideologically incompatible, the former was willing to cut deals with the latter to advance the economic and social interest of farmers, and so the two parties formed a governing coalition in 1936. The third bourgeois party, the liberal People's Party, prioritized a cautious foreign policy, with peace as the most important goal. Some People's Party members and newspapers were quite conservative, while others were dedicated anti-Nazis and argued for a liberal refugee policy and free press, and criticized the concessions made to Germany during the first years of the war.

Parties of the radical right and left in Sweden were unstable. In 1929, the Communist Party divided into two. Both splinter parties were weakened as a result of the split and they both lost votes in the parliamentary election in 1936. Sweden's Communist Party was backed by the Soviet Union and influenced by representatives from the Comintern. The Communist Party was strongly criticized for supporting the Molotov–Ribbentrop non-aggression agreement of August 1939 and the Soviet Union in the Winter War against Finland. After the German attack on the Soviet Union in June 1941, the communists again became anti-Nazis and their popularity with the electorate grew. There were four parties in Sweden with fascist or Nazi ideologies. Two of them were founded in the 1920s. The Swedish Nazis became more active when Hitler's National Socialists took power in Berlin in 1933. Although they organized large rallies and attracted a lot of public attention, these parties failed to garner support in elections. In the general election of 1936, the Nazi parties failed to get as many votes as they had members. Together, the Nazi parties attracted about 1 per cent of the votes, a result that led all but one of them to dissolve, while the remaining party tried to distance itself from the German National Socialists and stressed its Swedish character.

The failure of Nazi groups to gain much ground in Sweden is somewhat paradoxical. After all, during the 1920s and 1930s, racism, anti-Semitism and xenophobia were widespread in Sweden. Leading politicians spoke about the value of preserving the Swedish people as a racially pure national collective, and warned about the alleged dangers of foreigners and an influx of refugees. Attitudes to Jews fleeing Nazi oppression, among both politicians and civil servants, were coloured by the idea that Jews belonged to an alien people or race. Anti-Semitic stereotypes were expressed publicly. However, in Swedish public life, there were limits. When one member of the Farmers' Party confessed in a debate in parliament that he was an anti-Semite, he was criticized for overstepping the boundary of what was politically and socially acceptable. To express worries about the so-called 'Jewish question' and to argue that Jews in Germany (or in Sweden) had too much power was one thing, but to declare that you were an outright anti-Semite was quite another. When anti-Semitism in Germany expressed itself in open violence against Jews, even Swedish politicians with anti-Semitic sympathies disassociated themselves from such behaviour.[1]

After the outbreak of the Winter War between Finland and the Soviet Union in November 1939, the Social Democrats, the Farmers' Party, the Right Party and the People's Party formed a Grand Coalition, which remained in office until the summer of 1945. A coalition of national unity not only guaranteed all four political parties some influence on government policy, but also meant that they shared the responsibility for unpopular decisions. The Social Democratic Party retained the most influential Cabinet posts, such as Minister of Finances and Minister of Social Affairs, including responsibility for the police and the newly established security police. The leaders of the other parties were appointed to the less important posts, such as Minister of Education and Minister of Communications and Transport. To hold the contentious post of Minister of Foreign Affairs at a time of national emergency, the government

---

1 Klas Åmark, *Att bo granne med ondskan. Sveriges förhållande till nazismen, Nazityskland och Förintelsen* (Stockholm: Bonniers, 2011); Klas Åmark, *Hundra år av välfärdspolitik. Välfärdsstatens framväxt i Norge och Sverige* (Umeå: Borea, 2005), ch. 3.

appointed the non-party-political senior diplomat Christian Günther, a civil servant known for his prudence and pragmatism.[2]

Swedish foreign trade and trade policy, 1938–1945

From the late nineteenth century, Swedish industrialization was built on cheap hydroelectric power, abundant supplies of high-quality iron ore for export and domestic use by Sweden's prosperous engineering industry, and vast forests that were used to produce timber, pulp and paper. However, Sweden almost completely lacked two key industrial raw materials, coal and oil. Export-oriented Swedish industry became more and more dependent on foreign trade when the world began to recover from the Great Depression in the late 1930s. In 1938, Germany, Britain and the United States accounted for almost 60 per cent of Swedish foreign trade. Sweden bought large quantities of coal and coke from Poland, traded with Latin America and developed trade links with South Asia. Once war in Europe broke out, Sweden entered into trade talks with the two main belligerents in Northern Europe, Britain and Germany. Leading Swedish politicians believed that a neutral country such as Sweden had the right to trade according to its needs. According to them, Sweden had the right to export timber to Britain and iron ore to Germany, even though these two great powers were at war with each other. Not surprisingly, British negotiators, concerned about tightening the blockade of Germany, took issue with this point of view, while the Germans, concerned about guaranteeing the Third Reich's important source of iron ore, did not object to Sweden's trade in timber with Britain, so long as the iron ore continued to arrive in Germany.

Sweden needed to import coal and coke and other goods from Germany and German-occupied Poland. To guarantee the import of coal, the Swedes were prepared to sell as much iron ore and other important goods to Germany as was needed to pay for their imports. In complex talks with the belligerent powers, the Swedish government concluded advantageous agreements with both Germany and Britain. The latter country agreed that Sweden could export about 10 million tons of iron ore a year to Germany. This export was crucial for Germany's war economy until the summer of 1940, when France fell and Germany obtained control of the iron ore mines in Alsace-Lorraine. Even so, Swedish iron ore remained especially valuable

2 Åmark, *Att bo*, pp. 82–7.

because it contained 60 per cent iron, as compared to only 30 per cent in French ore (though Swedish ore contained a high proportion of phosphor, making it less suitable for high-quality metal).[3]

On 9 April 1940, Germany launched a surprise invasion of Denmark and Norway. Denmark capitulated immediately, while the fighting in Norway continued for about two months. For Hitler and the German high command, one key reason for invading Norway was to protect the import of Swedish iron ore, partly exported via Narvik in northern Norway, a harbour free from ice in winter time; it was also to prevent the British from cutting off the iron trade by occupying northern Norway and then the Sweden iron-ore mines. For Sweden, the German assault meant a dramatic change in the conditions for Swedish foreign trade. The Germans laid mines in the Skagerrak, the sea between Norway and Denmark, to keep the British navy out of the Baltic Sea. As a consequence, Swedish trade with countries outside of Continental Europe became impossible without German permission, while the British blockade of Germany tightened. Thus Sweden needed permission from both countries to import and export goods by sea.

After complex negotiations with Berlin, safe conduct for a limited Swedish trade was established in 1941. Sweden could import small quantities of goods, such as oil, petrol, rubber and grain from the United States and South America. Swedish trade with Britain had ceased in June 1940, after the fall of France, while trade with countries occupied by Germany, such as the Netherlands and France, was restricted. The Swedish wood industry was forced to sell its products to Germany instead of Britain and the United States. Germany used the new strategic situation to raise the prices on its exports, especially on coal. After the Japanese attack on Pearl Harbor and the German declaration of war on the United States in December 1941, Germany stopped all Swedish trade with the United States. By 1943, Swedish foreign trade was reduced from its 1938 volume by 50 to 60 per cent. About half of this trade was directly with Germany. In close cooperation with business leaders, the Swedish state imposed controls to ensure a steady supply of raw materials to industry and food for the population.

3 Klaus Wittman, *Schwedens Wirtschaftsbeziehungen zum Dritten Reich 1933–1945* (Munich: Oldenbourg Verlag, 1978); Martin Fritz, 'Ekonomisk neutralitet under andra världskriget. En fråga om praktisk politik', in Stig Ekman (ed.), *Stormaktstryck och småstatspolitik: aspekter på svensk politik under andra världskriget* (Stockholm: LiberFörlag, 1986); Martin Fritz, Birgit Karlsson, Ingela Karlsson and Sven Nordlund, *En (o)moralisk handel: Sveriges ekonomiska relationer med Nazityskland* (Stockholm: Forum för levande historia, 2006).

Although, militarily, Germany was far superior to Sweden, the economic relationship was more balanced. Swedish iron ore was vital to Germany's war economy. In 1939, 41 per cent of the total German consumption of iron was imported from Sweden; in 1943, the figure was 27 per cent.

As long as the export of iron ore continued, Germany had no reason to attack Sweden and the Swedes had some leverage over Berlin. Sweden could negotiate advantageous trade terms from Germany. While the civilian population in Germany had to freeze during the cold winters of 1941 and 1942 because of lack of coal, the Swedes managed rather well, thanks to German coal and coke. The Swedish steel industry, which required huge quantities of German coal to make steel, continued production throughout the war.[4] In their vision of a *Grossraumwirtschaft* (greater economic space – a plan for German dominance of the European economy), German economic planners wanted countries such as Sweden to be reduced to raw material suppliers for German industry, but the Swedes resisted German efforts to depart from a market relationship for their trade.[5] However, the economic relationship between Sweden and Germany was not just about trade.

The Nazi persecution of the Jews was extended to Sweden through German influence on Swedish business. When it became necessary for German state employees to prove that they were pure Aryans, those with Swedish relatives had to prove that they too were not Jews. Swedish law could not prevent the demands of German officials for information about the ethnic or religious identity of either German or Swedish citizens. The Germans used that information to demand exclusion of Jews from Swedish companies trading with the Third Reich, to discharge Jews from Swedish businesses owned by Germans, and to prevent German citizens from marrying Jews in Sweden.[6]

4 Fritz, 'Ekonomisk'; Peter Hedberg, *Handeln och betalningarna mellan Sverige och Tyskland 1934–1945. Den svensk-tyska clearingepoken ur ett kontraktsekonomiskt perspektiv* (Uppsala: Acta Universitatis Upsaliensis, 2003). For further information about Swedish foreign trade, see Statistisk årsbok 1946, table 114; Pierre Aycoberry, *The Social History of the Third Reich, 1933–1945* (New York: The New Press, 1999), p. 218.
5 Birgit Karlsson, *Egenintresse eller samhällsintresse: Nazityskland och svensk skogsindustri 1933–1945* (Lund: Sekel, 2007).
6 Sven Nordlund, *Affärer som vanligt. Ariseringen i Sverige 1933–1945* (Lund: Sekel, 2009); Anders Jarlert, *Judisk 'ras' som äktenskapshinder i Sverige. Effekten av Nürnberglagarna i Svenska kyrkans statliga funktion som lysningsförrättare 1935–1945* (Lund: Sekel, 2006).

Swedish neutrality after Norway's occupation

The German attack on Norway of 9 April 1940 surprised Stockholm. With great daring, German forces swept into Norway's big coastal towns and advanced up the Oslo fjord toward the capital. The Norwegian royal family and the government fled Oslo and made their way to London, where a Norwegian government-in-exile was established.[7] The Swedish government had made no plans or preparations for a German occupation of Norway, which left Sweden vulnerable to a German blockade. It was equally unprepared for the sort of pressures that Germany would now place on Sweden's neutrality.

Not long after the fighting in Norway ceased, Germany demanded that Sweden allow German troops on leave from Norway to travel by railway back and forth through Sweden to Germany. Berlin also wanted to transport munitions and other materials through Sweden to build the Norwegian part of their Fortress Europe. On 8 July 1940, Stockholm and Berlin concluded an agreement about what was to be called 'leave traffic', which permitted the Germans to send one train a day in each direction, with 500 unarmed soldiers. Publicly, the Swedish government maintained that leave traffic was compatible with Sweden's neutrality, but Prime Minister Hansson confided to his diary the harsh truth: 'So our dear and strict neutrality was broken because of the realization that it would be unreasonable in the present situation to risk war'.[8]

Hitler feared that Britain would try to interrupt Germany's supply of Swedish iron ore by attacking through Norway. As a result, the German occupation army in Norway grew to over 400,000 men. This large occupation force increased Berlin's demand for 'leave traffic' through Sweden. In the autumn of 1940, the Germans were granted the right to send two trains a day in each direction, carrying 2,000 through Sweden. In 1942, German soldiers made 850,000 trips through Sweden. Since there were no railway connections in Norway between Trondheim and Narvik, Germany was also allowed to transport soldiers and munitions from Trondheim in Norway on Swedish railways, up to Narvik in northern Norway. This land route was safer than sea transport along the Norwegian coast, which could be attacked by the British navy. Sweden's granting to Germany of access to its territory

7 Even Lange, *Kampen om felles mål*, vol. XI: *Aschehougs Norges historie* (12 vols., Oslo: Aschehoug, 1997), pp. 62–75.
8 Åmark, *Att bo*, ch. 3; Ulf Larsson (ed.), *Per Albin Hansson's anteckningar och dagböcker, 1929–1946* (Stockholm: Kungl Samfundet, 2011), 18 June 1940.

and railways, which facilitated the German occupation of Norway, underscores the extremely difficult compromises Stockholm had to make in negotiating its neutrality in the period of Germany's ascendancy in Europe.[9]

The midsummer crisis, 1941

While the German attack on Denmark and Norway came as a surprise for the Swedes, the Swedish Defence Staff was extremely well informed about the German military preparations for an attack on the Soviet Union on 22 June 1941. After the German occupation of Norway, the Germans had demanded the right to use Swedish telegraph lines from Oslo through Sweden to Berlin. To protect this secret traffic from interception by British or Swedish intelligence, the Germans employed an electro-mechanical cipher and teleprinter machine (*Geheimschreiber*) to encrypt and decode it. The brilliant young Swedish mathematician, Arne Beurling, single-handedly broke the German code and designed a decipher machine to read it. Until the summer of 1942, the Swedes deciphered most of the telegrams sent between Oslo and Berlin, which included daily communications from the German high command of the armed forces (*Oberkommando der Wehrmacht* – OKW). Swedish intelligence thus followed Germany's preparations for Operation BARBAROSSA as they unfolded, and they knew the hour for the assault two days in advance. Swedish officials, including Prime Minister Hansson and his Foreign Minister Günther, also knew that Germany had made no preparations to attack Sweden, but that Berlin intended to make fresh demands on Sweden's neutrality.[10]

The political crisis over the German demands, generally called the midsummer crisis (*Midsommarkrisen* in Swedish), is the most well-known and debated political crisis in Sweden during the Second World War. The most important demand the Germans made was to transport the fully equipped 163rd Infantry Division, stationed in Norway, through Sweden to southeast Finland, in order to fight the Red Army. Thanks to excellent intelligence, Prime Minister Per Albin Hansson and his Foreign Minister Christian Günther had ample forewarning of the impending crisis. Hansson expected disagreement in the coalition government about how to reply to Berlin. Sweden's politicians agreed that such an action would definitely be a breach

9 Åmark, *Att bo*, chs. 3, 4.
10 Bengt Beckman, *Codebreakers: Arne Beurling and the Swedish Crypto Program During World War II* (Providence, RI: American Mathematical Society, 2002).

of Sweden's neutrality. In a crisis such as this, the convention was that the government would consult the political parties in the parliament to share the responsibility for unpopular decisions. The three non-socialist parties could be expected to accept the German demands, but for quite different reasons. The Right Party wanted to support Finland, while the Farmers' Party and the People's Party prioritized peace. On the other hand, several of Hansson's Social Democratic colleagues in the government wanted to reject Berlin's demands. In a private conversation with King Gustav V about the situation, Hansson found the political leverage he needed to compel his Social Democratic colleagues into acquiescing to the German demands. According to Hansson, the King, who still retained formal power as head of state and head of government, said that he would not be party to a refusal of German demands. The Prime Minister interpreted this to mean that he would abdicate and thus provoke a constitutional crisis if the government sent a refusal to Berlin. Even though the leaders of the other parties did not take this threat seriously, Hansson exploited the King's alleged threat to abdicate as an argument in inter-party discussions. When Gustav V learned about what Hansson had done, he was somewhat surprised about how his words had been interpreted by Hansson, but he was not displeased.

Nonetheless, in Prime Minister Hansson's Social Democratic Party, the debate about Germany's new demands continued for some time. Powerful government ministers, such as Minister of Finance Ernst Wigforss and Minister of Social Affairs Gustav Möller, wanted to reject Berlin's demands. After hours of debate, the party made two decisions. First, it voted (159 for and 2 against) to refuse Berlin's demands. Then the party voted (72 votes for, 59 against and 30 abstentions) to agree to Germany's demands if the non-socialist parties continued to demand a positive answer to Germany. When the government met again, Hansson made no effort to convince the other parties to change their positions, and thus the government decided to accept Germany's demands. Not surprisingly, many of Hansson's Social Democratic Party colleagues were upset at what they regarded as the Prime Minister's political double-dealing.

The debates during the midsummer crisis were not just about Germany's demands, but also about Sweden's identity and role as a neutral. Many Social Democrats mistrusted Minister of Foreign Affairs Günther. They wanted to limit the scope for future concessions to Berlin and declared that the transit of the 163rd Division should be looked upon as a one-time concession. Günther, at this time strongly supported by the Right Party leader Gösta Bagge and Sweden's ambassador in Berlin, Arvid Richert, argued that

Sweden should not only make concessions, but should actively cooperate with Berlin, on the grounds that this would place Sweden in a strong position in the Baltic region after Germany won the war. If Sweden was forced into the war, Bagge wanted to join Finland in the war against the Soviet Union. On the other hand, many Social Democrats and anti-Nazi liberals believed that if Sweden was forced into the war, it should join its Nordic brothers, Denmark and Norway, in the fight against the Nazi regime.[11]

The cancellation of 'leave traffic', 1943

The entry of the United States in December 1941, after the Japanese attack on Pearl Harbor, and the Allied victories in the battles at El Alamein and Stalingrad in 1942–43, marked the downward turn in the fortunes of the Axis powers. These dramatic events, however, had no immediate and direct impact on Sweden's relations with Germany. Swedish exports to Germany continued, as did leave traffic. What began to shift Swedish opinion and Sweden's neutrality policy was events in Norway.

The German Reichskommissar Joseph Terboven governed occupied Norway. Vidkun Quisling's Nazi party National Unity was the only legal political party in Norway, and its senior members served as Cabinet ministers in the occupation regime. During 1942, the German occupation policy was tightened. Many opponents of the occupation were arrested, some were executed, while others were sent to Sachsenhausen concentration camp in Germany. Many Norwegian priests refused to follow the directives of the occupation regime and preferred to be dismissed. Also, many schoolteachers refused to join the Nazi-controlled teachers' union and endured arrest and forced labour rather than indoctrinating their pupils in Nazi ideology.[12]

The enforcement in Norway of a more brutal German occupation policy was observed carefully in Sweden. Norwegian refugees came to Sweden in growing numbers, with harrowing stories. From the end of 1942, knowledge of the situation in Norway became linked to the political debate in Sweden about German leave traffic. Liberal newspapers and some trade unions protested against leave traffic because it supported the Germans in Norway. Prime Minister Hansson defended the government policy of allowing the

11 Åmark, *Att bo*, ch. 4; John Gilmour, *Sweden, the Swastika and Stalin: The Swedish Experience in the Second World War* (Edinburgh University Press, 2010), pp. 67–71; Sven Radowitz, *Schweden und das 'Dritte Reich' 1939–1945* (Hamburg: Reinhold Krämer Verlag, 2005), ch. 5.
12 Lange, *Kampen*, pp. 75–97.

Germans to use Swedish territory to transport their troops for periods of leave. What concerned him, in the spring of 1943, was not so much the threat of German military action against Sweden if leave traffic was cancelled, but German trade sanctions, including the cancellation of an agreed shipment of 90,000 tons of oil, and the resulting unemployment. Confronting Germany would also require the mobilization of the army, which would be costly and would interfere with the collection of the harvest. Once the oil had safely arrived and the grain was collected, then the government was prepared to cancel the agreement.[13]

On 16 June 1943, the government decided, in principle, to cancel leave traffic, but it was not until 29 July that Foreign Minister Christian Günther informed the Germans that the transit traffic with soldiers and war equipment had to be stopped. By then, German soldiers had made more than 2 million journeys through Sweden. In 1942, leave traffic corresponded to 6 per cent of all railway passenger traffic in Sweden. The Germans had paid approximately 85 million Swedish crowns for this traffic, which today is equal to around 200 million euros.[14] After the cancellation of leave traffic, Germany had difficulties with transportation to and from the northern parts of Norway because of attacks by the British navy. Gradually, the Swedish government also cancelled a number of other agreements with Berlin, about transit for civilians and wounded German soldiers, and courier aeroplanes. Finally, on 8 May 1944, all of the special rights that Berlin had obtained from Sweden came to an end.

Sweden, Finland and the Soviet Union

The Non-Aggression Pact signed by Molotov and Ribbentrop in August 1939 was the starting point not only for the German attack on Poland, but also for a Soviet offensive against its western neighbours. The Soviet Union attacked Poland and occupied the eastern parts of that country. The Baltic states were forced to sign cooperation agreements with the Soviet Union, which, in the spring of 1940, were followed by the Red Army's full occupation of these countries, and their incorporation into the Soviet Union. In October 1939, the Soviet Union demanded concessions from Finland, especially territory

---

13 Rune Karlsson, *Så stoppades tysktågen. Den tyska transiteringstrafiken i svensk politik 1942–1943* (Stockholm: Allmänna förlaget, 1974); Åmark, *Att bo*, ch. 4.

14 Kent Zetterberg, 'Den tyska transiteringstrafiken genom Sverige 1940–1943', in Ekman (ed.), *Stormaktstryck*, pp. 97–118.

close to Leningrad, the second biggest city in the country. The Finnish government refused to meet Soviet demands, and on 30 November, the Soviet Red Army attacked Finland. Militarily, the Soviet Union was superior to Finland, but the Finnish army was superior when it came to winter warfare. After some months of fighting, the Soviet superiority in numbers produced results, and Finland was forced to conclude a peace agreement, according to which Finland lost more than the Soviets had demanded in autumn 1939.[15]

The Swedish government chose not to declare Sweden neutral in this war, but only a non-belligerent. This decision permitted a huge flow of Swedish aid to Finland. The Swedish state gave Finland large quantities of weapons – 86,000 rifles and 45 million bullets, 415 heavy infantry weapons with 110,000 cartridges, 216 artillery pieces with 170,000 shells and 32 fighter planes. The government also allowed a corps of 7,000 volunteers to be organized to fight in Finland. During 1940, Finland received 310 million Swedish crowns, which, at the time, corresponded to 70 per cent of the Finnish state budget for that year.[16]

During the autumn of 1940, the inner Cabinet in Helsinki, headed by the Supreme Commander Gustav Mannerheim, decided to cooperate with Germany against Russia. When Germany attacked the Soviet Union in June 1941, the Finnish army was fully mobilized and there were about 200,000 German soldiers stationed in the northern parts of Finland. The Finnish government waited three days after the German attack before declaring war on the Soviet Union. The Finns labelled this new war the 'Continuation War' – that is, a continuation of the defensive Winter War – in order to provide legitimacy for their offensive action.[17]

Sweden's relationship with Finland during the Continuation War differed from that of the Winter War. Many Swedes thought that Finland, this time, had acted rashly in aligning itself with Germany. In the coalition government, the Right Party leader Gösta Bagge supported helping Finland, while the People's Party leader Gustav Andersson, and some of the Social Democratic ministers, opposed such suggestions. In any case, 1,500 Swedes volunteered to fight for Finland, many of whom had far-right sympathies.

15 Olli Vehviläinen, *Finland in the Second World War: Between Germany and Russia* (Gordons-ville, Va.: Palgrave Macmillan, 2002), chs. 3, 4.
16 Alf W. Johansson, *Per Albin och kriget. Samlingsregeringen och utrikespolitiken under andra världskriget* (Stockholm: Norstedts Akademiska, 2007); Wilhelm Carlgren, *Swedish Foreign Policy During the Second World War* (London: Benn, 1977), ch. 2; Gilmour, *Sweden*, pp. 36–41.
17 Vehviläinen, *Finland*, chs. 5, 6; Henrik Meinander, *Finlands historia* (4 vols., Esbo: Schildt, 1999), vol. IV, pp. 227–67.

Crucially, the Swedish state supplied Finland with 317 million Swedish crowns' worth of food and other commodities of importance to Finland's war effort, during the period 1941 to 1944. Sweden also provided temporary care for 70,000 refugee children from Finland.[18]

Sweden and the Western powers

Sweden's relationship with Britain, the United States and France was of quite a different character from that with Germany. In February 1940, Britain and France demanded permission to send troops via Narvik through northern Sweden to assist Finland in the Winter War, a demand that Stockholm refused. During 1943 and 1944, Sweden's relations with the Western powers became tense. In trade negotiations, the British and Americans demanded that Sweden stop the German army's leave traffic through Sweden and reduce its exports to Germany and the Axis powers, including Finland. As a result, the German-Swedish trade agreement, concluded in January 1944, stated that Sweden would reduce its iron ore export to Germany by 30 per cent.

From the spring of 1943, the United States and Britain demanded more determinably that Sweden cut other aspects of its trade with Germany. The Americans complained that Swedish ball bearings were used in the production of German tanks and also in fighter aircraft that attacked US bombers over Germany. The Swedish Ball Bearing Company's (*Svenska Kullagerfabriken*) subsidiaries in Germany were responsible for a large portion of German production, while Swedish exports of ball bearings represented about 10 per cent of Germany's total production. US representatives argued, especially during the months before the invasion in Normandy, that Swedish ball bearings were used in German fighters and therefore contributed to the death of American soldiers. They tried to force the Swedish Ball Bearing Company to stop its export, and even threatened to bomb the Swedish factory in Gothenburg 'by mistake'.[19] Sweden accepted limits on its export to Germany in future, but did not want to break the existing agreements, for fear of retaliation: 'A small state's most valuable protection in an evil world is the sanctity of agreements and such a country cannot afford to treat existing agreements as "scraps of paper"', declared the State Secretary for Foreign Affairs, Erik Boheman.[20]

18 Johansson, *Per Albin*; Carlgren, *Swedish Foreign Policy*, ch. 6; Gilmour, *Sweden*, ch. 5.
19 Wittman, *Schwedens*, pp. 368–77.
20 Carlgren, *Swedish Foreign Policy*, pp. 133–68; Fritz, 'Ekonomisk'; Alf W. Johansson, 'Sverige och västmakterna 1939–1945', in Ekman (ed.), *Stormaktstryck*, pp. 117–69.

In the middle of 1943, with Germany in retreat on many fronts, the coalition government and, especially, Prime Minister Hansson wanted to return to a policy of strict neutrality. At the same time, more anti-Nazi and pro-Allied liberal and Social Democratic politicians wanted Sweden to act more favourably toward the Allies. For Prime Minister Hansson, however, such a policy would have demonstrated that Swedish foreign policy was purely opportunistic.

At the same time, many Swedes realized that Sweden's international goodwill was tarnished because of the concessions it had made to Germany during the dark days of the war. During the last year of the war and afterwards, Sweden therefore had good political and moral reasons to engage in international humanitarian relief. Close cooperation between the state, interest organizations (e.g. producers' organizations, employers' associations, trade unions) and voluntary organizations was established to administrate this relief. Sweden contributed large sums for humanitarian activities and reconstruction work, especially in Norway and Finland – altogether, 1.5 billion crowns during the period 1939–50. For example, during the years 1942–44, Swedish ships were used to transport about 715,000 tons of grain and other foodstuffs from the USA, Canada and Argentina to the starving Greek population, supporting about 1.8 million Greeks. During the last months of war in the Netherlands, starvation threatened, and Sweden delivered 15,000 tons of food. After the war, Swedish organizations were serving daily portions of soup to 120,000 children in Germany, 70,000 children in Austria and 25,000 in Romania and Hungary. Sweden also financed the building of children's hospitals in Norway and Poland.[21]

Sweden's press policy

A few days after the Nazi seizure of power in Germany in January 1933, the chief editor of the liberal paper *Göteborgs Handels-och Sjöfarts-Tidning*, Torgny Segerstedt, wrote: 'To force the politics of the whole world to engage itself with such a character, that is unforgiveable. Herr Hitler is an insult.' The newly appointed German Minister without Portfolio, Hermann Göring, protested forcefully in a telegram to the paper. At first, the editorial staff

---

21 Ann Nehlin, *Exporting Visions and Saving Children: The Swedish Save the Children Fund* (Linköping University, 2009); *Sveriges internationella hjälpverksamhet 1939–1950: en redogörelse från Svenska kommittén för internationell hjälpverksamhet och Svenska Europahjälpen* (Stockholm: utg., 1957).

thought it was a joke, but when the telegram proved to be genuine, it was framed and proudly displayed. Göring was known to be a friend of Sweden, for he had been married to Karin von Kantzow, a member of the Swedish nobility, who had died in 1930. In the 1920s, Göring had spent time in Sweden, and he continued to follow Swedish developments.

In August 1940, Göring demanded to see a Swedish government representative. The banker Jakob Wallenberg was sent for a five-hour meeting. Göring declared that the enemies of Sweden in the Nazi regime were gaining ground because of the attitudes of the Swedish press. Leading Germans did not care about the left-wing papers, but they were troubled by the negative attitudes in the more influential papers. He warned that it was hazardous for Sweden if the government did not do anything substantial to achieve a major change. The German Embassy in Stockholm followed about ninety Swedish papers and journals and, until the spring of 1943, often complained about them to the Swedish Foreign Ministry. When a new German ambassador was appointed, these kinds of complaints stopped.[22] So what could the government do, and what did it do?

Even during the war, there was no formal censorship of the press in Sweden, controlling the papers before they were printed. During the 1930s, Prime Minister Hansson and the Social Democratic Minister of Foreign Affairs Rickard Sandler urged the press to be cautious when commenting on foreign powers, especially in reference to Germany. However, the strongly anti-Nazi papers cared little about what the ministers said. During the 1930s, the only legal measure the government could use against printed publications was prosecution and trial before a nine-person jury. If the paper lost, the legally responsible publisher was sentenced to a couple of months in jail. During the war, thirty-eight prosecutions against the press were made, and of these, the papers were absolved in half the cases. Often, the publishers of communist papers were convicted. In a number of these cases, the papers were accused of having criticized Finland during the Winter War. Nazi newspapers were also prosecuted, but they were convicted less often than the communist ones.[23]

In the autumn of 1939, the Minister of Justice, K. G. Westman, introduced a new state measure against the press and printed books. According to the

22 Åmark, *Att bo*, ch. 6; Bagge's diary, 28 August 1940, in Kersti Blidberg and Alf W. Johansson (eds.), *Gösta Bagges minnesanteckningar 1939–1941*, Kungl. Samfundet (Stockholm: Elanders, 2013), pp. 135–7; Daniel B. Roth, *Hitler's Brückenkopf in Schweden. Die deutsche Gesandtschaft in Stockholm 1933–1945* (Berlin: LIT Verlag, 2009). ch. I 3 B.
23 Åmark, *Att bo*, ch. 6.

Freedom of the Press Act of 1810, the state could confiscate an issue of a
newspaper or a book that had caused friction with foreign states. The statute
had long fallen into disuse, but from late 1939 until the autumn of 1943,
Westman and Foreign Minister Günther invoked it 315 times. However,
this measure was not very efficient, since the confiscation could only be
made after the paper was published, and also usually distributed to its
subscribers.[24]

While the Germans usually complained about the influential mainstream
Swedish papers, the government most often confiscated left-wing papers,
such as the communist daily *Ny Dag* and the syndicalist paper *Arbetaren*
(a whistle-blower during the war, which had disclosed Nazi influence within
the Swedish police, for example), as well as a number of very small and
seldom-read papers. 'There grows an edge of weed around the loyal Swedish
press', Günther declared, and it was this weed he and Westman wanted to
get rid of.[25]

A major reason for confiscations was that the papers or books had
published what at the time was called 'atrocity propaganda'.[26] About one-
third of the confiscations were said to be measures against 'atrocity propaganda', but were, in fact, often examples of information about Nazi terror
and persecution of its political opponents and the Jews. On 13 November
1942, the government decided to confiscate a book called *Polens martyrium*
(*Poland's Martyrdom*), which contained information from the Polish government-in-exile in London on the situation in occupied Poland. In Sweden, the
book was published by the publishing company Trots allt!. The motive for
the confiscation was 'disagreement with a foreign state'. The publishing
company had already published a booklet with information from the same
source, which the Germans had complained about, and which had been
confiscated, but no German complaints about the book *Poland's Martyrdom*
have been found. In fact, this publication contained matter-of-fact information about the German occupation regime in Poland. The information in the
book had been smuggled out of Poland by a small group of Swedish
businessmen, especially the engineer Sven Norrman, who had stayed in
Warsaw after the German occupation. Risking their lives, they brought
information about the German persecution of the Poles and Polish Jews to

24 Ibid.; Gilmour, *Sweden*, ch. 8.
25 Åmark, *Att bo*, ch. 6.
26 At the time, the word *grymhetspropaganda* was used, a rather odd translation of the
    German concept from the First World War, *Greuelpropaganda*.

Sweden and handed it over to representatives of the Polish resistance in Stockholm, which then sent it to London, where it was first published.[27]

In March 1940, the parliament decided on a new law, according to which the government could ban the transportation of newspapers on public trains and buses for six months at a time. The transport ban was first used against the communist press, but also for a shorter period against the strongly anti-Nazi journal *Trots allt!* and once against a far-right paper. The Communist Party used a number of methods to avoid the consequences of the transport ban, but there is no doubt that the lack of distribution hit their newspaper revenue hard.

In 1940, the independent authority, the State Board of Information, was established. The board issued secret instructions to the press, the so-called 'grey slips', about what they were recommended to publish and not to publish. Many of the slips were uncontroversial instructions – for example, that the papers should not publish information about the ice in the Baltic Sea, about the Swedish defence or about which roads fugitives from Norway had used. But the instructions concerning the publication of negative information about the states involved in the war were controversial, and also show how the concept 'atrocity propaganda' was understood by Swedish authorities:

> [E]ach belligerent state considers all statements about acts of violence and abuse against civilians as very serious allegations, not to say as a serious insult against the military power in question. Therefore, it is of the utmost importance that such statements are not publicized, when it is natural that statements of this kind cannot be accepted by the accused party as fully backed by evidence. Especially in the present situation, this represents a serious danger for our country to reproduce statements and information of this kind.[28]

In 1941, the government also established a new special authority, the Press Committee, with representatives from the more influential newspapers, with the task of issuing warnings to papers that printed articles that created problems with foreign states. Altogether, sixty-six warnings were issued, in some cases to bigger and more influential newspapers.

Some measures used by the Swedish government were pre-emptive – for example, when leading ministers tried to convince the editors and journalists to not speak out against Germany, in order not to irritate Hitler and other

27 Åmark, *Att bo*, pp. 223–7.
28 Hans Dahlberg, *I Sverige under 2:a världskriget* (Stockholm: Bonnier 1983), p. 226. This slip was issued on 22 May 1940.

1 Naples during Hitler's state visit, 8 May, 1938.

2 Adolf Hitler makes a speech during a cornerstone-laying ceremony to mark the start of construction of the Volkswagen factory at Fallersleben, June, 1938. In the foreground is the prototype Volkswagen car designed by Professor Dr F. Porsche and handmade by the Mercedes-Benz car factory.

3 Representatives of twenty-six United Nations at Flag Day ceremonies in the White House to reaffirm their pact, Washington DC, July, 1942. Seated, left to right: Dr Francisco Castillo Najera, Ambassador of Mexico; President Roosevelt; Manuel Quezon, President of the Philippine Islands; and Secretary of State Cordell Hull.

4 The famous Soviet sculpture *Worker and Kolkhoz Woman*, by Vera Mukhina, stands on display in Moscow on 4 December 2009, the day of its official re-opening. The giant 24.5m stainless steel sculpture was created for the 1937 World's Fair in Paris and has recently undergone refurbishment.

ВИКТОР ИВАНОВ - 1941г

ЗА РОДИНУ,
ЗА ЧЕСТЬ, ЗА СВОБОДУ!

5 A Second World War Soviet propaganda poster by V. Ivanov, depicting the Red Army and Air Force on the attack, January, 1941. The text reads: 'For The Motherland, For Honour, For Freedom'.

5 REASONS WHY THE ALLIES WILL WIN

1. The Allies have greater man-power.

2. The Allies have greater air-power.

3. The Allies have greater sea-power.

4. The Allies have greater machine-power.

5. The Allies have greater resources.

THIS IS THE SIGN OF VICTORY FOR THE ALLIES

6 Propaganda poster: 5 reasons why the Allies will win. The poster depicts the flags of various Allied nations, including Great Britain, the USSR, the USA, Greece, Czechoslovakia, Norway, France, Belgium, the Netherlands, Luxembourg, Yugoslavia, Poland and China.

7 A German poster from the Second World War depicts German soldiers with swastika flags against the words *Ein Kampf, ein Sieg!* ('One fight, one victory!'), 30 January, 1943. It is the ten-year anniversary of the *Machtergreifung*, the rise to power of the Nazi Party in Weimar Germany.

8 Special correspondents from Japan, Sweden and Switzerland listening to the
explanations of a German soldier on the battlefield of Kharkov-Izium. Kharkov, June, 1942.

9 Buchenwald concentration camp: barrack accommodation for prisoners at Buchenwald.
Photograph taken after liberation by troops of the US Third Army, April, 1945.

10 A German girl is overcome as she walks past the exhumed bodies of some of the 800 slave workers murdered by SS guards near Namering, Germany. They were laid out by arriving Allied troops, so that townspeople could view the work of their Nazi leaders. Photograph by Corporal Edward Belfer, 17 May, 1945.

11 'The Nuremberg Trial, 1946'. Oil painting by Dame Laura Knight RA. On the right are two benches of accused Nazi leaders, with lawyers in front of them and white-helmeted military police behind. In the background the painting metamorphoses into a depiction of rubble and damaged buildings, leading towards a burning horizon.

12 Indicted Japanese war criminals standing to attention in the dock of the Singapore Supreme Court at the beginning of their trial in 1946.

13 Honour reception for British Prime Minister Neville Chamberlain, upon his arrival at Oberwiesenfeld airport on the way to a meeting with Adolf Hitler to discuss German threats to invade Czechoslovakia, 28 September 1938.

14 Japanese Navy Admiral Kichisaburo Nomura sitting with the United States Secretary of State, Cordell Hull, Washington DC, February, 1941.

15 (foreground, left to right) Foreign Minister of Germany, Joachim von Ribbentrop, Soviet leader Joseph Stalin and Foreign Minister Viacheslav Molotov pose for a photo at the signing ceremony in Moscow of the German-Soviet Treaty of Non-Aggression, 23 August, 1939.

16 Ambassador Kintomo Mushanokoji signs the Anti-Comintern pact in Berlin,
25 November, 1936. To his left is Joachim von Ribbentrop, future German Foreign Minister.

17 Saburo Kurusu, Galeazzo Ciano and Adolf Hitler at the signing of the Axis Pact in
Berlin, 27 September, 1940. Joachim von Ribbentrop is speaking.

18 Potsdam (Berlin) Conference of the leading statesmen of the three Allied powers, the
USSR, Great Britain and the United States, 17 July to 2 August 1945, in Cecilienhof and
Babelsberg. The Potsdam Agreement set out the international legal issues for building a
peaceful, democratic German state and the policy of the Allies against Germany.
Shown here from left to right: Winston Churchill, Harry S. Truman, Joseph Stalin.

19 Winston Churchill shares a joke with Marshal Stalin (with the help of Pavlov, Stalin's
interpreter, just visible left) in the conference room at Livadia Palace during the Yalta
Conference, February, 1945.

20 The meeting of the Spanish dictator Francisco Franco and Adolf Hitler in October 1940, at Hendaye near the Spanish-French border.

21 Swedish volunteers with the Finnish Army in the Soviet-Finnish war, 3 January, 1940.

22 Norwegian Waffen-SS volunteers of the Nordland Regiment, August, 1942.

23 German soldiers marching through a town in Holland during the Second World War, May, 1940.

24 A boat carrying people during the escape across the Oresound of 7,000 Danish Jews, who fled to safety in neighbouring Sweden, 1943.

25 A Polish Red Cross nurse captured during the German invasion of September 1939.

26 A group of Frenchwomen, who had been accused of collaborating with the Germans, stripped down to their underwear, some with heads shaved, as part of their public humiliation, December, 1944.

27 Resistance fighters gathering in Boussoulot, Haute-Loire (France), in 1941–42. This was the first paramilitary group to be formed in the region.

28 Photo taken at the instant bullets from a French firing squad hit a Frenchman who had collaborated with the Germans.

29 A little boy in Naples helps support a friend who lost a leg and walks with a crutch,
August, 1944.

30 'Signor Prigile, an Italian partisan in Florence'. British troops were ordered to avoid fighting with the Germans within Florence. Italian partisans occupying the Fortezza da Basso exchanged fire with snipers who remained after the German forces evacuated the city in August, 1944.

31 Group of fairly well-equipped male and female resistance fighters in Greece, October 1944.

32 Josip Broz, aka Marshal Tito (right), at his headquarters, with the Croatian Partisan leader Vlado Bakarić (left), and Edvard Kardelj (centre), Yugoslavia, July, 1944.

33 Members of an international commission and the foreign press invited by the German government, observe the exhumation of a Polish officers at Katyn, in occupied Russia, during the summer of 1943. Three years earlier, after the Soviet annexation of eastern Poland, the NKUD had murdered and buried thousands of men here.

34 Units of the Red Army on the streets of Vilno (Vilna), capital of Lithuania, which was annexed by Poland between 1920 and 1939, occupied by the Soviet army in September 1939, and annexed with the rest of Lithuania to the USSR in 1940.

35 Lieutenant of a Soviet tank unit lectures Vilno inhabitants about the lives of workers in the USSR, October, 1939.

36 Evacuees entering Chongqing, the capital of Nationalist China, in 1941 or 1942. By the end of the war nearly a million and a half people lived here.

37 Shanghai (China), refugees fleeing the city. The men wearing the swastika are possibly members of the Red Swastika Society, an organization that provided relief services to victims of the war, 1937.

38 This young Chinese boy died when he fell from a refugee train during flight from the Japanese invaders in eastern China, c.1942.

39 Corporal H. E. Webster, from Calcutta, working at a typewriter, while serving with the Auxiliary Territorial Service in East Lancashire.

40 Mule handlers of the Royal Indian Army Service Corps parade with drawn swords, 16 November, 1940.

41 Vichy: internment camp for colonial troops, 1940–43.

42 General de Gaulle, the Bey of Tunis and General Mast in the courtyard of the Bey's summer palace, Carthage, Tunisia, January, 1943.

43 Indian soldiers at the mosque in Woking, Surrey, November 1941. Dating from 1889, this was the first mosque to be built in Britain.

44 Delegates attending United Nations Monetary and Financial Conference at Bretton Woods, New Hampshire to plan for post-war reconstruction.

leading German politicians; others were sanctions used after the publication of objectionable views or facts, but formal censorship was never introduced. Ministers such as Hansson, Günther and Westman demanded loyalty from the Swedish press. Hansson stated that there was an important difference between loyal and disloyal criticism. He did not want Swedish citizens to take sides in the war and engage themselves strongly for one or the other side, since strong opinions would make Swedish foreign policy (dependent on successful negotiations with the great powers) more difficult.[29]

The Swedish press and the Holocaust

What did the world outside know about the Nazi persecution of the Jews? In a world at war, the press of the neutral states becomes particularly important in the international communication of news. Within the Swedish press, coverage of the German persecution of Jews before the war differed according to political affiliation and the resources available. Convinced anti-Nazi papers – some of them liberal, others Social Democratic or left-wing – often published articles about German violence and terror. In the openly pro-German and pro-Nazi papers, the coverage was rudimentary and grossly distorted. They did publish articles about German violence toward Jews, but they blamed Jews for provoking the violence.

Many Swedish papers, especially the smaller ones, were quite dependent on the news agency Tidningarnas Telegrambyrå, which was collectively owned by the Swedish press. The agency declared that it wanted to give the Swedish public an all-round picture of the events, and 'in this work we try to avoid everything which can cause irritation with the belligerents or in other ways hurt Swedish interests'. With such ambitions, it is no surprise that the information about the Holocaust became a severe shock for many Swedes.[30]

During the first years of the war, Swedish papers only sporadically covered treatment of the Jews in Germany. In 1942, detailed reports were published about the mass murder of European Jews. In October that year, the Swedish-Jewish historian Hugo Valentin published a major article in the anti-Nazi paper *Göteborgs Handels-och SjöfartsTidning*, entitled 'The War of

---

29 Åmark, *Att bo*, ch. 6; for an example of Hansson's view, see Larsson (ed.), *Albin Hansson*, 4 February 1942.

30 Elisabeth Sandlund, 'Beredskap och repression (1936–1945)', in Gunilla Lundström, Per Rydén and Elisabeth Sandlund (eds.), *Den svenska pressens historia III. Det moderna Sveriges spegel (1897–1945)* (4 vols., Stockholm: Ekerlids förlag, 2001), p. 286.

Extermination Against the Jews'. The real breakthrough in awareness of what was happening, however, came when the Germans started to arrest the Jews in Norway (of which more below). The Swedish press reacted with broad indignation against the arrests, since Norwegian Jews were regarded as almost Nordic brothers, and their fate concerned Swedes much more than the reports about what was happening in Poland, the Baltic states and the Soviet Union.

When, in April 1945, the United States and Britain liberated the concentration camps in Buchenwald and Bergen-Belsen, the Swedish press published shocking reports about the situation in the camps and photographs of starving inmates. These articles offered a concrete and realistic picture of the cruelty, terror and mass murder of a kind that had not been available earlier in the Swedish press. Since Swedish papers could conduct interviews with concentration camp prisoners who arrived with the White Buses (see below) even from Auschwitz, they could provide more realistic information about different German camps than, for example, the British press at the same time.[31]

Swedish refugee policy

In the course of the 1930s, Swedish policy on refugees became more restrictive. In early 1939, a heated debate had taken place about a proposal that Sweden should receive ten German Jewish doctors. In the first half of 1945, in contrast, there were more than 210,000 refugees and evacuees staying in Sweden, without any major debate about the size of the Swedish refugee reception. The change came late. It was not until 1942 and 1943 that the number of refugees in Sweden grew rapidly. The largest groups of refugees arrived between the summer of 1944 and the summer of 1945.[32]

In the 1930s, the refugees who applied for permission to transit or stay in Sweden (until the outbreak of the war, German citizens had the right to stay in Sweden for three months without a visa) all came from Germany, or, in the last years of the 1930s, from Greater Germany, including Austria and parts of Czechoslovakia. About 80 per cent were Jews, and the remainder were political refugees. The Swedish Aliens Act, revised in 1937, gave

---

31 Åmark, *Att bo*, ch. 7; Antero Holmila, *Reporting the Holocaust in the British, Swedish and Finnish Press, 1945–50* (Basingstoke: Palgrave Macmillan, 2011).

32 Klas Åmark, 'Sweden and the Refugees, 1933–1945', in Mikael Byströnm and Pär Frohnert (eds.), *Reaching a State of Hope: Refugees, Immigrants and the Swedish Welfare State, 1930–2000* (Lund: Nordic Academic Press, 2013).

political refugees a better chance of obtaining a residence permit than Jews, and they could not be sent back to Germany. The Social Democratic government, working closely with the labour movement's refugee relief, preferred Social Democratic refugees to communists and syndicalists. Sweden did not recognize ethnic oppression as a valid reason to obtain a residence permit: Jews were said to merely 'feel discomfort' in Germany, rather than a threat to their life. Sweden also gave priority to those refugees who intended to stay in Sweden for a limited time and then continue to other receiving countries.[33]

After the German occupation of Norway in April 1940, Norwegians started to cross the border into Sweden. Nordic 'brothers' were a quite different category than Jews and political refugees from Germany. A growing number of these Norwegians were allowed to stay. Most Norwegians were young men, who felt threatened by the Germans – for example, because they had taken part in the resistance movement. Some of them got the chance to continue their journey to the United Kingdom to fight against Germany.

In October 1942, German police in Norway started to arrest Norwegian Jews. The arrests continued in November, and 774 Jews were sent to Auschwitz, where many of them were killed immediately on arrival. Only thirty-four survived the war. The Swedish Ministry for Foreign Affairs was rather slow to realize what was going on, and it was only in November that attempts to save Norway's Jews began. The Norwegian resistance also set about smuggling Jews over the border to Sweden. In total, some 1,100 Jews fled from Norway into Sweden, about 150 of whom were Jewish refugees living in Norway.[34]

In September 1943, Hitler ordered action against the Danish Jews. On this occasion, however, leading Germans leaked news of the planned arrests to the Danes. The Swedish government hurried to announce that all Jews living in Denmark were welcome in Sweden. Most Jews went into hiding, and a major rescue operation got under way to transport Danish Jews to Sweden, usually in small fishing boats. About 7,800 persons arrived in Sweden in October and November 1943. Of them, around 5,700 were Danish Jews,

33 Statens Offentliga Utredning 1936:53, *Utredning angående revision av bestämmelserna om utlännings rätt att här i riket vistas och därmed sammanhängandespörsmål* (Stockholm: Norstedts, 1936), p. 57.
34 Irene Levin, *Flukten. Jödenes flukt til Sverige under annen verdenskrig* (Oslo: HL-senteret, 2007).

1,400 were Jewish refugees who had been staying in Denmark and about 700 were Danes who chose to follow their Jewish spouses to Sweden.[35]

The famous Swedish rescue operation in Budapest in the second half of 1944 was something completely new. On 19 March, German troops occupied Hungary. On 15 May, the last chapter of the Holocaust started, with the transportation of hundreds of thousands of Hungarian Jews to Auschwitz. After an initiative from the Americans, the young Swedish businessman Raoul Wallenberg was sent to Budapest in order to help the persecuted Jews. Since Hungary still was an independent state after the German occupation, formal diplomatic representation was possible, and there were also local Hungarian authorities to negotiate and make bargains with. Since the terror against the Jews was conducted in the open, diplomats from the neutral countries knew immediately what was happening. This was the first time that Sweden attempted a major rescue operation for Jews outside the Nordic countries. Thousands of protective passports were issued, and Wallenberg made many concrete efforts to protect and save Jews.[36]

From the 1930s, Sweden preferred to allow transit refugees to enter the country. In the last years of the war, Sweden continued to expect most new refugees to leave the country as soon as hostilities ended. The tens of thousands of Norwegian and Danish refugees returned to their home countries in the summer of 1945. The major exception was the refugees coming from the Baltic countries, most of whom arrived in the autumn of 1944. They had fled from Soviet occupation, and therefore could be expected to remain in Sweden. The Baltic refugees often comprised whole families, sometimes even three generations. Some of them, about 7,000, were Swedish-speaking. More than 30,000 refugees arrived in Sweden from the Baltic states, most of them from Estonia. This large influx of refugees, from countries that were not usually thought of as Nordic, marked a major change in Swedish refugee policy.[37]

In the spring of 1945, Count Folke Bernadotte, Vice-Chairman of the Swedish Red Cross, succeeded in reaching an agreement with the SS leader Heinrich Himmler, according to which the so-called White Buses were allowed to transport not only 7,000 Danes and Norwegians from German concentration camps to Sweden, but also 12,000 camp inmates of other

35 Åmark, *Att bo*, pp. 536–9; Bo Lidegaard, *Landsmän. De danska judarnas flykt i oktober 1943* (Stockholm: Albert Bonniers Förlag, 2013).
36 Bengt Jangfeldt, *The Hero of Budapest: The Triumph and Tragedy of Raoul Wallenberg* (London: Tauris, 2014).
37 Åmark, *Att bo*, ch. 15.

nationalities, many of them Jews. In the early summer of 1945, the Swedish government accepted, somewhat reluctantly, a request from the United Nations Refugee and Rehabilitation Administration to receive another 10,000 former camp prisoners for health care. The large majority were young women, often Jewish, from the concentration camp Bergen-Belsen.[38] During this rescue action, new and sudden possibilities arose which were immediately used by Swedes to help new groups of camp prisoners. At the same time, this rescue action entailed an impossible moral dilemma. When the leadership for the White Bus operation wanted to collect Scandinavian prisoners from the Neuengamme concentration camp outside Hamburg, the SS demanded that the buses should first transfer thousands of other very sick prisoners to another camp, and the Swedes complied.[39]

The Swedish authorities had learned that large-scale rescue efforts were possible. Tens of thousands of refugees could be received, cared for, housed, fed and given health care, without seriously threatening Sweden's welfare provision. The Swedish reception system proved to be both efficient and flexible. A new element in Swedish refugee policy in the last years of the war was a willingness among leading officials and citizens to seize opportunities. Their ability to help the victims depended on bargaining with the perpetrators.[40]

Sweden and the war criminals

At the end of the war, the Stockholm government publicly accepted the principle that war criminals could be extradited from Sweden, but they claimed there were no such people in the country. During the last year of the war, tens of thousands of refugees arrived in Sweden from the Baltic states, most of them from Latvia and Estonia. Swedish authorities became worried that Nazis, communists and collaborators would be among them. Therefore, the police questioned many of them on their arrival in Sweden. The policemen and security personnel who interrogated the refugees collected thorough and detailed information about what had happened in countries occupied by Germany, especially in Norway and the Baltic states. Hundreds of persons who were interrogated could be suspected to be war

38 Sune Persson, 'Vi åker till Sverige'. De vita bussarna 1945 (Stockholm: Fischer och Co, 2002); Åmark, Att bo, pp. 546–56.
39 Ingrid Lomfors, Blind fläck. Minne och glömska kring svenska Röda korsets hjälpinsats i Nazityskland 1945 (Stockholm: Atlantis, 2005).
40 Åmark, Att bo, ch. 15.

criminals. The unmistakable lack of interest of the Swedish security police in investigating the testimonies of war crimes more thoroughly may have been influenced by the idea that modern warfare was cruel and brutal and that the borderline between what was acceptable as normal warfare and what should be classified as war crimes was thin and unclear. Since the police at the time never followed up the initial interrogations with rigorous investigations, it is not possible today to decide how many war criminals were actually allowed to stay in Sweden.

There were several other reasons behind Swedish passivity in the pursuit of Nazi war criminals. Even if the government publicly declared that it accepted the Allies' policy on war criminals, neither the government nor the representatives of the Swedish legal system fully accepted the concept of a war crime and that war criminals should be brought to justice. When Minister of Social Affairs Gustav Möller argued that Sweden should not harbour war criminals, he thought primarily of the top Nazis. Moreover, the Swedish legal system was not framed to handle war crimes. Swedish law made it practically impossible to extradite persons who risked being sentenced to death. At the same time, until 1958, it was not possible for Swedish courts themselves to sentence foreign citizens who had committed crimes abroad. Sweden's role in the international war crime trials was very limited. Sweden neither contributed to the work to establish new laws and courts, nor took an active part in the work to find criminals and bring them to trial. Sweden extradited Norwegian and Danish quislings immediately after the war, but until recently, only one war criminal has been extradited. Sweden actually became a refuge for war criminals, where they were allowed to live without the threat of prosecution.[41]

Conclusion

Before the war in Europe, the Swedish government knew that it would need to negotiate the terms of Sweden's neutrality with the belligerents. A vulnerable neutral state could not decide what neutrality would mean on its own. In the autumn of 1939, negotiations began, first about trade. Swedish negotiators had to convince the representatives of the great powers to accept that Sweden would trade with both sides. Trade agreements normally lasted for one year, and therefore had to be renegotiated under

---

41 Mats Deland, *Purgatorium: Sverige och andra världskrigets förbrytare* (Stockholm: Atlas, 2010); Åmark, *Att bo*, ch. 16.

changing circumstances. Swedish trade policy was successful in maintaining Swedish trade, if one looks at it only from the Swedish viewpoint. On the other hand, this policy meant that Germany could import products essential for its war effort.

The terms for leave traffic and other concessions to German demands were also decided through complex negotiations. The same was true for Germany's use of Swedish territory for air and sea transport. Even the measures the government put in place to influence the press offered foreign states, particularly Germany, the opportunity to make demands on what could and could not be published in Sweden. Likewise, Sweden's relief operations to aid refugees and to carry through humanitarian relief actions to countries such as Greece and the Netherlands had to be negotiated with leading representatives of the Nazi regime.

The necessity to negotiate meant that Sweden had to accept the Nazi regime as the legitimate government of Germany, with the authority to conclude agreements and make them function. This was a hazardous assumption. Negotiating with gangsters, as Sweden's State Secretary for Foreign Affairs Erik Boheman once put it, meant that agreements could be violated at any time. The negotiating policy also meant that the Swedish government accepted that the great powers had the right to make claims on Sweden and to start negotiations about these claims. The Swedish negotiators and the Swedish government were well aware that negotiating was a risky business that involved unpleasant compromises, but it became the foremost method for the small state to protect itself against open violence and war.

PART III

*

OCCUPATION, COLLABORATION,
RESISTANCE AND LIBERATION

Introduction to Part III

RICHARD J. B. BOSWORTH AND JOSEPH A. MAIOLO

In the rugged, stony hills above Trieste can be found the *foibe*, natural deep sinkholes. These sites were used by all competing wartime forces in the area – fascist, Nazi, communist, Slovene, patriotic Italian – 'for the easy and quick burial' of those whom they killed. In such brutal actions, soldiers were repeating what the locals had done for decades or centuries, when secrecy was needed or the rules of the authorities were ignored.[1] A small tale of murder, it might seem, yet they are slayings which have not been, and are not, forgotten. If anything, the power of the memory of the *foibe*, disputed between rival political groups and ethnicities, has grown with time. Despite worthy attempts by expert historians to settle such issues as the wildly inflated numbers of the victims in some accounts, no peace about this past has been signed. This small history of a minor front of one of the Second World Wars can still spark shock waves through the communities involved, while local feelings have also been nationalized. In Italy in 2005, Silvio Berlusconi instituted 10 February as a National Memory Day for Exiles and the *Foibe*, making it the third Italian celebration of that nation's (disputed) memory of its war, in partnership or rivalry with 27 January, Holocaust Day, and 25 April, Liberation Day. Berlusconi is anything but an ideal history-maker. However, his political opponents have not resiled from the anti-'Slav' sentiments commonly expressed on 11 February and the crude nationaliza-tion of the past that is involved.

The story of the *foibe* is a reminder that 'the Second World War' is not a neat historical particle that can be confined to calendar dates between 1939 and 1945, and viewed as essentially a military or political fight between the armed forces at battle or the statesmen in charge of the domestic policy

---

1 José Pirjevec, *Foibe: una storia d'Italia* (Turin: Giulio Einaudi, 2009), pp. 138–9.

or diplomacy of this combatant or that. So, in this part of Volume II, our contributors will go beyond the states and polities in conflict to consider how the peoples of Europe, Asia and, indeed, the rest of the world experienced the war as it visited them. Here, therefore, are discussed many Second World Wars and the participation in them of men and women who were by no means simply defined by their nationality or the ideology of the state which formally controlled their lives. Here, gender, class, family, age, region, religion, occupation, as well as the chance of what aspect of the war most entered lives, matter as much as grand conflicts between democracy and authoritarianism, somehow defined. Here, indeed, were people's wars, individual, local, national and transnational.

Nick Stargardt introduces readers to such issues in his sensitive account of the Germans, the national grouping which felt more drastically the highs and lows of victory and defeat. Germans gave widespread consent to the ideological explanation for war of their Nazi masters, but eventually had to confront the bewilderment of its exposure as murder and genocide (and, often enough, ruthless incompetence). Stargardt emphasizes that his approach will not be that of 'old-fashioned history', whether diplomatic or military. Rather, he notes, he will focus on 'food and sex as issues which crossed all national boundaries in occupied Europe, were profoundly influenced by German actions and, in turn, became key to the changing moral values and commitments of occupied Europeans'. In this regard, Stargardt displays the deadly implications for the peasants and the city dwellers of all the Russias in Nazi procurement policies, marked as they were by 'the unregulated brutality of colonial rule'. Even in more gently administered Western Europe, Nazi management led to scarcity, while inadvertently sponsoring the Darwinism of the black market. Meanwhile, sometimes bathetically, Nazi racism had to supervise sex and yet could not reliably do so. 'In reality, policing neighbourhood relations was highly selective and therefore rather arbitrary.' And other societies, during and after battle, would also grapple with how 'horizontal collaboration' of whatever kind should be punished or understood.

William Hitchcock focuses on the West and on the experience of Europeans where Nazi racial theoretics did not damn those locals who were not Jewish to present or future extermination. Danes, Norwegians, Belgians, Dutch, the French and, especially after 8 September 1943 and the bungled establishment attempt to change sides, the Italians (and their various subnational groups), all looked to collaborate with the triumphant Third Reich, some with ideological effusion, most with the self-interest of community or individuals as prime impulse. To be sure, a minority of citizens of these states sought to oppose and 'resist' the Germans and their local friends, touching off a series of internecine struggles, which, however uneven in practical effect, framed much post-1945 politics. At least in the short term, 'Liberation', in these societies always achieved under the aegis of Anglo-American liberal democracy, mostly enhanced the clashes, with killing, either judicial or extrajudicial, and sometimes 'spontaneous' and personal, continuing into the summer months of 1945 and beyond. This afterglow of war ensured the survival of further memories of conflict that did not necessarily fit into cheap talk about a 'good war' or the seamless virtue of 'anti-fascism'. As with the *foibe*, such histories could nurture lingering nostalgia on the right in most European societies for fascism and other authoritarianism, cleansed of the cruder features of Nazism. Because of its anti-communism, such worldviews over the decades after 1945 were often blessed by that American capitalism which had really won the war.

Davide Rodogno turns to the less familiar topic of Italian occupations in Europe. (Its more drastically murderous activities in its empire, noted briefly here, win further space from David Motadel, later in this volume.) Rodogno's detail reminds us both of Germany's massive supremacy within the Axis and of the ruthless ambitions of Mussolini's lesser dictatorship, with its dream of its own version of empire and new order. Military, political, economic and social failure, and even the disdain with which local inhabitants often treated Fascist occupiers, so blatantly the 'ignoble seconds' of the Germans, Rodogno underlines, should not prevent historiographical reckoning with Italian perpetration, whether of the deed or in the mind. After all, 'at the extreme of Fascist imagining, national *spazio vitale* included the Iberian Peninsula, France, Switzerland and the Balkans, and extended far into Africa and Asia, indeed beyond the boundaries of the classical Roman Empire'. But Italians were speedy and united in refusing to face their national responsibility, certainly in the immediate post-war, when war crimes were scarcely prosecuted and any convicted soon amnestied. Nor has present-day Italy done much to fill this gap in comprehension of a violent past. In their own myths, and those of many foreigners, Italians, despite their wartime record of murder, are 'good people' (*brava gente*).

Gregor Kranjc explores the Balkans, a territory that endured Italian and German occupation, as well as liberation, except in Greece, by the Red Army and Stalin's commissars. Of all the post-war states, Yugoslavia was the least able to quell different readings of the meaning of collaboration and resistance (and of the officially denied multiple civil wars), debates that were re-ignited by the new wars of the 1990s. In the twenty-first century, that Yugoslavia which was once portrayed as a heroic ally on the ground of the Soviet-Western alliance in its overthrow of Nazi fascism has disappeared. Croatia (and with greater wartime complexity), Slovenia, Bosnia and Kosovo, polities that were granted some right to exist in Hitler's New Order, are back in business, despite 'losing' the 'good war'. Greece possessed, and possesses, a very different but no less embattled set of histories and memories, ones that still colour its recent fate as Europe's saddest victim of the 2008 neoliberal recession. As so often, simultaneously victims and perpetrators, Greeks, with the rise of 'Popular Association – Golden Dawn' (Λαϊκός Σύνδεσμος – Χρυσή Αυγή), have given serious support to a xenophobic and racist political movement, with a decidedly recalcitrant understanding of modern history as expressed in Greece's Second World War and its prolongation into the Civil War of 1946–49. In both Greece and Yugoslavia, then, 'ideological extremism' stained occupiers, resisters and collaborators, creating a wartime world of appalling civilian casualty, compared with the occupied nations of Western Europe. Here 'brutal...atrocities' were regularly inflicted on 'all opponents, real or potential', and the memory of such deeds has gone marching on.

If the Balkans were a centre of wartime death and destruction, and of their tormented legacy, the motley territories that composed the Soviet Union and so, in the Nazi mind, had fallen under the sway of that 'Judeo-Bolshevism' they were utterly determined to extirpate, were the prime killing fields of the Second World War, whether for soldiers or civilians. Here, almost 30 million died, the majority civilians, and the Nazis dreamed of the liquidation of as many more. Mark Edele examines how the Stalinist state, with its own pre-war murders and deep-seated social violence, and its massive contradictions about the definition of class and nation, fought the war. Its war-making varied in three phases: when in partnership via the Molotov–Ribbentrop Pact with the Nazis, 1939–41; in all but overwhelming defeat, 1941–42; or in rallying to bloody victory, 1943–45 (and beyond), across a vast sphere that ran from Berlin to Tabriz, and from Finnmark to Pyongyang. The USSR, Edele underlines, 'was a Eurasian empire fighting a Eurasian war'.

From the first, in Poland in 1939, the Red Army 'executed POWs, raped women, looted property (like later in Germany, Manchuria or Korea, wristwatches were popular trophies) and killed civilians'. Soviet forces never ceased 'marauding', despite the communist regime's desire to check and control its soldiery. Rape and murder, in other words, came from 'below' as much as 'above', and were by no means merely inspired by a desire to avenge the Germans' massacres in all the Russias after 1941. The Stalin regime had long been devoted to 'revolutionary violence', where 'targets', however capriciously defined, were punished by population transfer and death. 'Plunder' was another constant often uniting commissars and soldiers in the hope of gain. As Edele wryly remarks, 'as locals got to know these liberators, they often found "liberation" and "occupation" hard to distinguish'. Yet despite the commitment to 'scientific Marxism', the USSR lacked the radical drive of Nazism to extermination, and, Edele concludes, left a wartime story where 'different people were affected in different places and different times in different ways'. In turn, before and after the collapse of communism, the peoples of the region have disputed and still dispute their often vivid and profound memories of what the regime euphemistically called the 'Great Patriotic War'. In 2015, such battles continue most openly and viciously in Ukraine.

European historians have often been sadly Eurocentric, with quite a few major histories of the Second World War making little attempt to examine its Asian or African faces and tabulate the death toll in China or Ethiopia, for example. In this volume, however, Margherita Zanasi, Paul Kratoska and Ken'ichi Goto, Ashley Jackson, Martin Thomas and David Motadel all explore the fighting and its effects away from Europe. Zanasi's concentration is on Taiwan, Korea and China, all territories subjected to Japanese occupation, the first two as part of an empire (Taiwan seized in 1895 and Korea in 1910) that began before the First World War, and China as another of the war's sites of invasion and massacre, where the full death toll is still not accurately tabulated. In each society (Korea split into North and South after its own civil and ideological war, 1950–53), myths of resistance have been crucial in framing post-war government, however far their moralized certainties were from a wartime reality where collaboration and accommodation were at least as common as was armed opposition. Nor are the ghosts of war and occupation stilled today, when China and Japan (and Korea) contest the ownership of unpopulated islands in their surrounding seas, and politicians and people vigorously primp their nationalisms through evocation of the past war.

The situation is not so diverse in Southeast Asia, where certainly Thailand, and perhaps the Philippines, were, in 1939, the only independent states, but where, today, the empires of Britain, France and the Netherlands have vanished. The overlay of decolonization, a process naturally exposing metropolitan ignorance and tyranny, has left deep ambiguities in local meanings of the Second World War. Talk of 'Asian values', for example, contains ironic parallels with wartime Japanese rhetoric about a Greater East Asian

Co-Prosperity Sphere. Nor has the identification of usable pasts been made easier by the return of Japanese economic power to the region from the 1960s (now rivalled or excelled by China's flourishing). After all, the war regionally was vicious. Japanese violence, brutality and murder, despite variations over time and space, 'quickly put an end to open opposition, but...generated lasting resentment'. Here was a power that called itself 'Asian', yet was no better in its present and planned future governance than the area's European masters had been, and perhaps was worse. War, in sum, in its local complexity, often accelerated the creation of the new nation states, with their own flaws and contradictions. Yet it was not imperial and authoritarian Japan that had wanted this 'liberation'.

Britain's wartime leader, Winston Churchill, is still regularly hailed in his own country as the greatest hero. But his glory, even in his own mind, was confined to Europe. After all, he was the unreconstructed imperialist, who maintained: 'I did not become the King's First Minister to preside over the liquidation of the British Empire', and expostulated that India was 'the greatest war profiteer'.[2] The imperial governments over which he presided failed to stem the Bengal famine, which brought up to 4 million to an early grave in perhaps the most unremarked disaster of the Second World War (the vagueness and inadequacy of statistics, here and elsewhere in the non-European world, are themselves a lesson in the nature of imperialism, whether experienced from 'above or 'below'). Ashley Jackson has the formidable task of reckoning with the war's effects across a global stage where not all Britons, and certainly not Churchill, had accepted that the sun must soon set. 'Terror, mass migration, shortages, inflation, blackouts, air raids, massacres, famine, forced labour, urbanization, environmental damage, occupation, resistance, collaboration – all of these dramatic and often horrific phenomena shaped the war experience of Britain's imperial subjects', Jackson declares. The imperial British war afflicted people in Valletta as well as Calcutta, Jamaica as well as Diego Garcia. The ramifications were legion and could be unexpected, when, for example, sex workers crowded into the towns and ports of Sierra Leone, 'to be nearer to the market created by concentrations of Allied and imperial service personnel'; or when long-term dietary shifts occurred well up-country, under the often harsh requisitioning orders of the metropolis. All in all, Britain may have won its

---

2 David Reynolds, *In Command of History: Churchill Fighting and Writing the Second World War* (London: Allen Lane, 2004), pp. 195, 335.

Second World War in Europe, but it lost its larger contest with its imperial peoples (as well as with the triumphant Americans).

Ironically, given its utter defeat, however 'strange', France possessed an imperial history during the war and uneasily absorbed it after 1945 in ways that are not so different from 'victorious' Britain. As Martin Thomas makes plain, 'Greater France', beyond its European bounds, was vitiated by 'economic disruption, social protest and acute ethnic discrimination', each, wherever the national tricolour waved, manifested in 'World War, civil war and contested decolonization'. Given the 'fall of France' in Europe, the empire did have a peculiarity in becoming the site of the renewal of metropolitan 'faction fights' that, in the main, were 'curiously removed from the daily lives of colonial communities for whom more fundamental questions of food supply, underemployment and basic rights' dominated the everyday experience of war. Whereas Germany was the overweening enemy in Europe, the French empire suffered incursion not only from the Japanese and Italians, but also from the British, Americans and Soviets. Nor did battle end in 1945. Rather, imperial and civil wars and conflicts continued, in 1961, to reach the streets of Paris, when leftover police from Vichy murdered those they defined as their North African enemies and threw their bodies into the Seine.[3]

David Motadel brings this section of Volume II to a close in another chapter of massive range, demonstrating how, contrary to some legend, the (admittedly heterogeneous) 'Muslim world' experienced its own special Second World Wars. Here, again, the ideological battle between the Allies, whether liberal democrat or Soviet, and the Axis rubbed up against a reality where some 200 million Muslims lived under direct European rule, whether Western or Soviet. Egypt, Arabia, Iran and Turkey clung to greater or lesser formal independence, always likely to be conditioned by imperial 'advice' or military intervention, quite a bit of it bloody. Tens of thousands of Muslim soldiers fought in the armies of one side or the other.

Despite its commitment to Judeocide, a policy that pleased some Muslims, notably those already engaged in battle in Palestine, the Axis was rarely a credible 'liberator', even when the Nazis, for example, offered Muslims, notably those who viewed their special enemy as Russian Communists, a place in the Waffen-SS. However, the Germans' genocidal aims, against the Roma for example, could kill Muslim gypsies, even if, as Motadel indicates,

3 For graphic detail, see Jim House and Neil MacMaster, *Paris 1961: Algerians, State Terror, and Memory* (Oxford University Press, 2006).

the Germans 'had trouble distinguishing Muslim Roma from Tatars', and adroit identity transference did save some. Moreover, the Nazis' Italian allies, with their own deplorable record of murder in Libya contradicting regime chatter about Mussolini bearing aloft 'the Sword of Islam', were another complicating factor. So, on the other side, was Amharic Ethiopia, 'freed' by British (colonial) victory against the Fascist occupier, but also no gentle ruler of its Muslim peoples. Japan flirted with a pro-Muslim line in Asia, persuading the Tatar imam Abdurreshid Ibrahim, the 'patriarch of the Tokyo Mosque', to preach jihad against the Allies. But Japanese imperial schemes could scarcely be adjusted to genuine Muslim liberation, and Muslim Asians were often enough casualties of Tokyo's brutality. In sum, Motadel concludes, Muslims, like so many other peoples, had been 'victims, perpetrators and witnesses' of the wars that had irrupted into their lives after 1939 and did not necessarily cease in 1945. They, too, bore on their skins a killing that spread across the globe and has scarcely yet fallen into being dead history.

15

Wartime occupation by Germany

Food and sex

NICHOLAS STARGARDT

Introduction

The war Hitler had long envisaged – and openly canvassed in *Mein Kampf* – was Germany's eastward expansion into the Soviet Union. Destroying and taking over the Czechoslovak and Polish 'successor' states was both a means to that end and a goal in its own right. Their destruction began with Hitler's 'final' territorial demand for the Sudetenland in May 1938, continued with the occupation of the rest of the Czech lands in March 1939, and culminated in the attack on Poland on 1 September 1939, which brought Britain and France into the war. Hitler's goal of a German, continental empire in the European 'East' remained self-contradictory, blending images of colonial conquest and subjugation with the Pan-Germanist ideal of creating as large and ethnically homogeneous a Reich as possible. But in the West he had elaborated no real plans at all. The rapid conquests in Western Europe of April, May and June 1940 expanded German occupation to Denmark, Norway, Belgium, Luxemburg, the Netherlands and France, countries which were not the focus of German ambitions, but which promised far greater industrial resources. For four years, until the summer of 1944, most of Western and Eastern Europe lay under German occupation.

The speed and overwhelming military success of the Wehrmacht in the summer of 1940 led many West Europeans, including their political elites, to see the defeat of France as the effective end of the war: what mattered was to ensure the best terms of the post-war settlement and to use the opportunities available to embark on a process of 'national renewal'. This expectation conditioned the creation of broad-based and generally conservative political coalitions which formed the starting point for political 'cohabitation' and collaboration with the German occupiers in France, Belgium, Norway and the Netherlands. Denmark was different, in both the degree of political autonomy and the extent to which the Social Democratic Party was allowed to participate in general elections and wield power commensurate with its electoral mandate. As Mark Mazower has argued, the character of German rule varied across the continent. There were different models, from a relatively light 'advisory' one in Denmark, through more supervisory models in France and Belgium (including German military administration acting in parallel with the existing state bureaucracy), down to direct, colonial forms of governance in Poland and the occupied Soviet Union. And these models changed over time, becoming harsher and more punitive, as German demands grew and as resistance movements gained in confidence. The first cracks appeared in June 1941, when 'collaborationist' governments of Western Europe failed to give unilateral support for the German 'crusade against Bolshevism', prompting the Germans to promote local allies on the extreme right: by attempting to undermine some of their mainstream conservative collaborators in the Nether-lands and Norway, the Germans also tended to weaken their own hold over the West European elites. By 1942, the Wehrmacht had occupied Vichy too.[1]

The first wave of serious scholarship on occupied Europe tended to emphasize German economic exploitation and to look to the conscription of West European workers to work in Germany as a key motivation for joining the resistance.[2] A second wave of scholarship drew a direct line between the ideological hardening of German positions after 1941 and the rise of resistance, rightly drawing attention to the key successes of commun-ists in gaining wider legitimacy in regions of France, Italy, Greece and the Balkans, through their role in national resistance after June 1941.[3] While both interpretations raise issues of real importance, they have also come in for further revision, as historians have focused more on what it meant to live under occupation.[4] It has become clear, for example, that many of those

---

1 Mark Mazower, *Hitler's Empire: Nazi Rule in Occupied Europe* (London: Allen Lane, 2008); Martin Conway and Peter Romijn (eds.), *The War for Legitimacy in Politics and Culture, 1936–1946* (Oxford: Berg, 2008); H. R. Kedward, *Resistance in Vichy France* (Oxford University Press, 1978); G. Hirschfeld (ed.), *Nazi Rule and Dutch Collaboration* (Oxford University Press, 1988).

2 Alan Milward, *The New Order and the French Economy* (Oxford University Press, 1970); Czesław Madajczyk, *Polityka III Rzeszy w okupowanej Polsce* (Warsaw: Państwowe Wydawn, 1970).

3 S. J. Woolf, *Rebirth of Italy, 1943–50* (London: Longman, 1972); Paul Ginsborg, *A History of Contemporary Italy: Society and Politics, 1943–1988* (Harmondsworth: Penguin, 1990); Mark Mazower, *Inside Hitler's Greece: The Experience of Occupation, 1941–44* (New Haven, Conn.: Yale University Press, 2001).

4 Robert Gildea, Anette Warring and Olivier Wieviorka (eds.), *Surviving Hitler and Mussolini: Daily Life in Occupied Europe* (Oxford: Berg, 2006); Robert Gildea, *Marianne in Chains* (London: Macmillan, 2003).

driven into surviving on false papers – or without papers at all – in order to escape the labour drafts did not become political resisters, but vagrants or cheap and pliable farm workers; and that organizations which helped to hide them (for instance, trade unions and the Catholic Church in Belgium) did so with defensive motives: such acts of 'resistance' did not preclude accommodation and compromise in other areas. Instead of aligning all opposition to German demands with political resistance, it has become clear that, in Western Europe at least, friction led to negotiation, as both the occupied and the occupiers looked for ways to avoid a spiral of confrontation and violence. In the process, the historiography of occupied Europe has moved away from the rival ideological claimants to political leadership at a national level, and has come to focus, instead, on the ways in which more prosaic cultural, social and economic conflicts were transacted and negotiated, while Europe's Jews were being deported to their deaths.[5] Key among the economic assets which were being brokered were food and labour; among the cultural contacts and social forms of cohabitation, nothing was more freighted with ideological meanings but harder to regulate than sex. This chapter singles out food and sex as issues which crossed all national boundaries in occupied Europe, were profoundly influenced by German actions and, in turn, became key to the changing moral values and commitments of occupied Europeans.

Food

The German invasion of the Soviet Union in June 1941 was accompanied by a 'Hunger Plan', drafted by Herbert Backe, the State Secretary (later Minister) for Agriculture, to starve 20–30 million 'Slavs' to death in order to feed the German armies. Despite this overtly genocidal beginning, worse was to come. During 1942, German policy toward occupied Europe changed fundamentally. Food mattered as never before. Having staked everything on winning the Blitzkrieg in the Soviet Union, the Wehrmacht had seen itself almost destroyed in front of Moscow, and Backe had allowed food stocks to run low in the Reich. While the military crisis was still unresolved, German civilian administrators were plunged into a second crisis, as they were forced

---

to plan for a much longer war. Rations in Germany itself were cut sharply in April 1942, prompting the most rapid and drastic fall in the Nazi regime's popularity during the whole war. Six months later, German rations would be restored amid great fanfare by Hermann Göring, paid for by massive imports of food from occupied Europe, especially France, Poland and Ukraine.

The total deliveries of grain, meat and fats from France and the occupied Soviet territories more than doubled, from 3.5 million tonnes to 8.78 million tonnes over the same period. In the Kiev district of Ukraine, the greatest round of requisitioning during the whole occupation occurred ahead of the 1942 harvest itself: 38,470 tonnes of grain were collected in June 1942; the following month 26,570 tonnes; finally tailing off to a mere 7,960 tonnes in early August. The representative for Food and Agriculture for the Reichskommissariat Ukraine returned from a tour of inspection, content that the peasants of the district had no more grain, not even for seed. It had been an essentially military-style requisitioning operation, with detachments of the, mainly Ukrainian, Order Police descending on houses, mills, markets, gardens and barns to search for hidden stockpiles.[6] By 1942–43, Germany was drawing more than 20 per cent of its grain, 25 per cent of its fats and nearly 30 per cent of its meat from occupied Europe. While much of the French and Ukrainian supplies went directly to the Wehrmacht on the spot, the General Government, ruling over central and eastern Poland and western Ukraine, was shipping more than half of its deliveries of the rye and potatoes and two-thirds of the oats to the Reich.[7]

This was an unsustainable strategy. Over any longer period of time, the Reich could not suck both food and labour from its Polish and Soviet colonies. As in the First World War, so again now, successive labour drafts to work in Germany undermined local agriculture and harvest yields declined. The dynamic effects of transferring both food and labour to Germany pushed the new colonial supply zones into a spiral of starvation and increasing mortality. As in the first Soviet Five-Year Plan, so to those managing the German war economy, it did not matter if Ukrainian peasants starved or if agricultural output nosedived, so long as they delivered the food and labour needed for industry. But even Stalin had discovered in the 1930s that such a policy was unsustainable. In the second Five-Year Plan, Soviet industry had had to make net transfers to agriculture, establishing Motor

6 Berkhoff, *Harvest of Despair*, p. 122.
7 Karl Brandt, *Management of Agriculture and Food in the German-Occupied and Other Areas of Fortress Europe: A Study in Military Government* (Stanford University Press, 1953), pp. 610, 614.

Tractor Stations to make up for the loss of draught animals during forced collectivization. There was no sign that the Germans would ever have started investing in Polish or Ukrainian agriculture, to mitigate their enormous destructive efforts, except where the land was taken over by German 'colonists'.

The German 'east' was condemned to a spiral of economic decline, whose pace was accelerated by the unregulated brutality of colonial rule. By the autumn of 1942, German demands on the new harvest were becoming impossible to meet. Again, the postal censors and the SD (*Sicherheitsdienst* – SS security service) picked up the impact of requisitioning on the country-side. 'It's harvest time, and yet we have no bread', a woman wrote to relatives working in Germany. 'The guys gather stalks, and we mill this on the hand mill, to make some bread. This is how we live up to now, and we don't know what will be next'. In almost every household, private stills were set up and alcohol consumption soared. At least the grain they turned into alcohol could not be seized. 'They drink "for an occasion"', wrote a Volhynnian newspaper, and "without any reason". There used to be one inn for the entire village; now there is an inn in every third hut.'[8]

In poorer agricultural areas like Polissia, famine loomed and German actions changed gear completely. While German forces were still advancing eastward, a new and terrible war against the civilian population was beginning in the rear. On 2 September 1942, gendarmes and seventy Ukrainian police entered the village of Kaminka, east of Brest Litovsk, massacred the entire population and burned all the houses, leaving it as a warning to the surrounding district of the fate that awaited those who did not fulfil their delivery quotas or were suspected of supporting the partisans.[9] Exactly three weeks later, it was the turn of the village of Kortelisy, near Ratne. The District Commissioner of Kovel made a speech in German which an interpreter then translated: he had orders, he informed them, to burn them all alive in their homes for harbouring partisans, but he was going to commute the sentence to shooting. A total of 2,900 people were killed, not because any one of them had been a partisan, but as a demonstration of what awaited other villages which were tempted to give the partisans supplies or shelter. The next day, the village was burned to the ground. As a strategy of pacification through terror, practised across Eastern and Southern Europe, the number of villages burned would grow exponentially over the next two years.

8 Cited in Berkhoff, *Harvest of Despair*, p. 135.
9 Ibid., p. 134.

It would take time – and spiralling German terror – before peasants would see the partisans as liberators, rather than just another threat to their precarious lives, in which subsistence threatened continually to tip into famine. In 1942, partisan groups were still too weak and scattered to pose a serious threat to the Germans. Rather, the rival Polish, Jewish, Ukrainian and Soviet partisan groups forming in the forests expended more energy at this stage fighting each other for control of their base areas and the food supplies of the surrounding villages. And many-sided civil wars would rage for years after the Germans retreated. The economic, political and social collapse of Ukraine into a vortex of violence and inter-ethnic civil wars followed from the untrammelled German demands and the way in which they were imposed, without any compromise.

With different local starting points, parts of Belorussia, Greece, eastern Poland and Serbia and, later, Italy were all sucked into the orbit of German 'anti-partisan' actions, with their massive collective reprisals and spiralling violence. Although the balance of causes – military, political and economic – varied, they shared a common feature: the collapse of state authority. In Belorussia, Poland, Serbia and Ukraine, no autonomous national or local government had been tolerated and, reduced to mere 'auxiliaries', the local 'order police' eventually fragmented under the pressure. In Greece and Italy, the collapse of the state was more complicated, but the ruthlessness of German 'pacification' was still unlike anything practised in Western Europe: Oradour in France, and Lidice in Bohemia and Moravia, became memorials because they were unique exemplars of German brutality: by liberation, Belorussia could count over 600 villages destroyed and their populations massacred.[10]

In France, by contrast, the whole process of extracting food from farmers was transmitted through French intermediaries, even in regions like Brittany and the Loire, which came under German military administration from the start of the occupation. German and French officials negotiated and renegotiated quotas, from the centralized Vichy structures manned by the directors general of the *Ravitaillement*, all the way down to the mayors of individual rural communes. One of the great problems for the supply system was the illegal slaughter of livestock. From early in the occupation, new regulations

10 Martin Dean, *Collaboration in the Holocaust: Crimes of the Local Police in Belorussia and Ukraine, 1941–44* (Basingstoke: Macmillan, 2000); Chiari, *Alltag hinter der Front*; Christian Gerlach, *Kalkulierte Morde: die deutsche Wirtschafts- und Vernichtungspolitik in Weissrussland 1941 bis 1944* (Hamburg: Hamburger Edition, 2000); Mazower, *Hitler's Empire*.

were issued banning both butter-making and slaughter on farms, in order to promote large abattoirs and dairies, which, as in Britain, offered the authorities greater prospects of control. In France, this immediately ran into open hostility and private non-conformity. Even the new corporatist institutions invented by Vichy did not increase its control over the countryside, with the Peasant Corporation of Maine-et-Loire promptly electing an ordinary farmer rather than a Vichy official to lead it in the autumn of 1941. By this point, in a region like the Loire, local mayors frequently colluded with the protests of their constituents. A self-confident Conservative Catholic aristocrat, comte Henri de Champagny, well entrenched in the Vichy elite, had no compunction in unilaterally slashing the butter quota for his commune of Somloire in Anjou, from 375 to 50 kilos. Less well-connected mayors retreated to the age-old defence of the countryside, stubborn silence. Even the collective fines levied by the Germans for non-fulfilment of quotas often went unpaid for years – with relative impunity.

As German demands rose dramatically, finding the compromises and accommodations which kept the semblance of power and legitimacy intact would become increasingly difficult, even at the local level. By the spring of 1942, the sub-prefects were touring the Loire-Inférieure, urging the peasants to deliver their grain. Equally symbolic was the rediscovery of the language of the French revolution to express the anger of urban officials at the selfish parochialism of a Vendéan countryside: the Regional Prefect of Roussillon described the peasantry as '*affameurs*', deliberately starving the workers and small artisans of the town in pursuit of a 'spirit of lucre'. Such 'engrained individualism' of the peasant household presented a major challenge to his Pétainist conservative vision of 'solidarity and mutual aid on a national scale', even though the Marshal himself remained widely popular.[11]

In Ukraine, German demands on the countryside gradually destroyed the local organs of enforcement, leading to an anarchic and multidimensional civil war; in France, power drained away from the central state in a less dramatic, but still highly significant fashion. It was the local landlords and clerics who had met the invaders in 1940, who had guaranteed the safety of their citizens by offering themselves as hostages at the beginning of the occupation, and who, as local mayors, now tried to protect them against economic demands which they felt were illegitimate. As a similar process of official exhortation and communal recalcitrance was played out across

11 Gildea, *Marianne in Chains*, p. 126.

occupied Western Europe, local notables re-emerged as key actors, a victory of the *pays* over the *patrie*.

No surprise, then, that when it came to the black market, the authorities deemed it wiser to proceed with great caution and leniency. In Maine-et-Loire, only 15 per cent of cases brought resulted in fines, which were also set so low that they would scarcely deter illegal slaughter, with the local prefect urging a policy of exhortation rather than intimidation.[12]

The trades and ties of the black market were at their most dense at the local level, with butchers driving to the local farms of the Loire on their own account to stock up on meat for their shops. Dealing with those you knew minimized the risk of denunciation and established stable patterns of exchange at 'fair' prices.

The growth of the black market was, of course, a process in which Germans contributed directly as consumers. As entrepreneurial individuals, German civilian administrators, SS officers and ordinary soldiers had celebrated their conquests of 1940 and 1941 by buying stocks of goods hard to come by in the Reich. For the young infantryman Ernst Guicking, France was not just a cornucopia. Throughout the autumn of 1940, he sent parcels of wool and silk cloth home to his bride and took orders to local seamstresses.[13] A young actor at the German theatre in Prague, Wolf Goette, wrote home to take orders for furniture and antiques. With the abolition of the customs border between the Reich and the Protectorate of Bohemia and Moravia on 1 October 1940, one eyewitness saw German officers' luggage bulging with Czech 'furs, watches, medicines, shoes, in quite unimaginable quantities'.[14]

At a more modest level, a young soldier, devout Catholic and future novelist, Heinrich Böll, made a half-pound of coffee his first purchase in Rotterdam. Throughout the summer of 1940, he sent home letters about his regular 'coffee hunts', interspersed with 'butter travels', adding miscellaneous parcels with nail scissors, onions, make-up and a pair of women's shoes. By September, he noticed that the shops were being emptied of stock and that, although the Germans were paying for everything, it felt more like

---

12 Ibid., pp. 111, 126–32.
13 Ernst to Irene Guicking, 2, 7, 13 August, 3, 7 September 1940, in Irene Guicking and Jürgen Kleindienst (eds.), *Sei tausendmal gegrüsst. Briefwechsel Irene und Ernst Guicking 1937–1945* (CD-ROM, Berlin: JKL Publikationen, 2001).
14 Wilhelm Dennler, *Die böhmische Passion* (Freiburg: Dikreiter, 1953), p. 31; Götz Aly, *Hitlers Volksstaat: Raub, Rassenkrieg und nationaler Sozialismus* (Frankfurt am Main: S. Fischer, 2005), pp. 117–18.

'stripping a corpse'. Still, Böll kept a lookout for coffee.[15] At the Gare de l'Est in Paris, hordes of German soldiers staggering under enormous amounts of luggage, as they struggled to carry their own and their comrades' purchases home, became a daily sight, bringing a visual sense of the aggregation of the many small purchases which soon led to the French calling the Germans 'locusts' (*doryphores*).[16] In Ukraine, they would earn a new name, the 'eastern hyenas'.

Occasionally, too, German customs posts lifted a small corner of the curtain on the larger operations. They discovered, for instance that in 1940–41, a group of employees from the railway postal service were involved in running a weekly mail van to Paris, in order to bring back 'goods which are scarce in Paris like coffee, tea, cocoa, chocolate, cognac, champagne, wines, spirits, clothing, stockings, etc.' The employees met the returning train at Metz and accompanied their wagon back home to Nuremberg, where they disposed of most of the goods to other postal workers. The trade was fuelled by the illegal exchange of Reich Credit Chits.[17]

On the whole, it is much harder to trace the outlines of the larger-scale operations of the black market than the ad hoc family networks and trades. It is clear, however, that they existed, and they connected all sections of the German occupation administrations to the populations they were ruling. In Warsaw, a German edict banned the baking and sale of white bread from as early as 23 January 1940, but the shops and market stalls made a point of displaying it openly – and Germans also went there to buy it for themselves. The fleet of trucks bringing flour to Paris and Warsaw each day ran on petrol issued from German-controlled stocks, with permits purchased from corrupt officials within their respective military and civilian administrations. Occasionally, particular products revealed the pan-European extent of the deals being brokered with German officials. Before Christmas 1942, a large amount of poultry suddenly appeared on the Warsaw markets, no doubt diverted from shipments to Germany. In 1943, news leaked out that herrings – presumably shipped by the Wehrmacht's *Heringsweiterleitungsstelle* from Norway – were being sold in bulk to black market traders in Warsaw. Occasionally, the goods themselves revealed something of the scale of the

15 Aly, *Hitlers Volksstaat*, pp. 114, 118–19, 128; Heinrich Böll, *Briefe aus dem Krieg*, ed. Jochen Schubert (2 vols., Cologne: Kiepenheuer & Witsch, 2001), vol. 1, pp. 90, 101, 108, 111 (5 and 21 August, 4 and 7 September 1940).
16 Henri Michel, *Paris allemand* (Paris: A. Michel, 1981), p. 298.
17 Aly, *Hitlers Volksstaat*, pp. 115, 131–2; Böll, *Briefe aus dem Krieg*, pp. 407, 363, 406, 816, 417, 738, 908.

enterprise. In May 1943, it was tortoises. A whole consignment being sent from Greece or Bulgaria to Germany was offloaded on its way through Warsaw. Tortoises were a novelty. Though not part of traditional cuisine, they, too, were taken up by the black market and sold in street and market stalls throughout the city. But for weeks they were spotted crawling out from behind pillars and edging their way laboriously up steps, bringing a new spectacle to the streets.[18]

The process of economic fragmentation and regionalization overlaid a deeper and simpler divide – that between food surplus areas like the rich countryside of the Loire and areas of food deficit, sometimes in the same geographical region. Urban workers in the Loire region benefited from German demand for armaments, making ships' radios, tents, blackout material and camouflage netting, torpedo boats and destroyers, railway trucks and Heinkel 111 bombers, not to mention the huge projects constructing U-boat pens and Atlantic coastal fortifications. But urban wages, higher nominal rations and high employment did not protect them from a gradual but systematic shift of urban–rural trade. Even prosperous ports like Nantes and Saint-Nazaire, with thriving war industries, suffered from chronic food shortages and hunger.[19]

Worst off were the great cities. Vital as the family networks became in the struggle for survival, they could not fully replace the impersonal mechanisms of mass markets on which the enormous urban expansion of nineteenth-century cities had been built. In Paris, a 'riot', as the collaborationist press described it, broke out at the market at the rue de Buci on 31 May 1942, leaving two policemen dead. In the clampdown that followed, male communist militants who had helped to coordinate it were executed, while female suspects were sent to Ravensbrück concentration camp. This did not stop a similar – and also violent – protest erupting on 1 August at the rue Daguerre market. The right-wing L'Oeuvre daily duly proclaimed in its headlines that 'The second front stretches from the rue de Buci to the rue Daguerre', deriding both the protesters and the Allies, not to mention the 'terroristic' communists.[20] Such protests remained isolated incidents,

18 Tomasz Szarota, *Warschau unter dem Hakenkreuz: Leben und Alltag im besetzten Warschau 1.10.1939 bis 31.7.1944* (Paderborn: Schöningh, 1985), pp. 123–5; Aly, *Hitlers Volkstaat*, p. 123 on the establishment of the *Heringsweiterleitungsstelle* by the Wehrmacht at the end of 1942.
19 Gildea, *Marianne in Chains*, pp. 83–5.
20 Paula Schwartz, 'The Politics of Food and Gender in Occupied Paris', *Modern and Contemporary France* 7:1 (1999), 35–45.

however significant for the participants. The numbing reality remained the queue for official allocations, which increasingly ran short as supplies were diverted onto the black market.

Shortage remodelled social differences and shifted the value of assets. Across Europe, the countryside prospered from high demand brought about by a lack of overseas competition. In the Loire, some farmers saved enough during the war to buy their land, while in Saint-Mathurin the daughter of a deceased magistrate married the farmer who had courted her. Pre-war social snobbery gave way before his regular gifts of chops. Middle-class Parisians returned to areas, like Chinon, which they had come to know when their offices had been evacuated in 1940, while the bourgeois cycle-tourist, with double panniers, became a familiar sight in the countryside.[21] In the absence of motorized transport, the bicycle entered a golden age. Almost every town had at least one cycling club.[22] Most cyclists were increasingly concerned with mundane problems, like how to replace worn-out tyres when imported rubber had been choked off by the British naval blockade. A common, though slow and extremely bumpy, solution was to wire together lengths of garden hose.[23]

The logic of food surplus and deficit quickly imposed itself on the pan-European economy. The Netherlands and Denmark enjoyed a surplus, while Belgium, Norway and Greece all suffered from deficits. Left in charge of their own state, Danish administrators had adopted a pricing and rationing policy which encouraged farmers to increase the supply of pork, beef and milk and raise exports to Germany, without imposing harsh restrictions on domestic consumption or stimulating a black market. The outcome of this system of direct economic incentives was spectacular: with a population of 4 million, Denmark became an ever more important exporter to the German Reich, contributing some 10–12 per cent of its beef, pork and butter. By 1944, German cities may have drawn as much as a fifth of their meat supplies from Denmark, as other sources went into steep decline. The Netherlands, with its technically modern agricultural sector, remained important too, though it also had to adapt to the constraints of the British blockade. In the first two years of the war, Germany replaced Britain as the key export market for Dutch meat, but as the blockade halted the import of animal feed, Dutch

21 Gildea, *Marianne in Chains*, pp. 116–18.
22 Ibid., pp. 148–9, 27.
23 Reg Langlois (Jersey) and Daphne Breton (Guernsey), www.bbc.co.uk/history/ ww2peopleswar (accessed 5 December 2014), archive of stories, A3403946 and A4014091.

farmers switched increasingly to arable and greenhouse crops. By 1941, they had culled their herds to the point where they were able to export fodder themselves, as well as important supplies of fruit, vegetables, sugar and potatoes to Germany.[24]

Norway, Belgium and Greece all depended on large food imports. Nazi policy-makers, their reasoning based on a mix of racial and economic utility, regarded Norway as more 'Aryan' than the Reich and, in many other respects, the country was treated – by German standards – as a 'model' occupation. Yet even here, child mortality rates began to rise, and by the summer of 1942, German reports were noting that Norwegians were 'to a considerable extent under-nourished'.[25] In Belgium, imports from Germany were also never sufficient and only reached 17 per cent of the pre-war level.[26] As black market prices for food soared and wage rates remained fixed, there was a wave of labour unrest in those industries in which workers felt most secure and trade union structures remained intact. On 9–10 May 1941, there were strikes in the Belgian coal mines and steel mills, symbolically commemorating the first anniversary of the occupation. Keen to ward off any increase in communist influence, Belgian employers preferred to negotiate with the trade unions and agree to an 8 per cent wage rise, than to hand over the lists of militants which the German military authorities were demanding.[27] In France and Belgium, the memory of working-class hunger during the occupation was scarred deeply into collective common sense afterwards. At the time, the French trade union-run factory social committees and the Belgian factory councils spent so much of their efforts on trying to provide food, setting up works canteens and allocating allotments to dig, that they were dubbed 'potato committees'.[28]

Greece also had a food deficit and had depended on importing a third of its grain from Canada, the USA and Australia. In 1940–41, grain supplies plummeted to 40 per cent of their pre-war level, and within five months of the German occupation, the first famine broke out in occupied Europe.

24 Morgens Nissen, 'Danish Food Production in the German War Economy', in Frank Trentmann and Flemming Just (eds.), *Food and Conflict in Europe in the Age of the Two World Wars* (Basingstoke: Palgrave Macmillan, 2006), pp. 172–92; Voglis, 'Surviving Hunger', in Gildea et al. (eds.), *Surviving Hitler and Mussolini*, pp. 19–22.
25 Aly, *Hitlers Volksstaat*, p. 123.
26 Voglis, 'Surviving Hunger', pp. 21–2.
27 Robert Gildea, Dirk Luyten and Juliane Fürst, 'To Work or Not to Work', in Gildea et al. (eds.), *Surviving Hitler and Mussolini*, pp. 46–7.
28 Ibid., p. 50.

In Athens, the daily calorie intake dropped to 930, and over the next year, 40,000 died in the Athens-Piraeus area. Unlike Backe's successive 'Hunger Plans' for the Soviet Union, the Greek famine was an unintended consequence of German occupation, triggered by a fatal combination of military purchasing and requisitioning, alongside food hoarding by wholesale distributors. The famine was greatly exacerbated by the division of the country into three separate occupation zones – Italian, German and Bulgarian – each of which issued its own currency. Moreover, the Bulgarians prohibited all transports of grain out of Eastern Macedonia and Thrace, where 30 per cent of the pre-war grain had been grown. Even within the three occupation zones, physical and administrative obstacles were combining to fragment regional ties into ever smaller units. With damaged roads and requisitioned vehicles, transport networks collapsed. There was one train a day from Athens to the north, so that no more than 300–350 tonnes of food could reach the city each day by this means. As post and telecommunications broke down too, the integration of the national economy went into rapid reversal.[29]

It would have taken far more resilient state institutions and massive food aid to prevent the Greek famine. Neither the German military administrators on the spot, nor Backe's officials in the Reich Food Ministry in Berlin, were moved to provide much assistance. Germany would send 5,000 tonnes of grain; the Italians, severely short of food themselves, 10,000; and the third Axis occupying power, Bulgaria, nothing. By October 1941, things were already so bad that Greece's old enemy Turkey – officially neutral and within the British blockade zone – sent a relief ship with 1,100 tonnes aboard. It made four more crossings before sinking in January 1942. The famine was only finally relieved when Britain agreed to lift its blockade and permit Swedish vessels to bring Canadian grain to Greece under the supervision of the International Red Cross.[30] Whereas Belgium and Norway were of real economic and strategic importance, and counted as 'Germanic' and 'Aryan' nations, potential allies or even fellow citizens within an expanded German Reich, the philo-Hellenism of the German officers who set up their occupation administration in Athens in the spring of 1941 did not extend beyond the classical period. By the spring of 1942, German-language newspapers in

---

29 Mazower, *Inside Hitler's Greece*, pp. 23–72; Voglis, 'Surviving Hunger', pp. 23, 29–30; Violetta Hionidou, *Famine and Death in Occupied Greece, 1941–1944* (Cambridge University Press, 2006).
30 Voglis, 'Surviving Hunger', p. 24.

Greece began to deploy the language of urban parasites and 'useless eaters', which had so far been reserved within German parlance for the Jews.[31]

Genocide

On 6 August 1942, Hermann Göring chaired a meeting of officials from the occupied territories who were charged with putting Backe's European-wide food requisitioning demands into effect. Göring seems to have explicitly linked the food requisitioning with the murder of the Jews, as indeed Backe himself had a few weeks earlier, when he met with Hans Frank's officials from the General Government. Why did Backe, and, in all probability, Göring, refer to the genocide in connection with this second 'Hunger Plan'? Some historians have taken their interventions at face value as an announcement of policy, and argued that German food requirements became a major driver of the Holocaust. Ending the deployment of the Jews for forced labour and accelerating their murder, in this view, fits into an economic rationale of food rationing: the Jews were chosen to pay for the deliveries to the Reich.[32]

A different reading of these sources would suggest that Göring was not announcing a new policy to murder the Jews, but rather enlisting the fact of their murder for his immediate rhetorical purpose. The deportation and murder of the Slovakian, Dutch, French, Belgian and Polish Jews had already been in full swing for weeks, and the fact of their murder could hardly have come as news to anyone present. Göring's meeting in August was not the equivalent of the Wannsee Conference back in January 1942, where Heydrich had declared his ambition to 'evacuate' 11 million Jews. As Himmler told his own SS officials in Poland, the murder of the Jews was a 'political', not an economic decision.[33]

31 Mazower, Hitler's Empire, p. 280.
32 Christian Gerlach, Krieg, Ernährung, Völkermord: Forschungen zur deutschen Vernichtungs-politik im zweiten Weltkrieg (Hamburg: Hamburger Edition, 1998), pp. 168–9; Gerlach, Kalkulierte Morde, p. 672; Christoph Dieckmann, 'The War and the Killing of the Lithuanian Jews', in Ulrich Herbert (ed.), National Socialist Extermination Policies (New York and Oxford: Berghahn Books, 1999), pp. 210–39; Adam Tooze, The Wages of Destruction: The Making and Breaking of the Nazi Economy (London: Allen Lane, 2006), pp. 338–51; Lizzie Collingham, The Taste of War: World War Two and the Battle for Food (London: Allen Lane, 2011), pp. 204–13.
33 Christopher Browning, Nazi Policy, Jewish Workers, German Killers (Cambridge University Press, 2000), pp. 55–88.

Rather than announcing a new policy toward the Jews, it seems more likely that Backe and Göring were reminding their high-ranking audience of what they were already doing, in order to steel their nerves to take on a still greater challenge. They were not meeting to justify the murder of the Jewish *minority*, but rather to cajole German officials into doing something much more difficult, namely inflicting famine on the social *majority*. Imposing lethal levels of requisitioning on Poland and Ukraine meant taking on much larger sections of the population, with greater potential for armed resistance than the decimated and starving Jewish ghettoes. In this context, reference to the murder of the Jews may simply have served as a rhetorical and ideological prompt, to remind German occupation officials to stiffen their resolve and enact still 'harder' measures. Göring – who took overall responsibility for imposing the 1942 'hunger' plan – laid out the core argument with brutal clarity at the 6 August meeting:

> I have here before me reports on what you are expected to deliver... it makes no difference to me in this connection if you say that your people will starve. Let them do so, as long as no German collapses from hunger. If you had been present when the Gauleiter spoke here [yesterday], you would understand my boundless anger over the fact that we conquered such enormous territories through the valour of our troops, and yet our people have almost been forced down to the miserable rations of the First World War... I am interested only in those people in the occupied regions who work in armaments and food production. They must receive just enough to enable them to continue working.[34]

As so often in wartime Germany, Nazi public rhetoric followed a remarkably parallel path to what was being said behind closed doors. On Sunday 4 October 1942, Hermann Göring announced the full restoration of German rations, reversing the April cuts. In a speech appropriately billed to celebrate Harvest Thanksgiving, he assured Germans that 'we are feeding all of our troops from the occupied territories'. He also dwelt, at length, on the fact that this was, above all, a war against the Jews. Hammering home what would happen in the event of defeat, Göring spoke like a concerned father: 'German people, you [*Du*] must know: If the war is lost, then you are annihilated.' He went on to explain that 'This war is not the Second World War, this war is the Great Race War. Whether the German and Aryan stands

---

34 International Military Tribunal, *Trial of the Major War Criminals Before the International Military Tribunal, Nuremberg, 14 November 1945 – 1 October 1946* (Nuremberg: 1947–49), vol. XXXIX, doc. 170-USSR, pp. 384–412, cited in Tooze, *Wages of Destruction*, pp. 546–7.

here or whether the Jew rules the world, that is what it is about in the end and that is what we are fighting for out there.'[35]

How much the rest of occupied Europe cared about the fate of the Jews remains an open question: certainly less than people cared about German labour conscription, food delivery quotas, hostage-taking or reprisals for 'terrorist' acts of resistance. From July 1942 to March 1943, the trains deporting Jews from France departed amidst an eerie silence, quite different from the singing of the 'Marseillaise', raucous scenes and wildcat factory strikes that accompanied the forced drafts of French workers to Germany. But after they were gone, the fate of the Jews became a reference point of sorts, a worst-case scenario. In parts of Poland and Ukraine, where crowds had gathered to see the round-ups of Jews and to acquire the property they left behind in 1941 and 1942, the murder of the Jews soon became a yardstick for measuring their own possible fates. Through the summer and early autumn of 1942, SS units helped to requisition the Polish harvest. When they returned to drive Poles off the land and 'Germanize' villages in the Zamość district in November, the rumour soon spread that the Poles, too, would be sent to the gas chambers at Bełżec or Treblinka.[36]

In the cities of Ukraine, it was similar. When Kiev was occupied in September 1941, little sympathy or help had been extended when the Jews were immediately massacred in the ravine of Babi Yar. By 25 April 1942, the teacher L. Nartova could see no escape from the German-imposed blockade of food for the city. 'What can one do, how to live?' she asked her diary. 'They probably want to give us a slow death. Obviously it is inconvenient to shoot everybody'. By early autumn, after a year of German rule, Nartova chronicled the Kievan view from the queues: 'First they finished off the Yids, but they scoff at us for a whole year, they exterminate us every day by the dozens, they're destroying us in a slow death'.[37]

In Ukraine and Greece, famine and German 'anti-partisan' actions tipped whole regions of the countryside into civil wars, which extended for years beyond the end of the occupation. The destruction of state structures and socio-economic sinews during the occupation may well help to explain why

---

35 Peter Longerich, 'Davon haben wir nichts gewusst!' Die Deutschen und die Judenverfolgung, 1933–1945 (Munich: Siedler, 2006), pp. 203–4.
36 For rumours of extermination, see Czesław Madajczyk, Die Okkupationspolitik Nazideutschlands in Polen 1939–1945 (Cologne: Pahl-Rugenstein, 1988), p. 427; Dr Wilhelm Hagen to Adolf Hitler, 7 December 1942, in Kyril Sosnowski, The Tragedy of Children under Nazi Rule (Poznań: Zachodnia Agencja Prasowa, 1962), annex 29A, pp. 317–20.
37 Berkhoff, Harvest of Despair, pp. 183, 184.

this cycle of violence was so extreme, even after the Wehrmacht had retreated. In France or Belgium, the full brutality of German demands on food and labour was mitigated by the existence of national and local structures, able, for much of the occupation, to negotiate and ward off the worst of the German demands. For each institution involved, there were red lines, impositions which it would not accept: for the Catholic Church in France, that line finally came on 1 February 1944, with the conscription of unmarried women for labour in Germany. The Gallican Church's assembly of cardinals and archbishops felt moved to speak out, condemning this 'serious attack on family life and the future of our country, on the dignity and moral suscepti-bility of women and their providential vocation' – motherhood. The contrast with its own inaction over the deportation of the Jews was clear. These were not just moral positions. Silence was as calculated a negotiating position as protest, signalling areas of acquiescence in order to defend what really mattered.[38]

Sex

The lovers swapped photos before his departure to Vienna, from where André wrote to her, eagerly planning to visit at Christmas and promising her, 'I kiss your breasts a thousand times, we will do 69.'[39] It was not to be. During the Christmas holidays of 1943, her husband was the one who succeeded in getting leave from his anti-aircraft battery and André had to cool his ardour in Vienna. Undaunted, at the end of January 1944, André succeeded in having himself transferred to a job nearer to Berlin, only to find himself arrested soon after. His letter had fallen into the hands of the Gestapo, responsible – along with hunting communists, Freemasons, Jeho-vah's Witnesses who refused military service and Jews who did not turn up on the appointed date for deportation – for policing 'forbidden contact' between Germans and foreigners within the Reich.

André was in Germany as a French civilian worker and there was no actual ban on such relationships, although the fact that his lover was a married German woman gave the police an excuse to intervene. The investigation revealed a clandestine love story which had begun a year earlier, at the beginning of 1943, with Sunday trysts. André, it transpired, had in fact been a

---

38 Michèle Cointet, *L'Eglise sous Vichy, 1940–1945* (Paris: Perrin, 1998), p. 291.
39 Fabrice Virgili, *Naître ennemi: Les enfants de couples franco-allemands nés pendant la Seconde Guerre mondiale* (Paris: Payot, 2009), pp. 52–3.

French prisoner of war, one of the million sent to work in Germany after the armistice of 1940. Under lax guard, and helped by his lover to civilian clothes, it had not been difficult for him to escape. This was not so very unusual – perhaps as many as 200,000 other French prisoners did the same. But André was so smitten that no sooner had he arrived in France than he decided to return to Germany. André belonged to the relatively small minority who genuinely volunteered to work in the Reich, and he must have been one of the only ones to do so, not from economic motives, but, literally, out of love.

Unfortunately, for him, this was banned. In the complex knot of racial, military and political criteria, whereas relationships between Germans and French civilian workers were permitted, those with prisoners of war were prohibited. And then there was the small matter of André's escape. Soon after the capitulation of France, the Reich Security Main Office, under Heydrich, ordered 'that in accordance with the Führer's order, French, English and Belgian prisoners should, like the Polish prisoners of war, receive the death sentence in cases of sexual intercourse with German women and girls'. The Wehrmacht ignored Heydrich and, instead, followed the Geneva Convention, according to which representatives of the protecting powers were entitled to take part in the proceedings of the military courts and, more importantly, had to be informed of the verdict. Under article 92 of the military penal code, which covered cases of insubordination, they generally handed down prison terms of three years. These, too, might be lighter if it was believed that the woman had 'seduced' the man.[40] Conversely, if the woman was married to a soldier, then the sentence imposed by the military courts was usually heavier and involved sending the prisoner of war to the harsh Stalag at Graudenz. An estimated 7,000 to 9,000 internees were incarcerated in this fortress, where heavy labour, poor diet, exposure to the cold of winter and deficient hygiene took their toll.[41] André denied that he had had a sexual relationship in vain: his love letter had become incriminating evidence and he was sentenced to three years. We do not know how the German police treated his lover, though in other cases of this kind, much would have depended on the view of her husband.[42]

40 Ibid., pp. 86–7; Ulrich Herbert, *Hitler's Foreign Workers* (Cambridge University Press, 1997), pp. 129–30; Bernd Boll, '"...das gesunde Volksempfinden auf das Grobste verletzt": Die offenburger Strafjustiz und der "verbotene Umgang mit Kriegsgefangenen" wahrend des 2. Weltkriegs', *Die Ortenau* 71 (1991), 661.

41 Virgili, *Naître ennemi*, pp. 84–5.

42 Robert Gellately, *Backing Hitler: Consent and Coercion in Nazi Germany* (Oxford University Press, 2001), pp. 169–70.

The imperative of policing sex and the impossibility of doing so marked out the ways in which German notions of national purity and power were defined by gender and sex, as well as race, during the Second World War. In Nazi, but not only Nazi, eyes, the Fatherland was ultimately female: foreign men posed a clear threat. By the end of May 1940, there were 853,000 foreign workers in Germany, nearly two-thirds of whom were employed in agriculture, most of them Poles. For a regime which had made such an ideological fetish out of national – and racial – purity, this initial influx of farm labour could at least be depicted as a resumption of a tradition of drawing on seasonal Polish migrant labour. From June 1940, even before France's capitulation, the Gestapo began to hang Polish men in public. In early July, a report came in from Ingeleben near Helmstedt, where a Polish prisoner of war, who had been remanded in the military prison for sexual intercourse with a German woman, was handed over to the Gestapo and 'hanged from a tree as a warning to others'. Many others followed.[43]

Policing sex followed a pattern established since the Nuremberg Laws of 1935 had banned sex between 'Aryans' and Jews. Much depended on neighbours reporting home visits and acts of 'friendliness' in order to spot incipient cases of 'race defilement' or 'forbidden contact' before they came to fruition. Anything which involved the daily surveillance of neighbourhood relations depended on snooping and denunciation by quarrelsome neighbours, nosy block wardens, suspicious postmen, zealous work colleagues and, occasionally, spiteful in-laws. Not surprisingly, the number of denunciations was very large from the point of view of the small and undermanned Gestapo, and for most of the war would constitute the bulk of its caseload. Yet at the same time, only a very small number of Germans ever became denouncers or, for that matter, were ever denounced. Through its mass organizations, the Nazi state might, in principle, penetrate down into the ranks of concierges, porters and school children, but it lacked the active manpower to do more than demonstrate the risks of 'forbidden relations'. For the entire war, the Düsseldorf Gestapo generated a mere 165 such case files.[44]

By portraying itself as omnipresent, omniscient and omnipotent, the Nazi dictatorship was marketing its own 'totalitarian' claims as a form of deterrence. In reality, policing neighbourhood relations was highly selective and therefore rather arbitrary. Both the threat and the application of

43 Herbert, *Hitler's Foreign Workers*, pp. 61–4, 86–96, 132.
44 Gellately, *Backing Hitler*, pp. 155–66: he found 150 in Palatinate and 146 in Lower Franconia.

punishment carried a strong resonance of the public spectacle of exemplary justice of a pre-liberal and pre-enlightenment era. In the pre-war years, local Nazi activists had devised rituals of public degradation, parading the Jewish men who broke the Nuremberg Laws, who were mocked and made to run the gauntlet of the streets bearing placards describing their crime.[45] Continuing this reinvention of the 'rough music' of *charivari*, the police relied on local activists to inflict a ritual of humiliation on the German woman or, more rarely, man.

The public spectacle was designed to impress and deter two different constituencies, Poles and Germans, who were brought together in order to keep them apart. In Germany, the judicial norm for capital punishment was the guillotine, carried out by qualified public executioners, under judicial supervision in major prisons. Hanging had not gone through the Anglo-American scientific evolution of the long-drop and counter-weights resulting in instant rupture of the spinal column. It had remained, as it had been in the medieval and early modern periods, a dishonourable death by slow strangulation, and one from which, until 1944, Germans were generally exempt.[46] It was a further sign that within the same towns and villages of the Reich there were two orders, the one German and the other colonial. Dragooned into attending the executions, the local population of Polish forced labourers would be forced to walk past and view the body of the man, whom two of their number had been pressed into hanging. Whatever they thought and felt, they were wise enough to keep to themselves.

The Germans were free to attend and were voluble in their views. German reactions generally depended on what they thought of the case. One of the first executions, on 3 June 1940, of a civilian worker in Eiberg near Wattenscheid, 'met with disapproval' from the local population because the man had a reputation in the locality for being well behaved, hard-working and shy – and his offence had allegedly been to have 'put his hand up the skirt of a German girl on agricultural labour service'.[47] Often there were calls for the woman to be forced to attend the execution of her lover; not infrequently, for her to suffer the same fate, either because she was held to be the 'seducer' or because, as the kerbside judgement of a case in Regensburg would have it, 'the larger part of the city population actually

45 Michael Wildt, *Volksgemeinschaft als Selbstermächtigung: Gewalt gegen Juden in der deutschen Provinz 1919 bis 1939* (Hamburg: Hamburger Edition, 2007).
46 Richard J. Evans, *Rituals of Retribution: Capital Punishment in Germany, 1600–1987* (Oxford University Press, 1996).
47 Herbert, *Hitler's Foreign Workers*, p. 132.

apportioned the greater guilt to the German girl': for, it was said, 'the Polish man was simply satisfying his sexual need, while the German girl, from whom more could be expected than the Pole, had damaged the honour of the nation'.[48] More common was the sense that she should be punished because she had betrayed the 'honour of the German woman'.[49] In its guidelines of 1943, the Reich Ministry of Justice was merely repeating its basic axiom when it stated that 'German women who engage in sexual relations with prisoners of war have betrayed the front, done gross injury to their nation's honour, and damaged the reputation of German womanhood abroad'.[50] As it turned the intimate details of its citizens' sex lives into local news stories, the Nazi regime was reinventing a popular theatre of the gallows that nineteenth-century penal reformers had congratulated themselves on having banished.[51]

Building on the shaming rituals meted out to German women who 'defiled the race' by having relationships with Jewish men, shaving women's heads was intended to strip women of their sexuality. In so doing, they were being reminded that their bodies were not fully their own. Occasionally, men might be marched and pilloried too, like the unfortunate farm labourer August Kreidel, who was paraded through the streets of his Lower Franconian village, displayed at the marketplace to be jeered and humiliated by a crowd of 500, before being sent to Dachau for a three-month spell.[52] The only parallel to shaving women's hair among men were the scenes in which laughing groups of soldiers in the East cut off Jewish men's beards: both were gendered, and both used ridicule and mockery as a prelude to further violence. But here the parallels end: attacking male sexuality in this way was something only done to Jews and it was often a prelude to their murder. As a particularly gendered punishment, cutting off the hair was a public desexualization: the whole point of shaming women was that, after they had been punished, they would return to the same community, chastened and painfully aware that their neighbours would remember who they were long after their hair had regrown.

48 Robert Gellately, *The Gestapo and German Society: Enforcing Racial Policy, 1933–1945* (Oxford University Press, 1990), p. 243.
49 Gellately, *Backing Hitler*, pp. 179–80.
50 Cited in Christiane Rothmaler, 'Fall 29', in Justizbehörde Hamburg (ed.), '*Von Gewohnheitsverbrechern, Volksschädlingen und Asozialen': Hamburger Justizurteile im Nationalsozialismus* (Hamburg: Ergebnisse, 1995), p. 372.
51 Richard van Dülmen, *Theatre of Horror: Crime and Punishment in Early Modern Germany* (Oxford: Polity Press, 1990); Evans, *Rituals of Retribution*.
52 Gellately, *Backing Hitler*, pp. 173, 157–8.

Since the Germans subjected to such rituals were mainly women, female spectators also began to make their views of the double sexual standards heard. So, in early 1941, a number of women called out from the crowd watching a woman being paraded through the streets of Ebern, with a placard reading 'I sullied the honour of German womanhood'. According to the Security Service, they 'let it be known that they disapproved of this action. A few women also ventured to ask whether the same would be done to a man who had an affair with a French woman while in France'. While most women in the crowd, even those in the Nazi Party, joined in the criticism, 'a greater part of the population', presumably the male majority, 'welcomed the measure, and some demanded that a beating be added'.[53]

In small-town and rural Thuringia – a Lutheran heartland with a strongly pro-Nazi, German Christian provincial church – the new rituals quickly gained a popular following. As early as March 1940, the Jena higher court was complaining that it had become normal there to shave a woman's head, hang a placard on her proclaiming her crime and march her through the village, even before she was charged. On 15 November 1940, the town square of Eisenach in Thuringia filled to mock a German woman and her Polish lover, tied back to back against a post on a small platform in the centre of the marketplace. Above her shaven head, her placard proclaimed 'I let a Pole have me'; above his, 'I am a race-defiler'. In the photograph, mothers brought their young children to the front or lifted them up so that they could see too.[54] In Thuringia, even the Security Service of the SS baulked at the popular enthusiasm for attending public executions, shocked that 800–1,000 spectators in Hildburghausen flocked to watch the mass hanging of twenty Poles – and that was not counting the 600–700 women and children whom the police held back in the forest to prevent them attending.[55]

Not all parts of the Reich were as enthusiastic as German Christian Thuringia. Adverse, even hostile, reactions were reported from some Catholic areas, such as Würzburg or the Rhineland: there the Poles were co-religionists as well, and the industries of the Rhineland and the Ruhr had also attracted large-scale Polish migration; increasingly, the Gestapo itself advised against public executions in Catholic regions.[56] It was not only the huge freight being

---

53 Birthe Kundrus, 'Forbidden Company: Romantic Relationships between Germans and Foreigners, 1939 to 1945', *Journal of the History of Sexuality* 11:1 and 2 (2002), 210; also Rolf Hochhuth, *Eine Liebe in Deutschland* (Reinbek: Rowohlt, 1978), p. 63.
54 Virgili, *Naître ennemi*, pp. 88–9.
55 Gellately, *Backing Hitler*, p. 179; SD Bayreuth, 17 August 1942.
56 Gellately, *Backing Hitler*, pp. 174, 180, 160.

loaded onto the 'honour of German womanhood' or the double standard being applied to German men and women which led to dissent. The authorities, as well as the population as a whole, were confused about what kinds of relationships were permissible. Why was sex off-limits, though not forbidden, with men from the 'Aryan' countries, such as Denmark, Norway and the Netherlands, places where the Wehrmacht and SS positively encouraged – and supported – German soldiers who had children with local women? And then there were the exemptions made for 'racial inferiors' who happened to be Germany's national allies. Italy, Croatia, Romania, Spain, Hungary and Yugoslavia were all meant to be exempt, although the Weimar Gestapo wanted to stop relationships 'in view of our racial beliefs', and, in a small number of cases, the authorities actually did so. Italians, Croatians, Romanians, Spaniards, Hungarians and Ukrainians were categorized in a way that suited the German Foreign Ministry and offended the Reich Security Main Office and the Nazi Party. Hitler had encouraged Ukrainian and Belorussian nationalists as potential allies against Bolshevism, and, unlike Poles and Russians, Ukrainians were permitted to go to shops, cinemas, church and restaurants. Germans, accustomed to thinking of all 'easterners' as 'Russians', often struggled with these distinctions, leading to tragic results.[57]

In an attempt to mitigate the international public relations disaster at a time when Germany needed to keep its allies on side and persuade their citizens to volunteer to work in the Reich, Hitler banned the public shaming rituals and punishments altogether in October 1941.[58] It is impossible to quantify how many relationships were not reported. No witness to André's year-long comings and goings had denounced them. If a block of flats or a village closed ranks, then, like the dog (in Sherlock Holmes) which failed to bark, the relationships left no trace in the official records.

★★★

The obsession with sex was not just a German one. It formed a pan-European common sense of the Second World War, in which the enemy

---

57 Kundrus, 'Forbidden Company'; Annegret Hansch-Singh, 'Rassismus und Fremdarbeitereinsatz im zweiten Weltkrieg' (unpublished PhD thesis, Freie Universität, 1991), p. 139; Hans-Henning Kramer and Inge Plettenberg, *Feind schafft mit... Ausländische Arbeitskräfte im Saarland während des Zweiten Weltkrieges* (Ottweiler: Ottweiler Druckerei und Verlag, 1992), pp. 134–5.

58 Bormann directive, 31 October 1941, in Beatrice Heiber and Helmut Heiber (eds.), *Die Rückseite des Hakenkreuzes: Absonderliches aus den Akten des Dritten Reiches* (Munich: Deutscher Taschenbuch Verlag, 1993), pp. 234–5.

was always male and actively predatory, while one's own nation remained passive and female. After the war, officials in France boasted that Frenchmen had fathered 200,000 children in Germany. No doubt they were not considering possible claims for child support. Rather, this was a foundational, masculine code of national virility which held good across Europe, for German occupiers and national resistance movements alike: what they disagreed about was who was being screwed by whom.

The Polish resistance had immediately issued warnings that there would be plenty of room in the brothels for the women who took up with German men. But, like their campaign to boycott the downmarket love stories, adventure and war films authorized in Polish cinemas, warnings against 'horizontal collaboration', as it was disparagingly dubbed, also failed. Warsaw became a magnet for German soldiers on leave from the Eastern Front.[59] But even in more affluent Denmark, which had lost no men and where the Danish army and state remained intact, the glamour of victorious uniforms had a particular allure. In the military base and fishing port of Esbjerg on the western coast, some 3,000–4,000 German troops were added to a population of 32,000. As the German demand for the fish catch kept rising, so the number of young Danish men continued to rise too, leading to conflicts and resentment as it became clear that young women and teenage girls often preferred German to Danish men. By early August 1940, the local police chief was warning that there was general outrage among the town's young men at the 'German fraternization with the young Danish women in town and the way this fraternization takes place'.[60]

Unable to do anything about young women once they had come of age, the Danish authorities concentrated on those under eighteen, shrugging off pressure from the Germans to push the age of consent down to fifteen. In August 1940, one fourteen-year-old told police questioning her that it was unfair of them to pick up her and her friend, and that 'she did it [went with soldiers], because that's what all girls did, now they thought it was fun, so why shouldn't they?'[61] The pull of a free ticket to cafes, bars and restaurants became the stuff of peer-group envy; and, determined to prevent an epidemic of venereal disease, moral corruption and prostitution, the welfare

59 Szarota, *Warschau unter dem Hakenkreuz*, pp. 283, 181–5.
60 Lulu A. Hansen, '"Youth Off the Rails": Teenage Girls and German Soldiers – A Case Study in Occupied Denmark, 1940–1945', in Dagmar Herzog (ed.), *Brutality and Desire: War and Sexuality in Europe's Twentieth Century* (Basingstoke: Palgrave Macmillan, 2009), pp. 135–67.
61 Ibid., p. 150.

authorities and police kept on picking up girls in the parks and air-raid shelters and near the German military bases.[62]

Unlike young Danish fishermen, the Germans had a lot of free time. Military drill aside, the life of occupying troops was one of profound idleness, with abundant opportunities for courtship, friendships and hobbies which they would have had difficulty pursuing in civilian life. A Danish doctor, Grethe Hartmann, interviewed a group of Danish girls for her 1946 study, *The Girls They Left Behind*, and discovered that the most significant motive they gave for preferring Germans over Danes was that they had better, more courtly manners. A small number considered the Germans to be better lovers, showing, as one put it, 'consideration for the soul of the woman concerned'. And then there were those who fell in love.[63]

In the small Breton town of Morlaix, Aline noticed a new arrival at the Hôtel des Bains, where she waited on tables, in August 1940. He was Walter, and like many of the other Germans who came to eat in the restaurant, he was quartered in the hotel. Gradually, their chance conversations grew longer, with the help of his dictionary. That autumn, they fell in love. It was her first such encounter, and, as she told the historian Fabrice Virgili sixty-three years later, she could not pass the building where the hotel had been without remembering that time. The relationship lasted. For her twenty-third birthday, in January 1942, a Morlaix florist delivered twenty-three red roses. But Walter was tactful and more careful in public, changing out of uniform and wearing civilian suits and ties when they went out walking together. A photo she kept shows the couple together in front of a barn, respectably turned-out and looking rather older than their years. Interviewed at the age of eighty-four, Aline insisted, 'I did not do it because he was a German but because I loved him. That was all. Love knows no borders.' It may not have been an accident that she chose to confide in a sympathetic listener half her age.[64]

In August 1944, women deemed guilty of 'horizontal collaboration' would become the principal targets of communal violence. It was those who had formed durable relationships, entertained Germans in the privacy of their homes, rather than casually meeting them in public places, who faced particular condemnation and attracted a moral opprobrium which most male

62 Ibid., pp. 150–7.
63 Grethe Hartmann, *The Girls They Left Behind* (Copenhagen: Munkagaard, 1946), p. 61; and critical appraisal in Anette Warring, *Tyskerpiger: under besoettelse og retsopgør* (Copenhagen: Gyldendal, 1994).
64 Virgili, *Naître ennemi*, pp. 57–8.

collaborators, including those in positions of economic and political influ-ence, were spared.[65] Such judgements, with their common conviction that women's bodies belonged first to the nation and only then to themselves, encapsulated a particular kind of patriotism, shared by male-led resistance movements across Europe, by conservative elites seeking to accommodate the Germans and, when it came to German women back in the Reich, by German authorities too.

This was a sexual politics of the nation which cut across the politics of left and right and across the multiple differences between Western European experiences of occupation. However, it does not seem to have made the same impact on the occupied Soviet territories, though that absence may simply reflect the fact that historians have not yet asked these questions there, and that the Soviets imposed a taboo on the topic after the war. There was certainly no shortage of consenting sexual relationships within the occupied territories. If there is anecdotal evidence of consenting sexual relationships, there were also virtually no attempts to police rape. Uninhib-ited, male sexual violence became part of the trail left behind by the German armies and civilian administrators, alongside punishment beatings, execu-tions, looting and murder. By contrast, the Wehrmacht dealt severely with rape cases in the West.[66] In the occupied Soviet territories, no attempt was made to hold troops in check, let alone to engage with the moral categories of the occupied. This complete absence of shared moral and political space may also have prevented sexual relationships from occupying the symbolic public space that they took on in occupied and post-war Western Europe.

Conclusion

National and family values were enforced in wartime Germany by shaving women's heads. Across Europe, in the Channel Islands, Belgium, the Nether-lands, Denmark, Norway, France and Italy, when 'liberation' came, women's heads were again shaved in degrading public rituals, leaving the women with a social stigma which long outlasted the physical marks. The subjects of such vehement scorn and condemnation could retreat into silence and isolation. Some, like Aline, might look for private consolation by recalling memories of

65 Fabrice Virgili, *Shorn Women: Gender and Punishment in Liberation France* (Oxford: Berg, 2002); Warring, *Tyskerpiger*; Gildea, *Marianne in Chains*.
66 Regina Mühlhäuser, *Eroberungen. Sexuelle Gewalttaten und intime Beziehungen deutscher Soldaten in der Sowjetunion 1941–1945* (Hamburg: Hamburger Edition, 2010); Warring, *Tyskerpiger*, p. 131; Hansen, 'Youth Off the Rails', pp. 145–6.

love they might have avoided talking about to their own generation; a few managed even to forge relationships across post-war national borders to bring up their bi-national children. That stigma accompanied the children through childhood, schooling and often affected their life chances: it took sixty years before groups of them put their experience of discrimination on the political agenda – and that was in Norway, one of the most liberal and tolerant of Europe's democracies.[67]

In the Soviet territories, the Balkans and parts of Southern Europe, the German occupiers inflicted what they considered to be a species of 'colonial' rule. It was so ruthless that it tore the structures of state and society apart, inaugurating a spiral of civil war which outlasted the German occupation. In the West, the real contest was not the political one being waged between the collaborationist national governments and communist-led resistance move-ments for the soul of the nation. While the great cause of the *patrie* was fraying away, myriad small ties to the *pays* were becoming stronger and more complex. It was the local notables, landlords and clerics who had met the invaders in 1940, who had guaranteed the safety of their citizens by offering themselves as hostages at the beginning of the occupation, and who, as local mayors, now tried to protect them against economic demands which they felt were illegitimate. As a similar process of official exhortation and communal recalcitrance was played out across occupied Western Europe, it spelled a major reversal of the dominant trend of the previous hundred years toward the centralization of political legitimacy, which Max Weber had described as a key facet of 'modern' politics. The wartime trend to localizing struggles over legitimacy manifested itself not in the grand words of rival ideologies, but in the mundane strategies of black markets, sexual politics and family survival. Unsurprisingly, post-war democratic politics in the West and authoritarian communism in the East would be constructed around secure employment, stable prices and, above all, placing the family at the centre of welfare. Such family-centred populism, maintained over two gen-erations, testified most eloquently to the kind of 'people's war' most Euro-peans had endured and were determined to escape.

---

67 Anette Warring, 'Intimate and Sexual Relations', in Gildea et al. (eds.), *Surviving Hitler and Mussolini*, pp. 88–128; Kjersti Ericsson and Eva Simonsen (eds.), *Children of World War II: The Hidden Enemy Legacy* (Oxford: Berg, 2005); Virgili, *Naître ennemi*, pp. 60–3.

16

Collaboration, resistance and liberation in Western Europe

WILLIAM I. HITCHCOCK

Collaboration was both a German demand and a European response to catastrophic military defeat and occupation. The six nations considered here – Denmark, Norway, Belgium, the Netherlands, France and (with a rather different chronology) Italy – all developed some form of national administration with which to interact with their German overlords, often searching for a way to offer cooperation in return for a degree of national autonomy and a softening of the harsh hand of direct rule. The degree of collaboration – whether enthusiastic and efficient or dilatory and feckless – varied and was influenced by national, geographic and strategic considerations, as well as the ideological tendencies of the occupied peoples. Yet everywhere collaboration led to subordination and humiliation that spurred greater resistance as the war went on. The dynamic tension between collaboration and resistance inevitably shaped the experience of liberation, when the resistance forces and governments-in-exile sought to settle scores with their domestic enemies and shape the post-war political order.

The Germans set the terms of occupation in defeated Europe, but those terms were refracted through a prism of racial ideology as well as economic and strategic calculation, resulting in wide variation in occupation policies. Furthermore, within occupied states, the humiliation of defeat naturally discredited pre-war governments and elites, and opened the way to opportunists of varied ideological stripe to take power under the guise of collaboration. Thus in most occupied nations, a two-dimensional struggle began almost immediately: the struggle to adapt and perhaps resist the foreign occupation, and the internal struggle for power among competing political factions.

In some countries, small political factions welcomed the Nazi triumph as a prologue to the destruction of communism and decadent liberalism. Far more common reactions included shock, shame and humiliation, which translated quickly into subservience. Few people chose to fight the Germans through organized resistance, preferring to adapt to the new realities while protecting themselves, their families and their livelihoods. The scope of the German victory, the power of the Nazi war machine, the acquiescence of national leaders and the distant prospect of liberation made resistance seem futile. By contrast, a policy of waiting, hoping and keeping one's head down was natural and less likely to get one killed.

Over time, however, as the German occupation became more intrusive and demanding, and as the fortunes of war began to turn against the Third Reich, the appeal of resistance grew. The longer the war went on, the more the Germans had need of extracting resources and labour from their conquered territories – a process which, in turn, inflamed resentment and hatred of the German occupation. If resistance movements were slow to start, they mushroomed during the course of the war, so much so that by the final months of the war, resistance movements were large, in some cases operating as organized military formations, and acted as the vanguard of the postwar political administration. Yet resistance rarely translated into national political unity. Despite a common enemy in fascism, European resistance movements, especially those led by communists, remained loyal to ideological interests. Such partisan loyalty hobbled their military effectiveness, and certainly eroded any claim to speak for the nation. The politicized nature of the resistance would fuel decades of post-war controversy.

In the period 1944–45, these six nations were liberated by Anglo-American arms, working in conjunction with other Allied powers and local resistance movements. These were joyous days, but they were marred not only by the extraordinary ferocity of the fighting in the last year of the war, but also by the political factionalism that now spilled out into the open. The liberation period saw a brutal settling of scores, summary justice, the start of administrative purge trials and the bitter struggle to form new national governments. The clash was no longer with the Germans. Instead, resistance movements turned on one another, and against the governments-in-exile now laying claim to political power. And the new occupying powers – the Allied powers – also had post-war political ambitions that would decisively tip the balance away from the revolutions so ardently desired by some radical factions within the European underground movements. Now was born the thesis of a 'lost liberation' that would continue to roil post-war European politics for a generation.

Collaboration and resistance in Denmark and Norway

German occupation policy in Denmark and Norway was shaped by German racial ideology and strategic interests. Hitler viewed these Nordic states as potential future provinces of an expanded Reich; their population could easily be incorporated into Germany rather than suffer the fate that awaited the *Untermenschen* of the East. At the same time, Germany needed quick compliance from both nations in order to forestall a British invasion of Scandinavia and to guard its northern flank.

With the outbreak of war in September 1939, the Danish government reasserted its long-standing neutrality. As a consequence, when the Germans did invade Denmark on the morning of 9 April 1940, as part of their daring assault on Norway, the Danes had barely 20,000 troops in readiness. The Germans easily occupied ports, airfields and key road junctions, and presented the Danish government with a declaration of their goodwill: the German occupation would in no way rupture Danish sovereignty or political independence, if the Danes behaved themselves. King Christian X and the government immediately capitulated, and issued an appeal to the public for calm and good conduct. While such a supine response may have been precipitated by Germany's overwhelming power, it remains a hard fact that the Danish king, government and people did not raise a hand against the invaders.

There were certain benefits to such a cooperative attitude. Life in Denmark was not significantly disrupted in the first three years of the occupation. The standard of living remained comparatively high and the country did not suffer the war-related damage that accompanied the invasions of Poland or France. The King remained popular, a symbol of national unity and quiet defiance – though not yet resistance. The Danish government, made up of a unity Cabinet with representatives from the major parties, retained limited autonomy – enough to negotiate with the German occupation authorities. The Danish parliament continued to function. The social liberal parliamentarian Erik Scavenius, Foreign Minister and briefly Prime Minister, was the principal agent of Danish collaboration and led a technocratic government, whose purpose was to protect national sovereignty while cooperating with the German authorities. German interests were initially directed by a career diplomat with long experience in Denmark, Cecil von Renthe-Fink, who answered to the German Foreign Office. In November 1941, Foreign Minister Joachim von Ribbentrop could inform Hitler that no occupied country in Europe was as trouble-free or cooperative as Denmark.[1]

Although Hitler replaced Renthe-Fink with *SS-Gruppenführer* Karl Rudolph Best in October 1942, this protégé of Himmler nonetheless continued a

---

1 Norman Rich, *Hitler's War Aims*, vol. II: *The Establishment of the New Order* (2 vols., New York: Norton, 1973–74), p. 110.

relatively restrained policy in Denmark, and even allowed free parliamentary elections in March 1943 – elections that led to a thorough repudiation of the tiny Danish Nazi Party. Evidently, the lack of ideological conformity did not bother the Germans, as long as Denmark continued to provide food, military supplies, port facilities and labour for the German war machine, which it did. Until mid-1943, minor acts of resistance and the appearance of a small underground press did not seriously threaten the basic stability of the Danish-German arrangement.

The contrast with Norway is striking. The Germans invaded Norway on 9 April 1940, but King Haakon VII – the younger brother of Denmark's monarch – rejected a German ultimatum to surrender and made his way northward, to join British, French and Polish forces in Narvik which had launched a counter-attack. When the British withdrew on 7 June, the King and the Norwegian Cabinet followed them to London, and exile. On the day of the German invasion, the leader of the fascist Nasjonal Samling party, Vidkun Quisling, attempted a seizure of power, though this was met with incredulity by Norwegians and scepticism by the German invaders, as Quisling was an unimpressive figure and had almost no political base of support in the country. Hitler, angered that Norway had not followed the cooperative attitude of the Danes, appointed a Nazi Gauleiter, Josef Terboven, as *Reichskommissar* for Norway. Terboven put members of the Nasjonal Samling into leadership positions of key administrative departments, including Interior, Justice and Education, though he remained wary of the dubious Quisling. Over time, the Germans would augment the power of this fascist party and gradually allow Quisling a leading, if largely powerless, role. He was named Minister President in February 1942, officially Head of State, and remained in office until the end of the war. The real authority, however, lay with Terboven. Unlike his counterpart in Denmark, Terboven enjoyed the full powers of a conqueror and could govern by decree. Yet an iron hand was not initially necessary: with the departure of the King and Cabinet from the country, the Norwegian civil service cooperated efficiently, if unwillingly, with the German overlords.

Norwegians had courageously defied the invaders and they now paid the price. Unlike Denmark, Norway had to pay for the costs of the German occupation, a huge financial burden. All military materiel was immediately seized. The economy was fully geared toward German needs and the population was subject to labour service for the war effort. The country lost its all-important maritime trade with Britain and could no longer pay for imported foodstuffs on which it relied. The standard of living dropped sharply. Predictably, the heavy-handed tactics of the German occupiers in Norway provoked resistance earlier than in Denmark. By the summer of 1941, strikes and significant acts of sabotage were disrupting economic life in the country, and led to harsh reprisals and the expansion of the jurisdiction of the SS in the country. An internal resistance headquarters, the Milorg (Military Organization), emerged by late 1941 and was in contact with the government-in-exile as well as the British SOE. German penetration of underground networks limited the capabilities of armed resistance, though in February 1943, with British help, Norwegian commandos did sabotage the Vemork hydroelectric plant that was making heavy water for Germany's atomic bomb programme. Civilian resistance focused on the production of a large underground press and the creation of an internal civilian leadership, closely coordinated with the exiles in London.[2]

If Norway entered into resistance early, the Danes were slower to confront the occupier. In August 1943, with the war turning sharply against the Germans, Danish dockworkers in Odense went on strike; at the same time, the small Danish resistance, supplied by the British SOE, set off nationwide acts of sabotage. Some of these were substantial enough to threaten the transportation network and the economy itself. Berlin reacted swiftly, ordering *Gruppenführer* Best to impose full-scale military rule upon Denmark and to sweep away any vestige of Danish autonomy. Best and the Wehrmacht commander in Denmark disarmed the Danish army; the navy, however, scuttled many vessels rather than turn them over to the Germans, and some ships slipped away to Sweden, with their crews. The Danish government was disbanded and martial law declared. The SS now expanded its control. Communist political operatives, previously merely kept in jail, were deported to concentration camps. Jews were suddenly vulnerable to round-ups and deportation.

Danish resisters founded the Freedom Council in September 1943, and worked closely with SOE to organize sabotage and intelligence operations. In one of the more remarkable acts of national defiance to the New Order, the Council alerted Denmark's Jewish community to an impending round-up, and then organized the transport of over 7,000 Jews to Sweden in early October. Almost the entire Jewish community was saved. (At the same time, the resistance movement helped nuclear physicist Niels Bohr to flee to Sweden.) These actions, along with persistent, if small-scale, acts of sabotage

2 J. Andenaes, O. Riste and M. Skodvin, *Norway and the Second World War* (Lillehammer: Tanum-Norli, 1983).

after the Allied landings in June 1944, salvaged Denmark's national honour, which had been tarnished in the early years of the war.

Collaboration and resistance in Belgium and the Netherlands

Belgium was another nation on Germany's periphery for which neutrality was no protection at all from German invasion. Although the Belgians, who anticipated the German attack, mounted a reasonably stout defence with eighteen infantry divisions, they were no match for the combined air and ground assault the Germans launched on 10 May 1940. On 28 May, King Leopold III surrendered. This was a controversial decision: the elected government under Prime Minister Hubert Pierlot denounced it, for the King had not only surrendered the army of which he was Commander-in-Chief, but also turned over the nation to the invaders, a political act that required parliamentary ratification. The constitutional crisis endured for the duration of the war, as the Cabinet under Pierlot and Foreign Minister Paul-Henri Spaak formed a government-in-exile in London. The King chose to remain in the country, on the grounds that he must share the fate of his people. In November 1940, he met Hitler and hoped to secure a clear statement on the future independence of Belgium in Nazi Europe. Hitler refused any such guarantees, and Leopold returned to his splendid imprisonment in the opulent Royal Palace at Laeken.

Before leaving for exile, the government had delegated authority to the permanent civil service to administer all the departments and ministries during the crisis. Thus Belgium had no political leaders, but plenty of talented bureaucrats at the ready to keep the country going. Nothing could have served German purposes better. Hitler, with no clear idea in his mind about how to treat this hybrid (part-Germanic, part Francophone) state, chose to postpone matters and placed Belgium under military government, with General Alexander von Falkenhausen in command. He would remain in place until he was arrested in July 1944 for his ties to the anti-Hitler plotters. His principal deputy for administration was *SS-Gruppenführer* Eggert Reeder. The two men shared the goal of exploiting Belgium in the interests of the Reich, while limiting the scale of the occupation and keeping out interfering rival authorities from Berlin. As it happened, this suited Belgian interests as well. The civil service, industry and banking aligned themselves with German needs rapidly, and with a minimum of German pressure.

Just as the King opposed any prolonged armed resistance and refused to lead a government-in-exile, so too did Belgian industrial and banking leaders choose to make the best of the defeat and occupation. A small number of banks controlled most of the industrial economy and had done so for many decades. Within days of the capitulation, a group of bankers and industrialists gathered under the leadership of Alexandre Galopin, the governor of the largest bank in the country, the Société Générale de Belgique. Galopin's informal committee emerged as a kind of shadow government, working in tandem with the ministries and the occupation authorities. Given the dependence of the Germans upon continued Belgian economic productivity, the occupation authorities had no incentive to disrupt Belgian control of the economy. The Germans implemented a policy of placing orders for non-military iron and steel production with Belgian firms, and allowed the Belgians to fulfil these orders using their own methods and raw materials. But this trade was subsidized by the Belgian banks. In July 1940, the banking consortium paid the Germans 3 billion francs so that the Germans could use these funds to place orders in the economy and generate economic activity. This process of Belgian banks subsidizing economic activity through heavy occupation payments continued throughout the war.[3]

The Germans nimbly exploited not just Belgium's economy, but its ethnic divisions. Divided between the Dutch-speaking Flemish population and the French-speaking Walloons, the country was a fragile construct and the Germans used that to their advantage. They encouraged Flemish nationalism and found a willing servant in Staf de Clercq, the leader of the Flemish National Union (*Vlaamsch Nationaal Verbond*). This party, which before the war had attracted modest support even in Flanders, was avowedly pro-German and anti-Semitic; it favoured the union of Flanders with a greater Netherlands. Although Berlin had no interest in creating an autonomous Dutch-speaking entity, the Germans allowed de Clercq to nourish such hopes in exchange for his collaboration, which duly followed. Members of the Flemish National Union were given leading positions in municipal and local administration, and participated in the round-up of Belgian Jews, 25,000 of whom were deported. When de Clercq died in late 1942, he was succeeded by the mayor of Ghent, Hendrik Elias, an outspoken admirer of Hitler, who nonetheless opposed the full integration of Flanders into the

---

3 J. Gérard-Libois and José Gotovich, *L'an 40: La Belgique occupé* (Brussels: CRISP, 1971), pp. 169–84; John Gillingham, *Belgian Business in the Nazi New Order* (Ghent: Jan Dhondt Foundation, 1977), pp. 30–1, 67–8; Herman van der Wee and Monique Verbreyt, *A Small Nation in the Turmoil of the Second World War* (Leuven University Press, 2009), pp. 143–6, 202–5.

Reich. Far more fanatical in his desire for German victory and the integration of Belgium into the Reich was the bloodthirsty leader of Wallonia's Rexist Party, Léon Degrelle. Avowedly fascist, Degrelle immediately sought to curry favour with the German occupiers, and championed the formation of a Walloon brigade in the Waffen-SS, in which he served. Although the German occupation authorities initially denigrated the Walloons for their francophone ethnicity, Degrelle's movement drew much critical acclaim from Himmler. Degrelle received the Knight's Cross from Hitler himself.

The Belgian resistance was divided on ideological lines. The Front de l'Indépendence was communist-controlled, and a number of armed bands operated under its aegis. They took aim at leading collaborationists, gunning down mayors and police officials, despite the lethal reprisals these actions provoked. The Armée Secrète, meanwhile, included mostly military officers, whose loyalty to the discredited King was stronger than the government-in-exile would have liked. As in France, these underground movements gained notable traction once the German demands for more Belgian labour intensi-fied in 1943. Although never large, the Belgian resistance was especially valuable in securing for the Allies intelligence about German military dispos-itions along the Belgian coast, as well as in guiding downed Allied pilots out of the country and to safety. One such network, codenamed Comète and run by a twenty-four-year-old Red Cross volunteer named Andrée de Jongh, helped hundreds of fliers make it to Spain; but de Jongh was betrayed in the spring of 1943. After enduring torture by the Gestapo, she was sent to the Ravensbrück concentration camp. More common than this kind of active resistance was the general participation, after 1943, in sympathetic acts of support, whether in assisting underground newspapers, supplying food to those fleeing the labour round-ups, providing administrative help, false papers, money or shelter to those in need. These gestures, insignificant on an individual basis, could be knitted together into a broad picture of a nation increasingly determined to declare its opposition to German exploitation.

Compared to Belgium, the Netherlands endured a harsher fate during the war. Within days of the German invasion, the Dutch armed forces collapsed and the monarch, Queen Wilhelmina, and her government fled to London. But unlike Belgium, which remained under the rule of the military, the Netherlands was placed under civil rule and governed by an all-powerful *Reichskommissar* who served as Hitler's personal envoy. The Dutch were fated to be ruled by a clever and ruthless Nazi, Artur Seyss-Inquart, one of Hitler's Austrian countrymen who had played a crucial role in engineering the Anschluss. His chief aim was the eventual Nazification of the Netherlands and its incorporation into the Reich; yet such plans would have to await the end of the war. In the meantime, the Netherlands was treated like a well-stocked storehouse, ripe for German plundering.

As in Belgium, the majority of civil servants and bureaucrats in the Dutch government continued to work for the new occupation administration. And similar arrangements were established for the exploitation of Dutch industry by the German war machine: a central purchasing office was set up to buy up supplies of value to the Reich, which were paid for by overvalued marks, and the Dutch economy was gradually oriented entirely toward German needs. Labour recruitment followed the familiar pattern: initially voluntary, the Germans made registration for labour in the Reich compulsory in May 1943. By 1944, half of the Dutch industrial economy was working for Germany.

In the first year of the occupation, German policy focused on securing economic cooperation and political quiescence, thus opening the way for a degree of Dutch autonomy within the context of German rule. With the fall of France and the apparent German victory across Europe, Dutch political leaders chose the path of political accommodation with German rule. The initial architect of this policy was Hendrik Colijn, a conservative Calvinist parliamentarian who had been Prime Minister in the 1920s and 1930s. Colijn was a natural ally for Seyss-Inquart in this moderate phase of the occupation: though hostile to the Dutch fascists, Colijn was strongly anti-communist and could win the support of elites for his accommodationist policies. Colijn sang from sheet-music that was making the rounds in Western Europe at this moment: the German victory was complete; national independence could only be assured by cooperation with the new German master; and this arrangement might also offer possibilities for national renewal in the face of the collapse of Europe's liberal democratic institutions before the challenge of fascism. In July 1940, the leading political party leaders reluctantly agreed to the creation of a single national bloc called *Nederlandsche Unie* (NU) that would serve as the chief representative of the Dutch people to the occupation authorities. It was premised on a gamble: that speedy cooperation with the Germans would enhance Dutch autonomy and turn back the ambitions of the Dutch fascists. These hopes were inevitably dashed.

Seyss-Inquart rapidly grew disenchanted with NU precisely because of its success in rallying mass Dutch support: over a million members joined the movement in 1940 and it soon emerged as a potential source of nationalist resistance to German domination. In June 1941, despite having mouthed anti-communist slogans for over a year to curry favour with Seyss-Inquart, the NU refused to openly support the German invasion of the Soviet Union. Seyss-Inquart now saw the movement as a thinly disguised effort to reject Hitler's declared policy of full integration of the Netherlands into a greater Reich, so, in December 1941, he ordered it disbanded. Seyss-Inquart turned increasingly to the fascist alternative: Anton Mussert's National Socialist Movement (NSB), from now on the only legal political party in the country.

Mussert, a civil servant in the Department of Public Works in Utrecht, had founded the NSB in 1931. In the context of the economic crises and political divisions of the 1930s, the NSB's appeal was based on its anti-communism, nationalism and careful insistence on protection of private property. Despite some electoral support from white-collar workers, civil servants and rural landowners, the party never won more than a tiny fraction of Dutch support at the polls before 1940. Upon the German invasion in May, Mussert hoped his moment had come, but he was shunted off to the side by Seyss-Inquart, just as Terboven in Norway had ignored Vidkun Quisling's claims to a leadership role. Mussert worked diligently to prove his loyalty to Berlin: in August 1940, he penned a memorandum that called for Hitler to incorporate the Dutch, as well as the Swedes, Danes, Norwegians and Flemings, into the new Greater German Reich, while ensuring that Jews were eliminated. And Mussert happily volunteered the Dutch people for the work of waging war in, and colonizing, the East. Although Mussert himself was kept at arm's length for a time, the German rulers used members of the NSB to staff local administrative posts across the country, thus allowing deeper penetration of the fascists into the inner workings of Dutch society. Mussert's support for the German invasion of Russia and his prodding of NSB members to volunteer for the Waffen-SS further impressed the Germans, but worsened his support within the Netherlands. In December 1941, just as the NU was banned, Mussert, in Berlin, swore his 'loyalty unto death' to Adolf Hitler, a move that turned the Dutch people overwhelmingly against him. Although all real power in the occupied Netherlands remained in Seyss-Inquart's hands, Hitler did throw Mussert a crumb: he named him 'Führer of the Dutch people' and allowed him to form a Cabinet.

The German policy of elevating Mussert and the NSB to a position of influence profoundly agitated Dutch opinion and led to a spike in resistance activity. Since May 1940, resistance in the country had been negligible, with the notable exception of a two-day protest in February 1941 in reaction to the first Jewish round-ups in Amsterdam. But by 1943, with the increased prominence of the NSB, the Dutch resistance targeted collaborators for assassination, which in turn led to sharp German reprisals. In April 1943, the

Germans, increasingly anxious about a national resistance movement emerging, ordered all former members of the Dutch Army to report for internment in Germany, an act that triggered a major nationwide strike. The SS, under the control of Seyss-Inquart's colleague and rival *SS-Brigadeführer* Hanns Albin Rauter, savagely crushed the uprising, using lethal force on striking workers and hostages alike. There followed the imposition of compulsory labour service registration for all men aged eighteen to fifty. The effect of this policy was to push hundreds of thousands of young men into hiding and resistance. The opportunities for active military resistance against the Germans were limited in the Netherlands by its flat, densely settled topography and the lack of a *maquis* in which to hide. But small-scale acts, like assassinations, break-ins and sabotage now erupted across the country. Unfortunately, the SOE operation in the country was penetrated by the German *Abwehr*, and throughout 1942 and 1943, SOE agents, supplies and information fell into German hands.

Before June 1944, these resistance actions did little to hamper German control of the country, and were certainly ineffective in stopping the viciously thorough deportation of Dutch Jews carried out by Rauter and his men. As elsewhere in occupied Europe, Dutch Jews were hit first by the assault on their legal status, which denied them civil and political rights. In January 1941, all Jews had to register with local authorities; in June 1942, the round-ups began, on the pretext that Jews were to be assigned to work in Germany. In fact, they were sent to Auschwitz. By the end of 1942, 50,000 Dutch Jews had been sent to their deaths. Within the next eighteen months, an additional 60,000 Jews would follow them. This policy was fully supported by Seyss-Inquart, egged on by Himmler, and implemented with the full cooperation of the Dutch police, many of whose members were associates of the NSB. Seventy-five per cent of Dutch Jews were murdered in the Holocaust – the highest percentage of any Western European country.

The ordeal of France

There is a reason that historians of the Second World War keep turning back to France: the baffling complexities of the French response to occupation, from obsequious collaboration to heroic resistance, provide a window into the turmoil of a continent. With the defeat of French armed forces following the German invasion of May 1940, French President Albert Lebrun named vice premier and First World War hero Marshal Philippe Pétain as Prime Minister, with a mission to secure an armistice. He did so on 22 June 1940, to the enormous relief of the nation. The war had been a disaster, with 90,000 soldiers killed, an astonishing 1.5 million men taken prisoner and 6–8 million refugees fleeing south away from the front.[4] The armistice at least promised an end to the chaos. But the terms were harsh and non-negotiable: Alsace-Lorraine was sliced away by the Reich (and many of its young men drafted into the Wehrmacht), portions of northeastern France were removed from French control, and the northwest half of the country, including the Atlantic coastline, was placed under German occupation. The southern half of the country remained unoccupied. The French army was to be reduced to 100,000 men. Occupation costs were to be borne by the French government. The German Military Administration took command in Paris. The French government, assigned the duties of civilian administration of the nation, was allowed to establish its new capital in a small provincial town in the unoccupied zone known for its thermal baths: Vichy.

The most influential historian of these dark years of occupation, Robert Paxton, has written that 'collaboration was a French proposal that Hitler ultimately rejected'.[5] This assertion shocked readers in 1972; it has since become widely accepted. The French invented the idea of collaboration as a response to catastrophic defeat and as a strategy for survival in Hitler's New Order. In ruling France, the Vichy leaders reasoned, Germany would rely upon a French administration, and such dependence would increase France's bargaining power and open the way to a more balanced partnership. In order to maintain the French Empire, keep communism at bay, and enhance their own power, the leaders of the Vichy regime were willing to act as Hitler's junior partners. This gamble proved terribly wrong. German demands only intensified as the war continued, French autonomy was eroded rather than expanded, and the French public was not spared the harsh and brutal realities of living as a conquered people.

On 9 July 1940, the French National Assembly abolished the constitution and voted full powers to Pétain to draft a new one, providing his administration with a patina of legitimacy to which it clung for the rest of the war. Pétain assumed the office of Head of the French State, with Pierre Laval as premier. Vichy still maintained certain outward appearances of sovereignty: it controlled a large navy and an extensive colonial empire, and kept up

---

4 Julian Jackson, *The Fall of France: The Nazi Invasion of 1940* (Oxford University Press, 2003), pp. 174, 180.
5 Robert Paxton, *Vichy France: Old Guard and New Order, 1940–1944* (New York: Columbia University Press, 1972), p. 51.

diplomatic relations with other powers, notably the United States. In order to distance itself from the defeat and its alleged causes, the regime declared its intention to construct a new France on the rubble of the old. Thus a conservative, authoritarian and backward-looking regime invoked the language of renewal and revolution.

At the centre of Vichy's project of renewal lay collaboration: without success there, France could never secure greater autonomy and proceed down the road of moral revival. The initial architect of collaboration was Laval, who sought out contact with the Germans and proposed a new era of Franco-German conciliation. He proposed giving French support in the war against Britain in exchange for German recognition of French national and colonial sovereignty. On 22 and 24 October, Laval and Pétain met Hitler at Montoire-sur-Loir, soon after which Pétain announced his dedication to a policy of collaboration as a means to ease the burden of defeat, secure the release of POWs and bring normalcy to France's place in Europe. Laval, despite strenuous entreaties, was unable to win German concessions, and Pétain fired him in December, replacing him first with Pierre-Etienne Flandin and then with Admiral François Darlan, chief of the French navy, who urgently resumed the attempt to secure the status of partner in Hitler's New Order. Darlan's ambitions were those of a naval officer: he wanted to enhance French overseas power at the expense of Britain and was happy to play a junior role to Germany in order to do so. In May 1941, Darlan met Hitler and offered Germany the use of French military bases in Syria, Tunisia and Dakar, in exchange for a reduction in payments of the occupation costs and speedier repatriation of POWs. The Germans appeared to agree to this, but then reneged, unwilling to treat France as an equal. At no point were the Germans willing to accept partnership with France, despite Vichy's repeated offers of collaboration. Having failed with Darlan, Pétain cashiered him and reinstated Pierre Laval in April 1942. Laval continued his unceasing effort to win the favour of the Third Reich. On 22 June 1942, in a speech to mark the anniversary of the German invasion of the Soviet Union, Laval notoriously championed the Nazi struggle against communism, declaring: 'I desire victory for Germany because without it Bolshevism would establish itself everywhere.' In December 1942, after the success of the American landings in North Africa, Laval refused to change his tune: 'Victory for the Americans would be a triumph for Jewry and Communism. . . I, for my part, have made my choice.'[6]

6 Jean-Pierre Azéma, *From Munich to the Liberation, 1938–1944* (Cambridge University Press, 1984), p. 121.

If a formal partnership with Germany eluded the Vichy government, a series of economic arrangements did take hold during the occupation, and these were highly advantageous to Germany. Over the course of 1940–41, German authorities worked out purchasing agreements with numerous sectors of French industry to supply valuable raw and finished goods for the Reich. The Germans (after imposing a devaluation of the franc) bought up French textiles, bauxite, steel, aluminium, wool, leather goods and agricultural products; the French even built aircraft for the Luftwaffe. By the middle of the war, Germany was appropriating 40 per cent of French industrial production for its war effort. Over 15,000 French firms took contracts for the production of products destined for German consumption, and as many as 1.5 million workers were employed in supplying Germany's needs. Much of this commerce was in fact subsidized by the French themselves, through heavy occupation payments. While this arrangement kept French workers employed, it also sharply reduced the standard of living in France for the duration of the war.[7]

Had Vichy's collaboration been limited to the economic sphere, perhaps the regime would be considered merely another example of European accommodation to German victory. But Vichy went much further, using the defeat of 1940 as an excuse to move the nation into ideological harmony with the Third Reich. The regime swept away parliamentary structures and created a cult of personality around Pétain. Veterans were enrolled into a militarist grouping called the *Légion Française des Combattants* that served as a mass rally for the regime. Trade unions were gutted, the press was muzzled, Popular Front-era leaders were arrested and put on trial, communists were persecuted, and Jews were arrested, incarcerated and finally deported into German hands. Almost immediately upon the signing of the armistice, Vichy adopted anti-Jewish legislation, culminating in the *statut des juifs* of 3 October 1940, which stigmatized Jews and banned them from certain professions and public offices. From then on, Vichy pursued a state policy of anti-Semitism, evident in the creation of a Commissariat General for Jewish Affairs under the control of the anti-Semite Xavier Vallat, whose purpose was to cut away the Jewish presence from French life. In the summer of 1942, under increased pressure from Germany, Pierre Laval approved the deportation of foreign Jews living in France. By the end of the war, Vichy

---

7 Julian Jackson, *France: The Dark Years, 1940–44* (Oxford University Press, 2001), pp. 185–9; Philippe Burrin, *France under the Germans* (New York: The New Press, 1996), pp. 245–9.

authorities had deported 75,000 Jews from France; nearly all of them were murdered at Auschwitz.[8]

The government at Vichy was not the only site of collaboration with the German occupation. In occupied Paris, under the benevolent gaze of the Germans and beyond the control of Vichy, a number of extremist parties, embryonic before the war, seized upon the defeat to push their own interests and openly bid for the favour of the German occupiers. The ultra-nationalist *Parti Populaire Français* was led by Jacques Doriot, a former communist and Great War veteran, whose conversion to anti-communism was so zealous that he joined the *Légion des Volontaires Français contre le Bolchevisme* and fought with the Wehrmacht on the Russian Front, eventually winning an Iron Cross. A rival group, the *Rassemblement National Populaire* under Marcel Déat, attempted to organize workers into a fascist party. Both leaders hoped they might emerge as replacements for Pétain, but they never developed a mass following and were unable to persuade the Germans to bet heavily on them: the legitimacy of the Vichy regime was too valuable to the Germans to be jeopardized by trusting these marginal figures with real authority. Yet they served as a sad reminder that the bacillus of fascism circulated in the French body politic.[9]

With the Allied invasion of North Africa, as well as the reversals of German fortunes in Russia after Stalingrad, German demands on France grew in intensity. The Germans occupied the southern zone of France in retaliation, after French colonial forces, under Darlan's command, rallied to the Allies. Conditions across the country soon worsened. In February 1943, the Germans turned what had been a voluntary labour programme into a mandatory one: French workers were being sucked into forced labour to serve German needs. Over 700,000 French workers would wind up in harness in Germany. And Vichy created a new police force, the *Milice*, to hunt down shirkers and resisters. Its leader was Joseph Darnand, a notorious right-wing agitator, who accepted the rank of *Sturmbannführer* in the SS. The *guerre franco-française* was now in full swing.

The French resistance that Vichy and its *Milice* attempted to crush had many identities. Charles de Gaulle served as its traditionalist and non-communist face to the outside world: his broadcast of 18 June 1940 from

---

8 The essential study is Michael Marrus and Robert Paxton, *Vichy France and the Jews* (New York: Basic Books, 1981).
9 Bertram M. Gordon, *Collaborationism in France During the Second World War* (Ithaca, NY: Cornell University Press, 1980).

London called for Frenchmen to oppose the armistice, sustain the fight against Germany and build a movement from the empire with which to save France. He was, however, an unknown figure in the country and had no base of support. Few rallied to his side at first. He would emerge only in 1943 as the undisputed leader of the external Free France movement and a liberator in waiting. For the first year of the war, French men and women engaged in isolated acts of defiance and resistance across the country, usually without coordination or direction. After Hitler's invasion of the Soviet Union, the French communists joined the anti-German ranks and resistance took on a more militant and organized shape. But it remained heterodox. Communists, socialists, Catholics, Gaullists all shared a common enemy, yet nourished sharply divergent views of what kind of France they wished to see emerge from the war. In 1943, de Gaulle's emissary, Jean Moulin, created the National Council for the Resistance that served as an umbrella for various movements; its membership agreed on a broad post-war programme of social justice and institutional reforms, but members remained wary of one another, as well as of de Gaulle.

Forms of resistance varied, from publishing underground newspapers to staging work stoppages, from aiding downed Allied pilots to providing intelligence on German military dispositions. Sabotage, small-scale and insignificant in the early years, became widespread by 1944. The flourishing underground press – there were almost 1,000 separate clandestine publications in France during the war – gave voice to the breadth of anti-Vichy sentiment across the country. Titles such as *Combat*, *Libération-sud* and *Franc-Tireur* put out 150,000 papers with each print run. Without doubt, the creation of the forced labour service (*Service de Travail Obligatoire*) in February 1943 radicalized the situation and sent thousands of young men into the arms of the resistance. As their numbers grew and their actions became more daring, German and Vichy repression intensified. The German counter-espionage operations penetrated many resistance networks and took a heavy toll on their operations.

In February 1944, the resistance was bold enough to create an internal armed force, the *Forces Françaises de l'Interieur* (FFI), under the command of General Pierre Koenig. Despite enduring political and ideological differences within the armed resistance, by June 1944 the FFI possessed enough combat power to engage in the liberation of the country alongside Allied forces. With the help of parachuted 'Jedburgh' teams of professional military officers, French resistance groups aided considerably – how much is still a subject of dispute – in slowing German reinforcements into Normandy to meet the Allied invasion, as well as in securing French ports in the Mediterranean that were needed by the Allied invasion of southern France. Across the country, FFI units fought openly with Germans and with the *Milice* in the final months before the liberation. Over 20,000 FFI soldiers were killed.

The Resistance did not unite the country: rather, it gathered together many men and women who shared a profound hatred of the German occupier and its Vichy protégés. These resisters differed sharply on political questions, and sometimes these disagreements hobbled their effectiveness. After the war, the resistance movement signally failed to maintain its sense of a common purpose and broke up into competing political factions. Nonetheless, at a time of great national shame and an appalling loss of moral direction, small groups of French patriots kept the hope of a democratic and free France alive.

Germany's lost ally: Italy

As an ally of Hitler, Mussolini's Italy did not experience foreign occupation in the early years of the war, when Germany's war machine was sweeping across Europe. But in mid-1943, with the Allied invasion of southern Italy, the country began a long and bloody passage to liberation. The Anglo-American invasion of Sicily began on 10 July 1943. It took Allied troops just six weeks to clear Sicily of Germans, and in early September, British and American forces jumped over to the mainland to begin driving up the boot of Italy, reaching Naples by the end of the month. Then, 100 miles south of Rome, the Allies hit the Gustav line, a forbidding German defensive barrier that stopped the liberators in their tracks, cut the country in half, and turned the Allies into occupiers of Italy's southern half. For the next two years, British and American soldiers fought a bitter, slow-moving and costly effort to push the Germans out of central and northern Italy.

It might have worked out differently but for the bungling of the Italian leadership. On 25 July 1943, the Fascist Grand Council, under the influence of Count Dino Grandi, long a valued ally of Mussolini, but also a man who was strongly anti-German and wished to see Italy exit from the war, passed a vote to dismiss Mussolini. King Victor Emmanuel III, aware of the conspiracy and also anxious to ease Italy out of the war, was ready to replace the Duce with the former army chief, Marshal Pietro Badoglio, and to seek a separate peace with the Allies. The King, however, prevaricated over the terms of the surrender, while the Italian army melted away and the Germans began pouring troops into northern Italy. On 8 September, the King announced that Italy had surrendered to the Allies. The Germans, having anticipated this, seized Rome, and General Eisenhower was forced to scratch an airborne invasion plan to capture the capital. Instead, the King and the Marshal fled the invading Germans, and placed themselves under the protection of the British and Americans. The Germans captured and deported half a million Italian soldiers. They also rescued Mussolini from the jail in which the King had incarcerated him and placed him at the helm of a new puppet government in the northern, German-occupied half of Italy, now to be called the Italian Social Republic. In October, the impotent King redundantly declared war on Germany.[10]

Liberation brought little relief to the people of southern Italy; they exchanged one occupier for another. In Naples, where the British set up the headquarters of the Allied Military Government, food was in very short supply, the water mains cut off and the aqueduct destroyed by German sabotage. The sewers were badly damaged; there was no electricity; the ports needed to be cleared; and the whole distribution network for food and supplies was shattered due to lack of transportation. In circumstances like this, officials feared an epidemic of typhus, which was averted only by delousing virtually everyone in the city with heavy dustings of DDT. Malaria and smallpox also broke out. Both civilians and troops suffered especially from venereal disease, despite a system of regularized and licensed prostitution; Allied hospitals were treating 3,500 patients a month for VD alone. In Rome, which was finally taken by the Allies in June 1944, the daily bread ration had been fixed at 100 grams – about three thin slices – under the German occupation. The Allies tried to increase this to 200 grams, but had difficulty sustaining even that low figure. It was not without trying. In June to July 1944, the Allies shipped 10,000 tons of flour, grain, sugar, olive oil and soap into Rome alone, though one in three truckloads wound up on the black market. There were just too many mouths to feed: the city was swollen with 200,000–300,000 refugees, fleeing the fighting in the north. Allied armies were reluctant to use valuable military trucks for civilian uses, so the food problem persisted throughout the last years of the war. 'In these circumstances', wrote the official British historian, 'the comment was not infrequently heard that Rome had been better off under the German occupation'.[11]

---

10 The story may be followed in Elena Agarossi, *A Nation Collapses: The Italian Surrender of September 1943* (Cambridge University Press, 2000).

11 C. R. S. Harris, *Allied Military Administration of Italy, 1943–1945* (London: HMSO, 1957), pp. 85–91, 167–70, 193, Appendix IV, pp. 419–28.

But in the north, life under German occupation was decidedly worse than in the south. After the events of the summer of 1943, an Italian resistance emerged, slowly at first, made up of small bands of young men and women, many on the run from German forced-labour round-ups or military service on behalf of Mussolini's puppet regime. In the north, partisan bands slowly developed a political culture of their own, chiefly under the influence of the communists, who styled themselves Garibaldi Brigades, and the non-communist resistance in the 'Justice and Liberty' group, which soon emerged as the Action Party. The resistance was heterodox: ex-fascists, army officers, white-collar workers, Catholics affiliated with the Church-sponsored Catholic Action group, as well as socialists and liberals flowed into a variety of underground operations. These organizations, ideologically at daggers drawn, worked together in a loosely coordinated Committee of National Liberation for Upper Italy (CLNAI), which was based in Milan. It developed close contacts with the Committee for National Liberation in Naples and then Rome, which was acting as a provisional government. Over the last two years of the war, and especially in the last six months, this resistance grew to include 100,000 partisans, and their activities were aided by supplies of weapons and ammunition from the British SOE and the American OSS. They mined bridges, derailed German troop trains, picked off German sentries, deprived the Germans of mountainous territory and made life a persistent misery for the occupation forces. They also had to contend with the anti-partisan squads of Mussolini's puppet regime, whose brutality toward the resistance was notorious.

Their fight was a desperate one, under horrific conditions and savage German reprisals. When a partisan attack on a German troop column in Rome on 23 March 1944 killed thirty-two soldiers, Hitler ordered that the civilians be made to pay at the rate of ten Italians for every German killed. Field Marshal Albert Kesselring, in overall command of this theatre, promptly gave the order, and 335 Romans were rounded up, driven to the Ardeatine caves outside the city and shot. But he did not stop there. In June, Kesselring offered a gruesome pledge to his trained killers: 'The fight against the partisans must be carried on with all means at our disposal. I will protect any commander who exceeds our usual restraint in the choice and severity of the methods he adopts against the partisans.' This was an open invitation to his junior commanders to commit atrocities, and many obliged. In the early autumn of 1944, the SS stormed through northern Italy, killing 360 civilians at St Anna di Stazema in Lucchese; 107 civilians at Valla; 53 in San Terenzo; 108 at Vinca; and so on. On 29 September, two regiments of SS soldiers entered the small town of Marzabotto, near Bologna; 147 people who had taken shelter in the village church were dragged out into the cemetery and shot. The priest was among them. Over the next two days, the Nazis scoured the town and nearby villages, burning as they went. The final tally was 1,830, including five priests, two nuns and over a hundred children. In these circumstances, it is not surprising to find that many Italians set aside ideology and banded together in a widespread resistance movement, united by a deep abhorrence of fascism, both in its German and its Italian manifestations. This experience of occupation, resistance and war, as historian Paul Ginsborg has noted, 'gave rise to a myth of solidarity which was to be as potent and enduring as that of the Blitz in London'.[12]

A lost liberation?

The liberation of France began on 6 June 1944, with the Allied landings on the beaches of Normandy. The amphibious military operation, OVERLORD, brought over 100,000 Allied soldiers into France within twenty-four hours. Despite furious German resistance, the Allies formed defensible beachheads on the first day and, with the aid of overwhelming air power, built up a terrific assault force in Normandy that within thirty days of D-Day exceeded a million soldiers. The fighting in the summer of 1944 in Normandy was a brutal and bloody engagement, in which German troops, their backs to the wall, fought with extraordinary skill and tenacity, giving American and British troops a small taste of what Soviet soldiers had endured on the Eastern Front for three years. The combined Anglo-American force, whose naval, air, infantry and artillery power had been so carefully built up over the previous year, finally shattered a German army which, by the summer of 1944, could not make good the massive losses it sustained. The battle for Normandy was in fact the battle for France – once the Germans broke, in late August, the path to Paris was open. On 24 August, Allied troops, with the French 2nd Armoured Division marching at the lead, reached the gates of Paris.

The collapse of Vichy authority and the restoration of Republican legality in France occurred with stunning swiftness, considering the degree of civil strife France had endured for four years. On 25 August, General de Gaulle

12 Paul Ginsborg, *A History of Contemporary Italy: Society and Politics, 1943–1988* (London: Penguin, 1990), p. 21; David Ellwood, *Italy, 1943–1945* (New York: Holmes and Meier, 1985), pp. 75–8; G. Quazza, 'The Politics of the Italian Resistance', in Stuart J. Woolf (ed.), *The Rebirth of Italy, 1943–1950* (London: Longmans, 1972), pp. 1–29; Richard Lamb, *War in Italy, 1943–1945: A Brutal Story* (New York: Da Capo Press, 1993), pp. 56–68.

spoke from the balcony of the Hôtel de Ville in Paris, proclaimed the restoration of the Republic and French Empire, and installed a provisional government that was recognized as legitimate by the vast majority of the country. De Gaulle also tried to draw a veil over the past, claiming that French citizens had always been of good faith, and had always been united in their hatred of the enemy. But unity was not the watchword in the summer of 1944. FFI soldiers in newly liberated towns dished out drumhead justice to reputed collaborators; perhaps 10,000 people were executed by local bands of resistance and citizen action groups. Local townspeople engaged in ritual humiliations such as public beatings and head-shaving of women known to have consorted with German soldiers. The political scene, too, was unsettled: the heterodox resistance organizations believed de Gaulle owed them respect and a seat at the table in planning post-war France's resurrection. They would become bitterly disappointed, as the pre-war political parties swiftly asserted their authority and marginalized the resistance movements. The dream of a social revolution so ardently hoped for in the dark days of the occupation evaporated.

Vichy, too, evaporated, as if the whole affair was a bad dream. Marshal Pétain was hauled off by the retreating Germans to Schloss Sigmaringen in the Swabian Alps. Following the liberation of that region by American troops in April 1945, Pétain, eighty-nine years old and infirm, was put on trial in Paris for treason and condemned to death. De Gaulle commuted the sentence; Pétain lived, until 1951, in imprisoned isolation on the Île d'Yeu. His countrymen were uninterested in picking over the monstrous legacy of his government. A small number of leading Vichy officials were put on trial for treasonous acts: Pierre Laval, having tried and failed to kill himself with poison, was tied to a post and shot while still retching up his insides. But most high-ranking Vichy officials were let off the hook. The new Republic could not secure the loyalty of the nation's political elites by engaging in a thorough investigation of wartime politics. The Republic endured, and that was enough.

The liberation of Belgium occurred so quickly – the Germans pulled out of Belgium in early September 1944 during their retreat from France, so as to set up a new line of defence on the German border – that it denied the Belgians any claim to having liberated their own soil. Belgium's principal problem was its lack of a 'man of destiny' like de Gaulle to impose order: their king, Leopold III, had been shamed by his early capitulation and had been seized and deported to Germany in June 1944. The debate over his post-war fate became a subject of bitter dispute in the nation. The only legitimate authority was the government-in-exile of Hubert Pierlot, who was duly flown into Brussels in September by the British. But Pierlot had little standing among the resistance, and when, in October, he called for the disarmament of all resistance formations, thousands of well-armed communists defied him, threatening insurrection against any attempt to squash their radical demands for change. General Eisenhower had to parachute arms to the Belgian police in an effort to restore order.

Belgium, freed from occupation, was not yet free of the scourge of war. The German V-1 and V-2 rockets, aimed at Allied troop concentrations in Antwerp and Liège, took a terrible toll upon civilians in the autumn of 1944. And when Hitler launched his winter offensive in the Ardennes in December – what became the Battle of the Bulge – thousands of Belgian civilians were killed. The Ardennes offensive was stopped and turned back, but eastern Belgium was ravaged by the battle. Even after the retreat of the last German units in January 1945, Belgium faced a winter of food and coal shortages, worsened by the weakness of the central government, which continued to feud with the radical resistance groupings and which signally failed to undertake an effective purge of collaborators. As in France, the watchword was continuity rather than change, a return to pre-war structures rather than an embrace of the possibilities of renewal.

The rapid liberation of Belgium brought the Allies to the doorstep of the Netherlands, and when Operation MARKET GARDEN was launched on 17 September 1944, it appeared that the Dutch would be delivered from German occupation within days. The Dutch government-in-exile ordered a nationwide strike, in an effort to slow German military traffic, but within days it appeared that the attempt to seize bridgeheads across the Rhine had failed. Only a small slice of southern Holland was freed from German control, and the rest of the country, including the main cities of Amsterdam, The Hague and Rotterdam, remained under occupation until the end of the war. Although the Allied armies periodically launched attacks on the German lines in Holland – the First Canadian Army fought bitterly there – the major thrust of operations was eastward, away from Holland and into Germany proper. It would be months before the Allies fought their way northward, across the watery fingers of the Maas, Waal and Rhine Rivers. In retaliation for the Dutch strikes, *Reichskommissar* Seyss-Inquart placed an embargo on all food imports into the German-held areas. This marked the start of the gravest period of the war for the Netherlands: the 'hunger winter'. During the late winter and early spring of 1945, when life had revived in liberated Brussels and Paris, northwest Holland was a lifeless zone of darkness and hunger, a pitiful encampment of skeletal children and cadaverous people, surviving on tulip bulbs and beets. The Dutch people's deliverance did not come until the collapse of the Third Reich itself, by which time some 16,000 people had died of starvation, while countless others suffered from malnutrition and disease. The German command capitulated on 6 May to Allied forces; the Dutch resistance was not represented in the armistice discussions and was denied the chance of playing any role in the liberation of their country.

Denmark and Norway, too, had to await larger strategic developments before they could enjoy a return to freedom. The Soviet Red Army entered northern Norway in October 1944, in pursuit of German forces which were retreating out of Finland. Soviet authorities then allowed a small Norwegian force, under the command of the government-in-exile, to assist in liberating Finnmark, Norway's most northerly province. But Norway remained a sideshow for the broader Allied campaign against Germany, and despite persistent Norwegian calls for an Allied offensive there, it was not until the German surrender of 4 May on Lüneburg Heath to Field Marshal Montgomery that Norway was free. On 13 May, members of the government arrived from London to restore Norwegian sovereignty. The German capitulation of 4 May also brought liberation to Denmark.

In Italy, the liberation was a long time coming. The spring of 1944 saw a major offensive, DIADEM, designed to breach the Gustav line and take Rome, which fell to the Allies on 5 June. But with the success of the landings in Normandy the next day, the Allies shifted troops and resources away from the Italian campaign. In November, the Allied Commander in Italy, General Harold Alexander, announced the suspension of military activity for the winter. The Germans used this respite to unleash a savage campaign against resistance organizations across northern Italy, leading many of the communist resistance activists to suspect a deliberate Allied conspiracy to allow the Germans to wipe out radical resistance elements in the north before the end of the war.

Yet the resistance survived to play a significant and historically important role in the final liberation of Italy. With the resumption of Allied offensive operations in the spring of 1945, the Italian resistance movements launched uprisings across the north, playing a major role in the liberation. In April 1945, partisan groups as well as industrial workers in Turin, Bologna, Genoa and Milan closed down factories and engaged German troops in pitched battles, liberating one city after another, before the arrival of Allied formations. On 27 April, Mussolini, his mistress and members of his inner circle were arrested by communist partisans while attempting to cross into Switzerland. The following day, they were executed. Their bodies were trucked to Milan, then publicly displayed, hanging upside down, in the Piazzale Loreto, the same public square where the Germans occasionally displayed murdered partisans. On 2 May, the remaining Germans in Italy surrendered. Perhaps 45,000 partisans had died in these final battles of liberation. Despite this heroic contribution to the liberation of their nation, however, Italian resistance members were deeply divided among themselves, and remained a minority in a country which had embraced Fascism and tyranny for two decades and which would prove deeply reluctant to embrace the radical ideas nourished by the resistance for social justice and revolution. Once again, the resistance would find itself marginalized by powerful elites whose interests lay in stability and stasis.

The experience of defeat and occupation that these nations all endured (Italy excepted) triggered strikingly similar reactions from political elites as well as ordinary citizens. The speed and scope of the German invasion, the terrifying efficiency of the occupation, and the failures of the pre-war political structures to defend the nation, all contributed to a mood of defeatism and denial in Western Europe. From there, the first step to collaboration was an easy one, especially for political opportunists and outsiders, who now sought to use the German victory to pursue their own sinister ambitions. But after two or three years of being yoked to the German war effort, thousands of people entered into open resistance against the German New Order. It is true that their effectiveness was limited, even in a nation like Italy, where the resistance grew into the largest movement in Western Europe. Resistance provided a foundation on which a story of national resilience and defiance could be based. It remains a bitter reality, however, that because resistance was never widespread in the West, the revolutionary ambitions of the resistance movements gained little traction among the public. Instead, old elites fairly rapidly returned to positions of influence in post-war Western Europe, and their interests lay in a restoration of stability, economic reconstruction and a turning away from the bitter divisions of the war years. As the Cold War opened, and Western Europeans drew closer to the United States in a political and military partnership, the idealistic and revolutionary hopes of the resistance were hastily locked away, another casualty of the Second World War.

17

Wartime occupation by Italy

DAVIDE RODOGNO

This chapter explores the politics and policies of occupation by Fascist Italy during the Second World War (1940–43). It was in Albania, Greece, Yugoslavia and metropolitan France that Fascism's nationalist, imperialist and racist assumptions conflated, when territories of the so-called *spazio vitale* (space for control and expansion), the equivalent of the Nazi *Lebensraum*, fell under Italian rule for an ephemeral amount of time. This chapter illustrates the discrepancy between Fascism's ambitions and the reality of the occupation, and devotes particular attention to the Fascist authorities' grudging acceptance of the status of junior partner in the Axis and their attempts to pursue independent policies in the 'conquered' territories, despite the interference of the Nazis.

Italy entered the war on 10 June 1940. It won few victories on its own, and it was only thanks to the decisive role played by the German army that Italy managed to occupy or annex a number of European territories. In June 1940, it took control of some ten French towns, including Menton. Following Yugoslavia's defeat in April 1941, its territory was divided between Germany, Italy, Bulgaria, Hungary and Albania; Croatia became a formally independent state, Montenegro was administered by the Italian military, though the initial plan of the Fascist government was to turn it into a protectorate; the rump of Serbia came under German rule. Italy annexed Kotor and Split; Zara (Zadar), which had been an Italian possession since the end of the First World War, was enlarged by the addition of some of the surrounding area. Together, these three towns formed the *Governatorato della Dalmazia* (Government of Dalmatia), ruled by a civilian, Giuseppe Bastianini. The rich areas of Slovenia were annexed to the Reich, whereas Ljubljana and the southern part of the country were annexed to the Kingdom of Italy; the lands of the Kupano, including the town of Sušak, were joined to the province of Fiume (Rjeka). At the Vienna Conference (21–24 April 1941), Germany and Italy agreed that

Montenegro and Croatia would become protectorates of Rome. Kosovo, the western part of Yugoslav Macedonia – the rest going to Bulgaria – and Metohija were to be annexed to Albania. Officially, Germany did not impose any limitations on Italy's ambitions, but it nevertheless ensured that the Reich's economic and political interests in the Balkans did not come under the control of Rome or any of its satellite states. From the summer of 1941, Italy was its ally's underdog. The Axis powers occupied Greece after Germany intervened in April 1941. The Italian army, having tried unsuccessfully to defeat Greece from October 1940 to 23 April 1941, then occupied the whole of mainland Greece, with the exception of the wealthy province of Greek Macedonia and its capital Salonika, which was in German hands, and Thrace, which had been de facto annexed by Bulgaria. Italy also annexed the Ionian Islands, and occupied the Cyclades and the Southern Sporades. The Germans and Italians shared control over Athens and set up a collaborationist government, to help to overcome administrative paralysis. Coexistence between the occupying powers worked poorly, however, and there was no serious coordination between them in the military, political and economic realms. During the summer of 1941, following serious uprisings in response to the ruthlessness of the Ustaša (a Croat fascist movement and party), the Italian army occupied western and central Croatia, a large part of Bosnia and the whole of Herzegovina. Finally, on 12 November 1942, the Italian army occupied Corsica and eight departments to the east of the Rhône River in southeastern France, including the principality of Monaco. The Italian occupation of all these territories came to an end with the signing of the armistice on 8 September 1943.

Historiographical lacunae

For a long time, historians did not deem Fascism's military occupations and annexations in the Balkan peninsula and metropolitan France as being particularly significant for the history of the Second World War or of the Fascist regime. There was some research on specific resistance movements and Italy.[1] During the 1980s, the Italian Army Ufficio Storico published several volumes of official accounts.[2] Several protagonists brought out

---

1 See bibliographical essay.
2 Salvatore Loi, *Le Operazioni delle Unità Italiane in Jugoslavia (1941–43)* (Rome: USSME, 1978); Mario Montanari, *La Campagna di Grecia* (3 vols., Rome: USSME, 1980); Oddone Talpo, *Dalmazia. Una Cronaca per la Storia* (3 vols., Rome: USSME, 1985).

memoirs with apologetic intent, not particularly useful for the study of wartime occupations.[3] However, no study was made of Italian policy toward such minorities as the Vlachs of northern Greece or the Muslims of Bosnia. Not a single monograph examines the role of the *Carabinieri Reali* (the Italian military police), of the Blackshirts or even of the Fascist Party in the occupied territories. No comparative analysis of the administrative organization of annexed territories has yet been published.[4] Very little is known about the careers of civil servants who served in these territories. For instance, we ignore whether or not they had previous experiences in the colonial administration. Despite the National Bank (*Banca d'Italia*) archives being fully accessible and extremely well organized, the study of economic exploitation, financial and industrial policies is far from being advanced, especially when one compares this field of research with works on Nazism. Few studies deal with the educational policies and cultural penetration in the occupied territories.[5] The denationalization campaigns in Venezia Giulia – an area which, at the end of the First World War, included 327,000 Slovenes and 152,000 Croats – encompassing forced and brutal assimilation, are well known. However, only very recently has a historian related these Fascist actions to colonial policies.[6] The radicalization of reprisals against Yugoslav civilian populations – for example, in the establishment of concentration camps for these populations in Rab, Gonars, Renicci and elsewhere – has not yet been reviewed in regard to the long history of Italian anti-Slav racism.

The most plausible reason for the lack of interest in Fascist Italy's wartime occupations is their undeniable military, political, social and economic failure. Fascist Italy's unrealistic wartime objectives were never attained. Italy lost the war in 1943; Mussolini was evicted in July; General Pietro Badoglio signed the armistice with the Allies on 8 September. After that time, all Italian occupied territories fell under Nazi control. However, while the Nazis were involved in crucial battles against the Soviet Union and the Anglo-Americans they could not adequately replace the Italians. In the regions previously occupied by the latter, Nazi occupiers became harsher on local populations in a desperate attempt to maintain order. For obvious reasons,

3 Galeazzo Ciano, *Diary, 1937–1943: The Complete Unabridged Diaries of Count Galeazzo Ciano, Italian Minister for Foreign Affairs, 1936–1943* (New York: Enigma Books, 2002).
4 Jean-Louis Panicacci, *L'Occupation italienne. Sud-Est de la France, juin 1940–septembre 1943* (Presses Universitaires de Rennes, 2010).
5 Stefano Santoro, *L'Italia e l'Europa Orientale. Diplomazia Culturale e Propaganda 1918–1943* (Milan: Franco Angeli, 2005).
6 Roberta Pergher, 'Staging the Nation in Fascist Italy's "New Provinces"', *Austrian History Yearbook* 43 (2012), 98–115.

the memory of the Nazi occupation, especially the period 1943–45, is more distinct and vivid than the previous period, when the occupiers were Italians. Moreover, in 1940–41, Fascist Italy did not decide what territories to occupy. The Italians did not defeat the French, Yugoslav or Greek armies. Local populations often disdained the presence of Italian soldiers, and the flagrant encroachments and interferences of the Nazis within Italian-occupied territories led local populations and authorities to question Fascist leadership. Nonetheless, it is worth exploring how Italian policy produced famine in Greece, misery in Croatia, Bosnia-Herzegovina, Montenegro, Albania and Macedonia, where over 100,000 civilians were interned in prisons and concentration camps.[7] Italians were not benevolent occupiers; they were scarcely Mussolini's unwilling executioners and certainly did not endanger their lives to save occupied populations.

Imagined geographies and sociopolitical organization of the 'conquered' space

At the extreme of Fascist imagining, national *spazio vitale* included the Iberian Peninsula, France, Switzerland and the Balkans, and extended far into Africa and Asia, indeed beyond the boundaries of the classical Roman Empire. Eventually, all 'conquered' territories would have belonged the *comunità imperiale*, a poor translation of the English imperial commonwealth, ironically signalling the intellectual indebtedness of Fascism to British and French imperialism.

Fascism's European empire would have been organized according to the principle of the racial unity of the nation ('a single people for a single nation', as Mussolini liked to say). The government and institutions that Fascist 'dominators' would have imposed – violently – on each satellite would have depended on the latter's degree of 'civilization' and on the racial ranking, which, needless to say, would be decided by the 'civilizers'. Within the imperial community, the regime would have established a frontier – permeable for Italians, impenetrable for dominated populations – between the space reserved to the 'civilizers' and the rest. Admittedly, on the full extent of this space, Fascist authors, intellectuals and academics, ministerial experts and party dignitaries did not agree. According to some, it should have included the Maritime Alps, Savoy, Corsica, the Balearic Islands, the Ionian

---

7 Davide Rodogno, *Fascism's European Empire: Italian Occupation During the Second World War* (Cambridge University Press, 2006).

Islands, eastern Greece, Bosnia, Herzegovina, Slovenia, Dalmatia and southern Switzerland. According to others, the nucleus of the empire should have corresponded to the territories traditionally claimed by Italian nationalists: Dalmatia, the Ionian Islands, Nice and perhaps the Swiss Ticino. Beyond these areas lay further territory washed by the western and eastern Mediterranean – the 'Mare Nostrum' – and perhaps still more.

The most obvious opponent to such massive expansion was the evidently dynamic Nazi regime to which Italy found itself allied, but Italian commentators in the late 1930s generally ignored its penetration of the Balkans and Danube region. They refrained from analysis of how Italy might compete in such places and, especially, how it could be girded with the industrial and financial means necessary there. By implication, only military conquest could bring Italy this empire. But Italians preferred to stick to an academic line, whereby Germany and Italy would readily agree to split Europe into mutual spheres of influence.

Fascist 'civilization' would have set up a new order. Like other Western empires, the Fascist empire would have been centralized and would have had an emperor at its head – not the Italian monarch, but Mussolini. In this unrealistic and not particularly original – especially because of its obsessive reference to ancient Rome – situation, the dictator would have been able to get rid of his tactical alliance with traditional elites within Italy, the monarchy included. In practice, the never-to-be-admitted aim was to catch up with the British and French empires. In the process, Fascism assumed the superiority of Italian 'civilization' and race, from which it derived the inalienable right to have an empire, and the 'duty' to 'civilize' and 'dominate' its inhabitants. Fascism's imperial visions did not encompass the idea of the dominator mingling with dominated populations. In Europe, in Africa and Asia, this empire would have been based on a racial hierarchy, which would have been kept *ad libitum*. Emancipation and uplifting of dominated races would be limited, and identification of dominated races with the conquerors was excluded.

It is true that there were parallels between Nazi and Fascist discourse on demography and each dreamed of maximizing its own population. But the Nazis envisaged an end of Europe in the sense of a community of independent states. Even 'first ally' Italy would have lost its autonomy. Nazism was also fundamentally genocidal, both against the Jews as an internal enemy and against the Bolshevized and racially 'worthless' peoples of the East. Italy also contemplated forced displacements and mass expulsions. But its Europe, or rather Italy's sphere in Europe (and the world), was to be composed of protectorates and satellites without genocide. Fascism's vital space can be imagined as three concentric spheres: the first, often referred to as the *piccolo spazio*, was the core of the empire; the second, larger sphere would have included the European territories; the third sphere was that of African and Asian colonies. The sociopolitical organization of this space would have been hierarchical; the Italians would have dominated the Europeans; Africans, Asians and Jews would have been the pariahs of this imperial community. The Italian Jews would have been eliminated from the first sphere and the European Jewish communities would have disappeared from the second circle. They would have been displaced into the third sphere, somewhere in Africa or Asia.

The occupiers and their Duce

War had an essential place in Mussolini's worldview. For Mussolini, life was a perpetual struggle and the nation would be made through war and territorial expansion. As historian MacGregor Knox puts it, under the sign of perpetual struggle, internal and foreign policy, revolution and war merged. Internal consolidation was a precondition for foreign conquest, and foreign conquest was the decisive prerequisite for revolution at home.[8] Mussolini believed that Fascism's new religion would fashion Italians into a race of conquerors. Thanks to their faith in the Duce, the Italians, like the Romans before them, would dominate the Mediterranean once again.

When Italy entered the war in June 1940, the Fascist regime had enhanced its social engineering schemes: it had implemented a racist colonial legislation, radicalized the discriminatory legislation against Slav minorities, and promulgated anti-Semitic laws in 1938.[9] Nonetheless, for most Italians, the 'stay-at-home preference' (*politica del piede di casa*) and the 'bourgeois spirit' prevailed. Immediately following Italy's entry into the war, Mussolini was forced to admit that the Italians were a long way from being a race of conquerors. Fascism's domestic revolution was far from being achieved. The regime was still entangled with traditional and conservative institutions such as the Catholic Church and the monarchy. The new Fascist man, a warrior ready to die for the regime and his Duce, was not yet born.

8 MacGregor Knox, *Common Destiny: Dictatorships, Foreign Policy, and War in Fascist Italy and Nazi Germany* (Cambridge University Press, 2000), pp. 62, 109.
9 Michele Sarfatti, *The Jews in Mussolini's Italy: From Equality to Persecution* (Madison: University of Wisconsin Press, 2006).

The institutions entrusted by Mussolini to undertake this work, the party and the state, had proved unable to create the martial, violent, fearless and pitiless universe in which Italian children should have revelled. Younger generations of Italians were not ready for Fascism's total war. The tactical and temporary agreement with Italian conservative elites – the Vatican and the Italian Church, Italian financial and industrial elites, the monarchy and the army – allowed Mussolini to consolidate power.[10] However, it jeopardized Fascism's revolutionary aims and hindered it from matching the degree of fanaticism, violence, terror and radical social reorganization that took place, especially after 1938, in Nazi Germany.

Mussolini, however, was far from being a weak dictator. By 1940, he was head of government, Prime Minister, Secretary of State and Commander General of the *Milizia Volontaria per la Sicurezza Nazionale* (MVSN). He wielded, albeit by proxy, effective powers of command, and appropriated the king's prerogatives as commander of the nation's armed forces. Since 1933, he had been Chairman of the Supreme Defence Council and Minister of War, the Navy and the Air Force. In March 1938, together with the king, he was elevated to the rank of First Marshal of the Empire.

The Italian armed forces were not Mussolini's army.[11] Italian military elites were Fascists; they were also nationalists, conservatives and monarchists. As to Italian ordinary soldiers, their degree of fascistization is hard to assess. Many were illiterate, and the Italian army's confidential reports on privates' ideological beliefs are not sufficiently telling. Conversely, it is plausible to argue that Italian officers' and generals' ideological affinities with Fascism were numerous: they were revisionists as far as the Versailles Treaty was concerned; they wanted Italy to have a more prominent role in European affairs; they shared the idea of achieving a mission for the state and envisioned a hierarchical organization of Italian society; finally, many thought of war as a positive and ineluctable phenomenon in international relations. During the 1920s and 1930s, officers enthusiastically embraced colonial adventures. Italian military elites' military-technical, tactical and operational conservatism was consistent throughout the 1920s and 1930s, and even more deadening than that of their French counterparts. Until it was too late, the army neglected medium-size tanks; the navy disdained radar; and the air force opposed the all-metal monoplane fighter. Inadequate training,

10 Philippe Burrin, *Fascisme, nazisme et autoritarisme* (Paris: Seuil, 2000).
11 I paraphrase the title of Omer Bartov's book, *Hitler's Army: Soldiers, Nazis, and War in the Third Reich* (Oxford University Press, 1992).

doctrinal lethargy, administrative disorganization and the active discourage-
ment of individual creativity produced a junior officer corps with insufficient
capacity for command, and non-commissioned officers with an almost total
absence of initiative.[12]

Italian armed forces and the regime closely cooperated in the so-called
pacification of Libya, an Italian colony since 1911. When the Fascists replaced
the last liberal government, the latter had already begun a campaign of brutal
reprisals. Pacification took a decade and meant the killing or starvation of
local populations, especially in Cyrenaica, where the regime aimed at driving
the semi-nomadic tribes out of the most fertile lands of the Gebel, and at
exercising total political-military control over them. The *Regio Esercito* was
aware that this was part of a broader design to destroy the traditional society
of the cattle-raisers of the Gebel and convert them into a reserve of low-cost
and constantly available labour. General Rodolfo Graziani shared with Fascist
leaders the view of nomad societies as an imminent threat that ought to be
eradicated permanently. He viewed them as enemies of agriculture and
progress, as well as potential rebels. Graziani interned civilian populations
in concentration camps where living conditions were dire, and forcefully
expelled many others from the best areas of the Gebel to the pre-desert
borderlands. The survivors were condemned to barely subsistence-level
living conditions. According to historian Giorgio Rochat, around 100,000 of
them, about 50 per cent of the population, were deported, and 50,000 died
during the repression.[13] Continuities between liberal and Fascist imperial
policies explain the active involvement of the Italian military. Colonial ethnic
cleansing is far from being specific to Italian Fascism; what is specific to it is
the intimate connection between domestic and foreign policy, between the
implementation of racist colonial legislation and anti-Semitism or anti-Slav
legislation at home.

The Italian army used chemical weapons during this campaign, as it would
later do in the war against Ethiopia. In Libya, as well as in Ethiopia after 1935,
Italian armed forces (and in some cases, civilians too) did not respect the laws
of war and infringed conventions signed by Italy both during the war and in
its aftermath, when Ethiopian resistance was ruthlessly crushed. Crimes
committed by Italian soldiers and officers went unpunished, for they took

---

12 MacGregor Knox, 'Expansionist Zeal, Fighting Power, and Staying in Power in the
  Italian and German Dictatorships', in Richard Bessel (ed.), *Fascist Italy and Nazi
  Germany: Comparison and Contrasts* (Cambridge University Press, 1996), pp. 113–33.
13 Giorgio Rochat, *Guerre italiane in Libia e in Etiopia* (Treviso: Pagus, 1991), pp. 5–6, 84–5.

place with the authorization and in the presence of clear orders emanating from the political authorities and Mussolini. Forceful deportation of civilians also became an ordinary instrument for the maintenance of public and colonial order in Eritrea and Somalia, where the system of incarceration, the installation of a racially discriminatory system, inhuman treatment, lack of respect for persons and property, denial of impartial trial and torture were systematically enforced by Italian armed forces, under the direct responsibility of Mussolini and with the acquiescence of the Italian civilian population living in the colonies.[14]

In wartime occupied territories, the Italian armed forces executed the plans and policies emanating from Mussolini and his government. They did so because generals and highly ranked officers owed their careers to the regime or because they thought about career advantages. Some of them shared the regime's ideology; others obeyed out of dutiful consensus, which derived from their allegiance to King Victor Emmanuel III.[15] The latter had been actively involved in and shared Mussolini's foreign and imperial policy. The rigidity of service promotion procedures and the caste resistance of senior generals, who maintained a traditional gulf between officers and men, inhibited the injection of fresh Fascist blood into the higher reaches of the armed forces. Furthermore, Mussolini chose to consolidate his power by numerous changes of the guard, rather than by delegating authority to younger generations, supposedly more fascistized. The Italian armed forces lacked the degree of enthusiasm, ambition, initiative and radicalization which Hitler fostered in every sector of German society – the army and SS included. Revealingly, the MVSN, which incarnated better than any other Fascist organization the military spirit of Fascism, played a very minor role in the occupied territories, and the Blackshirts were regimented in the army and had no freedom of action. Nonetheless, even if the fascistization of the *Regio Esercito* (which, as the name indicates, still was the King's army) never reached the same level as the Nazification of the Wehrmacht, the Italian army was more a national Italian one, and therefore murderous in its way.

Mussolini exercised overriding decisional power and control as military leader; he was the pivot of a system as centralized and hierarchical as it was

---

14 Nicola Labanca, 'Colonial Rule, Colonial Repression and War Crimes in the Italian Colonies', *Journal of Modern Italian Studies* 9 (2004), 300–13; Angelo Del Boca, *Italiani Brava Gente?* (Vicenza: Neri Pozzi Editore, 2005), pp. 105–228.

15 Fortunato Minniti, 'Gli ufficiali di carriera dell'Esercito nella crisi del regime', in A. Ventura (ed.), *La società italiana dal 'consenso' alla Resistenza* (Venice: Marsilio, 1996), pp. 75–123.

dysfunctional and inefficient. This system enhanced the traditional lack of initiative of Italian military elites. It increased the lack of coordination between the army, the navy and the air force; it worsened the pervasive bureaucratic dysfunctions in civilian ministries with military duties (for instance, colonial viceroy and governors acted independently of the minister of the colonies).[16] The war was Mussolini's job; the Chief of General Staff (1940–43), General Pietro Badoglio, was nothing more than his subservient assistant. Mussolini's refusal to permit centralization outside his own person was supposed to demonstrate his infallibility as *condottiere*. When, in 1940–41, Fascist Italy started losing important battles in Europe and its African empire, the whole system collapsed, for, among other reasons, the myth of Mussolini's infallibility had allowed the military elites to deny responsibility for defeats and passively to accept military disasters. At the same time, paradoxically, the inertia of such a dysfunctional system proved to be remarkable. Hence policies and orders kept being executed until after the eviction of Mussolini in July 1943.

The political and military circumstances of the occupations

By the end of 1939, the Ethiopian, Spanish and Albanian operations had heavily affected the Italian military budget, its reserves of materiel and armaments. The 1935 war against Ethiopia had come at a price, for it was followed by an intense and expensive period of pacification. On 1 September 1939, vast-scale repression demanded the employment of 200,000 men, a number corresponding to the total of the Italian army in peacetime.[17] These military involvements drained resources, impossible for Italian industry to replace, needed for the development and modernization of the armed forces. Paradoxically, small successes in the wars that took place from 1935 to 1939, as well as the conservatism of the military elites and Mussolini's damaging centralization of all military powers, compromised the preparation for the European conflict to come. In 1939, and for many years after, Italy could have pursued only a very limited war, perhaps against Greece or Yugoslavia, certainly not against France or Great Britain. More importantly, Italy needed a strong ally.

16 Fortunato Minniti, 'Profili dell'iniziativa strategica italiana dalla non belligeranza alla guerra parallela', *Storia contemporanea* 23 (1987), 1113–97; Giorgio Rochat, *L'Esercito italiano in pace e in guerra* (Milan: Rara, 1991).
17 Giorgio Rochat, *Le guerre italiane 1935–1943. Dall'impero d'Etiopia alla disfatta* (Turin: Einaudi, 2005), p. 89.

On 22 May 1939, Italy and Germany signed the Pact of Steel. The Italian Minister for Foreign Affairs, Galeazzo Ciano, foolishly left the task of drawing up the treaty to the Germans, who contrived for its article 3 to place Italy at the mercy of Germany's decision when war would be declared. When Ciano made it plain that Italy would not be ready to enter the war until 1943, he received only vague reassurances from his counterpart Ribbentrop. No article, nor indeed any clause, of this alliance stipulated that Germany must not act before 1943, when, supposedly, Italy would be ready to wage war in Europe. The objective of the alliance was not stated, nor was any formal recognition made of Italy's and Germany's respective spheres of influence. There was no protocol that defined frontiers, apart from the declared inviolability of the Brenner, and no jointly defined military strategy.

Yet despite all the risks involved in the alliance, if Fascist Italy looked to gain total mastery of the Mediterranean, Nazi Germany was the only plausible ally. Since 1938, Berlin had economically and politically penetrated the whole Danube basin, which, with its Austrian communication routes, Romanian oil, Hungarian cereals and Yugoslav and Bulgarian minerals and timber, represented the only directly accessible source of raw materials for Italy. Rome was economically and politically excluded from the richest region of its alleged *spazio vitale*. Mussolini's counter was to occupy Albania, which, on 8 April 1939, became an Italian protectorate; it was a country that Fascist propaganda claimed had enormous economic potential. This coup was intended to demonstrate that Rome took its decisions regardless of Germany's wishes, and that it had not renounced its expansionist ambitions in the Balkans. At the same time, as a consequence of the impossibility of competing with Germany in the Balkans, Italy now had to focus on expansion elsewhere in the Mediterranean, which meant a probable showdown with London and Paris.

When, on 23 August 1939, the announcement of a German-Soviet Pact was made public, Mussolini informed Hitler that, if the conflict with Poland remained localized, Italy would give Germany the political and economic support that it requested. But if the conflict spread, Italy could not take any initiative unless Germany delivered the military supplies and raw materials that Italy required to resist an attack by the French and the British. Humiliated at being obliged to acknowledge Italy's lack of preparedness for war, the Duce proclaimed Italy's 'non-belligerence'. For six months, the Italian government anxiously observed German victories. On 10 March 1940, Mussolini informed Ribbentrop that Italy intended to wage a 'parallel war' in the Mediterranean, but it would do so only after Germany's western offensive had begun. A secret memorandum, circulated by Mussolini on 31 March 1940, confirmed that his policy was one of defence on land and attack in the Balkans, as well as a general maritime offensive, which was wholly incongruous given the lack of terrestrial objectives. The collapse of France persuaded Mussolini that the time had come for Italy to enter the war.

Despite its contradictions and inconsistency, the concept of the parallel war would become the cornerstone defining the attitude of the Italian authorities toward the Nazi ally, especially in the occupied territories. The doctrine of Italy's absolute freedom of action from Germany, the idea of waging a war that did not overlap or even mesh with the greater and more general conflict, signalled the attitude of a proud though unrealistic autonomy. Fascist Italy was not fighting for Germany, nor with Germany, but alongside Germany. Rome rejected any form of strategic collaboration with Berlin, so that the Fascists might demonstrate their military prowess to the German ally, to the nation and to the world. Should this strategy prove successful, Italy could cash it in at the peace table for territorial gains. Things went differently.

On 10 June 1940, Italy declared war against France and Great Britain. A week later, Hitler announced to Mussolini that France had sued for armistice. The Duce ordered Badoglio to attack France; the French defended themselves exceptionally well. The most 'brilliant' achievement by the Italian troops was the occupation of the town of Menton and of some small communes in the French Alps. On 24 June, Italy and France signed an armistice at Villa Incisa (Rome). Italy's demands were the creation of a thirty-mile demilitarized zone to the west of Italy's frontier and the military occupation of the communes conquered during the campaign. The uneasy military victory in the Alps made it impossible for Italy to sit at the peace table as an outright victor. On the African front, Italy's victories would be ephemeral and the East African empire would be lost by 5 May 1941, when the British triumphantly escorted the Emperor Haile Selassie into Addis Ababa. On 13 September, Graziani attacked the British positions in western Egypt and occupied Sidi el-Barrani, but the Italians failed to proceed further. Had they accepted the two armoured divisions offered by Hitler, events may have turned out otherwise. By February 1941, when the five divisions of the German Afrikakorps arrived in northern Africa under the command of General Erwin Rommel, the Italian troops had lost the whole of Cyrenaica, and the British had captured more than 130,000 soldiers, and disabled all the Italians' tanks and 1,000 of their aircraft.

Seeking a conspicuous success elsewhere, Mussolini informed Hitler that Italy was ready to launch an attack against Greece. The latter enjoined his ally not to undertake any military operations there. As absolute master of the economies of the Balkan countries, the Reich was concerned to keep the region out of the war, and it had no need – unlike Italy – to assert its hegemony in the concrete form of direct military occupation. Ever more dependent on Germany, Rome received no guarantees from Berlin that it would have access to the supplies – steel, oil and coal – essential for its prosecution of the war. Further reasons that precipitated the attack against Greece were the failure of operations against Britain, postponed *sine die* in September 1940, and the German occupation of Romania (on 12 October, and which the Italians had known about several weeks beforehand). These events increased Italian fears that the war was about to conclude with a negotiated peace between London and Berlin, from which Rome would be excluded. For this reason, heedless of Hitler's veto, Mussolini chanced his arm on achieving rapid victory in Greece. At a meeting on 15 October 1940, Mussolini and his closest advisors agreed that the occupation of Greece would be entirely straightforward. The military objective was possession of Greece's western coast, Zante, Cephalonia, Corfu and Salonika, then the complete occupation of the country. Italian generals dared not explain to Mussolini that Greece was impossible to defeat with the meagre military means allocated to the campaign (an expeditionary force of 60,000 men), or that the demobilization of 300,000 soldiers (between the end of 1940 and the beginning of 1941) would render any rapid reinforcement of the front in Greece practically impossible. The politicians, Ciano most of all, bore heavy responsibility for the miscalculation. The Greek campaign was an utter disaster.

Mussolini eventually resigned himself to accepting Germany military assistance. Six months after Italy's failed assault, Germany attacked Yugoslavia and Greece. Between 6 and 23 April, both countries were defeated. During the armistice meetings in Vienna, Italian plenipotentiaries suggested to the Germans that their respective spheres of influence might be established according to a rigid division of geographical zones (Yugoslavia and Greece to Italy, all the rest to the Germany); the Germans rejected the proposal and obliged their junior partner to accept the principle of each of the two powers' 'prevalence'[18] in a particular zone, so that Germany could

18 In Nazi parlance, 'prevalence' meant that there would be German troops and emissaries in Italian zones, and vice versa.

maintain a presence in those areas controlled by Italy. However much Fascist propaganda might proclaim the priority of Italy's interests in the Balkans, there was no doubt that the Reich had absolute superiority. Furthermore, as the Italian men on the spot would soon find out, in Slovenia, Croatia and Bosnia-Herzegovina lived tens of thousands of *Volksdeutschen*. Local populations spoke or understood German because of the Habsburg imperial legacy, and more easily fell prey to the propaganda of the Nazis, who seemed more efficient and better prepared to deal with occupied populations than the Fascists. Fascism's annexations in the eastern Adriatic exacerbated relations between Italy and Croatia, for the nationalist regime in Zagreb deemed these lands Croatian.

From 1941, Berlin could have obliged Rome to place the Italian army under the command of the Germans. Yet Berlin permitted Italy to occupy large areas of territory and to settle the political question and the boundary dispute with the Croats as it wished. Italy's negligible economic significance, but extensive sphere of military occupation gave Nazi propagandists an opportunity to rebut accusations of German hegemony, and to purvey the idea that the Axis allies were co-participants in the 'new order'. Between May 1941 and July 1943, Italy reluctantly accepted Germany's real supremacy. With only a narrow margin for initiative, but, paradoxically, thanks to the magnanimity of the Germans, Italy gained a nominal foothold in the Balkans. Italy would fight a war within the war, against its senior partner, as the partial 'conquest' of the *spazio vitale* had come about in circumstances that differed entirely from those envisaged by the regime. Once the Italians gained a foothold in the Balkans, and later in metropolitan France, they sought to carve out a broader role for themselves than their ally was willing to grant.

On 11 December, Italy and German declared war to the United States of America. From 1941 to 1943, Mussolini sent an Italian army to the Soviet Union. Around half of these 200,000 Italian soldiers died in battle, and many others were lost or taken prisoner. At the end of 1942, the Axis war effort in the Mediterranean was in disarray, while the capitulation of the German Sixth Army at Stalingrad on 31 January 1943 had marked a turning point in continental Europe as well. The question was no longer whether the Axis would lose the war, but when. It was the Allied landings in Africa – these being taken to be a crucial change of circumstances with respect to the armistice of 1940 – that induced Germany to occupy the whole of France and invite Italy to join the operations mounted on 11 and 12 November 1942. It was action by the Germans, not Italy's own military initiative, which enabled it to occupy almost all the territory as far as the Rhône originally intended for annexation. The Italian troops, given the task of maintaining the order established by the Germans, deployed themselves along the line of the Rhône, as well as in Corsica.

The occupations

Unlike the Germans, who were defeated after their conquests, the Italians were defeated in advance, but became conquerors of Greece, vast areas of Yugoslavia and metropolitan France. It was as difficult for the Italians to impose themselves as winners politically as it was militarily. They could have defended the annexed territories around Menton, Dalmatia and the Ionian Islands, and eventually put down what were still unorganized and uncoordinated resistance movements. The soldiers deployed in the Mediterranean territories conquered after 1940 numbered approximately 850,000, which amounted to two-thirds of all troops committed outside Italian borders. The Italian Second Army (known as *Supersloda*) was composed of over 10,000 officers and 225,000 men. The xiv Army Corps dispatched in Montenegro had almost 3,000 officers and 74,000 men. In Albania, Kosovo and western Macedonia, the Ninth Army counted on 5,000 officers and 113,000 soldiers. The Eleventh Army, of 6,000 officers and 130,000 men, occupied mainland Greece and many Greek islands. Finally, the Fourth Army occupied the French departments east of the Rhône with 7,300 officers and 143,000 men. The vii Army Corps was sent to Corsica.

The Balkans absorbed 650,000 men, and the occupation of southern France and Corsica required a further 200,000. Undoubtedly such a number, as well as those sent to the Soviet Union, weakened the defence of the peninsula. The deployment also required the adjustment of logistics and armaments to the new circumstances. For almost two years, Italian armies in occupied Europe fought a guerrilla warfare they were totally unprepared for, despite the experience of colonial veterans still in armed service. The extremely mobile and logistically agile enemy, who operated in small units and mingled with the civilian population after operations, caused great difficulties for the large Italian units burdened by heavy artillery. The difficulties were worsened by the excessive dispersal of forces in order to defend numerous logistical bases and communication routes, the slowness due to heavy and cumbersome equipment and the need to ensure that all supply lines were secure. Moreover, the enemy was often well informed about the deployment and movement of the Italian units and the operational intentions of their commanders, while the *Servizi Informazioni* (intelligence services), the worst among Western European countries, were incapable of furnishing timely and accurate information. With the evolution of the conflict, the average size of the Italian battalions, commanded by reservist officers, diminished to around 4,000 men, with weaponry and equipment rarely and inefficiently replaced, and increasingly less suited to the manifold requirements of the war.

Mussolini, his regime's party leaders, top-ranking civil servants and Royal Army officers refused to accept that Italy was nothing more than Germany's *brillant Sekundat*, the Axis's junior partner. They deemed Berlin's actions within the *spazio vitale* as illegitimate interferences, and reacted against them, even if, in practice, little could be done to amend the situation. All Italian occupied territories were economically exploited by Nazi Germany; local governments and local authorities were perfectly aware that Nazi Germany was calling the shots, and did not hesitate to play the Germans off against the Italians. One of the clearest examples of the tensions between the two Axis powers concerned the Italian authorities' decision not to hand in selected groups of foreign Jews, despite the reiterated demands of the German ally. This decision was not taken by Italian local authorities or by the government in Rome out of philo-Semitism or empathy. Instances proving Italian soldiers' anti-Semitism are numerous, and the anti-Semitic legislation of Fascist Italy was some of the harshest in Europe. Moreover, instances of expulsion from the newly annexed provinces are equally well documented; they took place even when Italian authorities were fully informed about the 'Final Solution'. The reasons why the Italian government resolutely refused to hand in thousands of foreign Jews to its German ally are explained by the context of the occupations. The Italian government, Mussolini included, wished to prove to Italian soldiers, occupied populations, local authorities, and even the collaborationist governments of Athens, Zagreb and Vichy, that Italy was in control of 'its' military occupied territories. This was a political, not a humanitarian decision; prestige and political opportunism rather than humanity explain it. Obviously, examples of 'good' Italians do exist and should not be forgotten. However, no rescue plans for foreign Jews were ever set up by Italian authorities, and there is no evidence whatsoever of a conspiracy led by Italian officers, against the regime, to save foreign Jews.

The considerable geographical extension of Italian wartime occupations meant that maintenance of law and order became a central feature of these occupations. One of the most significant documents pertaining to repression in the Balkans is General Roatta's *Circular Note 3C*. Roatta, Commander-in-Chief of *Supersloda*, circulated that document on 1 March 1942, before the partisans undermined the Italian occupation system. The document had a twofold purpose: it explained methods of repression to the Italian soldiers; and it was supposed to enlighten them on the attitude to be taken toward occupied populations, thereby revealing the way in which Italian military commands intended their troops to perceive (and be perceived by) such people. Roatta ordered his troops always to keep a warlike mentality and to repress all the qualities of the 'good Italian' (*il buon italiano* or *bono'taliano*). Soldiers had to behave fearlessly in all circumstances and harshly fight the enemy. Rebels had to be treated not according to the saying 'an eye for an eye, a tooth for a tooth', but instead according to a 'head for a tooth'. Roatta resorted to simple psychology: he threatened harsh punishments for those disobeying his orders; he aroused and incited his soldiers, diminished the enemy and pushed his troops to be extremely mistrustful of local populations. The General explained that relations between victorious nations and defeated populations had to be based on the concept of superior–inferior. In order to legitimize the occupiers' authority and to build a barrier between them and local populations, Roatta deliberately tried to instil into his soldiers' minds the idea that the partisan-enemy was a non-human, uncivilized barbarian. Consequently, civilians supporting the partisans were also inferior human beings; 'Bolshevik bandits', they represented a dangerous threat to Fascist civilization. Hence it was absolutely forbidden to fraternize with them.[19]

Roatta's document is not an exception, and similar guidelines were circulated in Greece and Albania. Roatta was not a more fervently Fascist general than many others. Comments on Balkan uncivilized populations were quite common, especially among officers who had served in the Italian colonies. Italian officers insisted on immediate and violent reaction to every hostile act. In April 1943, General Carlo Geloso – Commander-in-Chief of the Eleventh Army – proclaimed that in Greece, the enemy had exceeded the infamy of savages and the infamy of blood-drinking, sadist orgiastic beasts: the enemy was not a human being. Against these beasts and their accomplices, everything was allowed. Moral, juridical and military laws were not in force anymore; the occupiers could enforce a pitiless vengeance and the most brutal reprisals, and they did it. Repression and reprisals in the occupied territories show that, if the fascistization of the Italian Royal Army was a

---

19 M. Legnani, 'Il ginger del general Roatta, le direttive della II° Armata sulla repressione antipartigiana in Slovenia e Croazia', *Italia Contemporanea* 209–210 (December 1997 – March 1998), 156–74.

failure, especially when compared to the degree of Nazification of the Wehrmacht, Italian generals' attempt to dehumanize the other, both the partisan (as terrorists) and civilian populations (inferior human beings), cannot be minimized. It also shows that deeply rooted anti-Slav racism, as well as repressive practices in the colonies, had meaningful repercussions in wartime occupied territories. Many Italian civil servants and officers with administrative duties asserted the 'superiority' of Fascism and perceived occupied societies as 'uncivilized'. For instance, on 5 August 1942, *Carabinieri* General Giuseppe Pièche wrote a report on the Ustaša regime. He explained that morally defective individuals served in the Ustaša Movement. They were not faithful to Ante Pavelić as an act of political coherence or devotion because Balkan people could not rise to these virtues.

In the above-mentioned document, General Roatta wrote that the ongoing fight against the 'rebels' was a kind of colonial war. As in the colonies, any form of resistance had to be liquidated. To do so, massive internment and deportations of civilian populations and scorched-earth policies were necessary. They also fulfilled the Fascist ambition of de-Balkanization or *bonifica etnica* (ethnic cleansing, as we would say today), and anticipated the Italian colonization of eastern Adriatic annexed territories, and the most complete domination of all the territories that were not to be annexed to Italy. Roatta shared Fascism's imperial vision, according to which vast areas had to be emptied (cleared, evacuated). He admitted that it was a complicated and delicate operation, and that the military alone could not carry it out. This is why, in September 1942, he asked the Ministry of the Interior in Rome for help. He wished the latter to identify where to deport masses of civilians. Roatta's document distinguished between *regular* and *irregular* areas. The latter were those places where military operations against rebels were occurring. There, families whose 'males' (from sixteen to sixty years of age) were absent without any valid justification were to be interned in concentration camps. Moreover, in all *irregular* areas, Italian commanders had to designate a portion of the local population that were to be considered as suspect. The latter would be arrested and kept as hostages; if those responsible for any aggression committed against Italian military forces were not identified within forty-eight hours, the hostages were to be executed. The inhabitants of any house situated next to the place where an aggression or sabotage (railway, street, communication lines) had occurred were to be considered as co-responsible for such an act; they would be interned, their livestock confiscated and their houses destroyed.

Documents having similar contents circulated in the annexed territories. The operation referred to as 'disarmament of the population of Ljubljana' of February 1942 combined law and order objectives with preparation for the imminent colonization of a province which had no previous common past whatsoever with Italy. The xi Army Corps operating in Slovenia encircled the city of Ljubljana, making extensive use of barbed wire, photo-electric stations and checkpoints. Ljubljana rapidly became an enormous concentration camp. The occupiers rounded up civilians, and daily arrested dozens of civilians for several weeks. On 23 May 1942, in Fiume (Rjeka), Roatta met Mussolini. The latter reiterated that in a war, the best possible scenario was that the enemy was dead. Therefore, in the occupied territories, the Italians needed to have at their disposal numerous hostages to be executed when necessary. As to the Slovene question, Roatta suggested closing the borders of the province and then proceeding with the evacuation of the whole population living within two to two and a half miles east of the pre-1941 border with Italy. Police squads should constantly check borders and open fire against all those who attempted to cross them. Roatta estimated that 20,000–30,000 Slovenes (out of a province inhabited by 90,000–100,000 people in 1940) would have to be deported, and that their lands and properties should be given to families of Italian soldiers who had died during the war. In his view, such a policy could have been extended to Dalmatia. In June 1942, Italian authorities deported the unemployed, refugees, beggars, people who had no families, university students, teachers, employees of the Yugoslav administration, priests, and workers who had moved to Slovenia from the Italian region of Venezia-Giulia after 1922. From Italian archives, no information has emerged so far concerning the exact number of deportees arrested because they were directly or indirectly involved in resistance. It is plausible to argue that, given the objectives of the regime in Slovenia, many deportees were arrested and deported for purely political reasons. The report of a meeting held in Gorizia on 31 July 1942 shows that Mussolini argued that he was not at all opposed to a mass transfer of local populations.

Despite the ruthlessness of Fascist repression and reprisals, resistance operations increased. General Robotti de facto replaced Grazioli and set up seven operations between July and September 1942. According to Italian documents, partisans' losses amounted to 1,053 dead in action, 1,236 executed, 1,381 captured; Italian losses for the month of August amounted to 43 dead and 139 injured soldiers. Data indicate that Roatta's orders to treat rebels according to a 'head for a tooth' had been enforced. By November 1942, the 'Italian province of Ljubljana' was devastated; commercial and industrial activities were interrupted, communication routes were destroyed, social life was deeply affected (schools did not open) and there was a serious risk of famine. On 5 November 1942, General Robotti triumphantly announced that the enemy had lost 7,000 men. Unfortunately, we do not know how many civilians were killed during these operations, nor the number or circumstances of the civilian hostages killed in reprisal. In Dalmatia, the situation was similar to that in Slovenia. Thousands of civilians were sent to concentration camps. In July 1942, the Italian authorities informed the population that, if they abandoned their place of residence to join the resistance, they would be put on specific lists, and, when captured, they would immediately be executed, their families would be taken as hostages, and their property would be confiscated or sold. Furthermore, mayors of all villages had to actively collaborate in the search for and identification of 'rebels'; if reluctant to do so, they would be executed.

Methods of repression in the militarily occupied areas of Croatia were identical to those applied in Dalmatia and Slovenia. Local commanders ordered the destruction of every house and every rebel village, the deportation of civilian populations, including women, children, old people and adult men. They ordered troops to raze to the ground villages collaborating with the rebels. As an example of the consequences of this order, in May to June 1942, in the area surrounding the town of Ogulin, Italian soldiers destroyed 132 houses allegedly used by the partisans. The historian will hardly find evidence in the Italian archives of how many houses Italian soldiers destroyed without any proof that the village or the family in question had collaborated with the partisans. One does not yet know if military tribunals judged Italian soldiers responsible for burning down or razing to the ground houses or villages. In occupied Montenegro, military Governor General Alessandro Pirzio Biroli gave his troops the order to destroy villages and to take civilian hostages, even entire families. The latter were sent to concentration camps situated in Albania, whose sanitary and hygienic conditions were pitiful. At the end of 1941, Pirzio Biroli issued a proclamation amnestying 3,000 prisoners, who were free to go back to their villages. At the same time, the governor decided to keep a number of civilian hostages as guarantors of the Montenegrin behaviour. Every fortnight, a new group of hostages, whose names had to be proposed by mayors or representatives of local populations, would replace these hostages. The ceremony of exchange would be solemn and, on this occasion, Italian authorities would give further instructions to representatives of local populations. Pirzio Biroli specified that hostages would be treated well, would not have to work, would be properly fed, and that the hygienic conditions of their detention would be good. This decision was taken out of propaganda reasons, not because of a genuine humanitarian concern for local populations.

Italian repression in Greece, in 1941, was different from that in Yugoslavia. The Greek government protested when the Italian army took Greek civilians as hostages. In Yugoslavia, nobody could or wanted to protest. Yugoslav territories were either annexed to or militarily occupied by Italy; the Croat government took civilian hostages or executed them even more often than the Italians did, and the Germans did the same in occupied Serbia. When the resistance appeared in Greece, Italian repressive methods adjusted to the Yugoslav standard: execution of the 'bandits' (another term Italian occupiers used to indicate partisans); arrest of bandits' families and execution of all those who helped the bandits. No exceptions would be made for Greek political and clergy representatives. Moreover, abettors' houses and, if necessary, entire villages would have been burned out or destroyed (using 81 mm mortars) and entire populations would be displaced. By the end of 1942, the Eleventh Army command had issued new guidelines, specifying that soldiers should not hesitate to take hostages among rebels' relatives, especially if they were men and over eighteen years of age; if attacked, Italian soldiers were to counter-attack massively, using grenades and mortars. By the end of 1942, when Italian occupiers in the Balkan peninsula were aware that the war was lost, Roatta's motto – deploy massive forces and powerful means even in minor military operations – was fully applied all over the Balkan territories occupied by the Italian army. To the better organization and much improved efficiency of the partisans' attacks, the Italian occupiers replied with indiscriminate reprisals against civilian populations. In early 1943, the village of Domenikon, located in Thessaly, was razed to the ground and a massacre of civilians took place. When the Italian Chief-of-Staff in Rome asked for explanations for the execution of civilians, Geloso answered that intensification of rebellion, extreme mobility of rebels' bands and a high risk of an Allied invasion of Greece entailed reprisals. He explained that 'rebels' had no territorial objectives to protect, hence Italian troops had to punish civilian populations collaborating with 'bandits'. Furthermore, 'rebels' were not a regular army, they were not belligerents, and they systematically killed Italian privates and officers.[20] During the summer of 1943, even after the Allies landed in Sicily,

20 Davide Rodogno, *Fascism's European Empire*; and Lidia Santarelli, 'Muted Violence: Italian War Crimes in Occupied Greece', *Journal of Modern Italian Studies* 9 (2004), 280–99.

Italians in occupied Greece continued to execute reprisals on civilian populations, and even increased indiscriminate aerial bombing.

A further explanation of the Italian army repressions and reprisals in the Balkans is related to the pace of anti-partisan operations from the summer of 1942. First, Italian garrisons were now often attacked; second, the *irregular* areas extended considerably. During these operations, the conditions of Italian soldiers worsened. Devastation of fields, pillage of civilian provisions and supplies, and theft of cattle can be explained by the hardship the 'conquerors' experienced. The term was long and tough; Italian soldiers were rarely replaced. Tens of thousands of Italian soldiers were confronted with the horrors of war and the experience of death. They saw with their own eyes civilians slaughtered in Croatia; starving children, women and the elderly in Greece. They saw piled up corpses in the streets of Athens, shambles and human bodies, horribly mutilated, thrown into Balkan rivers. In this extremely brutal way, Italian soldiers became conscious of death, and began to interiorize violence. At the beginning, they were passive spectators of events they thought of as being outside their responsibility. Transition from adaptation to passive brutality to active brutality happened when death hit soldiers close enough, particularly when they began to kill, or saw their comrades killed by the partisans. This was often an unbearable part of their everyday existence. Some soldiers avenged themselves on partisans for having killed or tortured their friends. Revenge became a moral duty, even for soldiers who might have been reluctant to embrace Fascist ideology and propaganda. Aware that what had happened to comrades could happen to them at any moment, soldiers curled up in their shells, removing all trace of the atrocities they committed. For many of them, the experience of death awoke the survival instinct much more often than the idea to desert or to renounce fighting. From 1943, Italian soldiers waited for defeat, while hoping for their individual survival. This was a murderous hope, for violence and brutality followed the interiorization of violence, when Italian soldiers burnt down entire villages or undertook violent reprisals against civilian populations. Fascist war propaganda and the long-lasting Fascist campaign of hatred against Slav populations did play a role and contributed to enhance violence; however, excesses of Italian repression were not, as in the Nazi case, the actions of a victorious army and nation, but a reflex of Italian military weakness.

The fact that Fascist Italy's wartime occupations have been, for a long time, a parenthesis, or, at best, a wry account of the pathetic adventures of Italian soldiers abroad, contributed to the responsibilities of the Italians being overlooked, and, as we know, Italian war crimes and crimes against humanity went unpunished. More generally, the omission fed the myth of the *brava gente* (nice people), the Italians as benevolent occupiers, which still thrives today within Italy and beyond its frontiers.[21] Italian occupations were not a footnote in the history of the Second World War, at least not for the countries, societies and individuals that experienced them. The history of these wartime occupations is not that of the movie *Mediterraneo*, and it is certainly not the trivial love story of Captain Corelli and his mandolin.[22] Rather it is the history of the life and death of over 800,000 Italian soldiers, sent by their generals and the regime to 'win' a war, and who occupied vast territories for almost two years. A more accurate analysis of these events sheds a different light both on them and on the origins of the new world order that emerged at the end of the Second World War. It also contributes to explaining both continuities and ruptures between the liberal and Fascist eras, and between the latter and the Italian Republic, at least as far as civil servants and administrative structures are concerned.

21 See bibliographical essay.
22 In 1991, the movie directed by Gabriele Salvatores won the Oscar as Best Foreign Film. Louis de Bernières, *Captain Corelli's Mandolin* (London: Secker & Warburg, 1994). This best-selling novel became a Hollywood movie in 2001.

Administrative boundaries

Before the surrender of Italy

1. NDH (Under German and Italian occupation)
2. Occupied and annexed by Italy
3. Occupied by Italy and annexed to Albania
4. Occupied by Italy
5. Occupied and annexed by Hungary
6. Under German occupation; special status within Serbia
7. Under German occupation
8. Occupied and annexed by Bulgaria
9. Occupied and annexed by Germany
10. Occupied and annexed by Bulgaria 1941; occupied by Germany July 1943

Principal partisan activity in Yugoslavia and Greece during 1941 comprised open revolts of relatively short duration, most prominently in Serbia, Montenegro and Thrace. There was also smaller scale partisan activity across Yugoslavia more widely, as well as in Greek regions such as Crete, Macedonia and Epirus. In Yugoslavia, Communist Partisans played a prominent role during 1941; in Greece, EDES and EAM/ELAS did not become proactive until 1942. In different regions at different times during 1942-3, partisan activity against the occupiers comprised sabotage and other irregular actions, development of administration in 'liberated zones', and efforts to withstand Axis anti-partisan offensives. The Yugoslav regions in which such activities were most prominent during this period were Bosnia and Herzegovina, though to varying degrees there was also significant activity across other occupied Yugoslav regions, particularly in the rest of the NDH. The most prominent such regions in Greece were Macedonia, Epirus, Thessaly, the northern Peloponnese, and Evritania and central Greece. Partisan activity was becoming a countrywide phenomenon in both Yugoslavia and Greece during 1942-3, a trend that intensified further in 1944.

18.1 The Balkans under Axis occupation

Collaboration, resistance and liberation in the Balkans, 1941–1945

GREGOR KRANJC

The general story of Second World War resistance, collaboration and liberation in Greece and Yugoslavia is well known. Invaded by the Germans and their Axis allies in April 1941 (the Greeks having fought off an initial Italian invasion from Albania in October 1940), their armed forces quickly crumbled. Out of the ashes emerged two of the most significant armed and mostly communist-led resistance movements of the Second World War, instrumental in freeing vast areas of the countries' interior from Axis control and accelerating the Germans' withdrawal in 1944 and 1945. Yet the occupation of Greece and Yugoslavia was also marked by collaboration and treason. Fratricidal conflict, especially in Yugoslavia, claimed a significant share of the unbearably high civilian casualties. Liberation did not staunch the bloodshed, and it marked the start of a vicious historiographical debate over these events that persists to the present. What is remarkable is how similar, in many respects, the stories of collaboration, resistance and liberation were in these two states. Yet for all of their similarities, Yugoslavia and Greece took remarkably different paths at the war's end. One emerged as the doyen of East European communism, with its leader rivalling Stalin in regional influence. The other tore itself asunder in a brutal civil war, before emerging as a crucial ally in the West's strategy of containment of communism. Their divergent post-war stories betray the long tradition of great-power machinations in the region.

On 6 April 1941, Greece's and Yugoslavia's four years of Axis occupation were ushered in on the wings of devastating German bombers. Within three weeks, their governments had escaped abroad, while their armed forces capitulated and were dissolved by the occupiers. Yugoslavia was partitioned into more pieces by its victorious occupiers than any other occupied state in Europe. Slovene regions were trisected and annexed by Italians, Germans and Hungarians. Slices of Serbian territory were served to Hungary, Bulgaria and Italy's protectorate Albania, with the rest coming under German military command. Italy occupied Montenegro and annexed its coastal region, while a southern strip was annexed by Albania. Yugoslav Macedonia was mostly annexed by its covetous Bulgarian neighbour, while its western regions were ceded to Albania. Croatia, shorn of its Hungarian-annexed eastern regions and Italian-annexed portions of Dalmatia, but enlarged with the addition of Bosnia-Herzegovina, became an Axis-sponsored puppet state under the fascist Ustaša party. Belying its name, the Independent State of Croatia (*Nezavisna Država Hrvatska* – NDH) was partitioned into German and Italian spheres of influence. Greece was also partitioned, but into slightly more coherent German, Italian and Bulgarian sections. As in Yugoslavia, the Germans assumed the leading role in Greece's occupation, controlling critical ports and strategic areas, including Athens. However, unlike Yugoslavia, Greece was provided with a collaborating government – the Hellenic State – but it was to garner little loyalty and exercise even less real control over the country. Yugoslavia had no equivalent; outside Croatia, Yugoslavs were allowed to form administrations at various times in only fragmented pieces of their former country. Thus Greeks and Yugoslavs found themselves increasingly atomized in the wake of the invasion. With the exodus of pre-war governments, the collapse of many former state authorities and institutions, and the parcelling away of territory to the various Axis stakeholders, the choice of whether to collaborate or resist fell increasingly upon ordinary civilians, who, in turn, often based their decision upon local, familial and individual considerations. The rise of the resistance was, in part, an attempt to fill this vacuum of political representation – *to speak for* Yugoslavs and Greeks.

Armed resistance in Greece and Yugoslavia came to be dominated by two communist-led coalitions. In Yugoslavia, the National Liberation Partisan[1] Detachments sprang into action in various parts of the country shortly after the meeting of the Yugoslav Communist Party's (*Komunistička partija Jugoslavije* – KPJ) Politburo on 4 July 1941, which called upon its approximately 10,000 members to rise up against the occupiers.[2] Its Commander-in-Chief was the General Secretary of the Communist Party of Yugoslavia, Josip Broz Tito. The Communist Party of Greece (*Kommounistiko Komma*

1 Hereafter, 'Partisans' (with a capital 'P') denotes the Yugoslav Partisans, the official name of the armed wing of the communist-led Yugoslav National Liberation movement.
2 Walter Roberts, *Tito, Mihailović and the Allies, 1941–1945* (New Brunswick, NJ: Rutgers University Press, 1973), p. 24.

Elladas – KKE) spearheaded the National Liberation Front (*Ethniko Apeleftherotiko Metopo* – EAM), formed in September 1941, and its military arm, the Greek People's Liberation Army (*Ellinikós Laïkós Apeleftherotikós Stratós* – ELAS), activated in December 1941. Both movements emerged from humble and chaotic roots. Ideological conviction did send some fighters into the forest – the German attack on the Soviet Union in June 1941 was the clarion call devoted communists were awaiting. But conveying party orders faced serious obstacles in the terrorized and politically fragmented reality of 1941. The hardened left–right schism between competing resistance movements would take some time to arise from what was, in reality, a politically heterogeneous grouping of would-be resisters. Localized violence and conditions were just as important in pushing people into the resistance. The German attempt to ethnically cleanse 250,000 Slovenes, beginning in the summer of 1941, led to unrest in Slovenia, while the occupier-engineered famine that gripped Greece in the winter of 1941/42 gave rise to food riots and strikes that would provide recruits for the resistance. Generational characteristics helped too, as impatient and impulsive students defied occupational policies in both Yugoslavia and Greece, including conscription into Axis labour and military units.

The path from civilian life to armed resistance was a short one when sheer survival was at stake. The Ustaša's genocidal attacks had one of their victims – the Serb minority of the NDH – in open revolt by the summer of 1941, together with their brethren across the border in German-occupied Serbia. However, it was much more common for resistance to progress in stages: from a gradual disenchantment with the conditions of occupation, to more active, non-violent resistance, to finally seizing hold of a weapon. The forms of unarmed resistance were varied – listening to Allied broadcasts, laying wreaths on the tomb of the Unknown Soldier on the anniversary of Italy's attack upon Greece, painting 'Tito' slogans on walls and distributing anti-Axis leaflets. While important in promoting a sense of solidarity and defiance among the occupied, these examples of unarmed resistance were hardly unique to the Balkans. What distinguished Balkan resistance, particularly from its Western European counterparts, was the strength of its armed variant.

Historical and geographical factors helped to condition this response. The forests, cave-studded karst topography and inaccessible mountains of the Balkans provided significant hiding places. Indeed, areas controlled by the Yugoslav resistance were clustered in the west and centre of the country along its Alpine and Dinaric mountain spine, and petered out as the landscape levelled into the Pannonian plain in the east. The high mountains of Central Greece, Epirus and Macedonia also helped to cultivate resistance activity. Yet this rough terrain and its poverty also limited the size and mobility of the Partisan bands. Moreover, geography alone cannot explain the timing or the vigour of resistance. What explains the passivity of Yugoslavia's pro-royalist Četniks versus their Partisan competitors, who operated in equally inhospitable terrain?

The organized state, including its most recent interwar Greek and Yugoslav manifestations, had always had a weak impact on the impoverished rural and mountainous Balkan interior. Axis occupation policies did not appear to be any different. Following their lightning invasion in April, elite German units were promptly withdrawn to take part in Operation BARBAROSSA. Left behind were enemy garrisons that generally remained limited to larger strategic towns and transportation routes, which criss-crossed mostly unoccupied hinterlands. This hasty, patchy occupation provided the nascent resistance territory and opportunities to hide weapons and to organize. A coterie of Partisans, Četniks and demobilized Yugoslav soldiers took advantage of these favourable conditions as they overran much of western Serbia in the late summer of 1941.

The occupiers made up for their numerical weakness with brutal collective reprisal policies and aggressive 'policing campaigns' against these self-proclaimed liberated territories. Emblematic of this liberally applied terror was the 10 October 1941 order issued by the Wehrmacht's Commanding General in Serbia, General Franz Böhme, calling for the execution of one hundred Serb – and disproportionately Serbian Jewish – hostages for every German killed, and fifty for every German wounded by insurgents.[3] The same month, over 2,000 Serb civilians in Kragujevac were massacred in reprisal for a joint Četnik–Partisan ambush that killed fewer than a dozen Germans. This atrocity effectively shelved future Partisan–Četnik cooperation, confirming for the Četnik leader, Draža Mihailović, that a policy of immediate armed resistance was reckless, irresponsible and premature. Greeks had experienced their own Kragujevac a month earlier, when the Bulgarians executed some 2,200 people, including women and children, in the Greek Macedonian town of Drama, in reprisal for a KKE-led uprising that

---

3 Ben Shepherd, 'Bloodier then Boehme: The 342nd Infantry Division in Serbia, 1941', in Ben Shepherd and Juliette Pattinson (eds.), *War in a Twilight World: Partisan and Anti-Partisan Warfare in Eastern Europe, 1939–45* (Basingstoke and New York: Palgrave Macmillan, 2010), p. 194.

had killed thirty-five Bulgarian police, civil servants and local collaborators.[4] The Drama massacre had a 'huge restraining impact on the development of the resistance movement in both Eastern Macedonia and Western Thrace', and 'dealt a massive blow to the morale of the local population, shaking popular faith in the benefits of armed resistance'.[5] Thus terror bore some immediate results – in eastern Greek Macedonia, as in western Serbia, the fledgling resistance was largely suffocated by the end of 1941.

Indeed, until the capitulation of the Italians in September 1943, the true significance of Greek and Yugoslav resistance was measured less by their coordinated attacks on the occupiers than by their sheer ability to survive repeated Axis campaigns to eradicate them. Tito's Partisans alone endured five Axis offensives between the autumn of 1941 and the spring of 1943. Their survival was facilitated by a variance in Axis occupational policies that saw the Italians generally pursuing a less aggressive strategy, most evident in their willingness to look the other way as Jews sought refuge in regions under their control. Yet 'less aggressive' did not mean lenient. The Italians encircled the city of Ljubljana with barbed wire in 1942, to sever connections between resisters in the city and the countryside, while a network of Italian concentration camps imprisoned tens of thousands of Greek and Yugoslav civilians in deplorable conditions. Nevertheless, the Italians were cognizant of their own military weakness and the difficulties of suffocating the insurgency through force alone. They were thus more willing to 'contract out' their security responsibilities to collaborationist organizations or to competing resistance factions, which only added fuel to emerging civil wars.

With Mihailović's shift to passive resistance in late 1941, and the open collaboration of some Četnik units with Italian forces in a shared fight against the Partisans in 1942, Tito's movement was gradually monopolizing active armed resistance. While ELAS was the largest Greek resistance force by the spring of 1943, it had to share the liberation struggle with republican competitors. The most significant was the National Republican Greek League (*Ethnikos Dimokratikos Ellinikos Syndesmos* – EDES). Founded in the spring of 1942, it operated mostly in Epirus, the home region of its

---

4 Kevin Featherstone, Dimitris Papadimitriou, Argyris Mamarelis and Georgios Niarchos, *The Last Ottomans: The Muslim Minority of Greece, 1940–1949* (London: Palgrave Macmillan, 2011), p. 136.
5 Ibid.

leader, General Napoleon Zervas. Sharing EDES's anti-monarchist platform was the much smaller National and Social Liberation (*Ethnike kai Koinonike Apeleftherosis* – EKKA), based in Rumeli. The strength of the resistance was still limited before the critical year of 1943, numbering only some 20,000[6] fighters in Greece, while the more vigorous Partisans counted approximately 50,000–60,000 members.[7] These numbers also conceal regional weaknesses. No more than 500–1,700[8] resisters engaged the Bulgarian occupiers in Western Thrace, while only 852[9] Partisans were active in Serbia in June 1942.

Nevertheless, expanding liberated territory in Greece and Yugoslavia provided the resistance with more stable sources of food, shelter and recruits. In return, the resistance attempted to provide a makeshift government and a modicum of security in these regions. Indeed, as historian Steven Bowman noted, the Second World War 'was the watershed of modernity for the mountains of Greece', a claim that could also be applied to Yugoslavia.[10] The resistance provided some with their first experiences of schools, law courts, medical treatment, theatres and parliamentary assemblies. A female Greek villager reminisced that 'the government made beautiful things happen and we were raised to a higher level. The other governments had neglected the peasants. Beautiful things happened, like voting. I voted. And we helped in the local government in any way we could.'[11] As most of the resistance forces were wary of their respective governments-in-exile, who had persecuted communists in pre-war Yugoslavia, and communists and republicans in General Metaxas's Greece, liberated territory became a *tabula rasa* upon which a new post-war society would be built. The inequality of the old economic and social order would be overturned, or at the very least reformed, while interwar Serb hegemony – a stain still associated with the Četniks – would be replaced with a federally restructured Yugoslavia of equal national republics. The reach of the resistance also extended beyond liberated areas into firmly Axis-controlled territory. Underground national

6 The approximate strength of Greek guerrillas in July 1943: ELAS, 16,000 fighters; EDES, 3,000; and EKKA, 400, in Charles Shrader, *The Withered Vine: Logistics and the Communist Insurgency in Greece, 1945–1949* (Westport, Conn., and London: Praeger, 1999), p. 34.
7 Mark Mazower, *Hitler's Empire: How the Nazis Ruled Europe* (New York: Penguin, 2008), p. 484.
8 Featherstone et al., *The Last Ottomans*, p. 295.
9 Roberts, *Tito, Mihailović and the Allies*, p. 76.
10 Steven Bowman, *The Agony of Greek Jews, 1940–1945* (Stanford University Press, 2009), p. 162.
11 Janet Hart, *New Voices in the Nation: Women and the Greek Resistance, 1941–1964* (Ithaca, NY, and London: Cornell University Press, 1996), p. 210.

liberation committees gathered provisions for the Partisans, infiltrated the occupiers' administration and bureaucracy, and collected intelligence. They also identified (and at times executed) traitors, undermined recruiting campaigns for collaborationist or labour units, and channelled deserters and Jews into guerrilla ranks.

Yet ideological extremism was also a hallmark of the resistance. The introduction of collectivization into some liberated regions of Yugoslavia only increased the effectiveness of anti-communist propaganda. 'People's courts' could and did deliver rough justice. Historian Mark Mazower provided a haunting image, noting that EAM 'theatre troupes were presenting their plays in mountain villages where ELAS firing squads were executing prisoners'.[12] In the winter of 1941/42, Montenegro was the scene of brutal Partisan atrocities, 'against all opponents real or potential. . .[the] plunder of villages, the execution of captured Italian officers, of party "fractionalists" and even of "perverts"'.[13] Having earned the scorn of the local population, the Partisans were evicted from most of Montenegro in early 1942 by combined Četnik-Italian forces. Such initial failures helped to convince the KPJ and the KKE that the success of their movements would be contingent upon providing a wide enough ideological umbrella to accommodate local sentiments, including their religiosity. Many of their rural recruits did not have the faintest idea about communism. Indeed, anthropologist Janet Hart noted that 'EAM's success in mass organizing reinforced its tendency towards inclusiveness',[14] while the first Anti-Fascist Council of the People's Liberation of Yugoslavia (*Antifašističko Vijeće Narodnog Oslobođenja Jugoslavije* – AVNOJ) held in Bihać, Bosnia, in 1942 – an organization of the various national liberation committees in Yugoslavia – did not advocate a communist government, and reaffirmed the 'inviolability of private property and individual initiative in industry, trade and agriculture'.[15]

Thus resistance leaders were forced to accommodate and recognize the critical role civilians played in supporting armed guerrillas. Besides providing the basic necessities of life, the local population acted as couriers, guides and

---

12 Mark Mazower, *Inside Hitler's Greece: The Experience of Occupation, 1941–44* (New Haven, Conn., and London: Yale University Press, 1993), p. 286.

13 Stevan Pavlowitch, *Hitler's New Disorder: The Second World War in Yugoslavia* (New York: Columbia University Press, 2008), p. 105.

14 Hart, *New Voices*, p. 124.

15 Roberts, *Tito, Mihailović and the Allies*, p. 78.

the 'eyes and ears' that warned of coming Axis offensives. Yet harbouring the resistance was also a burden. The resistance ultimately requisitioned scarce food and manpower, in the name of the 'people', if civilians did not voluntarily satisfy these demands. In return, the Axis punished this support for 'bandits' with arson, summary executions, arrests and the plundering of any remaining provisions, turning some terrified villagers against the resistance. Lieutenant John Hamilton of the Office of Strategic Services (OSS) described such reprisals in Dalmatia in 1944:

> The majority of the farmers resent the high-handed manner in which the Partisans operate. Also, and this is the crux of the entire situation, it is the farmer or rather the civilian peasant and his family, who are doing the work and paying the penalty too. Partisan elements are billeted with the farmers everywhere. They feed the Partisans; they supply the Partisans with livestock, horses and wagons for transport. In return, they are left behind whenever there is an enemy drive through the country... This leaves the farmer holding the bag. The Germans, or local fascists, plunder his farm, rape his women, burn a few homes and move on. Then the Partisans return and the cycle is ready to commence anew.[16]

However, the peasants who lost everything in this cycle of violence were also potential recruits for the guerrillas, as Edvard Kardelj, Tito's right-hand man in Slovenia, declared: 'In war, we must not be frightened of the destruction of whole villages. Terror will bring about armed action.'[17] Such logic also applied to Greek villagers, who most often 'wanted nothing more than to be left alone; and it took a visit from German troops, burning and looting, to make them change their minds and look more tolerantly upon EAM's vision of social cooperation'.[18] Nevertheless, it is also misleading to view civilian support as simply a detached cost–benefit calculation, with the resistance valuated as a lesser evil than the occupiers. For an increasing number of occupied Greeks and Yugoslavs, the resistance was a source of pride, opportunity, adventure and a welcomed challenge to traditional life. This is perhaps best seen in the successful recruitment of women to the cause of the left-wing resistance. By war's end, some 2 million Yugoslav women had joined the ranks of the Partisans' Anti-Fascist Front of Women, while ELAS enlisted far more women into its ranks than Zervas's EDES, who, according

---

16 Report by 2nd Lieutenant John Hamilton, Hacienda Mission, folder 615/A, box 69, entry 144, record group 226, National Archives and Records Administration.
17 Nora Beloff, *Tito's Flawed Legacy: Yugoslavia and the West, 1939–84* (London: Victor Gollancz, 1985), pp. 75–6.
18 Mazower, *Inside Hitler's Greece*, p. 284.

to his niece, 'did not believe that women should take up arms and fight'.[19] Providing women with their first real voting rights was also critical to the Partisans' and ELAS's recruiting success. In short, while archival assessments of popular support for the resistance are often contradictory (and accurate conclusions are impossible in an era without public opinion polls), there is little doubt that without at least the passive acceptance of a significant portion of the local population, the Partisans and ELAS would not have been able to flourish to the extent that they did.

German military fortunes declined precipitously in 1943. Allied victories in North Africa and Stalingrad persuaded increasing numbers of Greeks and Yugoslavs that the end of Axis occupation was a real and imminent possibility. Rumours of a possible Anglo-American invasion of Nazi-occupied Europe through the Balkans appeared to be substantiated by Operation ANIMALS in June and July 1943, as the British Special Operations Executive (SOE) encouraged more active resistance, in part as a diversion for the Allied invasion of Sicily. Impressed by their potential to pin down Axis forces and disrupt their supply lines – as seen by the spectacular destruction of the Gorgopotamos railway viaduct, in a combined ELAS-EDES-British operation in November 1942 – both the British and the Americans had established contacts with the various Greek and Yugoslav resistance movements by the end of 1943. Anticipation of an Allied liberation had two immediate impacts on the resistance. Internally, it accelerated the imposition of stricter Communist Party control within ELAS and the Partisans. To non-communists within what had been rather politically diverse resistance coalitions, this was a worrying trend. As the Slovene dissident and former Partisan Edvard Kocbek noted, 'the [Communist] Party with its exclusiveness buried the meaning and might of the Liberation Front, as it took over the entire cadre'.[20] Externally, ELAS and the Partisans attempted to elbow out competing resistance organizations ahead of any Allied liberation, and thus to position themselves as viable alternatives to the return of governments-in-exile.

However, it was Italy's capitulation in September 1943 that decisively tipped the balance of power in favour of the Partisans and ELAS. As the most numerous and widespread resistance movements, they were best positioned to exploit the surrender of Italian arms – which they desperately needed – and to seize additional territory, thus bolstering recruitment.

---

19 Hart, *New Voices*, p. 212.
20 Boris Pahor and Alojz Rebula, *Edvard Kocbek: Pričevalec našega časa* (Trst: Zaliv, 1975), p. 133.

They also used their new-found strength to permanently sideline their rivals. In regions vacated by the Italians, Četniks and sundry pro-Italian collaborating units that had been fighting Tito's forces since late 1941 were mauled by the more disciplined Partisans. Buoyed by their success, and despite an aggressive German reoccupation of former Italian territory, the Partisans convened their historic second session of AVNOJ in Jajce, Bosnia, on 29 November 1943. AVNOJ was transformed into the highest legislative body in occupied Yugoslavia, and the authority of the government-in-exile was transferred to the newly created National Committee of Liberation of Yugoslavia, with Tito as its Prime Minister and Defence Minister. The Yugoslav King, Peter II, was prohibited from returning until a post-war referendum decided his future. While the Allies would not deal with the thorny question of two competing Yugoslav governments until 1944, they did reward Tito's military contributions by switching their materiel support from Mihailović to Tito's forces in December 1943. In Greece, ELAS accused EDES of collaboration, and attacked them in the autumn in the so-called First Round of the Civil War. Despite being on the verge of annihilation, EDES survived, in part because of the increased materiel support they received from the British, who saw them as a counter-weight to a possible communist takeover of Greece. Heightening British fears was ELAS's creation, in March 1944, of an administrative body for liberated Greece, the Political Committee of National Liberation (*Politiki Epitropi Ethnikis Apeleftherosis* – PEEA). While it did not claim to be a provisional government like AVNOJ, it 'clearly constituted a direct challenge to the authority of the government-in-exile in Cairo'.[21]

The resistance struggle had clearly entered a new phase by late 1943, in which the guiding principle was less about the defeat and eviction of the occupiers and more about positioning for post-war political power. Numerous SOE and OSS reports in 1944 criticized the Partisans and ELAS – as they had earlier chastised Mihailović – for inactivity against the Germans at the same time as they were readying themselves to settle 'internal' scores. Yet such accusations were only partially correct. While post-war political considerations were obviously growing in the sunset of German occupation, domestic opposition in the form of enhanced German-sponsored anti-communist collaborationist units was also absorbing an ever-increasing share of the resistance's attention.

---

21 Richard Clogg, *Greece 1940–1949: Occupation, Resistance, Civil War: A Documentary History* (Basingstoke and New York: Palgrave Macmillan, 2002), p. 14.

The true extent of wartime collaboration was pushed into the historio-graphical shadows in post-war Greece and Yugoslavia. This was due, in no small part, to the embarrassingly close links between the post-war Greek political order and collaborators, and because the ugly truth of widespread collaboration challenged the Titoist nation-building mantra of overwhelming popular resistance against the occupation. Despite Kardelj's claim that 'from the first day in our country, the occupier was welcomed with war',[22] collabor-ation, or at the very least accommodation, was initially a far more widespread reaction. Axis occupation was obviously cheered by German, Hungarian, Italian and Albanian minorities. Yet Ante Pavelić's Ustaša government was also initially welcomed by many Croatians. It earned the endorsement of the Zagreb Catholic Archbishop Alojzij Stepinac, not least because it promised prison sentences for swearing and draconian punishments for abortion. Sla-vophone Macedonians, who had been chafing under the interwar assimila-tionist pressures of the Serbs and Greeks, 'expect[ed] relief from the Bulgarians', who 'posed as liberators'.[23] Even the Greeks, who had already fought the Italians for six months prior to the April invasion, largely adhered to the call of the Hellenic State's first puppet prime minister to return to their 'homes, maintain your gratitude to the Fuhrer and apply yourselves to your peaceful endeavours'.[24] Indeed, 'reluctant accommodation to overwhelming force' was not unique to the Balkans, as historian Rab Bennet noted, but 'was a Europe-wide response' visible in other occupied states.[25]

Yet accommodation was not collaboration, which remains a slippery term to define. Its most extreme form, which a historian of Vichy France, Stanley Hoffman, described as 'an openly desired cooperation with, and imitation of, the occupying regime', was a relatively rare phenomenon in Greece and Yugoslavia.[26] Strictly Nazi-oriented or fascist parties did not score well electorally during the interwar era, despite the rightward shift of Greek and Yugoslav governments in the 1930s. Yet those that did exist were willing to assist the occupiers. The National Union of Greece, which had participated

22 Edvard Kardelj, *Pot nove Jugoslavije: Članki in govori iz narodnoosvobodilne borbe, 1941–1945* (Ljubljana: Državna založba Slovenija, 1946), p. 447.

23 Andrew Rossos, *Macedonia and the Macedonians: A History* (Stanford University Press, 2008), p. 186.

24 Neni Panourgiá, *Dangerous Citizens: The Greek Left and the Terror of the State* (New York: Fordham University Press, 2009), p. 50.

25 Rab Bennett, *Under the Shadow of the Swastika: The Moral Dilemmas of Resistance and Collaboration in Hitler's Europe* (London: Macmillan, 1999), p. 9.

26 Stanley Hoffman, *Decline or Renewal? France Since the 1930s* (New York: Viking, 1974), p. 27.

in the 1931 pogrom against Salonika's Jews, once again fanned anti-Semitism and assisted in the deportation of Salonika's approximately 50,000-strong Jewish community to Auschwitz in the spring of 1943.[27] In Athens, the National Socialist Patriotic Organization harassed Athens's Jews and recruited volunteers for German industry and the Russian front. Leaving aside for the moment the ultra-nationalist secessionist variant of fascism, the only noteworthy Yugoslav fascist movement which also advocated a unified Yugoslavia was Zbor (Rally), headed by Dimitrije Ljotić. With its stock-in-trade racism, anti-Semitism, corporatism and penchant for dictatorship, Zbor captured only 1 per cent of the vote in pre-war elections, yet nevertheless attracted covert German financial and organizational support. Zbor returned the favour after April 1941 by assisting the puppet administration of Serbia and forming the largest share of the 3,500-strong collaborationist Serbian Volunteer Corps, which fought the resistance in occupied Serbia.

The greater popularity of the Ustaša underscores the importance that ethnic grievances and rivalry played in fostering collaboration in Yugoslavia and, to a lesser extent, in Greece. Outlawed in the interwar era for advocating an armed Croat struggle to disassemble the Yugoslav state, the Ustaša sought the protection and assistance of Yugoslavia's covetous enemies – Italy, Bulgaria and Hungary. The Ustaša's hold on Croatian allegiances was very weak before 1941. Indeed, the Germans first approached Vladko Maček, leader of the popular interwar Croat Peasant Party, about forming a puppet government, and only when he refused were the unpredictable Ustaša foisted upon the ethnically mixed NDH. Yet there is no denying the strong initial support for the Ustaša. In the eyes of Croats, their country appeared to have been spared the fate of Serbs and Slovenes, and, what is more, was given a Croatian government, army and additional territory. The regime acquired the backing of the Peasant Party and the Catholic Church, while opportunities for administrative promotion at the expense of the Serbs were welcomed by many. However, the hope that Croatians would escape the horrors of occupation was destroyed in mere weeks, as the Ustaša unleashed their genocide against Serbs, Jews and Roma, which in turn fed the resistance. The Italians accelerated the Ustaša's increasingly ineffectual control over western Croatia by deploying Četniks against the Partisans, while Germany de facto occupied its half of Croatia, exploiting its economic and human resources in the interests of the Reich.

27 Irith Dublon-Knebel, *German Foreign Office Documents on the Holocaust in Greece (1937–1944)* (Tel Aviv University, 2007), p. 21.

Pre-existing ethnic tensions also fed collaboration in other regions of Yugoslavia. In the Vojvodina and the Banat, the favoured Hungarian and *Volksdeutsche* minorities monopolized local administration and policing. The Italians and, later, the Germans sought the administrative assistance of Montenegrin separatists known as Greens, who had never accepted Montenegro's 1918 decision to unify with Serbia. In Kosovo and western Macedonia, the Italians' pro-Albanian and anti-Slav policies attracted local Albanian collaborators. The Germans continued this arrangement after the Italian collapse, recruiting some 6,000 Albanians into the 21st Waffen-SS Division 'Skanderbeg'. Sandwiched between competing Croats and Serbs, some Bosnian Muslims were among the perpetrators of Ustaša-led atrocities against Serbs, while others were the victims of Serb reprisals. The Germans exploited this insecurity by recruiting over 20,000 Muslims for the first non-Germanic Waffen-SS division, the 13th Division 'Handschar', in 1943. The Bulgarians also attempted to organize a collaborationist movement out of Yugoslavia's disaffected Macedonians, the *kontračeti*, to fight the Partisans in Macedonia. However, by 1942, the initial honeymoon of pro-Bulgarian sentiments had dissipated in the 'forcible Bulgarianization' of Macedonians, and only some 200 *kontračeti* were recruited, who were, in turn, defeated and dispersed by the Partisans.[28]

While Greece's wartime history was not as ethnically convoluted as that of Yugoslavia, the unwillingness of post-war Greek governments and some scholars to recognize the ethnic intricacies of Greece has obscured the role ethnicity played in collaboration and resistance. Following Greek victories over the invading Italians in 1940, the Cham Albanian minority of Epirus were arrested, exiled and killed for their presumed collaboration with the Italians. The Chams repaid this brutality and that of 'a quarter of a century of treatment as second-class citizens under Greek rule' by collaborating administratively and assisting the Italian and German occupiers in subduing the Greek resistance.[29] With Bulgarian officers, the Germans and Italians created the *komitadži* movement from Greece's marginalized Slavophone Macedonian community, to defend their villages against incursions by the Greek resistance. '[M]ore anti-Greek and anti-Communist than pro-German, -Italian or -Bulgarian', the 10,000-strong *komitadži* would be neutralized by ELAS attacks and the appeal of the Slav-Macedonian National Liberation Front,

---

28 Rossos, *Macedonia and the Macedonians*, p. 188.
29 Robert Elsie and Bejtullah Destani, *The Cham Albanians of Greece: A Documentary History* (London: Tauris, 2013), p. xxxix.

a Slavophone Macedonian branch of ELAS, formed in October 1943 to win Macedonians' support.[30] The Italians also managed to recruit a few hundred Vlach auxiliaries to combat the resistance in the northern Pindus mountains, by promising autonomy and, perhaps most significantly, food.[31]

While ethnic grievances were far more pronounced a factor in shaping collaboration in the nationally combustive Balkans, the collaboration of former members of the political and military elite was not unlike similar trends in Western Europe. Among the most prominent were the three Prime Ministers of the Hellenic State: Georgios Tsolakoglou, Constantine Lotothe-topolous and Ioannis Rallis; the Prime Minister of the collaborating Serbian Government of National Salvation, Milan Nedić; and the President of the German-sponsored puppet administration of the formerly Italian-occupied Slovene Province of Ljubljana, Leon Rupnik. Few would have predicted their treasonous future careers before 1941. While they may have shared a certain admiration for German power, they had, in most cases, served their countries honourably. Tsolakoglou, Nedić and Rupnik were former generals, Lotothetopolous was a medical doctor, and Rallis was a royalist politician from a family with a long pedigree of political service to Greece. In a certain sense, they were all realists. Axis power was here to stay and they clearly believed that the best way to assist their countries, to borrow the words of the French collaborating leader Marshal Philippe Pétain, was 'to protect you from the worst. . .for if I could no longer be your sword, I wished to remain your shield'.[32] These men did not see themselves as traitors. Instead, they were, in Tsolakoglou's view, 'soldiers and patriots'.[33] Unlike the pre-war governments and their self-serving sectarian politicians, who fled to the safety and comfort of exile, they remained behind and were willing, in Rupnik's far less delicate words, to 'eat excrement' in order to protect their nations that were 'stuck between communist horrors and the occupiers' repression'.[34] Yet their twofold aim of moderating the demands of the occupiers while pacifying the resistance proved to be a Sisyphean task. None enjoyed the genuine public sympathy that Pétain achieved in the early

30 Rossos, *Macedonia and the Macedonians*, pp. 187–8.
31 John Koliopoulos, *Plundered Loyalties: Axis Occupation and Civil Strife in Greek West Macedonia, 1941–1949* (London: Hurst, 1999), pp. 82–4.
32 Stephen Gilliatt, *An Exploration of the Dynamics of Collaboration and Non-Resistance* (Lewiston, NY: Edwin Mellen Press, 1990), pp. 79–80.
33 Peter Davies, *Dangerous Liaisons: Collaboration and World War Two* (Harlow: Pearson Longman, 2004), p. 20.
34 Marjan Drnovšek, France Rozman and Peter Vodopivec (eds.), *Slovenska Kronika XX Stoletja, 1941–1995* (Ljubljana: Nova Revija, 1996), p. 57.

months of his collaboration, earned in part by the relatively correct behaviour of the Germans and concessions to French autonomy. Greeks and Yugoslavs were greeted by a different kind of German, as they endured hunger, executions, deportations and arrests, while Greek and Yugoslav political collaborators were often 'rewarded' for largely fruitless attempts at tempering the occupiers' behaviour by having their names attached to universally hated policies, such as the conscription of civilian labour. Moreover, their claims to be apolitical, 'guided only and solely by the purest of Greek [or Serbian, or Slovene] interest', must be treated with suspicion.[35] In particular, the political collaborators' intense hatred of communism pushed them and their security, intelligence and propaganda apparatuses into an ever-expanding role in suppressing the resistance. This decision to settle unresolved political or ideological feuds with the assistance of the occupiers marked their transformation into anti-partisan Axis auxiliaries. Despite their claims to the contrary, political collaborators did still wield the 'sword', but it was now pointed at their compatriots in the resistance.

Collaboration is ultimately an 'occupier-driven phenomenon', as historian Jan Gross described it.[36] If the occupier was unwilling to countenance collaboration with the occupied, then collaboration usually did not occur. However, the willingness of the occupiers to permit collaboration in Greece and Yugoslavia was also, to a certain extent, 'resistance-driven', and herein lies the amplified contribution of the harried resisters to Axis occupational policies in the Balkans. The occupiers' desire to crush the mostly communist-led resistance dovetailed with the anti-communist proclivities of a certain part of the Greek and Yugoslav establishment and their followers, helping to fuel collaboration and the internecine violence that inflicted such a brutal toll on the two nations. The Italians were most willing to foster collaboration, in part because they recognized their military weakness relative to the Germans, and in part because Italian Fascism did not share Nazism's racial obsessions in engaging with non-Italians. Italy's more 'liberal concepts' of occupation, which Italian Foreign Minister Galeazzo Ciano, in April 1941, hoped would 'have the effect of attracting sympathies for us' in occupied Slovenia, also had the unintended consequence of incubating the resistance.[37] Despite the fact that Italian 'liberalism' would be replaced by increasingly

35 Davies, *Dangerous Liaisons*, p. 48.
36 Jan T. Gross, 'Themes for a Social History of War Experience and Collaboration', in I. Deák, J. Gross and T. Judt (eds.), *The Politics of Retribution: World War II and Its Aftermath* (Princeton University Press, 2000), p. 24.
37 Galeazzo Ciano, *Ciano's Diary, 1939–1943* (London: Heinemann, 1947), pp. 334–6.

brutal counter-insurgency measures in 1942, the Italians also collaborated with local security forces. In Yugoslavia, the Italians created the Anti-Communist Voluntary Militia (*Milizia Volontaria Anti Comunista* – MVAC), the umbrella organization under which all armed anti-Partisan units were grouped. The largest contingent of the MVAC in the province of Ljubljana was the 6,000 members of the Village Guard (*vaške straže*). Most were recruited from supporters of the Catholic-oriented Slovene People's Party, the most popular pre-war Slovene party, who were incensed with Partisan assassinations of well-known figures from the Catholic right, whom the resistance accused of collaboration. The Italians seized upon similar schisms elsewhere in Yugoslavia, by early 1943 recruiting some 17,000 separatist-inclined Montenegrin auxiliaries, and another 20,000 Četniks in western Croatia, to fight their Partisan rivals.[38]

Hitler and the German high command were far more reluctant than the Italians to engage in military collaboration with the Greeks and Yugoslavs, although they accepted the administrative assistance provided by the Hellenic State and Nedić's puppet government in Serbia. While the Germans provided Nedić, as early as the summer of 1941, with a 10,000-strong gendarmerie (the nucleus of the future Serbian State Guard) and accepted the assistance of Ljotić's Serbian Volunteer Corps and Kosta Pećanac's errant Četniks, this was permitted primarily because the Germans needed more troops, in the wake of Operation BARBAROSSA, to suppress the Četnik–Partisan rebellion in western Serbia.[39] When the emergency passed in 1942, the Germans dissolved collaborating Četnik units and arrested some questionable officers, while simultaneously pressuring the Italians to end their collaboration with the Četniks. German suspicions were well grounded, as it was the immediate need to neutralize their communist-led rivals, not allegiance to Germany or Italy, which motivated the Četniks to accept the occupiers' truces and their arms. As for Nedić, the Germans prevented him from exercising any real control over the expanded Serbian State Guard.

By late 1943, Germany was forced to overcome its reluctance to engage in military collaboration in the Balkans, as it suffered defeats on European battlefields and an Italian capitulation that had emboldened the resistance and overstretched German resources. In the wake of the Italian departure

38 Jozo Tomasevich, *War and Revolution in Yugoslavia: Occupation and Collaboration* (Stanford University Press, 2001), pp. 143, 256.
39 Sabrina Ramet and Sladjana Lazić, 'The Collaborationist Regime of Milan Nedić', in Sabrina Ramet and Ola Listhaug (eds.), *Serbia and the Serbs in World War Two* (Houndmills: Palgrave Macmillan, 2011), p. 23.

from the province of Ljubljana, the Germans permitted the creation of the Slovene Home Guard – an anti-Partisan force that would more than double the size of its Village Guard predecessor – and the collaborating Provincial Administration, headed by Rupnik. The growing impotence of Pavelić, who was ridiculed by the Waffen-SS Major General Ernst Frick in early 1944 as the 'mayor of the city of Zagreb, excluding the suburbs', convinced the Germans to continue the Italian policy of collaborating with the more effective Četniks in anti-Partisan operations in the NDH.[40] Yet despite the various ceasefires with Mihailović's commanders, the distrust between Germans and Četniks did not disappear. Mihailović supporters were purged from Slovene Home Guard ranks in the spring of 1944, while the Germans provided 'only a trickle of additional supplies' to the Četniks in Serbia in 1944.[41] Clearly, each side was using the other for its own ends.

While Rallis had created the Greek Security Battalions in April 1943, it was the manpower shortage aggravated by the Italian capitulation in September that convinced the Germans of their usefulness in suppressing the resistance. Recruitment surged, fed in part by ELAS attacks, in the autumn of 1943, on EDES, whose mostly republican elements were attracted to the fervent anti-communism of the Battalions and their 'ostensible' anti-monarchist orientation.[42] The Security Battalions reached their maximum strength of 16,000 men by the summer of 1944.[43] Like the Četniks and some other anti-Partisan auxiliaries in Yugoslavia, they also retained pro-Allied and anti-German sympathies. With the defeat and departure of the Germans appearing, as a 1944 British report concluded, 'a foregone conclusion', collaboration with the Germans was understood by Rallis and some of his Battalionists as the 'least worst' option in defeating the far more serious threat of a communist revolution in Greece.[44] Nevertheless, the Security Battalions remained a German creation – they decided how large the units would become, their weapons and their objectives. Indeed, the Security Battalions were concentrated in the Peloponnesus to help forestall an Allied landing, and in Macedonia to secure the German evacuation route north to the Reich. While it is true that the Security Battalions recruited Greeks who had experienced ELAS

---

40 Tomasevich, *War and Revolution in Yugoslavia*, p. 324.
41 Ibid., p. 227.
42 Andre Gerolymatos, 'The Security Battalions and the Civil War', *Journal of the Hellenic Diaspora* 12:1 (1985), 19.
43 Stathis Kalyvas, 'Armed Collaboration in Greece, 1941–1944', *European Review of History* 15:2 (April 2008), 131.
44 Ibid., 134.

violence, they also attracted fascists, opportunists and ordinary criminals, who used the power of the Germans for material gain.[45]

There is little doubt that, by 1944, we enter what Mazower described as 'the murky atmosphere of underground "nationalist" politics, a highly duplicitous and dangerous world where resistance did not rule out collaboration, and where service alongside the Wehrmacht was justified on the grounds that it was necessary to save Greece [and Yugoslavia] from the Left'.[46] We also enter the 'highly duplicitous and dangerous world' of great-power politics. Churchill confirmed the laissez-faire attitude toward post-war political developments in Yugoslavia, which, according to Fitzroy Maclean – Churchill's personal representative to Tito – appeared to have been sealed by the November 1943 Tehran Conference decision to materially support the Partisans, during a tête-à-tête with Maclean: '"Do you intend to make Yugoslavia your home after the war?" he asked Maclean. "That being the case, the less you and I worry about the form of Government they set up, the better. That is for them to decide. What interests us is, which of them [Mihailović or Tito] is doing most harm to the Germans?"'[47] Yet as early as 1943 it appeared that the British indifference to post-war Yugoslav affairs would not extend to Greece. Greece was too important for protecting British sea communications and its interests in the Middle East (especially oil) from Soviet encroachment to make military effectiveness against the Germans the main criterion in deciding its post-war fate. The fingerprints of the British were everywhere in Greece and they remained, despite periodic crises, the strongest supporters of its government-in-exile. Alarmed by the republican and communist character of the resistance, the British 'effectively torpedoed' the August 1943 talks in Cairo between resistance representatives and the government-in-exile, confirming EAM–ELAS suspicions that the British would restore the King by force if necessary.[48] Relations further deteriorated when the British supported EDES in the conflict with ELAS in the autumn of 1943. Yet EAM–ELAS also unnerved the British with their establishment of PEEA in March 1944, made all the more ominous by the subsequent mutiny in the Greek government-in-exile's army in the Middle East, whose ringleaders demanded a government of national unity based on PEEA. No sooner had British forces helped to suppress the mutiny than word came of ELAS's liquidation of the

45 Andre Gerolymatos, 'The Role of the Greek Officer Corps in the Resistance', *Journal of the Hellenic Diaspora*, 11:3 (1984), 78.
46 Mazower, *Inside Hitler's Greece*, p. 329.
47 Roberts, *Tito, Mihailović and the Allies*, p. 174.
48 Clogg, *Greece 1940–1949*, pp. 12–13.

remnants of EKKA and its leader, Colonel Demetrios Psaros, in April. For the British, these developments revealed ELAS's plans to communize Greece, spurring Foreign Secretary Anthony Eden in May to offer the Soviets a free hand in Romania in return for Soviet non-interference in British designs for Greece, thus laying the groundwork for the 'percentages agreement' between Churchill and Stalin in October 1944. EAM's U-turn in July 1944, when it rejoined the Greek Government of National Unity headed by George Papandreou, which had been formed at the British-brokered conference in Lebanon in May, revealed both Soviet adherence to Eden's proposal and their successful pressure on EAM to comply with 'the need for the unity of the Allied front'.[49]

Thus, on the cusp of the liberation of Athens and Belgrade, the resistance's positioning for post-war influence had clearly harvested rather different results in Greece and Yugoslavia. The Allied-sponsored reconciliation between the Yugoslav government-in-exile and Tito in June 1944 played into the latter's hands. The resulting Šubašić government could not contain elements that were hostile to Tito; it recognized the decisions of the second AVNOJ Congress and pledged organizational support for the Partisans. In return, Tito agreed that the question of the monarchy would be decided by the people after the war, and that a future unity government would be composed of members of the government-in-exile and the National Committee of Liberation. By September, King Peter was pressured to cut ties with Mihailović and, without mentioning names, accused him and his followers of collaboration with the occupiers. In Greece, the situation was far less favourable for EAM–ELAS. Unlike the Šubašić government, the Lebanon agreement provided EAM with only one-quarter of the Cabinet posts in the Government of National Unity. The British also urged republican resistors and royalists to trade their old rivalry for a common struggle against EAM–ELAS, an endeavour made all the easier by Zervas's reconciliation with the monarchy. Indeed, by 1944, EDES no longer represented 'the anti-monarchist faction but had come to reflect a broad spectrum of right-wing forces opposed just as much to ELAS as to the Germans'.[50] Moreover, despite Zervas's 'close ties with the collaborationist government and even the Germans in an unofficial anti-Communist alliance', and the defection of some EDES members to the Security Battalions, the British did not cut

49 Lars Baerentzen, 'The Arrival of the Soviet Military Mission in July 1944 and KKE Policy: A Study of Chronology', *Journal of the Hellenic Diaspora* 13:3–4 (1986), 83, 96–7.
50 Gerolymatos, 'Role of the Greek Officer Corps', 78.

Zervas loose like Mihailović.[51] EAM–ELAS and the KKE were aware of these machinations and played a two-pronged approach – negotiating and working with the British and their rivals when necessary, yet also positioning for de facto control of Greece when the Germans retreated. Their acceptance of the British-brokered Caserta Agreement of 26 September, less than a month before the liberation of Athens, was evidence of this flexibility, as it demanded that all guerrilla forces be placed under the orders of the Greek Government of National Unity, which, in turn, was subordinated to the General Officer Commanding Allied Land Forces Greece, Lieutenant General Ronald Scobie.

Liberation of the Balkans from Axis occupation was a drawn-out affair. Athens and Belgrade were freed in October 1944, and some Greek islands and much of Slovenia only in May 1945. In the wake of the German retreat, Tito's forces seized control of much of Yugoslavia with relative ease, assisted by their Soviet comrades, who helped to liberate Belgrade and parts of eastern Yugoslavia. Tito's two priorities during this period were liquidating any remnant Četnik and other collaborating formations which had not fled with the Germans, and seizing the disputed ethnically mixed frontiers with Italy and Austria. His forces won the 'race for Trieste' on 1 May and entered Klagenfurt, the capital of Austrian Carinthia, on 8 May, sparking two of the first flashpoints of the Cold War. The German retreat – and that of a handful of utterly compromised Greek collaborators – from most of the Greek mainland in September and October was accelerated by Soviet penetrations into the eastern Balkans, Bulgaria's decision to switch sides in September, and the Battle for Belgrade, which threatened the main rail corridor north from Greece. Instead of harassing the retreating Germans, the Greek resistance seized their weapons and turned them on their internal opponents. EDES ethnically cleansed Cham villages, while ELAS targeted the Security Battalions and other collaborators, massacring hundreds in the Peloponnesus towns of Meligala and Kalamata in September. While EAM–ELAS stood by Caserta's definition of the Security Battalions as 'instruments of the enemy', the British and Greek governments pointed to Caserta's prohibition against guerrilla units taking the law into their own hands, ordering the Battalionists to be held as prisoners of war until Greek courts were established.

The scandal over the Meligala massacres underscores the existential question which confronted resistance movements across Europe that had

---

51 Keith Lowe, *Savage Continent: Europe in the Aftermath of World War II* (London: Viking, 2012), p. 303.

acquired power during the war largely through their own efforts and the authority of the gun: when the occupiers retreated, should they disband and allow national governments, often with the support of the Allied victors, to return to power, or should they remain intact to shape their countries' post-war destinies? In the wake of liberation, returning governments sought to reassert the 'ultimate authority of the modern state', which Judt defined as 'its monopoly of violence and its willingness to deploy force if necessary', over independent nuclei of armed authority and the rudimentary justice systems that they developed during the occupation.[52] In most Western and Central European countries, the resistance movements willingly stepped aside, often merging with established political parties and national armies to whom they professed allegiance during the occupation. This transition was often sweetened by broad amnesties for any fratricidal killings committed by the resistance during the war. Events were more complicated in Eastern Europe and the Balkans, where resistance forces such as EAM–ELAS and the Partisans had been at cross-purposes with their governments-in-exile, or, in the case of the Polish Home Army, the new Soviet-backed Polish government. However, unlike the Home Army, EAM–ELAS and Tito's Partisans were also strong enough to challenge the return of these governments. Indeed, the Partisan movement was the only European resistance force to seize post-war political power. The United Yugoslav Government that emerged in March 1945 was communist in everything but name. Tito's rough-and-tumble resistance fighters had been transformed into the conventional Yugoslav Army; the KPJ monopolized the makeshift politics and administration of liberated territories; and Partisan wartime intelligence had morphed into the feared Department of National Security (OZNA), whose task, according to Tito, was 'to strike terror into the hearts of those who did not like this sort of Yugoslavia'.[53] Tito's aims were not unlike European governments that returned in the wake of liberation – neutralize internal challenges to the state's monopoly on power. What set communist Yugoslavia apart was the persistent lethal force they employed in pursuing this aim. Not only were obvious collaborators targeted, but political parties and personalities that had not necessarily compromised themselves during the war, but were opposed to the communization of Yugoslavia, including members of the Catholic Church and the propertied class, were dragged in

52 Tony Judt, *Postwar: A History of Europe Since 1945* (New York: Penguin, 2005), p. 37.
53 John Lampe, *Yugoslavia as History: Twice There Was a Country* (Cambridge University Press, 2000), p. 227.

front of Yugoslav military and civilian courts and sentenced to varying degrees of punishment, from the nationalization of property and 'rehabilitative' hard labour to execution. Ethnic Germans and Italians who had not had the good sense to flee before liberation were arrested, executed and expelled en masse. Special punishment was reserved for the tens of thousands of Slovene Home Guards, Četniks, Ustaša, Croatian Home Guards (the regular armed forces of the NDH), Nedićists, Ljotićists and sympathetic civilians who fled north with the retreating Germans, in an attempt to surrender to the Allied forces in Italy and Austria. While those in Italy largely escaped punishment, the British forcibly repatriated most Yugoslav collaborators and some civilians from Austria in the second half of May, or blocked their entrance into Austria. Most were summarily executed by Tito's forces shortly upon their return. While the total number repatriated and killed has never been conclusively established, the most reliable statistics reveal that over 70,000 Yugoslavs were executed in connection with events in Austria, which does not include the thousands who died in the settling of scores elsewhere in Yugoslavia.[54]

While post-war political authority in Greece had been ceded to the British-backed Papandreou government that was sworn in on 23 October 1944 – a government that EAM–ELAS officially supported – the gulf between the two sides was not bridged with paper promises. EAM–ELAS was unconvinced that the Papandreou government, its army or its courts, composed of many of EAM–ELAS's opponents and critics, would protect its members, punish collaborators or give the resistance a political role commensurate to its wartime sacrifices. For their part, the Papandreou government and its British supporters were convinced that EAM–ELAS was unwilling to surrender its revolutionary goal of a communist Greece, and its continued reliance on People's Courts to pursue 'obvious collaborators', as well as 'royalists, nationalists and simply wealthy "bourgeois"', was evidence of this nefarious intent.[55] These tensions erupted into the open in November, as the deadline approached for the surrender of that which had ultimately underpinned EAM–ELAS's authority during the war – the gun. While EDES and Greek military units returning from the Middle East were also to disband in order to create a new national army that absorbed all wartime factions, the acting

54 Tomasevich, *War and Revolution in Yugoslavia*, pp. 763–5.
55 Mark Mazower, 'Three Forms of Political Justice: Greece, 1944–1945', in Mark Mazower (ed.), *After the War Was Over: Reconstructing the Family, Nation, and State in Greece, 1943–1960* (Princeton University Press, 2000), p. 27.

General Secretary of the KKE, Giorgos Santos, baulked, accusing Papandreou of acting in bad faith.[56] Despite Scobie's threat to defend the Papandreou government by force if necessary, EAM ministers resigned from the government on 2 December, setting the stage for the massive street protests that ultimately heralded the start of the *Dekemvriana*, the December battle for Athens between EAM–ELAS and British and Greek government forces. The initially outnumbered government forces recruited National Guard units, partly from right-wing militias and former Security Battalionists, who only a few weeks before seemed utterly compromised. Both sides committed war crimes, not sparing civilians as they settled the accumulated hatreds of the war years. Nor was the fighting confined to Athens – ELAS chased EDES out of its Epirus stronghold and solidified its control in some rural regions, while elsewhere National Guard vigilantes targeted EAM–ELAS's civilian sympathizers. Yet the fighting also squandered much of the goodwill and respect EAM–ELAS had earned from Greek civilians for its wartime resistance, while confusion reigned among some of their rank and file, who had joined the resistance to liberate their country from the hated occupiers and their domestic lackeys – not to shoot fellow Greeks or their British liberators.

EAM–ELAS was ultimately forced out of Athens, and in February it signed the Varkiza Agreement. Among its points was a renewed order for ELAS's demobilization and the creation of a Greek national army, an amnesty for political crimes committed in the recent fighting, and a promise to purge the civil and security services on the criteria of 'collaboration with the enemy'.[57] Unfortunately, the same suspicions accompanied Varkiza. ELAS dissolved, yet the KKE concealed part of its weaponry. Tainted by embarrassing links with wartime collaborators, the Greek government's promised purge of traitors 'petered out more quickly in Greece', according to Mazower, 'than anywhere else in Europe' – a leniency that did not extend to former EAM–ELAS fighters.[58] By the end of 1945, ten times more former resisters had been convicted by the courts than collaborators, packing prisons with those 'whose only crime was to have fought against the Germans'. These injustices and the still outstanding accounts from the occupation would help to fuel the bloody Greek civil war of 1946–49.

Liberation revealed the horrendous toll of Axis occupation. Over 1,000 Greek villages and one-third of Greece's national wealth were destroyed,

---

56 Clogg, *Greece 1940–1949*, p. 16.
57 Ibid., p. 189.
58 Mazower, *Inside Hitler's Greece*, p. 372.

while in Yugoslavia, one in five homes was destroyed, one-third of its industrial capacity, 60 per cent of its roads and 50 per cent of its livestock.[59] However, it is in human losses that the true cost of the occupation is measured. Since conventional warfare was relatively brief and the occupation was endured primarily by civilians, civilian deaths outnumbered military dead. While the numbers remain contested, the best estimates are between 1 million and 1.4 million Yugoslavs and approximately 430,000–550,000 Greeks.[60] Relative to total population, Yugoslavia and Greece ranked as the second and fourth worst war-affected countries, with one in eight and one in fourteen killed respectively.[61]

Moreover, in both Greece and Yugoslavia, the occupation removed much of the traditional political elite, sapping their ability to moderate the demands of the occupiers. Understood in this manner, the quicksand politics of occupation was a great experiment. It provided opportunities for new faces and forces – resisters and collaborators alike – to step into a national narrative that had been wiped clean by the invasion, in order to promote their own versions of what Greece and Yugoslavia should be. These versions were informed by pre-war political, ethnical and ideological schisms. However, the course of the occupation and its ferocious cycles of violence would also override pre-war factors, and divide and cleave them on the elementary questions of national and personal survival, the value of resistance, the definition of treason and, in the sunset of German domination, the postwar future of their states. The results were alliances – some expected, others novel – of resisters fighting collaborators, of resisters fighting resisters, but, too often, Greeks fighting Greeks and Yugoslavs fighting Yugoslavs. As Judt noted, 'it is one of the traumatic features of civil war that even after the enemy is defeated he remains in place'; indeed, the killing in the Balkans 'did not finish in 1945, with the departure of the Germans', but continued well after liberation until 1949.[62] And when the guns went silent, the pens continued. But it is altogether a different struggle now – one to understand the tortured history of Second World War collaboration, resistance and liberation in the Balkans.

59 Panourgiá, *Dangerous Citizens*, p. 62; Judt, *Postwar*, p. 17.
60 Judt, *Postwar*, p. 18; Tomasevich, *War and Revolution in Yugoslavia*, pp. 737–8.
61 Judt, *Postwar*, p. 18.
62 Ibid., p. 35.

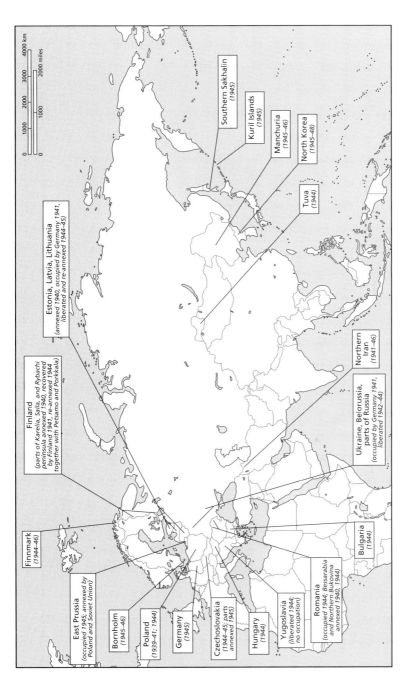

Finnmark
(1944–46)

East Prussia
(occupied 1945; annexed by
Poland and Soviet Union)

Bornholm
(1945–46)

Poland
(1939–41; 1944)

Germany
(1945)

Czechoslovakia
(1944–45; parts
annexed 1945)

Hungary
(1944)

Yugoslavia
(liberated 1944;
no occupation)

Romania
(occupied 1944; Bessarabia
and Northern Bukovina
annexed 1940, 1944)

Bulgaria
(1944)

Finland
(parts of Karelia, Salla, and Rybachi
peninsula annexed 1940, recovered
by Finland 1941, re-annexed 1944
together with Petsamo and Porkkala)

Estonia, Latvia, Lithuania
(annexed 1940, occupied by Germany 1941,
liberated and re-annexed 1944–45)

Northern
Iran
(1941–46)

Ukraine, Belorussia,
parts of Russia
(occupied by Germany 1941,
liberated 1942–44)

Tuva
(1944)

Southern Sakhalin
(1945)

Kuril Islands
(1945)

Manchuria
(1945–46)

North Korea
(1945–48)

0   1000   2000   3000   4000 km

0   1000   2000 miles

19.1 Advances of the Soviet Union by diplomacy and conquest, 1939–41

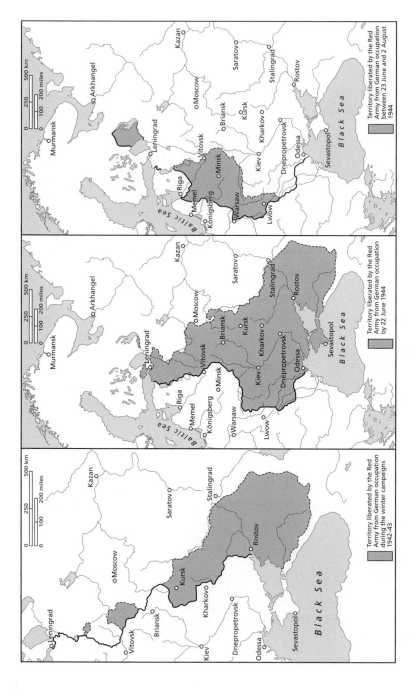

19.2 The process of Soviet liberation, 1943–44

Territory liberated by the Red Army from German occupation during the winter campaigns 1942–43

Territory liberated by the Red Army from German occupation by 22 June 1944

Territory liberated by the Red Army from German occupation between 23 June and 2 August 1944

Soviet liberations and occupations, 1939–1949

MARK EDELE

Soviet territorial change, 1939–1949

By early 1939, the Soviet Union encompassed eleven Union Republics covering one-sixth of the world's surface, inhabited by 167 million people, the third largest population after those of China and India.[1] In the north it bordered on Finland and the eastern tip of Norway; in the west, on Estonia and Latvia, Poland and Romania; in the south, on Turkey and Iran, Afghanistan and China, Tuva and Mongolia (Soviet satellites since the early 1920s), the Japanese puppet state of Manchukuo and Japanese-controlled Korea; in the east, the Soviets faced off the Japanese in the middle of the island of Sakhalin and across the small stretch of water separating the northernmost of the Kuril Islands from Kamchatka. Alaska lay toward the east, across the Bering Strait.

The Soviet Union began its expansion in 1939, a change in territory focusing on the north and the west: Eastern Poland was invaded in 1939; the Baltic republics, northern Bukovina, Bessarabia and parts of Finland were taken over in 1940. These occupations expanded the Soviet Union to sixteen republics, over 14 million square miles, and well over 190 million inhabitants.[2] In the south and the east, the Soviets did not move their borders for the time being, but defended them successfully in the undeclared border war with Japan (Battles of Lake Khasan in 1938 and Khalkhin Gol in 1939).

The expansion of 1939–40 was the first of five periods of territorial change, which would transform the Soviet Union from a besieged fortress into a superpower with an empire of satellites. The second period started with the

Research on this chapter was supported in part by an Australian Research Council Discovery Grant (DP130101215).

1 V. B. Zhiromskaia (ed.), *Vsesoiuznaia perepis' naseleniia 1939 goda. Osnovnye itogi. Rossiia* (Moscow: Blits, 1999), pp. 10–11; V. B. Zhiromskaia (ed.), *Naselenie Rossii v xx veke. Istoricheskie ocherki* (2 vols., Moscow: Rosspen, 2001), vol. II, p. 6.

2 Zhiromskaia (ed.), *Naselenie Rossii*, vol. II, pp. 7, 12, 61.

German attack on 22 June 1941, when the Soviets lost not only all they had acquired since 1939, but much else besides. By early 1942, Germany had occupied all of Poland, the Baltics, Belorussia and Ukraine, as well as a good part of European Russia, extending from just outside Leningrad in the north to close to Moscow and Stalingrad in the east, to Stavropol and Krasnodar in the south. Altogether, around a million square miles, or 9 per cent of the pre-war Soviet Union, were under Nazi occupation, an area which, before the war, had housed nearly 45 per cent of the Soviet population.[3] While territory after territory was lost, however, the Soviets continued to expand the reach of their armies in the occupation of northern Iran from 25 August 1941.

The third period – recovery of German-held Soviet territories – had prequels in the liberation of Rostov and Tikhvin in November and December of 1941 and the Battle of Moscow and the ensuing Soviet offensive in the winter of 1941–42. Liberation began in earnest, however, with the Battle of Stalingrad of 1942–43. By late 1944, most pre-1941 territories had been regained and the fourth period had begun: the wartime expansion of 1944–45. It encompassed not only much of Eastern Europe and, again, parts of Finland, but also Manchuria and northern Korea (from 9 August 1945), southern Sakhalin (from 11 August 1945) and the Kuril Islands (from 18 August 1945). Less well known are the occupations of the far northern part of Norway, the eastern Finnmark, from late October 1944, and of the Danish island of Bornholm in 1945, to say nothing of the annexation of Tuva in October 1944.

By early September 1945, then, the reach of the Red Army extended not only to Berlin, Prague and Vienna in the west, but also to Tabriz in the south, and Harbin, Mukden, Port Arthur and Pyongyang in the east, with Bornholm as a Baltic outpost in the northwest and the Finnmark as a bridgehead in the northeast. This high point of Soviet expansion by military means was consolidated in a fifth and final period, which began in late 1945. Northern Norway was abandoned in September 1945; Denmark's Bornholm, China's Manchuria and Iran's northern reaches in 1946; Korea in 1948; and Austria only in 1955. Having thus shortened the front lines, Stalin could consolidate the centre of the new Soviet empire: Europe. The Königsberg region, which had originally been subjected to the policy of organized plunder typical of occupied enemy territory, was annexed to the Russian Soviet Federative Socialist Republic in April 1946, renamed 'Kaliningrad region' in July, and settled with Soviet citizens between August 1946 and 1950. In a flanking move, Germans were

---

3 Ibid., p. 61; V. A. Zolotarev (ed.), *Velikaia Otechestvennaia. Istoriia Velikoi Pobedy 1941–1945 gg* (Moscow: Animi Fortitudo, 2005), p. 599.

expelled in 1947–49. This radicalization was mirrored by the changes in approach to other European satellites-in-the-making: in 1945–47, the 'people's democracies' came increasingly under communist control, before an abrupt shift to Stalinist dictatorship from September 1947.

These long-term trajectories are covered in other chapters of this history of the Second World War. Our task here is to look more closely at the practice of Soviet seizure of territory and populations, be it accompanied by liberation from foreign occupation or not. The most obvious feature of this process was the high level of physical force against people and their property. It took many forms: troop, revolutionary and economic violence. The origins of all these forms of force were complex, driven by a variety of actors, with divergent needs and multiple and changing aims. Stalin and the leadership were not the only agents of destruction. Troops in the field and their commanders often had their own agenda, and what the NKVD or the military occupation authorities did was not always neatly synchronized with the field army. This complexity becomes particularly clear if we assume a bird's-eye view which does not focus on one occupation *pars pro toto*. The Soviet Union was a Eurasian empire fighting a Eurasian war, and this chapter takes account of this fact. It begins by discussing the three types of violence and their distribution across all Soviet occupations before concluding with a discussion of the question of whether the labels 'occupation' or 'liberation' adequately describe the arrival of Red Army troops in a given territory.

Troop violence

The first category of violent behaviour, besides military violence to subjugate the enemy (including counter-insurgency against irregulars and terrorists), encompassed various forms of war crimes: the execution of prisoners of war, rape, plunder, murder of civilians and wanton destruction of enemy property. As these kinds of atrocities were particularly visible in Germany, many historians have explained them by the prior actions of the enemy – that is, as motivated by revenge and fuelled by hatred against those who had done likewise. However, Soviet troops behaved similarly in contexts where biblical invocations of an eye for an eye could not be mobilized as easily. During the 1939 campaign in Poland, Soviet troops and their field commanders, on their own initiative, executed POWs, raped women, looted property (like later in Germany, Manchuria or Korea, wristwatches were popular trophies) and killed civilians.[4] This experience worried the leadership enough to issue a stern warning to the troops fighting Finland, prohibiting 'requisitions from the population', as well as 'arbitrariness and lynch law'. Finnish soldiers, policemen and civilians 'who are guilty of counter-revolutionary acts against the Red Army' were to be handed over to the proper authorities rather than dealt with 'according to the personal judgement of some officer or another'.[5] Troops were also instructed to hold fire near settlements, in order to decrease the likelihood of civilian casualties – a somewhat ironic policy given the strategic air war against Helsinki.[6] In reality, excesses against civilians were made less likely by the Finnish evacuation of the front-line zones, but property crimes could at best be contained. Troops looted what they could, from bicycles to winter coats, shoes or children's clothes.[7] Likewise, during the first couple of days after the initial entry of Soviet troops into Iran in August 1941, 'many instances of looting by Red Army officers and soldiers' are documented.[8]

Marauding was a matter of course in Eastern Europe at the war's end. According to a Polish eyewitness on 1 August 1944, 'most of the stores had been looted first by the retreating Germans and then by the incoming Soviets'.[9] But the wild confiscation of property was not the worst of the matter, as military authorities knew well. In 1944, well before Stalin's much cited clash with the Yugoslav leadership over the question of rape, Soviet military commanders ordered that soldiers guilty of 'arbitrariness and excesses in relation to the population of Yugoslavia' were to be 'strictly punished'.[10] In the Baltic Military District, too, there were 'cases of violence, robbery, and other crimes', perpetrated by soldiers on the civilian

4 M. I. Mel'tiukhov, *17 sentiabria 1939. Sovetsko-pol'skie konflikty. 1918–1939* (Moscow: Veche, 2009), pp. 478–502.

5 Kombrig Gordov, Komissar Ivanov, 'Shifrofka No. 39419/39418/sh.' (29 November 1939), Tsentral'nyi Arkhiv Ministerstva oborony (hereafter TsAMO), fond 221, opis 263, delo 22, lists 222–3 (Library of Congress, Volkogonov papers, container 1, reel 1).

6 Alexander Chubaryan and Harold Shukman (eds.), *Stalin and the Soviet Finnish War, 1939–40* (London: Frank Cass, 2002), p. 60.

7 H. B. Elliston, *Finland Fights* (London: George G. Harrap, 1940), p. 330; Catherine Merridale, *Ivan's War. Life and Death in the Red Army, 1939–1945* (New York: Metropolitan Books, 2006), p. 80.

8 Jamil Hasanli, *At the Dawn of the Cold War: The Soviet-American Crisis over Iranian Azerbaijan, 1941–1946* (Lanham, Md.: Rowman & Littlefield, 2006), p. 204.

9 Zygmunt Klukowski, *Red Shadow: A Physician's Memoir of the Soviet Occupation of Eastern Poland, 1944–1956* (Jefferson, NC: McFarland & Co., 1997), p. 7.

10 Tolbukhin, Laiok, Anoshin to Military Council of 57th Army and Commander of IV Guards Cavalry Corps (14 October 1944), TsAMO, fond 243, opis 2912, delo 127, list 98 (Library of Congress, Volkogonov papers, container 1, box 1, folder 4).

population, as an order of Deputy Commissar for Defence General Bulga-
nin complained on 27 October 1945.[11] In Manchuria, 'the Russians' were 'the
wildest, most undisciplined bunch of soldiers, pillaging and raping', and
locals wondered if there were no 'military police in the Russian army'.[12]
The Chinese Communist Party protested that their alleged class allies
engaged 'in activities inconsistent with the practices of a proletarian army,
in particular raping women and depriving peasants of their livelihood'.[13]
Troops shot at random, took what they pleased and raped women, 'Japanese and Chinese alike. It did not matter to them'. As earlier in Poland or
Germany, Soviet soldiers in Manchuria were particularly interested in
acquiring wristwatches, wearing several on their arms at the same time.
As in Germany, too, the mass rapes led to mass abortions.[14] In Korea, Red
Army men also 'committed depredations against the Japanese and Koreans,
including rape and looting, on what appears to have been a wide scale and
which went quite beyond taking revenge against the enemy and its Korean
allies'.[15]

Troop violence on Soviet territory puts the widespread lawlessness in
much of the occupied territories in 1939, and then again in 1944–45, into yet
another context. The Soviet authorities struggled everywhere with controlling their troops. In late 1941, paratroopers in training had to subdue, with an
iron fist, the inmates of military hospitals terrorizing the town of Essentuki.[16]
Later in the war, during the transfer of combat personnel to the eastern front
with Japan in 1945, 'group binges, shootings, theft, burglary, [and] rape'
emanated from the echelons.[17] And once the war was over, during mass
demobilization of the European army, a trainload of disabled servicemen
raped and plundered their way through Poland and the Soviet Union,
not sparing a nurse unlucky enough to be in charge of their care. Attempts
to arrest drunken soldiers of demobilization echelons sparked riots and

11 Reprinted in V. A. Zolotarev (ed.), *Prikazy Narodnogo komissara oborony SSSR i Ministra vooruzhennykh sil SSSR 12 oktiabria 1945 g. – 1949 g.* (Moscow: Rosspen, 2011), pp. 13–14, quotation at p. 13.
12 Kazuko Kuramoto, *Manchurian Legacy: Memoirs of a Japanese Colonist* (East Lansing: Michigan State University Press, 1999), p. 62.
13 Brian Murray, 'Stalin, the Cold War, and the Division of China: A Multi-Archival Mystery', *Cold War International History Project Working Papers* 12 (1995), p. 3.
14 Kuramoto, *Manchurian Legacy*, pp. 64, 86, 90.
15 Bruce Cumings, *The Origins of the Korean War: Liberation and the Emergence of Separate Regimes, 1945–1947* (Princeton University Press, 1981), p. 388.
16 Grigorii Chukhrai, *Moia voina* (Moscow: Algoritm, 2001), pp. 62–3.
17 Shamarin (Kemerovo) to L. P. Beriia, not after 23 July 1945, State Archive of the Russian Federation (GARF) fond r-9401, opis 2, delo 98, lists 11–12, here: list 11.

armed altercations.[18] The end of mass demobilization in 1948 did not end the violence. On 11 September 1949, military sailors celebrated the Day of the Tank Forces in the central Russian town of Shcherbakov (today Rybinsk), by beating up local youth in the public gardens. On 25 September of the same year, a group of demobilized soldiers, just released from the Far Eastern 14th Army, arrived in Vladivostok, to roam the city drinking vodka, disturbing the peace and beating up a police officer.[19]

Given the pervasiveness of troop brutality, revenge for German atrocity alone clearly falls short as an explanation. Historians have offered the Stalinist way of war,[20] the brutality inherent in the Soviet political system,[21] sexual frustration fuelled by alcohol,[22] or the long-term brutalization of Soviet society in general[23] as alternative explanations to the revenge thesis. A comparative frame does indeed point to the emergence of troop violence, as it were, 'from below'. The Korean case is particularly instructive in this respect. As one historian has pointed out, the unimaginable losses in men and materiel in the European theatre of war forced the Soviets 'to recruit soldiers, young peasant men and women, just for the campaigns against the Japanese'. These green troops 'came into Korea lacking even uniforms and shoes in some cases and lived off the Korean land with no provisions for themselves'.[24] These shortages alone, and, more generally, the extreme poverty of the Soviet population, explain the plundering all the way back to the Poland campaign in 1939.

The high losses also help us to understand the prevalence of sexual violence: they undermined discipline and group cohesion. Recent research has stressed male bonding in wartime as a central aspect of rape warfare. Sexual violence is not an efficient, but instead an extremely costly form of war-making; it is seldom ordered from above, but frequently committed in

18 Mark Edele, *Soviet Veterans of the Second World War: A Popular Movement in an Authoritarian Society, 1941–1991* (Oxford University Press, 2008), pp. 26–8.
19 Orders from 30 September and 7 October 1949, in Zolotarev (ed.), *Prikazy Narodnogo komissara oborony*, pp. 455–8.
20 Andreas Hillgruber, *Zweierlei Untergang: Die Zerschlagung des Deutschen Reiches und das Ende des europäischen Judentums* (Berlin: Siedler, 1986), p. 35.
21 Joachim Hoffmann, *Stalins Vernichtungskrieg 1941–1945* (2nd rev. edn, Munich: Verlag für Wehrwissenschaften, 1996); Amir Weiner, 'Something to Die for, a Lot to Kill For: The Soviet System and the Barbarisation of Warfare, 1939–1945', in G. Kassimeris (ed.), *The Barbarization of Warfare* (New York University Press, 2006), pp. 101–25.
22 Antony Beevor, *The Fall of Berlin, 1945* (New York: Penguin, 2003).
23 Oleg Budnitskii, 'The Intelligentsia Meets the Enemy. Educated Soviet Officers in Defeated Germany, 1945', *Kritika: Explorations in Russian and Eurasian History* 10:3 (2009), 629–82.
24 Cumings, *Origins of the Korean War*, p. 388.

gangs, suggesting group dynamics as the centre of the explanation: 'sexual violence, and particularly gang rape, enables armed groups with forcibly recruited fighters to create bonds of loyalty and friendship from these initial circumstances of fear and mistrust'.[25] And indeed, the majority of Soviet soldiers were not fighting voluntarily; the Red Army had serious disciplinary problems and consistent trouble promoting the identification of soldiers with their units.[26] Rape was not ordered from above and could be prosecuted; many of the assaults happened in public settings, committed by frequently drunken gangs.[27] Part of the explanation, then, might lie in the role of sexual violence in the creation of primary groups within an otherwise fragmented military, which would also help to explain the observation that elite units, with a higher level of cohesion and purpose, were less prone to rape than second-grade infantry.[28]

However, such an explanation cannot replace the revenge thesis completely. True, rape was pervasive along the Red Army's path in Europe as much as in Asia; and even liberated Soviet women, deported earlier by the Germans as slave labour, were assaulted.[29] Recent research on crimes of other occupation forces, likewise, leads to the suspicion that the Red Army was not so untypical in this respect. However, and with full acknowledgement of the problematic nature of any quantitative data on such crimes, the available statistics do not support these impressions. The 300,000 Soviet troops who took part in the Belgrade Strategic Offensive Operation in 1944 committed, according to Yugoslav authorities, 121 cases of rape, a ratio of 0.0004 assaults per soldier. The Soviet forces invading East Prussia and Manchuria in 1945 were considerably bigger – just under 1.7 million each. In East Prussia, they committed maybe 1.1 million rapes, a ratio of 0.6 assaults per soldier – much higher than in Yugoslavia; in Manchuria, the order of magnitude is probably in the hundreds or maybe thousands rather than millions, and the ratio of assault per soldier is likely to be closer to the Yugoslav than the German case. US forces in Germany, meanwhile,

25 Dara Kay Cohen, 'Explaining Sexual Violence During Civil War' (unpublished PhD dissertation, Stanford University, 2010), p. iv.

26 Roger Reese, *Why Stalin's Soldiers Fought: The Red Army's Military Effectiveness in World War II* (Lawrence: University Press of Kansas, 2011).

27 Barbara Stelzl-Marx, *Stalins Soldaten in Österreich. Die Innensicht der sowjetischen Besatzung 1945–1955* (Vienna and Munich: Böhlau Verlag and Oldenbourg Verlag, 2012), pp. 415–20.

28 Manfred Zeidler, *Kriegsende im Osten. Die Rote Armee und die Besetzung Deutschlands östlich von Oder und Neisse 1944/45* (Munich: Oldenbourg, 1996), pp. 146–8.

29 See the reports in the Russian State Archive of Socio-Political History (RGASPI) fond 17, opis 125, delo 314.

numbered 1.6 million on 8 May 1945. They committed, according to reports received by the military authorities, 552 cases of rape, or 0.03 assaults per soldier – lower than the Soviets in East Prussia, but considerably higher than the Red Army in Yugoslavia. The rape allegations in Germany constituted over 60 per cent of all such accusations against American troops in the entire European theatre of operations between July 1942 and November 1945. Hence, it appears that Allied soldiers were more likely to rape German women than those of other nationalities; and the Red Army was particularly fierce among the occupiers of Germany.[30]

Troop violence, then, blemished all Soviet occupations, but nowhere did it reach the level it did in Germany and Austria. It emanated from below, was made possible by poor discipline and lack of control over troops by often insufficiently trained officers; it was enhanced by incomprehension and anger at better living conditions, a fury fuelled further by the callous treatment by superiors; its sexual component was organized by alcohol-fuelled male bonding in small primary groups, urged on by the seemingly universal desire to emasculate the enemy by despoiling 'his women'; it was further escalated, in the German case, by revenge for what had happened in the Soviet Union, a hatred smouldering because of personal experience, word of mouth and explicit wartime propaganda. Russian historians, then, are correct in claiming that such crimes were 'spontaneous' (*stikhiino*) rather than part of a policy imposed from above.[31] Most of the troop violence was illegal, normally not ordered by properly constituted authorities, and at times prosecuted.

Revolutionary violence

The same cannot be said about the second category of force against people. Revolutionary violence was directed from above, executed according to decrees with the force of law, and implemented by the state apparatus. It

30 Milovan Djilas, *Conversations with Stalin* (New York: Harvest Books, 1990), pp. 88–9; G. F. Krivosheev, *Soviet Casualties and Combat Losses in the Twentieth Century* (London: Greenhill Books, 1997), pp. 151–2, 154–5, 160–1; Barbara Johr, 'Die Ereignisse in Zahlen', in Helke Sander and Barbara Johr (eds.), *Befreier und Befreite. Krieg, Vergewaltigung, Kinder* (Frankfurt am Main: Fischer, 2005), pp. 46–73, here: pp. 58, 61; Konstantin Asmolov, 'Pobeda na Dal'nem Vostoke', in Igor' Pykhalov and Aleksandr Diukov (eds.), *Velikaia Obolgannaia voina. Obe knigi odnim tomom* (Moscow: Eksmo, 2009), pp. 718–41, here: p. 734; J. Robert Lilly, *Taken by Force: Rape and American GIs in Europe During World War II* (Houndmills: Palgrave Macmillan, 2007), p. 12; Mary Louise Roberts, *What Soldiers Do: Sex and the American GI in World War II France* (University of Chicago Press, 2013), pp. 320–1, n. 1.
31 Asmolov, 'Pobeda na Dal'nem Vostoke', p. 735.

aimed at breaking potential resistance by deportation or execution of alleged or real enemies. Depending on estimates, in the western borderlands in 1939–41, probably 350,000 and maybe as many as 535,000 people were deported.[32] In western Belorussia, this meant that over 13 per cent of Poles and nearly 5 per cent of Belorussians were forcibly moved east in 1939–41.[33] After the war, at least 296,282 alleged or real enemies were deported from Lithuania, Latvia, Estonia and western Ukraine alone – a population transfer similar in scale to its 1939–41 predecessor.[34] In the Baltics, larger numbers were deported in the second wave after 1945.[35]

Deportations sometimes assumed the character of ethnic cleansing. The post-war expulsion of Germans from the Kaliningrad region, as well as from Poland and Czechoslovakia (the latter driven by the national governments, but encouraged by the Soviets), the exchange of Ukrainians and Belorussians for Poles, Polish Jews and Romanians between the Soviet Union and the Polish and Romanian states in 1944–46, even the repatriation of Japanese residents from the Kurils in 1948, can all be seen as extensions of the practice of removing potential fifth columnists as part of security operations since the outbreak of the Sino-Japanese War in 1937: Soviet Koreans in 1937, Finns and Germans in 1941, Kalmyks and Karachais in 1943, Chechens, Ingush, Balkars, Crimean Tatars, Greeks and others in 1944. The far eastern Koreans in 1937 and the Caucasian and Crimean peoples in 1944 were deported *in toto*, while the share of Germans subject to the same policy was larger than the equivalent among Poles, Belorussians, Ukrainians and Balts. Meanwhile, Germans and Poles were more likely to survive the experience than the other victims, dying at a rate of about one in every ten, as compared to one in five for Soviet citizens deported east.[36] Those who survived swelled the ranks of 'special settlers' from just under 1 million in 1940 to 2.2 million by 1948, largely due to the wartime deportation of Soviet Germans (43 per cent), Caucasians (18 per cent) and Crimeans (9 per cent), followed by former

---

32 Alexander V. Prusin, *The Lands Between: Conflict in the East European Borderlands, 1870–1992* (Oxford University Press, 2010), p. 143.

33 Bernhard Chiari, *Alltag hinter der Front. Besatzung, Kollaboration und Widerstand in Weissrussland 1941–1944* (Düsseldorf: Droste, 1998), p. 46.

34 Alexander Statiev, *The Soviet Counterinsurgency in the Western Borderlands* (Cambridge and New York: Cambridge University Press, 2010), statistics at pp. 177, 178; Aigi Rahi-Tamm, 'Deportations in Estonia, 1941–1951', in Kristi Kukk and Toivo Raun (eds.), *Soviet Deportations in Estonia: Impact and Legacy. Articles and Life Histories* (Tartu University Press, 2007), pp. 9–52, here: p. 20.

35 Elena Zubkova, *Pribaltika i Kreml'. 1940–1953* (Moscow: Rosspen, 2008), pp. 127, 181.

36 Timothy Snyder, *Bloodlands: Europe Between Hitler and Stalin* (London: Bodley Head, 2010), pp. 332–3.

kulaks (7 per cent) and military collaborators with the Germans (6 per cent), as well as Ukrainian nationalists (4 per cent).[37]

Revolutionary violence thus returned at war's end, and large numbers died of exposure, hunger or disease during deportations, forced expulsions, while fleeing Soviet troops, or while locked up in concentration camps; another large pile of corpses accumulated as the result of counter-insurgency operations in the western borderlands. But there was also an important shift: the deliberately lethal version of revolutionary violence reached its peak not during or after the war, but at its start. The mass shootings of 21,857 Polish citizens in Katyn, Starobelsk and other camps in 1940 was one high-water mark of Soviet exterminationist violence against occupied populations.[38] Elsewhere, the numbers were lower, but still significant. In Estonia, 1,214 death sentences were passed in 1941 alone,[39] and close to 500 arrestees died while detained by the Soviets from 1940.[40] Once the Germans attacked, the killing escalated: more than 2,000 Estonian civilians were killed by the Soviet security forces between June and October 1941,[41] 11,319 prisoners were shot in the western borderlands, and another 1,080 died of other causes during their evacuation east.[42]

After the war, fewer people were executed outright. In Estonia, 143 people were sentenced to death in 1944–47, and another 28 in 1950–53.[43] In 1945 Lithuania, NKVD tribunals sat in judgment over 8,675 people, but sentenced only 468 of them to death.[44] In western Ukraine, more than 153,000 people were killed between 1944 and 1952,[45] but in their vast majority they must have been victims of counter-insurgency operations rather than mass executions:

37 NKVD reports from 24 June 1953 and 1 April 1948, in A. N. Dugin, *Neizvestnyi GULAG. Dokumenty i fakty* (Moscow: Nauka, 1999), pp. 99, 92–3.
38 A. Shelepin to N. S. Khrushchev, 3 March 1959, in Anna M. Cienciala, Natalia S. Lebedeva and Wojciech Materski (eds.), *Katyn: A Crime Without Punishment* (New Haven, Conn., and London: Yale University Press, 2007), pp. 332–3, here: p. 332.
39 Leo Oispuu (ed.), *Political Arrests in Estonia, 1940–1988 (§58)* (2 vols., Tallin: Estonian Repressed Persons Records Bureau, 1996), vol. i, D5.
40 *Estonia, 1940–1945: Reports of the Estonian International Commission for the Investigation of Crimes Against Humanity* (Tallin: Estonian Foundation for the Investigation of Crimes Against Humanity, 2006), p. xiii.
41 Ibid., pp. xiv, 360.
42 NKVD report on prison evacuations, 24 January 1942. In Dugin, *Neizvestnyi GULAG*, p. 22.
43 Oispuu (ed.), *Political Arrests*, D5.
44 Amir Weiner, *Making Sense of War: The Second World War and the Fate of the Bolshevik Revolution* (Princeton University Press, 2001), p. 153.
45 Resolution by Presidium of CPSU Central Committee, 26 May 1953, reprinted in V. Naumov and Iu. Sigachev (eds.), *Lavrentii Beriia. 1953. Stenogramma iul'skogo plenuma TsK KPSS i drugie dokumenty* (Moscow: Demokratiia, 1999), pp. 46–9, here: p. 47.

by May 1946, the tally of such dead stood at 110,825 in the entire western borderlands.[46] Further west, of the 119,743 people arrested in Germany between May 1945 and May 1949, a staggering 35 per cent died of malnutrition and disease in Soviet 'special camps', but fewer than 1 per cent were shot, while another 5 per cent were deported to the Soviet Union.[47] While there were also wild executions of presumed or real Nazis,[48] none of this approached the killing frenzy in Katyn, or even the panicked mass murder of prison inmates in the summer of 1941: if the former victimized over 21,000 Poles and the latter over 11,000 prisoners, in Germany between 1945 and 1955, under 3,000 Germans were sentenced to death by the Soviet victors.[49]

In contrast to the other two types of compulsion against people and their property discussed in this chapter, which were Eurasian in their distribution, revolutionary violence was predominantly a European phenomenon. In the east and south, only the Kurils and southern Sakhalin, but not Iran, China and North Korea, were subjected to these measures by the Soviets. The 1946 land reform in Korea did confiscate property from large landowners, but this distribution of property from rich to poor in the countryside was more or less bloodless. There were no deportations or even mass shootings here. In Manchuria, what could be considered revolutionary violence – robbing and killing of Japanese settlers – was perpetrated by local Chinese and Koreans during the initial chaos of liberation, not by Stalin's agents.

Economic violence

The third category of destructive behaviour – 'economic violence' – was again an all-Eurasian affair: the plundering of the occupied territories by troops acting on their own initiative, but also – and more consequentially – by agents of the Soviet state. As far as the former were concerned, the most spectacular result was Marshal Zhukov's dacha. According to the envious policeman who searched this property once the formerly celebrated hero had fallen out of favour in 1948, this weekend home contained 'an enormous amount of all kinds of goods and valuables', looking more like 'an antique shop or a museum', with all walls – 'even in the kitchen' – covered by

46 Prusin, *Lands Between*, pp. 210–11.
47 Ministry of Internal Affairs report, 9 May 1949, in Dugin, *Neizvestnyi GULAG*, p. 39.
48 Giles Macdonogh, *After the Reich: The Brutal History of the Allied Occupation* (New York: Basic Books, 2007), p. 210.
49 Andreas Hilger (ed.), *'Tod den Spionen!' Todesurteile sowjetischer Gerichte in der SBZ/ DDR und in der Sowjetunion bis 1953* (Göttingen: V&R unipress, 2006), p. 168.

'expensive artistic paintings'. Particularly scandalous was 'a huge painting with a representation of two naked women', taking pride of place in Zhukov's bedroom.[50] The art-loving commander was an extreme case, but other soldiers also brought back as much as they could, the volume of booty determined by a complex interaction of military rank, personal ingenuity and connections, moral rectitude, as well as time and place of military service.[51]

It is impossible to quantify the level of destruction brought by the collective results of such individual attempts at profiting from the war. Worse was the organized dismantling of infrastructure by representatives of the Soviet state. The extent of this kind of organized pillage varied from region to region. Temporary occupation followed by a handover to a different state encouraged a high level of expropriations. The city of Vilnius (Wilno) is a case in point. Polish territory since the early 1920s and occupied by the Soviets in 1939, it was subsequently handed over to Lithuania as part of the 10 October 1939 deal to station Soviet troops in the country (which turned out to be the first step to annexation by the Soviets). Even as negotiations of the handover were going on, the Soviets removed industrial equipment to the Soviet heartland. Schools and hospitals, too, were scavenged for whatever seemed valuable to occupiers intent on leaving. The decision to incorporate the Baltic countries into the Soviet Union was only made in 1940; hence the Soviet leadership in 1939 gave the order to scavenge as much as possible.[52] Likewise, in the part of Lithuania the Germans had called the *Memelgebiet* (Klaipeda region, evacuated by the Wehrmacht in 1944 and later annexed as Kaliningrad to the Soviet Union), 'the trophy brigades of the RA constantly plundered and devastated deserted farms',[53] and in defeated Germany, this kind of economic dismemberment was so pervasive that one historian interprets these reparations as a smokescreen for Germany's 'deindustrialization'.[54] It is indeed clear that there was a major policy shift from a 'smash-and-grab' occupation in 1945, intent on extracting

---

50 V. S. Abakumov to I. V. Stalin, 10 January 1948, in V. N. Khaustov, V. P. Naumov and N. S. Plotnikova, *Lubianka. Stalin in MGB SSSR. Mart 1946–mart 1953* (Moscow: Demokratiia, 2007), pp. 135–6.

51 Edele, *Soviet Veterans*, pp. 30–3.

52 Alfred Erich Senn, *Lithuania 1940: Revolution from Above* (Amsterdam and New York: Rodopi, 2007), pp. 53–4. On the timing of the decision, see Zubkova, *Pribaltika i Kreml'*, pp. 77–8.

53 A. L. Arbusauskaite, 'Soviet Occupation of Former East Prussia', in Anu Mai Koll (ed.), *The Baltic Countries Under Occupation: Soviet and Nazi Rule, 1939–1991* (Stockholm: Studia Baltica Stockholmiensia, 2003), pp. 17–46; here: p. 35.

54 Bogdan Musial, *Stalins Beutezug. Die Plünderung Deutschlands und der Aufstieg der Sowjetunion zur Weltmacht* (Berlin: Propyläen, 2010), pp. 251–7.

'as many riches as possible from Germany', to a more long-term strategy from late 1946, when the Soviets started to assume that eastern Germany would remain in their orbit for the time being.[55]

The precursors of this behaviour in 1939–41 weaken the case for the most obvious explanation: that these were reparations motivated by what the enemy had done. In Soviet-occupied Poland in 1939–41, observers wondered 'whether the Soviets had any coherent economic policy towards their newly-acquired territory...beyond denuding it of movable property'.[56] And once the Soviets had liberated Poland again at war's end, 'the bolsheviks [*sic*] not only rolled up some telephone cable of theirs' when they moved their troops out of a region, but dug up 'even prewar underground cables'.[57] Plunder, then, was not confined to the former enemy, but to the enemy's victims as well: Czechoslovakia was as much subjected to what Molotov called the 'laws of war' as was Hungary.[58] Occupied China was stripped as thoroughly as the German enemy, no matter that the Soviets dismantled here not an adversary, but, in the words of one historian, a 'putative ally'.[59] Even in North Korea, 'Japanese enterprises of military and heavy industry' were considered 'trophies of the Red Army, since all these enterprises to one degree or another worked for the Japanese army'. These factories 'must be transferred to the Soviet Union as partial payment of reparations', as a December 1945 document put it.[60]

Overall, however, the dismantling of infrastructure in Korea was on a much smaller scale than in Manchuria, indicating plans to stay longer in this new outpost of Soviet power.[61] And Germany was clearly the most important source of loot. Of the 809,500 train car loads extracted by 1 May 1947, 64 per cent came from Germany, 26 per cent from Poland (in post-war

55 Filip Slaveski, *The Soviet Occupation of Germany: Hunger, Mass Violence and the Struggle for Survival, 1945–1947* (Cambridge University Press, 2013), p. 43.

56 Keith Sword, 'Soviet Economic Policy in the Annexed Areas', in Keith Sword (ed.), *The Soviet Takeover of the Polish Eastern Provinces, 1939–41* (New York: St Martin's Press, 1991), pp. 86–101, here: p. 89.

57 Klukowski, *Red Shadow*, p. 73.

58 Austin Jersild, 'The Soviet State as Imperial Scavenger: "Catch Up and Surpass" in the Transnational Socialist Bloc, 1950–1960', *American Historical Review* 116:1 (2011), 109–32, here: 113.

59 Steven I. Levine, *Anvil of Victory: The Communist Revolution in Manchuria, 1945–1948* (New York: Columbia University Press, 1987), pp. 68–70, here: p. 69.

60 Kathryn Weathersby, 'Soviet Aims in Korea and the Origins of the Korean War, 1945–1950: New Evidence from Russian Archives', *Cold War International History Project Working Papers* 8 (1993), 20.

61 Kathryn Weathersby, 'Soviet Policy Toward Korea, 1944–1946' (unpublished PhD dissertation, Indiana University, 1990), pp. 225–8.

borders), just over 4 per cent from Manchuria, under 4 per cent from Austria, and less than 1 per cent each from Hungary and Czechoslovakia.[62] The Soviets displayed most restraint in Iran. In late September and early October 1941, they confiscated both goods and money owned by German firms operating in the region, but they did not aggressively dismantle infrastructure. Rather the opposite: at a time when the severest shortages of consumer goods marred the Soviet economy, on 10 June 1945, Stalin signed a secret document ordering the building of factories for confectionary, shoes, textiles and even silk in northern Iran. Together with serious propaganda work and the continued presence of the same number of troops long after the German threat to the nearby Caucasus had disappeared, this exertion of extremely rare resources indicates plans to unite occupied 'South Azerbaijan' with the neighbouring Soviet republic.[63]

At its extreme, economic violence also directly victimized human beings. On 16 December 1944, Stalin ordered the round-up of Germans in the 'liberated territories of Romania, Yugoslavia, Hungary, Bulgaria, and Czechoslovakia', and their deportation to work in the Donbass. This 'mobilization' was to include all men aged seventeen to forty-five and all women aged eighteen to thirty, and was to be organized by the NKVD.[64] By early February 1945, over 112,000 Germans were victimized in this manner, followed by over 155,000 deportees from Germany itself.[65]

'Occupation' or 'liberation'?

There is, thus, no lack of material to tell the history of Soviet occupation as a tale of overwhelming violence. The necessity of long-term counter-insurgency operations in much of the incorporated European territories proves that many in these societies did not welcome the Red Army. Meanwhile, the Soviets carefully avoided the term 'occupation' (okkupatsiia), which, along

62 Musial, Stalins Beutezug, p. 337.
63 Hasanli, At the Dawn of the Cold War, pp. 9, 63, 64; Tadeusz Swietochowski, Russia and Azerbaijan: A Borderland in Transition (New York: Columbia University Press, 1995), pp. 137–8.
64 Viktor Cherepanov, Vlast i voina. Stalinskii mekhanizm gosudarstvennogo upravleniia v Velikoi Otechestvennoi voine (Moscow: Izvestiia, 2006), pp. 315–16.
65 Pavel Polian, '"Westarbeiter". Internierung, Deportation und Ausbeutung deutscher Zivilisten aus Europa in der UdSSR', in Karl Eimermacher and Astrid Volpert (eds.), Verführungen der Gewalt. Russen und Deutsche im Ersten und Zweiten Weltkrieg (Munich: Wilhelm Fink Verlag, 2005), pp. 1261–97, esp. pp. 1282, 1292–3; and Pavel Polian, 'Die Internierung der Deutschen in Südosteuropa', in ibid., pp. 1342–60, esp. 1344, 1358–9.

with 'occupier' (*okkupant*), was reserved for the German and Japanese 'aggressors' (*zakhvatchiki*). When the Red Army marched into Poland in 1939, the troops were welcomed 'as liberators from the yoke of the gentry, from the yoke of the Polish landlords and capitalists', or so the official representation went.[66] To Finland, the Soviets came 'not as conquerors, but as liberators of the Finnish people from the oppression of the capitalists and the landlords', as a leaflet proclaimed during the Winter War (dropped, optimistically, together with bombs, over Helsinki).[67] The occupation of Iran did not 'constitute a military occupation', despite 'the presence of these [British and Soviet] forces on Iranian territory', as the somewhat strained formulation of the Tripartite Agreement of 29 January 1942 had it.[68] Later, Belgrade, Warsaw and Prague were 'liberated' (and commemorative medals were issued to that effect),[69] as were English, American and French POWs.[70] Even the Austrians turned out to be liberated by the Soviets.[71] The Red Army did not come to Hungary as a conqueror (*zavoevatel'nitsa*), but as a liberator (*osvoboditel'nitsa*) – a statement by Stalin, ironically contained in a document also ordering the removal of all industrial equipment unless needed by the army or indispensable for supplying the local population.[72] In a careful avoidance strategy, the commemorative medals for the Battles of Budapest, Königsberg, Vienna and Berlin did not, like those for Belgrade, Warsaw and Prague, speak of 'liberation'; instead, these enemy cities were 'captured' (*vziatie*).[73] In Germany, such subtleties were dropped in the naming of the Group of Soviet Occupation Forces (*Gruppa sovetskikh okkupatsionnykh voisk v Garmanii*), only renamed in 1949 as 'Group of Soviet Forces in Germany'.[74] Less ambiguous, war in the east was, again, a 'liberation' (*ozvobozhdenie*): 'Red Army soldier!', the

66 Vyacheslav Molotov at Supreme Soviet, 31 October 1939, in Jane Degras (ed.), *Soviet Documents on Foreign Policy*, vol. III: *1933–1941* (3 vols., London: Oxford University Press, 1953), pp. 388–400, here: p. 392.
67 Elliston, *Finland Fights*, p. 237.
68 Jody Emami-Yeganeh, 'Iran vs. Azerbaijan (1945–46): Divorce, Separation or Reconciliation?', *Central Asian Survey* 3:2 (1984), 1–27, here: 10.
69 *Pravda*, 10 June 1945, p. 2.
70 *Pravda*, 11 March 1945, p. 3.
71 Stavka directive 11055 of 2 April 1945, signed I. Stalin and A. Antonov, in *Russkii Arkhiv/ Velikaia Otechestvennaia* (hereafter RA/VO), vol. v, pt. 4, pp. 221–2, here: p. 222.
72 GKO resolution (27 October 1944), signed I. Stalin, Arkhiv Instituta Voenoi istorii Ministerstva oborony SSSR, fond 190, opis 232, delo 7, lists 1–7, here: list 2 (for liberation), list 6 (for removal of equipment) (Volkogonov papers, container 1, reel 1).
73 *Pravda*, 10 June 1945, p. 1.
74 M. I. Semiriaga, *Kak my upravliali Germaniei. Politika i zhizn'* (Moscow: Rosspen, 1995), pp. 22–3.

commanders of the First Far Eastern Front exclaimed on 9 August 1945, 'They know you in the west as a liberator, and you should be known likewise in the east – in China, in Manchuria and Korea.'[75]

As locals got to know these liberators, they often found 'liberation' and 'occupation' hard to distinguish. Even in formerly Soviet territories, liberated from a German occupation so violent that even victims of Stalin's policies eventually saw their own dictatorship as the smaller evil, the liberated had second thoughts. 'The local inhabitants for some reason do not come out and greet us', remembered a Red Army soldier later turned defector. 'They are torn by contradictory feelings... They are happy that we came: clearly, life under the Germans was not sweet. They fear us: clearly, they know that we bring with us not much that is positive.'[76] Indeed, formerly Soviet regions were reoccupied with sometimes stunning viciousness, including rape, armed robbery and the murder of civilians.[77] Everywhere, the security services got busy mopping up. In 1943, NKVD troops detained 931,549 soldiers and civilians behind the lines of the advancing Red Army. Over half of them were soldiers who had retreated without order, lost contact with their units, been in German captivity or were suspect for a range of other reasons; 349,034 civilians had run away from the defence industry or escaped from prison, avoided service in the Red Army, dodged deportation from the front-line region, had in one form or another broken the front-line regime, were devoid of documents or simply categorized as 'suspicious elements'. Most of those detained were released after interrogation by the NKVD, but 80,296 were arrested: agents of the enemy, those who had served in German police units, aiders and abettors of the Nazis, deserters, marauders and 'other criminal elements'.[78] Nowhere did the authorities trust those who had been under German occupation; instead, they brought in outsiders from the unoccupied Soviet heartland to staff the rebuilt apparatus. Purges of state and party from those contaminated by their survival of German rule soon followed. In the Caucasus and the Kalmyk steppe, distrust toward the locals became so excessive that entire populations were removed after the initial

75 RA/VO, vol. 7, pt. 1, pp. 345–6, here: p. 346.
76 Anonymous, 'V boiakh za Rodinu i za Stalina' (unpublished memoir, Bakhmeteff Archive, Columbia University Rare Book and Manuscript Library, typescript, 1951), p. 355.
77 Vladimir Daines, Shtrafbaty i zagradotriady Krasnoi Armii (Moscow: Eksmo, 2008), pp. 162–5, 254, 271, 290–1.
78 Beriia to Stalin and Molotov, 8 January 1944, in V. N. Khaustov et al. (eds.), Lubianka. Stalin in NKVD-NKGB-GUKR 'Smersh' 1939–mart 1946 (Moscow: Demokratiia, 2006), pp. 406–9, here: pp. 406–7.

counter-insurgency against local resisters. In retaliation for the militancy of a minority, the Soviet leadership deported the entire population, man, woman and child, old and young, communist and enemy, soldier and civilian.

We do not know if Khrushchev's claim is true that the Ukrainians escaped a similar fate 'only because there were too many of them and there was no place to which to deport them' – an assertion which caused 'laughter and animation in the hall' during the secret speech of 1956;[79] but we do know that in the post-war western borderlands, deportations were a more targeted part of counter-insurgency operations, combining military and intelligence operations against the underground with threats to the insurgents' kin and offers of amnesty for defectors. These were still massive operations, as we have noted above, but they were not uprooting an entire group based on ethnic markers.[80] Moreover, in sharp contrast to occupied non-Soviet territory, liberated Soviet regions were not subject to economic violence: with liberation imminent, Stalin's underground fighters were ordered 'to protect human and material resources';[81] and from August 1943, investment was concentrated on these regions.[82]

Outside territory incorporated directly into the Soviet state, violent occupation was embedded even more glaringly into a discourse of liberation. This tension between words and deeds has enabled one of the least helpful controversies of recent decades, pitting Eastern European intellectuals and their allies in Anglophone historiography against Russian nationalists. The former reinterpret what used to be the liberation from Nazi occupation into a violent (re-)occupation by a Soviet regime intent on genocide. This position requires an extremely flexible definition of 'genocide'.[83] Even the mass killings of Poles (Katyn) are best described as 'bordering on' the genocidal (since they physically eliminated much of the political, military and social elite of pre-war Poland), rather than fully fledged 'genocide'.[84] Russian

---

79 Nikita Khrushchev, speech to Twentieth Congress of the CPSU, 24–25 February 1956. www.marxists.org/archive/khrushchev/1956/02/24.htm (accessed 24 November 2014).

80 Statiev, *The Soviet Counterinsurgency*.

81 Kenneth Slepyan, *Stalin's Guerrillas: Soviet Partisans in World War II* (Lawrence: University Press of Kansas, 2006), p. 157.

82 Timothy Dunmore, *The Stalinist Command Economy: The Soviet State Apparatus and Economic Policy, 1945–53* (New York: St Martin's Press, 1980), pp. 36–9.

83 For an argument for widening the definition sufficiently, see Norman M. Naimark, *Stalin's Genocides* (Princeton University Press, 2010).

84 Mark Edele and Michael Geyer, 'States of Exception: The Nazi-Soviet War as a System of Violence, 1939–1945', in Michael Geyer and Sheila Fitzpatrick (eds.), *Beyond Totalitarianism: Stalinism and Nazism Compared* (Cambridge and New York: Cambridge University Press, 2009), pp. 345–95, here: p. 366.

nationalists, then, are on fairly firm ground when arguing that 'genocide' is misleading as an appellation for what occurred after 1945 in the 'liberated' territories. Less reasonably, these historians sometimes proceed to conclude that if there was no 'genocide', then there was no 'occupation' either.[85]

Clearly, the crude alternative between the labels of 'liberation' and 'occupation' cannot adequately describe the complex experiences on the ground. For one, different groups had differing perspectives, as Omer Bartov has pointed out for Ukrainians, Poles and Jews in Galicia.[86] Similar cases could be made elsewhere: wherever Soviet troops appeared, there were winners as well as victims. In Iran, according to an internal Soviet report of October 1941, some Azeri expressed relief about their liberation from Persian rule: 'We have been waiting for the Red Army to come for more than twenty years. Finally, our dream has come true. We want Soviet power'. Communist activists were liberated from prison, and local Kurds, exiled and detained under Reza Shah, could return to their native lands now under Soviet occupation.[87] In the Outer Mongolian town of Hailar, 'the local population, including a significant part of the Russians, meet the Soviet troops in a friendly fashion, calling the Red Army their liberator', or so a senior political officer reported on 17 August 1945.[88] In Manchuria, Japanese settlers died in the thousands, killed by Soviet soldiers, armed Chinese or their own hands; tens of thousands died of exposure, malnutrition and disease while fleeing the advancing Red Army.[89] Meanwhile, the local Chinese greeted their liberators from the Japanese yoke enthusiastically. Remembering his entry into Mukden, a Soviet commander wrote: 'I have never been greeted in this fashion in the west, not even on the day the war ended'.[90] He did not mention that these crowds were predominantly male, as women were either hiding or cross-dressing to avoid unwanted attention from the liberators.

85 For example, Aleksandr Diukov, 'Estonskii mif o "sovetskoi okkupatsii"', in Pykhalov and Diukov (eds.), *Velikaia Obolgannaia voina*, pp. 635–63.
86 Omer Bartov, 'Genocide in a Multi-Ethnic Town: Origins, Event, Aftermath', in Daniela Baratieri, Mark Edele and Giuseppe Finaldi (eds.), *Totalitarian Dictatorship: New Histories* (New York: Routledge, 2014), pp. 212–31, here: pp. 221, 222–3.
87 Natalia I. Yegorova, 'The "Iran Crisis" of 1945–46: A View from the Russian Archives', *Cold War International History Project Working Papers* 15 (1996), 5; Hasanli, *At the Dawn of the Cold War*, p. 37.
88 RA/VO, vol. 7, pt. 1, p. 354.
89 Louise Young, *Japan's Total Empire: Manchuria and the Culture of Wartime Imperialism* (Berkeley: University of California Press, 1998), pp. 408–11.
90 A. I. Kovtun-Stankevich, 'Komandant Mukdena', in Iu. V. Chudodeev (ed.), *Na kitaiskoi zemle. Vospominaniia sovetskikh dobrovol'tsev 1925–1945* (2nd rev. edn, Moscow: Nauka, 1977), pp. 416–37, here: p. 422.

Here, as elsewhere, gender, class, ethnicity, generation and politics all fractured populations confronted with arriving representatives of the Soviet state. Moreover, perceptions also changed over time and under the impact of the various forms of violence discussed above, but also of more constructive Soviet policies.

As a result, experiences were ambivalent to a degree hard to reconstruct seven decades later. Take the most straightforward case of Jews, both in 1939 and 1944–45, who often welcomed Red Army troops, because their arrival meant security from the German alternative further west, but also because, in 1939, the destruction of the pre-war Polish state and its replacement with the anti-anti-Semitic Soviet administration meant the opening of opportunities and the potential for personal advancement. However, Jews were also over-represented among craftsmen and traders, hence 'class enemies', hence disproportionally victimized by deportations. Jewish cultural and community organizations were also either liquidated or Sovietized by the new rulers.[91] Jewish refugees from German-occupied territories could find themselves arrested for illegal border crossing, sometimes accused of infiltration and espionage, and sent to the Gulag.[92] And in the Berlin of 1945, Holocaust survivors were not exempt from theft, rape or murder.[93]

On the other side of the ethno-ideological front line, Polish nationalists could feel rather ambivalent, as the experience of Dr Zygmunt Klukowski demonstrates, whose home town of Szczebreszyn was liberated by the Red Army on 26 July 1944. 'Now we are under a new occupation', he noted matter-of-factly some four months later in his diary. 'It reminds us of the times under German occupation.' Arrests of members of the Polish underground left him in a state of anxiety. 'There is so much circumstantial evidence against me', he wrote on 28 November 1944, 'that I feel worse than under the German occupation'. A few days later, his mood changed: 3 December was a 'joyous day...not seen since 1939'. The ability to hold a Polish cultural event, and one where he could participate and display his considerable collection of books, lifted his spirits, making him feel 'very happy... In spite of the repression...I clearly feel how different today's situation is from what we had under the German occupation. Under the Germans it was impossible to organize any type of Polish cultural enterprise'. This was not

---

91 Chiari, *Alltag hinter der Front*, p. 42.
92 Yosef Litvak, 'The Plight of Refugees from the German-Occupied Territories', in Sword (ed.), *Soviet Takeover*, pp. 57–70, here: pp. 58–60.
93 Macdonogh, *After the Reich*, p. 110; Atina Grossmann, *Jews, Germans, and Allies: Close Encounters in Occupied Germany* (Princeton University Press, 2007), pp. 63–4, 188.

to be the last of his mood swings: the offers of some carrots, along with the stick, led to considerable vacillations in his perception of the regime.[94]

In conclusion, several points about Soviet liberations and occupations need to be stressed. First, the war did not further brutalize Soviet population policies, but increased their scale; mass killing operations were replaced with counter-insurgency, deportations and regular policing. Despite their lethality, then, the Soviets had not been transformed into Nazis. Moreover, they did not blindly extend revolutionary violence wherever they went, but confined it to those territories they actually incorporated either into the Soviet Union proper, or into the new European empire of satellites. Nevertheless, as this chapter has stressed throughout, Soviet territorial expansion in the decade from 1939 was a violent process. The force used against people and their property was often massive, but complex in origin and diverse in effect. Different people were affected in different places and different times in different ways, with the effect that their experiences cannot be categorized by simple labels, such as 'liberation' or 'occupation'.

94 Klukowski, *Red Shadow*, pp. 3, 32–3, 38, 39–40.

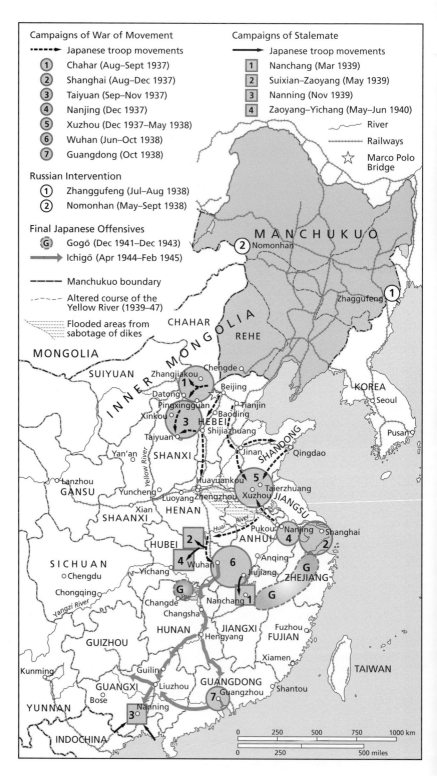

Campaigns of War of Movement

- - - ▶ Japanese troop movements
  (1) Chahar (Aug–Sept 1937)
  (2) Shanghai (Aug–Dec 1937)
  (3) Taiyuan (Sep–Nov 1937)
  (4) Nanjing (Dec 1937)
  (5) Xuzhou (Dec 1937–May 1938)
  (6) Wuhan (Jun–Oct 1938)
  (7) Guangdong (Oct 1938)

Russian Intervention

  (1) Zhanggufeng (Jul–Aug 1938)
  (2) Nomonhan (May–Sept 1938)

Final Japanese Offensives

  (G) Gogō (Dec 1941–Dec 1943)
  ▶   Ichigō (Apr 1944–Feb 1945)

— — — Manchukuo boundary

- - - - - Altered course of the
           Yellow River (1939–47)

Flooded areas from
sabotage of dikes

Campaigns of Stalemate

——▶ Japanese troop movements
  1 Nanchang (Mar 1939)
  2 Suixian–Zaoyang (May 1939)
  3 Nanning (Nov 1939)
  4 Zaoyang–Yichang (May–Jun 1940)

——— River
+++++ Railways
☆ Marco Polo
    Bridge

20.1 The Japanese invasion of central and southern China

Collaboration, resistance and accommodation in Northeast Asia

MARGHERITA ZANASI

The Japanese imperial expansion in Northeast Asia generated a wide spectrum of responses among the inhabitants of the occupied territories (Taiwan, Korea and China), ranging from tenacious armed resistance to collaboration with the occupying forces. Most of the local population, however, adopted various tactics of accommodation, forced to cope with deeply changed circumstances created by the Japanese occupation. Collaboration, resistance and accommodation remained sensitive issues in the post-war period. The political groups that emerged victorious from the ashes of the war integrated these issues into the construction of their political identities, claiming the mantle of resistance and presenting themselves as the only paladins of national interests. Post-war collaboration trials were often swiftly carried out, satisfying two different needs. The general population needed to see retribution being meted out to authoritarian leaders linked to the violent occupation. Many post-war governments, instead, used them to officially delegitimize and vilify alternative responses to the invading Japanese forces, to eliminate political opposition, and to establish a mythologizing narrative of the war that presented them as the beacon of morality and nationalism.[1]

'Resistentialism' – a black-and-white interpretation of the war based on the diametrical opposition between moral resisters and amoral collaborators – dominated the post-war narrative of the war globally.[2] This kind of narrative flattens the memory of the war experience by imposing a uniform

---

[1] Margherita Zanasi, 'Globalizing Hanjian: The Suzhou Trials and the Post-World War II Discourse on Collaboration', *American Historical Review* 113 (2008), 731–51; and Dongyoun Hwang, 'Wartime Collaboration in Question: An Examination of the Postwar Trials of the Chinese Collaborators', *Inter-Asia Cultural Studies* 6 (2005), 75–97.

[2] Henry Rousso, *The Vichy Syndrome: History and Memory in France Since 1944* (Cambridge, Mass.: Harvard University Press, 1991).

interpretative pattern. Its narrative of collaboration focuses on cases of callous opportunism, and extends the same moral judgement to the grey area of accommodation or to responses to Japanese forces based on alternative understandings of nationalism and resistance. Resistentialism also tends to cast the individual experience of each country into the same mould. In Northeast Asia, in fact, each country experienced occupation in its distinctive way, depending on a combination of Japanese policies and local conditions at the time of the invasion.

Although the central message of imperial propaganda remained the concept of the Greater East Asia Co-Prosperity Sphere – which represented Japan as the leader of East Asia's modernization efforts and struggle against Western imperialism – Japan's occupation strategies changed at different stages of its military expansion.[3] Taiwan and Korea – the focus of the first part of this chapter – fell to Japanese control in 1895 and 1910, respectively, and were organized into formal colonies. In these two countries, pre-war colonization deeply influenced local experiences of the Second World War. China – the focus of the second part – was occupied during the Pacific War (Japan's war of imperial expansion, from 1931 to 1945).[4] Here, the Japanese, rather than establishing colonies, relied on local 'client states', such as Manchukuo (1931–45), the Reformed Government (1938–40) and the Reorganized Nationalist Government (1940–45).[5]

Different local factors, such as the development of a mature nationalist movement in the pre-occupation period and deeply rooted expectations of independence, also influenced the way the local population responded to the invasion. Even in the post-war, although the language of resistentialism came to predominate official histories of the war through the region, views on

3 This theme was articulated first through the programme for an 'East Asian Federation' (1912), a 'New Order for Asia' (1938) and, ultimately, for a 'Greater East Asian Co-Prosperity Sphere' (1940). Peter Duus, 'Introduction', in Peter Duus, Ramon Hawley Myers, Mark R. Peattie and Wan-yao Chou (eds.), *The Japanese Wartime Empire, 1931–1945* (Princeton University Press, 1996), pp. xxi–xxvii; Janis Mimura, 'Japan's New Order and Greater East Asia Co-Prosperity Sphere: Planning for Empire', *The Asia-Pacific Journal: Japan Focus* 9 (5 December 2011), www.japanfocus.org/-Janis-Mimura/3657 (accessed 2 December 2014).
4 Duus, 'Introduction'. Taiwan and Korea have generally been identified as the 'original' colonies of the Japanese Empire. Recent historians, however, have begun to use that designation for areas annexed to Japan in much earlier stages of Japanese expansion, such as Hokkaido (1869), the Ryukyus (1879), the Karafuto islands (1904–5) and the Nan'yo South Pacific islands entrusted to Japanese mandate after the defeat of Germany in the First World War.
5 Saburo Ienaga, *The Pacific War: World War II and the Japanese, 1931–1945* (New York: Pantheon Books, 1978); Duus, 'Introduction'.

collaboration and resistance were significantly complicated, country by country, by such factors as Taiwanese resistance to the Chinese Nationalist government's post-war recovery of the island and the impact of the Cold War in Korea.

The colonies: Taiwan and Korea

In April 1895, at the end of the First Sino-Japanese War, the defeated Chinese Qing Dynasty ceded the island of Taiwan and the Penghu Islands (Pescadores) to Japan. The Japanese Empire was soon to expand with the colonization of Korea in 1910, which followed five years of de facto control begun with the 1905 Protectorate Treaty. The Japanese structure of the colonial administration and the policies it deployed in the two colonies were very similar. A Governor supervised the colonial government and a large police force, which was tightly integrated within the government administration, reaching down to grass-roots level in order to ensure the 'pacification' of local society. Both colonies were under a de facto police state.[6]

In both Taiwan and Korea, military and political resistance characterized the early stages of the Japanese occupation, but they decreased rapidly as the Japanese colonial government launched a swift and brutal repression, while tightening police control. In Taiwan, isolated uprising continued from around 1907 to 1915. At the same time, Taiwan's southern Hakka population and mountain tribes remained unruly and a cause of concern for the Japanese, who ended up encircling them with a security barrier, creating a virtual reservation for Taiwan's original inhabitants. In addition, the rural areas witnessed the sporadic activities of bandit resisters such as Liao Tianding. Considered by the Japanese police a mere criminal, Liao rose to legendary fame as a kind of Robin Hood resistance fighter, who not only outsmarted the enemy, but also took from the rich to give to the poor. Lately, historians have questioned Liao's nationalist motivations, tarnishing his reputation as a resistance fighter. Liao, however, remains a hero in popular memory. Enshrined in the Hanmin Ci temple, he is still an object of worship.[7]

---

6 Hui-yu Caroline Ts'ai, *Taiwan in Japan's Empire-Building: An Institutional Approach to Colonial Engineering* (New York: Routledge, 2009), esp. ch. 3: 'The Police as Lord', pp. 67–90.

7 I-lin Ho, 'Taiwanren de lishi yishi: "Yuyon shenshi" Gu Xiangrong yu "kangri ying-xiong" Liao Tianding', in Masahiro Wakabayashi and Micha Wu (eds.), *Kuajie de*

Despite tight police control, Korea witnessed a more coordinated polit-ical resistance, which was rooted in the nationalist movement developed in the pre-colonial period among young urban elites, and especially among the Christian, educational and intellectual communities. In 1919, a strand of Wilsonian utopianism, fuelled by resentment toward the colonial govern-ment's political discrimination, brought Korean urban intellectuals to organize against the Japanese authorities and launch the March First Move-ment, a wave of protests, strikes and business shutdowns that lasted until April.[8] In response, the Japanese police staged a brutal response that claimed the lives of hundreds of Koreans.[9] After the debacle of the March First Movement, most nationalist intellectuals fled abroad. Those who found refuge in Shanghai established the Korean Provisional Government (9 April 1919), under the leadership of Syngman Rhee. Their cause elicited little foreign support and the provisional government survived only for two years. Even after it was re-established in Chongching – the war capital of China's Nationalist government (1937–45), led by Chiang Kai-shek – it remained a powerless and short-lived organization.[10] Other Koreans crossed the border with Manchuria and north China and, after the Japanese takeover of Manchuria in 1931, joined the Chinese guerrilla units who fought against Japan at the Korean border.

During the 1930s and 1940s, organizations such as Singanhoe in Korea and the League for the Establishment of a Taiwan Parliament in Taiwan were still active. These organizations sought to advance the situation of the colonized people by working within the colonial system. Their progress, however, remained very limited, and both ended up disbanding due to increasing disappointment with liberal political options.

By the time East Asia became a new theatre of the Second World War (December 1941), Taiwan and Korea had already been Japanese colonies for a

Taiwanshi yanjiu: Yyu dongyashi de jiaocuo (Taibei Shi: Bozhongzhe wenhua youxian gongsi, 2004).

8 Erez Manela, 'Imagining Woodrow Wilson in Asia: Dreams of East–West Harmony and the Revolt against Empire in 1919', *American Historical Review* III (2006), 1327–51; Erez Manela, *The Wilsonian Moment: Self-Determination and the International Origins of Anticolonial Nationalism* (Oxford and New York: Oxford University Press, 2007); Adrian Buzo, *The Making of Modern Korea* (London: Routledge, 2007), chs. 1, 2.

9 Ken Wells, 'Between the Devil and the Deep: Nonpolitical Nationalism and "Passive Collaboration" in Korea During the 1920s', *Papers on Far Eastern History* 37 (1988), 125–47.

10 I refer here to the leader of the Nationalist government as Chiang Kai-shek, the most popular rendition of his Chinese name, rather than the alternative and most recent rendition of Jiang Jieshi.

few decades. Japan not only had the occasion to establish a powerful and repressive colonial administration – especially in Korea, which was directly under a military Governor, who did not share the same relatively enlightened view of colonization as the Taiwan Governor Goto Shinpei; it had also started assimilation policies and developed complex relationships with its colonial subjects. This long history of colonization influenced how Taiwanese and Korean people reacted to Japan's entrance into the Second World War, which, from their perspective, constituted just a new phase of their colonial experience.

Imperialism, modernity and the question of collaboration

Today, Taiwanese and Korean scholars approach the history of their countries in the period of Japanese domination from the perspective of colonial studies, rather than relying on the ideas of collaboration and resistance. They focus especially on 'the complex relationship that existed between nationalism, imperialism, and modernity in the post-WWI period'.[11] Taiwanese and Korean intellectuals and young urban reformers demonstrated a 'genuine interest' in modernity, even if represented by a colonial government.[12] Attracted by Japan's 'preternatural' modernization during the Meiji Restoration (1868–1912), they chose to study in Japan, becoming accustomed to the Japanese intellectual environment and supporting Japan's modernization drives.[13] At the same time, however, they began to experience frustration at Japanese discrimination against the colonized people.

Taiwanese participation in the colonial modernizing programme took various forms. Taiwanese doctors, for example, eagerly participated in medical reforms launched by the Japanese colonial state, which aimed at developing a network of local modern doctors. The Japanese expansion into China and Southeast Asia, however, brought a tightening of colonial control

---

11 Prasenjit Duara, *Sovereignty and Authenticity: Manchukuo and the East Asian Modern* (Lanham, Md.: Rowman & Littlefield, 2003), p. 1.
12 Koen de Ceuster, 'Wholesome Education and Sound Leisure: The YMCA Sports Programme in Colonial Korea', *European Journal of East Asian Studies* 2 (2003), 54; Tekashi Komagome, 'Colonial Modernity for an Elite Taiwanese, Lim Bo-seng: The Labyrinth of Cosmopolitanism', in Binghui Liao and Dewei Wang (eds.), *Taiwan Under Japanese Colonial Rule, 1895–1945: History, Culture, Memory* (New York: Columbia University Press, 2006), pp. 187–209; Andre Schmid, *Korea Between Empires, 1895–1919* (New York: Columbia University Press, 2002).
13 John Whittier Treat, 'Choosing to Collaborate: Yi Kwang-su and the Moral Subject in Colonial Korea', *Journal of Asian Studies* 71:1 (2012), 86.

over Taiwanese doctors. Ultimately, they became de facto tools of the Japanese Empire and were expected not only to cure 'the sick bodies, but also. . .to "cure" colonial bodies by spreading Japanese medical ideology'.[14] In this difficult situation, however, a collective identity began to take shape through 'submerged networks'. Through these networks, Taiwanese doctors constructed their identity based on the notion that the 'internalization of a modernist professional culture. . .rendered their ethnic boundaries particularly blurred'. In this context, many Taiwanese doctors chose to define themselves in terms of universal professional modernity rather than colonization or ethnicity.[15]

Taiwanese literature also came to reflect the urban intellectuals' interest in 'colonial modernity'. Especially active in Taiwan was the Taiwan Cultural Association – headed by Jiang Weishui – which sponsored theatre performances and literature that combined Chinese and Japanese new literary trends with studies of Taiwanese folklore.[16] This new cultural movement engendered a debate on the new and old literature, which some envisioned as a form of anti-Japanese resistance.[17] When, after the war, the Chinese nationalists regained control over Taiwan, they represented Jiang Weishui as a collaborator. Today, instead, Taiwanese scholars tend to perceive Jiang's negotiation between local identity and imperial modernity as the cradle of the Taiwanese nationalist movement. They consider both the medical and the literary communities' experiences with 'colonial modernity' as the foundation of a hybrid Taiwanese identity.[18]

Even entrepreneurs such as Gu Xianrong – still today one of the most infamous Taiwanese collaborators in popular memory – have recently been approached from the perspective of colonial modernity. One of the first to welcome the Japanese into Taibei, Gu maintained close relationships with the colonial authorities and was appointed to important positions within the colonial administration. Gu led the Japanese-sponsored modernization of the

14 Ming-cheng Miriam Lo, *Doctors Within Borders: Profession, Ethnicity, and Modernity in Colonial Taiwan* (Berkeley: University of California Press, 2002), p. 112.
15 Ibid., pp. 137–8.
16 Mei-er Huang, 'Confrontation and Collaboration: Traditional Taiwanese Writers' Canonical Reflection and Cultural Thinking on the Old–New Literature Debate During the Japanese Colonial Period', in Liao and Wang (eds.), *Taiwan Under Japanese Colonial Rule*, pp. 187–209.
17 Huang, 'Confrontation and Collaboration'.
18 Ping-hui Liao, 'Print Culture and the Emergent Public Sphere in Colonial Taiwan, 1895–1945', in Liao and Wang (eds.), *Taiwan Under Japanese Colonial Rule*, pp. 78–94.

sugar industry – at that time, a family-run, small-scale industry – overseeing the process of centralization of landownership and management, meanwhile amassing a personal fortune. Despite the negative memories still harboured by the older generation of Taiwanese, today Gu is perceived as a modernizing businessman, who realized that the colonial economic environment was a precious opportunity for developing the island's economy.[19]

Most controversial was the cultural assimilation aspect of the Japanese plans for the modernization of both colonies. In practice, assimilation consisted of the eradication of supposedly backward local habits, which were to be replaced with their modern Japanese equivalents. Assimilation policies intensified as Japan expanded its war efforts into China and Southeast Asia. At this time, both Taiwanese and Koreans were forced not only to abandon their culture and to embrace the official imperial Shinto religion, but also to discard their original names and adopt Japanese ones. The Japanese hoped that these policies would transform their colonial subjects into loyal Japanese citizens, ready to fight for the survival of the empire.

Many Taiwanese and Korean young modernizers supported the Japanese assimilation programme to various degrees, criticizing local traditional culture as stagnant and backward. While some expressed this support with attempts to integrate Japanese modernity into local culture, as exemplified by the Taiwan Cultural Association discussed above, others took assimilation to its extreme. This was the case with Korean writer Yi Kwang-su, still today the most infamous collaborator in Korean popular memory, together with Lee (Yi) Wang-yong, the official who signed the 1910 Japan–Korea Annexation Act. Educated in Japan since the age of thirteen, Yi Kwang-su was one among the 'many writers to find his literary and intellectual home in the Japanese colonial metropole'. Yi, however, took his pro-Japanese modernity position to the extreme, arguing not only for Korean writers to write in Japanese, but also for Koreans in general to forget they were Korean at all and to eagerly turn into Japanese. Leading by example, he was the first to take a Japanese name.[20]

Many voices participated in the debate on the identity of Korean literature and the choice of writing in the Korean or the Japanese language.[21] On the

---

19 Ho, 'Taiwanren de lishi yishi'.
20 Treat, 'Choosing to Collaborate', 87.
21 Nayoung Aimee Kwon, 'Colonial Modernity and the Conundrum of Representation: Korean Literature in the Japanese Empire', *Postcolonial Studies* 13 (2010), 421–39.

opposite extreme to Yi was a group of intellectuals who re-evaluated traditional Korean culture. They created a movement called 'culturalism', which became popular especially in Protestant circles. Culturalism postponed direct political confrontation with the colonial government in favour of a renewal of Korean culture, in preparation for a future independence. Disenchanted young urban intellectuals, however, came to question non-political nationalism and accused the culturalists of collaboration.[22]

A case illustrating the often blurred divide between resistance and collaboration, and the thorny entanglement of nationalism and modernity, can be found in the history of the YMCA in Seoul. The success of the YMCA rested on the fact that the sport-related activities of this organization served both Japanese and Korean goals. The Japanese saw physical education as part of mass mobilization directed to the construction of a Japanized modern Korea. The Koreans, for their part, viewed physical education as a tool to strengthen the nation as part of anti-Japanese nation building. They also perceived sporting competitions as an arena for symbolic victories against Japan. When Son Kijong won the marathon at the Berlin Olympics, outperforming Japanese participants, the Koreans felt they had scored one point against the invaders, disregarding the official Japanese interpretation that Son's victory was a success of the Japanese Empire. Because it served both these contradictory agendas, the YMCA was able to operate within the structure of Japanese rule until 1930.[23]

The cases of colonial modernity discussed above illustrate the variety of strategies adopted by both Taiwanese and Koreans in facing the colonial authorities. They also illustrate the importance and strength of the relationship between occupied and occupiers developed during the pre-war colonial period, which set the stage for the war experience in Taiwan and Korea.[24]

The war and post-war periods

The beginning of the Pacific War in 1931, and its coming together with the Second World War in December 1941, found the relationship between Japan and the colonized population in Taiwan and Korea already established. By this time, it was clear that decades of colonization had succeeded in

22 Michael Edson Robinson, *Cultural Nationalism in Colonial Korea, 1920–1925* (Seattle: University of Washington Press, 1988); Wells, 'Between the Devil and the Deep', 133, 135.
23 De Ceuster, 'Wholesome Education and Sound Leisure', 53–4.
24 Ts'ai, *Taiwan in Japan's Empire-Building*, p. 137; Ho, 'Taiwanren de lishi yishi'.

significantly 'pacifying' local society and compromising local identities. It is not surprising, therefore, that during the war the Japanese met with little resistance within the two colonies. The most prominent exception was a Korean armed movement, the *Uibyong* (Righteous Army), which had developed among resistance members who had fled Korea previously. The *Uibyong* remained active through the Pacific War, fighting at the border with Korea alongside Chinese nationalist and communist guerrilla units, and eventually with Soviet armed units.

During the war, many Taiwanese and Koreans joined the Japanese army. Some were forcibly recruited, while others joined voluntarily, often motivated by the fact that while in the army, although confined to the lower ranks, colonial subjects were treated exactly like Japanese soldiers and no longer discriminated against. Some Taiwanese were exploited for their knowledge of the Chinese language and used as interpreters and intermediaries with the local population in occupied China. A large number of Taiwanese and Koreans were forced into non-military services in support of the Japanese troops. The most infamous case of Japanese wartime exploitation of colonial subjects is the military's organization of 'comfort women'. These were mostly young girls, abducted from their homes and forced to serve as sex workers for Japanese soldiers. Many of them ended up being raped to death in the early days of their captivity. The horrors suffered by these girls have recently become an important topic in East Asian international relations.[25]

Korea's and Taiwan's colonial status also influenced the events that followed Japan's surrender in August 1945. Nationalist authorities from the Chinese mainland were uncertain whether to treat the Taiwanese as enemies, because of their long association with the Japanese Empire, or as fellow victims, since Taiwan had now rejoined China. Among the Taiwanese who remained stranded on the mainland, some were summarily executed by Chinese soldiers, while others were protected by the authorities and repatriated.[26] Many Taiwanese themselves were often not certain of their own citizenship. After decades of assimilation policies, they spoke Japanese better

---

25 Chunghee Sarah Soh, *The Comfort Women: Sexual Violence and Postcolonial Memory in Korea and Japan* (University of Chicago Press, 2008).

26 Jiu-Jung Lo, 'Trials of the Taiwanese as Hanjian or War Criminals and the Postwar Search for Taiwanese Identity', in Kai-wing Chow, Kevin Michael Doak and Poshek Fu (eds.), *Constructing Nationhood in Modern East Asia* (Ann Arbor: University of Michigan Press, 2001), pp. 279–316; Barak Kushner, 'Pawns of Empire: Postwar Taiwan, Japan and the Dilemma of War Crimes', *Japanese Studies* 30 (2010), 111–33.

than Chinese, but they suddenly found that they were required to be Chinese. The issue of citizenship was quite serious. The Taiwanese who were considered Japanese could be indicted for war crimes. If, instead, they were considered Chinese, they were liable to be accused of collaboration. Since Taiwanese collaborators ended up not being seriously prosecuted, while war criminals were, the resolution of the citizenship question could be costly.[27] Large sections of the Korean population also experienced similar uncertainties on their nationality and on the treatment they were to expect. An estimated 148 ethnic Koreans were tried for 'Japanese' war crimes.

In Taiwan, the prospect of reunification with the mainland caused a prompt shift in the target of local resistance, from Japan to the Chinese Nationalist regime.[28] Most Taiwanese resisted the Nationalists' persecution of local collaborators because they saw it as part of the Nationalists' attempt to rebuild Taiwan's identity in their image. They felt that they were imposing a narrative of collaboration and resistance that, even if appropriate for the Chinese experience, did not reflect local circumstances and the island's colonial experience.

In Korea, the fall of Japan raised high expectations for independence. The Allies, however, frustrated them, by deciding to create a system similar to that adopted in Germany. With the thirty-eighth parallel as the official divide, the USA came to control the southern part of the Korean peninsula, while the northern portion was entrusted to the Soviet Union. These political interferences complicated the post-war discourse on collaboration in both Koreas. The United States was particularly interested in maintaining stability in the south, even if it meant keeping in power an elite compromised by collaboration with the Japanese. In addition, US authorities were wary of those resisters who had taken part in armed guerrilla groups, whom they suspected of being Soviet agents. In this context, popular demands for bringing collaborators to trial were not heeded, and only a few Koreans who had worked as guards in concentration camps were tried.[29] The communist government in the north, instead, celebrated the anti-Japanese guerrillas and used them as a building block of its political legitimacy. It appears, however, that, in practice, this regime was not very thorough at

---

27 Lo, 'Trials of the Taiwanese'; Ts'ai, *Taiwan in Japan's Empire-Building*, pp. 137–40.
28 Lo, 'Trials of the Taiwanese', p. 280.
29 Koen de Ceuster, 'The Nation Exorcised: The Historiography of Collaboration in South Korea', *Korean Studies* 25 (2001), 211.

punishing collaborators, and was actually more accommodating to them than was the south.[30]

In the south, the issue of collaboration resurfaced during the 1980s democracy movement, which brought a resistantialist narrative of democracy to the front of the contemporary political arena. This movement ascribed the corruption and authoritarianism of the South Korean government to the persistence of collaborators among its ranks, while identifying its own democratic aspirations with the legacy of the resistance. In this context, bringing collaborators to trial was presented as an integral part of the democratization process.[31]

Taiwan's and Korea's colonial backgrounds, therefore, played an important role in shaping relations between the local population and the Japanese occupying forces during the Second World War, making it difficult to apply the categories of collaboration and resistance. In the post-war years, these categories came to play an important role in Korea due to a variety of factors, including the Allies' tendency to project the European experience over East Asia, as well as the development of the Cold War. In addition, a nationalist movement and a sense of national identity – sufficiently strong to envision a wartime Korean government in exile – had developed in the pre-war period, making it possible for the idea of national betrayal to surface. In Taiwan, on the other hand, nationalism did not have wide resonance, due to the island's status as a borderland and the weak identification with the Qing Empire at the time of Japanese occupation, as well as the complexity of its ethnic and cultural fabric. Arguably, a distinctive Taiwanese identity emerged under Japanese occupation, detaching the island from the Chinese nationalist discourse. Despite these differences, however, the common colonial background of Korea and Taiwan shaped the relationship between the local population and the Japanese occupying forces in ways that significantly differed from the Chinese experience of Japanese occupation.

China and the client states

Japan's victory in the Russo-Japanese War (1904–5) established Japanese supremacy in the Manchuria and Liaodong area, paving the way to a new wave of conquest. The Japanese army first occupied Manchuria (1931) and

---

30 B. R. Myers, *The Cleanest Race: How North Koreans See Themselves and Why It Matters* (Brooklyn, NY: Melville House, 2010), pp. 31–2.
31 De Ceuster, 'The Nation Exorcised'.

later pushed into China proper, ultimately leading to the Second Sino-Japanese War (1937–45). China remained the main focus of Japan's military operations until 1941, when Japan began its main push into Southeast Asia.

In China, Japan adopted a new strategy for maintaining control over the occupied areas. Instead of establishing formal colonies, it promoted the formation of client governments. These were ostensibly independent political entities, but in reality they were strictly under Japanese influence and worked in support of the empire's war effort. Japan abandoned this strategy in Southeast Asia, where it established military regimes directly controlled by the army. By that time, immediate and efficient mobilization of local resources had become an absolute priority and the client states had proved largely ineffective in this task.

The mode and goals of the Japanese occupation of China produced forms of collaboration and resistance that differed from those in colonial Taiwan and Korea, assuming a more decisive political and ideological nature than in the colonies. Anti-communism, which successfully resonated with a portion of local Chinese leaders, took centre stage, and colonial modernity remained in the background. One exception was Manchuria, where a few years of relative peace (1931–37) allowed the Japanese to promote a plan for economic development, which, at least in its early stages, proved quite successful. In China proper, which fell to the Japanese in 1937 and experienced a continuous state of war, the Japanese had little time for colonial modernization, an idea that sounded increasingly hollow as the war progressed. The mirage of modernity, however, continued to influence some Chinese intellectuals and reformers, especially those who had studied in Japan and admired its rapid transformation during the Meiji period. In this context, they attempted to negotiate with the colonial authorities to carve out opportunities for the modernization of China.

Resistance

War and post-war narratives of resistance in China were dominated by the Nationalists' and communists' highly partisan and mythologized interpretation of the war. Although these two parties had formed a United Front (1937–41) to fight against the Japanese, each claimed exclusivity over the nationalist mandate of resistance, a powerful source of political legitimacy in the post-war years.

The Chinese Nationalist Party (Guomindang – GMD) narrative focused mostly on the figure of Chiang Kai-shek, as the leader of 'Free China' and of the 'war of resistance against the Japanese', as the Second Sino-Japanese War is generally called in China. The GMD narrative was legitimized by US support.[32] The USA not only provided Chiang with military and financial aid, but also hailed him as the heroic leader of China's struggle against the Axis. Chiang and his wife, Soong Mei-ling, for example, made the front cover of *Time* magazine twice –on 1 March 1943 and 3 September 1945 – where they were celebrated as the symbols of China's resistance against Japan.

In the immediate post-war, Chiang staged a series of trials of the leaders of the client states, most prominently those of the Reorganized Nationalist Government (RNG), in order to consolidate his position as the supreme hero of Chinese resistance. At these trials, the prosecutors identified Chiang's war strategy as the only legitimate patriotic response to the Japanese invasion, condemning and delegitimizing all alternatives. The notion of 'collaborationist nationalism', which some leaders of client states claimed as the main inspiration for their actions, was immediately identified as unpatriotic collaborationism.[33] That at least some of the people who had lived in the occupied areas disagreed with Chiang's unilateral definition of nationalism was illustrated by the cheering crowd that greeted Chen Bijun – the wife of the recently deceased chairman of the RNG, Wang Jingwei – as she left the court where she had just been condemned to life imprisonment as the 'number one female traitor'.[34]

In reality, in the early stages of the war, Chiang's image as China's patriotic hero was rather tarnished. His credibility as a committed resister was undermined by his pre-war policy of appeasement of Japan, which was based on the principle that 'in order to resist on the external front, [China] must first pacify the country internally'. In Chiang's view, this formula prioritized eliminating the communists over resisting Japan, since he believed that the Japanese were a disease of the skin, while the communists were a disease of the heart.[35] It was not until December 1936 that Chiang, having

32 See, for example, Meizhen Huang, *Wangwei shiha jian: Wang Jingwei, Chen Gongbo, Zhou Fohai, Chu Minyi, Chen Bijun, Luo Junqiang, Wang Kemin, Wang Yitang, Liang Hongzhi, Li Shiqun* (Shanghai: Shanghai renmin chubanshe: Xinhua shudian Shanghai faxingsuo faxing, 1986); and Jing Zhang, *Shenxun Wangwei shihanjian* (Nanjing Shi: Jiangsu guji chubanshe: Jingxiao Jiangsusheng xinhua shudian, 1998).

33 Timothy Brook, 'Collaborationist Nationalism in Occupied Wartime China', in Timothy Brook and Andre Schmid (eds.), *Nation Work: Asian Elites and National Identities* (Ann Arbor: University of Michigan Press, 2000), p. 160.

34 Charles D. Musgrove, 'Cheering the Traitor: The Post-War Trial of Chen Bijun, April 1946', *Twentieth-Century China* 30 (2005), 3–27.

35 Parks M. Coble, *Facing Japan: Chinese Politics and Japanese Imperialism, 1931–1937* (Cambridge, Mass.: Council on East Asian Studies, Harvard University: distributed by Harvard University Press, 1991), p. 104. *Facing Japan* also offers a detailed discussion of Chiang's appeasement policies before 1936.

been kidnapped by the communists (the Xian Incident) – who had declared war on Japan as early as April 1932, in response to the invasion of Manchuria, and pushed for the end of Chiang's appeasement policy – agreed to his captors' request to establish a united front to fight the invader. In addition, although the Nationalist army had fought valiantly to protect Shanghai (Battle of Shanghai, August–October 1937) in the early stages of the war, Chiang adopted a strategy of retreat. This tactic rested on Chiang's long-term belief that a direct military confrontation with Japan would inevitably result in defeat for China. Since the early 1930s, Chiang had argued that, in the event of war, China should follow the tactic used by Russia against Napoleon – that is, exploiting the large size of the country to force the enemy to spread itself too thinly and collapse of its own accord. Accordingly, Chiang retreated to the interior, ultimately establishing his war capital in Chongqing (Sichuan). In Chiang's view, this retreat strategy was also a crucial for gaining precious time while waiting for the USA's intervention. Chiang had argued since the mid-1930s that only American military power could win the war for China.

The nationalist strategic retreat, however, proved very controversial. Many critics lamented that it left the Chinese population unprotected from the brutality of the Japanese army, a statement that appeared tragically confirmed by the Nanjing massacre. In November 1937, Nationalist troops hastily retreated from their pre-war capital, Nanjing, when faced with the advancing Japanese forces. Although the Nationalists would not have been able to protect the city for long, it appeared that their hasty retreat had set the stage for the six weeks of brutal killing, looting and raping that followed the fall of the city on 13 December 1937. Although Chiang's plans of strategic retreat and reliance on the US *deus ex machina* appeared foolish in 1937, they proved clairvoyant in December 1941, when the Japanese attacked Pearl Harbor and the USA entered the Second World War.

Despite rampant corruption, systemic military incompetence and dire living conditions – millions of refugees poured into Chongqing while the Japanese relentlessly bombarded it, adding to the already catastrophic shortage of food and shelter – Chongqing became, for many Chinese, a beacon of hope, and kept the idea of an independent Chinese nation alive. Chongqing also constituted a crucial base for sustained military resistance and for international aid. Its importance for the cause of China's independence is highlighted by the fact that the Japanese, although working with various client states in China proper, regarded Chongqing as the main threat to their occupation of China. Despite Prince Konoe's public rejections of the idea of negotiating with Chiang, behind the scenes Japan never gave up attempting to sign a peace agreement with him.

The communist base in Yanan (Shaanxi) also constituted a beacon of hope, especially for young urban nationalist and reformist intellectuals. While the Chinese Communist Party's (CCP) 1932 declaration of war against Japan had been mostly a symbolic gesture – in view of Yanan's distance from Manchuria – after 1937 the CCP was deeply engaged in heavy fighting, since its base was now directly threatened by the Japanese army. CCP resistance efforts developed in two main directions: direct military confrontations and underground activities in the occupied rural areas, aimed at creating support for the approaching CCP troops and organizing local resistance movements. In the case of direct military confrontation, the CCP armies – the New 4th Army operating south of the Yangzi River and the 8th Route Army based in Yanan – shared the brunt of the fighting, gaining a reputation among US personnel in China of being more effective and committed to fighting than the GMD.

The work of both the CCP armies and its underground agents in the occupied areas followed mass mobilization strategies. Promoting anti-Japanese feelings and some measure of land reform and class struggle, the CCP's political campaigns proved quite successful, generating wide support among the rural population. In the post-war period, the CCP stressed the success of this strategy, building a romanticized narrative of peasant nationalism and positive response to communist policies. This theme was picked up later by some Western scholars, such as Lucien Bianco and Chalmers Johnson, who viewed the war of resistance and the unity of nationalist goals between peasants and communists as crucial for the CCP's growth during the war, and for its later success in its quest for national control.[36]

Recent works, however, have challenged this romantic representation. The increased popular support for the CCP during the war appears to have been based on a wider variety of factors, which often departed from nationalist and revolutionary sentiments. In addition to a relaxation of class struggle and land reform, policies that alienated large sections of the rural population, the CCP mobilization tactics were often creative and apolitical. The communists, for example, compromised with bandit groups or secret societies that resisted Japan, as they had resisted traditionally any other external

---

36 Chalmers Johnson, *Peasant Nationalism and Communist Power: The Emergence of Revolutionary China* (Stanford University Press, 1962); Lucien Bianco, *Origins of the Chinese Revolution, 1915–1949* (Stanford University Press, 1971).

threats to the village.[37] Some peasants joined the CCP hoping to better their economic situation through land redistribution, or as a way to settle long-standing disputes within the village. Others undermined the Japanese war effort for basic economic reasons. Some peasants, for example, stopped growing rice because the Japanese forced them to sell their crops below market prices.[38] In other words, although the Japanese encountered fierce resistance in rural China, often such resistance was not an expression of loyalty to the Chinese nation and to socialism, but a more direct response to Japanese brutality and a sheer determination to survive. In spite of this resizing of the communist mythologizing narrative, communist and peasant resistance played a crucial role in weakening the Japanese army, undercutting its goals for resource extraction and, in general, disrupting its control over rural areas.

On the other hand, urban areas, which were more directly under Japanese control, became the centre of intricate networks of spies, resisters and saboteurs, making it difficult, at times, to understand who collaborated and who resisted. In the cosmopolitan city of Shanghai, white Russians tended to collaborate since they mostly shared Japan's anti-communism, while some left-wing Japanese spied for the Chinese communists. An intricate network of communist agents and Chongqing's spy rings, led by the infamous Dai Li, operated underground. The presence of foreign concessions further complicated this scene, since they provided refuge from the Japanese police and offered connections with foreign groups.[39] Policing came to require increasingly sophisticated techniques with the escalation of violence due to both pro-Japanese and anti-Japanese terrorism, and the conflating of crime and resistance as criminal gangs turned patriotic resisters.[40] This pattern was common to most of the occupied urban centres, including the then British colony of Hong Kong. Occupied by the Japanese on 25 December 1941, Hong

37 Linlin Wang, 'Another Way Out: The Wartime Communist Movement in Jiangsu, 1937–1945' (unpublished PhD dissertation, University of Texas, 2012); Donglan Huang, 'Revolution, War, and Villages: A Case Study on Villages of Licheng County, Shanxi Province During the War of Resistance against Japan', *Frontiers of History in China* 6 (2011), 95–116.
38 Christian Henriot, 'Rice, Power and People: The Politics of Food Supply in Wartime Shanghai (1937–1945)', *Twentieth-Century China* 26 (2000), 41–84.
39 Bernard Wasserstein, 'Ambiguities of Occupation: Foreign Resisters and Collaborators in Wartime Shanghai', and Joshua A. Fogel, 'The Other Japanese Community: Left-wing Japanese Activists in Wartime Shanghai', both in Wen-Hsin Yeh (ed.), *Wartime Shanghai* (London and New York: Routledge, 1998), pp. 24–41, 42–61.
40 Frederic E. Wakeman, *The Shanghai Badlands: Wartime Terrorism and Urban Crime, 1937–1941* (Cambridge and New York: Cambridge University Press, 1996).

Kong also experienced patterns of collaboration and resistance, developed along intricate lines of shifting roles of organized crime and local elites, as both the Chinese and the British attempted to manipulate the Japanese to secure their own survival. In this city, the Japanese also attempted to make the most of the anti-colonial theme of the Co-Prosperity propaganda, presenting themselves as the liberators from European imperialism. This strategy had very limited results, since it soon became clear that Japan's conquest actually ushered in even harsher patterns of subjugation and exploitation.[41]

Collaboration

Just as they have reappraised the GMD and CCP narratives of resistance, scholars have also taken a fresh look at issues of collaboration, going beyond Nationalist and communist resistantialism and focusing on the complexity of war experiences. A crucial issue brought up by these recent historiographical trends is the fragility of the Chinese national identity in the pre-war, which was characterized by competing visions of nationhood, anti-centralization movements led by the local elites who resisted the Nationalist government in its distant capital of Nanjing, a deep political fragmentation within the GMD itself, and the lingering culture of warlord-style politics.

This situation created the favourable conditions for the new Japanese strategy of co-opting local elites and establishing client states. In the border province of Manchuria, for example, warlord politics and the fragility of the GMD's narrative of national identity influenced the response to Japanese invasion among three dominant and competing groups. The first was led by the strongest among the local warlords, Zhang Xueliang. Zhang had joined forces with the GMD and promoted its nation-building reforms focused on political and administrative centralization, directly challenging the authority of the local elites, the second group. With the consolidation of Zhang's power, Ma Zhanshan, a minor warlord and the third competitor, also saw his power base shrink dramatically.

Against this background, when Zhang withdrew from Manchuria, faced with Japanese occupation, most members of local elites chose to collaborate. Encouraged by Japan's claim of supporting local autonomy, they hoped to regain power over local affairs and repel Nanjing's centralizing nation-building efforts. Ma Zhanshan, on the other hand, found himself once again excluded by the new political alliance and waged resistance against Japan

---

41 Philip Snow, *The Fall of Hong Kong: Britain, China, and the Japanese Occupation* (New Haven, Conn.: Yale University Press, 2003).

from the northern border region of Manchuria. Ma's choice to resist Japan, therefore, was motivated primarily by his political marginalization and his effort to preserve control over part of Manchuria. That the idea of nation and nationalist loyalty did not play a major role in Ma's decision to resist is illustrated by the fact that, on more than one occasion, Ma shifted his position. In 1931–32, for example, he joined the Japanese when relationships with other Chinese resistance groups soured and Japan's attitude toward him appeared to improve. Nationalism came to influence Ma's resistance rhetoric only at a later moment and in an indirect way, as he became the unwitting central figure of Nanjing anti-Japanese propaganda. Myriad newspaper accounts of Ma's resistance circulated all over China, depicting him as a nationalist hero and ignoring the less heroic reality of his motivations. Ma understood the advantages of this nationalist propaganda and exploited it to obtain support from both the GMD and international sources. Ma's eventual employment of nationalist slogans, therefore, was primarily a strategy to achieve local goals that actually differed from the centralizing nation-building plans of the GMD. In other words, both Ma's responses to the Japanese invasion and those of the local elites reflected the perspective of Manchuria as a borderland, geographically and politically at the margins of the Nationalist discourse of the nation.[42]

As the Japanese occupied Nanjing and the lower Yangzi valley, those who remained behind – from personal choice or because they were unable to evacuate – found it difficult to adhere to the romantic narrative of resistance spawned by the GMD. Collaboration emerged in three main areas: the client governments established by the political elites and motivated by national-level ideological and political issues; the minor local elites who faced a power vacuum and the task of reconstituting some semblance of administrative order in the occupied areas; and the economic elites who attempted to maximize their chances of economic survival through war devastation and Japanese control.

Dynamics and motivations for collaboration of the client states established in Nanjing differed from those in Manchuria, being focused on the idea of national salvation and directly reflecting issues of national political identity. The ideology of both the Reformed Government (RG, 1938–40) and the RNG (1940–45) reflected deep political disagreement over the path to nation building pursued by the Nationalist government, Chiang's retreat to the

42 Rana Mitter, *The Manchurian Myth: Nationalism, Resistance and Collaboration in Modern China* (Berkeley: University of California Press, 2000).

interior and the political vacuum that it created, and whether the war was already lost or there still was some possibility to overturn the Japanese occupation. The leaders of the RG based their choice on their belief that the war was lost and resistance would 'drive China into extinction'.[43] They therefore presented collaboration as a form of nationalism in direct competition to Chiang Kai-shek's, and aimed to return the nation to a 'purer [political] condition' than that envisioned by the GMD.[44] In the first draft of the RG political programme (February 1938), the three main RG leaders – Liang Hongzhi, Wen Zongyao and Chen Qun – specifically proposed the end of the GMD one-party leadership and stated their intention to sweep away the 'shallow doctrines of the former [regime]'.[45] The RG's founding manifesto also criticized the GMD's pre-war government for being corrupt, incompetent and having an overly pro-Western attitude. The current crisis, according to the manifesto, was the result of the Nationalist government's decision to fight Japan and to cooperate with the communists. Above all, the leaders of the RG accused the GMD of having retreated to the interior, leaving the Chinese people at the mercy of Japanese brutality.[46] This last point must have resonated deeply among the Chinese, since the memories of the Nanjing massacre were all too painfully fresh.

The RNG was led by Wang Jingwei, a prominent member of the pre-war Nationalist government. Wang had long opposed Chiang Kai-shek and his German-inspired vision of military nation building. He wanted to restore the GMD to civilian leadership and focus nation-building efforts on economic reconstruction, rather than military build-up. Before 1940, Wang had already attempted different strategies to undermine Chiang, including cooperating with warlords in an attempt to use their military power to overturn his opponent.[47]

Wang established the RNG in 1940, replacing the RG, in occupied Nanjing. At this time, Japan had launched a new policy, the new order in Asia. Admitting that Japan had held an unrealistic view of China, Japanese officials declared that they were ready to give China more autonomy, going as far as recognizing the validity of Sun Yat-sen's Three People's Principle – the

---

43 Brook, 'Collaborationist Nationalism', p. 160.
44 Ibid., p. 162.
45 Quoted in ibid., p. 173.
46 Ibid., p. 174.
47 Margherita Zanasi, *Saving the Nation: Economic Modernity in Republican China* (University of Chicago Press, 2006), pp. 159–90.

cornerstone of GMD's political ideology – as long as it was purged of anti-Japanese objectives.[48] The recognition of the Principles was essential for Wang's participation in a collaborationist government, since it allowed him to declare the RNG the legitimate embodiment of Nationalists' political heritage, and Chiang's government an aberrant variation. By using the term 'reorganized' in naming his client government, Wang also established a continuity with his long-time struggle against Chiang. Since 1929, Wang had been the leader of the GMD 'Reorganization Clique', which had mounted fierce opposition to Chiang.

In their programmes, therefore, both the RG and the RNG adopted the language of nationalism. Both governments justified collaboration as a way to preserve and protect the nation (a goal dubbed by Timothy Brook 'collaborationist nationalism'), and criticized Chiang's failure to protect the Chinese people from Japanese brutalities. As Gu Cheng, Minister of Information of the RG, argued, 'If the people do not survive, where is the nation?'[49]

Both collaborationist governments took on the 'difficult task of remaking the nation under collaboration'.[50] The RG's goal was to return China's political life to higher moral standards. Its political programme devoted most of its points to political and economic reconstruction, and to establishing an efficient and uncorrupt government with the interests of the people in mind.[51] The RNG, on the other hand, wanted to take back control over China's economic resources from the Japanese, believing such action to be crucial for launching economic development, becoming a modern nation and slowly shedding Japanese occupation.[52] The expectations of RG and RNG leaders for a genuine collaboration with the Japanese proved to be grossly over-optimistic. The reality of collaboration revealed the impossibility of carrying out the original objectives, and showed the weakness of the policy of attempting to engage in nation building while 'subordinating one's national identity to the hegemony of a foreign power'.[53] It is at this point that collaborators faced the reality of being instrumental in carrying out the repressing and exploitative agenda of the Japanese at the expense of the Chinese population.[54]

---

48 Brook, 'Collaborationist Nationalism', p. 177.
49 Quoted in ibid., p. 159.
50 Ibid., p. 179.
51 Quoted in ibid., p. 173.
52 Zanasi, Saving the Nation, pp. 159–90.
53 Brook, 'Collaborationist Nationalism', p. 186.
54 Margherita Zanasi, 'New Perspectives on Chinese Collaboration', The Asia-Pacific Journal: Japan Focus (2008), http://japanfocus.org/-Margherita-Zanasi/2828 (accessed 26 November 2014); and Zanasi, 'Globalizing Hanjian'.

Accommodation

In China, the Japanese not only sought the cooperation of some elements the national elites, but also attempted to build cooperation structures at the county level. After a generally brutal occupation, the Japanese would dispatch agents to carry out pacification and to establish local collaborationist administrative infrastructures. This strategy was relatively successful because, after a devastating occupation, millions of people found that cooperation was the only way of dealing with the new system established by the Japanese.[55] Under these circumstances, 'some Japanese and some Chinese negotiated working relationships under a new structure of authority', with the goal of re-establishing local functions crucial to everyday life, such as 'supplying food, organizing transportation, arranging security – the sort of matters that the local elites and local officials have to solve under any political dispensation'.[56]

These collaborationist administrations, however, did not always meet Japanese expectations. In Jiading county, for example, the Japanese were able to organize the local elites into self-government committees, but their members worked more to further their own interests than those of the Japanese. Gestures of collaboration, therefore, did not necessarily translate into effective support of Japanese goals.[57] On the other hand, complicities – 'a willingness to go along with the way things were, to accommodate and cohabit, because no other course seemed possible'[58] – could develop into a nuanced tripartite relationship between occupiers, occupied and third parties. This was the case of non-collaborationist Western communities. Members of the Nanjing International Committee negotiated between the Chinese and the Japanese during the brutal occupation of the city, and played a crucial role in the establishment of a Chinese collaborationist self-government committee. In this context, while not taking a direct position as either collaborators or resisters, the members of the international committee became complicit in establishing the first collaborationist network in Nanjing (which was soon to be replaced by the RG).[59] Complicities, however, also ended up forming 'a resilient web...running in many directions among

---

55 Timothy Brook, *Collaboration: Japanese Agents and Local Elites in Wartime China* (Cambridge, Mass.: Harvard University Press, 2005), p. 9.
56 Ibid., p. 7.
57 Ibid., ch. 3.
58 Ibid., p. 125.
59 Ibid., ch. 5.

many actors', and creating rivalries among different collaborationist groups and destabilizing the regime.[60]

The need to compromise with the Japanese, or with the client administration, and the challenges of survival in the occupied area, also affected urban entrepreneurs who faced complex choices. Only a small portion of Shanghai industries heeded Chiang's call to retreat to Free China – although that small portion was crucial for the survival of the GMD during the war. Most Shanghai capitalists – unable to move or fearful of the great risks involved in the evacuation process – remained in Shanghai, pursuing whatever survival strategies were available locally.[61] In general, 'most industrialists placed survival of the firm and family ahead of abstract concepts of nationalism', although nationalism did play a role.[62] Most Shanghai industrialists resisted cooperating with the Japanese as long as they could. This was possible as long as capitalists and entrepreneurs could find refuge in the foreign concessions where they could be shielded from Japanese threats. At this time, GMD agents exerted tremendous pressure on those who had remained behind, even resorting to the assassination of those who collaborated, to discourage any cooperation with the Japanese. It was only after Pearl Harbor and the end of the foreign concessions that the Chinese industrialists could no longer escape Japanese pressure for cooperation. This pressure increased dramatically in 1943, after Japan experienced significant military setbacks and decided to grant more economic authority to the RNG, in an attempt to increase China's economic production in support of the war efforts. At this time, the lack of opportunity to escape from Japanese jurisdiction, combined with more appealing offers from the RNG and the Japanese, including the return of confiscated property, led to an increase in cooperation among Chinese industrialists.[63]

A good example of this scenario is found in the Rong family group, one of the most prominent cotton textile and flour-processing magnates in the prewar period. Pursued by both the Japanese, who wanted the family to collaborate, and the GMD, who pressed them to move their mills to the interior, the Rongs decided to remain in Shanghai and operate the few mills

60 Ibid., ch. 6; Min Pan, *Jiangsu riwei jiceng zhengquan yanjiu* (Shanghai: Shanghai renmin chubanshe, 2006). Departing from Brook, Pan tends to focus more on opportunism and fears as the main reasons for collaboration: pp. 212–24.
61 Parks M. Coble, *Chinese Capitalists in Japan's New Order: The Occupied Lower Yangzi, 1937–1945* (Berkeley: University of California Press, 2003).
62 Ibid., p. 140.
63 Ibid.

in the foreign concessions that had not been taken over by the Japanese. A portion of the Rongs' mills in the nearby town of Wuxi, under the management of a son-in-law, however, did relocate, creating a schism in the family as much as an opportunity for a future reconciliation with the GMD. A delegation from the Shanghai branch of the family, in fact, was sent to Chongqing after 1941. Here, they registered the Shanghai mills with the GMD, and invested in a new factory that was to operate in Free China. Having bet on both the GMD and the Japanese, the Rong economic empire survived the war with relatively little damage.[64]

Most industrialists did not fare as well as the Rong family, however. Smaller industries had a harder time maximizing their chances of survival. Their responses to the Japanese occupation often depended on the state and nature of their business. For example, rubber manufacturers were predisposed to collaborate, as their industry, since its early days, had depended on Japanese supplies and was closely tied to Japan. Furthermore, because the Japanese military constituted their main market, rubber industrialists were willing to cooperate with them, although they were reluctant to share control of their businesses with Japanese partners. Other business families whose fortunes had declined before the war, such as the Nie family, chose to collaborate in an effort to regain some control over their lost enterprise. Despite the diversity of responses, however, most industrialists in the occupied areas attempted to avoid collaboration with the Japanese as long as they could, and started compromising only after 1943.[65]

By the post-war period, the Chinese discourse on collaboration and resistance had developed along lines similar to the European, focusing on political issues revolving around communism and on deep-rooted ideas of nation and national betrayal. Post-war collaboration trials also followed a similar path. As staged political events, they mythologized the narrative of the victor and delegitimized alternative narratives. The presence of client states also made it possible in China to criminalize political formations, as was done in Europe.[66] Local political culture and pre-war political debates that reflected China's particular issues, however, shaped collaboration and resistance choices for the Chinese people and influenced the mode of development of both responses.

---

64 Ibid., ch. 6.
65 Ibid., ch. 9.
66 Zanasi, 'Globalizing Hanjian'; Hwang, 'Wartime Collaboration in Question'.

Conclusion

Historians' understanding of collaboration and resistance has recently undergone deep changes, departing from a resistantialist narrative. This new approach is not motivated by a wish to absolve the brutal crimes perpetrated by the Japanese occupying forces or by their client states. It also does not want to deny that many collaborated for mere personal gain, even if they were conscious of the heavy price paid by the general population. Its goal is to gain a better understanding of the wide variety of responses to Japanese occupation and the factors that motivated them, including people's understanding of the crisis they faced and of the options they believed to be available to them at the time.

This approach is particularly important for the study of wartime Northeast Asia, where the Allies' Euro-centred narrative of collaboration and resistance has often been superimposed on local experiences, obscuring responses to Japanese occupation in the region that diverged significantly from reactions to the Nazi occupation in Europe. Even within Northeast Asia itself, reactions varied widely according to different Japanese policies and different local political and intellectual developments.

Lately, however, a few historians have challenged these new interpretative approaches, arguing that they tend to relieve collaborators of the responsibility for their actions. Consequently, a lively debate has developed, evaluating whether post-resistantialist historiography has gone too far in placing collaboration in a wider historical and cultural framework and has lost sight of ethical issues.[67]

---

67 Treat, 'Choosing to Collaborate'. For a debate on the issue of moral responsibility and collaboration, see 'Collaboration in War and Memory in East Asia: A Symposium', *The Asia-Pacific Journal: Japan Focus*, www.japanfocus.org/-timothy-brook/2798 (accessed 26 November 2014); the symposium was published in February 2012 in the *Journal of Asian Studies*, which centred around the article by Treat, 'Choosing to Collaborate'; for a discussion of the 'shield' defence, see Zanasi, 'Globalizing Hanjian'.

21

Japanese occupation of Southeast Asia, 1941–1945

PAUL H. KRATOSKA AND KEN'ICHI GOTO

When Japanese forces invaded Southeast Asia in 1941, local residents gave them a cordial, if somewhat wary reception. When Japanese generals came to Singapore in 1945 for a formal surrender ceremony, the waiting crowd screamed curses at them, using words the Japanese had routinely used to local residents during the occupation. People in Southeast Asia had come to detest the Japanese, and decades would pass before they were again welcome in the region. Japan presented the conquest as liberation from Western domination and the start of a new order based on Asian solidarity, but Southeast Asians experienced it as another version of foreign rule, accompanied by a sharp decline in living standards, restrictions on civil liberties, demeaning treatment, shortages, rampant inflation and propaganda rife with blatant lies.

Japan invaded Southeast Asia primarily to acquire oil. Territorial control of the region was incidental, although it suited Japan's ambition to build an autarchic empire. As early as the 1920s, Western military planners had identified Japan as the only serious potential threat to colonial dominance in Southeast Asia, and the policies of Japan's ultra-nationalist leaders caused great concern in the 1930s. Japan's alliance with Germany and Italy (September 1940) and the movement of Japanese troops into southern Vietnam (July 1941) prompted the United States and its allies to impose a total embargo on exports of oil to Japan, in an attempt to restrain Japanese ambitions. The Japanese needed fuel and other petroleum products to prosecute the Sino-Japanese War and to maintain their industrial capacity, and with no domestic supplies, political and military leaders viewed oil imports as crucial for the country's economic and military well-being. The situation provided the Western powers with a degree of leverage, but their effort to influence Japanese policy by withholding access to oil was a miscalculation that provided a powerful incentive for Japan's military thrust into Southeast Asia.

The oilfields of Sumatra offered a possible source of petroleum, but authorities in the Netherlands Indies (Indonesia) viewed Japan with suspicion, and the shipping lanes between Sumatra and East Asia were subject to interdiction from British Malaya, the Philippines and French Indochina. By 1941, political circumstances had shifted in ways that favoured Japan: Germany had occupied the Netherlands, French Indochina under Vichy France was no longer hostile, and Britain was preoccupied with the war in Europe. Nonetheless, Britain's Singapore naval base and American military forces in the Philippines still stood between Japan and free access to Indonesia's oil.

Japanese forces invaded Malaya and the Philippines on 8 December 1941, an action timed to coincide with the raid on Pearl Harbor in Hawaii across the International Dateline, where it was still 7 December. The initial attack caused extensive damage to US aircraft and bases in the Philippines; and two days later, Japanese aircraft sank two British warships, the *Repulse* and the *Prince of Wales*, off the east coast of Malaya, substantially reducing the threat posed by the Singapore naval base. British forces in Singapore surrendered on 15 February 1942, and by the end of May the Japanese controlled Southeast Asia.

Although Portugal was a neutral power, Japan invaded Portuguese Timor in February 1942. The island of Timor was strategically important as a base for an advance into Australia and a link with the South Pacific islands placed under Japanese control at the end of the First World War, as well as the Solomon and Aleutian Islands, Fiji, Samoa and Midway, which Japan conquered in its initial wave of conquests.

Japan had acquired a source of oil, but with it came a vast defence perimeter that faced hostile forces on all sides: British India to the west, Australia to the south, America to the east and China to the north. Supply lines were very long (Tokyo was 3,300 miles from Singapore, which was in turn 1,200 miles from Rangoon and 3,000 miles from New Guinea), and Japanese forces had to procure food and most other supplies from the territories they occupied. Oil aside, the region had limited value for Japan. The author of a planning document entitled 'Proposals for the Governance of Occupied Territories in the Southern Area of Operations' observed that 'The Philippines, if obtained, has very little to offer us, while at the same time increases our encumbrances'.[1] Much the same could be said of the rest of Southeast Asia, but with Japan's

1 Nakano Satoshi, 'Appeasement and Coercion', in Ikehata Setsuho and Ricardo Trota Jose (eds.), *The Philippines Under Japan: Occupation Policy and Reaction* (Quezon City: Ateneo de Manila University Press, 1999), p. 33.

Southern Army in control of the Philippines, the Malay peninsula, northern Borneo, Sumatra, Java and Burma, and the navy responsible for southern Borneo, the eastern part of the Indonesian archipelago and the islands of the South Pacific, military administrators and the civilian officials sent to support them now had to deal with the consequences of Japan's victories.

A document prepared in September 1942 by the Research Division of Japan's Naval Ministry includes two diagrams that illustrate some basic

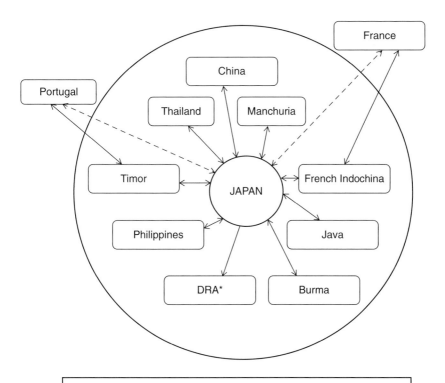

*Directly Ruled Areas, comprising former British territories excluding Burma, and the former Dutch East Indies excluding Java

21.1 Japanese navy conception of the Greater East Asia Co-Prosperity Sphere
21.1a: Japan as the centre of the GEACPS
21.1b: 'Side view' of the GEACPS (see overleaf)
Source: Doi Akira (gen. ed.), *Showa Shakai-Keizai Shiryo Shusei: Kaigunsho Shiryo* (Comprehensive Historical Material on Socio-economic Conditions in Showa Period: Materials of the Navy Department) (29 vols. plus one supplement, Tokyo: Institute of Oriental Studies [Daito Bunka Daigaku], 1992), vol. xvii, pp. 27–8. The original source is 'Daitoa Kyoeiken-ron' (On the Greater East Asia Co-Prosperity Sphere), prepared by the Research section of the Navy Department in 1943.

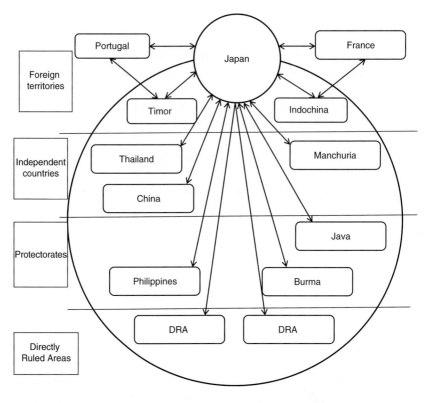

21.1 (cont.)

characteristics of Greater East Asia. In these drawings, Japan occupies the central position, and member states communicate directly with Japan, but not with each other. As the most developed island in the Dutch East Indies, Java is listed as a protectorate. The rest of the Indonesian archipelago and the Malay peninsula were categorized as Directly Ruled Areas. The compilers of the document remarked that 'in the future both French Indochina and Portuguese Timor should be placed under the guidance of the empire'.

Administration

It is a truism that no imperial power can succeed without local collaborators. Western colonial administrations created a new, Western-educated adminis-trative class to staff their bureaucracies, but they also relied heavily on support from local rulers, immigrant trading communities and ethnic minorities. In the 1930s, some anti-colonial activists, particularly on the left, saw Japanese ambitions as a threat to their own aspirations and offered to support the anti-fascist cause, but colonial authorities rebuffed these approaches, which they considered disloyal attempts to exploit a temporary weakness arising from the conflict taking shape in Europe.

The Japanese, like the Western powers that preceded them, needed local allies. A number of anti-colonial revolutionaries who had lived for many years in Japan as political exiles, among them Artemio Ricarte (b.1866), a general in the Philippine Revolutionary Army in the 1890s, the Sakdal leader Benigno Ramos (who was in Japan when his followers staged a rebellion in May 1935) and the Indian revolutionary Rash Behari Bose (b.1886), became involved in pro-Japanese activity in Southeast Asia, but their impact was limited. Southeast Asia's secular nationalists, most of whom were Western-educated advocates of democracy, self-determination and economic develop-ment, saw Japan's interest in the region as a positive development, and seemed ready to work with the new regime. However, their desire for an early transfer of power did not mesh well with Japanese objectives, and they were soon marginalized.

Civil servants who had worked for the former colonial regimes were viewed with suspicion, but replacing the existing administrative apparatus would have been difficult and time-consuming. A directive regarding the implementation of military administration stated that 'existing governmental organizations shall be utilized as much as possible, with due respect for past organizational structure and native practices'.[2] The Japanese removed British officers from positions of authority in Malaya and Burma, but tried retaining the services of Dutch officials in Indonesia, at least until sufficient numbers of Japanese administrators were in place and local members of staff were able to handle increased responsibilities. Dutch civil servants were apparently willing to cooperate, but they refused to swear allegiance to the emperor of Japan, and the Japanese soon abandoned the experiment. The fact that in Java alone there were nearly 15,000 European officials in 1940 indicates the magnitude of the staffing problem.[3]

As allies of Japan, French Indochina and Thailand escaped formal occupa-tion and retained their pre-war administrations, subject to varying degrees of

2 Harry J. Benda, James K. Irikura and Koichi Kishi, *Japanese Military Administration in Indonesia: Selected Documents*, Translation Series 6 (New Haven, Conn.: Yale University, Southeast Asia Studies, 1965), p. 1.
3 Shigeru Sato, *War, Nationalism and Peasants: Java Under the Japanese Occupation, 1942–1945* (St Leonard's, New South Wales: Allen & Unwin, 1994), p. 22.

interference. In French Indochina, Japan's goals were to maintain a supply base and a secure rear area, and to shut off the flow of supplies to nationalist forces in China. One scholar has described the arrangement in Indochina as the stationing of a garrison force rather than a true occupation, satisfying Japan's need for a staging area and a source of raw materials, and the French desire to retain their Indochinese territories at all costs.[4] In Thailand, Field Marshal Plaek Phibun Songkhram, Prime Minister from 1938 until 1944, made his cooperation conditional, asking the Japanese to pressure the French to return territories in Laos and Cambodia that the Thais had been forced to relinquish several decades earlier. Upon regaining the west bank of the Mekong River, Phibun bowed to the inevitable. He signed a treaty of alliance with Japan on 21 December 1941, and in January declared war against the Allied powers. As an independent nation allied with Japan, Thailand provided a possible model for other Southeast Asian countries, but the Thais were reluctant allies, acceding to requests to the extent necessary to mollify the Japanese, while secretly developing contacts with the Allied powers. When Thai support visibly flagged in 1943, the Japanese arranged the transfer of additional territories claimed by Thailand: two of Burma's Shan states (Kengtung and Mongpan) and the four northernmost Malay states (Kedah, Perlis, Trengganu and Kelantan). Apart from these changes, they generally maintained the territorial integrity of their conquests.

In 1935, the American colonial administration in the Philippines had ceded certain powers to an elected Commonwealth government, with a promise of independence in 1946, and the invasion disrupted Philippine progress toward that goal. Japan portrayed the war as a conflict between their forces and the United States, and tried to mobilize nationalist sentiment in support of the occupying forces, but many Filipinos saw the invasion as an attack on themselves as well as the Americans, and anti-Japanese feeling was strong. Japan's policy directive covering the Philippines stated that the goal was only to destroy American strongholds, and that the Japanese military should not directly govern the country.[5] In January 1942, before the conquest was complete, Prime Minister Tojo announced that Japan would grant independence to the Philippines. However, the President of the Philippine Commonwealth, Manuel Quezon, had already left the country to set up a government-in-exile, and pending further developments, an Executive

4 Masaya Shiraishi, 'La présence japonaise en Indochine, 1940–1945', in Paul Isoart (ed.), *L'Indochine Française, 1940–1945* (Paris: Presses Universitaires de France, 1982), p. 218.
5 Nakano, 'Appeasement and Coercion', pp. 31–2.

Commission headed by Jorge B. Vargas, Quezon's Executive Secretary, took charge of the administration.

In Burma, the British had introduced a system of parliamentary government in 1937 that gave local officials a degree of control over domestic affairs. Japanese agents contacted a nationalist group pressing for full independence, the Dobama Asi-ayone, and provided training on Hainan Island to a group of its members known as the Thirty Comrades. They re-entered the country with the Japanese army on 26 December 1941, recruited a Burma Independence Army (BIA) and set up Free Burmese Civilian Administrations (FBCA) as the invasion force moved northward. However, their ambitions went well beyond what the Japanese authorities were willing to countenance, and in June 1942 the Japanese replaced FBCA appointees with Peace Commissioners, many of whom were former members of the colonial civil service. The BIA also became a liability, owing to weak finances and poor discipline, and in July a much smaller Burma Defence Army (later renamed the Burma National Army) took its place. The head of the army was Aung San, one of the Thirty Comrades.

The Japanese studied the cultures and societies of Southeast Asia before the war, but most of the officials and soldiers sent to the region lacked local knowledge and language skills, and failed to respect local sensitivities. Moreover, military requirements were paramount and military officials overshadowed civilians. Seizaburo Okazaki, the first head of the military administration in Java, remarked, 'I did not usually consult with Hayashi [Hayashi Kyujiro, civilian advisor to the 16th Army] and when I did it was after I had made my decision'.[6]

At the start of the occupation, the Japanese used terror tactics to intimidate local populations, slapping or otherwise physically abusing residents who failed to pay homage to the emperor by bowing to Japanese sentries, and carrying out arrests and summary executions. These tactics quickly put an end to open opposition, but they generated lasting resentment. Having consolidated their grip on power, the Japanese tried to restore normal life and persuade residents to adjust to their new circumstances – for example, by learning and using the Japanese language – but normalcy was impossible while the war continued. By 1943, the region faced a growing list of intractable problems, among them shortages of food and consumer staples, widespread unemployment, a rising incidence of disease and soaring inflation.

6 George S. Kanahele, 'The Japanese Occupation of Indonesia: Prelude to Independence' (unpublished PhD dissertation, Cornell University, 1967), p. 283.

In an effort to deal with these issues, the Japanese sought the active support of residents in the occupied territories, abandoning the hard-line tactics of the early months of the occupation and working with local organizations to broaden their political base. In January 1943, premier Tojo announced that plans to grant independence to the Philippines and Burma would proceed. In August, a formal transfer of power took place in Burma, where the new government was headed by Ba Maw, Burma's first premier before the war. Intelligence assessments noted that a high proportion of the new officials had held responsible posts under the British and enjoyed a considerable degree of popular support. Ba Maw introduced a New Order Plan that called for reorganizing the administrative apparatus, mobilizing manpower and undertaking emergency tasks connected with the war. Burma was to have 'a single national structure', eliminating the relative autonomy formerly enjoyed by minority groups in outlying areas, and a single political party, Ba Maw's own Dobama Sinyetha Asi Ayon.[7] The dictatorial style and royalist pretensions associated with his 'supreme leadership' antagonized many Burmese, and the new government operated under many constraints. Japan retained control of foreign affairs, transport and communications, and food requisitioning, and placed advisors on committees concerned with war-related activities, including labour service, price control, agriculture and propaganda.[8] The Philippines received independence in October, and Jose P. Laurel, before the war a Senator and Supreme Court Justice, became President of what was known as the Second Philippine Republic. As in Burma, the new administration included many prominent pre-war political figures, and they, too, struggled to deal with continuing Japanese interference in government, a breakdown of basic services and public hostility to the occupation. Where Japan hoped independence for Burma would generate nationalist enthusiasm, its goal in the Philippines was to reduce the level of opposition, minimize Japanese responsibilities and place power in the hands of a non-hostile government.

Japan intended to retain Malaya and Indonesia as permanent parts of the empire, but starting in mid-1943, they created various advisory or consultative councils that ostensibly gave local residents a voice in government. In

---

7 Office of the Secretary General to the Nainggandaw Adipadi, 'A Review of the First Stage of the New Order Plan', National Archives of Burma (NAB), series 1/7, acc. no. 313.

8 Office of Strategic Services, Research and Analysis Branch (hereafter OSS R&A), no. 2015, 'Japanese Administration of Burma', 10 July 1944, US National Archives and Records Administration (NARA), RG226 E 136, box 52, folder 621, p. 25.

each country there were state or provincial councils and a central council. The central council for Malaya was inactive, but its counterpart in Java, the Chuo Sangi-in (Central Advisory Council), was a significant nationalist vehicle, although the Japanese restricted its freedom to act.

The new states are often dismissed as puppet regimes, but arguably they were more than that. The administrations had genuine popular appeal, but they could not overcome war-related hardships and suffered from their close association with Japan. The two countries reverted to their pre-war status when the war ended in 1945, but three years later, both the Philippines and Burma were independent, the first colonies in Southeast Asia to shake off foreign rule.

As part of the attempt to involve local residents in the war effort, the Japanese created national service associations, youth and women's groups, civil defence units, cultural bodies and ethnically based organizations such as the Overseas Chinese Association, the Indian Independence League and the Malay Welfare League. Neighbourhood associations (*tonarigumi*), which were linked to the lowest unit of the administration and recognized by the military authorities, became responsible for mobilization of manpower, air-raid drills and quasi-military activities. Local vigilance corps, such as the Keibodan in Indonesia, which claimed more than a million members by the end of the occupation, recruited and trained young men to assist in civil defence. Military auxiliaries known as *heiho*, found in Malaya, Sumatra, Burma, Java and Borneo (and in the Philippines under the name *yoin*), received military training and were formally part of the Japanese army, although they were used mainly as labourers. In addition, volunteer armies (*giyugun*) augmented regular Japanese military forces, and in Indonesia, Burma and the Philippines, the Japanese sanctioned and trained local armies. The names given to these forces, Indonesia's Volunteer Army of Defenders of the Fatherland, the Burma National Army and the Makapili (League of Patriotic Filipinos), suggest a nationalist rather than a pro-Japanese orientation.[9]

Greater East Asia

Japan's Greater East Asia propaganda invoked a pan-Asian identity (often described by the term *hakko ichiu* – eight corners of the world under the

---

9 Joyce Lebra, *Japanese-trained Armies in Southeast Asia* (Hong Kong: Heinemann Educational Books (Asia), 1977); Motoe Terami-Wada, 'Filipino Armies Under the Japanese Occupation', in Ikehata and Jose (eds.), *The Philippines Under Japan*, pp. 59–98.

same roof) and a corresponding Asian nationalism. In Java, for example, the Commander of the 16th Army, General Imamura Hitoshi, told Indonesians that they and the Japanese shared 'the same origin, the same ethnicity', a statement he claimed left Indonesians deeply moved because it conveyed the sense that they were part of a larger Asian community.[10] In Burma, a propaganda release asserted that 'The Nipponese, Burmese, Siamese, Indo-Chinese, Phillippinos [sic], all are Asiatics. They have historical connections in their manners, customs and have the same religious beliefs'. Using an analogy often deployed by the Japanese, the writer compared the Co-Prosperity Sphere to a family, saying: 'It is important to have parents in a household so also it is equally important to have somebody in the form of parents in Asia'. Asking rhetorically who was qualified to act as parents, he responded: 'After carefully surveying the situation, I sincerely think that I could find nobody else except the Nippons'.[11] Propaganda materials also promoted Japanese values, in particular *seishin* or Japanese spirit, a central but elusive concept that embraced discipline, tenacity, allegiance to country, austerity and thrift, and rejected the materialism and individualism of the West in favour of an Asian spiritualism. Japanese-language courses, newspapers and radio broadcasts, and public ceremonies all stressed these values.

The Japanese created a Ministry of Greater East Asia in November 1942, and a year later, in November 1943, staged a Greater East Asia Conference in Tokyo, intended as a summit for heads of 'independent' states within the Japanese Empire. Ba Maw represented Burma, and Jose P. Laurel attended for the Philippines, while the Thai Prime Minister sent a proxy. In a speech at the conference, Ba Maw stated: 'we must be aware that we who are born in Asia have a dual nationality – that is, we are nationals of our own country and at the same time we are nationals of Greater East Asia'.[12] Conference participants, he said later, responding to 'the call of common blood and homeland', had discovered their 'East Asiatic oneness'.[13] Political rhetoric aside, there was little basis for a shared identity in a region that included restive Muslim minorities in the Christian Philippines and Buddhist Thailand, a profusion of languages and religious beliefs in the Indonesian archipelago,

10 Yamamoto Moichiro, *Watashi no Indonesia Dai Juroku gun-jidai-no Kaiso* (Tokyo: Nihon-Indonesia Kyokai, 1979), p. 19.
11 The Rangoon Nipponese Military Information Bureau, Asiatic Progress News Bulletin no. 3, NAB, series 1/5, acc. no. 92.
12 Ito Takashi, Hirohashi Masamitsu and Katajima Norio (eds.), *Tojo Naikakusoridaijin Kimitsu-kiroku* (University of Tokyo Press, 1990), p. 327.
13 Nainggandaw Adipadi's Address to the Privy Council, delivered on Tuesday, 30 November 1943, NAB, series 1/7, acc. no. 313.

animist hill tribes in Burma, French Indochina and Malaya, and Chinese, Indian, Arab and other immigrant communities, all with strong cultural identities and histories of tension and conflict with other groups in the region.

There were substantial Indian communities in Malaya, southern Thailand and Sumatra, and more than a million Indians lived in Burma, where they made up more than half the population of Rangoon. The collapse of British rule sparked a large-scale withdrawal of Indians from the Burma Delta, triggered more by fear of the ethnic Burman population than of the Japanese, and a high proportion of the 400,000 or more people who made the arduous overland trek to British India were Indian.[14] The Japanese tried to cultivate Indian support by encouraging the independence struggle in India. A liaison unit, initially known as the Fujiwara Kikan (Fujiwara Organ) after its leader, Fujiwara Iwaichi, sponsored creation of an Indian Independence League (IIL),which became active in Thailand, Malaya and Burma, where members carried out propaganda work, espionage and sabotage on behalf of the Japanese. The Fujiwara Kikan also helped set up an Indian National Army (INA), which recruited local residents, as well as Indian soldiers who had been sent to reinforce British forces in Malaya shortly before the invasion. In 1944, when the INA took part in Japan's failed Manipur offensive along India's eastern frontier, British sources placed its total strength at around 28,000 soldiers, including 13,000 in Burma.[15]

The Chinese in Southeast Asia had staged a series of politically motivated boycotts of Japanese goods in the 1930s and were a significant source of support for China in the Sino-Japanese War, a history that shaped Japanese attitudes toward them. Particularly in Malaya, the Chinese community included many young, single, working-class men who were recent migrants and retained close ties with China, and the Japanese dealt with this group harshly, carrying out mass executions following a screening process. Other residents of Chinese descent came from families that had lived in Southeast Asia for generations and whose links with China had become attenuated. In Thailand and the Philippines, they had assimilated with the local population to such an extent that they no longer formed distinct communities; while in the Dutch East Indies and Malaya, they had developed distinctive hybrid

---

14 J. Russell Andrus, *Burmese Economic Life* (Stanford University Press, 1947), p. 35; Hugh Tinker, 'A Forgotten Long March: The Indian Exodus from Burma, 1942', *Journal of Southeast Asian Studies* 6:1 (March 1975), 2.

15 'Hikari Kikan', OSS R&A Report 8.N.D., 16 October 1944, NARA, RG226 E 19 XL13420.

identities. Chinese trading networks handled the movement and distribution of essential consumer goods and rice, and their disruption had serious adverse consequences across the region.

Religion

Much of the population of Southeast Asia was at least nominally Buddhist, Muslim or Christian, but religious practice was often syncretic and animist beliefs remained powerful. The Japanese presented themselves as a religiously tolerant people from a country steeped in Buddhism, but sympathetic to Islam and to Christianity. In reality, Japan had a long history of suppressing Christianity and little prior contact with Islam. Moreover, the idea that the Japanese emperor was a deity clearly clashed with Christian and Muslim monotheism, and the Japanese insistence that people bow in the direction of the emperor's palace in Tokyo – symbolically, if not literally standing with their backs to Mecca – caused great offence among Muslims. To facilitate their dealings with religious authorities, the Japanese attempted to bring all adherents of a particular religion within each country under the ambit of a single organization: the Maha Sangha for Buddhists in Burma, Masjumi for Muslims in the Indonesian archipelago, the Evangelical Church of the Philippines for Protestant denominations in the Philippines, and so on.

In December 1941, the Japanese Army's General Staff created a Religious Affairs Section that drew on the small Roman Catholic community in Japan to build ties with Catholic leaders in the Philippines. Its representatives protected church personnel and property, and promoted Filipinization of the clergy to develop a Catholicism 'free of Caucasian tint and Western aspects', but such was the prevailing hostility among the public at large that many Japanese came to view Filipino Catholics as inherently opposed to their rule.[16]

A Greater Japan Muslim League, established in 1938 to serve as an umbrella body for Muslim organizations in the Japanese Empire, attempted to position Islam as an anti-Western ideology and mobilize Muslim support for the war effort. A 1943 newspaper interview with Abdarashid Ebrahim, Imam of the Tokyo Mosque, described him as 'the respected patriarch of the Muslim world'. The article went on to draw a clumsy parallel between

16 Terada Takefumi, 'The Religious Propaganda Program for Christian Churches', in Ikehata and Jose (eds.), *The Philippines Under Japan*, p. 228. The quotation comes from a document written by Bishop Taguchi Yoshigoro about a proposed agreement with the Vatican regarding the Catholic Church in the Philippines.

Japan's military offensive and the struggle of the Prophet Mohammed: 'Nippon's cause in Dai Toa Senso [the Great East Asian War] is a sacred one and, in its austerity, is comparable only to the war carried out against the infidels by Prophet Mohammed in the past'.[17] The Japanese tried, without success, to get Muslim leaders to declare the conflict a holy war.

Buddhism in Japan was very different from the Theravada Buddhist tradition found in Southeast Asia, but Japan sought to build support by declaring itself a champion of Buddhism, and in July 1943 convened a Greater East Asia Buddhist Conference in Tokyo to reinforce this claim. However, the behaviour of Japanese soldiers at temples and in their dealings with Buddhist monks often offended religious sensibilities. In Thailand, for example, a serious clash (the Ban Pong Incident) erupted after Japanese soldiers slapped a Thai monk, not only failing to respect his religious status, but also violating a strongly held Thai feeling of reverence for the head.

The wartime economy in Southeast Asia

The Greater East Asia concept called for an integrated Co-Prosperity Sphere based on the industrial capacity of Japan and Manchuria, the manpower and markets of China, and the natural resources of Southeast Asia. An 'Outline of the Economic Policies toward the Southern Areas', adopted in December 1941, introduced a system of appointed enterprises that allowed nearly 1,300 Japanese companies to set up operations in army-occupied areas of Southeast Asia. The arrangement covered 525 firms engaged in industry, 224 in commerce and trade, 190 in agriculture, 133 in mining and 49 in forestry. More than three-quarters of these businesses were part of large conglomerates, including 240 from the Mitsui group and 125 from the Mitsubishi group.[18]

In an effort to control prices and reduce wasteful competition, the Japanese grouped local firms in the same line of business and gave these *kumiai* quasi-monopolies over the wholesale and retail trade in certain products, such as fish, vegetables, rice and cloth. The stated purpose was to improve economic

17 *Syonan Times*, 7 August 2603 [1943].
18 Kobayashi Hideo, '"Daitoa kyoeiken" to Nihon kigyo', in Wada Haruki, Goto Ken'i-chi, Kibata Yo'ichi, Kyondaru Cho, Yamamuro Sin'ichi and Kawashima Sin (eds.), *Higasi Ajia Kingendaishi* (10 vols., Tokyo: Iwanami Shoten, 2011), vol. vi; Hikita Yasuyuki, 'Japanese Companies' Inroads into Indonesia Under Japanese Military Domination', in Peter Post and Elly Touwen-Bouwsma (eds.), *Japan, Indonesia and the War* (Leiden: KITLV Press, 1997), pp. 134–76.

efficiency, but traders in the *kumiai* sabotaged these goals by manipulating markets and withholding goods. They made exorbitant profits, but contributed to shortages and a growing malaise.

In 1943, the Japanese abandoned the effort to build an integrated pan-Asian economic community in favour of economic decentralization and self-sufficiency, and made plans to set up industries in the region. The reason for the change lay in transport shortages, and particularly shipping. In December 1941, the Japanese army had 2,150,000 tons of shipping, but by December 1944 the figure had fallen to just 250,000 tons. In August 1943, the *Mainichi Shimbun* stated editorially that Japan's greatest concern was insufficient shipping capacity, which impeded 'the smooth flow of goods between the various regions of the Co-prosperity sphere', and forced officials 'to make unnatural self-sufficiency plans' to develop various regions separately and independently.[19] Fuel shortages also limited transport options. Japan procured less than half of the oil it expected from Indonesia, and the amounts dropped off sharply after 1943.[20] To compensate for the shortfall, the Japanese developed a process to extract oil from rubber, but rubber-based fuels and lubricants rapidly fouled the engines in which they were used.

In an effort to increase shipping capacity, Japan launched an ambitious programme to build wooden boats. Construction took place across the region, with the Mitsui and Mitsubishi corporations alone setting up thirty shipyards in connection with the project. Large quantities of cut timber were moved to the shipyards, but production was around 10 per cent of the target figure, and many boats were equipped only with sails because engines from Japan failed to arrive. The quality of the construction was poor, and to meet their quotas the shipyards used unseasoned timber. 'Even very soft woods...were employed and it was possible to see three or four different species in adjoining strakes, and all the seams gaping'.[21]

19 Sato, *War, Nationalism and Peasants*, p. 190; *Mainichi Shimbun*, 23 August 1943, quoted in 'Appreciation of Malaya: II – Post-Japanese Occupation', Malaysian National Archives (ANM), British Military Administration (Malaya), file 506/10.
20 Nenryo Konwa-kai (ed.), *Nihon Kaigun Nenryoshi gekan* (2 vols., Tokyo: Hara Shobo, 1972), vol. II, p. 944; United States Strategic Bombing Survey, Oil in Japan's War (Washington DC: Oil and Chemicals Division, United States Strategic Bombing Survey, 1946).
21 Situation Report on the Forest Department, Malaya, for September 1945, in ANM, Forests 30/1945; Paul H. Kratoska, *The Japanese Occupation of Malaya* (London: C. Hurst, 1998), pp. 161–5; Sato, *War, Nationalism and Peasants*, pp. 186–90; Iwatake Teruhiko, *Nanpogunseikano Keizaisisaku ge* (2 vols., Tokyo: Ryukei shosha, 1995), vol. II, pp. 281–3.

Banking and currency

To pay for goods and services, soldiers entering Southeast Asia carried military yen, and this currency was declared to be equal in value with Straits dollars, Javanese guilders, Thai baht, Indo-Chinese piasters and Burmese rupees (renamed kyat). The Japanese subsequently printed additional banknotes denominated in national currencies, again valued at parity with the Japanese yen. In principle, these currencies were interchangeable, but little foreign exchange took place.[22]

Japanese banks operating in Southeast Asia before the war, particularly the Yokohama Specie Bank, handled military accounts. In March 1942, Japan created a Southern Development Bank that provided credit to Japanese firms setting up operations in Southeast Asia, drawing on a military expense account to capitalize it. In April 1943, it became a bank of issue, printing banknotes and supplying funds to the government and the military.

Pre-war governments had taxed landholdings, commercial agriculture, mining, manufacturing and trade, but economic stagnation left wartime administrations with few sources of revenue, and they struggled to cover their expenses. For example, Burma's budget for 1943–44 placed estimated revenue at just over half of expenditure. To overcome such shortfalls, the Japanese borrowed large sums from local governments, a particular source of grievance in Thailand; and in the later stages of the occupation, they printed large quantities of money that lacked any sort of backing. Malaya's banknote circulation was $220 million in 1942 and nearly $5,000 million in August 1945; while in Burma the note circulation grew from 180 million rupees in 1940 to more than 1,300 million kyat when the war ended. There were similar rises in other occupied territories, and the result was massive price inflation. In Singapore, the cost of living increased more than seven-fold between December 1941 and December 1943, and by May 1945 was more than a hundred times greater than before the war. Prices in Rangoon increased seventeen-fold by December 1943, and had shot up to 1,800 times pre-war levels by August 1945.[23]

---

22 J. Russell Andrus, 'Burmese Economy During the Japanese Occupation', in *Burma During the Japanese Occupation* (2 vols., Simla: Government of India Press, 1944), vol. II, p. 231.

23 *Report of the Committee on Currency* (Rangoon: State Printing Presses, Burma, 1944), pp. 4–5, NARA RG226 E16 135452; *Financial and Economic Annual* (Rangoon, July 1943), cited in *Burma During the Japanese Occupation*, vol. II, p. 240; Kratoska, *The Japanese Occupation of Malaya*, pp. 202–3, 207, 213; Iwatake Teruhiko, *Nanpogunseikano Keizaisisaku ge*, pp. 541, 547; Shibata Yoshimasa, 'The Monetary Policy in the Netherlands East Indies Under the Japanese Administration', *Bijdragen tot de Taal-, Land-en Volkenkunde* 152:4 (1996), 699–724.

Consumer goods

As pre-war stocks of consumer goods dwindled and supplies went to the black market, it became difficult to purchase basic items such as cloth, matches, cooking oil, soap, salt and kerosene. Small-scale industries manufactured substitutes out of locally available raw materials, but the quality of these products was poor.

Cloth shortages were particularly serious, and across the region people tell stories of men working naked in their fields, or wearing clothes made from old gunny sacks or fibrous tree bark. In upland regions and northerly areas where temperatures fall to low levels in the winter months, the cloth shortage caused a great deal of hardship. The Japanese encouraged farmers to grow cotton on lands previously planted with other export crops, setting a target of 240,000 tons for Southeast Asia. In Burma, production was around 20,000 tons of raw cotton annually, and Japanese officials hoped to treble or quadruple that. In the Philippines, officials called for an increase from 30,000 to 1.25 million acres planted with cotton, and a harvest of nearly 100,000 tons. Planners anticipated bringing 120,000 idle spindles and 4,800 looms from Japan to develop the cloth industry in Southeast Asia, and delivered about one-third of this amount. Intelligence reports indicated that between 150,000 and 300,000 spindles reached Burma. However, the region produced poor-quality short-staple cotton, and too little of it to keep even this equipment fully occupied.[24]

Labour

Production of Southeast Asia's major export commodities – coffee, tea, abaca, sugar, palm oil and various minerals – far outstripped demand in the Japanese empire. Malaya and Indonesia, for example, produced more than a million tons of rubber in 1940, while Japan consumed less than 100,000 tons per year.[25] Many estates and mines closed, creating widespread unemployment not only for workers directly involved in production of export products, but also for those in ancillary businesses such as transport, insurance and warehousing. The Japanese suggested that people who were out of work should plant vegetables to feed themselves and others. A senior official in Malaya said, 'there is every prospect in growing foodstuffs and in

24 Sato, *War, Nationalism and Peasants*, pp. 76–7; Andrus, 'Burmese Economy During the Japanese Occupation', pp. 187–8; Nagano Yoshiko, 'Cotton Production Under Japanese Rule, 1942–1945', in Ikehata and Jose (eds.), *The Philippines Under Japan*, pp. 181–99.
25 Kratoska, *The Japanese Occupation of Malaya*, p. 225, n. 3.

rearing cattle and poultry', and that resistance to manual labour on the part of educated people was 'repugnant' to Nippon Seisin – Nipponese Fundamental Thought. 'We will have nothing to do with these people'.[26]

Construction projects, particularly repairs to roads, bridges and railways, eventually absorbed much of the surplus labour. The best known of these projects was a branch line linking the Thai and the Burmese railway systems, built to supply Japanese forces in Burma, but there were other railway projects in southern Thailand, Sumatra, Java and Borneo. The Japanese initially used prisoners of war to build the Thailand–Burma railway, but by 1943 they were recruiting workers locally. Burma created a 'sweat army' to service the railway, but the Thai government refused to conscript workers, and Japanese officials recruited labourers in Malaya for the Thai side of the line.

By the end of 1943, Southeast Asia was beginning to experience labour shortages. The Japanese responded with labour mobilization campaigns, and eventually turned to mass conscription. A Forced Labour Service Order took effect in the Philippines in November 1944, and around the same time, a 'Change of Trade Ordinance' in Malaya barred men from holding certain jobs that did not contribute to the war effort, a policy that led to increased female participation in the workforce.[27] Recruitment of 'labour warriors', or *romusha*, began in Java in October 1943. Most *romusha* worked on projects within the Indonesian archipelago, but some were sent to projects outside of Indonesia. By November 1944, the military directly employed more than 2.6 million Javanese workers, with another 10 million hired on a temporary basis. Death rates were extremely high, and when the war ended, vast numbers of displaced workers, many of them weakened, ill and without money, began trying to make their way back home.[28]

Food and nutrition

Before the war, imported rice accounted for 40 per cent of consumption in the Philippines, 50 per cent in Sarawak and the East Coast Residency of

---

26 Minutes, Meeting of District Officers, 5 November 2602 [1942], ANM, Batu Gajah 69/ 2602.

27 Paul H. Kratoska, *The Thailand–Burma Railway, 1942–1946: Documents and Selected Writings* (6 vols., London: Routledge, 2005); E. Bruce Reynolds, *Thailand and Japan's Southern Advance, 1940–1945* (New York: St Martin's Press, 1994), p. 171; OSS, Far Eastern Bureau (New Delhi), 'Malaya Under the Japanese', US National Archives file RG226 128585, March 1945.

28 Sato, *War, Nationalism and Peasants*, pp. 157–8; Paul H. Kratoska (ed.), *Asian Labor in the Wartime Japanese Empire* (Armonk, NY: M. E. Sharpe, 2005).

Sumatra, and 65 per cent in British Malaya and Ceylon. Mine and plantation workers, and residents of towns and cities, ate imported rice, but by the late 1930s many peasant farmers had abandoned rice cultivation to plant cash crops for export, and they too relied on food imports. In Malaya, for instance, the largely rural states of Kelantan and Pahang produced just 60 per cent of their rice requirements.

The great river deltas of Burma, Thailand and southern Vietnam exported more than 6 million tons of rice in 1940, far more than was needed to meet requirements in Southeast Asia, but after the conquest, fuel shortages and the lack of shipping limited the movement of rice to food deficit areas. Fighting in Burma caused the deaths of a large number of draft animals and destroyed many of the small boats used to carry rice from the fields to mills in port cities. Infrastructure in other rice-growing areas suffered little damage, but there, too, the lack of transport curtailed rice trading operations. The jute bags used to ship rice were also in short supply. Before the war, Burma alone imported around 52 million jute bags annually from India. With supplies from this source cut off, the Japanese pressed farmers to plant jute and other fibrous plants, but it was impossible to make up for the shortfall.

As price controls, forced sales and confiscation, and inflation made commercial rice cultivation increasingly unattractive, farmers reduced the area they planted, growing only enough rice for their own needs. Lower Burma was the world's largest rice exporter before the war. When the occupation ended, the planted area had fallen by more than half, and production by two-thirds. In Thailand, rice production remained close to pre-war levels, but exports fell from 1.9 million metric tons in 1939/40 to under 200,000 tons in 1945. The country was rumoured to hold vast stockpiles of rice, but this grain, if it ever existed, disappeared into the black market. In southern Vietnam, production declined after 1943, when Japanese army buying agents cut back on purchases and prices fell. Throughout Southeast Asia, nearly half a million acres of rice land went out of production between 1943 and 1945, and where rice fields were abandoned, canals and irrigation works deteriorated for want of maintenance.[29]

With imported rice increasingly unavailable, deficit areas had to rely on food produced locally. The result in many places was severe malnutrition.

29 Paul H. Kratoska, 'The Impact of the Second World War on Commercial Rice Production in Mainland South-East Asia', in Paul H. Kratoska (ed.), *Food Supplies and the Japanese Occupation in South-East Asia* (Houndmills and London: Macmillan Press, 1998), pp. 9–31.

More than half of the 2,500 calories the average person in Malaya consumed each day in 1940 came from imported foodstuffs, including rice, wheat and other cereals, pulses, sugar, eggs, condensed milk and milk powder. Rice imports, which amounted to 580,000 tons per year before the war, dropped by more than 50 per cent in 1942, and fell below 100,000 tons in 1945. The Japanese urged residents of cities and towns to plant gardens on open land, and encouraged them to move to the country to grow vegetables. Many of those who followed this advice knew nothing of farming, and they planted crops in unsuitable places, causing erosion that silted up waterways and worsened the problem of malaria by creating breeding sites for mosquitoes. Local production provided around 200 calories per person per day before the war, and 520 calories when the war ended, notwithstanding an aggressive Grow More Food campaign.[30] Malnutrition caused many deaths during the occupation, and deficiency diseases were common, as was stunted growth among young children.

Like Malaya, the Philippines imported rice before the war and experienced severe shortages of food during the occupation. The limited support for the Laurel government in the countryside complicated efforts to carry out rice purchase schemes, and guerrillas were active in farming areas. When food shortages reached crisis proportions in 1943, the government tried various expedients, including confiscation of rice stocks, but without much success. By the end of the occupation, much of the population could only acquire rice through the black market, and at exorbitant prices.[31]

In Malaya and the Philippines, the Japanese introduced fast-maturing strains of rice from Taiwan that made it possible to harvest two or even three crops per year. However, these varieties proved to be exceptionally vulnerable to padi blast disease and pest damage, and they required heavy fertilization as well as meticulous control of water levels. The yields in Malaya were less than one-third those of local varieties.[32]

In Vietnam, the worsening food situation led to famine in northern Vietnam, where possibly a million people died of starvation in 1945. The rice harvest was poor in 1944, and unusually severe winter weather limited production of secondary crops. Southern Vietnam had surplus grain, but

---

30 Kratoska, *The Japanese Occupation of Malaya*, pp. 247–83.
31 Ricardo T. Jose, 'The Rice Shortage and Countermeasures During the Occupation', in Ikehata and Jose (eds.), *The Philippines Under Japan*, pp. 197–214.
32 *Horaimai dan Taiwan Zairaimai* (Ipoh: Perak Shu Seicho, 2603), p. 1, copy in ANM, District Office Larut 114/2603 [1943]; 'Brief Report on Trials of Padi (Taiwan) by the Japanese in Perlis', 1945, ANM, British Military Administration file Perlis 43/1945.

bombers operating from US bases in China had destroyed road, rail and sea communications, making it impossible to ship rice from the south.[33]

In Java, the harvest fell sharply in the final years of the occupation, largely as a result of a policy that forced farmers to sell rice to the government at very low prices. There were also dramatic declines in the production of maize (down from 2.2 million tons in 1942 to under 1 million tons in 1945) and cassava (down from 8.7 million tons in 1942 to 3.1 million tons in 1945). The historian Louis de Jong has suggested that malnutrition and starvation directly or indirectly caused 2.5 million extra deaths during the occupation.[34]

Resistance to Japanese rule

As Japanese forces entered Southeast Asia in 1941, Britain's Special Operations Executive (SOE) organized stay-behind parties to operate in occupied territories and to organize local resistance groups, but the effort came very late and was seriously weakened by bureaucratic infighting. During the Occupation, SOE and the US Office of Strategic Services (OSS) had bases in China, India and Ceylon. The operations arm of SOE, Force 136, provided supplies to resistance groups in Burma and to the Malayan People's Anti-Japanese Army, and sent advisors to work with them. It also disseminated propaganda in occupied Southeast Asia, trained operatives to be dropped behind enemy lines, and developed a picture of conditions in the occupied territories by monitoring radio broadcasts, and interrogating fishermen and traders picked up from boats travelling along the coast.

Anti-Japanese resistance activity in occupied Southeast Asia fell into four categories:

1. Resistance movements that worked with the Allied powers, including USAFFE (US Armed Forces in the Far East) guerrillas in the Philippines, Force 136 in Malaya and Burma, and the Free Thai Movement.
2. Predominantly leftist anti-Japanese movements, such as the Viet Minh, the Hukbalahap in the Philippines, the Anti-Fascist Organization in Burma and the Malayan People's Anti-Japanese Army.

---

33 Nguyen The Anh, 'Japanese Food Policies and the 1945 Great Famine in Indochina', and Furuta Motoo, 'A Survey of Village Conditions During the 1945 Famine in Vietnam', both in Kratoska (ed.), *Food Supplies and the Japanese Occupation*, pp. 208–26, 227–37.
34 L. de Jong, *The Collapse of a Colonial Society: The Dutch in Indonesia During the Second World War* (Leiden: KITLV Press, 2002), p. 280.

3. Military forces trained by the Japanese that subsequently turned against Japanese rule, such as the Army for the Defence of the Fatherland (PETA) in Java and the Burma National Army.
4. Spontaneous resistance activity with socio-economic or cultural origins, such as an attack on Japanese forces at Lake Lanao in Mindanao (September 1942), the Kinabalu rebellion in Sabah (October 1943), the Singaparna peasant uprising in West Java (February 1944), and the Pontianak incidents in West Borneo in 1943 and 1944, which resulted in the execution of several hundred people, including twelve of the region's reigning sultans.[35]

Japanese propaganda in the Philippines suggested that resistance activity was pointless because the war would be settled elsewhere. 'Even if there are guerrillas launching attacks on the Japanese forces, such acts have absolutely no effect on the outcome of the war or the present situation in the Philippines. On the other hand, the retribution that will be taken by the Japanese military against such acts will not only cause trouble and suffering for the guerrillas, but also for innocent civilians.'[36] The South East Asia Command also discouraged activities likely to bring Japanese reprisals; and because of the strong communist presence in the resistance, Force 136 hesitated to supply arms and ammunition that might later be used against the Western powers. Guerrilla activity in Burma and the Philippines was important in the final stages of the occupation, but the resistance had little impact elsewhere.

In the Philippines, elements of USAFFE that had evaded capture recruited and trained guerrilla fighters, but following instructions issued by General Douglas MacArthur, they maintained a low profile pending the return of American forces. Other resistance groups took shape independently, the best known being the Hukbalahap (Hukbong Bayan Laban sa Hapon – People's Anti-Japanese Army), based on an alliance between the socialist and communist parties in central Luzon.

Before the fall of Burma, the British organized military levies in Burma's frontier areas, concentrating on the Karen, Kachin and Chin, three groups that had been active in the pre-war Burma Rifles, and in March 1943 they took steps to activate and strengthen the Northern (Kachin) and Western (Chin) Levies. Force 136 subsequently renewed contact with the Karen, and in February 1945 began arming and training Karen Levies. These fighters played

---

35 See articles in Paul H. Kratoska (ed.), *Southeast Asian Minorities in the Wartime Japanese Empire* (London: RoutledgeCurzon, 2002).
36 Nakano, 'Appeasement and Coercion', in Ikehata and Jose (eds.), *The Philippines Under Japan*, p. 46.

a crucial role in the British capture of the strong point of Toungoo.[37] In August 1944, a new broad-based Burmese organization, called the Anti-Fascist People's Freedom League (AFPFL), put out feelers to the Allies. Aung San, who took credit for bringing various parties together to form the AFPFL, said its direct aim was to gain independence for Burma.[38] On 27 March 1945, the Burma National Army changed sides, but in doing so, Aung San made it clear that he would cooperate with the Allied forces, but owed allegiance to a provisional government set up by the Anti-Fascist Organization seven months earlier. In May, Japanese forces withdrew from Rangoon, and Karen fighters are credited with killing more than 10,000 Japanese soldiers during the disorderly retreat that followed.

France established an intelligence organization in China in 1942, and in 1943, Britain's Special Operations Executive added a French Indochina Section. Between July 1944 and March 1945, General de Gaulle's provisional French government dropped personnel and supplies into Indochina, but the fact that the territories remained under French administration constrained resistance work.[39] In 1944, the Viet Minh Front of the Indochinese Communist Party, which had previously positioned itself as an opponent of fascism working in concert with other anti-fascist forces, announced its intention to create a government in opposition to both the Japanese and the French, and to resist any attempts by the British, the Americans, the USSR or China to intervene in post-war Vietnam.[40] Ho Chi Minh joined the Viet Minh in the border area in October 1944, and Vo Nguyen Giap took charge of Viet Minh military forces. They would prove to be a potent combination, but they did not act until the war ended, choosing instead to conserve their resources.

The end of the occupation

In December 1944, key Japanese and Filipino government personnel left Manila and took refuge in the mountains of northern Luzon. US forces attacked Manila in early February 1945, and the month-long battle that

---

37 Frontier Administration, NAB, series 1/1 (A), acc. no. 6277; Reorganisation of Burma Levies, NAB, series 1/1(A), acc. no. 6270; Paul H. Kratoska, 'The Karen of Burma Under Japanese Rule', in Kratoska (ed.), *Southeast Asian Minorities*, pp. 31–2.
38 'The Position on the Anti-Fascist People's Freedom League of Burma: A Statement by Major General Aung San', OSS R&A SEAC 26-R, 28 August 1945, NARA RG226 17592.
39 Claude Hesse d'Alzon, 'L'Armée française d'Indochine pendant la seconde Guerre Mondiale', in Isoart (ed.), *L'Indochine française*, pp. 113–26.
40 Phillippe Devillers, *Histoire de Viêt-Nam de 1940 à 1952* (Paris: Éditions du Seuil, 1952), p. 111.

followed caused immense damage to the city and left an estimated 100,000 Filipinos dead. Laurel was evacuated to Japan in March, and on 17 August, two days after the Japanese surrender, he declared that the Second Philippine Republic had ceased to exist.

With the collapse of the Vichy regime in 1944, a Japanese takeover of French Indochina became inevitable, but both sides hesitated to disturb the status quo. A major air raid against Vietnam on 12 January 1945 and Allied advances in the Philippines finally persuaded the Japanese that an invasion was imminent, and they carried out a *coup d'état* on 9 March 1945, which ended formal French rule. French soldiers were interned, but the Japanese instructed French civilians, apart from those in senior positions, to remain in their jobs, and most of them did so. Following the precedents set in Burma and the Philippines, the Japanese proceeded to grant independence to Laos, Cambodia and Vietnam, and recognized King Sisavangvong, King Norodom Sihanouk and Emperor Bao Dai as their respective rulers.

The Phibun government in Thailand fell in July 1944, and the new Prime Minister, Khuang Aphaiwong, cautiously tried to rebuild relations with the Allied powers without precipitating a Japanese takeover. The Japanese collapse in Burma, the coup in French Indochina, and deteriorating economic conditions within Thailand contributed to a tense and unstable situation. In May, the Free Thai movement proposed to stage an uprising against the Japanese, to be followed by an attack by the Thai army on the Japanese garrison force in Bangkok. The offer appears to have been an attempt to shore up political relations rather than to achieve any military goals, and it was shelved after Admiral Mountbatten gave instructions to postpone anti-Japanese attacks. With Japan's surrender, the Thai government declared that their declaration of war had been unconstitutional, and renounced their acquisitions of territory.[41]

In September 1944, Japan's new Prime Minister, Koiso Kuniaki, promised early independence for Indonesia and authorized the singing of the national anthem, 'Indonesia Raya', and displays of the red and white national flag. Thereafter the process stalled, but as the military situation deteriorated and the local population became more deeply mired in poverty, the Japanese found it increasingly difficult to maintain control. On 11 August 1945, the Southern Army approved an announcement of independence on 7 September, but Japan's unconditional surrender on 15 August left Indonesia's status

---

41 Reynolds, *Thailand and Japan's Southern Advance*, pp. 213, 222.

unresolved. In any case, Indonesian leaders were becoming convinced that 'independence made in Japan' would have little value. Responding to pressure from young radicals, Sukarno and Hatta issued a declaration of independence on 17 August. Ironically, this outcome suited the Japanese, who were by this time under orders to maintain the status quo until Allied troops arrived to take over, instructions they could not ignore but were loath to carry out.

The issue of collaboration

Guidance issued by the Supreme Allied Commander South East Asia warned that 'Pro-Japanese and anti-Allied opinions expressed publicly by prominent citizens during the Japanese Occupation should not be taken invariably at face value. Many such individuals have co-operated under pressure, and have acted as intermediaries on behalf of their respective communities'.[42] In some places, guerrillas attacked and killed individuals who had worked with the Japanese, but the Allied authorities showed little inclination to examine events during the occupation. The local political figures best able to help restore their authority and rehabilitate the region had participated in wartime administrations and were vulnerable to accusations of collaboration. Civil servants, who were equally at risk of being charged with collaboration, transferred their loyalty to post-war governments, maintaining a crucial element of continuity. The collaboration issue gained little traction except in the Philippines, where special People's Courts filed charges against more than 5,000 people and the issue lingered until 1948, when President Manuel Roxas granted an amnesty to all those charged except for cases that qualified as war crimes.[43]

Conclusion

Vice Admiral Lord Louis Mountbatten became Supreme Commander of a new South East Asia Command (SEAC) following the Quadrant Conference on Allied global strategy in August 1943. His military priorities were the recapture of Upper Burma to facilitate the movement of supplies into China, and seizure of the Andaman Islands to provide bases for bombing raids

---

42 SACSEA Security Intelligence for Planning Section, Proforma 'B' – Tactical: Malacca, NARA RG226 21414.

43 David Joel Steinberg, *Philippine Collaboration in World War II* (Ann Arbor: University of Michigan Press, 1967).

against Southeast Asian targets. As the campaign in the Pacific gathered momentum, Southeast Asia was increasingly marginalized. However, military activity in the region had an important political component, because Britain, the Netherlands and France wanted to regain the territories they previously controlled in the region before the war ended, in order to forestall anti-colonial pressure from the United States.

Japan's failure to satisfy the aspirations of people in the region and the hardships of the occupation had alienated the people of Southeast Asia, and they welcomed the end of the war and the departure of the Japanese. However, it quickly became apparent that there would be no restoration of the status quo ante. The occupation contributed to a new assertiveness in Southeast Asia, but the idea that Japan made an important contribution toward independence for the countries of Southeast Asia – a view that remains strong in some quarters in Japan – is not tenable. When the Japanese emperor visited Indonesia for the first time in 1991, the influential newspaper *Suara Pembaruan* carried an editorial (on 3 October) entitled 'Wound Healed, But Scar Remains', a headline that neatly encapsulated the lingering resentment in Southeast Asia of Japan's military occupation of the region.

22

The British Empire, 1939–1945

ASHLEY JACKSON

'A great Victory Parade was held in Colombo, at which some 3,500 representatives of all the services marched past in 35 minutes', wrote Admiral Lord Louis Mountbatten in his diary for 25 August 1945. As Supreme Allied Commander South East Asia, Mountbatten was proud of the size of his command, headquartered near Kandy in the highlands of Ceylon: 'At this rate the 1,380,000 men in SEAC [South East Asia Command] would take nearly 9 days and 9 nights to march past!', he noted with boyish pride. Ken Waterson, a lowlier member of the Royal Navy, was also in Ceylon at the time of the Japanese surrender and described the 'unreal atmosphere' that pervaded that memorable evening. When the news of the capitulation came through, he was on the middle watch aboard the destroyer *Relentless*, at anchor in Trincomalee harbour. The crew 'got up a singing party and took the ship's piano onto the quarterdeck', he recalled. 'There were rocket (distress flare) displays, jumping jacks and concerts. . . Ships were dressed, every colour of flag was flown. . . The dark night showed up illuminated Vs made up of coloured lightbulbs'. All the ships in harbour that night sounded their sirens, some spelling 'VJ' in Morse code; sailors got drunk and ships started firing rockets at each other and at the aircraft lined up on the deck of an aircraft carrier. Small fires broke out as awnings and gun covers caught fire, and this, in turn, led to hoses being used to dowse fires and the crews of neighbouring warships.[1]

Joyous sailors clambered over the superstructure of a British battleship in Sydney Harbour that same day; Swazi troops heard the news in North Africa; and crowds of civilians and service personnel thronged the streets of Ottawa and Toronto, as across the British Empire final victory was savoured. Yet

1 BBC World War II People's War Archive, A2237591. www.bbc.co.uk/history/ww2peopleswar/stories/91/a2237591.shtml (accessed 18 December 2014).

despite the celebrations, for the British Empire, the surrender of Germany and Japan would prove to be a pyrrhic victory. The astonishing essay in imperial power of the previous six years had brought on the climax of empire, the moment at which an overstretched system reached breaking point. Though mustering an unprecedented mobilization of imperial resources, the war plunged the British Empire into the abyss. Here, it was to find itself inadequately defended, bankrupted, buffeted by the currents of growing nationalism and communism, and dependent for survival upon a rival power, the United States of America, which placed the end of European colonialism high on its agenda.

The story of the British Empire's war, therefore, is one of imperial success in contributing toward Allied victory on the one hand, and egregious imperial failure on the other, as Britain struggled to protect people and to feed them, and failed to win the loyalty of colonial subjects – many of whom viewed the end of British rule with an indifference that shocked the British – or anti-British political leaders in Burma, Egypt, India, Iran, Iraq and Malaya, men prepared to court the enemy in their desperation to get the British out. Furthermore, Britain proved incapable of countering the corrosive effects of emerging anti-colonial superpowers that were ostensibly on the same side, or of cordoning off its own colonial affairs from the critical scrutiny of the newly founded United Nations.

With surprising parochialism, many accounts of 'Britain's war' neglect the imperial dimension that was an integral part of it. Furthermore, general histories of the Second World War – including ambitious edited volumes – often fail to capture the reliance that Britain placed upon colonial resources in prosecuting the war, and the war's impact on colonized peoples. This is part of a persistent imbalance that tends to marginalize the importance, say, of colonial food and raw materials for British larders and war industries, or the significance of imperial military formations, which were far more than just 'bolt-ons' to the British armed services. The importance of the imperial military contribution, and the Empire's role in producing the raw materials that fed Britain's global war effort, render these omissions striking. But more than this, the depth of the war's impact upon the territories and peoples of the British Empire – most of whom were 'at war' for no other reason than their colonized status – demands that this angle of vision become part of the standard British war story. Terror, mass migration, shortages, inflation, blackouts, air raids, massacres, famine, forced labour, urbanization, environmental damage, occupation, resistance, collaboration – all of these dramatic and often horrific phenomena shaped the war experience of Britain's imperial subjects. Air raids over Calcutta, Darwin, Mandalay, Singapore or Valletta, civilians fleeing the Japanese in Burma or evacuating Gibraltar, ARP wardens and rationing in Cape Town and Halifax, political ferment, enemy occupation, and the devastation of combat – the territories of the British Empire witnessed them all. This chapter explores a range of themes which offer an overview of the empire's war experience. They include an assessment of the imperial character of the 'British' war effort; the empire's contribution to Allied victory in terms of military formations, logistics and civilian labour; the colonial home front and the significance of colonial resources; the war as an engine of political and economic change; and the rise of American power in the empire.

An imperial state and an imperial war effort

The British Empire was an integrated economic, political and military zone, a veritable imperial state. In 1939, Britain was the

> only global power with interests in every continent and in theory the means to defend them. No other great power could match its combination of military (mainly naval) and economic strength or its latent ability to coerce its enemies. The intimidating scale of its territorial extent, including its self-governing member states and colonial possessions, made it hard to imagine the ultimate defeat of such a global leviathan.[2]

For Britain, the Second World War was an imperial conflict in four ways. First, the manner in which Britain fought the war was, to a significant extent, dictated by the geopolitical, logistical and resources logic of a global empire. Britain mobilized, strategized and fought imperially, using imperial military units, infrastructure and supply routes to fight campaigns in imperial zones, especially after Italy and Japan's entry into the war had made it a truly global struggle. It fought the war from the British Isles and from a network of imperial bases (in particular, Australia, Egypt and India, but also Canada, Ceylon, Singapore, South Africa and a host of smaller colonies). Be they bases for fuelling, victualling and ammunitioning warships and aircraft, docks or aerodromes, rest and recreation facilities, barracks and military headquarters establishments or intelligence-gathering posts linked to Bletchley Park, the empire provided the boards from which Britain's global war effort sprang.

---

2 John Darwin, *The Empire Project: The Rise and Fall of the British World System, 1830–1970* (Cambridge University Press, 2009), p. 476.

Second, it was an imperial war in that enemy and Allied powers alike sought to eradicate or diminish Britain's interests overseas. The Axis states wanted to conquer British colonies or replace British influence with their own in key non-European regions, while America and Russia sought to substitute British geopolitical, military and commercial power with their own. Third, it was an imperial war in the sense that a fundamental British duty was the defence of the empire and the trade and communications networks that invested it with life and substance. This was a view reinforced by the imperialist Prime Minister at the centre of the war effort, and the Tory majority in the House of Commons. This basic requirement was the subject of formalized pre-war planning and shaped the patterns of military procurement and force dispersal that governed the activities and dispositions of the empire's military formations, collectively known as imperial defence.[3]

Fourth, the Second World War was an imperial conflict because Britain depended upon imperial resources for its own survival and its ability to fight its enemies. Furthermore, as the war progressed and a dramatically altered post-war world hoved into view, Britain relied increasingly on imperial raw materials and dollar-earning potential to attempt to recover its economic independence. In a world where its power was visibly contracting, Britain came consciously to rely upon the retention of its empire, gathered closely about it like a shawl against the cold.

Britain's international political and strategic posture rested upon its alliance with the semi-autonomous Dominions, and its possession of India and a vast colonial empire. Britain was a unique belligerent, especially after its kindred imperial powers, France and Holland, had been defeated. No other power could call upon the resources that imperial statehood enabled Britain to command. It possessed within the empire significant inter-operable military forces, capable of rapid expansion, and a highly developed defensive and offensive infrastructure. It could recruit South Africans into the British Army, Jamaicans into the RAF, and Chitaggonians into the Merchant Navy, and possessed a treasure trove of strategic raw materials and other assets, envied by Britain's resource-hungry enemies.[4]

Being a part of an integrated imperial state conditioned the war experience of Britain and all of its colonies. It strongly influenced where British imperial

---

3 For an overview of the mechanisms of imperial defence, see Greg Kennedy (ed.), *Imperial Defence: The Old World Order, 1856–1956* (London: Routledge, 2008).

4 Raymond Dumett, 'Africa's Strategic Minerals During the Second World War', *Journal of African History* 26:4 (1985), 381–408.

forces fought – such as the Atlantic, Burma, East Africa, the Mediterranean, Southeast Asia and the Western Desert. It strongly influenced offensive and defensive priorities and military capabilities, the dispersal of resources and strategic prioritization, convoy and logistics routes. British power was imperial power; an empire of trade, commerce and global resources centred on Britain, cocooned by a system of imperial defence. The reverse side of this coin was that British weakness was imperial weakness, as perhaps was most graphically illustrated by the bankruptcy of the 'Singapore strategy', for so long brandished as a panacea for all the empire's defensive nightmares east of Suez. The British Empire suffered from the scourges that afflict all empires: overstretch, internal opposition and external rivalry. And despite Britain's experience of fighting global conflicts, the Second World War brought a novel dimension; for the first time, Britain faced first-class enemies not only in Europe and the Mediterranean, but in the Far East as well, and lost its chief strategic ally early in the conflict.

The sheer diversity of the imperial war effort is one of its most fascinating aspects. While much has been written about the war effort of the empire's more advanced territories (Australia, Canada, India, New Zealand and South Africa), a galaxy of 'lesser' colonies were also touched by the war in significant ways. Places as diverse as Borneo, the Cocos-Keeling Islands, Gibraltar, Sudan and Somaliland saw military action and were developed as military bases. The Gilbert Islands in the Pacific were occupied by the Japanese, as were the Andaman and Nicobar Islands in the Indian Ocean, many of the inhabitants murdered in the process. The war history of Diego Garcia, a tiny atoll in the Chagos archipelago, illustrates how even obscure 'outposts of empire' contributed to military operations and experienced distinct 'home front' challenges. In May 1941, it was decided to develop Diego Garcia and the Seychelles as way stations guarding vital Indian Ocean sea routes, and Addu Atoll in the Maldives as a secret fleet base in case Singapore was lost. To protect the sea lanes, surface, subsurface and air patrols were required, and this meant developing base facilities on remote islands, and, almost as importantly, denying them to the enemy. The decision to develop the island as a military base meant that its harbour, capable of accommodating ships up to the size of cruisers and light aircraft carriers, was equipped as a refuelling base. The island was kitted out for radio communications, as a wireless telegraphy network was cast across the Indian Ocean. Moorings and stores of fuel, ammunition and lubricants, sufficient to sustain flying-boats for a month of operations, were also built up, as Diego Garcia developed as an important base for operations, serving as part of a chain of islands across the ocean that provided anchorages for the operations of Catalina and Sunderland flying-boats. By 1944, the RAF was flying thirty sorties a month from the island. Ground forces as well as anti-aircraft batteries were needed to protect this burgeoning infrastructure, and the Diego Garcia garrison settled initially at around 500 men from Indian coastal batteries and engineer and grenadier units.

The military contribution and logistical network

The military contribution of the British Empire was a key facet of the 'British' war effort. In particular, the role of the (mainly land) forces of the 'white' Dominions and India was a definitive feature of the war and of the military power at the command of the British government. In terms of military manpower, India contributed nearly 2.5 million men, Canada over 1 million, Australia just under 1 million, South Africa 410,000, and New Zealand 215,000. The colonial empire produced over 500,000 uniformed service personnel, the majority of them from Africa. Few 'British' units – be they air force squadrons, fleets or divisions – were solely British; the Canadian navy became the third largest in the world, and Canada fielded an entire army as part of the Twenty-First Army Group on D-Day; armies such as the Eighth, Tenth, Twelfth and Fourteenth were entirely pan-imperial in their composition; units such as the King's African Rifles and Royal West African Frontier Force performed significant combat roles in East Africa and Burma; and Australians played a prominent role in Bomber Command's operations in Europe. While attention usually focuses on the larger imperial formations, such as the ANZAC divisions in the Western Desert or the Indian Army units in Burma, and while that attention increases the closer units were to front-line action, the picture of the empire's military contribution remains incomplete without reference to the host of smaller units, often engaged in essential 'rear echelon' (meaning behind the front line) military activities. These included units such as the Royal Indian Navy and the colonial naval forces of Kenya, Malaya and Trinidad; the East African Military Labour Service, the Arab Labour Corps, the 100,000 colonial subjects recruited into the Royal Pioneer Corps, and the numerous military units either created or expanded because of the war, such as the Aden Protectorate Levies, the Mauritius Defence Force, the Fiji Volunteer Corps and the Hong Kong and Singapore Garrison Artillery. Of the 32,000 Merchant Navy fatalities, over 5,000 of them were colonial subjects.

These military formations, organized into large regional commands, relied on a huge network of military bases provided by colonial territories, such as Cape Town, where nearly 6 million service personnel stopped off between the east and the west during the war. Their operations also depended on imperial air, land and sea routes in terms of logistics. Sea routes were crucial to the British Empire's war effort, and numerous colonial ports were used as bases for their defence or suffered enemy attention because of their strategic location. Air routes traversed the empire, such as the 'Takoradi air route' that ferried over 10,000 aircraft across Africa to the Middle East and India. The same was true of land lines of communication, such as the Burma and Ledo roads and the 'African Line of Communication' which moved goods overland to the Middle East fighting fronts. Sudan's road and rail network conveyed 80,000 imperial troops and 5,000 military vehicles, its airfields refuelling 15,000 aircraft transiting across Africa. The Donegal air corridor was a narrow stretch of Ireland that the Dominion's supposedly neutral government secretly allowed the RAF to traverse in order to shorten the distance between a base in Northern Ireland and the Atlantic Ocean. Colonies and Dominions trained scores of thousands of pilots for the RAF as part of the British Empire Air Training Scheme. Shipyards were developed in Canada, Ceylon and South Africa that were indispensable in refitting and repairing the thousands of merchant vessels and warships of the Merchant Navy and the Royal Navy and its colonial and Dominion partners.

Colonial home fronts

The concept of the home front is a familiar one in accounts of the British war effort, but it should also be applied to the territories of the British Empire because the war had significant, indeed sometimes profound, impacts upon the social, cultural and economic life of the empire's people. The war brought taxation, rationing, price controls and inflation, as well as profiteering. For some, it brought opportunity: military employment offered better wages, though many people were compelled to join the military or perform war-related jobs. Sex workers moved to towns in places such as Sierra Leone, to be nearer to the market created by concentrations of Allied and imperial service personnel. In territories such as India and South Africa, the war stimulated significant industrialization. But on the whole, consumption was reduced in the colonies, mirroring what was happening in Britain. Colonial home fronts were impacted by food shortages – sometimes leading to famine – and by dietary shifts, as staple foodstuffs such as rice disappeared from larders, and new ones, such as wheat, were introduced, requiring the deployment of 'nutrition demonstration units' offering bread-making lessons. The notorious Bengal famine of 1943 killed between 1.5 and 4 million people, and the presence of British and Russian occupying forces in Iran added to the food crisis of the Iranian population.

The Second World War was a war of strategic raw materials and competing labour demands. From the early days of conflict, the British government was thinking anxiously about colonial resources – including the need to deny those of French West Africa to the enemy (and secure them for itself) should France fall. The need to produce more food affected the whole empire; more food needed to be produced because less was being imported, and many regions needed to produce extra in order to feed concentrations of imperial troops, a relationship established, for example, between Britain's East African colonies and the enormous Middle East Command to its north, with a ration strength of up to a million personnel. Yet there were competing demands for labour – the imperial military had a voracious appetite for man- and woman-power, as too did war-related industries and business involved in producing essential raw materials. Many colonies walked the man- and woman-power tightrope; more women, children and old people were called upon to do what had previously been considered 'men's jobs'. War placed an enormous burden on colonial societies in terms of civil and military labour demands, the production of food and raw materials, and the operation of a global military and logistics system that depended on 'native' labour, including clearing ground for runways and constructing road networks and anti-tank defences.

New sources of colonial production were urgently developed once traditional sources had been taken by the Japanese; the loss of Malaya, for instance, led to a great expansion of Nigeria's tin industry, involving forced labour. With the loss of American and Dutch colonies in the East Indies, British African pyrethrum and sisal became highly sought-after. With the Japanese conquest of Britain's rubber plantations in Malaya, Ceylon rubber production soared, to the point where trees were slaughter-tapped to meet war demand; and Africa, which had accounted for only 1 per cent of global rubber output in 1939, was producing 30 per cent by 1945. Wartime demand for railway sleepers and other timber products rescued the Tanganyikan forestry industry, while in order to secure crucial oilfields and refineries, Britain invaded and occupied southern Iran and remilitarized Iraq. The war deepened the connection between colonial regions and the metropolitan and wider global economies. Britain benefited from the colonies as captive sources of supply in a time of great need. Regional marketing boards, such as the West African Supply Board, were created to rationalize the extraction of colonial products, such as palm oil, a priority commodity for the British fat ration. Bulk purchasing became widespread, and organizations such as the Middle East Supply Centre wielded enormous power in the import, export and distribution arrangements of huge regions.

War brought manifold disruptions, even to colonies far from the fighting fronts, such as Bechuanaland, landlocked in south central Africa, or Rodrigues in the middle of the Indian Ocean, where people prayed en masse to be delivered from the prospect of Japanese invasion. In Nigeria's Abeokutu district, struggles over foodstuffs between civilians and the military sharpened political tensions, as people sought to defend themselves in a new economic environment.[5] Freetown, meanwhile, by virtue of its status as a principal naval base and convoy mustering point, with up to 200 vessels in harbour during peak periods, experienced rapid urbanization. Its expansion and strategic importance caused the colonial government to attempt to stimulate a wartime mentality among the population, and also brought strikes among workers developing their collective bargaining power.

As an additional disruption to people's lives, the war caused significant migrations and shifting patterns of temporary settlement. Tens of thousands fled the Japanese advance from Burma into India, and similar numbers of Polish refugees crossed from the USSR into Iran and India via the Caspian Sea.[6] Thousands of civilians and military personnel fled the Dutch East Indies, Malaya and Singapore for Australia and Ceylon. Ceylon then became home to tens of thousands of African, Australian, British and Indian servicemen and women, initially in order to resist a possible Japanese attack, and then as it became a major base for military operations in Burma, Southeast Asia and the Indian Ocean. Bechuanaland lost 20 per cent of its adult male population to the army, and many more to the mines of South Africa, which were given permission to recruit despite the manpower shortage, because gold and minerals were considered vital war-related materials. Jews fleeing Central Europe were dispersed around

---

5 Judith Byfield, 'Feeding the Troops: Soldiers, Rice, and Economic Crisis in Abeokutu (Nigeria) During the Second World War', in Judith Byfield, Carolyn Brown, Timothy Parsons and Ahmad Sikaingi (eds.), *Africa in World War Two* (Cambridge University Press, 2015).
6 Anuradha Bhattacharjee, *The Second Homeland: Polish Refugees in India* (London: Sage, 2012).

the empire, having been denied access to Palestine, including 1,500 who spent the war as internees in Mauritius.[7] Gibraltar's civilian population was almost entirely evacuated in order to expedite its conversion into a military bastion; in Malta, Valletta's population fell from 21,000 to 6,000, and 35,000 houses were destroyed or damaged, with over 5,000 Maltese citizens killed or wounded. Thousands of European civilians fled Egypt and Malaya and headed for Australia, Ceylon and South Africa. The bombing of Calcutta caused people to flee, as did the April 1942 raids on Colombo and Trinco-malee. The Japanese bombing of Rangoon on 23 December 1941 caused an exodus of 75 per cent of the city's population. On Masirah Island at the mouth of the Persian Gulf,

> a considerable amount of trouble was encountered with the local inhabitants in connection with the unloading of stores for HM [His Majesty's] Forces stationed there. As a result, most of the people fled from the Island and only a few have since returned. There are, however, now several hundred Muscati and a few Aden labourers who have been brought to the Island for the work required by the British and US Forces there.[8]

A minor, yet representative example of the fact that any place, anywhere, gains strategic importance, and the lives of these few hundred marginalized people, disrupted by war, are as much a part of the war's story as are those of the people on the British home front.

Partly as a result of the multiple migrations of civilians and military personnel, the war fostered a range of cross-cultural contacts between indigenous people and outsiders, as well as significant environmental change. Some had the most profound consequences, such as the cargo cults of New Guinea and certain Melanesian islands. Overwhelmed with the material bounty of Japanese or Allied soldiers during their transient stay, when the occupiers departed, ceremonies and rituals developed in order to get the 'cargo' to return, often involving the crude manufacture of imitation docks or aerodromes, and transmitters made of wood and coconut.[9] Transnational relations had noticeable effects in other parts of the empire too: the enor-mous war effort of India, and the deep penetration of war-related activity,

---

7 See Genevieve Pitot, *The Mauritian Shekel: The Story of Jewish Refugees in Mauritius, 1940–1945* (London: Rowman & Littlefield, 2000).

8 The National Archives, Kew (TNA), CAB 66/66/3, Arabia – Acquisition of Masirah Island as a Permanent RAF Base, Memorandum by the Secretaries of State for Air and India, 29 May 1945.

9 See Holger Jebens (ed.), *Cargo, Cult and Culture Critique* (Honolulu: University of Hawaii Press, 2004).

reshaped military and civilian relations.[10] Widespread prostitution was one aspect of the gendered wartime economy, closely linked to the subcontinent's militarization and to the effects of the 1943 Bengal famine. Elsewhere, Nigerian prostitutes moved to the Gold Coast to take advantage of the influx of foreign troops.[11]

As well as the repercussions associated with the arrival of large numbers of soldiers, for civilians in many colonies the war's main effects were the reduction of supplies and the growing disruption brought by military activities. This had a range of effects, including changing use of land and buildings and an increase in the volume of traffic, both on land and in the air. In some colonies, tracts of land were taken over for the construction of military bases – barracks, airstrips and so on – or cordoned off as 'no go' areas reserved for military activities, such as jungle training and live firing exercises, including naval gunfire support. Vast swathes of bush and forest were cleared across the empire; coconut trees were bulldozed on the Cocos-Keeling Islands, so that pierced steel planking could be laid down for runways from which RAF aircraft could operate over occupied Southeast Asia, while Mountbatten's new South East Asia Command aerodrome in Ceylon destroyed 7,000 trees. Other land, meanwhile, was made over to food crops in an effort to boost self-sufficiency, given the shortage of shipping and available imports. In Bechuanaland, tribal chiefs were required to allocate communal 'war lands' and oblige their people to work them in order to build food reserves. In Ceylon, a sophisticated poster campaign associated growing food with supporting the war effort, and booklets on how to grow better crops were distributed, along with stickers and calendars encouraging ever greater agricultural endeavour. Special labour gangs, such as the Mauritius Civil Labour Corps and the Cochin State Civil Labour Unit, were recruited to perform war-related home front tasks. As in Britain, digging for victory became a major theme, encountered in the propaganda of the colonial state and in people's daily lives.

The extent to which the empire's home front experience mirrored that of Britain was evident in many ways, such as the requisitioning of buildings for military purposes. The National Museum of Ceylon in Colombo was commandeered as Army Headquarters, its collections damaged or lost in the

10 See Yasmin Khan, 'Sex in an Imperial War Zone: Transnational Encounters in Second World War India', *History Workshop Journal* 73:1 (2012), 240–58.
11 Carina Ray, 'Racial Politics of Anti-Prostitution Legislation: Sex Trade in British West Africa', in Byfield et al. (eds.), *Africa and World War Two*.

hasty removal and storage. The Gordon Memorial College on the banks of the Blue Nile in Khartoum was taken over for the same purpose, hampering the college's move toward university college status; students were obliged to evacuate King's College Lagos to make way for service personnel, leading to a student strike. In Colombo, schools and colleges were requisitioned for the Far East Combined Bureau, an intelligence outpost of Bletchley Park, and for the Eastern Fleet's large shore establishment. The Raffles Hotel in Singapore was taken over by the Japanese, then at the end of the war employed as a transit camp for liberated prisoners of war returning home. The headquarters building of the Hongkong and Shanghai Bank in Statue Square, Hong Kong, was employed as the headquarters of the Japanese army, the bank's operations moving to London for the duration. In Bangalore, Chinese evacuees from Malacca were ordered to leave their houses for 'so-called Military use'. A concerned Tan Cheng Lock, a prominent Chinese Malayan public figure, feared for his home-in-exile on Millers Road. Having fled his home in Singapore, his new home in Bangalore was threatened with requisition, the military already having taken over the grounds of the Theological College next door.[12] In Singapore, the clubhouse of the Ceylon Sports Club was used by the British Army to store drums of petrol, until dynamited the evening before the island surrendered. The Japanese military then built barracks on the site, and its playing fields were cultivated in order to grow banana, tapioca and sweet potato.[13]

Occupation and liberation (to the extent that genuine liberation was ever possible in the context of competing imperialisms) are essential themes in the study of the British Empire at war, because many British colonies either fell to the enemy or were threatened by them (most notably the Japanese, but also the Germans, Italians and Vichy French), and because the British occupied significant Italian and French colonial holdings in Africa and the Indian Ocean region, as well as acting as proxy colonial liberators on behalf of France and Holland in Indochina and the East Indies. The Gilbert and Solomon Islands and New Guinea in the Pacific, Hong Kong, Brunei, North Borneo, Sarawak, Labuan, Singapore, Malaya, Burma, parts of India, and the Andaman and Nicobar Islands were taken by the Japanese, British Somaliland, more briefly, by the Italians.

---

12 TCL Papers, Institute of South-east Asian Studies, Singapore, TCL 16/6, Tan Cheng Lock to Walter Fletcher, 1 March 1943.

13 National Archives of Singapore, CORD 002330, transcript of interview with Velayuther Ambiavagar.

Furthermore, many British colonies and ex-colonies were 'occupied' during the war by significant concentrations of Allied service personnel, including Australia, Ceylon, Egypt, Fiji, the Gold Coast, India, Iraq, Sierra Leone and the West Indies. 'Cairo still looks like an occupied city with camps all round it and in some of its parks', reported a British official in 1945.[14] Britain's occupation by hundreds of thousands of American service personnel was replicated across the empire, the presence of American units reflecting the republic's waxing power across the globe. The USA grew rapidly as a power in regions where the British traditionally claimed paramountcy. The September 1940 destroyers-for-bases agreement brought a growing American presence into parts of Newfoundland and the British West Indies; at one time, there were 20,000 Americans in Trinidad; over 10,000 in the Gold Coast, operating the air route across Africa to the Middle East; and 30,000 in Iran, as part of the new US Persian Gulf Command. Some British Pacific colonies were swamped with foreign soldiers too, and over a million Americans (including 100,000 African Americans) were based in Australia, 'over-sexed and over-paid' 'Yanks' stimulating the same kind of reaction as they did when billeted for lengthy periods near civilian populations in Britain.[15] Australian indigenous peoples and those of islands such as the New Hebrides wondered at the appearance, comportment and apparent affluence and power of African Americans. In Ceylon and Mauritius, meanwhile, local people were afraid of African troops, fearing their rumoured 'savagery' and even fleeing villages in order to avoid them.

Political change

While the traumas visited upon the French imperial structure because of metropolitan defeat were not shared by the British, local defeat in so many colonies irrevocably altered the basis of colonial rule once it had been re-established, and also fostered civil conflict in places such as Malaya, and between pro-Vichy and pro-Free French factions in Mauritius. The war greatly accelerated India's move toward independence, transformed the politics of Palestine, and brought demands for constitutional advance in

14 TNA, CAB 66/67/5, Imperial Security in the Middle East, 2 July 1945.
15 See Philip Bell and Roger Bell, *Implicated: The United States in Australia* (Melbourne: Oxford University Press, 1993). Fascinating recent work examines anti-racist and anti-colonial connections between Indians and African Americans. See Gerald Horne, *The End of Empires: African Americans and India* (Philadelphia, Pa.: Temple University Press, 2009).

colonies such as Ceylon and Nigeria. It is easy, from a metropolitan vantage point, to miss the tumult that war brought to many parts of the empire. On the political level, it transformed Britain's capacity to retain the empire because it destroyed the global preconditions upon which the British world system depended. On the ground in the colonies, war upset political relationships, increased the potency of nationalism, and strained the collaborative relations upon which British rule was based, as colonial intermediaries were asked to demand more of their people, and in turn demanded more of the British, and often took the opportunity to ask for political advancement in return.

From the Andaman Islands in the Indian Ocean to the Gilbert Islands in the Pacific, via the Malay barrier and Borneo, the British and their imperial allies were defeated by Japanese occupying forces, later to return as liberators. In attempting to expel the enemy, the British faced the awkward implications of arming movements resisting the Japanese that would later strive to eject the British, or working with forces, such as the Burma National Army, that had until recently fought for the enemy. The war also weakened (though by no means severed) Britain's political influence vis-à-vis the 'white' Dominions of Australia, Canada, New Zealand and South Africa. These were the core members of the British Commonwealth-Empire, technically independent since the Statute of Westminster, but dependent upon Britain in numerous ways, not least for their security. Ensuring the unity of the Commonwealth alliance had been a key consideration in the diplomacy leading to the declaration of war in September 1939. But the war speeded up the Dominions' push for greater autonomy within a redefined imperial framework, and Britain's inability to guarantee their security further loosened the ties that bound. Symbolizing this transforming relationship, Australia, Canada and New Zealand concluded formal defence treaties with America, the coming superpower, which excluded Britain.

The loss of political authority in conquered colonies was lethal for the future prospects of the British Empire. So, too, were some of the measures employed to win these territories back or foment resistance to Japanese invaders, such as arming and aiding (though never controlling) Chinese communist rebels of the Malayan People's Anti-Japanese Army, many of whom would later oppose the colonial regime during the Malayan Emergency. The occupation itself significantly altered the political landscape – for example, the authority of the Malayan kings, upon which the British sought to rebuild their rule, had been seriously diminished by Japanese policies. The same was true in Palestine, a territory where war completely undermined Britain's already precarious position. Here, military authorities allowed Jewish paramilitary and intelligence outfits a great deal of autonomy, to the chagrin of the Palestine government, in order to prepare the mandate for possible German attack. Before the war, the British had been trying to negotiate the Arab-Jewish tightrope, keen to use Palestine as a strategic base in case its position in Egypt became untenable. The Holocaust, adroit wartime manoeuvring by the Zionist movement, and the mounting gravity of the USA's voice in Palestinian affairs, meant that at the end of the war, British ambitions for the territory were in tatters. Rather than seeing Palestine as a potential base for the Middle East strategic reserve, the British now looked simply for a speedy exit from the Palestine imbroglio with the least possible dishonour, while salvaging the best possible relations with the region's Arab polities. Again indicating the way in which the war transformed relations between Britain and colonial and semi-colonial regions, London's gaze now came to rest on Libya as a base for British interests in the region.[16]

The war was also a game-changer for Britain's position in India. With the August offer (1940) and the Cripps offer (1942), promising post-war independence, London effectively abdicated control of the constitutional timetable. This was a novel and unforeseen eventuality born of the dire circumstances of early 1942, when imperial redoubts were crumbling east of Suez, Rommel was approaching Cairo, and Japanese forces had entered India. This situation, and the reliance on Muslim India for soldiers, also turned the prospect of a separate Pakistani state from a pipedream into a real political possibility.

The need to curb protest and ensure a clear field for military tasks led to 'war imperialism' – robust military and police actions considered necessary in terms of winning the war, but auguring ill for attempts to win the colonial peace. Such actions included imprisoning political opponents and threatening or deposing unhelpful rulers. Thus, in India, leading Congressmen were incarcerated and their activities outlawed; in Iraq, Britain overthrew Rashid Ali's government because of his anti-British and pro-Nazi predilections and his attack on British bases in his country; in Cairo, the Abdin Palace was surrounded by armoured cars, and the khedive offered the choice of signing a British-prepared abdication document or appointing a less pro-Nazi government. In order to protect its vital oil interests, in 1941, Britain invaded Iran in conjunction with the Russians, and deposed and exiled the Shah. Political

---

16 See Saul Kelly, *War and Politics in the Desert: Britain and Libya During the Second World War* (London: Society for Libyan Studies, 2010).

change caused by the war could be slow-burning; in Kenya, wartime food shortages enabled white settlers to farm their land profitably, and because of this, they gained greater political purchase over the colonial state. They were able to eject Kikuyu 'squatters' from their land, thus creating the conditions that led to the Mau Mau rebellion.

Mobilizing the empire to assist in Britain's fight against the Axis powers required bargaining with colonial elites and their people. In West Africa, there was a view among the educated elite, articulated in the region's vibrant African-owned press, that while fighting Hitler and racism was a logical thing to do, Africans should expect to see political advancement once the war had ended. The wording of the Atlantic Charter, signed by Churchill and Roosevelt in August 1941, was widely reported, and its expansive pledges to non-independent peoples duly noted, to Churchill's chagrin. U Saw, the Burmese leader, asked Churchill during a meeting in October 1941 to apply the Charter's third clause, the right to self-determination, in the case of Burma, in return for support during the war.

Propaganda activities were needed in order to try to win people's favour and active participation, and this required the construction of arguments about the benefits of British rule. Posters, leaflets and films devised under the aegis of the Crown Film Unit and the Ministry of Information were all deployed in pursuit of this, as were agents such as Freya Stark, battling Axis influence in Aden and Iraq. 'Partnership' replaced 'trusteeship' in the language of colonial administration, and Americans were targeted, Lord Hailey assigned the task of showing the sceptical ally how enlightened British rule really was.[17]

As the war developed, it was widely recognized that new constitutions were needed for politically advanced colonies such as Ceylon and Nigeria, and for those such as Burma which had been occupied. An indication of the speed of the political shifts caused by the war was the abortive nature of constitutions and political plans intended to be applied when the British regained their colonies from the Japanese. The Malayan Planning Unit was established in the War Office's Civil Affairs Directorate in July 1943, comprising nearly 300 military and civilian officials planning for the insertion of a British Military Administration once the Japanese had been evicted. It envisioned the post-war world, while Sir Reginald Dorman-Smith, Governor of Burma, sat in exile in the Indian hill station of Simla planning for the future.

---

17 Suke Wolton, *Lord Hailey, the Colonial Office, and the Politics of Race and Empire During the Second World War: The Loss of White Prestige* (Basingstoke: Macmillan, 2000).

Often, the meticulously crafted new constitutions were stillborn, such was the power and pace of the political demands tabled by increasingly articulate colonial politicians. In Ceylon, ministers had originally accepted the 1943 Declaration as a basis for interim reforms which would enable them to increase the war effort of Ceylon. But little more than a year later, Mr Senanayake, Leader of the State Council, said that he was 'no longer prepared to proceed on the basis of the 1943 Declaration, but wished to press for the grant of Dominion Status'. In making his 'plea', Senanayake said that he was expressing the views of 'the great majority of the people of Ceylon'. He was unwilling to sponsor the recommendations of the Soulbury Commission, responsible for constitutional advance in Ceylon, without something to show for his visit to Britain.[18] The May 1945 White Paper on Burmese constitutional advance offered a completely underwhelming three-stage programme of gradual political advancement, leading to possible independence no earlier than 1953. Burmese nationalists would not countenance it.

Demands for independence and pressure on the empire from outside occurred just as Whitehall came to appreciate fully how deeply Britain's economic recovery depended upon it, and how essential it was to Britain's status as a world power. The Middle East serves as an example of a region where these difficulties were starkly manifest. It was identified by the British government as essential to Britain's continued position as a world power. The Middle East abounded with 'vital' features and resources: Egypt and the Levant remained of great strategic importance; the region was a channel of communications, a strategic centre, the empire's main oil reservoir and, in the words of Sir Edward Bridges (Cabinet Office) and Sir Edward Grigg (Resident Minister Middle East), 'a region in which British political method must make good, if the British way of life is to survive'. The government considered it 'a region of life-and-death consequence for Britain and the British Empire'. But securing British interests here had become tougher as a result of the war. Political and financial conditions dictated policy: in pursuing British interests in the Middle East, for example, 'we are now entering an era in which political considerations will infallibly predominate'.[19] While military strength remained important, Bridges and Grigg told the War Cabinet, 'we shall not be able in peace to ride roughshod over political considerations as we have done at necessity in war'. Acknowledging

---

18 TNA, CAB 129/3, Cabinet, Ceylon Constitution, Report by the Lord Privy Seal, Chairman of the Colonial Affairs Committee, 23 October 1945.
19 TNA, CAB 66/67/5, Imperial Security in the Middle East, 2 July 1945.

the superpowers' new-found strength, and Britain's need for allies, the British government also recognized that its 'status and influence' depended upon its being the 'parent state' to the Commonwealth. Hard work lay ahead if this position was to be maintained in the Middle East, the report recognized, and Britain could not 'expect the sensitive young nationalist movements of the Middle East to accept direction and control from us merely because it is necessary to us'. People had to be persuaded and, using classic horse-and-rider imperial language, 'we must ride them with the loosest possible rein...humouring their national sensitivities in every possible way', especially by giving 'close attention to the trappings of national independence' and fielding 'American complaints against us'. But as the British were soon to discover, in the post-war climate, this was to be insufficient nourishment for a new, more powerful and increasingly globalized anti-colonialism.

The rise of other powers and the United Nations

Another factor weakening the empire was the rise of other powers, accelerated by the war, which threatened British imperial interests. One such power was China, though it was the USA's tremendous ascent in parts of the world previously dominated by Britain, including the Mediterranean and parts of Africa, Asia and the Middle East, that stood out. The war brought American competition for markets in many parts of the empire, demands for the termination of the old system of closed colonial economies, and the foundations of a new, American-led world order. It also brought a large military footprint, including hundreds of Flying Fortresses and Super Fortresses stationed in India. Churchill lamented the subordination of British strategy to American aims in places such as Burma, the Mediterranean and Southeast Asia, and clashed with Roosevelt over India's political future. In the Middle East, the USA encouraged state builders to 'transcend British tutelage en route to American-mandated post-colonial status'.[20] Anglo-American competition was visible in many parts of the world, such as the tussle over Venezuelan oil as two allied but rival commercial powers jockeyed for advantage; and in Saudi Arabia, where American petroleum rights were compromised by sterling area provisions.[21]

---

20 Simon Davis, 'The Middle East and World War Two', in Thomas Zeiler (ed.), *A Companion to World War Two* (Hoboken, NJ: Wiley Blackwell, 2012), pp. 317–21.
21 See Mark Seddon, 'Incorporating Corporations: Anglo-American Oil Diplomacy and Conflict Over Venezuela, 1941–1943', *Journal of Transatlantic Studies* 10:2 (2012), 134–49; and Davis, 'The Middle East and World War Two', for Saudi Arabia.

The USA's entry into previously exclusively British zones, often as a dominant partner, and its ambivalent or distinctly critical stance on British 'imperialism', created interfaces of friction all over the world. The High Commissioner in Pretoria, Sir Evelyn Baring, wrote that American influence in South Africa 'will produce many thorny problems for you [the British government]'.[22] The nationalists, Baring reported, look to the USA, not Britain. 'American influence is growing in many spheres of life. American ideas are welcomed by Nationalists who wish to be rid of the charge of being isolationists yet continue to hate the British'. The USA was all the rage, the High Commissioner noting, for example, that there was a demand for American cars which were 'far more suitable to rough conditions than British models'. Other examples of 'American infiltration' included the popularity of American expertise on the soil erosion question.

Whitehall monitored the 'receptioning' of Americans in the colonies. In the Pacific and the Caribbean, troubled waters had to be calmed at intergovernmental level, and prickly British officers or governors moved on in order to placate incoming Americans and smooth Allied relations. Such moves included the dispatch of Sir Bede Clifford from Mauritius to the governorship of Trinidad, where it was hoped that his pro-American outlook, American wife and personal friendship with the President would help resolve problems caused by the influx of American service personnel and senior commanders and the resistance of in situ British authorities.

At Yalta, Churchill 'declared that Britain would not permit the Empire to be placed in the dock and subjected to international examination'.[23] But the Yalta Protocol committed Britain to consult with the USA and China on colonial matters.[24] This was a familiar pattern toward the end of the war: Britain proclaiming in stentorian voice that the empire was not up for grabs, its future not negotiable, while all around its status in the international order was being renegotiated, despite attempts to ring-fence it from the unwelcome intrusions of external powers and 'busybody' organizations like the UN. The threat could also come from within the fold; though the British government was keen to ensure maximum unity with the Dominions in

22 TNA, CAB 129/2, Cabinet, Political Affairs in South Africa. Memorandum by Secretary of State for Dominion Affairs, 18 September 1945, letter from Sir Evelyn Baring (22 August 1945).
23 Piers Brendon, 'Churchill and Empire', in Brian Farrell (ed.), *Churchill and the Lion City: Shaping Modern Singapore* (National University of Singapore Press, 2011), p. 27.
24 TNA, CAB 66/64/8, War Cabinet, International Aspects of Colonial Policy, Memorandum by the Secretary of State for Foreign Affairs, 31 March 1945.

order to gain their support at international meetings such as the 1945 Council of Foreign Ministers, colonial politicians were themselves arguing for change.[25] India wanted out, and Australia and New Zealand 'strongly urged that the United Kingdom Government should take the lead in putting our Colonies under some measure of international trusteeship'. While the thrust of this drive was aimed at colonies being returned to France and Portugal, whose colonial record was considered less than ideal, it was necessary for Britain to comply too. It 'was just as important to do something to meet American criticism, however unjustified, of the Colonial activities of the Commonwealth'.[26] Frustrated British policy-makers pointed to alleged American double standards – for example, regarding the desire to retain islands prised from the Japanese by American arms. 'The one thing that matters is that the United States, while occupying the islands, should not appear to have theoretical sovereignty over them (for that would be Imperialism)'.[27] The British, for their part, were desperate to avoid 'throwing the whole Colonial Empire open to discussion by this motley assembly'.[28]

Conclusion

Appearances can be deceptive. Because the British Empire emerged from the debris of war intact, and because the first major decolonization did not take place until two years had elapsed between the guns falling silent and the lowering of the Union Flag in India, it might appear that the war did not significantly affect the British Empire. Nothing could be further from the truth. The war holed the British Empire below the waterline, and from 1945 on, it was a slowly sinking vessel that had been taking on water even before the conflict erupted. After that, it was all about managing decline and attempting to deal with the Cold War and retain a world role. Though there were bursts of imperial vigour after the war, not least the 'second colonial occupation' of Africa and Southeast Asia, they were born of now terminal weakness and the overwhelming need to rely on the empire, given that

25 TNA FO 800/443, Private Papers of Sir Ernest Bevin: Commonwealth and Colonial Territories, 1945–1946, Notes of Meeting in the Foreign Secretary's Room, 21 August 1945.
26 TNA, CAB 66/64/28, War Cabinet, International Aspects of Colonial Policy, Memorandum by the Secretary of State for Dominion Affairs, 10 April 1945.
27 TNA, CAB 66/63/55, War Cabinet, International Aspects of Colonial Policy, Memorandum by the Chairman of the Armistice and Post-War Committee, 28 March 1945.
28 TNA, CAB 66/64/8, War Cabinet, International Aspects of Colonial Policy, Memorandum by the Secretary of State for Foreign Affairs, 31 March 1945.

Britain had hit the buffers. Like a necromancer summoning his most puissant spell, the war educed the most remarkable display of imperial power, yet in that very effort enervated it to the point of collapse. This unravelling was aided by the demands of colonial peoples for a measure of the 'New Jerusalem' and enhanced democracy that the people of Britain were being offered as a reward for their wartime efforts.

Having said all that, this only became clear with hindsight. Looking forward from the vantage point of 1945 into an unknown future, it was all to play for, and British policy-makers set to the task with gusto. Yes, India had been offered independence and it was only a matter of time before it was granted. But the rest of the empire remained in tow, and the Dominions had not yet flown the nest, even though they were becoming far bolder in testing their wings. The determination on the part of the British government to ensure that the British Empire-Commonwealth remained a major force in global affairs remained strong too. Even though the war had irrevocably undermined the empire, some things took time to change. As the war was ending, the British government was manoeuvring to acquire new territory in order to protect its strategic interests. Libya was desired; so too was Masirah Island. The Secretaries of State for Air and for India recommended to the Cabinet that the government acquire a ninety-nine-year lease on the island from the Sultan of Muscat.[29] The island was valued as an air and naval base for patrolling the region, as a staging post on the South Arabian reinforcement and transport route to India, and as the hub of an air cover system also involving Aden, Bombay and Karachi. Brigadier Enoch Powell, meanwhile, was in Delhi as part of a planning team considering how to fight the next world war, against the USSR, using India as a strategic base.

Even though British rule remained in place throughout most of the empire, its geostrategic foundations had shifted. As Jan Smuts wrote to the Foreign Secretary in December 1945, 'in the Pacific in particular the UK will in future be largely dependent on the USA for the defence of British Commonwealth interests'.[30] The British Empire was beset by advancing threats. The international political landscape was visibly shifting to Britain's disadvantage, the country was bankrupt and nationalism stronger than ever before. Ultimately, the greatest threat came from Britain's allies and forces inside the empire, not from the enemies against which it had fought.

---

29 TNA, CAB 66/66/3, Cabinet, Arabia – Acquisition of Masirah Island as a Permanent RAF Base, Memorandum by the Secretaries of State for Air and India, 29 May 1945.
30 TNA, FO 800/443, Foreign Office to British Delegation Moscow, 21 December 1945.

The Foreign Office, in particular, was preoccupied, as the war's end came into sight, with the global implications of the emerging Cold War, adjusting to the protrusion of American power and the novel demands of the emergent United Nations, and dealing with Commonwealth, particularly Australian, desires for greater autonomy and greater consultation and cooperation. Metropolitan dependence on the empire for economic recovery was a symptom of war, leading to measures such as the 1945 Colonial Development and Welfare Act. It was a milestone piece of legislation, heralding a new policy regarding metropolitan investment in colonial development, a grand scheme to stimulate British recovery through more profitable colonial development policies.

Imperial territories, meanwhile, had been transformed by the war. Burma, for instance, had been devastated by two major military campaigns, laid waste by both sides, and its economy ruined. The High Commissioner in South Africa reported that rising gold prices started a boom that was given added impetus by war spending. This featured British government expenditure on provisions for convoys, investment in facilities for the South African branch of the British Empire Air Training Scheme, ship repairs, the receipt of large orders from members of the Eastern Group Supply Council, and demand for South African manufactured goods from adjoining territories deprived of overseas shipments.[31] By 1945, South Africa had become a creditor country and had built up a large number of secondary industries, notably state-owned steel, coal and iron. These developments, together with the problems associated with soil exhaustion, had led to a drift to the towns. Riots and racial divisions were becoming more intense, and pass laws and labour migration were key issues.

Chairing a session of the War Cabinet in April 1945, Winston Churchill welcomed Field Marshal Smuts, Peter Fraser (Prime Minister of New Zealand), Frank Forde (Australian Minister of Defence), Dr Herbert Evatt (Australia's Minister for External Affairs), Field Marshal Lord Wavell (Viceroy of India) and Sir Firoz Khan Noon (member of the Viceroy's Council and Indian delegate at the San Francisco Conference). The meeting reviewed the 'world situation', the Prime Minister stating that 'recent developments had caused him to reflect upon the future role of the British

---

31 The Eastern Group Supply Council was formed in Delhi in October 1940, aimed at joint war supply of munitions and stores for 'eastern group' colonies, to ensure fullest cooperation for war purposes and to relieve Britain of as much of the burden of overseas war production and supply as possible.

Commonwealth in world affairs'. It was a gloomy picture. Difficulties with the USSR were mounting, and American power was now 'vastly superior to our own'. These were the 'dominating facts in the world situation', and Britain could only hold its own by 'superior statecraft and experience and, above all, by the unity of the British Commonwealth of Nations'. Smuts, Jonah-like, pointed out the continued need for secure sea lines of communication – the empire's spinal column – but that, problematically, Britain was no longer the predominant naval power. Relations with the Dominions were increasingly ambiguous. The most dramatic development in Britain's modern imperial history was gathering pace too: at this Cabinet meeting, Wavell argued that India was the 'urgent' post-war problem, and that the prestige and power of the British Commonwealth would depend very largely on 'our having found a solution of the Indian problem' and launched it as an important player in world affairs.[32]

John Darwin writes that the 'strategic catastrophe of 1938 to 1942 and its devastating impact on the central elements of [the British world] system, were together so crushing that recovery (after 1945) was merely short-lived remission'.[33] Because of the war, Britain lost the vast bulk of its sterling assets, especially its dollars, wrecking the balance of payments; and its property empire was, to a large degree, liquidated. This forced Britain's retreat into a closed sterling zone and gravely damaged prospects of industrial modernization. The war transformed the terms of the Anglo-American relationship, making Britain dependent on the United States of America, a dependence only marginally offset by the value of Britain's contribution to a widening Cold War. The war also brought 'the lapse of Britain's claim to the (more or less) unconditional loyalty of the overseas dominions, and the irrecoverable offer of independence to India to meet the desperate emergency of 1942, marked the practical end of the British system created in the mid-nineteenth century'.[34]

---

32 CAB 65/52/1 WM (45), 39th Conclusions, Minute 1, Confidential Annex, 3 April 1945, Review of World Situation. Noon made a fascinating point, saying that when he 'reflected upon the magnitude of India's war effort, he was sometimes surprised that China should be generally regarded as the fifth of the Great Powers; and he wondered whether it might not prove wiser to look to India rather than China to play a leading role in world affairs in the East after the war'.

33 Darwin, The Empire Project, p. 649.

34 Ibid., p. 14.

23

France and its colonial civil wars, 1940–1945

MARTIN THOMAS

When France went to war in September 1939, it did so as a global imperial power. At this point, empire and its attendant social and cultural relationships, often collectively described by the short-hand term 'colonialism', were still part of the normative standards of global politics. France was only one of several European colonial powers. Other states, notably Japan and the United States, had also established more recent colonial empires of their own. The Soviet Union might be counted a Russian-led empire of sorts.[1] And imperial expansion was, of course, intrinsic to the coming global conflict. Six years later, the situation was much different. The French Empire emerged from the Second World War mired in crisis, and only partially intact. While it could be argued that economic disruption, social protest and acute ethnic discrimination were already endemic in numerous overseas territories of 'Greater France', all increased under the pressures of war. That pressure became manifest in different, but always disintegrative ways. Between 1939 and 1945, this empire experienced three types of armed conflict – world war, civil war and contested decolonization. Together, these violent currents would transform the empire's internal dynamics and the prospects for its continuation.

An empire at war with itself

Much of this was unanticipated by the empire's rulers before the calamitous French defeat of June 1940. Before then, the talk was of raw materials and

---

1 Ronald Grigor Suny, 'The Empire Strikes Out: Imperial Russia, "National" Identity, and Theories of Empire', in Ronald Grigor Suny and Terry Martin (eds.), *A State of Nations: Empire and Nation-Making in the Age of Lenin and Stalin* (Oxford University Press, 2001), pp. 23–57.

foodstuffs, additional human capacity, heightened colonial taxation revenue and strategic bases; in short, of the material basis of imperial power in war. These resources remained hugely significant to France's new rulers and their domestic opponents after the surrender to Germany, not least as they became central to the bargains made with the victorious occupiers. Of greater significance for colonial populations were the coercive means employed to mesh dependent territories into serving rival war efforts as the empire fractured. For much of the Second World War, fighting within colonial territory was Franco-French, part of an undeclared civil war between the Vichy regime and its ideological enemies. Once that civil war ended with liberation, Vichy's demise and the ascendancy of the resistance movements agitating for the restoration of democracy to mainland France, deeper, more intractable decolonization struggles between colonial peoples and French imperial authorities emerged from the shadows. The result was that by the summer of 1945, key French territories descended into conflicts that, in many ways, touched colonial lives more directly than the preceding World War. Any understanding of France's colonial Second World War hinges on explaining this dissonance between rulers and ruled.

The empire's governing elites were bitterly divided about the causes of France's defeat, about its implications for republican democracy, about the probable outcome of the war. Their argument concerned the complexion of French society; what adversity had revealed it to be and how to remake it. Measured by the objectives of its principal combatants, the French colonial civil war was not colonial at all. Rather, it was a conflict over who should determine the restoration of French independence and what should follow it. Equally, for colonial populations, the eventual liberation of France in 1944–45 was no liberation at all. Even when the wider war interceded, as, for instance, when Japanese forces occupied Southern Indochina in 1941, or when US and British imperial forces fought to expel Erwin Rommel's army from French North Africa in 1942–43, the quarrels between Vichy supporters and their resistance opponents predominated in French minds and actions.

Phrased differently, empire provided the terrain, but not the agenda for the French leadership contest fought out between 1940 and 1945. The upshot was that France's wartime faction fights, although substantially played out in colonial theatres, were peculiarly skewed toward a domestic struggle for power. Fought in the midst of colonial subjects and frequently exploiting them to do the actual fighting, this internecine struggle remained curiously removed from the daily lives of colonial communities, for whom more fundamental questions of food supply, under-employment and basic rights figured larger. Administrative elites obsessed with events in France, and their colonial subjects preoccupied by the local impact of a war not of their choosing – the disjuncture between the powerful and the disenfranchised in the French Empire stretched to breaking point. It was no coincidence that rebellion broke out in eastern Algeria on the very day that victory in Europe was celebrated – 8 May 1945.

Yet these points can only be taken so far. The colonial civil wars differed fundamentally from the struggle between resisters and collaborators in mainland France. Empire conflicts, albeit tied to fights for or against Vichy, were shaped by uniquely colonial factors: racial stratification and settler interests, economic shortage and geographical isolation, fear of overthrow by subject populations. France's colonial civil wars were also functionally dependent on the strategic choices of the Second World War's major combatants. This was a trend that began early. A fortnight after the Franco-German armistice of 22 June 1940, Britain attacked the French Mediterranean fleet at anchor in the Algerian port of Mers el-Kébir. Intended to nullify the risk of the French vessels falling into Axis hands, Royal Navy shelling killed 1,297 French sailors.[2] The inevitable cries of Perfidious Albion went up loudest among senior French naval commanders, several of whom – Jean-Marie Abrail, Jean Decoux, Jean-Pierre Esteva, Charles Platon and, of course, Jean-François Darlan – rose to prominence as ministers and colonial governors under Vichy. From North Africa to Indochina, the task of persuading French colonial administrations to join the Allied cause became all but impossible.[3]

Stronger imperial rivals made their presence felt elsewhere. While the fires of Mers el-Kébir smouldered, Japanese forces advanced southward into French-ruled Vietnam. Even the famous 'rallying' of black African territories to Charles de Gaulle's Free French movement, which began in earnest during late August 1940, rested on surreptitious British support. Subsequent

---

2 Martin Thomas, 'After Mers el-Kébir: The Armed Neutrality of the Vichy French Navy, 1940–1943', *English Historical Review* 112:447 (1997), 643–7. For Vichy propagandist responses, see Brett C. Bowles, '"La tragédie de Mers el-Kébir" and the Politics of Filmed News in France, 1940–1944', *Journal of Modern History* 76:2 (2004), 347–88.
3 Jean-Marie Abrail supervised the naval defence of Dunkirk, after which he was appointed Governor General of Algeria. At much the same time, Admiral Jean Decoux, Naval Commander in the Far East, became Governor of the Indochina Federation, a post he would hold until March 1945. Jean-Pierre Esteva served as Vichy Resident-Minister in Tunisia and received a life sentence in March 1945 for collaboration. Charles Platon became Vichy's Minister for Colonies. Jean-François Darlan rose furthest, becoming Vichy deputy premier, then Prime Minister and Commander of Vichy armed forces before his assassination by Gaullist resisters in Algiers on Christmas Eve, 1942.

changes of colonial allegiance proved similarly conditional on outside intervention. The outcomes of short, but bloody, armed confrontations between rival
administrative elites in Syria (1941), Madagascar, Somaliland and French North
Africa (1942), and Indochina (1945) were all determined by the foreign involvement that catalysed them. Reduced to its essence, the power of these outsiders
was this: Vichy existed only as long as it was expedient for Nazi Germany to
leave Marshal Pétain's regime in place, not just in unoccupied southern France,
but in much of French Africa as well. Meanwhile, Free France, as well as the
internal resistance groups fighting Vichy and its German and Italian overseers,
relied to varying degrees on Allied support: Anglo-American facilities, money
and war materiel for some; Soviet ideological inspiration for others.

Part military force, part quasi-government-in-exile, Free France was certainly committed to fighting the Axis powers.[4] But it operated beyond the
mainland for most of the war. Until mid-1943, its principal strategic assets
were in sub-Saharan Africa, President Franklin Roosevelt's US administration
blocking de Gaulle's move northward to 'liberated' Algiers following the
American landings in North Africa the previous November.[5] The Free
French should not be confused with the diverse civilian resistance networks
that emerged within metropolitan France. Ideologically situated to the left of
de Gaulle, these homeland resisters vied with Free France for power and
influence once the Vichy regime became more venal and collaborationist
from 1941 onward. Meanwhile, because their movement coalesced around
General de Gaulle in London and among his supporters in the colonies,
followers of Free France – a politically diverse group of armed forces
personnel, politicians, diplomats, bureaucrats and African colonial troops –
were often misleadingly described by the catch-all term 'Gaullists'.[6]

For some, support for the General and his unique vision of French
greatness – or *grandeur* – verged on the fanatical. For others, de Gaulle's
attractions were incidental to the more urgent priorities of fighting fascist

4 Edward Louis Spears papers, Middle East Centre archive, Oxford (hereafter MEC), box
  II/6, Note by Major Morton on Relations with the Free French, 6 January 1942.
5 Gloria Maguire, *Anglo-American Relations with the Free French* (Basingstoke: Macmillan,
  1995), pp. 118–19; Martin Thomas, *The French Empire at War, 1940–45* (Manchester
  University Press, 1998), pp. 159–64; Eric Jennings, *La France libre fut africaine* (Paris:
  Perrin, 2014), chs. 4–5.
6 The indispensable treatment of Free France and its followers is Jean-Louis Crémieux-
  Brilhac, *La France libre. De l'appel du 18 juin à la libération* (Paris: Gallimard, 1998). De
  Gaulle's and Pétain's military careers had been entwined since 1914, when the former
  served as a young Lieutenant in the 33rd Infantry Regiment, commanded, then, by
  Colonel Pétain. The link resumed in 1927, when, after Pétain's appointment as the
  French army's Chief of Staff, de Gaulle became his aide-de-camp.

occupation, ousting Vichy and restoring republican democracy to France. As for Free France's colonial troops, who campaigned arduously in North Africa, Italy and southern France, serving de Gaulle was, initially at least, as much circumstantial as deliberate. For what one historian dubs these 'soldiers of misfortune', it usually reflected the location of a particular garrison or the loyalties of its senior officers, not the political leanings of the rank and file.[7] The estimated 16,500 Free French military losses during campaigning in North Africa and Italy were primarily colonial. Villages in Morocco, Mali and Algeria, not Brittany, the Ardèche or the Pas-de-Calais, mourned the largest numbers of soldiers killed in French uniform after June 1940.[8]

The ambivalence within the Free French movement toward its symbolic figurehead points to other aspects of wartime France that bear emphasis. First, French people and society – at home and overseas – were as much politically as physically divided by the 1940 collapse. The circumstances of the defeat, the massive population exodus that preceded it, the removal of at least 1.65 million French POWs to Germany, and the carving of mainland France into occupied and unoccupied 'zones' turned people's worlds upside down.[9] The French population experienced warfare fitfully, first in May to June 1940, then following the Allied landings in northern and southern France in June and August 1944. In between times, their experiences of violence and loss derived from the consequences of occupation and population displacement. The absence of so many POWs, later compounded by German recruitment of 840,000 forced labourers, plus the forced enlistment of young men from Alsace into the Wehrmacht, weighed heavily. Worst of all, French Jews were systematically wiped out in the manner of their co-religionists and

---

7 Nancy Ellen Lawler, *Soldiers of Misfortune: Ivoirien Tirailleurs of World War II* (Athens: Ohio University Press, 1992). Losses among French African servicemen in the 1940 battle for France are discussed by Raphael Myron Echenberg, '"Morts pour la France": The African Soldier in France During the Second World War', *Journal of African History* 26 (1985), 263–80; Martin S. Alexander, 'Colonial Minds Confounded: French Colonial Troops in the Battle of France, 1940', in Martin Thomas (ed.), *The French Colonial Mind: Violence, Military Encounters, and Colonialism* (Lincoln: University of Nebraska Press, 2012), pp. 248–82; Raffael Scheck, *Hitler's African Victims: The German Army Massacres of Black French Soldiers in 1940* (Cambridge University Press, 2006).

8 Pieter Lagrou, 'The Nationalization of Victimhood: Selective Violence and National Grief in Western Europe, 1940–1960', in Richard Bessel and Dirk Schumann (eds.), *Life After Death: Approaches to a Cultural and Social History of Europe During the 1940s and 1950s* (Cambridge University Press, 2003), p. 249.

9 Hanna Diamond, *Fleeing Hitler: France, 1940* (Oxford University Press, 2008); Yves Durand, *La Captivité: histoire des prisonniers de guerre français, 1939–45* (Paris: FNCPG, 1980).

other persecuted groups in Eastern Europe.[10] Another cruel irony was that Allied bombing killed so many French civilians: the 600,000 tons of British and American bombs dropped on France resulted in an estimated 60,000 civilian deaths, a figure broadly comparable to the number of Britons killed in German raids on the United Kingdom.[11]

The Vichy state took shape amidst the chaos. Its authority was confirmed by National Assembly parliamentarians, who obligingly voted themselves out of office – and the Third Republic out of existence – by an overwhelming majority of 569 to 80 on 10 July 1940. Granted full powers by this act of political hara-kiri, the innate authoritarianism of Marshal Pétain's regime was set free at home and in the colonies.[12] Vichy signified what American historian Stanley Hoffman memorably dubbed 'the revenge of the minorities'. Right-wing anti-republicans, Catholic traditionalists and proto-fascists, the outsiders of the pre-war political system, moved to centre stage.[13] In a sweetly ironic twist, the regime's improvised Ministry of Colonies took up residence in Vichy's Hotel Britannique.[14] It is doubtful whether many French citizens or colonial subjects immediately grasped the implications of France's ideological lurch to the extreme right. Their lives thrown into confusion, the dominant emotion among the domestic population was bewilderment. Missing relatives, shortages and black market prices generated greater anxiety than high politics.[15]

Those prepared to express firm convictions or adopt life-changing positions for or against Vichy were a small minority. Some were ideologically motivated, welcoming the opportunity to build a disciplined, hierarchical society shorn of what they considered the decadent excesses of republican

10 Richard H. Weisberg, *Vichy Law and the Holocaust in France* (London: Routledge, 1997), ch. 6; Lagrou, 'Nationalization of Victimhood', pp. 248–9. Nearly 55,000 French Jews were sent to concentration camps during 1942 alone.
11 Lindsey Dodd and Andrew Knapp, '"How Many Frenchmen Did You Kill?" British Bombing Policy Towards France (1940–1945)', *French History* 22:4 (2008), 469–92, at 469.
12 Julian Jackson, *The Fall of France: The Nazi Invasion of 1940* (Oxford University Press, 2003), pp. 232–4; Nicholas Atkin, *Pétain* (Harlow: Longman, 1998), pp. 92–4.
13 Alice L. Conklin, Sarah Fishman and Robert Zaretsky, *France and its Empire Since 1870* (Oxford University Press, 2011), pp. 215–17; Stanley Hoffman, 'The Trauma of 1940: A Disaster and its Traces', in Joel Blatt (ed.), *The French Defeat of 1940: Reassessments* (Oxford: Berghahn, 1998), pp. 354–63.
14 Archives Nationales, Paris (hereafter AN), F60/307: Ministère des Colonies, Vichy: organization/administration, 1940–41.
15 Shannon L. Fogg, *The Politics of Everyday Life in Vichy France: Foreigners, Undesirables, and Strangers* (Cambridge University Press, 2009), pp. 19–55; Kenneth Mouré, 'Food Rationing and the Black Market in France (1940–1944)', *French History* 24:2 (2010), 262–82.

liberality.[16] Others felt compelled to keep fighting by the very opposite political and ethical attachments. Pre-eminent among them were communists. Their party outlawed back in September 1939, a month after Stalin's signature of the Nazi-Soviet Pact, communist supporters were driven underground well before the 1940 defeat.[17] If resistance organization came naturally to communist activists, others were animated by patriotic resolve, by personal loss or, as in the case of numerous Jewish families, by an ethno-religious background that placed them in mortal danger.[18] Settler communities in the empire, most with family or military connections 'back home', were also shattered by the defeat. But they had greater scope to express opinions than their kith and kin in France. Although their attachments were commensurately diverse, a high proportion welcomed Vichy's authoritarianism, which came with a pronounced racist tinge that celebrated settler virility and identified authentic French identity with whiteness.[19] Another point, then, is that colonial communities, marginal to pre-war French politics, became more intimately involved in the wartime struggle over France's long-term destiny.

Whatever the intensity of local involvement between territories, France's colonial civil wars were fundamentally the same. Their fraternal bitterness derived from irreconcilable visions of what France and its colonies represented, what their future should be, and how they should be run.[20] And lying beneath the surface of the Vichy–Free French contest for imperial control was the more intractable conflict between supporters of empire and their anti-colonial opponents among subject populations. Wartime Franco-French rivalry was thus inseparable from incipient decolonization. Colonial nationalist parties, religious associations, communist networks and other civil society groups, outlawed in the war years, emerged more cohesive and militant in their wake. Some, such as the Viet Minh coalition, took up arms during the war. Other nationalist organizations, such as Algeria's People's Party (*Parti du*

---

16 Peter Jackson, 'Recent Journeys Along the Road Back to France, 1940', *Historical Journal* 39:2 (1996), 497; Patrick Finney, *Remembering the Road to World War Two: International History, National Identity, Collective Memory* (London: Routledge, 2011), pp. 150–5.

17 David Wingeate Pike, 'Between the Junes: The French Communists from the Collapse of France to the Invasion of Russia', *Journal of Contemporary History* 28:3 (1993), 465–85.

18 Olivier Wieviorka, *Une certaine idée de la Résistance: Défense de la France, 1940–1949* (Paris: Editions du Seuil, 1995), pp. 20–3; Rod Kedward, *La Vie en bleu: France and the French Since 1900* (London: Penguin, 2005), pp. 272–4.

19 Conklin et al., *France and its Empire*, pp. 228–9; Francine Muel-Dreyfus, *Vichy and the Eternal Feminine* (Durham, NC: Duke University Press, 2001), pp. 97–124.

20 Intersections between local rivalries and national 'master narratives' of civil war are examined in Stathis Kalyvas, 'The Ontology of "Political Violence": Action and Identity in Civil Wars', *Perspectives on Politics* 1:3 (2003), 475–94.

Peuple Algérien – PPA), did so immediately the Second World War ended. Public protest assumed new forms, with organized labour, women's groups and youth movements especially prominent. All capitalized on the popular antagonism to French control, which the colonial civil wars had nourished.

The chronology of empire division

Few, though, predicted such irreconcilable division when war broke out in September 1939. Alongside the settler organizations that professed unflinching loyalty during the Phoney War, associations representing local notables, colonial veterans' groups and lower-tier administrators, many of them overseas citizens of Greater France, affirmed their readiness to serve the French cause. In Algeria, for instance, Cherrid Missoum, Secretary of the Algerian Muslim Congress youth wing, and local representatives of Algeria's proto-parliamentary financial delegations recognized the war's unifying potential.[21] Village elders, the Muslim ex-servicemen's association, and the leaders of Algeria's principal sufi orders identified with the fight against Nazism, suggesting that French assimilationist ideals might yet coalesce in the furnace of war.[22] Nowhere were the declarations of loyalty more pronounced than in the Mandates of Lebanon and Syria, where a varied chorus of elite voices saluted France's war. Endorsement from President Emile Eddé, the Maronite Patriarch Abdallah Khouri, and other Lebanese Christian Church leaders might be taken for granted. Across the border, the backing of Druze and Alawite chiefs, representatives of Syria's main compact minorities, was welcome. But endorsements from the Syrian National Bloc and the country's People's Party were positively effusive. Reacting to Prime Minister Edouard Daladier's 3 September 1939 war declaration, Jamal Mardam, leader of Syria's National Bloc, pronounced that 'To serve France is to serve the cause of humanity'.[23] Effusive, but prudent too, nationalist politicians stressed their loyalty in adversity, knowing that the Mandate's police were locking up communists and other dissidents.[24]

---

21 AN, F⁶⁰187/DA1, Algiers Chamber of Agriculture Motion Presented by M. Vagnon, December 1939; Cherrid Missoum to Daladier, 10 December 1939; no. 51054, Le Beau (Algiers) to Ministry of Interior/Cabinet, 28 May 1940.
22 'L'Afrique du Nord et la Guerre', *L'Afrique Française* 49:8–9 (September 1939), 212–13.
23 'Les populations du Levant sous mandat français et la Guerre', *L'Asie Française* 39:373 (September–October 1939), 275–7.
24 Service Historique de la Défense – Département de l'Armée de Terre (hereafter SHD-DAT), Archives de Moscou, C623/D1419, SEL note, 'Conversation avec M. Puaux', August 1939.

Empire loyalism, calculated or otherwise, conferred few short-term rewards. Neither Daladier's administration nor its successor under Paul Reynaud set much store on greater civil rights for colonial subjects or service personnel before defeat transformed the stakes involved. The war's initial impact was also felt differently in the colonies. State of siege regulations, tantamount to the imposition of martial law, were widely imposed at the outbreak of hostilities. Governors and local military commanders acquired unprecedented powers of summary arrest and detention. Political groups, whether avowedly anti-colonial or not, were increasingly constrained as imperial authorities moved to silence organized nationalist politics. Algeria's PPA and its Association of Reformist Ulamas were 'decapitated' by the incarceration of their senior leaders.[25] Detained politicians and clerics were joined by trade unionists, student leaders and other, less prominent figures that featured on colonial security services' notorious 'Carnet B' lists, which identified anyone suspected of sponsoring dissent – or 'anti-national' activity, as it was known.

Colonial repression in the Phoney War period, much like the mobilization of colonial military recruits, served strategic ends, but was racially constructed as well. Ethnic discrimination, though, was most widely felt in colonial rationing regulations. Foodstuff restrictions were particularly extensive in the cluster of Maghreb dependencies closest to the mainland. On 31 May 1938, the Ministry of Agriculture authorized the recently established National Wheat Office to stockpile a million tons of cereals in Morocco, Algeria and Tunisia.[26] It was a sensible precaution, but one whose allocation exposed the fundamental iniquity of colonial governance. Europeans would receive the bulk of high-quality soft wheat, adult settlers being allocated an annual 200 kilogram ration. Algeria's Muslims, reportedly 'accustomed' to a rougher diet, were assigned only 32 kilograms. Similar ratios were applied to meat, vegetable products, coffee and tea, which took average consumption patterns over the preceding two years as their benchmark. The result was a self-fulfilling prophecy. Settlers who ate well were to receive more; colonial subjects, on poorer, low-protein diets, faced harsher restrictions to come.[27]

---

25 Mahfoud Kaddache, 'L'opinion politique musulmane en Algérie et l'administration française (1939–1942)', *Revue d'Histoire de la Deuxième Guerre Mondiale* 114 (1979), 103–6.
26 SHD-DAT, 2N66/D1, no. 5159–2, Daladier to Henri Queuille, 6 September 1938.
27 SHD-DAT, 2N66/D1, no. 4739, 'Note de renseignements pour l'évaluation des besoins de la population civile en denrées de première nécessité', Algiers, 23 August 1938.

The case of rationing should give us pause when considering the wartime chronology of French imperial conflict. Empire disintegration continued inexorably over three wartime stages. From the Phoney War, through Vichy dominance in 1940–42, to the Free French ascendency cemented by de Gaulle's triumphal return to Paris on 25 August 1944, life remained very hard for colonial subjects. The three stages thus shared one point in common, despite the fact that French political leadership differed in each one. Throughout the war years, economic hardship, typified by foodstuff shortages and chronic price inflation, matched social exclusion and political repression in bearing more heavily on colonial lives than the progress of Allied campaigns or changes at the top of the colonial tree.

Again, French North Africa proves the point. The region is typically discussed in military histories of the war in relation to the aftermath of French defeat in 1940 and the outcome of Operation TORCH: the US takeover in Morocco and Algeria after only seventy-two hours of fighting in November 1942. But the French-ruled Maghreb was convulsed by other, deeper pressures of much longer standing. From the economic impact of conscription in the autumn of 1939, through the foodstuff crises and urban public health scares that sapped French capacity to overcome the material consequences of metropolitan defeat, French North Africa's war looked very different to the local administrators and wider populations that lived through it. Viewed in this way, the war years were most notable for the irreversible damage they wrought to economic stability and the hierarchies of colonial rule in North Africa. By the time General Maxime Weygand took over as Algeria's Governor General on 17 July 1941, living standards for the rural poor had declined precipitately. Fuel and foodstuffs were in short supply. The agricultural economy was profoundly disrupted. And average wages languished at subsistence level.[28]

Imperial contests: Vichy and Free France

Economic crisis proved no barrier to the embrace of Vichy's 'National Revolution' by colonial regimes. Most were enthused by the Pétainist cults of xenophobic ultra-nationalism, stricter social hierarchies, and a rural

---

28 TNA, FO 892/84, Ministry of Information, French Section Advisory Committee, Intelligence Report 39, 17 June 1941; *Journal Officiel* 197, 17 July 1941; Kenneth Mouré, 'Economic Choice in Dark Times: The Vichy Economy', *French Politics, Culture, and Society* 25:1 (2007), 108–30.

nostalgia flavoured with Catholic pro-natalism.[29] Peasant values, large families and veneration of conservative, often anti-republican institutions – the Catholic Church and the military foremost among them – came naturally to settlers and authoritarian administrators. Thus we find Jean Decoux, another Admiral catapulted to political prominence as Vichy's Governor of Indochina, promoting Pétainist youth movements in French Vietnam, celebrating the cult of Joan of Arc (Vichy's preferred symbol of patriotic self-sacrifice), and lauding the 'magnificent' fecundity of a settler couple from Tonkin, whose twelve children holidayed near the Governor's Palace in the Vietnamese hill station of Dalat.[30] The air of detachment from reality was hardly surprising when the realities in question were so alarming: the dual menace of a Japanese takeover and an incipient Vietnamese revolution impelled by French inability to satisfy the most basic needs of Indochina's peoples – for security and food.[31]

Across the French political divide, it is easier to see why senior Gaullists in London were determined to exploit the colonies when one remembers how few cards they had to play with their British patrons. And the British mission to the Free French National Committee was more than an intermediary, not merely relaying Gaullist economic requests for funds, supplies, shipping and other transport to the War Cabinet, but filtering out such demands when they conflicted with the overarching priorities of the Anglo-American supply boards that controlled the circulation of goods between Allied and imperial territories.[32]

British officialdom's enduring scepticism about de Gaulle and Free France as rulers of a revitalized French Empire was writ much larger across the Atlantic.[33] In February 1942, Maurice Dejean, Foreign Affairs Commissioner in the French National Committee, articulated a widely held view among Gaullist staff about the underlying reason behind the Roosevelt administration's enduring coolness toward Free France. The answer, Dejean insisted,

29 Eric Jennings, *Vichy in the Tropics: Pétain's National Revolution in Madagascar, Guadeloupe, and Indochina, 1940–1944* (Stanford University Press, 2001).

30 Eric Jennings, *Imperial Heights: Dalat and the Making and Undoing of French Indochina* (Berkeley: University of California Press, 2011), pp. 210–13; Eric Jennings, 'Conservative Confluences, "Nativist" Synergy: Reinscribing Vichy's National Revolution in Indochina, 1940–1945', *French Historical Studies* 27:4 (2004), 601–35.

31 Pierre Brocheux and Daniel Hémery, *Indochina: An Ambiguous Colonization, 1858–1954* (Berkeley: University of California Press, 2009), pp. 344–8.

32 TNA, FO 892/172, undated memo on functions of the British mission to the Free French National Committee.

33 Mario Rossi, 'United States Military Authorities and Free France', *Journal of Military History* 61:1 (1997), 49–64, especially 49–53.

lay in a secret US-Vichy deal whereby Pétain's regime agreed to minimize strategic concessions to Germany provided that the United States left Vichy's empire alone. US recognition of de Gaulle was allegedly withheld as part of the bargain.[34] The simpler reason for Washington's derision of Free France was that Roosevelt loathed de Gaulle, a man he considered pompous, autocratic and selfish.[35] But Dejean's conspiracy theory was less outlandish than it seemed. Roosevelt's special envoy, Robert Murphy, did agree with Admiral Darlan in March 1941 to trade US foodstuff convoys to Vichy for the promise (quickly broken) to limit collaboration with Germany, particularly in North Africa.[36] Murphy's talks marked the beginning of a longer-term association that climaxed in the so-called 'Darlan deal'. It left Vichy's former premier at the head of government in Algiers in return for the regime's acquiescence in Operation TORCH.[37]

De Gaulle's supporters were incandescent. Adrien Tixier and Pierre Mendès-France, later ministers in the post-war Fourth Republic, spent their war years in Washington trying to win support for the General. By mid-1942, both men were exasperated. The Americans did not understand what Free France stood for, they were hopelessly naive about the Vichy regime, and Roosevelt simply followed his instincts most of the time.[38] Excluded from TORCH planning, de Gaulle was even more incensed by American support of his new rival for leadership of the Free French, General Henri Giraud, in the limited handover of power that followed Darlan's assassination in Algiers on 24 December 1942.[39]

Operation TORCH also cast a spotlight on the changing economic balance of power in the Maghreb as the US invasion force moved rapidly eastward. Its supply needs took precedence over all else, and the Americans' dollar purchasing power put the French North African franc under strain. After TORCH, the Algiers authorities quickly negotiated a provisional franc–dollar exchange rate with the US Treasury Department. This, in turn, was supplanted at the Casablanca Conference by a stabilization accord that pegged

---

34 TNA, Political Warfare Executive files, FO 892/127, Maurice Dejean memo, 'Washington et Vichy', 4 February 1942.

35 Fredrik Logevall, *Embers of War: The Fall of an Empire and the Making of America's Vietnam* (New York: Random House, 2012), pp. 51–2.

36 France, Ministère des Affaires Etrangères (hereafter MAE), Guerre, 1939–1945, Londres, Comité National Français, vol. 299, Forces Françaises Libres, 2ème bureau, 'Projet d'accord franco-américain', 8 March 1941.

37 Arthur L. Funk, 'Negotiating the "Deal with Darlan"', *Journal of Contemporary History* 8:2 (1973), 81–117; Thomas, *The French Empire at War*, 159–90.

38 MAE, AP288, Maurice Dejean papers, vol. 24, Adrien Tixier to de Gaulle, 1 June 1942.

39 TNA, FO 892/174, Free French Press Service, de Gaulle communiqué, 2 January 1943.

the value of the franc throughout French Africa at fifty to the dollar.[40] Although the greater price stability that resulted was welcome to North Africans, the Casablanca economic agreements did not curb the overweening power of a local black market in which dollars reigned supreme, to the detriment of rural consumers least able to obtain them.[41]

One consequence was that, during the 1943–44 hiatus of transfers of executive power between Vichy and Free French administrations, the founding statutes of leading nationalist groups, including Algeria's *Amis du Manifeste et de la Liberté* and Morocco's *Hizb el-Istiqlal* (Constitution Party), cited poverty and economic exploitation as justifications for their anti-colonial platforms.[42] Likewise, Messali Hadj's PPA, still the major force in Algerian domestic politics, despite being banned outright since 1939, insisted that any ideological differences between Vichy and Gaullist tutelage were eclipsed by their shared colonialism, a phenomenon epitomized by ruthless wartime economic extraction. Whether Algeria's foodstuffs, minerals and other primary products were shipped to Marseilles and thence to Germany or to Allied ports, the essential fact was that Algerians, denied any democratic choice over participation in the war, went hungry. Messali received a fifteen-year sentence of forced labour from a Vichy military tribunal on 28 March 1941. So he might have been expected to welcome the advent of a Gaullist provisional government in Algiers, the French Committee of National Liberation (FCNL).[43] The nomenclature was telling. As Messali asked FCNL members on 11 October 1943, why should Algerians support French liberation when their own national freedom was denied?[44]

40 TNA, WO 204/239, Allied Civil Affairs memo, 'Dollar–Franc Rate of Exchange', 16 January 1943.
41 SHD-DAT, 2P12/D2, Vichy Secrétariat à la Guerre, Bulletin de Renseignements 64, 14 January 1943; James J. Dougherty, *The Politics of Wartime Aid: American Economic Assistance to France and French Northwest Africa, 1940–1946* (Westport, Conn.: Greenwood, 1978), pp. 4–5; Maguire, *Anglo-American Relations*, pp. 120–2. The French Committee of National Liberation negotiated a currency stabilization agreement with the British government that altered franc values throughout the African Empire, from 176.6 to 200 per pound, in February 1944: TNA, FO 371/40299, E1126/23/89, Spears Mission Summary 97, 19 February 1944.
42 'Manifeste du peuple algérien', in Jean-Charles Jauffret (ed.), *La Guerre d'Algérie par les documents* (2 vols., Vincennes: Service historique de l'Armée de terre, 1990), vol. 1, pp. 31–8; AN, F60/837, no. 685, Istiqlal executive memo, 'Au sujet des récentes réformes marocaines', 1 December 1944.
43 Jacques Simon (ed.), *Messali Hadj par les textes* (Paris: Editions Bouchène, 2000), doc. 17, Interview à *Combat*, 26 July 1946.
44 Ibid., doc. 14, Lettre aux membres du Comité de libération, 11 October 1943.

Meanwhile, to the east, US forces moved into Tunisia over the winter of 1942–43. Local sections of the country's dominant nationalist group, *Néo-Destour* (the 'new constitution' party) had been denuded by police harassment and long prison terms. The German authorities, hoping that party leader Habib Bourguiba and his followers would repudiate their erstwhile French persecutors, freed the *Néo-Destour* executive in January 1943. They were disappointed. Bourguiba denounced the Nazi occupation of Tunisia, thinking that his bravery might be acknowledged by de Gaulle's followers. This, too, proved a vain hope. Repression of nationalist activity resumed once Rommel's forces were evicted. During 1944, the Free French reimposed the ban on Bourguiba's party and ignored Tunisia's status as a protectorate with its own monarchical administration by enacting legislation that centralized political power under French authority. This signalled the beginning of Bourguiba's turn away from France toward the cultivation of Arab and US opinion, a strategy pursued until Tunisia achieved its independence in March 1956.[45]

North Africa's political violence in 1944 was gravest in Morocco. The ill-advised FCNL decision to arrest the four leaders of the *Hizb el-Istiqlal* on 29 January provoked rioting in Rabat, Salé and Fez, the death of at least forty protesters and the arrest of over 1,800 more.[46] As urban disorder became endemic in Morocco, even the Algiers authorities admitted that supply problems, unfair rationing and consequent shortages had become inseparable from nationalist dissent.[47] Perhaps inevitably, the nature and scale of Maghribi recruitment to the First French Army, which was meanwhile fighting northward through Italy, Corsica and southern France, compounded the friction between the Gaullist imperial establishment and its nationalist opponents. To the former, these units confirmed the unity of purpose between France and its North African subjects, even though the army's cadres were progressively 'whitened' the closer they got to the French capital. To the latter, the large numbers of North African army volunteers merely indicated how desperate they were for a steady income.[48] It was a

45 SHD-DAT, Fonds privés/Vichy, 1K592/1, Charles-Robert Ageron draft paper, 'Les mouvements nationalistes dans le Maghreb pendant la deuxième guerre mondiale'; AN, F60/883, no. 1890, General Charles Mast to Georges Bidault, 4 December 1945.
46 SHD-DAT, Fonds privés/Vichy, 1K592/1, Ageron draft paper, 'Les mouvements nationalistes'.
47 AN, Secrétariat Général du Gouvernement, F⁶⁰/835, Georges Spillmann, Directeur du Cabinet, to Georges Catroux, 12 December 1944.
48 SHD-DAT, Fonds privés, 1K650/D1, General Jean Richard papers, 'Vue d'ensemble sur la répartition des effectifs mobilisés en Afrique du Nord', February 1945; Claude

different story again for Algerian conscripts, among whom desertion rates climbed toward 20 per cent by July 1943, with some 11,119 out of 56,455 avoiding the call-up over the preceding six months.[49]

The Free French were hard-pressed to conceal the signs of unrest in their newly consolidated African empire. But the breakdown of colonial authority went furthest in a region still outside their control: the Indochina Federation. Admiral Decoux's faltering pro-Vichy government was isolated and starved of cash.[50] It was also threatened from three sides. For General Tsuchihashi's Japanese military administration, the bureaucratic convenience of leaving a bankrupt colonial regime in place became questionable.[51] For the regime's internal opponents, many of them loosely connected in the communist-dominated coalition that was the Viet Minh, the implosion of French colonial authority enhanced the prospects for a rapid seizure of power. Finally, for the Americans, it made sense to work with Viet Minh guerrillas, the sole group capable of mounting any serious local challenge to the Japanese.[52]

None of these three alternatives appealed to de Gaulle's supporters, of course. Without the resources to intervene independently in Indochina, and unable to 'turn' Decoux's government their way, de Gaulle's provisional government, newly installed in liberated Paris, could do little.[53] Observing the situation in Vietnam, the Gaullist military attaché in nationalist China conceded that the Indochina Federation had become 'a no man's land' for the major Allied powers. None dared intervene decisively lest they antagonize one another, or, far worse, trigger the Japanese takeover they all feared.[54] It was the Vietnamese who seized the initiative. By December 1944, Ho Chi Minh and Vo Nguyen Giap, the Viet Minh's leading strategic thinkers, had

d'Abzac-Epezy, 'Épuration, dégagements, exclusions. Les réductions d'effectifs dans l'armée française (1940–1947)', *Vingtième Siècle* 59 (1998), 66–9.

49 René Gallissot, *La République française et les indigènes: Algérie colonisée, Algérie algérienne (1870–1962)* (Paris: Editions de l'Atelier, 2006), p. 156. For fuller details of North African troop recruitment and morale in 1943–45, see Belkacem Recham, *Les Musulmans algériens dans l'armée française (1919–1945)* (Paris: L'Harmattan, 1996), pp. 236–72.

50 MAE, série Asie-Océanie 1944–1955, sous-série Indochine, vol. 30, 'Notes prises à la conférence de M. le Gouverneur-Général Laurentie sur l'Indochine', August 1945.

51 TNA, PREM 3/178/2, Chiefs of Staff sub-committee, 'Events in Indo-China Since 1939' March 1945.

52 Kiyoko Kurusu Nitz, 'Japanese Military Policy Towards French Indochina During the Second World War: The Road to the *Meigo Sakusen* (9 March 1945)', *Journal of Southeast Asian Studies* 14:2 (1983), 334–8.

53 Martin Thomas, 'Free France, the British Government and the Future of French Indo-China, 1940–45', *Journal of Southeast Asian Studies* 28:1 (1997), 141–4.

54 SHD-DAT, 4Q78/D5, no. 95, 'Perspectives d'évolution du conflit extrême-orient', 5 August 1944.

established the National Liberation Army of Vietnam, which operated from 'free zones' in the far north.[55] Choosing to overlook the Viet Minh's ideological leanings, the US and British special services – OSS and SOE – offered training and equipment for sabotage attacks on the Japanese.

Three months later, the Japanese struck back. The American reconquest of the Philippines in early 1945 alerted Japan's Supreme War Council to the possibility of similar US amphibious landings in Indochina. These might be supported, not just by the Viet Minh, but by Decoux's government as well. Tokyo therefore presented the Governor with an ultimatum. Place his administration and the French colonial garrison under Japanese command or face the consequences. Decoux's '*non*' spelt the end of French rule – albeit temporarily. Japanese units swept through Hanoi on the night of 9 March, killing scores of French bureaucrats and troops, and interning those unable to make a fighting retreat northward to China.[56] A puppet regime under Emperor Bao Dai was set up in Hue, Vietnam's imperial capital. Parallel monarchical regimes were re-established in Laos and Cambodia, which reverted to its pre-colonial title of Kampuchea. All three promptly declared 'independence' from France, under the approving gaze of General Tsuchihashi's occupation forces. From taxation systems to school curricula, symbols of French colonial power were hastily removed. Kampuchea's Prince Norodom Sihanouk even restored the Buddhist calendar and urged his subjects to abandon the use of Romanized script.[57]

The limits to this independence soon became tragically apparent in northern Vietnam, where the new authorities, under premier Tran Trong Kim, could not prevent heightened Japanese requisitioning, which destabilized the local rice market. Chronic price inflation made food of any kind unaffordable for the poorest labourers and their families. Famine took hold. It was especially devastating in the Red River Delta and two densely populated provinces of northern Annam.[58] Village populations collapsed. Some locked their doors, resolved to die together as a family. Others became famine

55 Stein Tønnesson, *Vietnam 1946: How the War Began* (Berkeley: University of California Press, 2009), pp. 21–2.
56 Logevall, *Embers of War*, pp. 84–7.
57 Pierre L. Lamant, 'Le Cambodge et la décolonisation de l'Indochine: les caractères particuliers du nationalisme Khmer de 1936 à 1945', in Charles-Robert Ageron (ed.), *Les Chemins de la décolonisation* (Paris: Centre national de la recherche scientifique, 1986), 189–99.
58 Ralph B. Smith, 'The Japanese Period in Indochina and the *coup* of 9 March 1945', *Journal of Southeast Asian Studies* 9:2 (1978), 290–1; Sugata Bose, 'Starvation Amidst Plenty: The Making of Famine in Bengal, Honan and Tonkin, 1942–45', *Modern Asian Studies* 24:4 (1990), 699–727.

refugees, begging on the streets of local towns and cities.[59] Starvation dominated North Vietnamese politics by early 1945. The faction fighting among the French colonial rulers was, at best, an irrelevance, at worst, an act of shocking insensitivity. Not surprisingly, the combination of Japan's military coup and the tragic shortcomings of its new surrogate authorities in Indochina enhanced the Viet Minh's legitimacy as a popular resistance movement. For the Western Allies, impatient to secure victory over Japan, as for Vietnamese, Cambodians and Laotians faced with punishing Japanese exactions, the Viet Minh counted for more than the French as summer arrived.

From wartime division to post-war crisis

With an empire wracked by violent internal division, the ebullience of French imperialism in 1945 seems puzzling.[60] Whereas, over the ensuing decades, Britain would adjust, albeit painfully, to America's new global dominance, successive French governments reacted in contrary fashion, equating retention of empire with resurgent international power. It was, after all, the colonies that made Free France credible, not just as a political force, but as a territorial entity. Even though, in terms of volume and value, French colonial trade improved sharply over the course of 1944, in purely monetary terms, France's empire was not generating foreign exchange revenues comparable to the sums derived from British territories.[61] So it was perhaps unsurprising that de Gaulle's senior advisors viewed imperial affairs in instrumental terms. In the months preceding the D-Day landings, this boiled down to a simple calculation: colonial reforms should enhance French power, not diminish it.[62]

In January 1944, the Governors of the Free French Empire assembled in Brazzaville, the sleepy Congolese capital of French Equatorial Africa, to consider the empire's post-war consolidation. The tenor of their discussions was deeply conservative. North Africa and Indochina – the regions where

59 David G. Marr, *Vietnam 1945: The Quest for Power* (Berkeley: University of California Press, 1995), pp. 96–107.
60 The following paragraphs draw on Martin Thomas, 'Divisive Decolonization: The Anglo-French Withdrawal from Syria and Lebanon, 1944–46', *Journal of Imperial and Commonwealth History* 28:3 (2000), 71–93, at 71–2.
61 AN, René Pleven papers, box 560AP/27, 'Commerce extérieur des premiers mois 1944', August 1944, and 'Situation économique du Sénégal en 1943 et 1944', 1944.
62 Martin Shipway, *The Road to War: France and Vietnam, 1944–1947* (Oxford: Berghahn, 1996), p. 90.

wartime disruption was greatest – were scratched from the conference agenda.[63] And plans for administrative restructuring, economic diversification and greater electoral representation in territories south of the Sahara were profoundly cautious, framed not in terms of preparation for independence, but the acquisition of a more francophone *personnalité politique* in individual colonies.[64] Put differently, wider citizenship rights, political responsibilities and improved living standards, however enacted once the war was over, were intended to make colonial peoples more French, not less so.

The 'colonial myth' that keeping empire intact was somehow pivotal to French grandeur was not confined to the Gaullist right, despite its self-proclaimed role as arch-defender of France's historical greatness. The imperialist reflex was prevalent throughout the political community in liberated France. Even the communist leadership, rhetorically anti-colonial to be sure, was not immune. Why? The unique circumstances of France's wartime defeat, liberation and reconstruction offer some explanation. France's acute weakness, compared with its major allies in 1945, nurtured the presumption that empire was fundamental to French recovery.[65] This view spanned the restyled French party-political spectrum. It was readily accepted by former resisters, erstwhile Vichyites and, it appears, newly enfranchised women voters. The acrimonious circumstances of France's eventual pull-out from Syria and Lebanon in 1944–46 helped turn presumption into dogma by the time the Indochina War broke out in December 1946.

Having negotiated (but not implemented) treaties of independence with the two Levant states in 1936, French governments exploited communal unrest and the outbreak of war in Europe to postpone consideration of a transfer of power. This pattern of obfuscation, justified by reference to internal disorder and France's primordial strategic requirements, continued during the war years, unaffected by the sequence of Vichy and Free French rule. France's imperial authority drained away regardless. In November 1943, Lebanese and Syrian parliamentarians took decisive steps toward unilateral declarations of independence that made French rule untenable. Local

63 AN, F60/889, Comité Français de Libération Nationale Secretariat note for de Gaulle, 'Conférence de Brazzaville', 5 January 1944.
64 Shipway, *The Road to War*, pp. 21–37.
65 Charles-Robert Ageron, 'La survivance d'un mythe: la puissance par l'Empire colonial, 1944–1947', *Revue Française d'Histoire d'Outre-Mer* 72 (1985), 388–97; D. Bruce Marshall, *The French Colonial Myth and Constitution-Making in the Fourth Republic* (New Haven, Conn.: Yale University Press, 1973).

opposition to it was overwhelming. And British determination to rebuild their Arab connections precluded support for a hated French administration.[66] The stern resistance of Syria's pro-Vichy garrison to a British-led imperial invasion force in June–July 1941 nourished British contempt for French sensibilities. So incensed were the Vichy authorities that they lobbied Hitler's government to authorize Luftwaffe raids against British Palestine's oil installations and urban centres.[67]

Beneficiaries of Syria's regime change over the summer of 1941, the Free French were no less suspicious of ulterior British motives. By 1944, the French Levant was critical to emerging British plans to redraw the boundaries of a 'Greater Syria' as part of a definitive Palestine partition.[68] De Gaulle raged against this scheming. It was, he said, tantamount to covert imperial warfare against an ally.[69] From its inception in July 1944, de Gaulle's provisional government railed against what were regarded as British diktats imposing withdrawal. Far from admitting the inevitability of a pull-out, throughout 1945 the Paris authorities interpreted British pressure for evacuation as a conspiracy to buy Arab friendship at French expense.[70] Meanwhile, in the fast-developing secret intelligence war between the two imperial powers, French security services began supplying arms and information to the Zionist terrorist groups *Irgun Tzva'i Le'umi* (National Military Organization) and the Stern Gang.[71]

Syria provoked the severest breakdown in Anglo-French imperial relations of the decolonization era. Last-ditch French efforts to stave off Syrian

---

66 Indispensable studies include William Roger Louis, *The British Empire in the Middle East, 1945–1951: Arab Nationalism, the United States and Postwar Imperialism* (Oxford: Clarendon Press, 1984); Philip S. Khoury, *Syria and the French Mandate: The Politics of Arab Nationalism, 1920–1945* (Princeton University Press, 1987); Aviel Roshwald, *Estranged Bedfellows: Britain and France in the Middle East During the Second World War* (Oxford University Press, 1990).

67 Haifa and Jaffa/Tel Aviv were hit, much as they had been by earlier Italian bombing raids between June and October 1940: see Nir Arielli, '"Haifa Is Still Burning": Italian, German and French Air Raids on Palestine During the Second World War', *Middle Eastern Studies* 46:3 (2010), 333–42.

68 MEC, Spears papers, box III/5, Sir J. Glubb, 'A Further Note on Peace Terms', 25 May 1943.

69 Gaullist suspicions are examined by Meir Zamir, 'The "Missing Dimension": Britain's Secret War Against France in Syria and Lebanon, 1942–45 – Part II', *Middle Eastern Studies* 46:6 (2010), 791–812.

70 Charles de Gaulle, *Mémoires de Guerre*, vol. III: *Le Salut, 1944–1946* (3 vols., Paris: Plon, 1959), pp. 781–95.

71 James Barr, *A Line in the Sand: Britain, France and the Struggle that Shaped the Middle East* (London: Simon & Schuster, 2012), pp. 253–97 and *passim*. The French security services were already funding the Stern Gang when two of its members assassinated Lord Moyne, Britain's Minister of State in the Middle East, on 6 November 1944.

and Lebanese independence were matched by countervailing British pressure to accelerate the process (an ironic counterpoint to subsequent British anger over US actions over Palestine). Faced with uncompromising nationalist opposition and Britain's decisive military presence, French evacuation was unavoidable. That it occurred only after bloodshed and amidst bitter acrimony between France and the nationalist governments in Damascus and Beirut was not. The venomous divisions between French and British authorities in the Middle East were partly to blame. So, too, was the reconstructed imperialism of the early Fourth Republic, which fed the mistaken presumption that France might yet salvage its position. This hard-line stance was doubly ironic in Syria, where the French had twice abandoned territory at the Mandate's northern margins in order to placate Kemalist Turkey – first in Cilicia in 1921, and second, in the sanjak of Alexandretta in 1938. Such pragmatism – and readiness to choose flight over fight – was forgotten amidst the fury of France's final withdrawal.[72]

For all sides involved, the material aspects to the Levant dispute – control over local security forces, provision for base rights and the recognition of French educational privileges – held particular symbolic value. To the Syrian and Lebanese authorities, the right to raise sovereign security forces was the yardstick of true independence.[73] For French negotiators, continued control over a handful of schools and military bases retained a cultural significance disproportionate to their material value. The unpopularity of the local French administration, the *délégation générale*, made a mockery of the high price placed by French negotiators on their cultural legacy in the Levant states, something that American, Arab League and United Nations observers found incomprehensible. But it was the violence that attended the Syrian endgame that utterly discredited French imperialism in the Middle East. Over two days on 29–30 May 1945, French artillery pounded the Damascus parliament building and its environs. The bombardment marked the culmination of three weeks of smaller-scale clashes in the capital, as French army reinforcements battled with Syrian security forces for control of the streets. The French commander, General Fernand Oliva-Roget, lost patience with this skirmishing and let loose his forces to

72 Sarah D. Shields, *Fezzes in the River: Identity Politics and European Diplomacy in the Middle East on the Eve of World War II* (New York: Oxford University Press, 2011), pp. 20–2, 114–24, 231–5.
73 SHD-DAT, 4H377/D6, Conférence de Chtaura, 22 February 1945.

teach the Syrians 'a good lesson'.[74] Hundreds died. North and West African colonial troops were quickly put to work burying Syrian gendarmes and other protestors in mass graves, making it impossible to calculate the numbers killed.[75] This bloody show of imperial defiance tipped the balance. Britain's Middle East Army Command, technically the ultimate military authority in the region, assumed full control in Syria, imposing martial law and confining the French garrison to its barracks. Negotiations over the terms of the French pull-out resumed, but their Mandate was already dead.[76]

The French coalition government, smarting from this humiliation, became doubly resolved to hang on elsewhere, whatever the expense involved. For the fact was that the human and material costs of maintaining the post-war empire fell on a country torn apart and traumatized by its 'dark years' of collaboration.[77] Imperial promises of new constitutional arrangements, development funding, inclusive governance and new eras of partnership hit the rocks when colonial voices turned this rhetoric of reform against colonial administrations, demanding that governments live up to pledges they were reluctant to keep.[78] Colonial disturbances of one kind or another became a constant feature in the post-war landscape, sometimes confined to the shadows of metropolitan politics, but occasionally jostling domestic or European issues out of the frame.

Conclusion

France moved in rapid succession from a nation defeated and occupied to one liberated and resurgent. A longer wartime constant was the state of undeclared civil war in its colonies. From June 1940 until Japan's final overthrow of the Vichyite regime in Hanoi on 9 March 1945, the French Empire was torn apart by an internecine war between the civil-military elites

---

74 Barr, *A Line in the Sand*, p. 291.
75 SHD-DAT, 4H360/D1, no. 1591/2S, Commandement Supérieur des Troupes du Levant memo, 1 June 1945; TNA, FO 371/45580, E5800/8/89, War Office Historical Record – Levant 29 May–11 June 1945. Estimates of the numbers killed in the bombardment range from 400 to 700.
76 SHD-DAT, 4H276/D3 EM-1, Instructions to Damascus Units, 29 July 1945; TNA, WO 201/1016, Brigadier J. G. Frere Reports to GHQ Middle East, 17–30 September 1945.
77 Julian Jackson, *France: The Dark Years, 1940–44* (Oxford University Press, 2001).
78 Frederick Cooper, 'Alternatives to Nationalism in French Africa, 1945–60', in Jost Düllfer and Marc Frey (eds.), *Elites and Decolonization in the Twentieth Century* (Basingstoke: Palgrave Macmillan 2011), pp. 113–15.

who ran it. Its endless factionalism antagonized the local notables essential to empire governance, presenting a golden opportunity for radical anti-colonial groups like Algeria's PPA and the Viet Minh resistance. The result was a crisis of colonial legitimacy that the French Empire never quite shook off. The Vichy–Free French antagonism was also sharpened by the weaknesses of each protagonist. Leaders on both sides of this Franco-French divide were acutely conscious of their relative powerlessness next to stronger European, American or Asian clients. It was these outsiders – British, American, German or Japanese – who controlled the wartime disposition of French colonial territory.

Nazi Germany, perhaps unrealistically, treated French North Africa as a strategic pawn until America took over following the TORCH landings of November 1942. And where Gaullist administrations refused to bend to American wishes, as in Pacific New Caledonia or the tiny islands of St Pierre and Miquelon off the Newfoundland coast, the political consequences of deeper US antagonism were greater than the *amour propre* satisfied by petty displays of French independence. Britain, meanwhile, pulled the key imperial levers in Syria and Lebanon after July 1941. British and Dominion forces also precipitated changes of administration, although not of underlying colonial conditions, in French Somaliland and Madagascar in 1942. Ultimately, though, it was Japan that did most to knock over France's house of colonial cards. Its occupation of Indochina, partial at first, total and brutal at last, catalysed the first of France's major fights against decolonization – an eight-year war against the Viet Minh that reverberated throughout Southeast Asia and the colonial world.[79]

Superficially at least, the French political figures determined to revitalize their empire immediately after the Second World War made unlikely imperialists. All professed republican ideals; most were ideologically left-of-centre. For the 1945 generation, the impetus was not to ignore the political fissures opened by the war, but to remodel imperial structures more fundamentally. African and Antillean deputies, such as the Senegalese Lamine Guèye and Léopold Senghor and the Guyanese Gaston Monnerville, used their positions as deputies in the newly elected French Constituent Assembly to call time on some of the worst injustices of the pre-war empire. Forced labour and arbitrary imprisonment were outlawed. Racially configured

79 MAE, série Asie-Océanie 1944–1960, sous-série Indochine, vol. 31, Comité d'Indochine Secrétariat notes, 21 April 1945.

voting systems were overhauled, if not quite abandoned.[80] But huge wartime debts and worsening East–West tensions transformed the economic and strategic context in which imperial rebuilding was supposed to occur, making it easier for French officials to spurn negotiated reform because of the overweening requirements of austerity and Cold War. Conflict and civil war in the French Empire were far from over.

80 Frederick Cooper, *Decolonization and African Society: The Labor Question in French and British Africa* (Cambridge University Press, 1996), pp. 184–93; Conklin et al., *France and its Empire*, pp. 250–1.

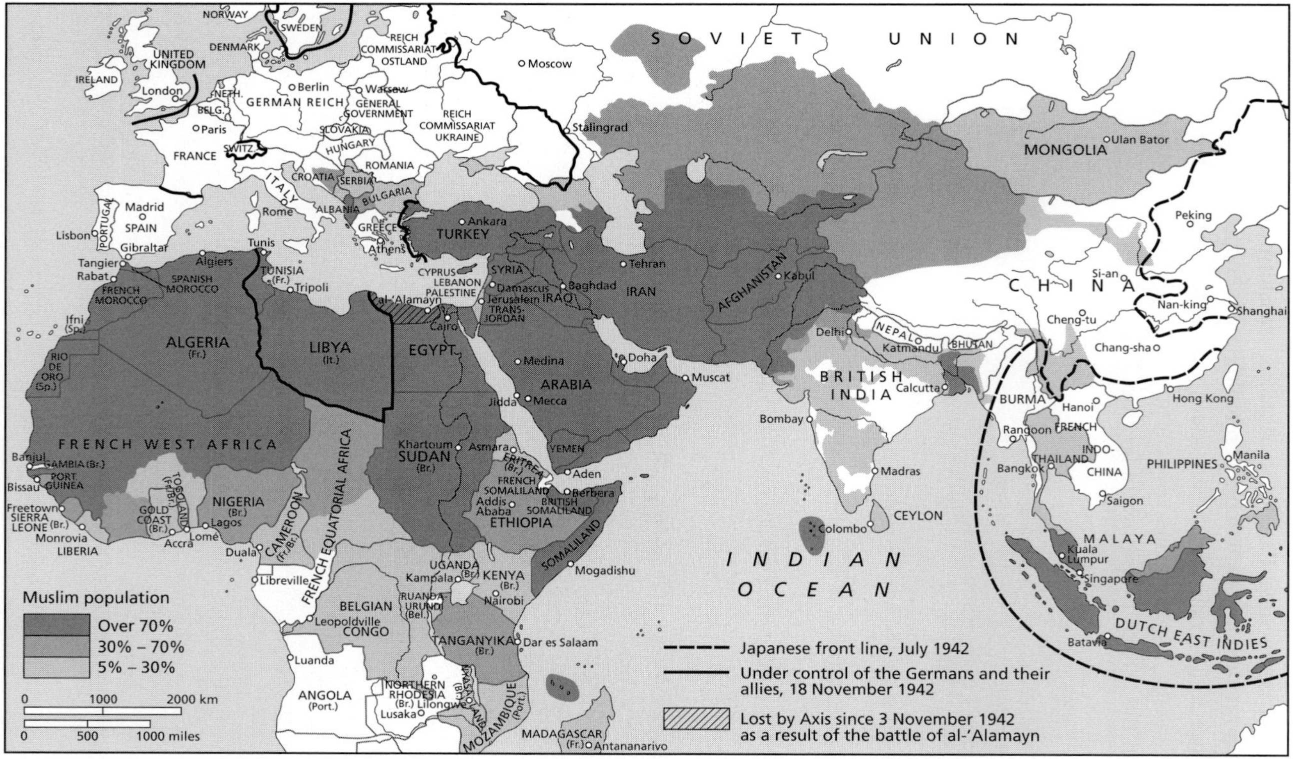

24.1 The Muslim world

Muslim population
Over 70%
30% – 70%
5% – 30%

Japanese front line, July 1942

Under control of the Germans and their allies, 18 November 1942

Lost by Axis since 3 November 1942 as a result of the battle of al-ʿAlamayn

24

The Muslim world in the Second World War

DAVID MOTADEL

Introduction

The Second World War had a momentous impact on the Islamic world. With the advance of Japanese troops into Southeast Asia, and the Italian and German military involvement in North Africa, the Balkans, Crimea and the Caucasus, Muslim-populated lands became front-line zones. At the same time, millions of Muslims who lived in the British, French and Dutch empires or under Soviet rule were drawn into the war. In the capitals of all major powers, officials believed the Islamic world to be politically and strategically significant, and, over the course of the conflict, increasingly engaged in policies and propaganda to win Muslim support.

The Islamic world has long been marginalized in historical accounts of the Second World War.[1] This is particularly striking if compared to studies on other global conflicts of the twentieth century. Muslim lands feature prominently in general histories of the First World War, with the jihad campaign of the Central Powers and the British-sponsored Arab Revolt; and the Cold War, when the Western powers came to see Islam as a bulwark against communism and supported Islamic movements across the world, a policy that culminated in the backing of the mujahidin during the anti-Soviet guerrilla war in Afghanistan.[2] This chapter is a first attempt to provide an

---

This chapter is based, in part, on David Motadel, *Islam and Nazi Germany's War* (Cambridge, Mass.: Harvard University Press, 2014).

1 I. C. B. Dear and M. R. D. Foot (eds.), *The Oxford Companion to World War II* (Oxford University Press, 1995), is a notable example.

2 Fritz Fischer, *Germany's Aims in the First World War* (New York: W. W. Norton, 1967), pp. 120–31; Hew Strachan, *The First World War* (London: Simon & Schuster, 2003), pp. 95–123; and David Stevenson, *1914–1918: The History of the First World War* (London: Allen Lane, 2004), pp. 115, 125; and, on the Cold War, John Lewis Gaddis, *The Cold War* (London: Allen Lane, 2005), pp. 208–11; and, more detailed, Odd Arne Westad, *The*

overview of the political history of the Islamic world in the war, assessing the impact of the conflict on Muslims across the world.

The following pages provide a sketch of the Second World War in a vast and highly heterogeneous region defined as the Muslim world. The geographical concept of the 'Muslim world' in itself, of course, is not unproblematic, and is used here only with reservations, as a shorthand term.[3] It should by no means imply an essentialist view of Muslim-populated lands. Indeed, although concise, the following pages make the heterogeneity of the Muslim world quite apparent, just as they reveal the diverse nature of the Second World War in different parts of the globe.

On the eve of the war, most of the world's Muslims were subjugated to foreign rule. Around 150 million between North Africa and Southeast Asia lived in the British and French Empires, and more than 20 million were governed by Stalin. In the capitals of Europe, Muslim populations were generally considered to be particularly prone to revolt. In the First World War, the Central Powers had even tried to stir up the Muslim subjects of their enemies' empires.[4] In the autumn of 1914, the Ottoman shaykh al-Islam – on behalf of the governments in Berlin and Constantinople – proclaimed jihad to mobilize the faithful for the war. Across the world, German and Ottoman emissaries spread pan-Islamic pamphlets, printed in Ottoman Turkish, Arabic, Persian, Urdu and Tatar, to incite, as the German emperor put it, 'the whole Mohammedan world to wild revolt'.[5] London, Paris and St Petersburg

Global Cold War: Third World Interventions and the Making of Our Times (Cambridge University Press, 2005), pp. 288–330.

3 Cemil Aydin, 'Globalizing the Intellectual History of the Idea of the "Muslim World"', in Samuel Moyn and Andrew Sartori (eds.), *Global Intellectual History* (New York: Columbia University Press, 2013), pp. 159–86. In this chapter, 'Muslim world' and 'Islamic world' refer to countries and territories with Muslim populations, either as majorities or significant minorities, without implying homogeneity, unity or any general characteristics.

4 Fischer, *Germany's Aims in the First World War*, pp. 120–31, was the first to study this campaign. Herbert Landolin Müller, *Islam, Gihâd ('Heiliger Krieg') und Deutsches Reich: Ein Nachspiel zur wilhelminischen Weltpolitik im Maghreb 1914–1918* (Frankfurt am Main: Peter Lang, 1992); Peter Hopkirk, *On Secret Service East of Constantinople: The Plot to Bring Down the British Empire* (London: John Murray, 1994); Donald McKale, *War by Revolution: Germany and Great Britain in the Middle East in the Era of World War I* (Kent, O.: Kent State University Press, 1998); Tilman Lüdke, *Jihad Made in Germany: Ottoman and German Propaganda and Intelligence Operations in the First World War* (Münster: Lit, 2005); Salvador Oberhaus, *'Zum wilden Aufstande entflammen': Die deutsche Propagandastrategie für den Orient im Ersten Weltkrieg am Beispiel Ägypten* (Saarbrücken: Müller, 2007); and Sean McMeekin, *The Berlin–Baghdad Express: The Ottoman Empire and Germany's Bid for World Power, 1898–1918* (London: Allen Lane, 2010), provide major accounts of the campaign for Islamic mobilization during the First World War.

5 Quoted in Fischer, *Germany's Aims in the First World War*, p. 121.

responded swiftly, denouncing not only the authority of the Ottoman caliph-
ate, but also supporting revolts in the sultan's volatile imperial hinterlands, and
promising their inhabitants independence.[6] To most Muslims, however, the
war did not bring liberation from foreign rule. The Versailles settlement
cemented a global order that placed most of the world's Muslims under direct
or indirect colonial rule, leaving many, as others in the non-European world,
deeply disillusioned.[7] In the interwar years, only a few countries with Muslim
majority populations were independent, most notably Kemalist Turkey, Pahlavi Iran and Hashemite (soon Saudi) Arabia. London and Paris took control of
the new mandates in the former Ottoman Levantine provinces, with France
ruling Syria and Lebanon, and Britain Palestine. Great Britain was, in fact, the
most potent power in the region, controlling Egypt, running a client state in
Transjordan, and exerting influence over the most important parts of the
Arabian Peninsula. A particularly symbolic new conflict emerged in British-
controlled Palestine, where Zionist mass migration antagonized Muslims,
leading to riots and revolts. North Africa, too, was under European imperial
rule, with France holding power in Algeria, Tunisia and Morocco, with the
exception of the northern coastal strip of Spanish Morocco, and Italy running a
repressive colonial regime in Libya. Most of the Muslim-inhabited regions of
sub-Saharan Africa were also ruled by Europeans, as were those of South and
Southeast Asia. In the Islamic borderlands of the newly established Soviet
Union, too, hopes for independence were crushed.

Throughout the interwar period, the Muslim world was shaken by anti-
imperial upheaval. Anti-colonial nationalism rose, particularly among urban
elites. Islamic movements, often led by religious authorities, continued to be
among the most widespread and potent forces of anti-imperial resistance, just
as they had been in the nineteenth century. In the 1920s and 1930s, British,
French, Dutch, Italian and Soviet authorities were continuously confronted

6 William L. Cleveland, 'The Role of Islam as Political Ideology in the First World War',
  in Edward Ingram (ed.), *National and International Politics in the Middle East: Essays in
  Honour of Elie Kedourie* (London: Frank Cass, 1986), pp. 84–101; and, more generally on
  British-sponsored revolt in the Arab hinterlands, Eliezer Tauber, *The Arab Movements in
  World War I* (London: Routledge, 1993); Haifa Alangari, *The Struggle for Power in Arabia:
  Ibn Saud, Hussein and Great Britain, 1914–1924* (Reading: Ithaca Press, 1998); and James
  Barr, *Setting the Desert on Fire: T. E. Lawrence and Britain's Secret War in Arabia, 1916–1918*
  (New York: W. W. Norton, 2008); and, on the Ottoman-Russian borderlands, Michael
  A. Reynolds, *Shattering Empires: The Clash and Collapse of the Ottoman and Russian
  Empires, 1908–1918* (Cambridge University Press, 2011).
7 Erez Manela, *The Wilsonian Moment: Self-Determination and the International Origins of
  Anticolonial Nationalism* (New York: Oxford University Press, 2007).

with rebel groups, calling for jihad against foreign intrusion.[8] There were uncountable local Islamic resistance movements, ranging from the warriors of the Sanusi order, who called for jihad against Italy's occupation of Cyrenaica, to Mahdist groups in sub-Saharan Africa, to Muslim rebels confronting Soviet troops and local party cadres in the mountains of the northern Caucasus. In 1919–24, the pan-Islamic Khilafat revolt shook British India. At the same time, urban Islamic protest movements emerged, most famously Egypt's Muslim Brotherhood, which, founded in 1928, soon became a mass movement and inspired political and religious leaders from West Africa to Southeast Asia.

War zones

Although Muslim territories remained at the fringes of the Second World War, they saw some of the bloodiest fighting.[9] The first region with a Muslim majority population that became a war zone was North Africa.[10] In the autumn of 1940, in his quest to establish an Italian empire in the Mediterranean, Mussolini attacked British-controlled Egypt. By the end of the year, Italian troops, under the command of the sinister Marshal Rodolfo Graziani, were more and more on the defensive. To prevent the humiliation of his ally, Hitler finally decided to support the Italians, sending Rommel's Afrikakorps in early 1941. Over the following two years, German and Italian

8 Rudolph Peters, *Islam and Colonialism: The Doctrine of Jihad in Modern History* (The Hague: Mouton, 1979), pp. 39–104; Nikki R. Keddie, 'The Revolt of Islam, 1700 to 1993: Comparative Considerations and Relations to Imperialism', *Comparative Studies in Society and History* 36:3 (1994), 463–87, esp. 481–5; and David Motadel, 'Islam and the European Empires', *Historical Journal* 55:3 (2012), 831–56, esp. 841–51, provide overviews.
9 Much of the Islamic history of the war is also colonial history; see Martin Thomas, *The French Empire at War, 1940–1945* (Manchester University Press, 1998); and Chantal Metzger, *L'empire colonial français dans la stratégie du Troisième Reich (1936–1945)* (2 vols., New York: Peter Lang, 2002), for France; and R. D. Pearce, *The Turning Point: British Colonial Policy, 1938–48* (London: Frank Cass, 1982); Ashley Jackson, *The British Empire and the Second World War* (London: Continuum, 2006); Christopher A. Bayly and Tim Harper, *Forgotten Armies: Britain's Asian Empire and the War with Japan* (London: Allen Lane, 2004); and, for a concise overview, Keith Jeffery, 'The Second World War', in Judith M. Brown and Wm. Roger Louis (eds.), *The Oxford History of the British Empire*, vol. IV: *The Twentieth Century* (5 vols., Oxford University Press, 1999), pp. 306–28, for Britain. Rheinisches Journalistenbüro (ed.), *'Unsere Opfer zählen nicht': Die Dritte Welt im Zweiten Weltkrieg* (Hamburg: Assoziation A, 2005), provides a good overview of the struggle for the non-European world during the Second World War.
10 Martin Kitchen, *Rommel's Desert War: Waging World War II in North Africa, 1941–1943* (Cambridge University Press, 2009), provides a comprehensive account of the military events in North Africa.

troops fought in Tunisia, the Libyan Desert and on the fringes of Egypt, where they advanced to the small desert train station al-'Alamayn (El Alamein), only 150 miles west of Cairo. Following the crushing defeat there by Montgomery's Eighth Army in the autumn of 1942, the Italian-German army was quickly pushed back. Around the same time, in Operation TORCH, Anglo-American troops landed in Algeria and Morocco to put further pressure on the remains of Rommel's forces. The Germans and Italians retreated to Tunisia, where they capitulated.

The populations in the North African war zones suffered considerably. Particularly bleak was the situation in Italian Libya.[11] Already before the war, the country had experienced brutal colonial oppression, and the incursion of Italian settlers, causing much discontent among the population. In fact, ever since the conquest of Libya in 1911, imperial rule had been challenged by local resistance movements, most importantly the Sanusi order, which had been the strongest native political force in Cyrenaica. Although the Italians had crushed Sanusi resistance in the early 1930s, marked by the public hanging of the legendary Sanusi commander 'Umar al-Mukhtar, the movement's leader, Sayyid Muhammad Idris al-Sanusi, had escaped to Egypt and was now, at the height of the Second World War, rallying his followers again.[12] A group of Sanusi warriors, fighting in the Sanusi Arab Force (later Libyan Arab Force), advanced alongside the British army into Cyrenaica, and when German troops were defeated and Italian rule destroyed, London decided to make the Sanusi leader king of post-colonial Libya.

Vichy rule in North Africa – Tunisia, Algeria and Morocco – would not last either.[13] When pushed out of Libya in late 1942, German and Italian troops occupied parts of Tunisia, although they depended largely on the French administration. The Bey of Tunis – Muhammad VII al-Munsif – remained formally in power, even receiving a German delegation on the occasion of the 1942 *'Id al-Adha*, the feast of sacrifice marking the end of the annual hajj season. Accused of Axis collaboration, he was later dethroned by the Allies and replaced by Lamine Bey, the last Bey of Tunis. During the war years, the

---

11 Patrick Bernhard, 'Behind the Battle Lines: Italian Atrocities and the Persecution of Arabs, Berbers, and Jews in North Africa During World War II', *Holocaust and Genocide Studies* 26:3 (2012), 425–46; and, more generally on Italian colonial rule in Libya, Claudio G. Segrè, *Fourth Shore: The Italian Colonization of Libya* (University of Chicago Press, 1974).

12 Saul Kelly, *War and Politics in the Desert: Britain and Libya During the Second World War* (London: Silphium, 2010).

13 Christine Levisse-Touzé, *L'Afrique du Nord dans la guerre 1939–1945* (Paris: Albin Michel, 1998).

population in Tunisia suffered under repressive Vichy policies, and even more under the brief but brutal German-Italian occupation. In the rest of French North Africa, Algeria and Morocco, the situation was only marginally better, and most welcomed enthusiastically the Anglo-American invasion and the end of Vichy rule.

Egypt, behind the eastern front lines, too, became part of the North African war zone, with the west of the country being turned into a major battlefield, and Axis aircraft flying raids on targets in the hinterland. Anxious about anti-colonial revolts, the British strengthened their control and censorship, which, in turn, fuelled anti-British resentment even more, and led to a state of internal crisis. When, in early 1942, King Faruq resisted London's requests to dismiss the incumbent government, which Whitehall deemed unreliable, British tanks took to 'Abdin Palace, forcing the monarch to give in. The events sparked anti-British student protests across Cairo.[14] 'They demonstrated in the streets, chanting slogans like "Advance Rommel!" as they saw in a British defeat the only way of getting their enemy out of the country', Anwar al-Sadat, stationed as a young officer in the capital, later recalled.[15] Still, overall, the situation remained under control. No major uprisings broke out, and following the victory at al-'Alamain, the popular mood was shifting toward the Allies again.

As Axis and Allied troops clashed in North Africa, the Middle East became increasingly embroiled in the war.[16] The region was important not only because of its oilfields, but also, and perhaps even more importantly, because of its geopolitical location. After the invasion of the Soviet Union in the summer of 1941, Hitler's generals drew up plans to advance from the Maghrib into the Mashriq, uniting with German troops breaking through from the Caucasus. Around the same time, Berlin became embroiled in the failed coup led by Rashid 'Ali al-Kilani in Iraq, dispatching a special military mission to Baghdad.[17] Al-Kilani and his co-conspirators, the four officers known as the

14 Charles D. Smith, '4 February 1942: Its Causes and its Influence on Egyptian Politics and on the Future of Anglo-Egyptian Relations, 1937–45', *International Journal of Middle East Studies* 10:4 (1979), 453–79, esp., on the pro-Axis protests, 468.

15 Anwar el-Sadat, *In Search of Identity* (London: William Collins, 1978), pp. 31–2.

16 George Kirk, *The Middle East in the War* (Oxford University Press, 1952), remains the classic; see also, on German policies and propaganda, Bernd Philipp Schröder, *Deutschland und der Mittlere Osten im Zweiten Weltkrieg* (Göttingen: Muster-Schmidt, 1975); and, focusing on the Arab world, Heinz Tillmann, *Deutschlands Araberpolitik im Zweiten Weltkrieg* (Berlin, East: Deutscher Verlag der Wissenschaften, 1965); Łukasz Hirszowicz, *The Third Reich and the Arab East* (London: Routledge, 1966); and Jeffrey Herf, *Nazi Propaganda to the Arab World* (New Haven, Conn.: Yale University Press, 2009).

17 Bernd Philipp Schröder, *Irak 1941* (Freiburg: Rombach, 1980).

'Golden Square', were stopped by British military force. Al-Kilani fled to Berlin. At once, British and Free French troops occupied Vichy Syria and Lebanon, while Anglo-American and Soviet soldiers marched into Iran, accusing the Riza Shah of sympathies for Hitler, and replacing him with his politically inexperienced son Muhammad Riza Pahlavi.[18] The Middle East was now under firm Allied control, and would remain so until Victory Day. The sporadic attempts of German intelligence officers to foster subversive activities and conduct sabotage in the region, particularly in Palestine and Iran, were widely ineffective. Overall, with the exception of the events in Iraq, no major popular anti-Allied revolts shook the region during the war. The two most important states in the Middle East that remained independent – Turkey and Saudi Arabia – though courted by Berlin, Rome and Tokyo, were drawing nearer to the Allied camp as the tide of the war turned against the Axis.[19]

One of the Muslim areas most neglected in the historiography of the Second World War is the Islamic borderlands of the Soviet Union.[20] When Hitler's armies conquered Crimea in the autumn of 1941, and advanced into

18 Geoffrey Warner, *Iraq and Syria 1941* (London: Davis-Poynter, 1974); Anthony Mockler, *Our Enemies the French: Being an Account of the War Fought Between the French and the British: Syria 1941* (London: Leo Cooper, 1976); and Aviel Roshwald, *Estranged Bedfellows: Britain and France in the Middle East During the Second World War* (New York: Oxford University Press, 1990), on Syria and Lebanon; and Miron Rezun, *The Iranian Crisis of 1941: The Actors, Britain, Germany and the Soviet Union* (Cologne: Böhlau, 1982); Richard A. Stewart, *Sunrise at Abadan: The British and Soviet Invasion of Iran, 1941* (New York: Praeger, 1988); and Jana Forsmann, *Testfall für die 'Grossen Drei': Die Besetzung Irans durch Briten, Sowjets und Amerikaner 1941–1946* (Cologne: Böhlau, 2010), on Iran. On the relations between Nazi Germany and Iran, see Djalal Madani, *Iranische Politik und Drittes Reich* (Frankfurt am Main: Peter Lang, 1986).

19 Lothar Krecker, *Deutschland und die Türkei im Zweiten Weltkrieg* (Frankfurt am Main: Vittorio Klostermann, 1964); Johannes Glasneck and Inge Kircheisen, *Türkei Brennpunkte der Orientpolitik im Zweiten Weltkrieg* (Berlin: Deutscher Verlag der Wissenschaften, 1968); Zehra Önder, *Die türkische Aussenpolitik im Zweiten Weltkrieg* (Munich: Oldenbourg, 1977); and, more generally, Selim Deringil, *Turkish Foreign Policy During the Second World War: An 'Active' Neutrality* (Cambridge University Press, 2004), for Turkey; and for Saudi Arabia, see note 16 above.

20 Patrik von zur Mühlen, *Zwischen Hakenkreuz und Sowjetstern: Der Nationalismus der sowjetischen Orientvölker im Zweiten Weltkrieg* (Düsseldorf: Droste, 1971); and Andrej Angrick, *Besatzungspolitik und Massenmord: Die Einsatzgruppe D in der südlichen Sowjetunion 1941–1943* (Hamburg: Hamburger Edition, 2003); and, on Caucasus, Joachim Hoffmann, *Kaukasien 1942/43: Das deutsche Heer und Orientvoelker der Sowjetunion* (Freiburg: Rombach, 1991); and, on Crimea, Michel Luther, 'Die Krim unter deutscher Besatzung im Zweiten Weltkrieg', *Forschungen zur Osteuropäischen Geschichte* 3 (1956), 28–98; and Norbert Kunz, *Die Krim unter deutscher Herrschaft 1941–1944: Germanisierungsutopie und Besatzungsrealität* (Darmstadt: Wissenschaftliche Buchgesellschaft, 2005). David Motadel, 'Islam and Germany's War in the Soviet Borderlands, 1941–1945', *Journal of Contemporary History* 48:4 (2013), 784–820, provides a general account of German engagement with Muslims in these areas.

the Caucasus in the summer of 1942, some of Moscow's Muslim-populated areas turned into front-line zones. On the Crimean peninsula, held by the Wehrmacht until 1944, the Germans ruled a quarter of a million Sunni Tatars. In the northern Caucasus, they briefly occupied the Muslim valleys of Karachai-Circassia and Kabardino-Balkaria, even advancing to the fringes of Chechnya, though never taking Grozny. Having felt suppressed under Soviet rule, which had brought forced economic collectivization and religious persecution, parts of the Muslim population now welcomed the Germans as liberators. Behind the frontlines, particularly in Chechnya-Ingushetia and, to a lesser extent, Karachai-Circassia and Kabardino-Balkaria, anti-Soviet uprisings broke out. In a special mission, a Wehrmacht command was parachuted behind the front lines of Chechnya to incite and unite the rebels, though to little avail.[21] Among the most determined and efficient rebel groups were those led by religious leaders, such as the guerrillas of Shaykh Qureish Belkhoroev in the mountains of Ingushetia and eastern Ossetia, who kept up their fight until 1947. Anxious to pacify the volatile front regions, the Germans did not miss the opportunity to exploit this hostility. In both the Caucasus and Crimea, the army command made substantial efforts to win the Muslims over as collaborators. In the bigger cities of Crimea, the Tatars were permitted to form so-called 'Muslim Committees' to administer some aspects of their affairs, and 20,000 of them were recruited into German auxiliary units to fight partisan insurgency on the peninsula. Furious about the collaboration, Stalin, after the reconquest of the areas, ordered the deportation of the Muslim minorities (along with the Volga Germans and Kalmyks): Crimean Tatars, Karachais, Balkars, Chechens and Ingush.

On the European fringes of the Islamic world, in the Balkans, the war had no less severe effects on the Muslim population. Although the Axis invasion of the Kingdom of Yugoslavia in spring 1941 was welcomed by many Muslims who had felt repressed under Orthodox Serbian hegemony, the years that followed brought unimaginable misery.[22] While the Germans

---

21 Günther W. Gellermann, *Tief im Hinterland des Gegners: Ausgewählte Unternehmen deutscher Geheimdienste im Zweiten Weltkrieg* (Bonn: Bernard und Graefe, 1999), pp. 107–27.

22 The most comprehensive work remains Jozo Tomasevich, *War and Revolution in Yugoslavia, 1941–1945: Occupation and Collaboration* (Stanford University Press, 2001), esp. pp. 466–510; see also, on Bosnia in particular, Enver Redžić, *Bosnia and Herzegovina in the Second World War* (New York: Frank Cass, 2005); Enver Redžić, *Muslimansko Autonomaštvo i 13. SS Divizija: Autonomija Bosne i Hercegovine i Hitlerov Treći Rajh* (Sarajevo: Svjetlost, 1987); Marko Attila Hoare, *Genocide and Resistance in Hitler's*

occupied Serbia, the Muslim-populated regions fell under the administration of the Italians (Montenegro), the Bulgarians (Macedonia) and, most crucially, the newly created Croatian Ustaša state (Bosnia and Herzegovina). Ruling the largest part of Yugoslavia's Muslim population, Ante Pavelić's Ustaša regime tried formally to accommodate Islam in the new state. Soon, however, the Muslims became embroiled in the civil war between the Ustaša regime, Tito's communist Partisans and Draža Mihailović's Orthodox Serbian Četniks. The Partisans clashed with both Ustaša forces and Četniks, while the Četniks, in the quest for a Serbian kingdom, fought Ustaša troops and Tito's Partisans. The Muslim population was attacked by all three parties. When the Ustaša sent Muslim army units to fight Partisans and Četniks, the Muslim civilian population soon became targets of retaliatory attacks from both. Unable to pacify the country, the Ustaša often did not intervene in these attacks, and in some cases the regime punished Muslim villages whose leaders had agreed to local ceasefires with the insurgents. Muslims made some attempts to form self-defence militias, but these, too, on the whole, were unable to protect the population. As a consequence, more and more Muslim leaders in Bosnia and Herzegovina began advocating independence. Some of them turned to Hitler, asking for Muslim autonomy under the Third Reich's protection. The Wehrmacht and, more importantly, the SS, which in early 1943 became increasingly involved in Croatia again, to prevent the civil war eroding Axis power in the region, saw in the Muslims trustworthy allies, and began to court them. The Germans launched a massive propaganda campaign, consulted with Muslim leaders, and recruited almost 20,000 Muslims into the infamous SS Handžar Division. In contrast, Bulgarian occupation authorities in Macedonia, and the Italians in Montenegro and Albania (already occupied by Mussolini in 1939), made no significant attempts to reach out to the Muslim population.[23] In the Sandžak area, the mountain belt between Montenegro and Serbia, the Italians had

Bosnia: The Partisans and the Chetniks, 1941–1943 (Oxford University Press, 2006); and Marko Attila Hoare, *The Bosnian Muslims in the Second World War: A History* (London: Hurst, 2013). David Motadel, 'The "Muslim Question" in Hitler's Balkans', *Historical Journal* 56:4 (2013), 1007–39, provides an account of German policies towards the Muslim populations.

23 Bernd J. Fischer, *Albania at War 1939–1945* (London: Hurst, 1999); Hubert Neuwirth, *Widerstand und Kollaboration in Albanien 1939–1944* (Wiesbaden: Otto Harrassowitz, 2008), for Italian and German engagement with the Muslims of Albania; and Mary C. Neuburger, *The Orient Within: Muslim Minorities and the Negotiation of Nationhood in Modern Bulgaria* (Ithaca, NY: Cornell University Press, 2004), pp. 48–54, 183–4; and Kevin Featherstone, Dimitris Papadimitriou, Argyris Mamarelis and Georgios Niarchos, *The Last Ottomans: The Muslim Minority of Greece, 1940–1949*

repeatedly turned a blind eye to Četnik raids on Muslim villages. When the Germans became involved in these regions – especially after Rome's withdrawal from the Balkans in the autumn of 1943 – they made advances to these Muslim populations as well. In the Epirus area of northwestern Greece, which had also been ruled by the Italians, Wehrmacht authorities sought the cooperation of the Albanian Muslim Cham minority.[24] Overall, however, German patronage only worsened the situation of the Balkans' Muslims. They suffered massacres, expulsion and hunger, and, after the war, were stigmatized as collaborators. In Tito's new socialist state in Yugoslavia and in Enver Hoxha's People's Republic of Albania, Islamic institutions were attacked. Accused of collaboration, the Muslim Chams of Epirus were targeted by Greek nationalist militias, who raided their villages, killed many and expelled the survivors to Albania.

In both the Balkans and the Soviet borderlands, Muslims were immediately affected by the Holocaust. In the first months of the war on the Eastern Front, many Muslim prisoners of war were executed by the SS on the assumption that their circumcision proved that they were Jewish.[25] At a high-level conference of the representatives from the Wehrmacht, the SS and the Ministry for the Occupied Eastern Territories in the summer of 1941, a fierce argument broke out about these executions, particularly a case in which hundreds of Muslims, possibly Crimean Tatars, had been killed because they were taken for Jews. Reinhard Heydrich subsequently sent out a directive cautioning the SS Einsatzgruppen that 'circumcision' did not constitute satisfactory 'proof of Jewish descent'.[26] On the Muslim fringes of the Soviet Union, however, Himmler's killing squads still had difficulties distinguishing Muslims from Jews. When beginning to exterminate the Jewish populations in the Caucasus and Crimea, they encountered three

(New York: Palgrave Macmillan, 2011), esp. pp. 91–157, for the Bulgarian engagement with Muslims in the war.

24 Mark Mazower, 'Three Forms of Political Justice: Greece, 1944–1945', in Mark Mazower (ed.), *After the War Was Over: Reconstructing the Family, Nation and State in Greece, 1943–1960* (Princeton University Press, 2000), pp. 24–41, here: pp. 24–6; and Hermann Frank Meyer, *Blutiges Edelweiss: Die 1. Gebirgs-Division im Zweiten Weltkrieg* (Berlin: Ch. Links, 2008), *passim*.

25 Raul Hilberg, *The Destruction of the European Jews* (London: W. H. Allen, 1961), pp. 222–3; Hans Adolf Jacobsen, 'The Kommissarbefehl and Mass Executions of Soviet Russian Prisoners of War', in Martin Broszat, Hans Buchheim, Hans-Adolf Jacobsen and Helmut Krausnick (eds.), *Anatomy of the SS State* (London: Collins, 1968), pp. 505–35, here: pp. 529–30; and Christian Streit, *Keine Kameraden: Die Wehrmacht und die sowjetischen Kriegsgefangenen 1941–1945* (Stuttgart: Deutsche Verlags-Anstalt, 1978), p. 98.

26 Quoted in Streit, *Keine Kameraden*, p. 98.

Jewish communities who had long lived closely alongside the Muslim population: the Karaites and Krymchaks in Crimea, and the Judeo-Tats in the Caucasus.[27] While the Karaites were classified as ethnically Turkic and the Tats as Muslims, the Krymchaks were considered Jewish and killed.

When the Germans began murdering Europe's gypsies, they soon had to decide about the fate of many Muslim Roma. Indeed, a major part of the Roma of Crimea was Islamic, and for centuries had assimilated with the Tatars.[28] Tatar leaders showed solidarity with their co-religionists, asking the occupation authorities to spare them. Many Muslim Roma pretended to be Tatars. As the Germans had trouble distinguishing Muslim Roma from Tatars, some – estimates range around 30 per cent – survived. During his interrogation at the *SS Einsatzgruppen* trial, Otto Ohlendorf, who had been in command of the SS killing units in Crimea, explained that the screening of 'gypsies' on the peninsula had been complicated by the fact that many Roma had been followers of Islam: 'That was the difficulty, because some of the gypsies – if not all of them – were Moslems, and for that reason we attached a great amount of importance to not getting into difficulties with the Tartars and, therefore, people were employed in this task who knew the places and the people'.[29] Similarly, Muslims in the Balkans were affected by the perse-cution of the Roma, as here, too, many Roma were of the Islamic faith. Eager to integrate Muslims into their new state, Ustaša officials excluded the Muslim Roma from persecution.[30] The protection of these so-called

27 Mühlen, *Zwischen Hakenkreuz und Sowjetstern*, pp. 49–51; and Angrick, *Besatzungspolitik und Massenmord*, pp. 326–31, 612; and, on the Karaites and Krymchaks in particular, Kunz, *Die Krim unter deutscher Herrschaft*, pp. 187–94; and Kiril Feferman, 'Nazi Germany and the Karaites in 1938–1944: Between Racial Theory and Realpolitik', *Nationalities Papers* 39:2 (2011), 277–94; and, on the Judeo-Tats in particular, Hoffmann, *Kaukasien*, p. 439; and Rudolf Loewenthal, 'The Judeo-Tats in the Caucasus', *Historia Judaica* 14 (1952), 61–82, here: 79.

28 Martin Holler, *Der nationalsozialistische Völkermord an den Roma in der besetzten Sowjet-union (1941–1944)* (Heidelberg: Dokumentations-und Kulturzentrum Deutscher Sinti und Roma, 2009), pp. 91–101; and Mikhail Tyaglyy, 'Were the "Chingené" Victims of the Holocaust? Nazi Policy Toward the Crimean Roma, 1941–1944', *Holocaust and Genocide Studies* 23:1 (2009), 26–53, here: 37–9, 41, 43–4.

29 'Extracts from the Testimony of Defendant Ohlendorf', in *Trials of War Criminals Before the Nuernberg Military Tribunals under Control Council Law No. 10*, vol. IV: *The Einsatzgruppen Case* (Washington DC: Government Printing Office, 1949–53), pp. 223–312, here: p. 290.

30 Tomasevich, *War and Revolution in Yugoslavia*, p. 609; Karola Fings, Cordula Lissner and Frank Sparing, '. . .einziges Land, in dem Judenfrage und Zigeunerfrage gelöst': Die Verfolgung der Roma im faschistisch besetzten Jugoslawien 1941–1945* (Cologne: Rom, 1992), p. 20; Michael Zimmermann, *Rassenutopie und Genozid: Die nationalsozialistische 'Lösung der Zigeunerfrage'* (Hamburg: Christians, 1996), p. 285; David M. Crowe, 'Muslim Roma in the Balkans', *Nationalities Papers* 28:1 (2000), 93–128, here: 97–8; Mark Biondich,

'white gypsies' led to a massive increase in the number of conversions of Christian Roma to Islam, though these conversions were eventually officially prohibited. In other parts of the Balkans, too, their religious affiliation gave Muslim Roma some protection.

Throughout the war, the Axis powers spread anti-Jewish hate propaganda across the Islamic world. It is impossible to generalize about the attitudes of the Muslim population in the Balkans and the Eastern territories toward the genocide of the Jews, nor is it possible to make general statements about the responses of the Muslim majorities in the Maghrib to Vichy and fascist discrimination and persecution of their Jewish neighbours. Actual reactions on the ground ranged, as elsewhere, from collaboration and profiteering to empathy and, in some cases, solidarity with the victims. There are examples of Muslims who saved their Jewish neighbours. Among the most famous is the case of the Albanian Muslims who helped many of their Jewish country-men.[31] Another prominent example is Sultan Muhammad V of Morocco, who showed solidarity with his Jewish subjects targeted by the Vichy's anti-Jewish laws.[32] In North Africa and the Middle East, the war years saw a rise in anti-Zionist, and indeed anti-Jewish, resentment. On the local level, however, relations between Jews and Muslims were often complex, depending on the social and political conditions.[33] There were no major anti-Jewish riots during the war, with the exception of the 1941 pogrom in Iraq, known as *farhud*, when, after the failed al-Kilani coup, a Muslim mob attacked Jewish houses and shops, killing 179.[34] It is noteworthy, finally, that in both the Balkans and North Africa, some Jews tried to escape persecution through conversion to

'Persecution of Roma-Sinti in Croatia, 1941–1945', in Paul A. Shapiro and Robert M. Ehrenreich (eds.), *Roma and Sinti: Under-studied Victims of Nazism* (Washington DC: Center for Advanced Holocaust Studies, 2002), pp. 33–47, here: pp. 37–8; Donald Kenrick and Grattan Puxon, *Gypsies Under the Swastika* (Hatfield: University of Hertfordshire Press, 2009), pp. 99, 101; and, on German conceptions of the 'white gypsies', Sevasti Trubeta, '"Gypsiness", Racial Discourse and Persecution: Balkan Roma During the Second World War', *Nationalities Papers* 31:4 (2003), 495–514, here: 505–6.

31 Norman Gershman, *Besa: Muslims Who Saved Jews in World War II* (Syracuse University Press, 2008).

32 Robert Assaraf, *Mohammed V et les Juifs du Maroc à l'époque de Vichy* (Paris: Plon, 1997).

33 Michel Abitbol, *The Jews of North Africa During the Second World War* (Detroit, Mich.: Wayne State University Press, 1989); Michael M. Laskier, *North African Jewry in the Twentieth Century: The Jews of Morocco, Tunisia and Algeria* (New York University Press, 1994), pp. 55–83; and Robert Satloff, *Among the Righteous: Lost Stories from the Holocaust's Long Reach into Arab Lands* (New York: Public Affairs, 2006), provide overviews of the fate of Jews in North Africa during the Second World War.

34 Hayyim J. Cohen, 'The Anti-Jewish Farhūd in Baghdad, 1941', *Middle Eastern Studies* 3:1 (1996), 2–17.

Islam. In the Balkans, a number of Jews even succeeded in escaping, disguised as Muslims, some of them fleeing wearing the Islamic veil.[35]

In South and Southeast Asia, the Second World War affected some of the world's largest Muslim populations. The Muslims of British India were, from the outset, considered to be of utmost importance by Whitehall.[36] Throughout the war, British authorities fought uprisings along the Northwest Frontier, organized by the Pashtu rebel leader Mirza Ali Khan, known as the Fakir of Ipi.[37] Calling for jihad against the empire, his guerrillas launched attacks against the imperial infrastructure, and clashed with contingents of the British Indian Army. Through their missions in Kabul, both Italian and German emissaries tried to support the rebels, supplying money, weapons and ammunition. The majority of India's Muslims, however, remained loyal to the empire. British officials tried their best to court Muslims, with Lord Linlithgow, Viceroy and Governor General of India, assuring Muhammad Jinnah, head of the Muslim League, that 'His Majesty's Government' had 'friendly and sympathetic relations with all Muslim Powers'.[38] The Muslim League, the largest Muslim organization of the country, backed the war effort, although their leaders used the situation to push for partition.[39] The war, in fact, significantly strengthened Muslim separatism in India, resulting in the foundation of Pakistan in 1947.

Beyond India, in the Southeast Asian war zones – particularly in British Malaya, invaded by Japanese troops in late 1941, and in the Dutch East Indies, occupied in the spring of 1942 – millions of Muslims were directly confronted with the horrors of war.[40] Although Japanese authorities in Malaya were

---

35 Robert J. Donia, *Sarajevo: A Biography* (London: Hurst, 2006), pp. 174, 176–9; and, on Jewish conversions to Islam, see also Tomasevich, *War and Revolution in Yugoslavia*, pp. 543–4; Redžić, *Bosnia and Herzegovina in the Second World War*, pp. 78, 172; and Redžić, *Muslimansko Autonomaštvo i 13. SS Divizija*, p. 20.

36 Johannes H. Voigt, *India in the Second World War* (New Delhi: Arnold-Heinemann, 1987); and, on Axis policies towards India, Reimund Schnabel, *Tiger und Schakal: Deutsche Indienpolitik 1941–1943* (Vienna: Europa, 1968); Milan Hauner, *India in Axis Strategy: Germany, Japan, and Indian Nationalists in the Second World War* (Stuttgart: Klett-Cotta, 1981); and Jan Kuhlmann, *Netaji in Europe* (New Delhi: Rupa, 2012).

37 Milan Hauner, 'One Man Against the Empire: The Faqir of Ipi and the British in Central Asia on the Eve of and During the Second World War', *Journal of Contemporary History* 16:1 (1981), 183–212.

38 Quoted in Stanley Wolpert, *Jinnah of Pakistan* (New York: Oxford University Press, 1984), p. 186.

39 Ibid., pp. 171–246.

40 Harry J. Benda, *The Crescent and the Rising Sun: Indonesian Islam under the Japanese Occupation, 1942–1945* (The Hague: W. van Hoeve, 1958), on the occupation of the Dutch East Indies; and Abu Talib Ahmad, *Malay-Muslims, Islam and the Rising Sun, 1941–1945* (Selangor: Royal Asiatic Society, 2003), on the occupation of British Malaya.

keen to ally with the local population and involved many Malay in the administration, their occupation grew more brutal as the war went on, bringing economic hardship, violence and slave labour. Similarly, in the occupied Dutch East Indies, where most had initially welcomed the Japanese as liberators from European colonial rule, hopes for a better life were soon shattered by forced labour and famine. In both areas, the rise of Muslim guerrilla resistance led to ruthless Japanese reprisals.

Movements

One of the most dominant political issues across the Muslim world during the war was the question of national independence from imperial rule. Here, as elsewhere, anti-colonial nationalists saw the war as an opportunity to achieve self-determination; and they had to decide on which side to stand in a conflict that would shape the future world order. Both Axis and Allied powers tried to engage with the question of national independence – and both struggled with the problem of credibility.

Imperial Japan and Nazi Germany, and even, though to a lesser extent, Fascist Italy and Vichy France, engaged in anti-colonial propaganda. Across Southeast Asia, Tokyo spread its pan-Asian slogans against European imperialism, promising a bright future within the Greater East Asian Co-Prosperity Sphere. Although many anti-colonial leaders in the region initially welcomed the Japanese conquest, their hopes were soon shattered, as it became clear that the occupiers pursued their own imperial goals. Rome, too, was quick to proclaim, when invading Egypt in the summer of 1940, that 'Italian action on the Cyrenaican border is directed exclusively against the English', and that Italy only 'wants to be a significant factor in the liberation of Egypt and of the entire Arab world from British domination'.[41] Similarly, when German-Italian troops marched into Tunisia in late 1942, Mussolini made overtures to the Néo-Destour and to Habib Bourguiba, freeing the politician – with Nazi support – from a Vichy prison in France, and staging a reception for him in Rome; yet all to no avail: after his return to Tunis, and following the Axis defeat in the Maghrib, Bourguiba quickly sided with the Allies. It is hardly surprising that Italy's slogans found little resonance, given the country's own colonialist record. The Germans also raised the hopes of nationalist

---

41 Quoted in Nir Arielli, *Fascist Italy and the Middle East, 1933–40* (New York: Palgrave Macmillan, 2010), p. 178.

movements, from North Africa to the Middle East to Central Asia. In the war years, nationalists and anti-colonial leaders from across the Muslim world came to Berlin, where they published papers and became involved in German war propaganda. In the Muslim world itself, too, some nationalists, like al-Kilani and the 'Golden Square', or al-Sadat and his comrades from Egypt's revolutionary 'Free Officers' group, threw in their lot with the Germans. In the end, the hopes of these nationalists were shattered. Axis slogans remained empty propaganda, designed to destabilize the hinterlands of the enemy. Mussolini's Italy and Pétain's France had their own schemes for North Africa and the Middle East, while Hitler was not willing to give definite statements on national independence to the Muslims in these regions, the southern Soviet Union or elsewhere.

The Allies, in contrast, felt easier in giving out promises for self-determination, promoting the war as a struggle for freedom and democracy against tyranny and dictatorship. The Atlantic Charter, issued in the summer of 1941, guaranteed the 'rights of all peoples to choose the form of government under which they will live'.[42] These words obviously conflicted with the realities in most parts of the Islamic world, where Muslims were subjugated to imperial regimes based on inequality and exploitation, not to mention the Allied invasions of Syria, Lebanon, Iraq, Iran and Libya. Still, the war offered anti-colonial leaders the opportunity to press for concessions. While many were unsuccessful, cooperation during the war brought some closer to independence – most notably, of course, nationalists in Libya and Pakistan. In any case, in most parts of the Muslim world, the conflict further facilitated anti-colonial nationalism and marked the beginning of decolonization.

As the war engulfed more and more areas populated by Muslims, both Axis and Allied powers also began to see Islam as strategically significant. Islam had proven, or so it seemed, a potent political mobilizing force in anti-imperial revolts. Considering Islam as the Achilles heel of the European empires and the Soviet Union, the Axis powers organized a massive religiously charged propaganda campaign – employing Islamic rhetoric, slogans and imagery – and religious policies – engaging with religious authorities and institutions – in order to provoke unrest in their enemies' hinterlands. Already in the spring of 1937, Mussolini had ordered that he be publicly presented with a bejewelled 'Sword of Islam' (which had been made in Italy)

---

42 Quoted in Jeffery, 'The Second World War', p. 314.

at a ceremony in Tripoli, symbolically promoting himself as the protector of the Muslim world.[43] Italy, the Duce proclaimed, would always respect the 'laws of the Prophet'. 'Mussolini is travelling through Africa and thereby is paying homage to Islam. Very clever and cunning. Paris and London are immediately suspicious', Goebbels noted in his diary.[44] Throughout the war, Fascist Italy launched a massive propaganda campaign across the Islamic world, glorifying Mussolini as a 'protector of Islam'.

Germany, as in the First World War, engaged in an even more significant campaign for Islamic mobilization. On all fronts, from the Sahara Desert to the Balkan peninsula to the Soviet borderlands, the Germans promoted the Third Reich as the friend of Muslims and defender of their faith against allegedly common enemies – the British Empire, communists and Jews.[45] Nazi authorities founded several Muslim institutions, such as the Berlin 'Islamic Central Institute', inaugurated in 1942, and enlisted religious leaders to rally Muslim support. Among them were authorities from Eastern Europe, such as the Lithuanian Mufti Jakub Szynkiewicz of Vilna, who propagated Hitler's New Order in the Eastern territories; from Southeastern Europe, such as the Bosnian dignitary Muhamed Pandža of the Sarajevo 'ulama, who became an ally of the Germans in the Balkans; and from the Arab world, such as the Moroccan cleric and pan-Islamic activist Taqi al-Din al-Hilali, who became one of Berlin's major Muslim broadcast propagandists. The most famous among them, of course, was the peacock-like Mufti of Jerusalem, Amin al-Husayni, who had come to Berlin in 1941, where he was received by Hitler in the New Reich Chancellery, and soon began calling on the faithful to wage holy war on the side of the Axis.[46] On the ground, in the

43 John L. Wright, 'Mussolini, Libya, and the Sword of Islam', in Ruth Ben-Ghiat and Mia Fuller (eds.), *Italian Colonialism* (New York: Palgrave Macmillan, 2005), pp. 121–30, 123–5; and more generally, Manuela A. Williams, *Mussolini's Propaganda Abroad: Subversion in the Mediterranean and the Middle East, 1935–1940* (London: Routledge, 2006), esp. p. 205; and Arielli, *Fascist Italy and the Middle East*, esp. pp. 1, 97–8.
44 Elke Fröhlich (ed.), *Sämtliche Fragmente*, pt. 1, vol. IV: *Die Tagebücher von Joseph Goebbels* (3 pts., 27 vols., Munich: K. G. Saur, 2000), pp. 50–1 (14 March 1937).
45 Motadel, *Islam and Nazi Germany's War*; and, for some aspects of this policy, Gerhard Höpp, 'Der Koran als "Geheime Reichssache": Bruchstücke deutscher Islampolitik zwischen 1938 und 1945', in Holger Preissler and Hubert Seiwert (eds.), *Gnosisforschung und Religionsgeschichte: Festschrift für Kurt Rudolph zum 65. Geburtstag* (Marburg: Diagonal, 1994), pp. 435–46.
46 Joseph B. Schechtman, *The Mufti and the Fuehrer: The Rise and Fall of Haj Amin el-Husseini* (London: Thomas Yoseloff, 1965); Jennie Lebel, *The Mufti of Jerusalem Haj-Amin El-Husseini and National-Socialism* (Belgrade: Cigoja, 2007); and Klaus Gensicke, *The Mufti of Jerusalem and the Nazis: The Berlin Years, 1941–1945* (London: Vallentine Mitchell, 2011), provide accounts of the collaboration of the Mufti with the Germans.

Muslim war zones, German troops were ordered to respect religion when dealing with Muslims. As early as 1941, the Wehrmacht distributed the military handbook *Der Islam* among its soldiers in North Africa, to train them to behave properly toward the locals. On the Eastern Front, in the Caucasus and Crimea, army authorities ordered the rebuilding of mosques and madrasas and the re-establishment of religious holidays and celebrations, all with the intention of undermining Soviet rule.

An equally sustained attempt to instrumentalize Islam was made by Japan, seeking to mobilize Asia's Muslims against Britain, the Netherlands, China and Soviet Russia.[47] Although Japan had begun its political engagement with Islam in the 1930s – the Tokyo Mosque and the 'Greater Japan Islamic League' were both founded in 1938 – it intensified these policies when advancing through Southeast Asia. During the invasion of the Dutch East Indies, Japanese agents contacted local Muslim leaders to support the Japanese incursion, and, after the occupation, military authorities made extensive efforts to co-opt the local 'ulama. Japanese officials supplied political texts to imams to be read out in their Friday sermons, and instructed them to offer prayers for Tokyo's victory. In the spring of 1943, Islamic religious leaders from the occupied territories were summoned to a conference in Singapore, at which Japanese propagandists proclaimed that Tokyo was the true protector of Islam. A second conference of religious leaders was organized in late 1944, in Kuala Kangsar on the Malay peninsula. From the Japanese capital, the Tatar imam Abdurreshid Ibrahim, the 'patriarch of the Tokyo Mosque', preached jihad against the Allies. 'Japan's cause in the Greater East Asia War is a sacred one and in its austerity is comparable to the war carried out against the infidels by the Prophet Muhammad in the past', he announced in the summer of 1942.[48]

In their efforts to appeal to Islamic sentiment, by the middle of the war the Axis faced competition not only from the British, but also from the Americans and the Soviets, all promising to defend Islam and to protect the

---

47 Benda, *The Crescent and the Rising Sun*, on the East Indies; and Ahmad, *Malay-Muslims, Islam and the Rising Sun*; as well as Abu Talib Ahmad, 'Research on Islam and Malay-Muslims During the Japanese Occupation of Malaya, 1942–45', *Asian Research Trends* 9 (1999), 81–119; and Abu Talib Ahmad, 'Japanese Policy Towards Islam in Malaya During the Occupation: A Reassessment', *Journal of Southeast Asian Studies* 33:1 (2002), 107–22, on Malaya. Selçuk Esenbel, 'Japan's Global Claim to Asia and the World of Islam: Transnational Nationalism and World Power, 1900–1945', *American Historical Review* 109:4 (2004), 1140–70, offers insights into the origins of Japan's engagement with Islam.

48 Anonymous, 'Japan Muslims Confident of Nippon Victory', *Shanghai Times*, 14 June 1942.

faithful. For the Allies, Islam was both a potential threat in their own Muslim territories and a powerful instrument that could be employed in political warfare. Churchill took Islamic anti-imperialism very seriously, urging that Britain 'must not on any account break with the Moslems'.[49] During the war, London made significant efforts to strengthen its ties with the world of Islam. British authorities opened the East London Mosque, and the Churchill War Cabinet decided to build the London Central Mosque in Regent's Park, to demonstrate the empire's respect for Islam.[50] Pamphlet and radio propaganda drew on sacred texts – the Qur'an and the Hadith – to legitimize Muslim loyalty to London.[51] The *Frankfurter Zeitung* lamented that London was trying with 'great effort' to turn the Islamic world against the Third Reich, accusing 'British propaganda' of exploiting the Qur'an to prove 'an ideological affinity between Islam and democracy'.[52] On the ground, British officials employed various local religious figures, among them, for instance, the Mufti of Tripoli, who, in early 1943, made a public statement praising Churchill and Great Britain.[53] After the 1941 invasion of Vichy Levant, the powerful Mufti of Lebanon, Shaykh Muhammad Tawfiq Khalid, had already openly called the faithful to support the Allies.[54]

London was particularly anxious to control the Islamic leaders and movements in Egypt, not only because of the country's proximity to the North African front line, but also because its religious establishment was considered influential beyond Egyptian borders. Still, most of the traditional 'ulama refrained from making public political statements. The Mufti of Egypt, Shaykh 'Abd al-Majid Salim, was one of the country's main proponents of political neutrality.[55] His even more influential rival, Muhammad Mustafa

49 Winston S. Churchill, *The Second World War*, vol. IV: *The Hinge of Fate* (6 vols., London: Cassell, 1951), pp. 185–6, quoting a letter from Churchill to Roosevelt of 4 March 1942.
50 Humayun Ansari, *The Infidel Within: Muslims in Britain since 1800* (London: Hurst and Co., 2004), pp. 134, 342 (East London Mosque), 134, 341 (London Central Mosque); and, more detailed on the London Central Mosque, A. L. Tibawi, 'History of the London Central Mosque and the Islamic Cultural Centre 1910–1980', *Die Welt des Islams* 21:1–4 (1981), 193–208.
51 Neville Barbour, 'Broadcasting to the Arab World: Arabic Transmissions from the BBC and Other Non-Arab Stations', *Middle East Journal* 5 (1951), 57–69; and Seth Arsenian, 'Wartime Propaganda in the Middle East', *Middle East Journal* 2 (1948), 417–29.
52 Anonymous, 'Die arabische Welt sammelt ihre Kräfte: Strömungen und Gegenströmungen im ersten Kriegsjahr', *Frankfurter Zeitung*, 25 May 1941.
53 Motadel, *Islam and Nazi Germany's War*, p. 113.
54 Götz Nordbruch, *Nazism in Syria and Lebanon: The Ambivalence of the German Option, 1933–1945* (London: Routledge, 2009), pp. 120–2.
55 Jakob Skovgaard-Petersen, *Defining Islam for the Egyptian State: Muftis and Fatwas of the Dār Al-Iftā* (Leiden: Brill, 1997), pp. 159–70.

al-Maraghi, the elderly rector of al-Azhar, followed the same line.[56] The political activities of Azhari students – many of whom were more radical and pro-Axis – were closely controlled by the authorities. While the traditional 'ulama abstained from making political statements about the war, popular Islamic revivalist movements, most importantly the Muslim Brotherhood, fervently opposed to British imperialism, were more receptive to advances from enemies of their enemies.[57] During the war, some factions of the Muslim Brotherhood, by then Egypt's biggest Islamic organization, did not hide their sympathies for the Axis. Concerned, the British kept the group under firm control. Its newspapers were temporarily banned, a number of its branches closed, its meetings monitored and some of its leaders arrested. Hasan al-Banna was put under pressure, and even briefly taken into custody, before finally giving in and openly pledging his loyalty to the rulers.

Following Operation TORCH, officials in Washington, too, grew concerned about Islam. The US War Department trained its troops in how to interact positively with Muslims on the ground, and prepared manuals designed to instruct soldiers in the basics of the Islamic faith. The American military also discovered religion as an instrument of propaganda. Following the landing of GIs in Algeria and Morocco, the US Office of Strategic Services distributed religious pamphlets that called for a 'great Jihad of Freedom' against Rommel's army in North Africa.[58] At the same time, Washington broadcast Qur'an readings in its propaganda programmes to North Africa and the Middle East several times every day.

Even the Kremlin, which had brutally suppressed the Muslim faith (along with other religions) in the interwar years, changed its policy in 1942, establishing four Soviet Muslim councils or 'spiritual directorates'.[59]

---

56 Costet-Tardieu Francine, *Un réformiste à l'Université al-Azhar: Œuvre et pensée de Mustafâ al-Marâghi (1881–1945)* (Paris: Karthala, 2005), pp. 169–75.

57 Richard P. Mitchell, *The Society of the Muslim Brothers* (London: Oxford University Press, 1969), pp. 19–34; Brynjar Lia, *The Society of the Muslim Brothers in Egypt: The Rise of an Islamic Mass Movement, 1928–1942* (Reading: Ithaca Press, 1998), pp. 256–69; and Gudrun Krämer, *Hasan al-Banna* (New York: Oneworld, 2010), pp. 61–5, provide accounts of the role of the Muslim Brotherhood in the Second World War.

58 Quoted in Anthony C. Brown, *Oil, God, and Gold: The Story of Aramco and the Saudi Kings* (Boston, Mass.: Houghton Mifflin, 1999), pp. 104–5.

59 Walter Kolarz, *Religion in the Soviet Union* (London: Macmillan, 1961), pp. 425–8; Alexandre Bennigsen and Chantal Lemercier-Quelquejay, *Islam in the Soviet Union* (London: Pall Mall, 1967), pp. 165–74; Hans Bräker, *Kommunismus und Weltreligonen Asiens: Zur Religions- und Asienpolitik der Sowjetunion*, vol. I: *Kommunismus und Islam: Religionsdiskussion und Islam in der Sowjetunion* (2 vols., Tübingen: Mohr, 1969), pp. 121–35; and Galina M. Yemelianova, *Russia and Islam: A Historical Survey* (New York: Palgrave Macmillan, 2002), pp. 120–4.

New mosques were built, Islamic congresses were organized, and Moscow started tolerating Muslim religious practices – ultimately, even permitting loyal Muslims to go on the hajj pilgrimage, which had been banned before the war. Desperate for total military mobilization for the Great Patriotic War, Stalin's propaganda appealed to the religious feelings of Muslims and called for jihad against the German invaders. Addressing the faithful from the 'Central Muslim Spiritual Directorate', headquartered in Ufa, Abdurrahman Rasulaev, the 'red mufti', called for a united defence against the Axis aggressors.[60] Hitler's aim was 'to exterminate the Moslem faith', he warned. This was a direct response to Germany's propaganda campaign on the Muslim fringes of the Soviet Union. For the Allies, Islam was both a potential threat and an important source of human manpower. Their religious policies and propaganda were directed toward mobilizing their empires, and sought to counter-balance Axis policies and propaganda.

Muslim soldiers fought on all sides. Tens of thousands served in the Red Army.[61] Only in the case of the Chechens did Moscow order a temporary recruiting stop, as the Soviets deemed them to be untrustworthy. Even more Muslims stood under British command.[62] Muslims, in fact, constituted the largest religious group of the British Indian Army, which grew to about 2.25 million men during the war. Across the world, Muslims fought in British contingents. In Palestine, about 9,000 Muslims were recruited into British Army units. Muslims also served under British command in the legendary Arab Legion of Transjordan, which was employed in different regions of the Middle East. Likewise, the French army enlisted thousands of Muslim colonial soldiers, especially from North and West Africa, who first fought for the Third Republic during the battle for France, and later in the Free French forces, which, in fact, consisted primarily of colonial troops. From French North Africa alone, no fewer than 233,000 men were

60 Abdurrahman Rasulaev, Appeal, 18 July 1941, printed in Stanley Evans, *The Churches of the USSR* (London: Cobbett, 1943), p. 158.
61 J. Otto Pohl, *Ethnic Cleansing in the USSR, 1937–1949* (Westport, Conn.: Greenwood, 1999), pp. 75, 82, 113; and, on the case of the Chechens, Abdurahman Avtorkhanov, 'The Chechens and the Ingush During the Soviet Period and its Antecedents', in Marie Bennigsen Broxup (ed.), *The North Caucasus Barrier: The Russian Advance Towards the Muslim World* (London: Hurst, 1992), pp. 146–94, here: pp. 179–80.
62 Philip Mason, *A Matter of Honour: An Account of the Indian Army – Its Officers and Men* (London: Jonathan Cape, 1974), pp. 471–527; and the contributions in Alan Jeffreys and Patrick Rose (eds.), *The Indian Army, 1939–47: Experience and Development* (Farnham: Ashgate, 2012), provide insights into the history of the British Indian Army. Godfrey Lias, *Glubb's Legion* (London: Evans Bros, 1956), is an account of the Arab Legion.

recruited – 134,000 Algerians, 73,000 Moroccans and 26,000 Tunisians.[63] Chasing Hitler's armies back into the Reich, they fought in the Maghrib, in Corsica and in the Elbe, in Rome and at Monte Cassino, in Marseille and in Alsace-Lorraine.

As their military situation worsened, the Axis powers, too, made efforts to enlist Muslims, promising them that they would be fighting to liberate their homes from foreign suppression. Muslims served in Japanese ranks and in Mussolini's army. The most spectacular effort to mobilize Muslims, however, was made by the Germans, who, from 1941, recruited tens of thousands of Muslims into the Wehrmacht and the SS.[64] Most of these soldiers came from the Soviet Union, though many were also enlisted in the Balkans, and some were from the Middle East and North Africa. They were organized in formations such as the Wehrmacht's Muslim Eastern Legions, the Arab contingent of the Wehrmacht, the East Muslim SS Division and SS units in the Balkans, most notably the Bosnian Handžar Division. Some fought for the liberation of their countries from non-Muslim and imperial rule. Most, however, had more pragmatic reasons for entering the German ranks. Almost all of the Muslim soldiers from the Eastern territories were recruited in prisoner-of-war camps, where the conditions were so miserable that only service in the German army seemed to offer a chance of surviving the war. Muslim volunteers from the Balkans simply hoped to protect their villages with German arms from Partisan and Četnik attacks, and perhaps to gain independence. In the end, Hitler's Muslim soldiers fought on all fronts – they were employed in Stalingrad, Warsaw and Milan, and even in the defence of Berlin. Nazi officials granted them numerous religious concessions and made significant efforts to provide religious care and propagandistic indoctrination. The religious calendar and religious laws, such as ritual slaughter, were taken into account. Propaganda was spread in the form of booklets, pamphlets and military journals. An important role in the units was played by military mullahs, who were responsible not only for spiritual care, but also for political propaganda. Initially, imams who served in the Wehrmacht units were educated at the University of

63 Belkacem Recham, 'Les Musulmans dans l'armée française, 1900–1945', in Mohammed Arkoun (ed.), *Histoire de l'Islam et des Musulmans en France du Moyen Age à nos jours* (Paris: Albin Michel, 2006), pp. 742–61, here: pp. 748–53; and, focusing on Algerian soldiers, Belkacem Recham, *Les Musulmans algériens dans l'armée française (1919–1945)* (Paris: L'Harmattan, 1996), pp. 175–274; and, focusing on Moroccan soldiers, Moshe Gershovich, 'Scherifenstern und Hakenkreuz: Marokkanische Soldaten im Zweiten Weltkrieg', in Gerhard Höpp, Peter Wien and René Wildangel (eds.), *Blind für die Geschichte? Arabische Begegnungen mit dem Nationalsozialismus* (Berlin: Klaus Schwarz, 2004), pp. 335–64.
64 Motadel, *Islam and Nazi Germany's War*, pp. 217–312.

Göttingen. Later, they were also trained at the so-called SS imam school that was founded in the small town of Guben in Brandenburg, and at the SS mullah school that opened in Dresden. By the end of the war, tens of thousands of Muslims had fallen in battle, used as cannon fodder by all major powers.

Conclusion

While thousands of Muslims had fought for the Axis, many more had served in the ranks of its enemies. Hitler was convinced, nevertheless, that the entire Islamic world had been prepared to side with the Third Reich. 'All Islam vibrated at the news of our victories' and Muslims had been 'ready to rise in revolt', he told his private secretary, Martin Bormann, in the last months of the war, in the Berlin bunker.[65] 'Just think what we could have done to help them, even to incite them, as would have been both our duty and our interest!' Instead, he fumed, Germany had too long respected Italian and Vichy interests in the Muslim world, which had hindered a 'splendid policy with regard to Islam'.[66] And yet, even though Hitler had hoped to involve Muslims even more in the war, the conflict had still shaped the Islamic world more than any other conflict of the twentieth century.

This chapter has provided a broad-brush overview of the political history of Muslim-populated lands in the Second World War. Muslims were involved on most fronts. They were victims, perpetrators and witnesses. Overall, the war had a lasting impact on the Muslim world. It shaped some who would later emerge as the most important Muslim political leaders of the twentieth century, including Anwar al-Sadat and Habib Bourguiba; it helped others to rise to power, such as Idris al-Sanusi and Muhammad Jinnah; and it brought about the fall of some eminent political figures, like Muhammad al-Husayni of Palestine, Muhammad VII al-Munsif Bey of Tunisia and Riza Shah of Iran; most importantly, though, across the lands of Islam, it shaped the lives of millions of ordinary people.

---

65 François Genoud (ed.), *The Testament of Adolf Hitler: The Hitler-Bormann Documents, February–April 1945*, trans. R. H. Stevens, introd. H. R. Trevor-Roper (London: Cassell, 1961), pp. 69–75 (17 February 1945), quotation at pp. 70–1.

66 Ibid.

Bibliographical essays

1 The Axis
Germany, Japan and Italy on the road to war
Robert Gerwarth

Comparative histories of the Axis

The comparative literature on the German and Italian dictatorships is considerably more developed than the scholarship comparing wartime Japan with Fascist Italy or Nazi Germany, partly because of Western historiography's 'Eurocentric' tendencies, and partly because the two regimes in Berlin and Rome had more in common than they did with wartime Japan. One of the few exceptions is the recent PhD thesis by Reto Hofmann, which explores the impact of Mussolini's rise to power on intellectual debates in Japan: Reto Hofmann, 'The Fascist Reflection: Japan and Italy, 1919–1950' (unpublished PhD thesis, Columbia University, 2010). Another book that keeps the wider context in focus is Harry Harootunian, *Overcome by Modernity: History, Culture, and Community in Interwar Japan* (Princeton University Press, 2000). For comparative studies on Germany and Italy, see, among others, Richard Bessel (ed.), *Fascist Italy and Nazi Germany: Comparisons and Contrasts* (Cambridge University Press, 1996). MacGregor Knox, *To the Threshold of Power, 1922/33: Origins and Dynamics of Fascist and National Socialist Dictatorships* (2 vols., Cambridge University Press, 2007), vol. I. On the three 'leaders' of wartime Germany, Italy and Japan, see the magisterial works of Ian Kershaw, *Hitler* (2 vols., London: Allen Lane, various edns); R. J. B. Bosworth, *Mussolini* (London: Arnold, 2002); and H. P. Bix, *Hirohito and the Making of Modern Japan* (New York: HarperCollins, 2000). All three books succeed in weaving together biographical perspectives with general accounts of the societies that shaped their leaders' lives.

The road to (and reality of) the Second World War

General comparative histories of the Axis are rare and commonly exclude Japan. For a good general global account of the Second World War that covers both European and Asian theatres of the war, see Gerhard L. Weinberg, *A World at Arms: A Global History of World War II* (2nd edn, Cambridge University Press, 2005). On the Pacific theatre of war, see, too, John Dower, *War Without Mercy: Race and Power in the Pacific War* (New York: Pantheon Books, 1986). A very reliable account of Japan's road to war is Akira Iriye, *The Origins of the Second World War in Asia and the Pacific* (London and New York: Longman, 1987). A short, but very useful account of the genesis of the international crisis of the 1930s is provided by Richard J. Overy, *The Interwar Crisis, 1919–1939* (Harlow: Pearson, 1994).

The Axis's empire-building

On attempts at empire-building by wartime Germany, see Mark Mazower, *Hitler's Empire: How the Nazis Ruled Europe* (New York and London: Penguin Press, 2008). Japan's imperialist dreams and practices are analysed in Louise Young, *Japan's Total Empire: Manchuria and the Culture of Wartime Imperialism* (Berkeley: University of California Press, 1998); and Yoshihisa Tak Matsusaka, *The Making of Japanese Manchuria, 1904–1932* (Cambridge, Mass.: Harvard University Press, 2001). On Italy, see the account of Davide Rodogno, *Fascism's European Empire: Italian Occupation During the Second World War* (Cambridge University Press, 2008). For a comparative perspective on Nazi Germany and Fascist Italy, see Aristotle Kallis, *Fascist Ideology: Territory and Expansionism in Italy and Germany, 1922–1945* (London: Routledge, 2000).

2 Western Allied ideology, 1939–1945
Talbot Imlay

For a survey of the war aims of the various belligerent powers, see Victor Rothwell, *War Aims in the Second World War: The War Aims of the Major Belligerents, 1939–45* (Edinburgh University Press, 2005). Much of the best work on Allied war aims appears in specialist studies, focusing on specific countries. For France up to its defeat in 1940, see Jean-François Crémieux-Brilhac, *Les Français de l'An 40* (2 vols., Paris: Gallimard, 1990); the opening section of Julian Jackson, *France: The Dark Years, 1940–1944* (Oxford University Press, 2001); and Kevin Passmore, *The Right in France from the Third Republic to Vichy* (Oxford University Press, 2013). Valuable biographies of French leaders include Elisabeth du Réau, *Edouard Daladier, 1884–1970* (Paris: Fayard, 1993); and Thibault Tellier, *Paul Reynaud: Un indépendant en politique, 1878–1966* (Paris: Fayard, 2005). On Reynaud's liberalism, see Stefan Grüner, *Paul Reynaud (1878–1966): biographische Studien zum Liberalismus in Frankreich* (Munich: Oldenbourg, 2001). Two studies that consider British and French policies together are Talbot C. Imlay, *Facing the Second World War: Strategy, Politics, and Economics in Britain and France, 1938–1940* (Oxford University Press, 2003); and P. M. H. Bell, *France and Britain, 1900–1940: Entente and Estrangement* (London: Longman, 1996).

For Britain, the best study of Neville Chamberlain's policy is R. A. C. Parker, *Chamberlain and Appeasement: British Policy and the Coming of the Second World War* (London: St Martin's Press, 1993); see also Robert Self, *Neville Chamberlain: A Biography* (Burlington, Vt.: Ashgate, 2006). Biographies of Winston Churchill are legion, but among the most useful are Richard Toye, *Churchill's Empire: The World that Made Him and the World He Made* (London: Macmillan, 2010); and Martin Gilbert's multi-volume biography, *Winston S. Churchill*, especially vol. VI: *Finest Hour, 1939–1941* (New York: Houghton Mifflin Company, 1983) and vol. VII: *Road to Victory, 1941–1945* (New York: Houghton Mifflin Company, 1986); but also worth reading is David Reynolds, *In Command of History: Churchill Fighting and Writing the Second World War* (London: Allen Lane, 2004). For the Labour leader Clement Attlee, see Trevor D. Burridge, *Clement Attlee: A Political Biography* (London: Jonathan Cape, 1985). For wartime British domestic policy, see the classic study by Angus Calder, *The People's War: Britain, 1939–45* (London: Jonathan Cape, 1969), as well as José Harris, *William Beveridge: A Biography* (Oxford University Press, 1977). For Labour, see Stephen Brooke, *Labour's War: The Labour Party During the Second World War* (Oxford University Press, 1992); and Trevor Burridge, *British Labour and Hitler's War* (London: Deutsch, 1976).

For the United States, there are countless studies of Roosevelt. Among those that stand out are Warren F. Kimball, *The Juggler: Franklin Roosevelt as Wartime Statesman* (Princeton University Press, 1991); and Robert Dallek, *Franklin D. Roosevelt and American Foreign Policy, 1932–1945* (New York: Oxford University Press, 1979). On American wartime domestic policy, see David M. Kennedy, *The American People in World War II* (New York: Oxford University Press, 1999); and William O'Neill, *A Democracy At War: America's Fight at Home and Abroad in World War II* (Cambridge, Mass.: Harvard University Press, 1995). For a more critical perspective, see Paul A. C. Koistinen, *Arsenal of World War II: The Political Economy of American Warfare, 1940–1945* (Lawrence: University Press of Kansas, 2004); and Patrick Hearden,

Architects of Globalism: Building a New Order During World War II (Fayetteville: University of Arkansas Press, 2002).

For excellent studies of Anglo-American wartime relations, see Warren F. Kimball, *Forged in War: Roosevelt, Churchill, and the Second World War* (New York: W. Morrow, 1997); Christopher Thorne, *Allies of a Kind: The United States, Britain, and the War Against Japan, 1941–1945* (Oxford University Press, 1979); and Wm. Roger Louis, *Imperialism at Bay, 1941–1945: The United States and the Decolonization of the British Empire* (Oxford: Clarendon, 1977).

3 The Soviet Union and the international left
Silvio Pons

General accounts of the Soviet Union during the Second World War focus almost exclusively on military aspects, on the home front, on the regime's evolution and on diplomatic issues, while paying poor attention to Moscow's political and ideological relations with the international left. A partial exception is G. Roberts, *Stalin's Wars: From World War to Cold War, 1939–1953* (New Haven, Conn., and London: Yale University Press, 2006). More information can be found in single chapters of histories of the Comintern. See, in particular, K. McDermott and J. Agnew, *The Comintern: A History of International Communism from Lenin to Stalin* (London: Macmillan, 1996); S. Wolikow, *L'Internationale communiste (1919–1943). Le Komintern ou le rêve déchu du parti mondial de la révolution* (Paris: Les Éditions de l'Atelier, 2010). For a documentary collection on the relations between the Comintern and communist parties in the years 1939–43, see N. S. Lebedeva and M. M. Narinskii (eds.), *Komintern i Vtoraia Mirovaia Voina* (2 vols., Moscow: Pamiatniki Istoricheskoi Misly, 1994–98). A key source on the period 1939–45 is Georgi Dimitrov's diary, which is edited in many languages: see *The Diary of Georgi Dimitrov 1933–1949*, introduced and edited by I. Banac (New Haven, Conn., and London: Yale University Press, 2003). See also A. Dallin and F. I. Firsov (eds.), *Dimitrov and Stalin, 1934–1943: Letters from the Soviet Archives* (New Haven, Conn., and London: Yale University Press, 2000).

Significant studies based on archival documents have been published in the last twenty years on bilateral relations between Moscow and single communist parties in Europe in the last phase of the war and in the early post-war era. On East Central Europe, see, in particular, K. Kersten, *The Establishment of Communist Rule in Poland, 1943–1948* (Berkeley and Los Angeles: University of California Press, 1991); M. Mevius, *Agents of Moscow: The Hungarian Communist Party and the Origins of Socialist Patriotism, 1941–1953* (Oxford University Press,

2005); V. Dimitrov, *Stalin's Cold War: Soviet Foreign Policy, Democracy and Communism in Bulgaria, 1941–48* (London: Palgrave Macmillan, 2008). On East Southern Europe, see P. J. Stavrakis, *Moscow and Greek Communism, 1944–1949* (Ithaca, NY: Cornell University Press, 1989); A. Gerolymatos, *Red Acropolis, Black Terror: The Greek Civil War and the Origins of Soviet-American Rivalry, 1943–1949* (New York: Basic Books, 2004). The memories of Milovan Djilas are an important source on Yugoslav communism and also on Stalin's thinking: M. Djilas, *Conversations with Stalin* (New York: Harcourt, Brace and World, 1962); M. Djilas, *Wartime* (New York: Harcourt Brace, 1980). On Western Europe, see Ph. Buton, *Les lendemains qui déchantent. Le Parti communiste français à la Libération* (Paris: Presses de la Fondation Nationale des Sciences Politiques, 1993); S. Pons, *L'impossibile egemonia. L'URSS, il PCI e le origini della guerra fredda (1943–1948)* (Rome: Carocci, 1999); E. Aga Rossi and V. Zaslavsky, *Togliatti e Stalin. Il Pci e la politica estera italiana negli archivi di Mosca* (Bologna: Il Mulino, 2007). For a comprehensive account of resistance movements in Southern Europe, the main reference remains *Resistance and Revolution in Mediterranean Europe 1939–1948*, edited by T. Judt (London and New York: Routledge, 1989).

On the relations between Moscow and the Chinese Communist Party in wartime, see M. M. Sheng, *Battling Western Imperialism: Mao, Stalin, and the United States* (Princeton University Press, 1997). See also the relevant chapter of *The Rise to Power of the Chinese Communist Party: Documents and Analysis*, edited by T. Saich (Armonk, NY, and London: M. E. Sharpe, 1996). For an account of communist policies in India, see D. N. Gupta, *Communism and Nationalism in Colonial India, 1939–45* (New Delhi: Sage, 2008).

For an overview of European socialist parties in wartime, see the relevant chapter of G. Eley, *Forging Democracy: The History of the Left in Europe, 1850–2000* (New York: Oxford University Press, 2002). On the Labour Party, see T. D. Burridge, *British Labour and Hitler's War* (London: André Deutsch, 1976); S. Brooke, *Labour's War: The Labour Party During the Second World War* (Oxford: Clarendon Press, 1992).

4 The propaganda war
Jo Fox

There is no comprehensive account of propaganda during the Second World War covering the experience of all belligerents. General studies of the wider history of propaganda often devote chapters to the war, the best examples being Susan Carruthers's *The Media at War* (Basingstoke: Palgrave, 2011); and P. M. Taylor's *Munitions of the Mind* (Manchester University Press, 1995).

Single nation studies tend to dominate the historiography, although, more recently, scholars have begun to explore the transnational dimensions of the propaganda war – on British assaults on US neutrality, for example, in Susan Brewer's *To Win the Peace* (Ithaca, NY: Cornell University Press, 1997), and Nicholas J. Cull's *Selling War: The British Propaganda Campaign Against American 'Neutrality' in World War II* (Oxford University Press, 1995); or on Nazi attempts to disrupt British influence in the Middle East in Jeffrey Herf's *Nazi Propaganda for the Arab World* (New Haven, Conn.: Yale University Press, 2009). Works by David Welch (notably, *The Third Reich: Politics and Propaganda* (London: Routledge, 2002)) and Aristotle Kallis (*Nazi Propaganda and the Second World War* (Basingstoke: Palgrave, 2005)) remain useful starting points for the study of Nazi wartime propaganda, while Corey Ross's more recent monograph situates Goebbels' campaigns within a wider chronological framework (*Media and the Making of Modern Germany: Mass Communications, Society, and Politics from the Empire to the Third Reich* (Oxford University Press, 2008). Jeffrey Herf's *The Jewish War* is essential and provocative reading for any student of Nazi anti-Semitic propaganda. Barak Kushner offers a sophisticated interpretation of the Japanese *shisosen* in *The Thought War. Japanese Imperial Propaganda* (Honolulu: University of Hawaii Press, 2006). The most recent, and indeed comprehensive, account of the role of propaganda in the Soviet Union is provided by Karel C. Berkhoff in *Motherland in Danger: Soviet Propaganda During World War II* (Cambridge, Mass., and London: Harvard University Press, 2012).

Steven Casey's compelling discussion of the relationship between propaganda and Roosevelt's policy-making (*Cautious Crusade: Franklin D. Roosevelt, American Public Opinion, and the War Against Nazi Germany* (Oxford University Press, 2001)) might usefully be read alongside the more recent research by Mordecai Lee on Robert Horton, Director of the Division of Information in the Executive Office of the President from 1941 (*Promoting the War Effort: Robert Horton and Federal Propaganda, 1938–1946* (Baton Rouge: Louisiana State University Press, 2012)), and James T. Sparrow's assessment of American public opinion in *Warfare State: World War II Americans and the Age of Big Government* (Oxford University Press, 2011). Allan M. Winkler's *The Politics of Propaganda: The Office of War Information, 1942–1945* (New Haven, Conn., and London: Yale University Press, 1978) remains the standard history of the OWI. Michael J. Sproule's *Propaganda and Democracy: The American Experience of Media and Mass Persuasion* (Cambridge University Press, 1997) provides a thought-provoking account of the tensions between propaganda and liberal democratic traditions somehow lacking in the literature on British campaigns. While Ian McLaine's *Ministry of Morale: Home Front Morale and the Ministry of Information in World War II* (London: Allen and Unwin, 1979) remains the standard reference work, there is undoubtedly a need for an updated history of Britain's MoI that draws in more recent scholarship revealing its 'carefully concealed connections', which rarely appear in existing accounts (one example being Valerie Holman's *Print for Victory* (London: British Library, 2008)).

5 Reporting from the battlefield
Censorship and journalism
Steven Casey

This subject lacks a comprehensive single account that draws together the experience of all the leading belligerents. Instead, a number of synthetic accounts of the media–military relationship since the mid-nineteenth century contain sections on the Second World War, including Philip Knightley, *The First Casualty: The War Correspondent as Hero and Mythmaker, from Crimea to Iraq* (Baltimore, Md.: Johns Hopkins University Press, 2004), which is organized chronologically; and Joseph J. Matthews, *Reporting the Wars* (Minneapolis: University of Minnesota Press, 1957), which is arranged thematically. Susan L. Carruthers, *Military and Media at War* (Basingstoke: Palgrave Macmillan, 2011), and Mark Pedelty, *War Stories: The Culture of Foreign Correspondents* (New York: Routledge, 1995), both adopt a more conceptual or theoretical approach to military–media relations, and are extremely useful.

With no book exploring the global war as a whole, the most relevant works concentrate on the experience of single belligerents. Georg Schmidt-Scheeder, *Reporter Der Hölle: Die Propaganda-Kompanien Im 2. Weltkrieg* (Stuttgart: Motorbuch, 1977), is a good starting point for exploring the German correspondents who worked for the *Propaganda-Kompanien*. Daniel Uziel, *The Propaganda Warriors: The Wehrmacht and the Consolidation of the German Home Front* (New York: Peter Lang, 2008), tries to place their activity in a broader institutional perspective. Aristotle Kallis, *Nazi Propaganda and the Second World War* (Basingstoke: Palgrave Macmillan, 2005), Gerald Anthony Kirwin, "Nazi Domestic Propaganda and Popular Response, 1943–45" (University of Reading PhD, 1979), and David Welch, *The Third Reich: Politics and Propaganda* (London: Routledge, 1993), all explore the role of Goebbels, and how war reporting connected with the overall Nazi propaganda campaign. The basic outline of Japanese censorship policies can be found in Richard H. Mitchell,

Censorship in Imperial Japan (Princeton University Press, 1983). David C. Earhart, *Certain Victory: Images of World War Two in the Japanese Media* (London: M. E. Sharpe, 2008), offers an excellent account of how battlefield images were relayed to the Japanese public. Barak Kushner, *The Thought War: Japanese Imperial Propaganda* (Honolulu: University of Hawaii Press, 2006), places these efforts in broader perspective.

On the other side, Ian McLaine, *Ministry of Morale: Home Front Morale and the Ministry of Information in World War II* (London: George Allen & Unwin, 1979), and Michael Balfour, *Propaganda in War, 1939–1945* (London: Routledge, 1979), remain useful starting points for understanding the basic British framework. Michael Sweeney's two books, *Secrets of Victory: The Office of Censorship and the American Press and Radio in World War II* (Chapel Hill: University of North Carolina Press, 2001), and *The Military and the Press: An Uneasy Truce* (Evanston, Ill.: Northwestern University Press, 2006), provide the same function for the American experience. The appendix in Forrest C. Pogue, *The Supreme Command* (Washington DC: Office of the Chief of Military History, 1954), contains an interesting essay on Eisenhower's press relations after D-Day. Steven Casey, *When Soldiers Fall: How Americans Have Confronted Combat Losses from World War I to Afghanistan* (New York: Oxford University Press, 2013), contains two chapters on how the US military and media reported battlefield death.

The Soviet experience is best recounted in Karel Berkhoff, *Motherland in Danger: Soviet Propaganda During World War II* (Cambridge, Mass.: Harvard University Press, 2012). Antony Beevor and Luba Vinogradova (eds.), *A Writer at War: Vasily Grossman with the Red Army, 1941–1945* (London: Pimlico, 2006), provides a compelling – and frequently chilling – account.

6 International organizations
Patricia Cravin

Two studies are key to understanding the place of international organizations in Roosevelt's war aims, and the ways in which this changes with the advent of President Truman: Warren Kimball, *The Juggler: Franklin Roosevelt as Wartime Statesman* (Princeton University Press, 1994); and Robert C. Hilderbrand, *Dumbarton Oaks: The Origins of the United Nations and the Search for Postwar Security* (Chapel Hill: University of North Carolina Press, 1990). The intellectual antecedents of twentieth-century international organizations are the topic of recent historical interest. Mark Mazower's *Governing the World: The History of an Idea* (London: Penguin, 2013) serves as a general introduction to the Anglo-American perspective; while Glenda Sluga, *Internationalism in the Age of Nationalism* (Philadelphia: Pennsylvania University Press, 2013), and Daniel Lacqua (ed.), *Internationalism Reconfigured: Transnational Ideas and Movements Between the Wars* (London: I. B. Tauris, 2011), demonstrate the flowering in new research and stress the importance of intellectual contribution to notions of global governance from those marginalized in national politics. These groups include anti-colonial activists, feminists, anti-slavery campaigners and those fighting for the rights of the child. The essays brought together by Abigail Green and Vincent Viaene (eds.), *Religious Internationals in the Modern World: Globalization and Faith Communities Since 1750* (London: Palgrave Macmillan, 2012), offer a pioneering account of the importance and legacies of religious internationalism.

In the study of international relations, the history of international organizations has been a significant theme since the founding of the discipline. Here, important work includes Cornelia Navari, *Internationalism and the State in the Twentieth Century* (London: Routledge, 2000); and Andrew Hurrell, *On Global Order: Power, Values and the Constitution of International Society* (Oxford University Press, 2007).

For the wartime record of the League of Nations and the ways in which it shaped the genesis of new organizations of global governance, see Patricia Clavin, *Securing the World Economy: The Reinvention of the League of Nations, 1920–1946* (Oxford University Press, 2013). Egon Ranshofen-Wertheimer stresses the significance and novelty of the world's first international bureaucracy for the development of the institutions forged in the war in his classic study of *The International Secretariat: A Great Experiment in International Administration* (New York: Columbia University Press, 1945). For the work of the International Labour Organization in the war, see Eddy Lee, Lee Swepston and Jasmien van Daele, *The ILO and the Quest for Social Justice, 1919–2009* (Geneva: International Labour Organization, 2009); while Susan Pedersen offers a historiographical overview of this fast-developing field in Susan Pedersen, 'Back to the League of Nations', *American Historical Review* 112:4 (2007), 1091–117.

For further insight into the ideas, practices and people who underpinned the development of new economic and financial organizations, see Robert Skidelsky's magisterial *John Maynard Keynes*, vol. III: *Fighting for Britain, 1937–1946* (London: Macmillan, 2000); the now classic study by John G. Ikenberry, 'A World Economy Restored: Expert Consensus and the Anglo-American Postwar Settlement', *International Organization* 46:1 (winter, 1992), 289–321; and on trade, Douglas A. Irwin, Petros C. Mavroidis and Alan

O. Sykes, *The Genesis of Gatt* (Cambridge University Press, 2008). On the (surprising) survival of the Bank of International Settlements, see Gianni Toniolo, *Central Bank Cooperation at the Bank for International Settlements, 1930–1973* (Cambridge University Press, 2005). For an assessment of these organizations' contribution to global stability after 1945, see Ngaire Woods, *The Globalizers: The IMF, the World Bank and their Borrowers* (Ithaca, NY: Cornell University Press, 2006). For the aspirations to organize food production and distribution on an international basis, see Luciano Tosi, *Alle Origini della FAO. Le relazioni tra L'Istituto Internazionale di Agricoltura e la Società della Nazioni* (Rome: Angeli, 1991); James Vernon, *Hunger: A Modern History* (Cambridge, Mass.: Harvard University Press, 2007); and Frank Trentmann and Just Fellming (eds.), *Food and Conflict in Europe in the Age of the Two World Wars* (New York: Palgrave Macmillan, 2006).

For the organization of international health, see Iris Borowy, *Coming to Terms with World Health: The League of Nations Health Organization, 1921–1946* (Frankfurt am Main: Peter Lang, 2009); Sunil Amrith, *Decolonizing International Health: India and Southeast Asia, 1930–1945* (London: Palgrave Macmillan, 2006); and offering a rare recognition of the importance of Latin American participation, Paul Weindling, 'The League of Nations Health Organization and the Rise of Latin American Participation', *História, Ciências, Saúde – Manguinhos* 13:3 (2006), 1–14. For an introduction into the emergence of the United Nations Relief and Rehabilitation Administration's work, see Jessica Reinisch and Elizabeth White (eds.), *The Disentanglement of Populations: Migration, Expulsion and Displacement in Post-War Europe, 1944–9* (London: Palgrave Macmillan, 2011).

7 Nazi genocides
Jürgen Matthäus

While historiography has confirmed Raul Hilberg's early understanding of the Holocaust as a highly organized project that involved broad strata of German society, scholars continue to grapple with problems posed by all genocides: how do groups and individuals come to participate in the perpetration of mass murder? What are the interrelations between historic events and their post-genocidal impact? If there is consensus among scholars working from different angles on Nazi crimes, it is on the need for multi-causal explanations and interdisciplinary approaches. Despite a vast, continuously growing body of literature, no coherent picture has yet emerged that depicts the issue in all its historical dimensions and ongoing consequences.

This overview covers but a small fraction of the scholarly production since the 1990s, with special focus on more recent empirical findings and remaining desiderata, while excluding the sea of publications on the aftermath of the Holocaust in terms of its memorialization and representation. For broader overviews, see Dan Stone, *Histories of the Holocaust* (Oxford University Press, 2010); David Bankier and Dan Michman (eds.), *Holocaust Historiography in Context: Emergence, Challenges, Polemics and Achievements* (New York: Berghahn Books, 2008). Publications already mentioned in this chapter's footnotes are not explicitly referenced here.

To date, comparatively few monographic studies exist that analyse the murder of the European Jews on a solid empirical basis in the context of other forms of mass violence. Robert Gellately and Nathan Stoltzfus, *Social Outsiders in Nazi Germany* (Princeton University Press, 2001), look at a broad range of 'outgroups', as does Michael Burleigh and Wolfgang Wippermann's still relevant *The Racial State: Germany, 1933–1945* (Cambridge University Press, 1991). On the persecution of Sinti and Roma, Michael Zimmermann's *Rassenutopie und Genozid. Die nationalsozialistische 'Lösung der Zigeunerfrage'* (Hamburg: Christians, 1996) is the standard reference work; while Henry Friedlander's *The Origins of Nazi Genocide: From Euthanasia to the Final Solution* (Chapel Hill: University of North Carolina Press, 1995), analyses the Third Reich's racial policies against 'gypsies', hospital patients and the disabled. Guenther Lewy, *The Nazi Persecution of the Gypsies* (Oxford University Press, 2000), argues against the assumption of an extermination programme analogous to the murder of Jews. Donald Bloxham, *The Final Solution: A Genocide* (Oxford and New York: Oxford University Press, 2009), reflects on the Holocaust against the background of mass violence in Europe from the late nineteenth century, and presents insights into key structural features of modern genocide. Useful compilations of different cases are provided by Robert Gellately and Ben Kiernan (eds.), *The Specter of Genocide: Mass Murder in Historical Perspective* (New York: Cambridge University Press, 2003); and Fritz Bauer Institut and Sybille Steinbacher (eds.), *Holocaust und Völkermord. Die Reichweite des Vergleichs* (Frankfurt am Main and New York: Campus, 2012). Doris Bergen, *War and Genocide: A Concise History of the Holocaust* (Lanham, Md.: Rowman & Littlefield, 2003), and Dieter Pohl, *Verfolgung und Massenmord in der NS-Zeit 1933–1945* (Darmstadt: Wissenschaftliche Buchgesellschaft, 2003) offer most valuable overviews.

In addition to the process character of Nazi mass violence, space has been identified as a key concept for the better understanding of wartime events.

Among recent attempts to establish a geohistorical framework, especially in Eastern and Southeastern Europe, are Holly Case, *Between States: The Transylvanian Question and the European Idea During World War II* (Stanford University Press, 2009); Timothy Snyder, *Bloodlands: Europe Between Stalin and Hitler* (New York: Basic Books, 2010); and Alexander V. Prusin, *The Lands Between: Conflict in the East European Borderlands, 1870–1992* (Oxford University Press, 2010). These studies intersect with others that focus on the interplay between national and colonial histories, either broadly, like Mark Levene, *Genocide in the Age of the Nation-State*, vol. 1: *The Meaning of Genocide* (London and New York: Tauris, 2005), Michael Mann, *The Dark Side of Democracy: Explaining Ethnic Cleansing* (Cambridge University Press, 2005), Mark Mazower, *Hitler's Empire: Nazi Rule in Occupied Europe* (London: Allen Lane, 2008), and A. Dirk Moses (ed.), *Empire, Colony, Genocide* (New York: Berghahn, 2008); or with reference to special historical settings, for example, Wendy Lower, *Nazi Empire-Building and the Holocaust in Ukraine* (Chapel Hill: University of North Carolina Press, 2005), or Edward B. Westermann, *Hitler's Ostkrieg and the Indian Wars: Comparing Conquest and Genocide* (Norman: University of Oklahoma Press, forthcoming).

While the comparative integration of Nazi genocides into broader analyses of mass violence has only started, Holocaust studies have evolved into a burgeoning, highly specialized field. Overview studies on the history of Nazi Germany have increasingly highlighted the regime's crimes, and the Holocaust plays a large role in published biographies of members of the Nazi elite – for example, Ian Kershaw's two-volume *Hitler, 1889–1945* (London: Allen Lane, 1998 and 2000); Peter Longerich, *Heinrich Himmler* (Oxford University Press, 2012); and Robert Gerwarth, *Hitler's Hangman: The Life of Heydrich* (New Haven, Conn.: Yale University Press, 2011). National, regional or local case studies with a focus on Holocaust perpetration are too numerous to list here, but the following are groundbreaking: Dieter Pohl, *Nationalsozialistische Judenverfolgung in Ostgalizien 1941–1944. Organisation und Durchführung eines staatlichen Massenverbrechens* (Munich: Oldenbourg, 1996); Radu Ioanid, *The Holocaust in Romania: The Destruction of Jews and Gypsies under the Antonescu Regime, 1940–1944* (Chicago, Ill.: Ivan R. Dee, 2000); and Christoph Dieckmann, *Deutsche Besatzungspolitik in Litauen 1941–1944* (Göttingen: Wallstein, 2011). Scholarship on the subject has reached a stage at which synthetic studies offer concise overviews and cutting-edge interpretations, together with introductions into the historiography and orientation regarding archival and published sources – for example, Peter Longerich, *Holocaust: The Nazi Persecution and Murder of the Jews* (Oxford

University Press, 2010); Hans Mommsen, *Auschwitz, 17. Juli 1942. Der Weg zur europäischen 'Endlösung der Judenfrage'* (Munich: DTV, 2002); and Dieter Pohl, *Holocaust. Die Ursachen – das Geschehen – die Folgen* (Freiburg: Herder, 2000). Up-to-date bibliographic overviews can also be found at www.ushmm.org/research/research-in-collections/search-the-collections/ bibliography (accessed 3 November 2014) and in the bibliographic sections of the journal *Holocaust and Genocide Studies*.

The prevailing interpretation of the Holocaust as emblematic for the Third Reich's history is reflected in studies that have stressed the important function of outgroup stigmatization for the regime's success in creating societal coherence – for example, Michael Wildt, *Hitler's Volksgemeinschaft and the Dynamics of Racial Exclusion: Violence Against Jews in Provincial Germany, 1919–1939* (New York, Berghahn 2012); Thomas Kühne, *Belonging and Genocide: Hitler's Community, 1918–1945* (New Haven, Conn.: Yale University Press, 2010); and Peter Fritzsche, *Life and Death in the Third Reich* (Cambridge, Mass.: Belknap Press, 2008). Earlier publications, most notably Robert Gellately, *The Gestapo and German Society: Enforcing Racial Policy, 1933–1945* (Oxford University Press, 1991), and Gerhard Paul and Klaus-Michael Mallmann (eds.), *Die Gestapo im Zweiten Weltkrieg. 'Heimatfront' und besetztes Europa* (Darmstadt: Wissenschaftliche Buchgemeinschaft, 2000), leave no doubt that Hitler's regime rested not only on terror, but also on its ability to attract support from among Germany's elites and significant parts of the wider public. Further empirical research is needed to establish the social reality behind the propaganda notion of the 'people's community' and its relevance for Nazi crimes.

Generalizations also seem premature in regard to the importance of economic factors. Participation in acts of violence and expectations of material gain helped to grease the process of persecution, yet the debate triggered by Adam Tooze, *The Wages of Destruction: The Making and Breaking of the Nazi Economy* (London: Viking, 2007), and Götz Aly, *Hitler's Beneficiaries: Plunder, Race War, and the Nazi Welfare State* (New York: Metropolitan, 2007), points to the varying importance of economic considerations on the macro- and micro-level throughout the Third Reich's history. Nazi planners frequently invoked food and other shortages in conjunction with debates about what to do with outgroups; yet as much as the ruthless extraction of resources for feeding the Home Front was part and parcel of Germany's war policy, the fact remains that 'useless eaters' and 'the unwanted' are sui generis ideological categories. Similarly, the role of forced labour as a means of exploitation and mass murder needs to be assessed more fully, following Peter Hayes, *Industry and Ideology: IG Farben in the Nazi Era* (Cambridge University Press, 2001), and Michael Thad Allen, *Hitler's Slave Lords: The Business of Forced Labour in Occupied Europe* (Stroud: Tempus, 2004).

Motivation has been the focal point of an evolving subfield of 'perpetrator studies' since Christopher Browning's groundbreaking *Ordinary Men: Reserve Police Battalion 101 and the Final Solution in Poland* (New York: HarperCollins 1992). His book, followed by Daniel J. Goldhagen's *Hitler's Willing Executioners: Ordinary Germans and the Holocaust* (New York: Knopf, 1996), as well as the controversy about the crimes of the Wehrmacht, have either drawn on or prompted important studies into individual and group behaviour – for example, Hans Safrian, *Eichmann's Men* (Cambridge and New York: Cambridge University Press, 2010); Rolf-Dieter Müller and Gerd R. Ueberschär (eds.), *Hitler's War in the East, 1941–1945: A Critical Assessment* (New York: Berghahn Books, 2009); and Edward B. Westermann, *Hitler's Police Battalions: Enforcing Racial War in the East* (Lawrence: University Press of Kansas, 2005). More broadly, see Harald Welzer, with Michaela Christ, *Täter. Wie aus ganz normalen Menschen Massenmörder werden* (Frankfurt am Main: S. Fischer, 2005); and James Waller, *Becoming Evil: How Ordinary People Commit Genocide and Mass Killing* (Oxford University Press, 2002). The issue of perpetration is related to new findings on the question of what 'ordinary Germans' knew during the Third Reich about the 'Final Solution', as reflected in Peter Longerich, *'Davon haben wir nichts gewusst!' Die Deutschen und die Judenverfolgung 1933–1945* (Munich: Siedler, 2006), and Bernward Dörner, *Die Deutschen und der Holocaust. Was niemand wissen wollte, aber jeder wissen konnte* (Berlin: Propyläen, 2007).

A combination of traditional historiographic bias and the prevalence of perpetrator studies has delayed research into groups neglected in their role as active historical agents. Since the book by Dalia Ofer and Lenore J. Weitzman (eds.), *Women in the Holocaust* (New Haven, Conn., and London: Yale University Press, 1998), gender studies on the Holocaust have produced significant findings; see, most recently, Myrna Goldenberg and Amy Shapiro (eds.), *Different Horrors, Same Hell: Gender and the Holocaust* (Seattle: University of Washington Press, 2013). The interrelation between war, mass violence and gender is addressed in Gisela Bock (ed.), *Genozid und Geschlecht. Jüdische Frauen im nationalsozialistischen Lagersystem* (Frankfurt am Main and New York: Campus, 2005); Regina Mühlhäuser, *Eroberungen. Sexuelle Gewalttaten und intime Beziehungen deutscher Soldaten in der Sowjetunion 1941–1945* (Hamburg: Hamburger Edition, 2010); and Insa Eschebach and Regina

Mühlhäuser, *Krieg und Geschlecht. Sexuelle Gewalt im Krieg und Sex-Zwangsarbeit in NS-Konzentrationslagern* (Berlin: Metropol, 2008). On women as part of the persecutory system, see Gudrun Schwarz, *Eine Frau an seiner Seite. Ehefrauen in der 'SS-Sippengemeinschaft'* (Hamburg: Hamburger Edition, 1997); stressing female perpetration is Wendy Lower, *Hitler's Furies: German Women in the Nazi Killing Fields* (Boston, Mass.: Houghton Mifflin Harcourt, 2013). Few books, among them Deborah Dwork, *Children with a Star: Jewish Youth in Nazi Europe* (New Haven, Conn.: Yale University Press, 1991), and Patricia Heberer, *Children During the Holocaust* (Lanham, Md.: AltaMira Press, 2011), address the fate of children and adolescents, while research on the elderly is still lacking.

The rapid expansion of Holocaust studies since the 1990s has helped to soften the long-standing scholarly divide between perpetrator- and victim-focused research. Dan Michman, *Holocaust Historiography – A Jewish Perspective: Conceptualizations, Terminology, Approaches and Fundamental Issues* (London and Portland, Oreg.: Vallentine Mitchell, 2003), identifies past developments and future trends. Saul Friedländer's two-volume *Nazi Germany and the Jews* (New York: HarperCollins, 1997 and 2007) has served as a model for similar attempts at integrating victim and perpetrator narratives, yet other options await further exploration. Those persecuted during the Nazi era have produced important sources during or after the war that attest not only to the forms and consequences of victimization, but also to the behaviour and mentality of persecutors and bystanders, as shown by Mark Roseman, 'Holocaust Perpetrators in Victims' Eyes', in Christian Wiese and Paul Betts (eds.), *Years of Persecution, Years of Extermination: Saul Friedländer and the Future of Holocaust Studies* (London: Continuum, 2010), pp. 81–100; Mark Roseman, *A Past in Hiding: Memory and Survival in Nazi Germany* (London: Metropolitan Books, 2000); see also Samuel D. Kassow, *Who Will Write Our History? Emanuel Ringelblum, the Warsaw Ghetto, and the Oyneg Shabes Archive* (Bloomington: Indiana University Press, 2007); Alexandra Garbarini, *Numbered Days: Diaries and the Holocaust* (New Haven, Conn.: Yale University Press, 2006). For the study of Nazi crimes in general, and their ramifications in the fields of law, politics and memory, Omer Bartov, Atina Grossmann and Mary Nolan (eds.), *Crimes of War: Guilt and Denial in the Twentieth Century* (New York: New Press, 2002); Donald Bloxham, *Genocide on Trial: War Crimes Trials in the Formation of Holocaust History and Memory* (Oxford University Press, 2001); Christopher R. Browning, *Remembering Survival: Inside a Nazi Slave-Labor Camp* (New York: W. W. Norton & Co., 2010); Lawrence Douglas, *The Memory of Judgment: Making Law and*

History in the Trials of the Holocaust (New Haven, Conn.: Yale University Press, 2001); and Annette Wieviorka, *The Era of the Witness* (Ithaca, NY: Cornell University Press, 2006), have highlighted the specificity, potential and limitations of survivor accounts.

8 War crimes trials
Donald Bloxham and Jonathan Waterlow

At the international level in Europe, the UN War Crimes Commission is examined in Arieh J. Kochavi, *Prelude to Nuremberg: Allied War Crimes Policy and the Question of Punishment* (Chapel Hill: University of North Carolina Press, 1998). Bradley F. Smith's enduring *The Road to Nuremberg* (New York: Basic Books, 1981) is excellent on the pre-history of the IMT case, with an American focus. John Tusa and Ann Tusa, *The Nuremberg Trial* (London: Macmillan, 1983) is more British-focused; Claudia Moisel, *Frankreich und die deutschen Kriegsverbrechen* (Göttingen: Wallstein, 2004), considers the French relationship to the trial. George Ginsburgs examines the Soviet side in *Moscow's Road to Nuremberg: The Soviet Background to the Trial* (The Hague: Martinus Nijhoff, 1996); and Francine Hirsch's article, 'The Soviets at Nuremberg: International Law, Propaganda, and the Making of the Postwar Order', *American Historical Review* 113 (2008), provides thought-provoking analysis of the Soviets' role at the IMT. N. S. Lebedeva's edited document collection, *SSSR i Niurnbergskii protsess: Neizvestnye i maloizvestnye stranitsy istorii* (Moscow: Mezhdunarodnyi fond 'Demokratiia', 2012), offers a detailed, archivally based summary. Telford Taylor, *Anatomy of the Nuremberg Trial* (London: Bloomsbury, 1993), is as good as any other overall account of the IMT trial. For the NMT programme, see (especially from the legal perspective) Kevin Jon Heller, *The Nuremberg Military Tribunals and the Origins of International Criminal Law* (Oxford University Press, 2011); and (more from the historical perspective) Kim C. Priemel and Alexa Stiller (eds.), *NMT: Die Nürnberger Militärtribunale zwischen Geschichte, Gerechtigkeit und Rechtschöpfung* (Hamburg: Hamburger Edition, 2013).

On national trial programmes in Europe, Robert Sigel, *Im Interesse der Gerechtigkeit: die Dachauer Kriegsverbrecherprozesse* (Frankfurt: Campus, 1992), and Tomaz Jardim, *The Mauthausen Trial: American Military Justice in Germany* (Cambridge, Mass.: Harvard University Press, 2012), respectively, consider the American 'Dachau' series and one case within that series. French trials are considered by Claudia Moisel, *Frankreich und die deutschen Kriegsverbrechen* (Göttingen: Wallstein, 2004). Soviet policy is considered in

Andreas Hilger, Mike Schmeitzner and Ute Schmidt (eds.), *Sowjetische Militärtribunale* (2 vols., Cologne: Böhlau, 2003). Most of the other relevant European states' trial policies are covered by chapters in Norbert Frei (ed.), *Transnationale Vergangenheitspolitik: Der Umgang mit deutschen Kriegsverbrechern in Europa nach dem Zweiten Weltkrieg* (Göttingen: Wallstein, 2006). Devin O. Pendas considers the case of German-run courts east and west in 'Transitional Justice and Just Transitions: The German Case, 1945–1950', *European Studies Forum* 38 (2008), 57–64. Donald Bloxham, *Genocide on Trial: War Crimes Trials and the Formation of Holocaust History and Memory* (Oxford University Press, 2001), considers the prosecution of crimes against Jews in the post-war period.

Neil Boister and Robert Cryer, *The Tokyo International Military Tribunal: A Reappraisal* (Oxford University Press, 2008), and their documentary accompaniment, *The Tokyo International Military Tribunal: Judgment and Documents* (Oxford University Press, 2008), are good starting points from the legal perspective on the most prominent Asian trial. Yuma Totani, *The Tokyo War Crimes Trial: The Pursuit of Justice in the Wake of World War II* (Cambridge, Mass.: Harvard University Asia Center, 2008), and Madoka Futamura, *War Crimes Tribunals and Transitional Justice: The Tokyo Trial and the Nuremberg Legacy* (Abingdon: Routledge, 2008), blend legal and historical perspectives. On the controversial Yamashita case, see A. Frank Reel, *The Case of General Yamashita* (University of Chicago Press, 1949). Philip Piccigallo's idiosyncratic *The Japanese on Trial: Allied War Crimes Operations in the East, 1945–1951* (Austin: University of Texas Press, 1979) surveys the broad vista, but is more a starting than an end point for further investigation into the different national trial programmes in East Asia.

9 Europe
The failure of diplomacy, 1933–1940
Peter Jackson

The literature on international politics during the 1930s is vast and grows almost daily. The following is only a brief introduction to this literature and should be consulted in addition to the secondary sources cited in the chapter notes. The best overall guide is the magisterial two-volume study by Zara Steiner, *The Lights that Failed: European International History, 1919–1933* (Oxford University Press, 2005) and *The Triumph of the Dark: European International History, 1933–1939* (Oxford University Press, 2011). P. M. H. Bell's *The Origins of the Second World War in Europe*

(3rd edn, London: Longman, 2007) remains indispensable. Richard Overy's *The Inter-War Crisis* (2nd edn, London: Longman, 2007) is valuable for its emphasis on the relationship between ideology, political economy and international relations. Among the many useful collections of essays on various aspects of the topic are Frank McDonough (ed.), *The Origins of the Second World War: An International Perspective* (London: Bloomsbury, 2011); Robert Boyce and Joseph Maiolo (eds.), *The Origins of World War Two: The Debate Continues* (London: Palgrave, 2003); and Patrick Finney (ed.), *The Origins of the Second World War* (London: Arnold, 1997). On German foreign policy, Gerhard Weinberg's two-volume *Foreign Policy of Hitler's Germany* (University of Chicago Press, 1970 and 1984) has yet to be superseded. Zach Shore, *What Hitler Knew: The Battle for Information in Nazi Foreign Policy* (Oxford University Press, 2004), provides an interesting and original perspective, as does Adam Tooze, *The Wages of Destruction: The Making and Breaking of the Nazi Economy* (London: Penguin, 2007). On the diplomacy of Fascist Italy, see MacGregor Knox, *Mussolini Unleashed* (Cambridge University Press, 1982); Robert Mallet, *Mussolini and the Origins of the Second World War* (London: Palgrave, 2003); and Bruce Strang, *On the Fiery March: Mussolini Prepares for War* (Westport, Conn.: Praeger, 2003). All three reject the more traditional view put forward by Italian historians that Fascist policy was essentially 'realist' in its inspiration. On the foreign policy of the Soviet Union, see Michael Carley, *Silent Conflict: A Hidden History of Early Soviet-Western Relations* (New York: Rowman & Littlefield, 2014), for the earlier period. Key sources for Soviet policy in the 1930s are Sarah Davies and James Harris, *Stalin's World: Dictating the Soviet Order* (New Haven, Conn.: Yale University Press, 2014); Silvio Pons, *Stalin and the Inevitable War, 1936–1941* (London: Cass, 2002); Sabine Dullin, *Men of Influence: Stalin's Diplomats in Europe, 1930–1939* (Edinburgh University Press, 2008); Geoffrey Roberts, *The Soviet Union and the Origins of the Second World War* (London: Macmillan, 1997); and the still useful Jonathan Haslam, *The Soviet Union and the Struggle for Collective Security in Europe, 1933–1939* (London: Macmillan, 1984). On French diplomacy, see, especially, Robert Young, *France and the Origins of the Second World War* (London: Macmillan, 1996), as well as his earlier *In Command of France: French Foreign Policy and Military Planning* (Cambridge, Mass.: Harvard University Press, 1978). Young's sympathetic interpretation of the dilemmas facing French policy stands in contrast to the Gaullist-inspired accounts of Jean-Baptiste Duroselle in his classic study, *France and the Nazi Threat: The Collapse of*

French Diplomacy, 1932–1939 (New York: Enigma, 2004). Anthony Adamthwaite, *France and the Coming of the Second World War, 1936–1939* (London: Cass, 1977), is rich in anecdotes, but lacking in systematic analysis. This is not the case with Martin Thomas's superb 'Appeasement in the Late Third Republic', *Diplomacy and Statecraft* 19:3 (2008), 566–607. Among the vast array of secondary work on British appeasement, the most relevant for the topic addressed in this chapter are R. A. C. Parker, *Chamberlain and Appeasement: British Policy and the Coming of the Second World War* (London: Macmillan, 1993); Michael Roi, *Alternative to Appeasement: Sir Robert Vansittart and Alliance Diplomacy* (Westport, Conn.: Praeger, 1997); Gaines Post, Jr., *Dilemmas of Appeasement: British Deterrence and Defence* (Ithaca, NY: Cornell University Press, 1993); Robert Self, *Neville Chamberlain: A Biography* (London: Ashgate, 2006); and the relevant chapters in Keith Neilson and Thomas Otte, *The Permanent Under-Secretary for Foreign Affairs, 1854–1946* (London: Routledge, 2009). On historiographical issues, Patrick Finney, *Remembering the Road to World War Two: International History, National Identity, Collective Memory* (London: Routledge, 2010), is full of useful insights. Excellent studies of the effects of the Civil War in Spain (which have not received the attention they deserve in this chapter) are Glyn Stone, *Spain, Portugal and the Great Powers, 1931–1941* (London: Palgrave, 2005); and Christian Leitz and Joe Dunthorne (eds.), *Spain in an International Context, 1936–1939* (Oxford: Berg, 1999). On the role of Eastern Europe, see Anita Prazmowska, *Eastern Europe and the Origins of the Second World War* (London: Macmillan, 2000); and Pior Wandycz, *The Twilight of French Eastern Alliances, 1926–1936* (Princeton University Press, 1988). On Franco-British relations, see the excellent works of Daniel Hucker, *Public Opinion and the End of Appeasement in Britain and France* (London: Ashgate, 2011); Talbot Imlay, *Facing the Second World War: Strategy, Politics and Economics in Britain and France, 1938–1940* (Oxford University Press, 2003); Michael Dockrill, *British Establishment Perspectives on France, 1936–1940* (London: Macmillan, 1999); and Martin Thomas, *Britain, France and Appeasement* (Oxford: Berg, 1996). The best single study of the final months of peace remains D. C. Watt, *How War Came: The Immediate Origins of the Second World War* (London: Pimlico, 1989). On the failure to negotiate a 'grand alliance', see Michael Carley, *The Alliance that Never Was and the Coming of World War II* (Chicago, Ill.: Ivan R. Dee, 1999); and Keith Neilson, *Britain, Soviet Russia and the Collapse of the Versailles Order* (Cambridge University Press, 2006).

10 Asia-Pacific
The failure of diplomacy, 1931–1941
Peter Mauch

Readers interested in reading further on this topic should, in the first instance, consult the notes in the text. There are also a number of excellent historiographical essays and bibliographic works. These include the relevant chapters in Robert L. Beisner's two-volume *American Foreign Relations Since 1600: A Guide to the Literature* (Santa Barbara, Calif.: ABC Clio, 2003); and Sadao Asada's *Japan and the World, 1853–1952: A Bibliographic Guide to Japanese Scholarship in Foreign Relations* (New York: Columbia University Press, 1989). Readers should also consult Michael A. Barnhart, 'The Origins of the Second World War in Asia and the Pacific: Synthesis Impossible?' *Diplomatic History* 20 (1996), 241–60.

For more recent scholarship on pre-Pearl Harbor US policy and diplomacy, see David Reynolds, *From Munich to Pearl Harbor: Roosevelt's America and the Origins of the Second World War* (Chicago, Ill.: Ivan R. Dee, 2002). There are also instructive essays in Edward J. Marolda (ed.), *FDR and the US Navy* (New York: Palgrave, 1998). Concerning the Anglo-American alliance, see Mark A. Stoler, *Allies in War: Britain and America against the Axis Powers, 1940–1945* (New York: Oxford University Press, 2005); and Mark A. Stoler, *Allies and Adversaries: The Joint Chiefs of Staff, the Grand Alliance, and US Strategy in World War II* (Chapel Hill: University of North Carolina Press, 2000). Among recent international histories is Evan Mawdsley, *December 1941: Twelve Days that Began a World War* (New Haven, Conn.: Yale University Press, 2011); and also Gerhard Weinberg, *A World at Arms: A Global History of World War II* (Cambridge University Press, 1994).

For two groundbreaking studies of the financial, commercial and economic path to war, see Edward S. Miller, *Bankrupting the Enemy: The US Financial Siege of Japan before Pearl Harbor* (Annapolis, Md.: Naval Institute Press, 2007); and Haruo Iguchi, *Unfinished Business: Ayukawa Yoshisuke and US-Japan Relations, 1937–1953* (Cambridge, Mass.: Harvard University Asia Center, 2003). For recent works on pre-Pearl Harbor Japanese policy and diplomacy, see Sadao Asada, *From Mahan to Pearl Harbor: The Imperial Japanese Navy and the United States* (Annapolis, Md.: Naval Institute Press, 2006); Peter Mauch, *Sailor Diplomat: Nomura Kichisaburō and the Japanese-American War* (Cambridge, Mass.: Harvard University Asia Center, 2011); Masato Kimura and Tosh Minohara (eds.), *Tumultuous Decade: Empire, Society, and Diplomacy in 1930s Japan* (Toronto University Press, 2013); Eri Hotta, *Japan 1941: Countdown to Infamy* (New York: Knopf, 2013); and Takeo Iguchi, *Demystifying Pearl Harbor: A New Perspective from Japan* (Tokyo: International House of Japan, 2010). See also Peter Mauch, *Tojo* (Cambridge, Mass.: Harvard University Press, forthcoming). The Japanese emperor and his role in Japan's path to war continues to polarize scholarship. For one side of the debate, see Herbert P. Bix, *Hirohito and the Making of Modern Japan* (New York: HarperCollins, 2000). For the other side of the debate, see Noriko Kawamura, 'Emperor Hirohito and Japan's Decision to Go to War with the United States: Reexamined', *Diplomatic History* 31:1 (2007), 51–79; and Ikuhiko Hata, *Hirohito: The Showa Emperor in War and Peace*, ed. Marius Jansen (Folkestone: Global Oriental, 2007).

11 The diplomacy of the Axis, 1940–1945
Norman J.W. Goda

The best overview of Axis wartime diplomacy is Gerhard L. Weinberg, *A World at Arms: A Global History of World War II* (2nd edn, New York: Cambridge University Press, 2005). Also essential is *Das deutsche Reich und der Zweite Weltkrieg* (10 vols., Stuttgart: Deutsche Verlags-Anstalt, 1979–2008), which covers all aspects of Germany's war, from diplomacy to economics to operations. At this printing, most volumes have been translated and published by Clarendon Press, under the title *Germany and the Second World War*.

For German-Japanese relations, the essential volumes are Bernd Martin, *Akten zur deutschen auswärtigen politik, 1918–1945* (new edn, Hamburg: Nikol Verlag, 2001); and, from the Japanese perspective, Gerhard Krebs, *Japans Deutschlandpolitik, 1935–1941: Eine Studie zur Vorgeschichte des pazifischen Krieges* (2 vols., Hamburg: Gesellschaft für Natür und Völkerkunde Ostasiens, 1984). See also the articles in John William Morley (ed.), *Japan's Road to the Pacific War* (5 vols., New York: Columbia University Press, 1976–94). There are many good books on Italian-German relations, most notably MacGregor Knox, *Mussolini Unleashed, 1939–1941: Politics and Strategy in Fascist Italy's Last War* (New York: Cambridge University Press, 1982); MacGregor Knox, *Hitler's Italian Allies: Royal Armed Forces, Fascist Regime, and the War of 1940–1943* (New York: Cambridge University Press, 2000). Books on the smaller Axis powers, their military and economic relationship with the Germans and each other, and their part in the 'Final Solution', are cited in the footnotes for this chapter.

Printed primary sources include diplomatic records of the German Foreign Ministry in *Akten der deutsche auswärtigen Politik*. Series D covers the years from 1937 to 1941 and is translated as *Documents on German Foreign Policy*.

Series E covers the years from 1941 to 1945. Italian records are printed in the Italian Foreign Ministry series *I Documenti Diplomatici Italiani*, particularly Series 9 and 10, which cover the war years. Documents concerning the diplomacy of the 'Final Solution' are in the aforementioned volumes, as well as Henry Friedlander and Sybil Milton, *Archives of the Holocaust: An International Collection of Selected Documents* (21 vols., Westport, Conn.: Garland Press, 1987–99).

12 The Diplomacy of the Grand Alliance
David Reynolds

Victor Rothwell, *War Aims in the Second World War: The War Aims of the Major Belligerents* (Edinburgh University Press, 2005), is a useful overview. On Anglo-American relations, see David Reynolds, *The Creation of the Anglo-American Alliance: A Study in Competitive Cooperation, 1937–1941* (London: Europa, 1981); and Christopher Thorne, *Allies of a Kind: The United States, Britain and the War against Japan, 1941–1945* (London: Hamish Hamilton, 1978). For American policy, see Warren F. Kimball, *The Juggler: Franklin Roosevelt as Wartime Statesman* (Princeton University Press, 1991), and his *Forged in War: Roosevelt, Churchill, and the Second World War* (New York: William Morrow, 1997); also the insightful study by Steven Casey, *Cautious Crusade: Franklin D. Roosevelt, Public Opinion and the War against Nazi Germany* (Oxford University Press, 2004). For contrasting views of Stalin's leadership, see Vojtech Mastny, *Russia's Road to the Cold War: Diplomacy, Warfare and the Politics of Communism, 1941–1945* (New York: Columbia University Press, 1979); and Geoffrey Roberts, *Stalin's Wars: From World War to Cold War, 1939–1953* (New Haven, Conn.: Yale University Press, 2006). See also Robin Edmonds, *The Big Three: Churchill, Roosevelt and Stalin in Peace and War* (London: Hamish Hamilton, 1986); and David Reynolds, *From World War to Cold War: Churchill, Roosevelt and the International History of the 1940s* (Oxford University Press, 2006). Professor Vladimir Pechatnov is preparing a full edition of Stalin's correspondence with Roosevelt and Churchill, in collaboration with David Reynolds. For background, see V. O. Pechatnov, 'How Soviet Cold Warriors Viewed World War II: The Inside Story of the 1957 Edition of the Big Three Correspondence', *Cold War History* 14:1 (2014), 109–25. On wartime conferences, see Keith Sainsbury, *The Turning Point: Roosevelt, Stalin, Churchill, and Chiang-Kai-Shek, 1943. The Moscow, Cairo, and Teheran Conferences* (Oxford University Press, 1986); Fraser J. Harbutt, *Yalta 1945: Europe and America at the Crossroads* (Cambridge University Press,

2010); S. M. Plokhy, *Yalta: The Price of Peace* (New York: Viking, 2011). Underlying cultural attitudes are explored in Eduard Mark, 'October or Thermidor? Interpretations of Stalinism and the Perception of Soviet Foreign Policy in the United States, 1927–1947', *American Historical Review* 94:4 (1989), 937–62; P. M. H. Bell, *John Bull and the Bear: British Public Opinion, Foreign Policy and the Soviet Union, 1941–1945* (London: Edward Arnold, 1990); and Martin H. Folly, *Churchill, Whitehall and the Soviet Union, 1940–45* (London: Macmillan, 2000).

13 Spain
Betting on a Nazi victory
Paul Preston

The biggest obstacle to a study of Spain's role in the war is the paucity of diplomatic documents in Madrid, most of which were carefully purged after 1945. Fortunately, a substantial body of primary sources from other countries is available in published form. There are official collections of the German, American, Italian and Portuguese diplomatic documents, and a smattering in *British Documents on Foreign Affairs: The Foreign Office Confidential Print*, pt. 3: *The Second World War* (76 vols., Bethesda, Md.: University Publications of America, 1997–99).

There are also some extremely useful memoirs by the Spanish and Italian Ministers of Foreign Affairs, Serrano Suñer and Ciano, and by the British, American, Portuguese and Vichy French ambassadors – Maurice Peterson (*Both Sides of the Curtain* (London: Constable, 1950)), Samuel Hoare (*Ambassador on Special Mission* (London: Collins, 1946)), Carlton J. H. Hayes (*Wartime Mission in Spain* (New York: Macmillan, 1945)), Pedro Teotónio Pereira (*Correspondência de Pedro Teotónio Pereira para Oliveira Salazar*, vol. III: *1942* (Lisbon: CLNRF, 1990)) and François Piétri (*Mes années d'Espagne, 1940–1948* (Paris: Plon, 1954)). Important accounts by more junior officials include those by the Spanish press attaché in Berlin, Ramón Garriga (*La España de Franco: las relaciones con Hitler* (2nd edn, Puebla, Mexico: Jorge Alvarez Editor, 1970)); a senior Foreign Office functionary, Jose María Doussinague (*España tenía razón* (Madrid: Espasa Calpe, 1949)); Italy's ex-ambassador Roberto Cantalupo (*Fu la Spagna. Ambasciata presso Franco. Febbraio–Aprile 1937* (Milan: Mondadori, 1948)); and the second-in-command at the American Embassy, Willard L. Beaulac, *Career Ambassador* (New York: Macmillan Company, 1951). That perceptive volume is bizarrely contradicted by Beaulac's wildly pro-Franco apologia, *Franco: Silent Ally in World War II*

(Carbondale: Southern Illinois University Press, 1986). Needless to say, the usual caveats about memoirs apply.

Moving on to secondary sources, there are wide-ranging overviews in the following: Stanley G. Payne, *Franco and Hitler: Spain, Germany, and World War II* (New Haven, Conn., and London: Yale University Press, 2008); David Wingeate Pike, *Franco and the Axis Stigma* (London: Palgrave Macmillan, 2008); Paul Preston, *Franco: A Biography* (London: HarperCollins, 1993); and Javier Tusell, *Franco, España y la II guerra mundial: entre el Eje y la neutralidad* (Madrid: Temas de Hoy, 1995).

Among accounts centring largely on the Spanish point of view, two of the more important stress Franco's imperialist ambitions as key to his policy during the war: Gustau Nerín and Alfred Bosch, *El imperio que nunca existió: la aventura colonial discutida en Hendaya* (Barcelona: Plaza y Janés, 2001); and Manuel Ros Agudo, *La gran tentación: Franco, el imperio colonial y los planes de intervención en la Segunda Guerra Mundial* (Barcelona: Styria de Ediciones, 2008). Others that have concentrated on the economic dimension of Spain's relations with the Third Reich are Jordi Catalan, *La economía española y la segunda guerra mundial* (Barcelona: Ariel, 1995); Rafael García Pérez, *Franquismo y Tercer Reich: las relaciones económicas hispano-alemanas durante la segunda guerra mundial* (Madrid: Centro de Estudios Constitucionales, 1994); and José Luis Rodríguez Jiménez, *Los esclavos españoles de Hitler* (Barcelona: Editorial Planeta, 2002). Best of all is Denis Smyth's perceptive 'The Moor and the Money-lender: Politics and Profits in Anglo-German Relations with Francoist Spain 1936–1940', in Marie-Luise Recker (ed.), *Von der Konkurrenz zur Rivalität: Das britische-deutsche Verhältnis in den Ländern der europäischen Peripherie 1919–1939* (Stuttgart: Steiner Verlag, 1986). For a recent overview, see Xavier Moreno Juliá, *Hitler y Franco: diplomacia en tiempos de guerra (1936–1945)* (Barcelona: Editorial Planeta, 2007).

From the German perspective, two of the earliest secondary accounts that remain of paramount importance are Charles B. Burdick, *Germany's Military Strategy and Spain in World War II* (Syracuse University Press, 1968); and Klaus-Jörg Ruhl, *Franco Spanien im Zweiten Weltkrieg. Franco, die Falange und das Dritte Reich* (Hamburg: Hoffman und Campe Verlag, 1975). A more recent account can be found in Christian Leitz, *Economic Relations Between Nazi Germany and Franco's Spain, 1936–1945* (Oxford University Press, 1996).

Allied attitudes toward Spain are examined in two elegant volumes on British policy: Denis Smyth, *Diplomacy and Strategy of Survival: British Policy and Franco's Spain, 1940–41* (Cambridge University Press, 1986), and Richard Wigg, *Churchill and Spain: The Survival of the Franco Regime, 1940–45* (London:

Routledge, 2005); and in two volumes by the Catalan historian Joan Maria Thomàs, *Roosevelt and Franco During the Second World War: From the Spanish Civil War to Pearl Harbor*, and *Roosevelt, Franco and the End of the Second World War* (London: Palgrave Macmillan, 2008, 2011).

Italian policy is analysed in Massimiliano Guderzo, *Madrid e l'arte della diplomazia. L'incognita spagnola nella seconda guerra mondiale* (Firenze: Manent, 1995); and Javier Tusell and Genoveva García Queipo de Llano, *Franco y Mussolini: la política española durante la segunda guerra mundial* (Barcelona: Editorial Planeta, 1985). The perspective of France is in Michel Catala, *Les relations franco-espagnoles pendant la deuxième guerre mondiale. Rapprochement nécessaire, réconciliation impossible, 1939–1944* (Paris: Éditions L'Harmattan, 1997); Matthieu Séguéla, *Pétain-Franco: les secrets d'une alliance* (Paris: Albin Michel, 1992); and Philippe Simonnot, *Le secret de l'armistice* (Paris: Plon, 1990).

On espionage and sabotage carried out by both sides in Spain, see the superb overview by Manuel Ros Agudo, *La guerra secreta de Franco, 1939–1945* (Barcelona: Editorial Crítica, 2002). His research in Spanish military archives reveals the extent of serious anti-British and -French planning. See also Jesús Ramírez Copeiro del Villar, *Huelva en la segunda guerra mundial: espías y neutrales* (Huelva: Jesús Ramírez Copeiro del Villar, 1996); Denis Smyth, *Deathly Deception: The Real Story of Operation Mincemeat* (Oxford University Press, 2010); and Smyth's articles, 'Les Chevaliers de Saint-George: la Grande-Bretagne et la corruption des généraux espagnols (1940–1942)', *Guerres mondiales et conflits contemporains* 162 (April 1991), 29–54, and 'Screening "Torch": Allied Counter-Intelligence and the Spanish Threat to the Secrecy of the Allied Invasion of French North Africa in November 1942', *Intelligence and National Security* 4:2 (April 1989), 339–44.

There is a growing bibliography on Spain and the Holocaust. Essential works are Haim Avni, *Spain, the Jews and Franco* (Philadelphia, Pa.: The Jewish Society of America, 1982); Isabelle Rohr, *The Spanish Right and the Jews, 1898–1945: Antisemitism and Opportunism* (Brighton: Sussex Academic Press, 2007); and Bernd Rother, *Spanien und der Holocaust* (Tubingen: Max Niemeyer, 2001). On Spanish victims, see the pioneering work by David Wingeate Pike, *Spaniards in the Holocaust: Mauthausen, the Horror on the Danube* (London: Routledge, 2000).

On the Blue Division sent by Franco to fight in Russia, there is a large memoir literature by protagonists. The best overviews are Xavier Moreno Julià's balanced *La División Azul: sangre española en Rusia, 1941–1945* (Barcelona: Editorial Crítica, 2004); and Gerald R. Kleinfeld and Lewis A. Tambs, *Hitler's Spanish Legion: The Blue Division in Russia* (Carbondale: Southern

Illinois University Press, 1979). Despite an uninhibited anti-Russian tone, this earlier volume makes use of important German documentary material.

14 Sweden
Negotiated neutrality
Klas Åmark

Two major research programmes have dominated the historiography of Sweden in the Second World War: *Sverige under andra världskriget* (SUAV, 'Sweden During the Second World War', 1965–78), and *Sweden's Relations to Nazism, Nazi Germany and the Holocaust* (SweNaz, 2000–11). The SweNaz programme published an overview of earlier research, including the research of the SUAV project, in Stig Ekman and Klas Åmark (eds.), *Sweden's Relations to Nazism, Nazi Germany and the Holocaust: A Survey of Research* (Stockholm: Almqvist & Wiksell International, 2003). In the introductory chapter, the SUAV project leader, Stig Ekman, presented the debate between the two interpretations that had dominated both the historical research and the public debate. The first interpretation saw Swedish policy in the light of 'small state realism' – in other words, a small neutral state had to make unpleasant moral compromises to prevent being drawn into the war by more powerful neighbours. The second interpretation criticized Sweden's concessions to Germany on moral grounds. The SweNaz programme also published a bibliography of German research on Sweden and Nazi Germany: Patrick Vonderau, *Schweden und das nationalsozialistische Deutschland* (Stockholm: Almqvist & Wiksell International, 2003).

More recent Nordic historiography is presented in Henrik Stenius, Mirja Österberg and Johan Östling (eds.), *Nordic Narratives of the Second World War: National Historiographies Revisited* (Lund: Nordic Academic Press, 2011). See also Helle Bjerg, Claudia Lenz and Erik Thorstensen (eds.), *Historicizing the Uses of the Past: Scandinavian Perspectives on History, Culture, Historical Consciousness and Didactics of History Related to World War II* (Bielefeld: Transcript, 2011).

During the last decade, some more general works have been published. Sven Radowitz studied, especially, the military aspects of relations between Germany and Sweden in *Schweden und das 'Dritte Reich' 1939–1945* (Hamburg: Reinhold Krämer Verlag, 2005). John Gilmour wrote the first extensive summary in English, *Sweden, the Swastika and Stalin: The Swedish Experience in the Second World War* (Edinburgh University Press, 2010), in which he argued for the 'small-state realistic' paradigm. Klas Åmark, who was the coordinator of the SweNaz programme, published a broad synthesis of the results from that programme, but also of much of the earlier research, in an attempt to transcend the two paradigms; this was *Att bo granne med ondskan. Sveriges förhållande till nazismen, Nazityskland och Förintelsen* [*Living as Neighbour to Evil: Sweden's Relations to Nazism, Nazi Germany and the Holocaust*] (Stockholm: Bonniers, 2011).

In research of the last fifteen to twenty years, topics related to Sweden and the Holocaust have been treated extensively. Most important has been the research on Swedish refugee politics, recently summarized in Mikael Byström and Pär Frohnert (eds.), *Reaching a State of Hope: Refugees, Immigrants and the Swedish Welfare State, 1930–2000* (Lund: Nordic Academic Press, 2013). In 2012, one hundred years since the birth of Raoul Wallenberg, a number of bibliographical books about him and his rescue mission in Budapest for Hungarian Jews were published, among them Bengt Jangfeldt, *The Hero of Budapest: The Triumph and Tragedy of Raoul Wallenberg* (London: Tauris, 2013). Some aspects of the Swedish press and the Holocaust are analysed by Antero Holmila in *Reporting the Holocaust in the British, Swedish and Finnish Press, 1945–1950* (Basingstoke: Palgrave Macmillan, 2011). There is not much written about Swedish humanitarian and relief work during and after the war, but see Ann Nehlin, *Exporting Visions and Saving Children: The Swedish Save the Children Fund* (Linköping University, 2009).

15 Wartime occupation by Germany
Food and sex
Nicholas Stargardt

The study of Europe under German occupation began with the political history of resistance and collaboration. Path-breaking work by scholars such as Alan Milward, Robert Paxton, H. R. Kedward and Czesław Madajczyk in the early 1970s set the standard of scholarship for the next fifteen to twenty years: Robert Paxton, *Vichy France: Old Guard and New Order 1940–44* (London: Barrie & Jenkins, 1972); Alan Milward, *The New Order and the French Economy* (Oxford University Press, 1970); Czesław Madajczyk, *Polityka III Rzeszy w okupowanej Polsce* (Warsaw: Państwowe Wydawn, 1970); H. R. Kedward, *Resistance in Vichy France* (Oxford University Press, 1978); Vojtech Mastny, *The Czechs under Nazi Rule: The Failure of National Resistance, 1939–42* (New York: Columbia University Press, 1971). An important later contribution to these approaches is G. Hirschfeld (ed.), *Nazi Rule and Dutch Collaboration* (Oxford: Berg, 1988).

The later 1980s and early 1990s saw the rise of new scholarship on the role of the German army in massacring civilian populations in occupied Europe, especially Eastern and Southern Europe, with the work of Omer Bartov and Christian Streit opening the way to considering the relationship between German terror, resistance and civil war: Christian Streit, *Keine Kameraden: die Wehrmacht und die sowjetischen Kriegsgefangenen 1941–1945* (Stuttgart: Deutsche Verlags-Anstalt, 1978); Omer Bartov, *Hitler's Army: Soldiers, Nazis and War in the Third Reich* (Oxford University Press, 1991); Mark Mazower, *Inside Hitler's Greece: The Experience of Occupation, 1941–44* (New Haven, Conn.: Yale University Press, 1993).

The decade 1990–2000 also saw a new historiographic recognition of the centrality of the Holocaust, and an increasing awareness of its importance to the history of the non-Jewish populations of occupied Europe. Interestingly, work on the experience at the time went hand-in-hand with scholarship on the cultural repression of the memory of the deportation and murder of the Jews in the post-war decades. Among important works in this area are: Henry Rousso, *The Vichy Syndrome: History and Memory in France Since 1944* (Cambridge, Mass.: Harvard University Press, 1991); István Deák, Jan Gross and Tony Judt (eds.), *The Politics of Retribution in Europe: World War II and its Aftermath* (Princeton University Press, 2000); Jan Gross, *Neighbors: The Destruction of the Jewish Community in Jedwabne, Poland* (Princeton University Press, 2001); Robert Moeller, *War Stories: The Search for a Usable Past in the Federal Republic of Germany* (Berkeley: University of California Press, 2001); Richard Bessel and Dirk Schumann (eds.), *Life after Death: Approaches to a Cultural and Social History of Europe During the 1940s and 1950s* (Cambridge University Press, 2003); Pieter Lagrou, *The Legacy of Nazi Occupation: Patriotic Memory and National Recovery in Western Europe, 1945–1965* (Cambridge University Press, 2000).

Many new regional and national studies appeared, especially in areas where archives only became open to scholars after the collapse of the Soviet Union in 1990 (and then sometimes only for a relatively short time): Bernhard Chiari, *Alltag hinter der Front: Besatzung, Kollaboration und Wider-stand in Weissrussland 1941–1944* (Düsseldorf: Droste Verlag, 1998); Christian Gerlach, *Kalkulierte Morde: die deutsche Wirtschafts-und Vernichtungspolitik in Weissrussland 1941 bis 1944* (Hamburg: Hamburger Edition, 2000); Martin Dean, *Collaboration in the Holocaust: Crimes of the Local Police in Belorussia and Ukraine, 1941–44* (Basingstoke: Macmillan, 2000); Karel Berkhoff, *Harvest of Despair: Life and Death in Ukraine under Nazi Rule* (Cambridge, Mass.: Harvard University Press, 2004); Wendy Lower, *Nazi Empire-Building and the Holocaust in Ukraine* (Chapel Hill: University of North Carolina Press,

2005); Thomas Sandkühler, *'Endlösung' in Galizien: der Judenmord in Ostpolen und die Rettungsinitiativen von Berthold Beitz, 1941–1944* (Bonn: Dietz, 1996); Christoph Dieckmann, *Deutsche Besatzungspolitik in Litauen 1941–1944* (Göttingen: Wallstein, 2011).

The most important single overview on the murder of the Jews is Saul Friedländer, *The Years of Extermination: Nazi Germany and the Jews, 1939–1945* (London: Weidenfeld & Nicolson, 2007). At the same time as interest was spreading outward, there has been increasing awareness of the extent to which other Europeans experienced the war in Germany, drawn there through the recruitment of foreign labour: Ulrich Herbert, *Hitler's Foreign Workers* (Cambridge University Press, 1997).

The movement of populations, with millions of German men stationed in occupied Europe and European women working in Germany, has been treated in studies on gender, violence and sexuality: Fabrice Virgili, *Shorn Women: Gender and Punishment in Liberation France* (Oxford: Berg, 2002); Kjersti Ericsson and Eva Simonsen (eds.), *Children of World War II: The Hidden Enemy Legacy* (Oxford: Berg, 2005); Fabrice Virgili, *Naître ennemi: Les enfants de couples franco-allemands nés pendant la Seconde Guerre mondiale* (Paris: Payot, 2009); Regina Mühlhäuser, *Eroberungen: sexuelle Gewalttaten und intime Beziehungen deutscher Soldaten in der Sowjetunion 1941–1945* (Hamburg: Hamburger Edition, 2010); Dagmar Herzog (ed.), *Brutality and Desire: War and Sexuality in Europe's Twentieth Century* (Basingstoke: Palgrave Macmillan, 2009).

Among the new studies of Western Europe, particularly remarkable are: Robert Gildea, *Marianne in Chains* (London: Macmillan, 2003); Julian Jackson, *France: The Dark Years, 1940–1944* (Oxford University Press, 2001); Richard Bosworth, *Mussolini's Italy: Life Under the Dictatorship, 1915–1945* (London: Allen Lane, 2005).

A number of innovative attempts have been made to write the history of occupation across Europe by focusing on a particular theme: for German policy and its war economy, there are: Adam Tooze, *The Wages of Destruction: The Making and Breaking of the Nazi Economy* (London: Allen Lane, 2006); Götz Aly, *Hitler's Beneficiaries: How the Nazis Bought the German People* (London: Verso, 2007); and Mark Mazower, *Hitler's Empire: Nazi Rule in Occupied Europe* (London: Allen Lane, 2008).

Looking at the changing character of political legitimacy are Martin Conway and Peter Romijn (eds.), *The War for Legitimacy in Politics and Culture, 1936–1946* (Oxford: Berg, 2008). With a focus on everyday life are Robert Gildea, Anette Warring and Olivier Wieviorka (eds.), *Surviving Hitler and Mussolini: Daily Life in Occupied Europe* (Oxford: Berg, 2006); and Lizzie

Collingham, *The Taste of War: World War Two and the Battle for Food* (London: Allen Lane, 2011). Scholars are also increasingly aware of the significance of the Allied air war for occupied Europe: Claudia Baldoli, Andrew Knapp and Richard Overy (eds.), *Bombing, States and Peoples in Western Europe, 1940–1945* (London: Continuum, 2011); and Richard Overy, *The Bombing War: Europe 1939–1945* (London: Allen Lane, 2013).

16 Collaboration, resistance and liberation in Western Europe
William I. Hitchcock

One of the best surveys of Europe under German occupation, based on extensive study of German sources, is Norman Rich, *Hitler's War Aims* (2 vols., New York: Norton, 1973–74). An ambitious recent synthesis is Mark Mazower, *Hitler's Empire: Nazi Rule in Occupied Europe* (New York: Penguin, 2008). In German, a central starting point is the multi-volume series edited by Werner Röhr, *Europa unterm Hakenkreuz* (8 vols., Berlin: Hutig, 1988–94). A suggestive collection of original essays on European society is Robert Gildea, Anette Warring and Olivier Wieviorka (eds.), *Surviving Hitler and Mussolini: Daily Life in Occupied Europe* (Oxford: Berg, 2006).

For Denmark, an excellent recent analysis is Joachim Lund, 'Denmark and the "European New Order", 1940–42', *Contemporary European History* 13:2 (2004), 305–21; on Norway, J. Andenaes, O. Riste and M. Skodvin, *Norway and the Second World War* (Lillehammer: Tanum-Norli, 1983), is brief but essential. A narrative account is given in Richard Petrow, *The Bitter Years: The Invasion and Occupation of Denmark and Norway* (New York: William Morrow, 1974).

Belgium has been carefully examined by economic historians: Herman van der Wee and Monique Verbreyt, *A Small Nation in the Turmoil of the Second World War* (Leuven University Press, 2009). Daily life is examined in Jacques de Launay and Jacques Offergeld, *La Vie Quotidienne des Belges sous l'Occupation* (Brussels: Legrain, 1982). Also useful on the mechanics of occupation: J. H. Geller, 'The Role of Military Administration in Occupied Belgium', *Journal of Military History* 63:1 (1999), 99–125.

On the Netherlands, Gerhard Hirschfeld, *Nazi Rule and Dutch Collaboration: The Netherlands under German Occupation* (Oxford: Berg, 1988), is excellent, and can be supplemented by Werner Warmbrunn, *The Dutch Under German Occupation* (Stanford University Press, 1963).

The essential volume on France is now Julian Jackson, *France: The Dark Years, 1940–44* (Oxford University Press, 2001); though Robert Paxton, *Vichy*

France: Old Guard and New Order, 1940–1944 (New York: Columbia University Press, 1972), merits careful reading. The scope of collaborationist agendas in France is captured in G. Hirschfeld and P. March (eds.), *Collaboration in France* (Oxford: Berg, 1989). Philippe Burrin, *France Under the Germans* (New York: The New Press, 1996), and Richard Vinen, *The Unfree French* (London: Allen Lane, 2006), are original and bracing.

Italy's anomalous wartime history has been treated well in Richard Lamb, *War in Italy: A Brutal Story, 1943–1945* (New York: St Martin's Press, 1994); and David W. Ellwood, *Italy, 1943–45* (Leicester University Press, 1985). For post-war political controversies, see Philip Cooke, *The Legacy of the Italian Resistance* (Basingstoke: Palgrave Macmillan, 2011).

Excellent essays on the resistance can be sampled in Bob Moore (ed.), *Resistance in Western Europe* (Oxford: Berg, 2000). Older, but still invaluable work that adopts a transcontinental perspective includes Henri Michel, *The Shadow War* (New York: Harper and Row, 1972); Jorgen Haestrup, *European Resistance Movements, 1939–1945* (Odense University Press, 1981); and M. R. D. Foot, *Resistance: An Analysis of European Resistance to Nazism* (London: Eyre Methuen, 1976).

For a sombre portrait of the liberation period, see William Hitchcock, *The Bitter Road to Freedom* (New York: Free Press, 2008); and Keith Lowe, *Savage Continent: Europe in the Aftermath of World War II* (New York: St Martin's Press, 2012).

17 Wartime occupation by Italy
Davide Rodogno

As far as Italian archives are concerned, many problems hinder the consultation of several collections. The *Carabinieri* archives are inaccessible; the documents of the *Guardia di Finanza* for the Second World War are contained in a few brief folders. The Ministry of Foreign Affairs – Commercial Affairs series exists, but is not accessible. The archives of Italian military tribunals, located at the Archivio Centrale dello Stato (ACS, Rome) are not indexed, whereas the Italian soldiers' correspondence, located at the Ufficio Storico dello Stato Maggiore dell'Esercito Italiano, is not accessible because of Italian privacy legislation. Documents on the Under-Secretariat for Albanian affairs are not consultable, hampering research on Italian rule over Albania. As research by Jean-Louis Panicacci shows, departmental archives in metropolitan France contain important material: *L'Occupation italienne: Sud-Est de la France, juin 1940–septembre 1943* (Paris: Presses Universitaires de

Rennes, coll. 'Histoire', 2010). This is also the case for the documentation pertaining to the ex-Yugoslav territories now located in the national archives of Croatia (Zagreb), Serbia (Belgrade) and Slovenia (Ljubljana). Recent research undertaken in Albanian archives by Michele Sarfatti shows that further documents are to be found in Tirana: Michele Sarfatti, 'Tra uccisione e protezione. I rifugiati ebrei in Kosovo nel marzo 1942 e le autorità tedesche, italiane e albanesi', *Rassegna Mensile di Israel* 76:3 (2010), 223–42; and Laura Brazzo and Michele Sarfatti (eds.), *Gli ebrei in Albania sotto il fascismo. Una storia da ricostruire* (Florence: Giuntina, 2010).

The area under Italian occupation that has drawn more attention is that of the ex-Yugoslav territories. The first studies date back to the 1970s and 1980s: Giacomo Scotti, *Le Aquile delle Montagne Nere: storia dell'Occupazione e della Guerra Italiana in Montenegro (1941–1943)* (Milan: Mursia, 1987); and Giacomo Scotti, *Bono Taliano. Gli italiani in Jugoslavia (1941–1943)* (Milan: La Pietra, 1977). See also Teodoro Sala and Enzo Collotti, *Le Potenze dell'Asse e la Jugoslavia* (Milan: Feltrinelli, 1974). Among more recent publications, the following are noteworthy: Marco Dogo, *Kosovo* (Lungro di Cosenza: C. Marco, 1992); Marco Cuzzi, *L'Occupazione Italiana della Slovenia (1941–1943)* (Rome: Ufficio Storico Stato Maggiore dell'Esercito, 1998); and Eric Gobetti, *L'Occupazione Allegra. Gli Italiani in Jugoslavia (1941–1943)* (Rome: Carocci, 2007) Documentary collections by Slovene historian Tone Ferenc are of crucial importance, among them: *La Provincia 'Italiana' di Lubiana. Documenti 1941–1942* (Udine: Istituto Friulano per la Storia del Movimento di Liberazione, 1994). The Italian occupation of Greece is far less explored than that of the ex-Yugoslav territories. Mark Mazower's excellent *Inside Hitler's Greece: The Experience of Occupation, 1941–1944* (New Haven, Conn.: Yale University Press, 2001) mentions, *en passant* only, the role of Italy. Sheila Lecoeur has devoted an entire monograph to the island of Syros, using Italian and Greek sources: *Mussolini's Greek Island: Fascism and the Italian Occupation of Syros in World War II* (London: Tauris, 2009).

On Italian war crimes, literature in Italian is extensive. See, for instance, the excellent study by Filippo Focardi, *L'Immagine del 'cattivo tedesco' e il mito del 'bravo italiano'. La costruzione della memoria del fascismo e della Seconda Guerra Mondiale in Italia* (Padova: Il Rinoceronte, 2005); Filippo Focardi, *Criminali di guerra in Libertà. Un Accordo Segreto tra Italia e Germania Federale, 1949–55* (Rome: Carocci, 2008); Joze Pirjevic (ed.), *Foibe* (Turin: Einaudi, 2009). In English: Arieh J. Kochavi, *Prelude to Nuremberg. Allied War Crimes Policy and the Question of the Punishment* (Chapel Hill: University of North Carolina Press, 1998); Effie G. H. Pedaliu, 'Britain and the "Hand-Over" of Italian War

Criminals to Yugoslavia, 1945–48', *Journal of Contemporary History* 39 (2004), 503–29; Filippo Focardi and Lutz Klinkhammer, 'The Question of Fascist Italy's War Crimes: The Construction of Self-Acquitting Myth (1943–1948)', *Journal of Modern Italian Studies* 9 (2004), 330–48; and Michele Battini, 'Sins of Memory: Reflections on the Lack of an Italian Nuremberg and the Administration of International Justice After 1945', *Journal of Modern Italian Studies* 9 (2004), 349–62.

On Italian armed forces, see the classic study by Lucio Ceva, *Le forze armate* (Turin: Utet, 1981). Enzo Collotti has written quite extensively on the 1930s and on the military occupations. Among his studies is Enzo Collotti, 'Sulla politica di repressione italiana nei Balcani', in Luigi Paggi (ed.), *La memoria del nazismo nell'Europa di oggi* (Florence: La Nuova Italia, 1997), pp. 182–208. In English, emphasizing the comparative dimension between Fascism and Nazism, see the following titles by MacGregor Knox: *Mussolini Unleashed, 1939–1941: Politics and Strategy in Fascist Italy's Last War* (Cambridge University Press, 1982); *Common Destiny: Dictatorship, Foreign Policy, and War in Fascist Italy and Nazi Germany* (Cambridge University Press, 2000); and *Hitler's Italian Allies: Royal Armed Forces, Fascist Regime, and the War of 1940–1943* (Cambridge University Press, 2000). The works of military historian Giorgio Rochat are of crucial importance, among them: *Guerre italiane in Libia e in Etiopia* (Treviso: Pagus, 1991); and *L'esercito italiano in pace e in guerra* (Milan: Rara, 1991).

18 Collaboration, resistance and liberation in the Balkans, 1941–1945
Gregor Kranjc

Few works compare resistance, collaboration and liberation in Greece and Yugoslavia specifically, but see Stanley Payne, *Civil War in Europe, 1905–1949* (Cambridge University Press, 2011); and Philip Minehan, *Civil War and World War in Europe: Spain, Yugoslavia, and Greece, 1936–1949* (New York: Palgrave Macmillan, 2006). For shared atrocities, see Paul Mojzes, *Balkan Genocides: Holocaust and Ethnic Cleansing in the Twentieth Century* (Lanham, Md.: Rowman & Littlefield, 2011). On Italian occupation policies, see Davide Rodogno, *Fascism's European Empire: Italian Occupation During the Second World War* (Cambridge University Press, 2006); and H. James Burgwyn, *Empire on the Adriatic: Mussolini's Conquest of Yugoslavia, 1941–1943* (New York: Enigma Books, 2005). For German counter-insurgency, see Ben Shepherd, *Terror in the Balkans: German Armies and Partisan Warfare* (Cambridge, Mass.: Harvard

University Press, 2012). For two excellent general studies on resistance, collaboration and liberation in occupied Greece and Yugoslavia, see Mark Mazower, *Inside Hitler's Greece: The Experience of Occupation, 1941–44* (New Haven, Conn., and London: Yale University Press, 1993); and Jozo Tomasevich, *War and Revolution in Yugoslavia: Occupation and Collaboration* (Stanford University Press, 2001); see also Stevan Pavlowitch, *Hitler's New Disorder: The Second World War in Yugoslavia* (New York: Columbia University Press, 2008); and Richard Clogg, *Greece 1940–1949: Occupation, Resistance, Civil War: A Documentary History* (Basingstoke and New York: Palgrave Macmillan, 2002). On the shifting policies of EAM–ELAS and the Partisans, see Melissa Bokovoy, *Peasants and Communists: Politics and Ideology in the Yugoslav Countryside, 1941–1953* (Pittsburgh, Pa.: University of Pittsburgh Press, 1998); and Haris Vlavianos, *Greece, 1941–49: From Resistance to Civil War. The Strategy of the Greek Communist Party* (Basingstoke and New York: Palgrave Macmillan, 1992). For a concise, theoretical understanding of Greek collaboration, see Stathis Kalyvas, 'Armed Collaboration in Greece, 1941–1944', *European Review of History* 15:2 (April 2008), 129–42. For ethnic-specific studies on collaboration, resistance and liberation in Yugoslavia, see Gregor Kranjc, *To Walk with the Devil: Slovene Collaboration and Axis Occupation, 1941–1945* (University of Toronto Press, 2013); Sabrina Ramet and Ola Listhaug (eds.), *Serbia and the Serbs in World War Two* (Houndmills: Palgrave Macmillan, 2011); Andrew Rossos, *Macedonia and the Macedonians: A History* (Stanford University Press, 2008); Marko Attila Hoare, *Genocide and Resistance in Hitler's Bosnia: The Partisans and the Chetniks, 1941–1943* (Oxford University Press, 2006). For similar approaches in Greece, see Kevin Featherstone, Dimitris Papadimitriou, Argyris Mamarelis and Georgios Niarchos, *The Last Ottomans: The Muslim Minority of Greece, 1940–1949* (London: Palgrave Macmillan, 2011); Steven Bowman, *The Agony of Greek Jews, 1940–1945* (Stanford University Press, 2009); John Koliopoulos, *Plundered Loyalties: Axis Occupation and Civil Strife in Greek West Macedonia, 1941–1949* (London: Hurst, 1999). For women's contributions to resistance and collaboration, see Kevin Passmore (ed.), *Women, Gender and Fascism in Europe, 1919–45* (Manchester University Press, 2003); Janet Hart, *New Voices in the Nation: Women and the Greek Resistance, 1941–1964* (Ithaca, NY, and London: Cornell University Press, 1996); Barbara Jancar-Webster, *Women and Revolution in Yugoslavia, 1941–1945* (Denver, Colo.: Arden Press, 1990). On liberation and post-war retribution, see the panoramic view presented in Keith Lowe, *Savage Continent: Europe in the Aftermath of World War II* (London: Viking, 2012); and Mark Mazower (ed.), *After the War Was Over: Reconstructing the Family, Nation, and State in Greece, 1943–1960*

(Princeton University Press, 2000). The controversy over the British repatri-
ations of collaborators from Austria to Yugoslavia is carefully addressed in
Christopher Booker, *A Looking-Glass Tragedy: The Controversy over the Repatri-
ations from Austria in 1945* (London: Duckworth, 1997). While many of the
aforementioned works include sections on the historiography and memory
of resistance, collaboration and liberation, see also Nikos Marantzidis and
Giorgos Antoniou, 'The Axis Occupation and Civil War: Changing Trends in
Greek Historiography, 1941–2002', *Journal of Peace Research* 41:2 (March 2004),
223–31.

19 Soviet liberations and occupations, 1939–1949
Mark Edele

This chapter has profited from attempts to overcome the Eurocentrism of
much of the literature on the Second World War. See, for example Evan
Mawdsley, *World War II: A New History* (Cambridge University Press, 2009),
or Antony Beevor, *The Second World War* (New York: Back Bay Books, 2012).
Histories of the Soviet war, meanwhile, remain focused on the European
story, giving short shrift to Asia, if they do not ignore it altogether. An
exception is a sketch by Mark Harrison in James R. Millar (ed.), *Encyclopedia
of Russian History* (4 vols., New York: Macmillan, 2004), vol. IV, pp. 1683–92.
Diplomatic historians are more likely to give the Asian theatre its due. See, in
particular, Geoffrey Roberts, *Stalin's Wars: From World War to Cold War,
1939–1953* (New Haven, Conn., and London: Yale University Press, 2006);
Jonathan Haslam, *The Soviet Union and the Threat from the East, 1933–1941:
Moscow, Tokyo, and the Prelude to the Pacific War* (Pittsburgh, Pa.: University of
Pittsburgh Press, 1992); and David Wolff, 'Stalin's Postwar Border-making
Tactics', *Cahiers du Monde russe* 52:2–3 (2011), 273–91. An intentionalist inter-
pretation of Stalin's empire-building in east and west, as well as at home, is
Robert Gellately, *Stalin's Curse: Battling for Communism in War and Cold War*
(Oxford University Press, 2013).

Useful bird's-eye views on the liberations and occupations in Eastern
Europe and the 'western borderlands' are offered by Dietrich Beyrau,
Schlachtfeld der Diktatoren. Osteuropa im Schatten von Hitler and Stalin (Göttin-
gen: Vandenhoeck & Ruprecht, 2000); Alexander V. Prusin, *The Lands
Between: Conflict in the East European Borderlands, 1870–1992* (Oxford University
Press, 2010); and Timothy Snyder, *Bloodlands: Europe Between Hitler and Stalin*
(London: The Bodley Head, 2010). The classic studies of the occupation of
Poland in 1939 are Jan T. Gross, *Revolution from Abroad: The Soviet Conquest of*

Poland's Western Ukraine and Western Belorussia (expanded edn, Princeton University Press, 2002); and Keith Sword (ed.), *The Soviet Takeover of the Polish Eastern Provinces, 1939–41* (New York: St Martin's Press, 1991). A detailed case study is Alexander Brakel, *Unter Rotem Stern und Hakenkreuz: Baranowicze 1939 bis 1944. Das westliche Weissrussland unter sowjetischer und deutscher Besatung* (Paderborn: Schöningh, 2009). The state-of-the-art on Katyn is Anna M. Cienciala, Natalia S. Lebedeva and Wojciech Materski (eds.), *Katyn: A Crime Without Punishment* (New Haven, Conn., and London: Yale University Press, 2007). On the Baltics, see Mart Laar, *War in the Woods: Estonia's Struggle for Survival, 1944–1956* (Ann Arbor, Mich.: Compass Press, 1992); David Wolff and Gael Moullec, *Le KGB et les pays Baltes 1939–1991* (Paris: Belin, 1999); and Elena Zubkova, *Pribaltika i Kreml'. 1940–1953* (Moscow: Rosspen, 2008). On the prisoner executions in 1941, see Bogdan Musial, *'Konterrevolutionäre Elemente sind zu erschiessen'. Die Brutalisierung des deutsch-sowjetischen Krieges im Sommer 1941* (2nd edn, Berlin and Munich: Propyläen, 2001).

Three essential studies on Iran are Louse Fawcett, *Iran and the Cold War: The Azerbaijan Crisis of 1946* (Cambridge University Press, 1992); Tadeusz Swietochowski, *Russia and Azerbaijan: A Borderland in Transition* (New York: Columbia University Press, 1995); and Jamil Hasanli, *The Soviet-American Crisis over Iranian Azerbaijan, 1941–1946* (Lanham, Md.: Rowman & Littlefield, 2006). Important Russian-language contributions include N. I. Egorova, '"Iranskii krizis" 1945–1946 gg. po rassekrechennym arkhivnym dokumentam', *Novaia i noveishaia istoriia* 3 (1994), 24–42; and N. I. Egorova, '"Iranskii krizis" 1945–1946 gg.: vzgliad iz rossiiskikh arkhivov', in M. M. Narinskii (ed.), *Kholodnaia voina. Novye podkhody, novye dokumenty* (Moscow: RAN, 1995), pp. 294–314.

On the Soviet war against Japan, see David Holloway, 'Jockeying for Position in the Postwar World: Soviet Entry into the War with Japan in August 1945', in T. Hasegawa (ed.), *The End of the Pacific War: Reappraisals* (Stanford University Press, 2007), pp. 145–88; and Tsuyoshi Hasegawa, *Racing the Enemy: Stalin, Truman, and the Surrender of Japan* (Cambridge, Mass.: Harvard University Press, 2005). For an operational history of the Manchurian campaign, see David M. Glantz, *Soviet Operational and Tactical Combat in Manchuria, 1945: 'August Storm'* (London: Frank Cass, 2003). On the occupations in Asia, see John J. Stephan, *The Kuril Islands: Russo-Japanese Frontier in the Pacific* (Oxford: Clarendon Press, 1974); John J. Stephan, *Sakhalin: A History* (Oxford: Clarendon Press, 1971); Mariya Sevela, '"How Could You Fear or Respect Such an Enemy?" The End of World War II on

Sakhalin', in Bert Edström (ed.), *The Japanese and Europe: Images and Perceptions* (Richmond: Japan Library, 2000), pp. 172–92; Steven I. Levine, *Anvil of Victory: The Communist Revolution in Manchuria, 1945–1948* (New York: Columbia University Press, 1987); Charles K. Armstrong, *The North Korean Revolution, 1945–1950* (Ithaca, NY, and London: Cornell University Press, 2003); and Ronald H. Spector, *In the Ruins of Empire: The Japanese Surrender and the Battle for Postwar Asia* (New York: Random House, 2007).

On ethnic cleansing, see Terry Martin's seminal article, 'The Origins of Soviet Ethnic Cleansing', *Journal of Modern History* 70:4 (1998), 813–61; also J. Otto Pohl, *Ethnic Cleansing in the USSR, 1937–1949* (Westport, Conn.: Greenwood Press, 1999); and Norman M. Naimark, *Fires of Hatred: Ethnic Cleansing in Twentieth-Century Europe* (Cambridge, Mass., and London: Harvard University Press, 2001). On the deportation of Germans to forced work in the Soviet Union, see Georg Weber, Renate Weber-Schlenther, Armin Nassehi, Oliver Sill and Georg Kneer, *Die Deportation von Siebenbürger Sachsen in die Sowjetunion 1945–1949* (3 vols., Cologne: Böhlau Verlag, 1995). On Soviet deportations more generally, see Pavel Polian, *Ne po svoei vole. . . istoriia i geografiia prinuditel'nykh migratsii v SSSR* (Moscow: OGI, 2001); N. Vert [Nicolas Werth] and S. V. Mironenko, *Istoriia stalinskogo GULAGa. Konets 1920-kh – pervaia polovina 1950-kh godov*, tom 1: *Massovye repressii v SSSR* (7 vols., Moscow: Rosspen, 2004); and N. L. Pobol' and P. M. Polian (eds.), *Stalinskie deportatsii 1928–1953, Rossiia XX vek. Dokumenty* (Moscow: Demokratiia, 2005).

Three complementary studies of the Red Army are David M. Glantz, *Colossus Reborn: The Red Army at War, 1941–1943* (Lawrence: University Press of Kansas, 2005); Catherine Merridale, *Ivan's War: The Red Army, 1939–1945* (London: Faber & Faber, 2005); and Roger R. Reese, *Why Stalin's Soldiers Fought: The Red Army's Military Effectiveness in World War II* (Lawrence: University Press of Kansas, 2011). On the violence in Germany in 1944–45, still unsurpassed are Norman Naimark, *The Russians in Germany: A History of the Soviet Zone of Occupation, 1945–1949* (Cambridge, Mass.: Belknap Press, 1995); and Manfred Zeidler, *Kriegsende im Osten. Die Rote Armee und die Besetzung Deutschlands östlich von Oder und Neisse 1944/45* (Munich: Oldenbourg, 1996); now flanked by Atina Grossmann, *Jews, Germans, and Allies: Close Encounters in Occupied Germany* (Princeton University Press, 2007); Ian Kershaw, *The End: Hitler's Germany, 1944–45* (London: Allen Lane, 2011); and Filip Slaveski, *The Soviet Occupation of Germany: Hunger, Mass Violence and the Struggle for Survival, 1945–1947* (Cambridge University Press, 2013). On Austria, see Barbara Stelzl-Marx, *Stalins Soldaten in Österreich. Die Innensicht der sowjetischen Besatzung 1945–1955* (Vienna and Munich: Böhlau and Oldenbourg, 2012). Brave contributions by Russian historians include Pavel N. Knyschewskij [Knyshevskii], *Moskaus Beute. Wie Vermögen, Kulturgüter und Intelligenz nach 1945 aus Deutschland geraubt wurden* (Munich: Olzog, 1995); Gennadij Bordjugow [G. Bordiugov], 'Wehrmacht und Rote Armee – Verbrechen gegen die Zivilbevölkerung. Charakter, Grundlagen und Bewusstsein von Menschen unter Kriegsbedingungen', in Karl Eimermacher and Astrid Volpert with Gennadij Bordjugow (eds.), *Verführungen der Gewalt. Russen und Deutsche im Ersten und Zweiten Weltkrieg* (Munich: Fink, 2005), pp. 1213–60; and Oleg Budnitskii, 'The Intelligentsia Meets the Enemy: Educated Soviet Officers in Defeated Germany, 1945', *Kritika: Explorations in Russian and Eurasian History* 10:3 (2009), 629–82. A sceptical view of an emblematic Soviet atrocity is provided by Bernhard Fisch, *Nemmersdorf, Oktober 1944: Was in Ostpreussen tatsächlich geschah* (Berlin: Edition Ost, 1997). The mass dying in Soviet camps in Germany is analysed by Natalja Jeske, 'Versorgung, Krankheit, Tod in den Speziallagern', in Sergej Mironenko, Lutz Niethammer, Alexander von Plato, Volkhard Knigge and Günther Morsch (eds.), *Sowjetische Speziallager in Deutschland 1945 bis 1950* (2 vols., Berlin: Akademie Verlag, 1998), vol. I, pp. 189–223. A first stab at a comparative history of the violence of occupation by all four Allied powers is Giles Macdonogh, *After the Reich: The Brutal History of the Allied Occupation* (New York: Basic Books, 2007); on rape, in particular, see Jeffrey Burds, 'Sexual Violence in Europe in World War II, 1939–1945', *Politics and Society* 37:1 (2009), 35–74. On the extent to which Soviet behaviour was radicalized by German example, see Mark Edele, 'Learning from the Enemy? Entangling Histories of the German-Soviet War, 1941–1945', in D. Baratieri, M. Edele and G. Finaldi (eds.), *Totalitarian Dictatorship: New Histories* (London: Routledge, 2014), pp. 190–211.

On the reconstruction of liberated Soviet territories, see David Marples, *Stalinism in Ukraine in the 1940s* (Basingstoke: Palgrave Macmillan, 1992); Kees Boterbloem, *Life and Death Under Stalin: Kalinin Province* (Montreal, London, and Ithaca, NY: McGill-Queen's University Press, 1999); Katrin Boeckh, *Stalinismus in der Ukraine. Die Rekonstruktion des sowjetischen Systems nach dem Zweiten Weltkrieg* (Wiesbaden: Harrassowitz Verlag, 2007); Jeffrey W. Jones, *Everyday Life and the 'Reconstruction' of Soviet Russia During and After the Great Patriotic War, 1943–1948* (Bloomington, Ind.: Slavica Publishers, 2008); and Karl Qualls, *From Ruins to Reconstruction: Urban Identity in Soviet Sevastopol After World War II* (Ithaca, NY, and London: Cornell University Press, 2009).

On liberation as reoccupation, see Sanford R. Lieberman, 'The Re-Sovietization of Formerly Occupied Areas of the USSR During World War II', in Sanford R. Lieberman, David E. Powell, Carol R. Saivetz and Sarah M. Terry (eds.), *The Soviet Empire Reconsidered: Essays in Honor of Adam B. Ulam* (Boulder, Colo.: Westview Press, 1994), pp. 49–67; Hiroaki Kuromiya, *Freedom and Terror in the Donbass: A Ukrainian-Russian Borderland* (Cambridge University Press, 1998); Nicolas Werth, 'A State Against Its People: Violence, Repression, and Terror in the Soviet Union', in S. Courtois and N. Werth (eds.), *The Black Book of Communism: Crimes, Terror, Repression* (Cambridge, Mass.: Harvard University Press, 1999), esp. pp. 216–31; Amir Weiner, *Making Sense of War: The Second World War and the Fate of the Bolshevik Revolution* (Princeton University Press, 2001); Alexander Statiev, 'The Nature of Anti-Soviet Armed Resistance, 1942–1944: The North Caucasus, the Kalmyk Autonomous Republic, and Crimea', *Kritika: Explorations in Russian and Eurasian History* 6:2 (2005), 285–318; and Jeffrey Burds, 'The Soviet War Against "Fifth Columnists": The Case of Chechnya, 1942–4', *Journal of Contemporary History* 42:2 (2007), 267–314.

20 Collaboration, resistance and accommodation in Northeast Asia
Margherita Zanasi

Historians of Taiwan mostly focus their attention on the relationships between local communities and Japanese occupation forces in the pre-war period, since they perceive the Second World War as an organic extension of the colonial experience (1895–1945). Historian Hui-yu Caroline Ts'ai has written extensively on issues of collaboration in this context. Her works include *Japanese Colonial Engineering in Taiwan, 1895–1945* (London: Routledge, 2008) and *Taiwan in Japan's Empire-Building: An Institutional Approach to Colonial Engineering* (New York: Routledge, 2009). Ming-cheng Miriam Lo, *Doctors Within Borders: Profession, Ethnicity, and Modernity in Colonial Taiwan* (Berkeley: University of California Press, 2002), is also an influential example of this approach. Although focused on Manchuria, historian Prasenjit Duara's *Sovereignty and Authenticity: Manchukuo and the East Asian Modern* (Lanham, Md.: Rowman & Littlefield, 2003) also discusses issues of colonial modernity and local nation building.

The complexity of the issue of resistance in Taiwan is aptly illustrated in Paul R. Katz's article, 'Governmentality and Its Consequences in Colonial Taiwan: A Case Study of the Ta-pa-ni Incident of 1915', *Journal of Asian Studies*

64 (2005), 387, which focuses on the interconnection between anti-Japanese uprisings and local religious beliefs and practices.

The predicament of Taiwanese after the fall of the Japanese Empire is the subject of Jiu-Jung Lo, 'Trials of the Taiwanese'; and Barak Kushner, 'Pawns of Empire: Postwar Taiwan, Japan and the Dilemma of War Crimes', *Japanese Studies* 30 (2010), 111–33.

For a general discussion of Taiwan under Japanese occupation, see Harry J. Lamley, 'Taiwan Under Japanese Rule, 1895–1945: The Vicissitude of Colonialism', in Murray A. Rubinstein (ed.), *Taiwan: A New History* (Armonk, NY, and London: M. E. Sharpe, 2007).

Korea specialists also tend to focus on the colonial experience as a whole (1910–45). One of the most influential writers in this field is historian Koen de Ceuster, author of 'The Nation Exorcised: The Historiography of Collaboration in South Korea', *Korean Studies* 25 (2001), 207–42, and 'Wholesome Education and Sound Leisure: The YMCA Sports Programme in Colonial Korea', *European Journal of East Asian Studies* 2 (2003), 53–88. Recent works also include Nayoung Aimee Kwon, 'Colonial Modernity and the Conundrum of Representation: Korean Literature in the Japanese Empire', *Postcolonial Studies* 13 (2010), 421–39. For a general discussion of Korea under Japanese occupation, see chapters 1 and 2 of Adrian Buzo, *The Making of Modern Korea* (London: Routledge, 2007).

Rana Mitter, *The Manchurian Myth: Nationalism, Resistance and Collaboration During the Manchurian Crisis, 1931–1933* (Berkeley: University of California Press, 2000), was the first scholarly work to deconstruct stereotypical resistantialist images of collaboration in the China region, by revealing the weakness of the idea of nationhood in the borderlands. Timothy Brook, *Collaboration: Japanese Agents and Local Elites in Wartime China* (Cambridge, Mass.: Harvard University Press, 2005), also greatly contributed to producing a nuanced understanding of issues of collaboration and accommodation, by shifting attention away from the higher echelons of the political leadership to explore the wide range of accommodation/collaboration dynamics that emerged at the local level. The diversity and complexity of forms of collaboration and resistance in China and the lack of clear dividing lines between the two are further explored in Parks M. Coble, *Chinese Capitalists in Japan's New Order: The Occupied Lower Yangzi, 1937–1945* (Berkeley: University of California Press, 2003).

Post-war collaboration trials have also attracted the attention of historians. For a discussion on this topic, see Margherita Zanasi, 'Globalizing Hanjian: The Suzhou Trials and the Post-World War II Discourse on Collaboration',

American Historical Review 113 (2008), 731–51; and Dongyoun Hwang, 'Wartime Collaboration in Question: An Examination of the Postwar Trials of the Chinese Collaborators', *Inter-Asia Cultural Studies* 6 (2005), 75–97.

Resistance and collaboration followed different lines of development in urban and rural areas. Frederic E. Wakeman, *The Shanghai Badlands: Wartime Terrorism and Urban Crime, 1937–1941* (Cambridge and New York: Cambridge University Press, 1996), and Wen-Hsin Yeh (ed.), *Wartime Shanghai* (London and New York: Routledge, 1998) offer an interesting discussion of Shanghai under Japanese occupation and the complex network of resistance, crime and collaboration that characterized this cosmopolitan city. As for the rural areas, the two works that best represent the theory of the rise of the CCP and peasant nationalism are Chalmers Johnson, *Peasant Nationalism and Communist Power: The Emergence of Revolutionary China* (Stanford University Press, 1962); and Lucien Bianco, *Origins of the Chinese Revolution, 1915–1949* (Stanford University Press, 1971).

This chapter does not include a discussion of the response of Chinese writers to Japanese occupation, a subject that is addressed by Poshek Fu, *Passivity, Resistance, and Collaboration: Intellectual Choices in Occupied Shanghai, 1937–1945* (Stanford University Press, 1993).

For a debate on the issue of moral responsibility and collaboration, see the symposium, 'Collaboration in War and Memory in East Asia: A Symposium', *The Asia-Pacific Journal: Japan Focus*, www.japanfocus.org/-timothy-brook/2798 (accessed 26 November 2014); as well as the debate centred around John Treat's article 'Choosing to Collaborate: Yi Kwang-Su and the Moral Subject in Colonial Korea', *Journal of Asian Studies* 71:1 (2012), 81–102: Timothy Brook, 'Hesitating Before the Judgment of History', *Journal of Asian Studies* 71:1 (2012), 103–14; Michael D. Shin, 'Yi Kwang-su: The Collaborator as Modernist Against Modernity', *Journal of Asian Studies* 71:1 (2012), 115–20; John Whittier Treat, 'Seoul and Nanking, Baghdad and Kabul: A Response to Timothy Brook and Michael Shin', *Journal of Asian Studies* 71:1 (2012), 121–5.

21 Japanese occupation of Southeast Asia, 1941–1945
Paul H. Kratoska and Ken'ichi Goto

Much of the written record of the occupation was destroyed at the end of the war, including a substantial amount intentionally destroyed by the Japanese military immediately after Japan's capitulation. As a result, historical accounts of the war years have depended very heavily on documentation collected or created by the Allied powers.

The Japanese government arranged for former senior officers to write accounts of major campaigns in which they participated, and these statements were published in a 102-volume *Senshi Sosho* (War History Series). English translations were subsequently made by the US Army Center of Military History. In the absence of operational records, these early post-war accounts rely heavily on the memories of the authors.

In addition to Japanese-language collections, like the twenty-nine-volume *Showa Shakai-Keizai Shiryo Shusei* (Comprehensive Historical Material on Socio-economic Conditions in Showa Period), general editor Doi Akira (Tokyo: Institute of Oriental Studies [Daito Bunka Daigaku], 1983–99), five collections of translated documents and related materials present first-hand information on Japanese policies in Southeast Asia: Harry J. Benda, James K. Irikura and Koichi Kishi, *Japanese Military Administration in Indonesia: Selected Documents*, Translation Series 6 (New Haven, Conn.: Yale University, Southeast Asia Studies, 1965); Mauro Garcia (ed.), *Documents on the Japanese Occupation of the Philippines* (Manila: Philippine Historical Association, 1965); Joyce Lebra, *Japan's Greater East Asia Co-Prosperity Sphere in World War II* (Kuala Lumpur: Oxford University Press, 1975); Akira Oki and Anthony Reid (eds.), *The Japanese Experience in Indonesia: Selected Memoirs of 1942–1945*, Monographs in International Studies, Southeast Asia Series 72 (Athens: Ohio University, Center for International Studies, Center for Southeast Asian Studies, 1986); Frank N. Trager, *Burma: Japanese Military Administration, Selected Documents, 1941–1945* (Philadelphia: University of Pennsylvania Press, 1971).

In the immediate aftermath of the occupation, a number of accounts appeared written by authors who drew on first-hand experience, but who had meagre documentary evidence. One early study that transcended these limitations was Harry J. Benda, *The Crescent and the Rising Sun: Indonesian Islam Under the Japanese Occupation, 1942–1945* (The Hague: W. van Hoeve, 1958). In 1980, Alfred W. McCoy (ed.), *Southeast Asia Under Japanese Occupation*, Monograph Series 22 (New Haven, Conn.: Yale University, Southeast Asia Studies), reassessed key issues and marked the beginning of a new generation of scholarship on occupied Southeast Asia. Over the next three decades, scholars prepared books and articles based on newly released archival material, and for each major country there is now at least one work providing a solidly grounded account, written with a level of detachment.

For Burma, Robert H. Taylor, *Marxism and Resistance in Burma, 1942–1945*, which is published together with Thein Pe Myint, *Wartime Traveler* (Athens:

Ohio University Press, 1984), explains the Burmese response to the occupation; and a more recent publication by Kei Nemoto, *Reconsidering the Japanese Military Occupation in Burma, 1942–45* (Tokyo University of Foreign Studies, 2007), utilizes both Burmese and Japanese source materials.

For Malaya and Singapore, Paul H. Kratoska, *The Japanese Occupation of Malaya, 1941–1945* (London: C. Hurst, 1997), describes the occupation based largely on archival sources. Abu Talib Ahmad, *Malay-Muslims, Islam, and the Rising Sun, 1941–1945* (Kuala Lumpur: Malaysian Branch of the Royal Asiatic Society, 2003), looks at Islamic policy; and Cheah Boon Kheng, *Red Star Over Malaya: Resistance and Social Conflict During and After the Japanese Occupation of Malaya, 1941–46* (4th edn, Singapore: NUS Press, 2012), considers the activities of the Malayan Communist Party.

An early standard work on the Philippines is Teodoro A. Agoncillo, *The Fateful Years: Japan's Adventure in the Philippines, 1941–45* (2 vols., Manila: R. P. Garcia, 1965). An edited work by Ikehata Setsuho and Ricardo Trota Jose, *The Philippines Under Japan: Occupation Policy and Reaction* (Quezon City: Ateneo de Manila University Press, 1999), offers updated accounts of key issues. Theodore Friend, *The Blue-Eyed Enemy: Japan Against the West in Java and Luzon, 1942–1945* (Princeton University Press, 1988), provides a perceptive comparison, based on an extraordinarily rich set of sources in a wide range of languages.

For Indonesia, volume 11 of Louis de Jong's massive *Het koninkrijk der Nederlanden in de Tweede Wereldoorlog* deals with the Netherlands Indies (12 vols., 's-Gravenhage: Staatsuitgeverij, 1984); a portion of volume 11B has been translated into English and published as *The Collapse of a Colonial Society: The Dutch in Indonesia During the Second World War* (Leiden: KITLV Press, 2002). Shigeru Sato, *War, Nationalism and Peasants: Java Under the Japanese Occupation, 1947–1945* (St Leonards, New South Wales: Asian Studies Association of Australia in association with Allen & Unwin, 1994), describes the socio-economic situation. Ken'ichi Goto, *'Returning to Asia': Japan–Indonesia Relations, 1930s–1942* (Tokyo: Ryukei Shyosha, 1997), explains the background to the Japanese thrust into Southeast Asia; and Benedict Anderson, *Java in a Time of Revolution: Occupation and Resistance, 1944–1946* (Ithaca, NY, and London: Cornell University Press, 1972), discusses the aftermath. Peter Post (gen. ed.), William H. Frederick, Iris Heidebrink and Shigeru Sato (eds.), *The Encyclopedia of Indonesia in the Pacific War* (Leiden: Brill, 2010), contains extensive detail on the war years.

The definitive work on Thailand is E. Bruce Reynolds, *Thailand and Japan's Southern Advance, 1940–1945* (New York: St Martin's Press, 1994), which uses both Japanese and Thai sources, while Direk Jayanama's *Thailand and World War II*, translated and edited by Jane Keyes (Chiang Mai: Silkworm Books, 2008), presents a Thai perspective on events.

A significant account of French Indochina is Paul Isoart (ed.), *L'Indochine française, 1940–1945* (Paris: Presses Universitaires de France, 1982). David G. Marr, *Vietnam 1945: The Quest for Power* (Berkeley: University of California Press, 1995), presents a detailed explanation of wartime events that is unlikely ever to be superseded.

22 The British Empire, 1939–1945
Ashley Jackson

A persistent problem in the historiography of the war is that the scale of colonial participation, and the impact of the war on colonial societies, is underplayed. Only local studies by specialists working on, say, an individual country or region, or a particular colonial raw material, seem able to capture adequately this level of wartime experience – which then, as often as not, suffers from the reverse problem; not being linked to the broader military, political and strategic scholarship on the war. There are other problems too, including the common disjuncture between military historians and historians of empire and colonial societies. Ignorance (sometimes even contempt) of one side and what it brings to the study of war is often displayed by the other. Furthermore, the mismatch in both scholarly knowledge and public knowledge can be astonishing: historians of Africa, for example, have long understood the extent of the dependence of the Allied war effort on African resources, but the subject receives little attention in general histories of the war, and the consequences of this dependence upon African communities is largely ignored.

The most comprehensive bibliography of works relating to the British Empire during the war appears in Ashley Jackson, *The British Empire and the Second World War* (London: Continuum, 2005) (reproduced, and updated, on the website of the British Empire at War Research Group, http://britishempireatwar.org – accessed 28 November 2014). Other books that address empire-wide themes include Nicholas Mansergh's *Survey of British Commonwealth Affairs: Problems of Wartime Cooperation and Post-War Change, 1939–1952* (London: Frank Cass, 1958), and Andrew Stewart's *Empire Lost: Britain, the Dominions, and the Second World War* (London: Continuum, 2008), both focusing on the politics of the imperial relationship, the theme of a special issue of the *Journal of Imperial and Commonwealth History* 40:1

(2012). Christopher Somerville's *Our War* (London: Weidenfeld and Nicolson, 1998) and Richard Aldrich's *The Faraway War* (London: Corgi, 2010) offer oral testimony from imperial theatres and colonial subjects.

Among the most salient themes in the literature are colony- and Dominion-level studies: while the larger territories have received a great deal of attention within the framework of well-developed national histories of the war, and specific official histories of the conflict produced by the governments of Britain, India and the former Dominions, a surprising number of other former colonies, generally with less developed national histories, have also had books devoted to their wartime experiences. These include Bechuanaland, Ceylon, Egypt, the Gold Coast, Hong Kong, India, Jamaica, Kenya, Malaya, Malta, Mauritius, Nigeria, Palestine, the Seychelles and Singapore. Jonathan Vance, *A Maple Leaf Empire: Canada, Britain, and Two World Wars* (Oxford University Press, 2012), and Peter Dean (ed.), *Australia 1942: In the Shadow of War* (Cambridge University Press, 2012), are good examples of comprehensive accounts addressing strategic, military and home front themes.

There are then regional studies looking at the war's impact on indigenous societies. Christopher Bayly and Tim Harper's *Forgotten Armies: Britain's Asian Empire and the War with Japan* (London: Allen Lane, 2004) memorably covers Southeast Asia. David Killingray and Richard Rathbone, *Africa and the Second World War* (Basingstoke: Macmillan, 1986); Richard Osborne, *World War II in Colonial Africa: The Death Knell of Colonialism* (Indianapolis, Ind.: Riebel-Roque, 2001); and Judith Byfield, Carolyn Brown, Timothy Parsons and Ahmad Sikaingi (eds.), *Africa and World War Two* (Cambridge University Press, 2015), cover the African continent. Judith Bennett's innovative *Natives and Exotics: World War Two and Environment in the Southern Pacific* (Honolulu: University of Hawaii Press, 2009), adds an exciting angle of vision in another colonized region; and Jean André Baptiste, *War Cooperation and Conflict: The European Possessions in the Caribbean, 1939–1945* (Westport, Conn.: Greenwood Press, 1988), examines the West Indies. Other works examine strategic plans, such as H. P. Wilmott's work on British strategizing east of Suez; and numerous works address theatres of conflict or particular campaigns that had a strong imperial dimension, such as the Battle of the Atlantic, the Burma campaign and the 'China-Burma-India' theatre, the Malaya and Singapore campaigns, the Western Desert, and the role of Malta in the Mediterranean contest.

Another distinct category relates to the armed forces of the empire, including numerous works on the Indian Army and the Dominions

(Alan Jeffreys, Iain Johnston, F. W. Perry, Douglas Delaney), and histories of units such as the King's African Rifles, the Eastern Fleet and the British Pacific Fleet. David Killingray, *Fighting for Britain: African Soldiers in the Second World War* (Woodbridge: James Currey, 2010), looks more generally at the experiences of African soldiers.

New approaches to studying the empire at war are occasionally encountered, such as the five chapters on the empire at war in Lee Grieveson and Colin MacCabe (eds.), *Film and the End of Empire* (Basingstoke: Palgrave, 2011); and it is to be hoped that more studies such as Boon Kheng Cheah's classic *Red Star Over Malaya: Resistance and Social Conflict During and After the Japanese Occupation of Malaya* (Singapore University Press, 1983) will get us closer to the 'underneath of things', the view of the war through the eyes of colonial peoples, a view recently developed further in Yasmin Khan's *India's War* (London: Bodley Head, 2014).

23 France and its colonial civil wars, 1940–1945
Martin Thomas

There remains an imbalance between the relative paucity of published work on the French colonial empire between 1939 and 1945, and the wealth of secondary literature on France's experience of the Second World War, much of which focuses, quite understandably, on questions of defeat, resistance and collaboration. Three exceptions that nonetheless prove the rule are Jacques Cantier and Eric T. Jennings (eds.), *L'Empire colonial sous Vichy* (Paris: Odile Jacob, 2004); Jérôme Ollandet, *Brazzaville, capitale de la France libre: Histoire de la résistance française en Afrique (1940–1944)* (Paris: L'Harmattan, 2013); and Martin Thomas, *The French Empire at War, 1940–45* (Manchester University Press, 1998). Some of the most informative studies in English and French are thus to be found in works of imperial historians and area studies specialists focused on particular colonies, regions or issues. North Africa and Indochina tend to predominate here, outstanding examples being Jacques Cantier, *L'Algérie sous le régime de Vichy* (Paris: Odile Jacob, 2002); and David G. Marr, *Vietnam 1945: The Quest for Power* (Berkeley: University of California Press, 1997). Annie Rey-Goldzeiguer's *Aux origines de la guerre d'Algérie 1940–1945: De Mers-el-Kébir aux massacres du nord-constantinois* (Paris: Editions la Découverte, 2002), and, above all, Jean-Pierre Peyroulou's *Guelma, 1945: Une subversion française dans l'Algérie coloniale* (Paris: Editions la Découverte, 2009) offer indispensable accounts connecting wartime deprivation and intercommunal frictions to the outbreak of rebellion in eastern Algeria in May 1945.

French colonial territories in West Africa and the Caribbean have attracted more attention in relation to three phenomena: the impact of colonial recruitment and colonial soldiering on local societies; the export of Vichy's ideological schema to the colonies; and the reconfiguration of local identities and political attachments consequent on the preceding two factors. Key works here include Nancy E. Lawler, *Soldiers of Misfortune: Ivoirien Tirailleurs of World War II* (Athens: Ohio University Press, 1992); Gregory Mann, *Native Sons: West African Veterans and France in the Twentieth Century* (Durham, NC: Duke University Press, 2006); Jacqueline Woodfork, *Senegalese Citizens, Subjects, and Soldiers: Intersecting Identities in the Second World War* (Lincoln: University of Nebraska Press, 2014); Ruth Ginio, *French Colonialism Unmasked: The Vichy Years in French West Africa* (Lincoln: University of Nebraska Press, 2006); and Eric T. Jennings, *Vichy in the Tropics: Pétain's National Revolution in Madagascar, Guadeloupe, and Indochina, 1940–1944* (Stanford University Press, 2002).

General surveys of the modern French colonial empire that pay considerable attention to the Second World War's legacies include Martin Shipway, *Decolonization and its Impact* (Oxford: Blackwell, 2008); Martin Thomas, L. J. Butler and Bob Moore, *Crises of Empire: Decolonization and Europe's Imperial Nation States, 1918–1975* (London: Bloomsbury, 2008); and Alice L. Conklin, Sarah Fishman and Robert Zaretsky, *France and its Empire Since 1870* (New York: Oxford University Press, 2011).

Finally, it seems appropriate to finish by highlighting the work done on Nazi massacres of French colonial troops during the 1940 battle for France, as well as an important study of those who survived as colonial prisoners of war thereafter. Raffael Scheck, *Hitler's African Victims: The German Army Massacres of Black French Soldiers in 1940* (Cambridge University Press, 2006), and Armelle Mabon, *Les prisonniers de guerre 'indigenes': Visages oubliés de la France occupée* (Paris: Editions la Découverte, 2010), stand out in this context.

24 The Muslim world in the Second World War
David Motadel

The history of the 'Muslim world in the Second World War' does not yet form a coherent field of research. Scholars interested in the subject must consult studies on different parts of the Muslim world. On the North African war zone, for the military history, see Martin Kitchen, *Rommel's Desert War: Waging World War II in North Africa, 1941–1943* (Cambridge University Press,

2009); on the political situation in Libya, Saul Kelly, *War and Politics in the Desert: Britain and Libya During the Second World War* (London: Silphium, 2010); on the suffering of Libya's local population, Patrick Bernhard, 'Behind the Battle Lines: Italian Atrocities and the Persecution of Arabs, Berbers, and Jews in North Africa During World War II', *Holocaust and Genocide Studies* 26:3 (2012), 425–46; and, focusing on French North Africa, Christine Levisse-Touzé, *L'Afrique du Nord dans la guerre 1939–1945* (Paris: Albin Michel, 1998). The classic account of the Middle East in the war remains George Kirk, *The Middle East in the War* (Oxford University Press, 1952). Bernd Philipp Schröder, *Deutschland und der Mittlere Osten im Zweiten Weltkrieg* (Göttingen: Muster-Schmidt, 1975), looks at the German involvement in the region. Notable regional studies are, on the Levant, Aviel Roshwald, *Estranged Bedfellows: Britain and France in the Middle East During the Second World War* (New York: Oxford University Press, 1990); on Iran, Richard A. Stewart, *Sunrise at Abadan: The British and Soviet Invasion of Iran, 1941* (New York: Praeger, 1988); and, on Turkey, Selim Deringil, *Turkish Foreign Policy During the Second World War: An 'Active' Neutrality* (Cambridge University Press, 2004).

The effects of the war on the Muslim population of the Soviet southern borderlands have been examined by Patrik von zur Mühlen, *Zwischen Hakenkreuz und sowjetstern: Der Nationalismus der Sowjetischen Orientvölker im Zweiten Weltkrieg* (Düsseldorf: Droste, 1971); and, more specifically on the Caucasus, Joachim Hoffmann, *Kaukasien 1942/43: Das deutsche Heer und Orientvoelker der Sowjetunion* (Freiburg: Rombach, 1991); and, on Crimea, Norbert Kunz, *Die Krim unter Deutscher Herrschaft 1941–1944: Germanisierungsutopie und Besatzungsrealität* (Darmstadt: Wissenschaftliche Buchgesellschaft, 2005), esp. pp. 213–17.

The history of Muslims in the wartime Balkans is documented in the comprehensive account of Jozo Tomasevich, *War and Revolution in Yugoslavia, 1941–1945: Occupation and Collaboration* (Stanford University Press, 2001), pp. 466–510; for Bosnia, Enver Redžić, *Bosnia and Herzegovina in the Second World War* (New York: Frank Cass, 2005); and Marko Attila Hoare, *The Bosnian Muslims in the Second World War: A History* (London: Hurst, 2013); and, for Albania, Bernd J. Fischer, *Albania at War, 1939–1945* (London: Hurst, 1999).

A comprehensive historical account of India's Muslims during the Second World War remains to be written, although some insights are provided by Johannes H. Voigt, *India in the Second World War* (New Delhi: Arnold-Heinemann, 1987); and, on Axis policies, by Milan Hauner, *India in Axis Strategy: Germany, Japan, and Indian Nationalists in the Second World War*

(Stuttgart: Klett-Cotta, 1981). Harry J. Benda, *The Crescent and the Rising Sun: Indonesian Islam Under the Japanese Occupation, 1942–1945* (The Hague: W. van Hoeve, 1958), and Abu Talib Ahmad, *Malay-Muslims, Islam and the Rising Sun, 1941–1945* (Selangor: Royal Asiatic Society, 2003), are excellent accounts of Muslims during the Japanese occupation of the Dutch East Indies and British Malaya.

Both Benda and Ahmad give insights into Japan's policies toward Islam, while Selçuk Esenbel, 'Japan's Global Claim to Asia and the World of Islam: Transnational Nationalism and World Power, 1900–1945', *American Historical Review* 109:4 (2004), 1140–70, explored the origins of this policy. Italy's engagement with the world of Islam has been assessed by John L. Wright, 'Mussolini, Libya, and the Sword of Islam', in Ruth Ben-Ghiat and Mia Fuller (eds.), *Italian Colonialism* (New York: Palgrave Macmillan, 2005), pp. 121–30; and Germany's campaign for Islamic mobilization has been studied by David Motadel, *Islam and Nazi Germany's War* (Cambridge, Mass.: Harvard University Press, 2014). On the Axis collaboration of the Mufti of Jerusalem, see Klaus Gensicke, *The Mufti of Jerusalem and the Nazis: The Berlin Years, 1941–1945* (London: Vallentine Mitchell, 2011).

Motadel, *Islam and Nazi Germany's War*, also provides a comprehensive account of the history of Muslim soldiers in Hitler's armies. Generally, the history of Muslims who fought in Allied and Axis forces during the war has remained neglected. Some insights are provided by Philip Mason, *A Matter of Honour: An Account of the Indian Army – Its Officers and Men* (London: Jonathan Cape, 1974), pp. 471–527, for the British Army; by Godfrey Lias, *Glubb's Legion* (London: Evans Bros, 1956), looking at the legendary Transjordan Arab Legion; and for the French forces, by Belkacem Recham, 'Les Musulmans dans l'armée française, 1900–1945', in Mohammed Arkoun (ed.), *Histoire de l'Islam et des Musulmans en France du Moyen Age à nos jours* (Paris: Albin Michel, 2006), pp. 742–61; and, focusing on Algerian soldiers, Belkacem Recham, *Les Musulmans algériens dans l'armée française (1919–1945)* (Paris: L'Harmattan, 1996), pp. 175–274. Bringing this research together, this chapter is a first attempt to provide an overview of the impact of the Second World War on Muslims around the world, but a comprehensive account remains to be written.

Index

Italy (cont.)
surrender of 81, 438
suspicion of Germany 22, 282–3
Taranto naval attack 282–3, 336
territorial losses 28–9
Trieste question 85
Tripartite Pact 22, 38, 269–74, 276–7, 281
in Tunisia 295
Two Red Years (*biennio rosso*) 30–1
venereal disease 428–9
Versailles, Treaty of 442
war crimes by 25–6, 443–4, 451–7
war and world politics 226–7
wartime myths 379
wartime objectives 438–9
and world opinion 242
and Yugoslavia 282–4, 436–7, 450–1
see also **Mussolini, Benito**
ITO (International Trade Organization) 156
Iwo Jima 133, 136

Jackson, Robert H. 184, 187, 198
Japan
Anti-Comintern Pact 21–4, 225–6, 231, 238, 240–1, 263–4
assimilation policies 515
atomic bombs 41, 299, 322
Axis global strategy failures 39–42
Borneo, invasion of 287
Buddhism 545
in Burma 294
Celebes, invasion of 287
censorship 120
charismatic leadership 26–7
China, occupation of 35–7, 120, 212–13, 255–60, 280–1, 293, 509–11
see also **Manchuria**
civil servants in occupied territories 537
collaboration with 509, 514–15, 518–19, 525–31, 536–7
comfort women 517
common Axis ideologies 24–7
defence perimeter 534–6
Draft Understanding 272
economic recession 33–4
Emperor System 26–7
expansionist/empire-building policy 25–6, 34–5, 280–1, 304, 509–11
fascism from above 26
fascist regime variations 24–5
genocide 25–6
German-Japanese relations 22–4, 269
and German/Soviet peace proposal 294

Gilbert Islands, invasion of 287
Greater East Asia propaganda 541–4
Greater East Asian Co-Prosperity Sphere 286–7, 381–2, 545–6
Guam, invasion of 287
Hainan, occupation of 268–9
and Hitler–Stalin Pact 24, 269
Hong Kong, invasion of 287
ideological view of 14–15
Imperial Rule Assistance Association 39
and Indian Ocean 293–4
Indochina, occupation of 273–4, 280–1, 286–7
international relations 22–3
Java, invasion of 287
journalism 120, 136
kamikaze attacks 136–7
Korea, occupation of 509–19
and League of Nations 29
League of Nations membership 145, 255–6
liberation-occupation ideology 7–9
London Naval Conference (1935) 262–3
Malaya, invasion of 287, 534
Manchukuo puppet state 255–6
Manchuria, occupation of 35, 212–13, 280–1, 293, 519–20
Manchurian Incident 35–7, 120, 255–60
Marco Polo Bridge Incident 213, 264–5
media control 120
as military ally 38–9
military auxiliaries 541
military expansion 39
and Muslims 621
Nanjing 36–7, 69–70, 267–8, 529–30
national service associations 541
naval codes 127–8
New Guinea, invasion of 287
new order 34
occupation strategies 510, 519–20, 536–41
oil supplies 38–9
Peace Preparation Commission 28
Pearl Harbor 39, 51, 102, 126–7, 148, 213, 253–5, 271–2, 287, 534
perceived betrayal by Hitler 269
Philippines, invasion of 287, 534
political radicalization 33–4
post-Paris Peace Conference 28–9
post-war rehabilitation 204
pre-war ideology 1–5
press publicity 136
propaganda 98–9, 113–14, 131
race equality proposal 29
racist policy 25–6